Introducing the Interactive Companion Web site for *Essentials of Sociology, 4/e*

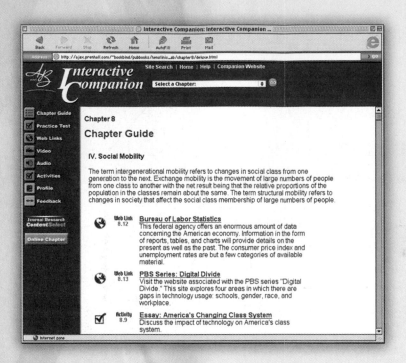

With the purchase of a new copy of Henslin's *Essentials of Sociology: A Down-to-Earth Approach, 4/e*, you'll get access to this PIN-code protected Web site FREE of charge. The Allyn & Bacon Interactive Companion Web site represents an exciting new study tool that uses the latest in multimedia to review, enrich, and expand upon key concepts presented in its companion textbook.

Using chapter highlights as its organizing structure, the Interactive Companion helps you apply what you've learned by presenting you with hundreds of links to audio and video clips, Web sites, activities, and practice tests. These links are annotated with brief descriptions that help you understand the value and purpose of each type of media in the context of the chapter.

Everything you need is right here at your fingertips!

ACTIVATE YOUR PIN.

How will you benefit from using the Interactive Companion Web site?

✓ **Provides you with frequent feedback on your learning progress to perform better on tests.**

✓ **Offers highly interactive ways for you to engage with the textbook content.**

✓ **Adds variety to course materials and helps you study more effectively.**

✓ **Helps you to think critically about the information presented to you in the textbook and on the Web site.**

✓ **Gives you access to the latest information related to the textbook topics via the Web.**

"*A major advantage of the Web site is that it allows students to connect with a wealth of learning support any time and any place. Professors can create a vast array of assignments and projects, knowing that all students — those in dorms and those commuting from home miles away, those with easy access to libraries and those who are more isolated — have the resources to complete the assignments and projects.*"

Anita Woolfolk
Educational Psychology Professor
The Ohio State University

your fellow students are saying the online materials for Henslin:

This Web site is one of the best I have ever worked with, and it has helped me succeed in my Sociology class here at my school. Thank you for such a wonderful source of learning!
Megan, age 20

Thanks for the study guide and practice tests. They both helped me prepare for my lecture exams. I look forward to my final exam, knowing that I've prepared using your site.
Bill, age 34

I think that this site is a great addition to the textbook. It helps me prepare for my exams and discussions in class. It is a different way of learning the material, and everything is outlined in such a way that things are very easy to find.
Mary, age 20

The interactive Web site for this book is a terrific achievement. **I got one of two A's in my class because I prepared for the test using this Web site.**
Brent, age 18

We formed a study group in our class, **virtually everyone uses the Web site,** and everyone is receiving good grades. Keep up the good work!!
Fatima, age 28

Everything you need is right here at your fingertips!

ACTIVATE YOUR PIN.

Easy navigation that lets you study the way you want!

1. Each chapter begins with an attention-grabbing opener. **Click on the associated audio icon and you'll hear questions or issues framed around the chapter opener;** this allows you to hear as well as read about new concepts.

2. **Chapter learning objectives are linked to the various topic areas,** allowing you to go directly from what you need to learn in the chapter to the media assets that will help you learn this new information.

3. **Each topic area ends with an activity** that is a review of key terms. These are created as flash card exercises — allowing you to reinforce the information that you've learned from that section of the book.

4. **Every chapter ends with three items:**

   a. **Concept Check Activity** which asks you to match terms and concepts in the chapter with their definitions.

   b. **"Closing Thoughts"** in which you revisit the opening scenario and consider the situation in light of what you've learned in the chapter.

   c. **Practice Test,** which promotes self-regulation and self-monitoring, two key elements of successful learning.

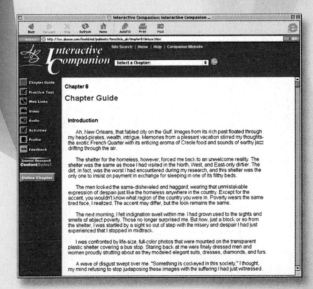

Additional chapter offered to you exclusively online!

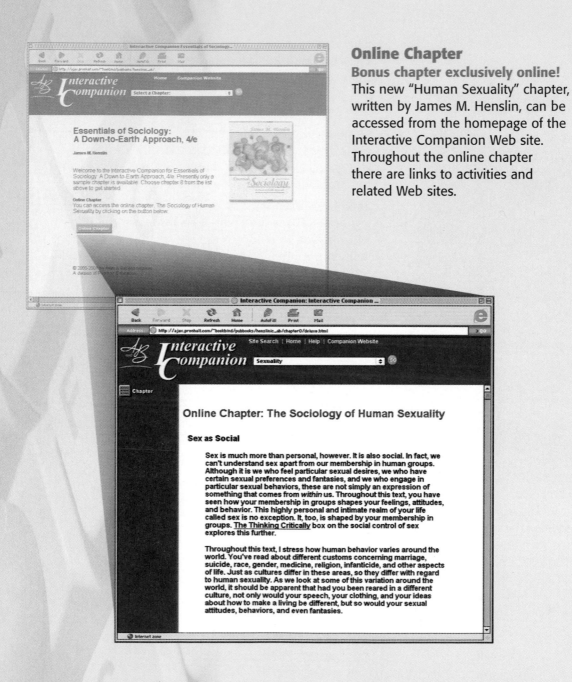

Online Chapter

Bonus chapter exclusively online!

This new "Human Sexuality" chapter, written by James M. Henslin, can be accessed from the homepage of the Interactive Companion Web site. Throughout the online chapter there are links to activities and related Web sites.

Everything you need is right here at your fingertips!

ACTIVATE YOUR PIN.

Interactive ways to prepare for that in-class exam and research paper!

Practice Test

Click on a **"Practice Test"** icon and you'll be able to test your understanding of the chapter material by completing a self-scoring practice test. You'll receive immediate results and feedback from your test, allowing you to review your weak areas in preparation for the actual in-class exam.

> " I think it's great. You can take practice tests so that when you really get tested, you already know what to expect. I think it really contributes to your learning. "
> **Gloria, age 27**

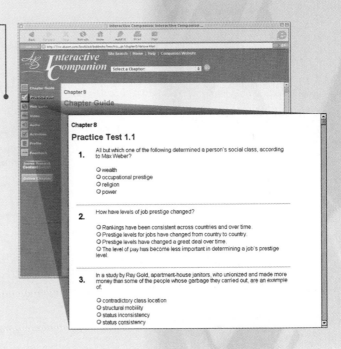

Web links

With the benefit of an Internet connection, by clicking on the **"Web links"** icon you'll jump to current Web sites that provide you with additional information about the specific topics you're studying. Web links are continuously monitored and updated by Allyn & Bacon, so you'll always have the most current sites to access. This is a great resource for you to utilize when writing a research paper!

> " These Web links help me find quality internet resources for the types of assignments required for class. "
> **Debra, age 22**

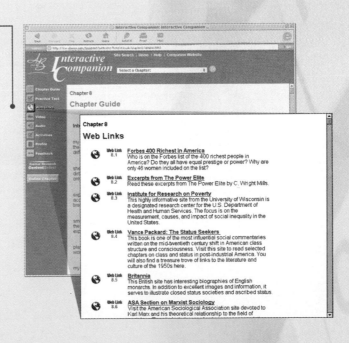

Information comes alive when you see it and hear it!

Video

Click on a **"Video"** icon and you'll be captivated by the **sights and sounds of video segments directly related to the material you just read.** These compelling video segments come from leading television news sources.

> *The audio, feedback, and videos help me understand each chapter.*
> **Janel, age 40**

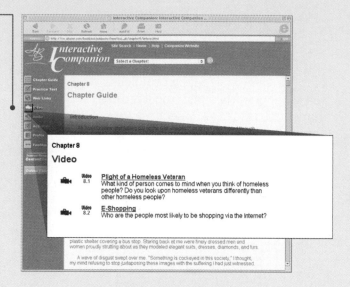

Audio

Click on an **"Audio"** icon and you'll hear either the author of the textbook or a specialist in the field speaking directly about concepts in the book. Often **the "voice" will add background information or give examples –** material that enhances and extends the chapter material.

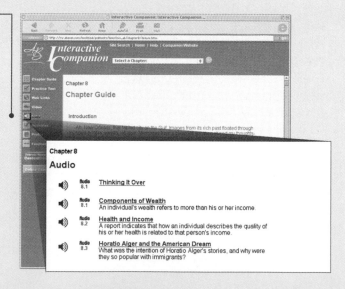

Everything you need is right here at your fingertips!

ACTIVATE YOUR PIN.

Activities give you more opportunities to test your level of understanding!

Activities

Click on an **"Activities"** icon and you can complete interesting activities directly related to the information presented in the textbook. **You'll be asked to research, discuss, think critically, and more!**

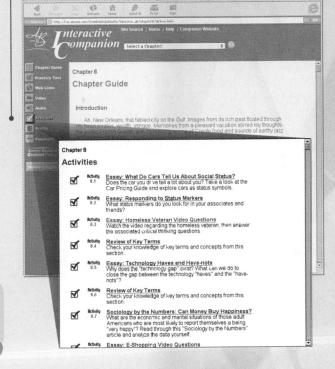

> *I enjoyed using the Web site! The matching games and the vocabulary terms helped me the most.*
> **Andy, age 18**

Profile

By entering your profile on the site, you can avoid retyping it every time you need to submit homework. Once saved, the information will appear automatically whenever it's required.

Feedback

We are always looking to improve and expand upon the information and technology we offer you. If you have any suggestions, questions or technical difficulties, please contact us through the feedback feature on the site.

More online resources to help you get a better grade!

ContentSelect for Sociology

The task of writing a research paper just got much less daunting! NEW from Allyn & Bacon — customized discipline-specific online research collections. Each database contains 25,000+ articles, which include content from over 100 leading peer-reviewed sociology journals plus selected news magazines. Sophisticated keyword search coupled with a simple and easy-to-use interface will give you a competitive course advantage by providing you with a relevant and flexible research tool. You no longer have to spend hours culling through irrelevant results from other less sophisticated databases! This incredible research tool is FREE for the entire year, and can be accessed from the password-protected Web site available with this book. Visit **www.ablongman.com/techsolutions** for more details.

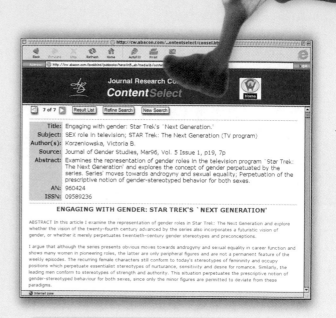

This powerful research tool will cut down on the amount of time you spend finding relevant information for your research papers.

Everything you need is right here at your fingertips!

ACTIVATE YOUR PIN.

ESSENTIALS OF

Sociology

A DOWN-TO-EARTH APPROACH

FOURTH EDITION

James M. Henslin

Southern Illinois University, Edwardsville

Allyn and Bacon
Boston ▪ *London* ▪ *Toronto* ▪ *Sydney* ▪ *Tokyo* ▪ *Singapore*

Editor-in-Chief, Social Sciences: Karen Hanson
Series Editor: Jeff Lasser
Editorial Assistant: Andrea Christie
Marketing Manager: Judeth Hall
Signing Representative: Ward Moore
Cover Administrator: Linda Knowles
Composition and Prepress Buyer: Linda Cox
Manufacturing Buyer: Megan Cochran
Photo Researcher: Myrna Engler
Fine Art Researcher: Laurie Frankenthaler
Editorial-Production Service: The Book Company
Text and Cover Designer: Carol Somberg, Delgado Design, Inc.
Page Layout: Omegatype Typography, Inc.
Copyeditor: Kathy Smith

Library of Congress Cataloging-in-Publication Data

Henslin, James M.
  Essentials of sociology : a down-to-earth approach / James M. Henslin. – 4th ed.
    p. cm.
  Includes bibliographical references and index.
  ISBN 0-205-33713-9
  1. Sociology.   I. Title.

HM586 .H43 2002
301–dc21

2001018894

Chapter Opener Art Credits

Chapter 1: *Second Circle Dance* by Phoebe Beasley, 1987. Collage, 36" × 36". © Phoebe Beasley/Omni-Photo Communications.

Chapter 2: *Robed Journey of the Rainbow Clan* by Helen Hardin, 1976. Acrylic. © Helen Hardin 1976. Photo © Cradoc Bagshaw 2002.

Chapter 3: *Making Mud Pies* by Diane Davis, 2000. Watercolor, 8" × 11". © Diane Davis/Omni-Photo Communications.

Chapter 4: *Congregating People* by Bernard Bonhomme, 1997. Digital image. © Bernard Bonhomme/SIS.

Chapter 5: *Les Flaneurs* by Jean-Pierre Stora, 1995. Oil on canvas, 61" × 50". © The Grand Design/SuperStock.

Chapter 6: *Prison* by Alan E. Cober. © Alan E. Cober/SIS.

Chapter 7: *Tea Pickers* by Senaka Sennayake, 20th century. Oil on canvas. © SuperStock.

Chapter 8: *Beg* by Graham Dean, 1991. Colored dyes, 71 cm. × 53 cm. © Graham Dean/CORBIS.

Chapter 9: *Watts 1963* by Kerry James Marshall, 1995. Acrylic collage on canvas, 114 × 135 inches. Collection of the St. Louis Museum of Art. Courtesy of Jack Shainman Gallery, New York City.

Art and photo credits continue on page PC-1, which is a continuation of this copyright page.

To my son, Paul,
who is inheriting a world not of his making.
May his contributions to it be of value to those who follow.

Brief Contents

Contents

PART I The Sociological Perspective

PART II Social Groups and Social Control

5 SOCIAL GROUPS AND FORMAL ORGANIZATIONS 104

6 DEVIANCE AND SOCIAL CONTROL 128

PART III Social Inequality

7 SOCIAL STRATIFICATION IN GLOBAL PERSPECTIVE   152

PART IV Social Institutions

12 MARRIAGE AND FAMILY 300

13 EDUCATION AND RELIGION 328

PART V Social Change

Boxed Features

Thinking Critically

Sociology and the New Technology

Guide to Social Maps

To the Student from the Author

Welcome to sociology! I've loved sociology since I was in my teens, and I hope you enjoy it, too. Sociology is fascinating because it holds the key to so much understanding of social life.

If you like to watch people and try to figure out why they do what they do, you will like sociology. Sociology pries open the doors of society so you can see what goes on behind them. *Essentials of Sociology: A Down-to-Earth Approach* stresses how profoundly our society and the groups to which we belong influence us. Social class, for example, sets us on a path in life. For some, the path leads to better health, more education, and higher income, but for others it leads to poverty, dropping out of school, and even a higher risk of illness and disease. These paths are so significant that they affect our chances of making it to our first birthday, as well as of getting in trouble with the police. They even influence how our marriage will work out, the number of children we will have—and whether or not we will read this book in the first place.

When I took my first course in sociology, I was "hooked." Seeing how marvelously my life had been affected by these larger social influences opened my eyes to a new world, one that has been fascinating to explore. I hope that this will be your experience also.

From how people become homeless to how they become presidents, from why people commit suicide to why women are discriminated against in every society around the world—all are part of sociology. This breadth, in fact, is what makes sociology so intriguing. We can place the sociological lens on broad features of society, such as social class, gender, and race-ethnicity, and then immediately turn our focus on the small-scale level. If we look at two people interacting—whether quarreling or kissing—we see how these broad features of society are being played out in their lives.

We aren't born with instincts. Nor do we come into this world with preconceived notions of what life should be like. At birth, we have no ideas of race-ethnicity, gender, age, or social class. We have no idea, for example, that people "ought" to act in certain ways because they are male or female. Yet we all learn such things as we grow up in our society. Uncovering the "hows" and the "whys" of this process is also part of sociology's fascination.

One of sociology's many pleasures is that as we study life in groups (which can be taken as a definition of sociology), whether those groups be in some far-off part of the world or in some nearby corner of our own society, we constantly gain insights into our own selves. As we see how *their* customs affect *them,* effects of our own society on us become more visible.

This book, then, can be part of an intellectual adventure, for it can lead you to a new way of looking at your social world—and in the process, help you to better understand both society and yourself.

I wish you the very best in college—and in your career afterward. It is my sincere hope that *Essentials of Sociology: A Down-to-Earth Approach* will contribute to that success.

James M. Henslin, Professor Emeritus
Department of Sociology
Southern Illinois University, Edwardsville

P.S. I enjoy communicating with students, so feel free to comment on your experiences with this text. Because I travel a lot, it is best to reach me by e-mail: henslin@aol.com

Also, you may want to look at the Website for this text: www.ablongman.com/henslin

To the Instructor from the Author

Remember when you first got "hooked" on sociology, how the windows of perception opened as you began to see life-in-society through the sociological perspective? For most of us, this was an eye-opening experience. This text is designed to open those windows onto social life, so students can see clearly the vital effects of group membership on their lives. Although few students will get into what Peter Berger calls "the passion of sociology," we at least can provide them the opportunity.

Sociology is like a huge jigsaw puzzle. Only very gradually do the intricate pieces start to fit together. As they do so, our perspective changes as we shift our eyes from the many small, disjointed pieces onto the whole that is being formed. Although this analogy is imperfect, it indicates a fascinating process of sociological discovery. Of all the endeavors we could have entered, we chose sociology because of the ways in which it joins together the "pieces" of society and the challenges it poses to "ordinary" thinking. To share the sociological perspective with students is our privilege.

As instructors of sociology, we have set formidable tasks for ourselves—to teach both social structure and social interaction, and to introduce students to the main sociological literature, to both the classic theorists and contemporary research. And we would like to accomplish this in ways that enliven the classroom, encourage critical thinking, and stimulate our students' sociological imagination. Although formidable, these goals are attainable. This book, based on many years of frontline (classroom) experience, is designed to help you reach these goals. Its subtitle, *A Down-to-Earth Approach,* is not proposed lightly. My goal is to share the fascination of sociology with students, and thereby make your teaching more rewarding.

Over the years, I have found the introductory course especially enjoyable. It is singularly satisfying to see students' faces light up as they begin to see how separate pieces of their world fit together. It is a pleasure to watch them gain insight into how their social experiences give shape to even their innermost desires. This is precisely what this text is designed to do—to stimulate your students' sociological imagination so they can better perceive how the "pieces" of society fit together—and what this means for their own lives.

Filled with examples from around the world as well as from our own society, this text helps make today's multicultural, global society come alive for the student. From the international elite carving up global markets to the intimacy of friendship and marriage, the student can see how sociology is the key to explaining contemporary life—and his or her own place in it.

In short, this text is designed to make your teaching easier. There simply is no justification for students to have to wade through cumbersome approaches to sociology. I am firmly convinced that the introduction to sociology should be enjoyable, and that the introductory textbook can be an essential tool in sharing the discovery of sociology with students.

THE ORGANIZATION OF THIS TEXT

The text is laid out in five parts. Part I focuses on the sociological perspective, which we introduce in the first chapter. We then look at how culture influences us in Chapter 2, examine socialization in Chapter 3, and compare macrosociology and microsociology in Chapter 4.

Part II, which focuses on groups and social control, adds to the students' understanding of how significantly social groups influence our lives. In Chapter 5, as we examine the different types of groups, we also look at the fascinating area of group dynamics. Then, in Chapter 6, we focus on how groups "keep us in line" and sanction those who violate their norms.

In Part III, we examine how social inequality pervades society and how those inequalities have an impact on our lives. Because social stratification is so significant, I have written two chapters on this topic. The first (Chapter 7), with its global focus, presents an overview of the principles of stratification. The second (Chapter 8), with its emphasis on variations in social class, focuses on stratification in U.S. society. After establishing this broader context, in Chapter 9 we examine inequalities of race and ethnicity, and in Chapter 10 those of gender and age.

Part IV makes students more aware of how social institutions encompass their lives. In Chapter 11, we look at how the economy and politics are our overarching social institutions. In Chapter 12, we examine the family, and in Chapter 13 we turn our focus on education and religion. Throughout, we look at how these social institutions are changing, and how their changes, in turn, influence our orientations and decisions.

With its focus on broad social change, Part V provides an appropriate conclusion for the book. Here we examine why our world is changing so rapidly, as well as catch a glimpse of what is yet to come. In Chapter 14, we analyze trends in population and urbanization, sweeping forces in our lives that ordinarily remain below our level of awareness. Our focus on technology, social movements, and the environment in Chapter 15 then takes us to the "cutting edge" of vital changes that engulf us all.

*T*HEMES AND FEATURES

Six central themes run throughout the text: globalization, cultural diversity, down-to-earth sociology, critical thinking, sociology and the new technology, and the theme new to this edition—the growing influence of the mass media on our lives. Let's look at these six themes.

Globalization

The first theme, globalization, explores the impact of global issues. The new global economy, for example, which has intertwined the fates of nations, vitally affects our lives. The globalization of capitalism influences the kinds of skills and knowledge we need, types of work available to us, costs of the goods and services we consume, and even whether our country is at war or peace. In addition to the strong emphasis on global issues that runs throughout this text, I have written a separate chapter on global stratification. I have also featured global issues in the chapters on social institutions and the final chapters on social change: technology, population, urbanization, social movements, and the environment.

What occurs in Russia, Japan, and China, as well as in much smaller nations such as the various parts of the former Yugoslavia, has direct and far-reaching

consequences on our own lives. Consequently, in addition to this global focus that runs throughout the text, the second theme, Cultural Diversity, also has a strong global emphasis.

Cultural Diversity in the United States and Around the World

The second theme, cultural diversity, has two primary emphases. The first is cultural diversity around the world. Gaining an understanding of how social life is "done" in other parts of the world often challenges our taken-for-granted assumptions of social life. At times, learning about other cultures gives us an appreciation for the life of other peoples; at other times, we may be shocked at some aspect of another group's way of life (such as female circumcision) and come away with a renewed appreciation of our own customs.

To highlight this sub-theme, I have written a series of boxes on worldwide diversity. The boxed features, here and throughout the text, are one of my favorite features of the book. They are especially valuable for introducing the provocative and controversial materials that make sociology such a lively activity. Among the boxed features that stress this sub-theme of cultural diversity around the world are an examination of human sexuality in Mexico and Kenya (Chapter 6), selling brides in China (Chapter 10), female circumcision in Africa (Chapter 10), love and arranged marriage in India (Chapter 12), infanticide in China (Chapter 14), and the destruction of the rain forests and indigenous people in Brazil (Chapter 15).

The second emphasis is cultural diversity in the United States. In this sub-theme, we examine groups that make up the fascinating array of people who compose the United States. Among the boxes I have written with this sub-theme are the significance of language— Spanish and English in Miami, and the terms people choose for their own racial-ethnic self-identification (both in Chapter 2), the resistance of social change by the Amish (Chapter 4), how Tiger Woods represents a significant change in racial-ethnic identification (Chapter 9), Islam as the new religious neighbor (Chapter 13), our shifting racial-ethnic mix (Chapter 14), and the Million Man March (Chapter 15).

Looking at cultural diversity—whether it be in the United States or in other regions of the world—often challenges our own orientations to life. To see that there are so many varieties of "doing" social life is to highlight the arbitrariness of our own customs—and our customary ways of thinking. These contrasts help students develop their sociological imagination. They are better able to see connections among key sociological concepts such as culture, socialization, norms, race-ethnicity, gender, and social class. As your students' sociological imagination grows, they can attain a new perspective on their own experiences—and a better understanding of the social structure of U.S. society.

Down-to-Earth Sociology

As many years of teaching have shown me, all too often textbooks are written to appeal to the adopters of texts rather than to the students who must learn from them. Thus, a central concern in writing this book has been to present sociology in a way that not only facilitates understanding but also shares its excitement. During the course of writing other texts, I often have been told that my explanations and writing style are "down-to-earth," or accessible and inviting to students—so much so that I have used this phrase as the book's subtitle. The term is also featured in my introductory reader, *Down to Earth Sociology*, 11th edition (New York: Free Press, 2001).

This third theme is highlighted by a series of boxed features that explore sociological processes that underlie everyday life. In these Down-to-Earth sociology boxes, we consider such issues as improper and fraudulent social research (Chapter 1), "written gestures" ("emoticons") being used in e-mail (Chapter 2), the relationship between heredity and environment (Chapter 3), how sports shape male identity in such a way that it makes intimate relationships difficult for men (Chapter 3), how the United States is being "McDonaldized" (Chapter 5), lifestyles of the super-rich (Chapter 8), how voice is used to practice racial discrimination in the rental market (Chapter 9), Louisiana's controversial covenant marriage (Chapter 12), the gentrification of Harlem (Chapter 14), and corporate welfare (Chapter 15).

This third theme is actually a hallmark of the text, as my goal is to make sociology "down to earth." To help students grasp the fascination of sociology, I continuously stress sociology's relevance to their lives. To reinforce this theme, I avoid unnecessary jargon and use concise explanations and clear and simple (but not reductive) language. I often use student-relevant examples to illustrate key concepts, and I have based several of the chapters' opening vignettes on my own experiences in exploring social life. That this goal of sharing sociology's fascination is being reached is evident from the many comments I receive from instructors and students alike that the text helps make sociology "come alive."

Critical Thinking

The fourth theme, critical thinking, focuses on controversial social issues and engages students in examining the various sides of those issues. These sections, titled "Thinking Critically," can enliven your classroom with a vibrant exchange of ideas. Among the issues addressed are our tendency to conform to evil authority, as uncovered by the Milgram experiments (Chapter 5); bounties paid to kill homeless children in Brazil (Chapter 7); social class inequality in the treatment of mental and physical illness (Chapter 8); racial segregation (by choice) on college campuses (Chapter 8); a consideration of quality of life and our potential to increase our life span (Chapter 10); and abortion as a social movement (Chapter 15).

Because these Thinking Critically sections are based on controversial social issues that either affect the student's own life or are something that he or she is vitally interested in, they stimulate critical thinking and lively class discussion. They also lend themselves especially well to debates and small-group discussion. For a full listing of this feature, see p. xv.

Sociology and the New Technology

The fifth theme, sociology and the new technology, investigates an aspect of social life that has come to be central to our existence. We welcome these new tools, for they help us to be more efficient at doing our tasks, from making a living to communicating with people on the other side of the globe. The significance of the new technology goes far beyond the tools and the ease and efficiency they bring to our tasks, however. The new technology also penetrates our being—it shapes our thinking, leading to changed ways of viewing life. We are in the midst of a social revolution that will leave few aspects of our lives untouched.

This theme is introduced in Chapter 2, where technology is defined and presented as a major aspect of culture. It is then discussed throughout the text. Examples include the implications of technology for maintaining global stratification (Chapter 7); how the consequences of technology differ by social class (Chapter 8); how technology outpaces norms (Chapter 10); how technology led to social inequality in early human history and how it now may lead to world peace—and to Big Brother

(Chapter 11). The final chapter (15), "Technology, Social Change, and the Environment," concludes the book with a focus on this theme.

To highlight this theme, I have written a series of boxes on how technology is changing society and affecting our lives. Among these are the potential of computers to replace the human species (Chapter 2), how for some people virtual friendship is replacing their flesh-and-blood friends (Chapter 4), the appearance of a new group, electronic communities (Chapter 5), cyberslacking and cybersleuthing (Chapter 5), the digital divide (Chapter 8), how technology is restructuring work (Chapter 11), and unusual reproduction (Chapter 12).

The Mass Media and Social Life

New to this edition is a sixth theme, how the mass media influence social life. In this theme, we stress how the media affect our behavior and permeate our thinking. We consider how they even penetrate our consciousness to such a degree that they have an impact on how we perceive our own bodies. As your students consider this theme, they should begin to see the mass media in a different light, which should further stimulate their sociological imagination.

In addition to this theme running through the text, I have also written a series of boxed features to make it more prominent for students. Among these are an analysis of why Native Americans like Western novels and movies even though Indians are usually portrayed as victims (Chapter 2), the influence of computer games on images of gender (Chapter 3), the worship of thinness—and how this affects our own body images (Chapter 4), the issue of censoring high-tech pornography (Chapter 6), slavery in today's world (Chapter 7), preaching hatred and online censorship (Chapter 9), finding pleasure in the pain of others (Chapter 10), stimulating greed to stimulate the economy (Chapter 11), and God on the Net (Chapter 13).

On Sources and Terms

Sociological data are found in an amazingly wide variety of sources, and this text reflects that variety. Cited throughout this text are standard journals such as the *American Journal of Sociology*, *Social Problems*, and *Journal of Marriage and the Family*, as well as more esoteric journals such as the *Bulletin of the History of Medicine*, *Chronobiology International*, and *Western Journal of Black Studies*. I also have drawn heavily from standard news sources, especially the *New York Times* and *Wall Street Journal*, as well as more unusual sources such as *El País*. In addition, I cite unpublished papers by sociologists.

Finally, a note on terms. Although still in use, the terms First World, Second World, and Third World are severely problematic. Even though unintentional, to say First World inevitably connotes superiority of some sort—a sort of coming in first place, with other nations following in lesser, inferior positions. To substitute the terms Most Developed Countries, Less Developed Countries, and Least Developed Countries carries the same ethnocentric burden. These terms indicate that our economic state is superior: *We* are "developed," but *they* are not. To overcome this problem, I use neutrally descriptive terms: the Most Industrialized Nations, the Industrializing Nations, and the Least Industrialized Nations. These terms do not carry an ethnocentric value burden, for they indicate only that a nation's amount of industrialization is measurable and relative, without a connotation that industrialization is desirable.

Supplements for the Instructor

Instructor's Manual. For each chapter in the text, the Instructor's Manual provides: a "chapter-at-a-glance" grid that coordinates use of other supplements; a chapter summary; learning objectives; a lecture outline; a list of what's new in the Fourth Edition; key terms with page references; classroom discussion topics and activities; and suggestions for guest lecturers.

Test Banks. The test banks contain several thousand questions in multiple choice, true-false, short answer, and essay formats. Many of the multiple choice questions test the students' ability to apply what they've learned to new situations.

Computerized Testing. Allyn and Bacon Test Manager is an integrated suite of testing and assessment tools for Windows and Macintosh. You can use Test Manager to create professional-looking exams in just minutes by selecting questions from the database, editing questions, or by writing your own questions. Course management features include a class roster, gradebook, and item analysis. Test Manager also has everything you need to create and administer online tests.

Call-In Testing. Allyn and Bacon can create tests for you and have a finished, ready-to-duplicate test on its way to you by mail or fax within 48 hours.

Allyn and Bacon Interactive Video for Introductory Sociology, and Video User's Guide. This custom video features television news footage on both national and global topics. The up-to-the-minute video segments are great to launch lectures, spark classroom discussion, and encourage critical thinking. A user's guide provides detailed descriptions of each video segment, specific tie-ins to the text, and suggested discussion questions and projects.

Allyn and Bacon Transparencies for Introductory Sociology. This package includes over 100 color acetates featuring illustrations both from the text and from other sources.

PowerPoint Presentation. A PowerPoint presentation created for this text provides hundreds of ready-to-use graphic and text images. The presentation is available on a cross-platform CD-ROM. PowerPoint software is not required to use this program; a PowerPoint viewer is included to access the images.

Digital Media Archive for Sociology. This CD-ROM for Windows and Macintosh contains media elements that you can use to create electronic presentations in the classroom. It includes hundreds of original images, as well as selected art from Henslin's texts and other Allyn and Bacon sociology texts. It gives you a broad selection of graphs, charts, and maps that illustrate key sociological concepts. For classrooms with full multimedia capability, it also contains video segments and links to sociology Web sites.

Learning by Doing Sociology: In-Class Experiential Exercises (Linda Stoneall). This manual offers step-by-step procedures for in-class activities, contains suggestions for managing experiential learning, and provides trouble-shooting tips. It contains twenty-two exercises on a broad range of topics typically covered in the introductory sociology course.

The Blockbuster Approach: A Guide to Teaching Sociology with Video (Casey Jordan, Western Connecticut State University). This manual describes hundreds of commercially available videos that can help you present sociological ideas and themes, and provides sample assignments.

Doing Sociology with Student CHIP: Data Happy!, Third Edition (Gregg Lee Carter, Bryant College). The exercises in this workbook, which explore major sub-fields of sociology, provide students the opportunity to use real data to explore sociological questions.

A&B Video Library. Qualified adopters may select from a wide variety of high quality videos from such sources as Films for the Humanities and Sciences and Annenberg/CPB.

Online Distributed Learning Options. For your on- or off-campus distributed learning courses, this text is available in special packages that provide the course management features of popular commercial platforms, combined with additional teaching and learning resources that complement the book. Choose from three types of courses: WebCT, Blackboard, and Course-Compass, our own nationally hosted system.

Supplements for Students

Study Guide Plus. This manual provides learning objectives, key terms, self-tests, and glossaries. Students who need special language assistance will find a glossary to help them learn idioms and colloquialisms.

Practice Tests. This manual of self-tests with answer justifications helps students prepare for quizzes and exams.

Allyn and Bacon Quick Guide to the Internet for Sociology. This reference guide, updated annually, introduces students to the basics of the Internet and the World Wide Web. It lists hundreds of URLs for sites that are useful for the study of sociology.

The Essential Sociology Reader (Robert Thompson, Minot State University). This brief anthology consists of sixteen original sociological articles.

Careers in Sociology, Second Edition (W. Richard Stephens, Greenville College). This supplement examines how people who are working as sociologists entered the field, and how a degree in sociology can be a preparation for careers in such areas as law, gerontology, social work, and computer specialties.

About the Website for This Edition

Students who visit the Companion Website that accompanies the Fourth Edition (www.ablongman.com/henslin) will find an online study guide that has practice tests, learning objectives, and links to useful sociology sites on the Internet. But that's just the beginning. Using a PIN code that is distributed with the text, students can log onto their own Interactive Companion, an area of premium content that complements their textbook and will enrich their study of sociology. In addition to hundreds of additional online learning activities, the Interactive Companion contains a brand new chapter, "The Sociology of Human Sexuality," written by text author Jim Henslin. It also gives students access to ContentSelect, a searchable database of thousands of articles in leading sociology journals. Adopters of the Fourth Edition will receive the Interactive Companion Teaching Tool, a printed guide to the Website, with suggestions for integrating it into the classroom. This Website will continue to grow, with new features and information being added regularly.

ACKNOWLEDGMENTS

The gratifying response to the third edition indicates that my efforts at making sociology down to earth have succeeded. The years that have gone into writing this text are a culmination of the many more years that preceded its writing—from graduate school to that equally demanding endeavor known as classroom teaching. No text, of course, comes solely from its author. Although I am responsible for the final words on the printed page, I have depended heavily on feedback from instructors who used the first three editions. I am especially grateful to

Sandra L. Albrecht *The University of Kansas*
Kenneth Ambrose *Marshall University*
Alberto Arroyo *Baldwin-Wallace College*
Karren Baird-Olsen *Kansas State University*
Linda Barbera-Stein *The University of Illinois*
Richard D. Clark *John Carroll University*
John K. Cochran *The University of Oklahoma*
Russell L. Curtis *University of Houston*
John Darling *University of Pittsburgh—Johnstown*
Ray Darville *Stephen F. Austin State University*
Nanette J. Davis *Portland State University*
Paul Devereux *University of Nevada*
Lynda Dodgen *North Harris Community College*
James W. Dorsey *College of Lake County*
Helen R. Ebaugh *University of Houston*
Obi N. Ebbe *State University of New York—Brockport*
Margaret C. Figgins-Hill *University of Massachusetts—Lowell*
David O. Friedrichs *University of Scranton*
Richard A. Garnett *Marshall University*

Norman Goodman *State University of New York—Stony Brook*
Anne S. Graham *Salt Lake Community College*
Donald W. Hastings *The University of Tennessee—Knoxville*
Michael Hoover *Missouri Western State College*
Charles E. Hurst *The College of Wooster*
Mark Kassop *Bergen Community College*
Alice Abel Kemp *University of New Orleans*
Dianna Kendall *Austin Community College*
Ross Koppel *University of Pennsylvania*
Gary Kiger *Utah State University*
Patricia A. Larson *Cleveland State University*
Abraham Levine *El Camino Community College*
John J. Malarky *Wilmington College*
Ron Matson *Wichita State University*
Armaund L. Mauss *Washington State University*
Evelyn Mercer *Southwest Baptist University*
Robert Meyer *Arkansas State University*
Beth Mintz *University of Vermont—Burlington*
Craig J. Nauman *Madison Area Technical College*
W. Lawrence Neuman *University of Wisconsin—Whitewater*
Charles Norman *Indiana State University*
Laura O'Toole *University of Delaware*
William Patterson *Clemson University*
Phil Piket *Joliet Junior College*
Adrian Rapp *North Harris Community College*
Howard Robboy *Trenton State College*
Walt Shirley *Sinclair Community College*
Marc Silver *Hofstra University*
Michael C. Smith *Milwaukee Area Technical College*
Roberto E. Socas *Essex County College*
Susan Sprecher *Illinois State University*
Randolph G. Ston *Oakland Community College*
Kathleen Tiemann *University of North Dakota*
Larry Weiss *University of Alaska*
Douglas White *Henry Ford Community College*
Stephen R. Wilson *Temple University*
Stuart Wright *Lamar University*
Meifang Zhang *Midlands Technical College*

I also wish to thank the reviewers of this edition:

William Danaher *College of Charleston*
Laura Siebuhr *Centralia College*
Lisa Waldner *University of Houston-Downtown*
Patricia Masters *George Mason*
Dick Jobst *Pacific Lutheran University*
Kent Sandstrom *University of Northern Iowa*

David Kyle *University of California-Davis*
Mike Lindner *Gloucester County College*
Annette Prosterman *Our Lady of the Lake
    University*
Tom DeDen *Foothill College*
Cecile Lycan *Spokane Community College*
Bonita Sessing Matcha *Hudson Valley Community
    College*
Tracy Tolbert *California State University*

I am also indebted to the fine staff of Allyn and Bacon. I wish to thank Karen Hanson, who saw the initial merits of this project and has given it strong support; Jeff Lasser, who is making his impact with the development of supplemental online sites; Hannah Rubenstein, who made vital contributions to earlier editions of the text on which this one is based; Judy Fiske for constantly hovering over detail after detail—and supporting my many suggestions; Kathy Smith for copy editing; Myrna Engler for photo research; and, finally, but far from least, Dusty Friedman, who always does such a capable job of overseeing both the routine and the urgent. I have tried their patience at times, I know, but somehow we work together beautifully as a team. The students are the bene-ficiaries of our combined efforts, whom we constantly kept in mind as we prepared this edition.

Since this text is based on the contributions of many, I would count it a privilege if you also would share with me your teaching experiences with this book, including any suggestions for improving the text. Both positive and negative comments are welcome. It is in this way that I learn.

I wish you the very best in your teaching. It is my sincere desire that *Essentials of Sociology: A Down-to-Earth Approach* contributes to that success.

Jim Henslin

James M. Henslin, Professor Emeritus
Department of Sociology
Southern Illinois University, Edwardsville

I welcome your correspondence. E-mail is the best way to reach me: henslin@aol.com

About the Author

James M. Henslin, who was born in Minnesota, graduated from high school and junior college in California and from college in Indiana. Awarded scholarships, he earned his Master's and doctorate degrees in sociology at Washington University in St. Louis, Missouri. After this, he was awarded a postdoctoral fellowship from the National Institute of Mental Health, and spent a year studying how people adjust to the suicide of a family member. His primary interests in sociology are the sociology of everyday life, deviance, and international relations. Among his more than a dozen books is *Down to Earth Sociology* (Free Press), now in its eleventh edition, a book of readings that reflects some of these sociological interests. He also has published widely in sociology journals, including *Social Problems* and *American Journal of Sociology*.

While a graduate student, James Henslin taught at the University of Missouri at St. Louis. After completing his doctorate, he joined the faculty at Southern Illinois University, Edwardsville, where he is Professor Emeritus of Sociology. He says, "I've always found the introductory course enjoyable to teach. I love to see students' faces light up when they first glimpse the sociological perspective and begin to see how society has become an essential part of how they view the world."

Henslin enjoys spending time with his wife, reading, and fishing. His two favorite activities are writing and traveling. He especially enjoys living in other cultures, for this brings him face to face with behaviors and ways of thinking that he cannot take for granted, experiences that "make sociological principles come alive."

Chapter 1

Phoebe Beasley, Second Circle Dance, 1987

The Sociological Perspective

Even from the glow of the faded red-and-white exit sign, its faint light barely illuminating the upper bunk, I could see that the sheet was filthy. Resigned to another night of fitful sleep, I reluctantly crawled into bed, tucking my clothes securely around my body like a protective cocoon.

The next morning, I joined the long line of disheveled men leaning against the chain-link fence. Their faces were as downcast as their clothes were dirty. Not a glimmer of hope among them.

No one spoke as the line slowly inched forward. When my turn came, I was handed a styrofoam cup of coffee, some utensils, and a bowl of semiliquid that I couldn't identify. It didn't look like any food I had seen before. Nor did it taste like anything I had ever eaten.

My stomach fought the foul taste, every spoonful a battle. But I was determined. "I will experience what they experience," I kept telling myself. My stomach reluctantly gave in and accepted its morning nourishment.

The room was eerily silent. Hundreds of men were eating, each immersed in his own private hell, his head awash with disappointment, remorse, bitterness.

As I stared at the styrofoam cup of coffee, grateful at least for this small pleasure, I noticed what looked like teeth marks. I shrugged off the thought, telling myself that my long weeks as a sociological observer of the homeless were finally getting to me. "That must be some sort of crease from handling," I concluded.

I joined the silent ranks of men turning in their bowls and cups. When I saw the man behind the counter swishing out styrofoam cups in a washtub of water, I began to feel sick to my stomach. I knew then that the jagged marks on my cup really had come from a previous mouth.

How much longer did this research have to last? I felt a deep longing to return to my family—to a welcome world of clean sheets, healthy food, and "normal" conversations. ■

*T*HE SOCIOLOGICAL PERSPECTIVE

Why were these men so silent? Why did they receive such despicable treatment? What was I doing in that homeless shelter? After all, I hold a respectable, secure, professional position, and I have a home and family.

Sociology offers a perspective, a view of the world. The *sociological perspective* (or imagination) opens a window onto unfamiliar worlds, and offers a fresh look at familiar worlds. In this text you will find yourself in the midst of Nazis in Germany, chimpanzees in Africa, and warriors in South America. But you also will find yourself looking at your own world in a different light. As you view other worlds, or your own, the sociological perspective enables you to gain a new vision of social life. In fact, this is what many find appealing about sociology.

The sociological perspective has been a motivating force in my own life. Ever since I took my first introductory course in sociology, I have been enchanted by the perspective that sociology offers. I have thoroughly enjoyed both observing other groups and questioning my own assumptions about life. I sincerely hope the same happens to you.

Seeing the Broader Social Context

The **sociological perspective** stresses the social contexts in which people live. It examines how these contexts influence people's lives. At the center of the sociological perspective is the question of how groups influence people, especially how people are influenced by their **society**—a group of people who share a culture and a territory.

To find out why people do what they do, sociologists look at **social location,** the corners in life that people occupy because of where they are located in a society. Sociologists look at jobs, income, education, gender, age, and race as significant. Consider, for example, how being identified with a group called *females* or with a group called *males* when we are growing up affects our ideas of who we are and what we should attain in life. Growing up as a male or a female influences not only our aspirations, but also how we feel about ourselves and how we relate to others in dating and marriage and at work.

Sociologist C. Wright Mills (1959) put it this way: "The sociological perspective enables us to grasp the connection between history and biography." By history, Mills meant that each society is located in a broad stream of events. Because of this, each society has specific characteristics—such as its ideas of the proper roles of men and women. By biography, Mills referred to the individual's specific experiences in society. In short, people don't do what they do because of inherited internal mechanisms, such as instincts. Rather, *external* influences—our experiences—become part of our thinking and motivations. The society in which we grow up, and our particular corners in that society, lie at the center of our behavior.

Consider a newborn baby. If we were to take the baby away from its U.S. parents and place it with a Yanomamo Indian tribe in the jungles of South America, you know that when the child begins to speak, his or her words will not be in English. You also know that the child will not think like an American. He or she will not grow up wanting credit cards, for example, or designer jeans, a new car, and the latest video game. Equally, the child will unquestioningly take his or her place in Yanomamo society—perhaps as a food gatherer, a hunter, or a warrior—and he or she will not even know about the world left behind at birth. And, whether male or female, the child will grow up assuming that it is natural to want many children, not debating whether to have one, two, or three children.

Examining the broad social context in which people live is essential to the *sociological perspective,* for this context shapes our beliefs and attitudes and sets guidelines for what we do. From this photo, you can see how distinctive those guidelines are for the Yanomamo Indians who live on the border of Brazil and Venezuela. How have these Yanomamo men been influenced by their group? How has your behavior been influenced by your groups?

This brings us to *you*—to how your social groups have shaped your ideas and desires. Over and over in this text you will see that the way you look at the world is the result of your exposure to certain groups. I think you will enjoy the process of self-discovery that sociology offers.

THE ORIGINS OF SOCIOLOGY

Tradition Versus Science

Just how did sociology begin? In some ways it is difficult to answer this question. Even ancient peoples tried to figure out social life. They, too, asked questions about why war exists, why some people become more powerful than others, and why some become rich. However, they often based their answers on superstition, myth, or even the position of the stars, and did not *test* their assumptions.

Science, in contrast, requires the development of theories that can be tested by systematic research. Measured by this standard, sociology only recently appeared on the human scene. It emerged about the middle of the nine-

teenth century, when social observers began to use scientific methods to test their ideas.

Sociology grew out of social upheaval. The Industrial Revolution had just begun, and masses of people were moving to cities in search of work. Their ties to the land—and to a culture that provided them with ready answers—were broken. The cities greeted them with horrible working conditions: low pay; long, exhausting hours; dangerous work. To survive, even children had to work in these conditions; some were even chained to factory machines to make certain they could not run away. Life no longer looked the same, and tradition, which had provided the answers to social life, no longer could be counted on.

Tradition was to suffer further blows. The success of the American and French revolutions encouraged people to rethink social life. New ideas arose, including the conviction that individuals possess inalienable rights. As this new idea caught fire, many traditional Western monarchies gave way to more democratic forms. People found the ready answers of tradition inadequate.

About this same time, the *scientific method*—using objective, systematic observations to test theories was being tried out in chemistry and physics. Many secrets that had been concealed in nature were uncovered. With tradition no longer providing the answers to questions about social life, the logical step was to apply the scientific method to these questions. The result was the birth of sociology.

Auguste Comte and Positivism

This idea of applying the scientific method to the social world, known as **positivism,** apparently was first proposed by Auguste Comte (1798–1857). With the French Revolution still fresh in his mind, Comte left the small, conservative town in which he had grown up and moved to Paris. The changes he experienced, combined with those France underwent in the revolution, led Comte to become interested in what holds society together. What creates social order, he wondered, instead of anarchy or chaos? And then, once society does become set on a particular course, what causes it to change?

As he considered these questions, Comte concluded that the right way to answer them was to apply the scientific method to social life. Just as this method had revealed the law of gravity, so, too, it would uncover the laws that underlie society. Comte called this new science **sociology,** "the study of society" (from the Greek *logos,* "study of," and the Latin *socius,* "companion," or "being with others"). Comte stressed that this new science not only would discover social principles but also would apply them to social reform. Sociologists would reform the entire society, making it a better place to live.

To Comte, however, applying the scientific method to social life meant practicing what we might call "armchair philosophy"—drawing conclusions from informal observations of social life. He did not do what today's sociologists would call research, and his conclusions have been abandoned. Nevertheless, Comte's insistence that we must observe and classify human activities in order to uncover society's fundamental laws is well taken. Because he developed this idea and coined the term *sociology,* Comte often is credited with being the founder of sociology.

Herbert Spencer and Social Darwinism

Herbert Spencer (1820–1903), who grew up in England, is sometimes called the second founder of sociology. Spencer disagreed profoundly with Comte that sociology should guide social reform. He was convinced that no one should intervene in the evolution of society. Spencer thought that societies evolve from lower ("barbarian") to higher ("civilized") forms. As generations pass, he said, the most capable and intelligent ("the fittest") members of the society survive, while the less capable die out. Thus,

This eighteenth-century painting (artist unknown) depicts women from Paris joining the French Army on its way to Versailles on October 5, 1789. The French Revolution of 1789 not only overthrew the aristocracy but upset the entire social order. With change so extensive, and the past no longer a sure guide to the present, Auguste Comte began to analyze how societies change, thus ushering in the science of sociology.

Auguste Comte (1798–1857), who is identified as the founder of sociology, began to analyze the bases of the social order. Although he stressed that the scientific method should be applied to the study of society, he did not apply it himself.

Karl Marx (1818–1883) believed that the roots of human misery lay in the exploitation of the proletariat, or propertyless working classes, by the capitalist class, those who own the means of production. Social change, in the form of the overthrow of the capitalists by the proletariat, was inevitable from Marx's perspective. Although Marx did not consider himself a sociologist, his ideas have profoundly influenced many in the discipline, particularly conflict theorists.

The French sociologist Emile Durkheim (1858–1917) contributed many important concepts to sociology. His systematic study comparing suicide rates among several countries revealed an underlying social factor: People are more likely to commit suicide if their ties to others in their communities are weak. Durkheim's identification of the key role of *social integration* in social life remains central to sociology today.

over time, societies improve. There is a steady march toward progress, and helping the lower classes interferes in this natural process. The fittest members will produce a more advanced society—unless misguided do-gooders get in the way and help the less fit survive.

Spencer called this principle "the survival of the fittest." Although Spencer coined this phrase, it usually is attributed to his contemporary, Charles Darwin, who proposed that organisms evolve over time as they adapt to their environment. Because they are so similar to Darwin's ideas, Spencer's view of the evolution of societies became known as *social Darwinism*.

Like Comte, Spencer was more of a social philosopher than a sociologist. Also like Comte, Spencer did not conduct scientific studies. He simply developed ideas about society. Eventually, after gaining a wide following in England and the United States, Spencer's ideas about social Darwinism were discredited.

Karl Marx and Class Conflict

The influence of Karl Marx (1818–1883) on world history has been so great that even the *Wall Street Journal*, that staunch advocate of capitalism, has called him one of the three greatest modern thinkers (the other two being Sigmund Freud and Albert Einstein).

Marx, who came to England after being exiled from his native Germany for proposing revolution, believed that the engine of human history is **class conflict.** He said that the *bourgeoisie* (the controlling class of *capitalists*, those who own the means to produce wealth—capital, land, factories, and machines) are locked in conflict with the *proletariat* (the exploited class, the mass of workers who do not own the means of production). This bitter struggle can end only when members of the working class unite in revolution and throw off their chains of bondage. The result will be a classless society, one free of exploitation, in which everyone will work according to their abilities and receive according to their needs (Marx and Engels 1848/1967).

Marxism is not the same as communism. Although Marx supported revolution as the only way that the workers could gain control of society, he did not develop the political system called *communism*. This is a later application of his ideas. Indeed, Marx himself felt disgusted when he heard debates about his insights into social life. After listening to some of the positions attributed to him, he shook his head and said, "I am not a Marxist" (Dobriner 1969b:222; Gitlin 1997:89).

Emile Durkheim and Social Integration

The primary professional goal of Emile Durkheim (1858–1917), who grew up in France, was to get sociology recognized as a separate academic discipline. Up to this time, sociology was viewed as part of history and economics. Durkheim achieved this goal when he received the first academic appointment in sociology, at the University of Bordeaux in 1887 (Coser 1977).

Durkheim had another goal: to show how social forces affect people's behavior. To accomplish this, he conducted rigorous research. Comparing the suicide rates of several European countries, Durkheim (1897/1966) found that each country's suicide rate was different and that each remained remarkably stable year after year. He also found that different groups within a country had different suicide rates and that these, too, remained stable from year to year. For example, Protestants, males, and the unmarried killed themselves at a higher rate than did Catholics, Jews, females, and the married. From this, Durkheim drew the insightful conclusion that suicide is not simply a matter of individuals here and there deciding to take their lives for personal reasons. Rather, *social factors underlie suicide,* and this is what keeps those rates fairly constant year after year.

Durkheim identified **social integration**, the degree to which people are tied to their social group, as a key social factor in suicide. He concluded that people with weaker social ties are more likely to commit suicide. This factor, he said, explained why Protestants, males, and the unmarried have higher suicide rates. It works this way, Durkheim argued: Protestantism encourages greater freedom of thought and action, males are more independent than females, and the unmarried lack the ties and responsibilities of marriage. In other words, because their social integration is weaker, members of these groups have fewer of the social ties that keep people from committing suicide.

A hundred years later, Durkheim's work is still quoted. His research was so thorough that the principle he uncovered still applies: People who are less socially integrated have higher rates of suicide. Even today, those same categories of people that Durkheim identified—Protestants, males, and the unmarried—are more likely to kill themselves.

From Durkheim's study of suicide, we see the principle that was central in his research: Human behavior cannot be understood simply in individualistic terms; we must always examine the social forces that affect people's lives. Suicide, for example, appears at first to be such an intensely individual act that psychologists should study it, not sociologists. Yet, as Durkheim illustrated, if we look at human behavior (such as suicide) only in individualistic terms, we miss its *social* basis.

Max Weber and the Protestant Ethic

Max Weber (Mahx VAY-ber) (1864–1920), a German sociologist and a contemporary of Durkheim, also held professorships in the new academic discipline of sociology. With Durkheim and Marx, Weber is one of the most influential of all sociologists, and you will come across his writings and theories in the coming chapters.

Let's take a brief look at one of those theories now. Weber disagreed with Marx's claim that economics is the central force in social change. That role, he said, belongs to religion. Weber (1904/1958) theorized that the Roman Catholic belief system encouraged Roman Catholics to hold onto traditional ways of life, while the Protestant belief system encouraged its members to embrace change. Protestantism, he said, undermined people's spiritual security. Roman Catholics believed that because they were church members they were on the road to heaven. Protestants, who did not share this belief, turned to outside "signs" that they were in God's will. Financial success became the major sign that God was on their side. Consequently, Protestants began to live

Max Weber (1864–1920) was another early sociologist who left a profound impression on sociology. He used cross-cultural and historical materials to trace the causes of social change and to determine how extensively social groups affect people's orientations to life.

frugal lives, saving their money and investing the surplus in order to make even more. This, said Weber, brought about the birth of capitalism.

Weber called this self-denying approach to life the *Protestant ethic.* He termed the readiness to invest capital in order to make more money the *spirit of capitalism.* To test his theory, Weber compared the extent of capitalism in Roman Catholic and Protestant countries. In line with his theory, he found that capitalism was more likely to flourish in Protestant countries. Weber's conclusion that religion was the central factor in the rise of capitalism was controversial when he made it, and it continues to be debated today. We'll explore these ideas in more detail in Chapter 13.

SEXISM IN EARLY SOCIOLOGY

Attitudes of the Time

As you may have noticed, we have discussed only male sociologists. In the 1800s, sex roles were rigidly defined, with women assigned the roles of wife and mother. In the classic German phrase, women were expected to devote themselves to the four *K's: Kirche, Küchen, Kinder,* und *Kleider* (church, cooking, children, and clothes). Trying to break out of this mold often brought severe social disapproval.

Few people, male or female, received any education beyond basic reading and writing. Higher education, for the rare few who received it, was reserved for men. A handful of women from wealthy families, however, did pursue higher education. A few even managed to study sociology, although the sexism that was so deeply entrenched in the universities stopped them from obtaining advanced degrees or becoming professors. In line with the times, their research was almost entirely ignored.

Harriet Martineau

A classic example is Harriet Martineau (1802–1876) who was born into a wealthy English family. When Martineau first began to analyze social life, she would hide her writing beneath her sewing when visitors arrived, for *writing was "masculine" and sewing "feminine"* (Gilman 1911:88). Martineau persisted in her interests, however, and she eventually studied social life in both Great Britain and the United States. In 1837, two or three decades before Durkheim and Weber were born, Martineau published

Interested in social reform, Harriet Martineau (1802–1876) turned to sociology, where she discovered the writings of Comte. An active advocate for the abolition of slavery, she traveled widely and wrote extensively.

Society in America, in which she reported on this new nation's customs—family, race, gender, politics, and religion. Despite her insightful examination of U.S. life, which is still worth reading today, Martineau's research met the fate of that of other early women sociologists and, until recently, has been ignored. Instead, she is known primarily for translating Comte's ideas into English.

SOCIOLOGY IN NORTH AMERICA

Early History: The Tension between Social Reform and Sociological Analysis

Transplanted to U.S. soil in the late nineteenth century, sociology first took root at the University of Kansas in 1892; at Atlanta University, then an all-black school, in 1897; and at the University of Chicago in 1899. It was not until 1922 that McGill University gave Canada its first department of sociology. Harvard University did not open a department of sociology until 1930, and the University of California at Berkeley didn't have one until the 1950s.

Initially, the department at the University of Chicago, which was founded by Albion Small (1854–1926), dominated sociology. (Small also founded the *American Journal of Sociology* and was its editor from 1895 to 1925.) Members of this first sociology department whose ideas continue to influence today's sociologists include

Robert Park (1864–1944), Ernest Burgess (1886–1966), and George Herbert Mead (1863–1931), who developed the symbolic interactionist perspective, which we will examine later.

Jane Addams and Social Reform

Although many North American sociologists combined the role of sociologist with that of social reformer, none was so successful as Jane Addams (1860–1935). She came from a privileged background and attended The Women's Medical College of Philadelphia, dropping out because of illness. On one of her many trips to Europe, Addams was impressed with the work being done on behalf of London's poor. From then on, she tirelessly worked for social justice, concentrating on housing, education, and the working conditions of the poor, especially immigrants. In 1889, Addams co-founded Hull-House, located in the midst of Chicago's slums. Hull-House was open to people who needed refuge— immigrants, the sick, the aged, the poor. Sociologists from the nearby University of Chicago were frequent visitors at Hull-House. With her piercing insights into the exploitation of workers and how peasant immigrants adjust to city life, Addams strived to bridge the gap between the powerful and powerless. Her efforts at social reform were so outstanding that in 1931 she was a co-winner of the Nobel Peace Prize, the only sociologist to ever win this coveted award.

Jane Addams, 1860–1935, a recipient of the Nobel Peace Prize, tirelessly worked on behalf of poor immigrants. With Ellen G. Starr, she founded Hull-House, a center to help immigrants in Chicago. She was also a leader in women's rights (women suffrage) and in the peace movement.

W(illiam) E(dward) B(urghardt) Du Bois (1868–1963) spent his lifetime studying relations between African Americans and whites. Like many early North American sociologists, Du Bois combined the role of academic sociologist with that of social reformer. He was also the editor of *Crisis,* an influential journal of the time.

W. E. B. Du Bois and Race Relations

Another sociologist who combined sociology and social reform is W. E. B. Du Bois (1868–1963), the first African American to earn a doctorate at Harvard. After completing his education at the University of Berlin, where he attended lectures by Max Weber, Du Bois taught Greek and Latin at Wilberforce University. He then went to Atlanta University in 1897, where he remained for most of his career.

Although Du Bois was invited to present a paper at the 1909 meetings of the American Sociological Society, he was too poor to attend. When he could afford to attend subsequent meetings, discrimination was so prevalent in the United States that he was not permitted to eat or stay at the same hotels as the white sociologists. Later in life, when Du Bois had the money to travel, the U.S. State Department feared that he would criticize the United States and refused to give him a visa (Du Bois 1968).

Du Bois' lifetime research interest was relations between whites and African Americans, and he published a book on this subject *each* year between 1896 and 1914. The Down-to-Earth Sociology box on the next page is taken from one of his books. Du Bois' insights into race relations were heightened by personal experiences. For example, he once saw the fingers of a lynching victim on display in a Georgia butcher shop (Aptheker 1990).

At first, Du Bois was content to collect and interpret objective data. Later, frustrated at the continuing exploitation of blacks, Du Bois turned to social action. Along with

Sociology

Down-to-Earth

EARLY NORTH AMERICAN SOCIOLOGY: DU BOIS AND RACE RELATIONS

The writings of W. E. B. Du Bois, which read as though they were written by an accomplished novelist rather than by a sociologist, have been neglected in sociology. To help remedy this omission, I reprint the following excerpts from pages 66–68 of *The Souls of Black Folk* (1903). In this book, Du Bois analyzes changes that occurred in the social and economic conditions of African Americans during the thirty years following the Civil War. For two summers, while he was a student at Fisk, Du Bois taught in a log-hut, segregated school "way back in the hills" of rural Tennessee. The following excerpts help us understand conditions at the end of the 1800s.

It was a hot morning late in July when the school opened. I trembled when I heard the patter of little feet down the dusty road, and saw the growing row of dark solemn faces and bright eager eyes facing me. There they sat, nearly thirty of them, on the rough benches, their faces shading from a pale cream to deep brown, the little feet bare and swinging, the eyes full of expectation, with here and there a twinkle of mischief, and hands grasping Webster's blue-black spelling-book. I loved my school, and the fine faith the children had in the wisdom of their teacher was truly marvelous. We read and spelled together, wrote a little, picked flowers, sang, and listened to stories of the world beyond the hill.

On Friday nights I often went home with some of the children—sometimes to Doc Burke's farm. He was a great, loud, thin Black, ever working, and trying to buy the seventy-five acres of hill and dale where he lived; but people said that he would surely fail and the "white folks would get it all." His wife was a magnificent Amazon, with saffron face and shiny hair, uncorseted and barefooted, and the children were strong and barefooted. They lived in a one-and-a-half-room cabin in the hollow of the farm near the spring.

I liked to stay with the Dowells, for they had four rooms and plenty of good country fare. Uncle Bird had a small, rough farm, all woods and hills, miles from the big road; but he was full of tales—he preached now and then—and with his children, berries, horses, and wheat he was happy and prosperous. Often, to keep the peace, I must go where life was less lovely; for instance, Tildy's mother was incorrigibly dirty, Reuben's larder was limited seriously, and herds of untamed insects wandered over the Eddingses' beds.

Best of all, I loved to go to Josie's, and sit on the porch, eating peaches, while the mother bustled and talked: how Josie had bought the sewing-machine; how Josie worked at service in winter, but that four dollars a month was "mighty little" wages; how Josie longed to go away to school, but that it "looked like" they never could get far enough ahead to let her; how the crops failed and the well was yet unfinished; and, finally, how "mean" some of the white folks were.

For two summers I lived in this little world. . . . I have called my tiny community a world, and so its isolation made it; and yet there was among us but a half-awakened common consciousness, sprung from common joy and grief, at burial, birth, or wedding; from common hardship in poverty, poor land, and low wages, and, above all, from the sight of the Veil* that hung between us and Opportunity. All this caused us to think some thoughts together; but these, when ripe for speech, were spoken in various languages. Those whose eyes twenty-five and more years had seen "the glory of the coming of the Lord," saw in every present hindrance or help a dark fatalism bound to bring all things right in His own good time. The

(continued)

Sociology *(continued)*

Down-to-Earth

mass of those to whom slavery was a dim recollection of childhood found the world a puzzling thing: it asked little of them, and they answered with little, and yet it ridiculed their offering. Such a paradox they could not understand, and therefore sank into listless indifference, or shiftlessness, or reckless bravado. There were, however, some—such as Josie, Jim, and Ben—to whom War, Hell, and Slavery were but childhood tales, whose young appetites had been whetted to an edge by school and story and half-awakened thought. Ill could they be content, born without and beyond the World. And their weak wings beat against their barriers—barriers of caste, of youth, of life; at last, in dangerous moments, against everything that opposed even a whim. ■

* "The Veil" is shorthand for the Veil of Race, a reference to how race colors human relations. Du Bois' hope was that "sometime, somewhere, men will judge men by their souls and not by their skins." (p. 261)

Jane Addams and others from Hull-House, he founded the National Association for the Advancement of Colored People (NAACP) (Deegan 1988). Continuing to battle racism both as a sociologist and as a journalist, he eventually embraced revolutionary Marxism. At age 93, dismayed that so little improvement had been made in race relations, he moved to Ghana, where he is buried (Stark 1989).

Talcott Parsons and C. Wright Mills: Theory Versus Reform

During the 1940s, the emphasis shifted from social reform to social theory. Talcott Parsons (1902–1979), for example, developed abstract models of society that greatly influenced a generation of sociologists. Parsons' detailed models of how the parts of society harmoniously work together did nothing to stimulate social activism.

C. Wright Mills (1916–1962) deplored the theoretical abstractions of this period, and he (1956) urged sociologists to get back to social reform. He saw the coalescing of interests on the part of a group he called the *power elite*—the top leaders of business, politics, and the military—as an imminent threat to freedom. Shortly after Mills' death, the United States entered the turbulent era of the 1960s and 1970s. Interest in social activism was sparked, and Mills' ideas became popular among a new generation of sociologists.

The Continuing Tension and the Rise of Applied Sociology

The apparent contradiction of these two aims—analyzing society versus working toward its reform—created a tension in sociology that is still with us today. Some sociologists believe that their proper role is to analyze some aspect of society and to publish their findings in sociology journals. Others say this is not enough—sociologists have an obligation to use their expertise to try to make society a better place in which to live, to help bring justice to the poor.

Somewhere between these extremes has emerged **applied sociology,** the use of sociology to solve problems. One of the first attempts at applied sociology—and one of the most successful—was one I just mentioned, the founding of the National Association for the Advancement of Colored People. Today's applied sociologists work in a variety of settings. Some work for business firms to solve problems in the workplace. Others investigate social problems such as pornography, rape, environmental pollution, or the spread of AIDS. The Down-to-Earth Sociology box on the next page gives an idea of the wide variety of settings in which applied sociologists work.

Applied sociology is not the same as social reform. It is an application of sociology in some specific setting, not an attempt to rebuild society, as early sociologists envisioned. Consequently, a new tension has emerged in sociology. Sociologists who want the emphasis to be on social reform say that applied sociology doesn't even come close to this. It is an application of sociology, but not an attempt to change society. Others, who want the emphasis to remain on discovering knowledge, say that when sociology is applied, it is no longer sociology. If sociologists use sociological principles to help prostitutes escape from pimps, for example, is it still sociology?

Sociology

SOCIOLOGISTS AT WORK: WHAT APPLIED SOCIOLOGISTS DO

Applied sociologists work in a wide variety of areas—from counseling children to making software programs more "user friendly." To give you an idea of this variety, let's look over the shoulders of three sociologists.

Leslie Green, who does marketing research at Vanderveer Group in Philadelphia, Pennsylvania, earned her bachelor's degree in sociology at Shippensburg University. To develop marketing strategies to get doctors to prescribe a particular drug, her company invites physicians to meet in groups and discuss prescription drugs. Green sets up the meetings, locates moderators for the discussion groups, and arranges payment to the physicians who participate in the research. "My training in sociology," she says, "helps me in 'people skills.' It helps me to understand the needs of different groups, and to interact with them."

Laurie Banks, who received her master's degree in sociol-

ogy from Fordham University, works for the New York City Health Department, where she analyzes vital statistics. As she examined death certificates, she found that some areas of the city had high rates of cancer. With its high rate of stomach cancer, a Polish neighborhood stood out. The Centers for Disease Control traced the cause to eating large amounts of sausage. In another case, Banks compared birth certificates and school records. She found that problems at birth—low birth weight, lack of prenatal care, and birth complications—were linked to low reading skills and behavior problems in school.

Ross Koppel, whose doctorate is from Temple University, runs his own research company, Social Research Corporation, in Philadelphia. His work, too, is filled with variety—from studying how an increase in fares would affect the use of public transportation to survey-

ing the customers of a credit card company so the company can understand its market. In one case, Koppel was asked to evaluate the services that unemployed workers received when a steel mill closed down. He found that the services and training were not very helpful. Too many workers were retrained in a single field, such as air conditioner repair, and the local market was flooded with more specialists than it could use. When Koppel testified before Congress, he recommended that displaced workers be trained to match the needs of the local labor market.

From just these few examples, you can catch a glimpse of the variety of work that applied sociologists do. Some applied sociologists work for corporations, some work for government and private agencies, and others operate their own firms. Note that you do not need a doctorate in order to work as an applied sociologist. ■

*T*HEORETICAL PERSPECTIVES IN SOCIOLOGY

Facts never interpret themselves. In everyday life, we interpret what we observe by using "common sense." We place our observations (our "facts") into a framework of more-or-less related ideas. Sociologists place their observations in a conceptual framework called a *theory*. A **theory** is a general statement about how some parts of the world fit together and how they work. It is an explanation of how

two or more "facts" are related to one another. By providing a framework in which to place observations, each theory interprets reality in a distinct way.

Sociologists use three major theories: symbolic interactionism, functional analysis, and conflict theory. Let's first examine the main elements of these theories. Then let's see how each theory helps us to understand why the divorce rate in the United States is so high.

Symbolic Interactionism

We can trace the origins of **symbolic interactionism** to the Scottish moral philosophers of the eighteenth century, who noted that people evaluate their own conduct by comparing themselves with others (Stryker 1990). This perspective was brought to sociology by Charles Horton Cooley (1864–1929), William I. Thomas (1863–1947), and George Herbert Mead (1863–1931). Let's look at the main elements of this theory.

Symbols in Everyday Life Symbolic interactionists study how people use symbols to establish meaning, develop their views of the world, and communicate with one another. Without symbols, our social life would be no more sophisticated than that of animals. For example, without symbols we would have no aunts or uncles, employers or teachers—or even brothers or sisters. I know that this sounds strange, but it is symbols that define for us what relationships are. There would still be reproduction, of course, but no symbols to tell us how we are related to whom. We would not know to whom we owe respect and obligations, or from whom we can expect privileges—the stuff that our relationships are made of.

Think of it like this: If you think of someone as your aunt or uncle, you behave in certain ways, but if you think of that person as a boyfriend or girlfriend you behave quite differently. It is the symbol that tells you how you are related to others—and how you should act toward them.

Symbols not only allow relationships to exist, but they also allow society to exist. Without symbols, we could not coordinate our actions with those of other people. We could not make plans for a future date, time, and place. Unable to specify times, materials, sizes, or goals, we could not build bridges and highways. Without symbols, there would be no movies or musical instruments. We would have no hospitals, no government, no religion. The class you are taking could not exist—nor could this book.

In short, symbolic interactionists analyze how our behaviors depend on the ways we define ourselves and others. They study face-to-face interactions; looking at how people work out their relationships, how they make sense out of life and their place in it. They point out that even the *self* is a symbol, for it consists of the ideas we have about who we are. And the self is a changing symbol; as we interact with others, we constantly adjust our views of who we are based on how we interpret the reactions of others. We'll get more into this later.

Applying Symbolic Interactionism To explain the U.S. divorce rate (see Figure 1.1 on page 15), symbolic

interactionists look at how people's ideas and behavior change as symbols change. They note that until the early part of the last century, people thought of marriage as a sacred, lifelong commitment. Divorce was seen as an immoral, harmful action, a flagrant disregard for public opinion.

Then, slowly, the meaning of marriage began to change. In 1933, sociologist William Ogburn observed that personality was becoming more important in mate selection. In 1945, sociologists Ernest Burgess and Harvey Locke noted the growing importance of mutual affection, understanding, and compatibility in marriage. Gradually, people's views changed. No longer did they see marriage as a lifelong commitment based on duty and obligation. Instead, they began to see marriage as an arrangement, often temporary, that was based on feelings of intimacy. The meaning of divorce also changed. Once a symbol of failure, it now became an indicator of freedom and new beginnings. When the stigma was removed from divorce, a strong barrier that had prevented people from breaking up their marriages was shattered.

Symbolic interactionists also note a change in related symbols—from marital roles to parenthood—and they point out that none of these changes strengthens marriage. For example, what is the "proper role" of a husband or wife today? Previously, due to tradition, each knew what was expected, but today the matter is confusing. As they work out their own arrangements, couples try to balance conflicting expectations, and many flounder in the process. Although couples find it a relief not to have to conform to what they consider to be burdensome notions, those expectations (or symbols) did provide a structure that made marriages last. When these symbols changed, that structure was weakened, making marriage more vulnerable to divorce.

Similarly, ideas of parenthood and childhood used to be quite different. Parents had little responsibility for their children beyond providing food, clothing, shelter, and moral guidance. And this was only for a short time, for children began to contribute to the support of the family early in life. Among many people, parenthood is still like this. In Colombia, for example, children of the poor often are expected to support themselves by the age of eight or ten. In advanced industrial societies, however, we assume that children are vulnerable beings who must depend on their parents for financial and emotional support for many years—often until they are well into their twenties. That this is not the case in many cultures often comes as a surprise to Americans, who assume that their situation is some sort of natural arrangement.

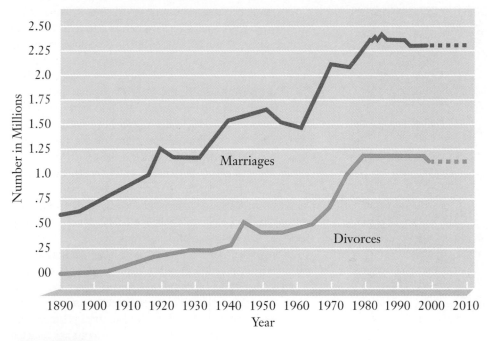

Figure 1.1   U.S. MARRIAGE, U.S. DIVORCE

Source: Statistical Abstract 1999:155: earlier editions for earlier years. The broken lines indicate the author's estimates.

The greater responsibilities that we assign to parenthood place greater burdens on couples, and with them, more strain on marriage.

Symbolic interactionists, then, look at how changing ideas (or symbols) put pressure on today's married couples. No single change is *the* cause of our divorce rate, but, taken together, these changes provide a strong "push" toward divorce.

Functional Analysis

The central idea of **functional analysis** is that society is a whole unit; it is made up of interrelated parts that work together. Functional analysis, also known as *functionalism* and *structural functionalism,* is rooted in the origins of sociology. Auguste Comte and Herbert Spencer viewed society as a kind of living organism. Just as a biological organism has parts that must function together, they wrote, so does society. Like an organism, if society is to function smoothly, its various parts must work together in harmony.

Emile Durkheim also saw society as being composed of many parts, each with its own function. When all the parts of society fulfill their functions, society is in a "normal" state. If they do not fulfill their functions, society is in an "abnormal" or "pathological" state. To understand society, then, functionalists say we need to look at both *structure* (how the parts of a society fit together to make the whole) and *function* (what each part does, how it contributes to society).

Robert Merton and Functionalism Robert Merton dismissed the organic analogy, but he did maintain the essence of functionalism—the image of society as a whole composed of parts that work together. Merton used the term *functions* to refer to the beneficial consequences of people's actions: They help keep a group (society, social system) in equilibrium. In contrast, *dysfunctions* are consequences that harm society. They undermine a system's equilibrium.

Functions can be either manifest or latent. If an action is *intended* to help some part of a system, it is a *manifest function*. For example, suppose that the government becomes concerned about our slowing rate of childbirth. Congress offers a $10,000 bonus for every child born to a married couple. The intention, or manifest function,

Sociologists who use the functionalist perspective stress how individualization and urbanization undermined the traditional functions of the family. Before industrialization, members of the family worked together as an economic unit. As production moved away from the home, it took with it first the father and, more recently, the mother. One consequence is a major dysfunction, the weakening of family ties. This scene was painted by Master of Serrone, Foligno, Italy.

of the bonus is to increase childbearing. Merton pointed out that people's actions also can have *latent functions*— *unintended* consequences that help a system adjust. Let's suppose that the bonus works, that the birth rate jumps. As a result, the sale of diapers and baby furniture booms. Because the benefits to these businesses were not the intended consequences, they are latent functions of the bonus.

Of course, human actions can also hurt a system. Because such consequences usually are unintended, Merton called them *latent dysfunctions.* Let's suppose that the government has failed to specify a "stopping point" with regard to its bonus system. To collect the bonus, some people keep on having children. The more children they have, however, the more they need the next bonus to survive. Large families become common, and poverty increases. The welfare bill skyrockets, taxes

jump, and the nation erupts in protest. Because these results were not intended, and because they harmed the social system, they represent latent dysfunctions of the bonus program.

Applying Functional Analysis Now let's apply functional analysis to the U.S. divorce rate. Functionalists stress that industrialization and urbanization undermined the traditional functions of the family. For example, prior to industrialization the family was a sort of economic team. On the farm, where most people lived, each family member had jobs or "chores" to do. The wife was in charge not only of household tasks, but also of raising small animals, such as chickens. Milking cows, collecting eggs, and churning butter were also her responsibility—as were cooking, baking, canning, sewing, darning, washing, and cleaning. Female children helped her. The husband was responsible for caring for large animals, such as horses and cattle, for planting and harvesting, and for maintaining buildings and tools. Male children helped him. *Together* they formed an economic unit in which each depended on the others for survival.

The functions that bonded family members to one another also included educating the children, teaching them religion, providing home-based recreation, and caring for the sick and elderly. To see how sharply family functions have changed, look at this example from back in the 1800s:

> When Phil became sick, he was nursed by Ann, his wife. She cooked for him, fed him, changed the bed linen, bathed him, read to him from the Bible, and gave him his medicine. (She did this in addition to doing the housework and taking care of their six children.) Phil was also surrounded by the children, who shouldered some of his chores while he was sick.

> When Phil died, the male neighbors and relatives made the casket while Ann, her mother, and female friends washed and dressed the body. Phil was then "laid out" in the front parlor (the formal living room), where friends, neighbors, and relatives paid their last respects. From there, friends moved his body to the church for the final message, and then to the grave they themselves had dug.

As you can see, the family used to have more functions. Families even handled many aspects of life and death that we now assign to outside agencies. Similarly, economic production is no longer a cooperative, home-based effort, with husbands and wives depending on one another for their interlocking contributions to a mutual endeavor. In contrast, today's husbands and wives earn individual paychecks and function as separate components of an impersonal, multinational, and even global system. When outside agencies take over family functions, this weakens the "ties that bind." Marriages become more fragile, and divorce rates increase.

Conflict Theory

Conflict theory provides a third perspective on social life. Unlike the functionalists, who view society as a harmonious whole, with its parts working together, conflict theorists stress that society is composed of groups that engage in fierce competition for scarce resources. Although alliances or cooperation may prevail on the surface, beneath that surface is a struggle for power.

Karl Marx, the founder of conflict theory, witnessed the Industrial Revolution that transformed Europe. He saw that peasants who had left the land to seek work in cities had to work for wages that barely provided enough to eat. The average worker died at age 30, the average wealthy person at age 50 (Edgerton 1992:87). Shocked by this suffering and exploitation, Marx began to analyze society and history. As he did so, he developed **conflict theory.** He concluded that the key to human history is class struggle. In every society, some small group controls the means of production and exploits those who are not in control. In industrialized societies the struggle is between the *bourgeoisie,* the small group of capitalists who own the means to produce wealth, and the *proletariat,* the mass of workers who are exploited by the bourgeoisie.

When Marx made his observations, capitalism was in its infancy, and workers were at the mercy of their employers. Workers had none of what we take for granted today—the right to strike, minimum wages, eight-hour days, coffee breaks, five-day work weeks, paid vacations and holidays, medical benefits, sick leave, unemployment compensation, Social Security. Marx's analysis reminds us that these benefits came not from generous hearts, but by workers forcing concessions from their employers.

Conflict Theory Today Some current conflict sociologists use conflict theory in a much broader sense. Ralf Dahrendorf (b. 1929) sees conflict as inherent in all relations that involve authority. He points out that authority, or power that people consider legitimate, permeates every layer of society—whether that be a small group, an organization, a community, or the entire society. People in positions of authority try to enforce conformity, which, in turn, creates resentment and resistance. The result is a constant struggle throughout society to determine who has authority over what (Turner 1978).

Another sociologist, Lewis Coser (b. 1913), pointed out that conflict is most likely to develop among people who are in close relationships. They have worked out ways to distribute responsibilities and privileges, power and rewards. Any change in this arrangement can lead to hurt feelings, to bitterness and conflict. Even in intimate relationships, then, people are in a constant balancing act, with conflict lying just beneath the surface.

Applying Conflict Theory To explain why the U.S. divorce rate is high, conflict theorists focus on how men's and women's relationships have changed. For millennia, women have been dominated by men. They had few alternatives than to accept their exploitation. Today, however, with industrialization, women can meet their basic survival needs outside of marriage. Industrialization also has fostered a culture in which females participate in social worlds beyond the home. Consequently, today's women refuse to bear burdens that earlier generations accepted as inevitable, and they are much more likely to dissolve a marriage that becomes intolerable— or even unsatisfactory.

In short, the traditional imbalance of power between men and women, which had been taken for granted, changed as women gained power, especially through the paycheck. One consequence is higher divorce rates as wives strive for more equality and husbands resist their efforts. From the conflict perspective, then, the increase in divorce is not a sign that marriage has weakened, but, rather, a sign that women are making headway in their historical struggle with men.

Levels of Analysis: Macro and Micro

A major difference among these three theoretical perspectives is their level of analysis (see Table 1.1 on the next page). Functionalists and conflict theorists focus on the **macro level;** that is, they examine large-scale patterns of society. In contrast, symbolic interactionists focus on the **micro level,** on **social interaction**—what people do when they are in one another's presence.

To make this distinction between micro and macro levels clearer, let's return to the example of the homeless with which we opened this chapter. To study homeless people, symbolic interactionists would focus on the micro level. They would analyze what homeless people do

Table 1.1

MAJOR THEORETICAL PERSPECTIVES IN SOCIOLOGY

Perspective	Usual Level of Analysis	Focus of Analysis	Key Terms	Applying the Perspective to the U.S. Divorce Rate
Symbolic Interactionism	Microsociological—examines small-scale patterns of social interaction	Face-to-face interaction; how people use symbols to create social life	Symbols Interaction Meanings Definitions	Industrialization and urbanization change marital roles and lead to a redefinition of love, marriage, children, and divorce.
Functional Analysis (also called functionalism and structural functionalism)	Macrosociological—examines large-scale patterns of society	Relationships among the parts of society; how these parts are *functional* (have beneficial consequences) or *dysfunctional* (have negative consequences)	Structure Functions (manifest and latent) Dysfunctions Equilibrium	As social change erodes the traditional functions of the family, ties weaken and the divorce rate increases.
Conflict Theory	Macrosociological—examines large-scale patterns of society	The struggle for scarce resources by groups in society; how dominant elites use power to control the less powerful	Inequality Power Conflict Competition Exploitation	When men control economic life, the divorce rate is low because women find few alternatives to a bad marriage; the rising divorce rate reflects a shift in the balance of power between men and women.

when they are in shelters and on the streets. They would also analyze their communications, both their talk and their **nonverbal interaction** (gestures, silence, use of space, and so on). The observations I made at the beginning of this chapter about the silence in the homeless shelter, for example, would be of interest to symbolic interactionists.

This micro level, however, would not interest functionalists and conflict theorists. They would focus instead on the macro level. Functionalists would examine how changes in the parts of society have increased homelessness. They might look at how changes in the family (smaller, more divorce) and economic conditions (higher rents, fewer unskilled jobs, loss of jobs overseas) cause homelessness among people who are unable to find jobs and have no family to fall back on. For their part, conflict theorists would stress the struggle between social classes, especially how the policies of the wealthy force certain groups into unemployment and homelessness. That, they point out, accounts for the disproportionate number of African Americans who are homeless.

Putting the Theoretical Perspectives Together

Which theoretical perspective should we use to study human behavior? Which level of analysis is the correct one? As you have seen, these theoretical perspectives provide contrasting pictures of human life. In the case of divorce, those interpretations are quite different from the commonsense understanding that two people were simply "incompatible." Because each theory focuses on different features of social life, each provides a distinctive interpretation. Consequently, it is necessary to use all three theoretical lenses to analyze human behavior. By combining their contributions, we gain a more comprehensive picture of social life.

How Research and Theory Work Together

Theory cannot stand alone. As sociologist C. Wright Mills (1959) so forcefully argued, if theory isn't connected to research, it will be abstract and empty. It won't represent the way life really is. It is the same for research. Without theory, Mills said, research is also of little value; it is simply a collection of meaningless "facts."

Research and theory, then, go together like a hand and glove. Every theory must be tested, which requires research. And as sociologists do research, they often come up with surprising findings. Those findings must be explained, and for that we need theory. As sociologists study social life, then, they combine research and theory. Let's turn now to how sociologists do research.

DOING SOCIOLOGICAL RESEARCH

Around the globe, people make assumptions about the way the world "is." *Common sense,* the things that "everyone knows are true," may or may not be true, however. It takes research to find out. To test your own "common sense," read the Down-to-Earth Sociology box below.

Regardless of the topic that we want to investigate, we need to move beyond guesswork and common sense. We want to *know* what is really going on. To find out, sociologists do research on just about every aspect of social life. Let's look at how they do their research.

A Research Model

As shown in Figure 1.2 on page 21, scientific research follows eight basic steps. This is an ideal model, however, and in the real world of research some of these steps may run together. Some may even be omitted.

1. *Selecting a topic.* First, what do you want to know more about? Let's choose spouse abuse as our topic.

2. *Defining the problem.* The next step is to narrow the topic. Spouse abuse is too broad; we need to focus on a specific area. For example, you may want to know why men are more likely than women to be the abusers. Or perhaps you want to know what can be done to reduce domestic violence.

3. *Reviewing the literature.* You must review the literature to find out what is already published on the problem. You don't want to waste your time rediscovering what is already known.

4. *Formulating a hypothesis.* The fourth step is to formulate a **hypothesis,** a statement of what you expect to find according to predictions that are based on a theory. A hypothesis predicts a relationship between or among **variables,** factors that vary, or change, from one person or situation to another. For example, the statement "Men who are more socially isolated are more likely to abuse their wives than are men who are more socially integrated" is a hypothesis.

Down-to-Earth *Sociology*

ENJOYING A SOCIOLOGY QUIZ— SOCIOLOGICAL FINDINGS VERSUS COMMON SENSE

Some sociological findings support commonsense understandings of social life, while others contradict them. Can you tell the difference? To enjoy this quiz, complete *all* the questions before turning the page to check your answers.

1. *True/False* More U.S. students are killed in school shootings now than ten or fifteen years ago.

2. *True/False* The earnings of U.S. women have just about caught up with those of U.S. men.

3. *True/False* When faced with natural disasters such as floods and earthquakes,

people panic and social organization disintegrates.

4. *True/False* Rapists are mentally ill.

5. *True/False* Most people on welfare are lazy and looking for a handout. They could work if they wanted to.

6. *True/False* Compared with women, men maintain more eye contact while they are conversing.

7. *True/False* The more available alcohol is (as measured by the number of places to buy alcohol per one hundred people), the more alcohol-related injuries and fatalities occur on U.S. highways.

8. *True/False* Couples who live together before marriage are usually more satisfied with their marriages than couples who do not live together before marriage.

9. *True/False* When husbands of working wives get laid off from work, most take up the slack and increase the amount of housework they do.

10. *True/False* Students in Japan are under such intense pressure to do well in school that their suicide rate is about double that of U.S. students. ■

Sociology

SOCIOLOGICAL FINDINGS VERSUS COMMON SENSE— ANSWERS TO THE SOCIOLOGY QUIZ

1. *False*   More students were shot to death at U.S. schools in the early 1990s than now (National School Safety Center, 2000). See the box on school shootings on page 340.

2. *False*   Over the years, the income gap has narrowed, but only slightly. On average, full-time working women earn only 65 to 70 percent of what full-time working men earn. This low figure is actually an improvement, for in the 1970s women's incomes averaged about 60 percent of men's. (See Figure 10.6, page 252.)

3. *False*   Following disasters, people develop *greater* cohesion, cooperation, and social organization to deal with the catastrophe.

4. *False*   Sociologists compared the psychological profiles of prisoners who had been convicted of rape and prisoners who had been convicted of other crimes. Their profiles were similar. Like robbery, rape is a learned behavior (Scully and Marolla 1984, 1985).

5. *False*   Most people on welfare are children, the old, the sick, the mentally and physically handicapped, or young mothers with few skills. Fewer than 2 percent meet the common stereotype of an able-bodied man.

6. *False*   Women maintain considerably more eye contact (Henley et al. 1985).

7. *False*   Researchers in California compared the number of alcohol outlets per one hundred people with the alcohol-related highway injuries and fatalities. Counties in which alcohol was more readily available did not have more alcohol-related injuries and fatalities (Kohfeld and Leip 1991).

8. *False*   The opposite is true. The reason, researchers suggest, is that many couples who marry after cohabiting are less committed to marriage in the first place—and a key to marital success is firm commitment to one another (Larson 1988).

9. *False*   Most husbands of working wives who get laid off from work *reduce* the amount of housework they do. See page 307 for an explanation.

10. *False*   The suicide rate of U.S. students is about double that of Japanese students (Haynes and Chalker 1997). ■

Your hypothesis will need **operational definitions,** that is, precise ways to measure the variables. In this example, you would need operational definitions for three variables: social isolation, social integration, and spouse abuse.

5. *Choosing a research method.* The means by which you collect your data is called a **research method.** Sociologists use six basic research methods, which are outlined in the next section. You will want to choose the method that will best answer your particular questions.

6. *Collecting the data.* When you gather your data, you have to take care to assure their **validity;** that is, your operational definitions must measure what they are intended to measure. In this case, you must be certain that you really are measuring social isolation, social integration, and spouse abuse—and not something else. Spouse abuse, for example, seems to be obvious. Yet acts that some people consider to be abuse are not considered abuse by others. Which will you choose? In other words, your operational definitions must be so precise that no one has any question about what you are measuring.

You must also be sure your data are reliable. **Reliability** means that if other researchers use your operational definitions, the findings will be consistent. If your operational definitions are sloppy, husbands who have committed the same act of violence might be included in some research but be excluded in other studies. You would end up with erratic results.

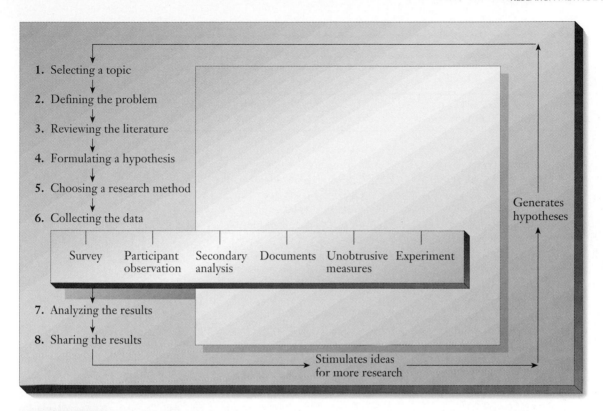

1. Selecting a topic
2. Defining the problem
3. Reviewing the literature
4. Formulating a hypothesis
5. Choosing a research method
6. Collecting the data

| Survey | Participant observation | Secondary analysis | Documents | Unobtrusive measures | Experiment |

7. Analyzing the results
8. Sharing the results

Generates hypotheses

Stimulates ideas for more research

Figure 1.2 **THE RESEARCH MODEL**

Source: Modification of Fig. 2.2 of Schaefer 1989.

You might show a 1 percent rate of spousal violence, but another researcher finds it to be 20 percent. This would make your research unreliable.

7. *Analyzing the results.* You can choose from a variety of techniques to analyze the data you gathered. If a hypothesis has been part of your research, it is during this step that you will test it. (Some research, especially that done by participant observation, is exploratory. You may know so little about the setting you are going to research that you cannot even specify the variables in advance.) Using a computer will allow you to perform tests on your data that used to take days, or even weeks. The basic programs that sociologists and many undergraduates use are Microcase and the Statistical Package for the Social Sciences (SPSS).

8. *Sharing the results.* To wrap up your research, you will write a report to share your findings with the scientific community. You will review how you did your research, including your operational definitions. You will also show how your findings fit in with the published literature, and how they support or refute the theories

that apply to your topic. As Table 1.2 on the next page illustrates, sociologists often summarize their findings in tables.

Let's look in greater detail at the fifth step and examine the research methods that sociologists use.

RESEARCH METHODS

As we review the six research methods (or "research designs") that sociologists use, we will continue our example of spouse abuse. As you will see, the method you choose will depend on the questions you want to answer. Because you will want to know what "average" is in your study, the ways to measure average are discussed in Table 1.3 on page 23.

Surveys

Let's suppose you want to know how many wives are abused each year. Some husbands are also abused, but

Table 1.2

HOW TO READ A TABLE

Comparing Violent and Nonviolent Husbands

Based on interviews with 150 husbands and wives in a Midwestern city who were getting a divorce.

Husband's Achievement and Job Satisfaction	Violent Husbands $n = 25$	Nonviolent Husbands $n = 125$
He started but failed to complete high school or college.	44%	27%
He is very dissatisfied with his job.	44%	18%
His income is a source of constant conflict.	84%	24%
He has less education than his wife.	56%	14%
His job has less prestige than his father-in-law's.	37%	28%

Source: Modification of Table 1 in O'Brien 1975.

A table is a concise way of presenting information. Because sociological findings are often presented in tabular form, it is important to understand how to read a table. Tables contain six elements: title, headnote, headings, columns, rows, and source. When you understand how these elements work together, you know how to read a table.

1. The *title* states the topic of a table. It is located at the top of the table. What is the title of this table? Please determine your answer before looking at the correct answer below.

2. The *headnote* is not always included in a table. When it is, it is located just below the title. Its purpose is to give more detailed information about how the data were collected or how data are presented in the table. What are the first seven words of the headnote of this table?

3. The *headings* tell what kind of information is contained in the table. There are three headings in this table. What are they? In the second heading, what does $n = 25$ mean?

4. The *columns* present information arranged vertically. What is the fourth number in the second column and the second number in the third column?

5. The *rows* present information arranged horizontally. In the fourth row, which husbands are more likely to have less education than their wives?

6. The *source* of a table, usually listed at the bottom, provides information on where the data shown in the table originated. Often, as in this instance, the information is specific enough for you to consult the original source. What is the source for this table?

Some tables are much more complicated than this one, but all follow the same basic pattern. To apply these concepts to a table with more information, see Table 9.2 on page 224.

Answers

1. Comparing Violent and Nonviolent Husbands
2. Based on interviews with 150 husbands and
3. Husband's Achievement and Job Satisfaction, Violent Husbands, Nonviolent Husbands
   The *n* is an abbreviation for number, and $n = 25$ means that 25 violent husbands were in the sample.
4. 56%, 18%.
5. Violent husbands
6. A 1975 article by O'Brien (listed in the References section of this text).

let's assume you are going to focus on wives. An appropriate method would be the **survey,** asking people a series of questions. Before you begin your research, however, you must deal with the practical matters that face all researchers. Let's look at these problems.

Selecting a Sample Ideally, you might want to learn about all wives in the world. Obviously, your resources will not permit such a study, and you must narrow your **population,** the target group that you are going to study.

Table 1.3

THREE WAYS TO MEASURE "AVERAGE"

The Mean

The term *average* seems clear enough. As you learned in grade school, to find the average you add a group of numbers and then divide the total by the number of cases that were added. For example, assume that the following numbers represent men convicted of battering their wives:

```
   321
   229
    57
   289
   136
    57
 1,795
```

The total is 2,884. Divided by 7 (the number of cases), the average is 412. Sociologists call this form of average the *mean*.

The mean can be deceptive because it is strongly influenced by extreme scores, either low or high. Note that six of the seven cases are less than the mean.

Two other ways to compute averages are the median and the mode.

The Median

To compute the second average, the *median*, first arrange the cases in order—either from the highest to the lowest or the lowest to the highest. In this example, the arrangement will produce the following distribution:

```
    57
    57
   136
   229
   289
   321
 1,795
```

Then look for the middle case, the one that falls halfway between the top and the bottom. That figure is 229, for three numbers are lower and three numbers are higher. When there is an even number of cases, the median is the halfway mark between the two middle cases.

The Mode

The third measure of average, the *mode*, is simply the cases that occur the most often. In this instance the mode is 57, which is way off the mark. Because the mode is often deceptive, and only by chance comes close to either of the other two averages, sociologists seldom use it. In addition, it is obvious that not every distribution of cases has a mode. And if two or more different numbers appear with the same frequency, you can have more than one mode.

Let's assume that your resources allow you to investigate spouse abuse only on your campus. Let's also assume that your college enrollment is large, so you won't be able to survey all the married women who are enrolled. Now you must select a **sample,** individuals from among your target population. How you choose a sample is critical, for your choice will affect the results of your study. For example, to survey only women enrolled in introductory sociology courses, or only those in advanced physics classes, would produce skewed results.

Because you want to generalize your findings to your entire campus, you need a sample that is representative of the campus. How do you get a representative sample?

The best is a **random sample.** This does *not* mean that you stand on some campus corner and ask questions of any woman who happens to walk by. *In a random sample, everyone in your population has the same chance of being included in the study.* In this case, because your population is every married woman enrolled in your college, all married women—whether first-year or

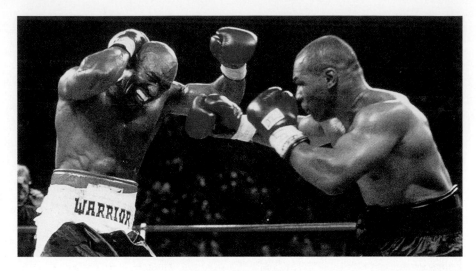

Because sociologists usually cannot interview or observe every member of a group they wish to study, such as the spectators at this boxing match between heavyweight world champion Evander Holyfield and Mike Tyson, they must select a sample that will let them generalize to the entire group. The text explains how samples are selected.

graduate students, full- or part-time—must have the same chance of being included in your sample.

How can you get a random sample? First, you need a list of all the married women enrolled in your college. Then you assign a number to each name on the list. Using a table of random numbers, you then determine which of these women become part of your sample. (Random numbers are available on tables in statistics books, or they can be generated by a computer.)

Because a random sample represents the population—in this case married women enrolled at your college—you can generalize your findings to all the married women students on your campus, whether they were included in the sample or not.

What if you wanted to know only about certain subgroups, such as freshmen and seniors? You could use a **stratified random sample.** You would need a list of the freshmen and senior married women. Then, using random numbers, you would select subsamples of each group. This would allow you to generalize to all the

freshmen and senior married women at your college, but you would not be able to draw any conclusions about the sophomores or juniors.

Asking Neutral Questions After you have decided on your population and sample, your next task is to make certain that your questions are neutral. Your questions must allow **respondents,** the people who respond to a survey, to express their own opinions. Otherwise you will end up with biased findings, which are worthless. For example, if you were to ask, "Don't you think that men who beat their wives should go to prison?" you would be tilting the answers toward agreement with a prison sentence. For other examples of flawed research, see the Down-to-Earth Sociology box on the next page.

Types of Questions You also must decide whether to use closed- or open-ended questions. **Closed-ended questions** are followed by a list of possible answers. This format would work for questions about someone's

Improperly worded questionnaires steer respondents toward answers that are not their own, thus producing invalid results.

Doonesbury © 1989 G. B. Trudeau. Reprinted with permission of Universal Press Syndicate. All rights reserved.

Sociology

LOADING THE DICE: HOW *NOT* TO DO RESEARCH

The methods of science lend themselves to distortion, misrepresentation, and downright fraud. Consider the following information. Surveys show that

- *Americans overwhelmingly prefer Toyotas to Chryslers.*
- *Americans overwhelmingly prefer Chryslers to Toyotas.*
- *Americans think that cloth diapers are better for the environment than disposable diapers.*
- *Americans think that disposable diapers are better for the environment than cloth diapers.*

Obviously such opposites cannot be true. In fact, *both* sets of findings are misrepresentations, although each does come from surveys conducted by so-called independent researchers. These researchers, however, are not independent and objective.

It turns out that some consumer researchers load the dice. Hired by firms that have a vested interest in the outcome of the research, they deliver the results their clients are looking for. There are six basic ways of loading the dice.

1. **Choose a biased sample.** If you want to "prove" that Americans prefer Chryslers over Toyotas, interview unemployed union workers who trace their job loss to Japanese imports. You'll get what you're looking for.

2. **Ask biased questions.** Even if you choose an unbiased sample, you can phrase questions in such a way that most people see only one logical choice. The diaper survey just cited is a case in point. When disposable diaper companies paid for the survey, the researchers used an excellent sample, but they worded the question this way: "It is estimated that disposable diapers account for less than 2 percent of the trash in today's landfills. In contrast, beverage containers, third-class mail and yard waste are estimated to account for about 21 percent. Given this, in your opinion, would it be fair to ban disposable diapers?"

Is it surprising, then, that 84 percent of the respondents said that disposable diapers are better for the environment than cloth diapers? Similarly, when the cloth diaper companies funded its survey, the wording of their questions loaded the dice in their favor.

Consider the following finding, which is every bit as factual as those just cited:

- *80 percent of Americans support foreign aid.*

It is difficult to get 80 percent of Americans to agree on anything, but as loaded as this question was it is surprising that there was *only* 80 percent agreement. Incredibly, the question was phrased this way: *"Should the U.S. share at least a small portion of its wealth with those in the world who are in great need?"*

This question is obviously designed to channel people's thinking toward a predetermined answer—quite contrary to the standards of scientific research.

3. **List biased choices.** Another way to load the dice is to use closed-ended questions that push people into the answers you want. Consider this finding:

- *U.S. college students overwhelmingly prefer Levis 501s to the jeans of any competitor.*

Sound good? Before you rush out to buy Levis, note what these researchers did: In asking students which jeans would be the most popular in the coming year, their list of choices included *no other jeans* but Levis 501!

4. **Discard undesirable results.** Researchers can simply keep silent about findings they find embarrassing, or they can continue to interview samples until they find one that matches what they are looking for.

As I've stressed in this chapter, research must be objective if it is to be scientific. Obviously, none of the preceding results qualifies. The underlying problem with the research cited here—and with many surveys bandied about in the media as fact—is that survey research has become big business. Simply put, the vast sums of money offered

(continued)

Sociology (continued)

Down-to-Earth

by corporations have corrupted some researchers.

The beginning of the corruption is subtle. Paul Light, dean at the University of Minnesota, put it this way: "A funder will never come to an academic and say, 'I want you to produce finding X, and here's a million dollars to do it.' Rather, the subtext is that if the researchers produce the right finding, more work—and funding—will come their way." He adds, "Once you're on that treadmill, it's hard to get off."

The first four sources of bias are inexcusable, intentional fraud. The next two

sources of bias reflect sloppiness—which is also inexcusable in science.

5. **Misunderstand the subjects' world.** This route can lead to errors every bit as great as those just cited. Even researchers who use an adequate sample, word their questions properly, and offer adequate choices can end up with skewed results. They may, for example, fail to anticipate that people may be embarrassed to express an opinion that isn't "politically correct." For example, surveys show that 80 percent of Americans are environmentalists. Most Americans,

however, probably are embarrassed to tell a stranger otherwise. Today, that would be like going against the flag, motherhood, and apple pie.

6. **Analyze the data incorrectly.** Even when researchers strive for objectivity, the sample is good, the wording is neutral, and the respondents answer the questions honestly, the results can still be skewed. The researchers may make a mistake entering data into their computers. This, too, of course, is inexcusable in science. ■

Sources: Based on Crossen 1991; Goleman 1993; Barnes 1995.

age (the possible answers would reflect a series of age ranges), but it wouldn't work for many other items. For example, how could you list all possible opinions that people hold regarding what causes spouse abuse? The alternative is **open-ended questions**, which allow people to answer in their own words. Although open-ended questions allow you to tap the full range of people's opinions, they make it difficult to compare answers. For example, how would you compare these answers to the question, "What do you think causes men to abuse their wives?"

"They' re sick."

"I think they must have had problems with their mother."

"We ought to string them up!"

Establishing Rapport Will victims of abuse really give honest answers to strangers? The answer is yes, but first you must establish **rapport** ("ruh-pour"), a feeling of trust, with your respondents. We know from studies of rape that once rapport is gained (often by first asking nonsensitive questions), victims will talk about very personal, sensitive matters.

To go beyond police statistics, each year researchers interview a random sample of 100,000 Americans.

They ask them if they have been victims of burglary, robbery, and so on. After establishing rapport, the researchers ask about rape. They find that rape victims will talk about their experiences. The national crime survey shows that the actual incidence of rape is *three* times as high as the official statistics (*Statistical Abstract* 1999: 212).

Participant Observation

In **participant observation** (also called *fieldwork*), the researcher *participates* in a research setting while *observing* what is happening in that setting. Obviously this method does not mean that you would be present during abuse. But if you wanted to learn how abuse has affected the victims' hopes and goals, their dating patterns, or their relationship with their spouse, you could use participant observation.

For example, if your campus has a crisis intervention center, you may be able to observe abuse victims from the time they first report the attack through their participation in counseling. With good rapport, you may even be able to spend time with victims in other settings, observing other aspects of their lives. Their statements and interactions with others may be the keys that

Domestic abuse is one of the most common forms of violence. Until recently, it was treated by the police as a private family matter. Shown here are police pulling a woman from her bathroom window, where she had fled from her armed husband, who was threatening to shoot her.

help you unlock answers about how the abuse has affected their lives. This, in turn, may allow you to make suggestions about how to improve college counseling services.

Secondary Analysis

If you were to analyze data that someone else has already collected, you would be doing **secondary analysis.** For example, if you were to examine the original data from a study of women who had been abused by their husbands, you would be doing secondary analysis.

Documents

Documents, or written sources, include books, newspapers, bank records, immigration files, and so on. To study spouse abuse, you might examine police reports to find out how many men in your community have been arrested for abuse. You might also use court records to find out what proportion of those men were charged, convicted, or put on probation. If you wanted to know about the social and emotional adjustment of the victims, however, these documents would tell you nothing. Other documents, though, might help answer such questions. For example, a crisis intervention center might have records that contain key information. Or the center might ask victims to keep diaries that you can study later.

Unobtrusive Measures

Researchers sometimes use **unobtrusive measures** to observe people who do not know they are being studied. To use this technique, you could go to a battered women's shelter. There you could secretly tape conversations among the women, as well as their telephone calls. Or you could use a one-way mirror to observe their interactions, or even videotape them. As may be obvious, although such unobtrusive measures might yield rich data, professional ethics prohibit such a study.

"Anthropologists! Anthropologists!"

A major concern of sociologists and other social scientists is that their research methods do not influence their findings. Respondents often change their behavior when they know they are being studied.

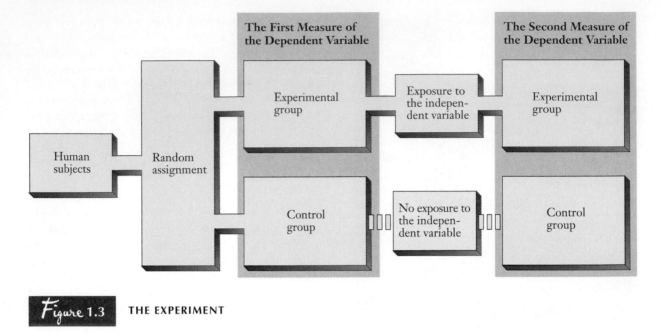

Figure 1.3   **THE EXPERIMENT**

Experiments

Let's suppose that you want to know if therapy for abusers actually works. You could conduct an **experiment** to find out. No one yet knows how to change abusers, and such experiments are badly needed.

Let's suppose that a judge likes your idea, and she gives you access to men who have been arrested for spouse abuse. You would randomly divide your subjects into two groups. (See Figure 1.3 above.) Those in the **experimental group** would be exposed to the independent variable; that is, they would attend therapy sessions. Those in the **control group** would not go to therapy. You would have to divide the men randomly in order to assure that their individual characteristics (number of arrests, severity of crimes, jail time, education, race, age, and so on) are evenly distributed between the groups.

Your **independent variable,** something that causes a change in another variable, would be therapy. Your **dependent variable,** the variable that is changed, would be the men's behavior: whether or not they abuse women after they get out of jail. To make that determination, you would need to rely on a sloppy operational definition: either reports from the wives, or whether or not the men are rearrested for abuse. This is sloppy because some of the women will not report the abuse, and some of the men who abuse will not be caught. Yet it may be the best you can do.

Let's assume that you choose rearrest as your operational definition. If you find that the men who received therapy are less likely to be rearrested for abuse, you can attribute the difference to the therapy. If you find no difference in rearrest rates, you can conclude that therapy was ineffectual. If you find that the men who received the therapy have a *higher* rearrest rate, you can conclude that the therapy backfired

ETHICS IN SOCIOLOGICAL RESEARCH

In addition to choosing an appropriate research method, we must also follow the ethics of sociology, which center on assumptions of science and morality (American Sociological Association 1997). Research ethics require openness (sharing findings with the scientific community), honesty, and truth. Ethics clearly forbid the falsification of results. They also condemn plagiarism, that is, stealing someone else's work. Another ethical guideline is that research subjects should not be harmed by the research. Ethics also require that sociologists protect the anonymity of people who provide private information. Finally, although not all sociologists agree, it generally is considered unethical for researchers to misrepresent themselves.

Sociologists take these ethical standards seriously. To illustrate the extent to which they will go to protect their respondents, consider the research conducted by Mario Brajuha.

Protecting the Subjects: The Brajuha Research

Mario Brajuha, a graduate student at the State University of New York at Stony Brook, was doing participant observation of restaurant work. He lost his job as a waiter when the restaurant where he was working burned down—due to a fire of "suspicious origin," as the police said (Brajuha and Hallowell 1986). When detectives learned that Brajuha had taken field notes, they asked to see them. Because he had promised to keep his information confidential, Brajuha refused. The district attorney then subpoenaed the notes. Brajuha still refused to hand them over. The district attorney then threatened to send Brajuha to jail. By this time, Brajuha's notes had become rather famous, and certain unsavory characters—perhaps those who had set the fire—also began to wonder what was in them. They, too, demanded to see them—accompanying their demands with threats of a different nature. Brajuha found himself between a rock and a hard place.

For two years Brajuha refused to hand over his notes, even though he grew anxious and had to appear at several court hearings. Finally, the district attorney dropped the subpoena. When the two men under investigation for setting the fire died, so did the threats to Brajuha, his wife, and their children.

Misleading the Subjects: The Humphreys Research

Sociologists agree on the necessity to protect respondents, and they applaud the professional manner in which Brajuha handled himself. Although there is less agreement that researchers should not misrepresent themselves, sociologists who violate this norm can become embroiled in ethical controversy. Let's look at the case of Laud Humphreys, whose research forced sociologists to rethink and refine their ethical stance.

Laud Humphreys, a classmate of mine at Washington University in St. Louis, was an Episcopal priest who decided to become a sociologist. For his Ph.D. dissertation, Humphreys (1970, 1971, 1975) decided to study social interaction in "tearooms," public restrooms where some men go for quick, anonymous sex with other men.

Humphreys found that some restrooms in Forest Park, just across from our campus, were tearooms. He began a participant observation study by hanging around these restrooms. He found that in addition to the two men having sex, a third man—called a "watchqueen"—served as a lookout for police and other unwelcome strangers. Humphreys took on the role of watchqueen, not only watching for strangers but also watching and systematically recording what the men did.

Humphreys decided that he wanted to know more about the regular lives of these men. For example, what was the significance of the wedding rings that many of the men wore? He hit on an ingenious technique. Many of the men parked their cars near the tearooms, and Humphreys recorded their license numbers. A friend in the St. Louis police department gave Humphreys each man's address. About a year later, Humphreys arranged for these men to be included in a medical survey conducted by some of the sociologists on our faculty.

Disguising himself with a different hairstyle and clothing, and driving a different car, Humphreys visited their homes. He interviewed the men, supposedly for the medical study. He found that they led conventional lives. They voted, mowed their lawns, and took their kids to Little League games. Many reported that their wives were not aroused sexually or were afraid of getting pregnant because their religion did not allow them to use birth control. Humphreys concluded that heterosexual men were also using the tearooms for a form of quick sex.

This study stirred controversy among sociologists and nonsociologists alike. Humphreys was severely criticized by many sociologists, and a national columnist even wrote a scathing denunciation of "sociological snoopers" (Von Hoffman 1970). As the controversy grew more heated and a court case loomed, Humphreys feared that his list of respondents might be subpoenaed. He gave me the list to take from Missouri to Illinois, where I had begun teaching. When he called and asked me to destroy it, I burned it in my backyard.

Was the research ethical? This question is not decided easily. Although many sociologists sided with Humphreys—and his book reporting the research won a highly acclaimed award—the criticisms mounted. At first, Humphreys vigorously defended his position, but five years later, in a second edition of his book (1975), he stated that he should have identified himself as a researcher.

Values in Sociological Research

Max Weber raised an issue that remains controversial among sociologists. He declared that sociology should be **value free.** By this he meant that a sociologist's **values**—personal beliefs about what is good or worthwhile in life—should not affect research. Instead, he said, we need objectivity, total neutrality, for if values influence research, sociological findings will be biased.

Objectivity as an ideal is not a matter of debate in sociology. All sociologists agree that no one should distort data to make them fit preconceived ideas or values. It is equally clear, however, that, like everyone else, sociologists are members of a particular society at a given point in history and are, therefore, infused with values of all sorts. These values inevitably play a role in our research. For example, values are part of the reason that one sociologist chooses to do research on the Mafia, while another turns a sociological eye on kindergarten students.

To overcome the distortions that values can cause, and that unwittingly can become part of our research, sociologists stress **replication,** the repetition of a study by other researchers to compare results. If values have influenced research findings, replication by other sociologists should uncover this problem and correct it.

Despite this consensus, however, values remain a hotly debated topic in sociology (Denzin 1997; Orlans 1999). This debate illustrates again the tension in sociology that we discussed earlier—the goal of analyzing social life versus the goal of social reform. Some sociologists are convinced that research should be directed along paths that will help reform society, that will alleviate poverty, racism, sexism, and so on. Other sociologists lean strongly toward **basic** (or **pure) sociology,** research that has no goal beyond understanding social life and testing social theories. They say that nothing but their own interests should direct sociologists to study one topic rather than another.

In the midst of this controversy, sociologists study the major issues facing our society at this crucial juncture of world history. From racism and sexism to the globalization of capitalism—these are all topics that sociologists study, and that we will explore in this book. Sociologists also examine face-to-face interaction—talking, touching, gestures, clothing. These, too, will be the subject of our discussions in the upcoming chapters. This beautiful variety in sociology—and the contrast of going from the larger picture to the smaller picture and back again—is part of the reason that sociology holds such fascination for me. I hope that you also find this variety appealing as you read the rest of this book.

SUMMARY AND REVIEW

■ The Sociological Perspective

What is the sociological perspective?
The **sociological perspective** stresses that people's social experiences—the groups to which they belong and their experiences within these groups—underlie their behavior. C. Wright Mills referred to this as the intersection of biography (the individual) and history (social factors influencing the individual). Pp. 4–5.

■ The Origins of Sociology

When did sociology first appear as a separate discipline?
Sociology emerged as a separate discipline in the mid-1800s in western Europe, during the onset of the Industrial Revo-

lution. Industrialization affected all aspects of human existence—where people lived, the nature of their work, how they viewed life, and interpersonal relationships. Early sociologists who focused on these social changes include Auguste Comte, Herbert Spencer, Karl Marx, Emile Durkheim, and Max Weber. Pp. 5–9.

■ Sexism in Early Sociology

What was the position of women in early sociology?
Sociology appeared during a historical period of widespread sexism. Consequently, few women received the advanced education required to become sociologists, and those who did, such as Harriet Martineau, were ignored. P. 9.

■ Sociology in North America

When were the first academic departments of sociology established in the United States?

The earliest departments of sociology were established in the late 1800s at the universities of Kansas, Atlanta, and Chicago. During the 1940s, sociology was dominated by the University of Chicago. Today, no single university or theoretical perspective dominates. Pp. 9 –10.

U.S. sociology has experienced tension between **pure** or **basic sociology,** in which the aim is to analyze society, and attempts to use sociology to reform society. Today, these contrasting orientations exist dynamically side by side. **Applied sociology** is the use of sociology to solve problems. Pp. 10–13.

■ Theoretical Perspectives in Sociology

What is a theory?

A **theory** is a statement about how facts are related to one another. A theory provides a conceptual framework for interpreting facts. P. 13.

What are sociology's major theoretical perspectives?

Sociologists use three primary theoretical frameworks to interpret social life. **Symbolic interactionism** examines how people use symbols to develop and share their views of the world. Symbolic interactionists usually focus on the **micro level**—on small-scale, face-to-face interaction. **Functional analysis,** in contrast, focuses on the **macro level**—on large-scale patterns of society. Functional theorists stress that a social system is made up of various parts. When working properly, each part contributes to the stability of the whole, fulfilling a function that contributes to the system's equilibrium. **Conflict theory** also focuses on large-scale patterns of society. Conflict theorists stress that society is composed of competing groups that struggle for scarce resources. Pp. 13–18.

Because no single theory encompasses all of reality, at different times sociologists may use any or all of the three theoretical lenses. With each perspective focusing on certain features of social life, and each providing its own interpretation, their combined insights yield a more comprehensive picture of social life. P. 18.

What is the relationship between theory and research?

Theory and research depend on one another. Sociologists use theory to interpret the data they gather. Theory also generates questions that need to be answered by research, while research, in turn, helps to generate theory. Theory without research is not likely to represent real life, while research without theory is merely a collection of empty facts. P. 18.

■ Doing Sociological Research

Why do we need sociological research when we have common sense?

Common sense is unreliable. Research often shows that commonsense ideas are very limited or false. Pp. 19–20.

What are the eight basic steps in sociological research?

1. Selecting a topic
2. Defining the problem
3. Reviewing the literature
4. Formulating a **hypothesis**
5. Choosing a research method
6. Collecting the data
7. Analyzing the results
8. Sharing the results

These steps are explained on pp. 19–21.

■ Research Methods

How do sociologists gather data?

To gather data, sociologists use six **research methods** (or research designs): **surveys, participant observation, secondary analysis, documents, unobtrusive measures,** and **experiments.** Pp. 21–28.

■ Ethics in Sociological Research

How important are ethics in sociological research?

Ethics are of fundamental concern to sociologists, who are committed to openness, honesty, truth, and protecting their subjects from harm. The Brajuha research on restaurants and the Humphreys research on "tearooms" illustrate ethical issues of concern to sociologists. Pp. 28–29.

What value dilemma do sociologists face?

Max Weber stressed that social research should be **value free:** The researcher's personal beliefs must be set aside in order to permit objective findings. Like everyone else, however, sociologists are members of a particular society at a given point in history and are infused with **values** of all sorts. To overcome the distortions that values can cause, sociologists stress **replication,** the repetition of a study by other researchers in order to compare results. Values present a second dilemma for researchers—whether to do research solely to analyze **basic** (or **pure**) **sociology** or in order to reform harmful social arrangements. P. 30.

Where can I read more on this topic?

Suggested readings for this chapter are listed on page SR-1.

YOUR INTERACTIVE COMPANION WEB SITE

Your Interactive Companion Web Site includes practice tests, with feedback, and online learning activities with video, audio, and Weblinks. Your access code for this Web site is provided with this text.

GLOSSARY

applied sociology sociology that is used to solve problems—from the micro level of family relationships to the macro level of war and pollution (p. 12)

basic (or **pure**) **sociology** sociological research whose only purpose is to make discoveries about life in human groups, not to make changes in those groups (p. 30)

class conflict Karl Marx's term for the struggle between owners (the bourgeoisie) and workers (the proletariat) (p. 7)

closed-ended questions questions followed by a list of possible answers to be selected by the respondent (p. 24)

conflict theory a theoretical framework in which society is viewed as being composed of groups that compete for scarce resources (p. 17)

control group the group of subjects not exposed to the independent variable (p. 28)

dependent variable a factor that is changed by an independent variable (p. 28)

documents in its narrow sense, written sources that provide data; in its extended sense, archival material of any sort, including photographs, movies, and so on (p. 27)

experiment the use of control groups and experimental groups and dependent and independent variables to test causation (p. 28)

experimental group the group of subjects exposed to the independent variable (p. 28)

functional analysis a theoretical framework in which society is viewed as a whole unit, composed of interrelated parts, each with a function that, when fulfilled, contributes to society's equilibrium; also known as *functionalism* and *structural functionalism* (p. 15)

hypothesis a statement of the expected relationship between variables according to predictions from a theory (p. 19)

independent variable a factor that causes a change in another variable, called the *dependent variable* (p. 28)

macro-level analysis an examination of large-scale patterns of society (p. 17)

micro-level analysis an examination of small-scale patterns of society (p. 17)

nonverbal interaction communication without words through gestures, silence, use of space, and so on (p. 18)

open-ended questions questions that respondents are able to answer in their own words (p. 26)

operational definition the way in which a variable in a hypothesis is measured (p. 20)

participant observation (or **fieldwork**) research in which the researcher *participates* in a research setting while *observing* what is happening in that setting (p. 26)

population the target group to be studied (p. 22)

positivism the application of the scientific method to the social world (p. 6)

random sample a sample in which everyone in the target population has the same chance of being included in the study (p. 23)

rapport a feeling of trust between researchers and subjects (p. 26)

reliability the extent to which data produce consistent results (p. 20)

replication repeating a study in order to test its findings (p. 30)

research method (or **research design**) one of six procedures sociologists use to collect data: surveys, participant observation, secondary analysis, documents, unobtrusive measures, and experiments (p. 20)

respondents people who respond to a survey, either in interviews or by self-administered questionnaires (p. 24)

sample the individuals intended to represent the population to be studied (p. 23)

secondary analysis the analysis of data already collected by other researchers (p. 27)

social integration the degree to which people are tied to their social groups (p. 7)

social interaction what people do when they are in one another's presence (p. 17)

social location the groups people belong to because of their location in history and society (p. 4)

society a group of people who share a culture and a territory (p. 4)

sociological perspective an approach that seeks to understand human behavior by placing it within its broader social context (p. 4)

sociology scientific study of society and human behavior (p. 6)

stratified random sample a sample of specific subgroups of the target population in which everyone in the subgroups has an equal chance of being included in the study (p. 24)

survey collecting data by having people answer a series of questions (p. 22)

symbolic interactionism a theoretical perspective that focuses on how people use symbols to establish meaning, develop their views of the world, and communicate with one another (p. 13)

theory a general statement about how some parts of the world fit together and how they work; an explanation of how two or more facts (or variables) are related to one another (p. 13)

unobtrusive measures observing people in such a way that they do not know they are being studied (p. 27)

validity the extent to which an operational definition measures what was intended (p. 20)

value free the view that a sociologist's personal values or biases should not influence social research (p. 30)

values ideas about what is good or worthwhile in life; attitudes about the way the world ought to be; the standards by which people define what is desirable or undesirable, good or bad, beautiful or ugly (p. 30)

variable a factor thought to be significant for human behavior, which varies from one case to another (p. 19)

Chapter 2

Helen Hardin, Robed Journey of the Rainbow Clan, 1976

Culture

I had never felt heat like this before. If this was northern Africa, I wondered what it must be like closer to the equator. Sweat poured off me as the temperature soared past 110° Fahrenheit.

As we were herded into the building—which had no air-conditioning—hundreds of people lunged toward the counter at the rear of the building. With body crushed against body, we waited as the uniformed officials behind the windows leisurely examined each passport. At times like this I wondered what I was doing in Africa.

When I first arrived in Morocco, I found the sights that greeted me exotic—not far removed from my memories of *Casablanca, Raiders of the Lost Ark,* and other movies that over the years had become part of my collective memory. The men, the women, and even the children did wear those white robes that reached down to their feet. What was especially striking was that the women were almost totally covered. Despite the heat, they wore not only full-length gowns, but also head coverings that reached down over their foreheads, and veils that covered their faces from the nose down. All you could make out were their eyes—and every eye the same shade of brown.

And how short everyone was! The Arab women looked to be, on average, 5 feet, and the men only three or four inches taller. As the only blue-eyed, blonde, 6-foot-plus person around, and the only one wearing jeans and a pullover shirt, in a world of white-robed short people, I stood out like a sore thumb. Everyone stared. No matter where I went, they stared. Wherever I looked, I found brown eyes watching me intently. Even staring back at those many dark brown eyes had no effect. It was so different from home, where, if you caught someone staring at you, the person would immediately look embarrassed and glance away.

And lines? The concept apparently didn't even exist. Buying a ticket for a bus or train

35

meant pushing and shoving toward the ticket man (always a man—no women were visible in any public position), who just took the money from whichever outstretched hand he decided on.

And germs? That notion didn't seem to exist here either. Flies swarmed over the food in the restaurants and over the unwrapped loaves of bread in the stores. Shopkeepers would considerately shoo the flies away before handing me a loaf. They also offered home delivery. I still remember watching a bread vendor deliver an unwrapped loaf to a woman who stood on a second-floor balcony. She first threw her money to the bread vendor, and he then threw the unwrapped bread up to her. Only, his throw was off. The bread bounced off the wrought-iron balcony railing and landed in the street, which was filled with people, wandering dogs, and the ever-present burros. The vendor simply picked up the loaf and threw it again. This certainly wasn't his day, for he missed again. But he made it on his third attempt. And the woman smiled, as she turned back into her apartment, apparently to prepare the noon meal for her hungry family.

Now, standing in the oppressive heat on the Moroccan-Algerian border, the crowd once again became unruly. Another fight had broken out. And once again, the little man in uniform appeared, shouting and knocking people aside as he forced his way to a little wooden box nailed to the floor. Climbing onto this makeshift platform, he shouted at the crowd, his arms flailing about him. The people became silent. But just as soon as the man left, the shoving and shouting began again as the people clamored to get their passports stamped.

The situation had become unbearable. His body pressed against mine, the man behind me decided that this was a good time to take a nap. Determining that I made a good support, he placed his arm against my back and leaned his head against his arm. Sweat streamed down my back at the point where his arm and head touched me.

Finally, I realized that I had to abandon U.S. customs. I pushed my way forward, forcing my frame into every square inch of vacant space that I could create. At the counter, I shouted in English. The official looked up at the sound of this strange tongue, and I thrust my long arms over the heads of three people, shoving my passport into his hand. ■

WHAT IS CULTURE?

What is culture? The concept is sometimes easier to grasp by description than by definition. For example, suppose you meet a young woman who has just arrived in the United States from India. That her culture is different from yours is immediately evident. You first see it in her clothing, jewelry, makeup, and hairstyle. Next you hear it in her speech. It then becomes apparent by her gestures. Later, you may hear her express unfamiliar beliefs about the world or about what is valuable in life. All of these characteristics are indicative of **culture,** the language, beliefs, values, norms, behaviors, and even material objects that are passed from one generation to the next.

In northern Africa, I was surrounded by a culture quite alien to my own. It was evident in everything I saw and heard. The **material culture**—such things as jewelry, art, buildings, weapons, machines, and even eating utensils, hairstyles, and clothing—provided a sharp contrast to what I was used to seeing. There is nothing inherently "natural" about material culture. That is, it is no more natural (or unnatural) to wear gowns on the street than it is to wear jeans.

I also found myself immersed in a contrasting **nonmaterial culture,** that is, a group's ways of thinking (its beliefs, values, and other assumptions about the world) and doing (its common patterns of behavior, including language, gestures, and other forms of interaction). North African assumptions about crowding to buy a ticket and staring in public are examples of nonmaterial culture. So are U.S. assumptions about not doing either of these things. Like material culture, neither custom is "right." People simply become comfortable with the customs they learn during childhood, and—as in the case of my visit to northern Africa—uncomfortable when their basic assumptions about life are challenged.

Culture and Taken-for-Granted Orientations to Life

To develop a sociological perspective, it is essential to understand how culture affects people's lives. Although meeting someone from a different culture may make us aware of culture's pervasive influence, attaining the same level of awareness regarding our own culture is quite another matter. *Our* speech, *our* gestures, *our* beliefs, and *our* customs are usually taken for granted. We assume they are "normal" or "natural," and we almost always follow them without question. As anthropologist Ralph Linton (1936) remarked, "The last thing a fish would ever notice would be water." So also with people: Except in unusual circumstances, the effects of our own culture generally remain imperceptible to us.

Yet culture's significance is profound; it touches almost every aspect of who and what we are. We came into this life without a language, without values and morality, with no ideas about religion, war, money, love, use of space, and so on. We possessed none of these fundamental orientations that we take for granted and that are so essential in determining the type of people we are. Yet at this point in our lives, we all have acquired them. Sociologists call this *culture within us.* These learned and shared ways of believing and of doing (another definition of culture) penetrate our being at an early age and quickly become part of our taken-for-granted assumptions concerning normal behavior. *Culture becomes the lens through which we perceive and evaluate what is going on around us.* Seldom do we question these assumptions, for, like water to a fish, the

framework from which we view life remains largely beyond our ordinary perception.

The rare instances in which these assumptions are challenged, however, can be upsetting. Although as a sociologist I should be able to look at my own culture "from the outside," my trip to Africa quickly revealed how fully I had internalized my own culture. My upbringing in Western industrialized society had given me strong assumptions about aspects of social life that had become deeply rooted in my being—staring, hygiene, and the use of space. But in this part of Africa these assumptions were useless in helping me get through daily life. No longer could I count on people to stare only surreptitiously, to take precautions against invisible microbes, or to stand in line in an orderly fashion, one behind the other.

As you can tell from the opening vignette, I personally found these different assumptions upsetting, for they violated my basic expectations of "the way people *ought* to be"—although I did not even know how firmly I held these expectations until they were so abruptly challenged. When my nonmaterial culture failed me—when it no longer enabled me to make sense out of the world—I experienced a disorientation known as **culture shock.** In the case of buying tickets, the fact that I was several inches taller than most Moroccans and thus able to outreach almost everyone helped me adjust partially to their different ways of doing things. But I never did get used to the idea that pushing ahead of others was "right," and I always felt guilty when I used my size to receive preferential treatment.

An important consequence of culture within us is **ethnocentrism,** a tendency to use our own group's ways of doing things as the yardstick for judging others. All of us learn that the ways of our own group are good, right, proper, and even superior to other ways of life. As sociologist William Sumner (1906), who developed this concept, said, "One's own group is the center of everything, and all others are scaled and rated with reference to it."

Ethnocentrism has both positive and negative consequences. On the positive side, it creates in-group loyalties. On the negative side, ethnocentrism can lead to harmful discrimination against people whose ways differ from ours.

The many ways culture affects our lives fascinates sociologists. In this chapter we'll examine more explicitly just how profoundly culture affects everything we are. This will serve as a basis from which you can start to analyze your previously unquestioned assumptions of reality and thus help you gain a different perspective on social life and your role in it.

■ **In Sum** To avoid losing track of the ideas under discussion, let's pause for a moment to summarize, and in some instances clarify, the principles we have covered:

1. There is nothing "natural" about material culture. Arabs wear gowns on the street and feel it is natural to do so; Americans do the same with jeans.

2. There is nothing "natural" about nonmaterial culture; it is just as arbitrary to stand in line as to push and shove.

3. Culture becomes a lens through which we see the world and obtain our perception of reality.

4. Culture provides implicit instructions that tell us what we ought to do in various situations; it provides a fundamental basis for our decision making.

5. Culture also provides a "moral imperative"; that is, the culture that people internalize seems "right" and other ways "wrong." (I, for example, deeply believed that it was wrong to push and shove to get ahead of others.)

6. Coming into contact with a radically different culture challenges our basic assumptions of life. (I experienced culture shock when I discovered that my deeply ingrained cultural ideas about hygiene and the use of space no longer applied.)

7. Although the particulars of culture differ from one group of people to another, culture itself is universal. That is, all people have culture. There are no exceptions. A society cannot exist without developing shared, learned ways of dealing with the demands of life.

8. All people are *ethnocentric,* which has both positive and negative consequences.

Practicing Cultural Relativism

To counter our tendency to use our own culture as the standard by which we judge other cultures, we can practice **cultural relativism;** that is, we can try to understand a culture on its own terms. Cultural relativism is looking at how the elements of a culture fit together, without judging those elements as superior or inferior to one's own way of life.

Because we tend to use our own culture to judge others, cultural relativism presents a challenge to ordinary thinking. For example, most U.S. citizens appear to have strong feelings against raising bulls for the purpose of stabbing them to death in front of crowds that shout "Olé!" According to cultural relativism, however, bullfighting must be viewed from the framework of the culture in which it takes place—*its* history, *its* folklore, *its* ideas of bravery, and *its* ideas of sex roles.

You still may regard bullfighting as wrong, of course, because U.S. culture, so deeply ingrained in us, has no history of bullfighting. We all possess culturally specific ideas about cruelty to animals, ideas that have evolved slowly and match other elements of our culture. Consequently, practices that once were common—cock fighting, dog fighting, bear-dog fighting, and so on—have been gradually weeded out (Bryant 1993).

None of us can be entirely successful at practicing cultural relativism; we simply cannot help viewing a contrasting way of life through the lens that our own culture provides. Cultural relativism, however, is an attempt to refocus that lens and thereby appreciate other ways of life rather than simply asserting, "Our way is right."

Although cultural relativism is a worthwhile goal and helps us avoid cultural smugness, this view has come under attack. Anthropologist Robert Edgerton, in a provocative book, *Sick Societies* (1992), points out that some cultures endanger their people's health, happiness, or survival. He suggests that we develop a scale for evaluating cultures on their "quality of life," much as we do for U.S. cities. He also asks why we should consider cultures that practice female genital mutilation, gang rape, wife beating, or that sell daughters into prostitution as morally equivalent to those that do not. Cultural values that result in exploitation, he says, are inferior to those that enhance people's lives.

Edgerton's sharp questions and incisive examples bring us to a topic that comes up repeatedly in this text—the disagreements that arise among scholars as they confront changing views of reality. It is such questioning of assumptions that keeps sociology interesting.

COMPONENTS OF SYMBOLIC CULTURE

Sociologists sometimes refer to nonmaterial culture as **symbolic culture** because its central component is the symbols that people use. A **symbol** is something to which people attach meaning and which they then use

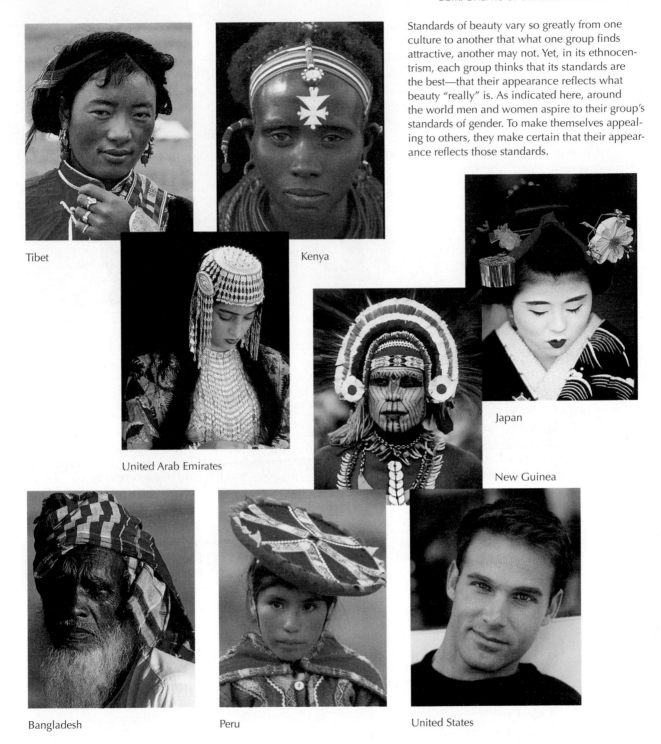

Standards of beauty vary so greatly from one culture to another that what one group finds attractive, another may not. Yet, in its ethnocentrism, each group thinks that its standards are the best—that their appearance reflects what beauty "really" is. As indicated here, around the world men and women aspire to their group's standards of gender. To make themselves appealing to others, they make certain that their appearance reflects those standards.

Tibet

Kenya

Japan

United Arab Emirates

New Guinea

Bangladesh

Peru

United States

to communicate. Symbols are the basis of nonmaterial culture. They include gestures, language, values, norms, sanctions, folkways, and mores. Let's look at each of these components of symbolic culture.

Gestures

Gestures, which involve using one's body to communicate with others, are useful shorthand ways to convey messages without using words. Although people in every culture of the world use gestures, the meaning of those gestures may change completely from one culture to another. North Americans, for example, communicate a succinct message by raising the middle finger in a short, upward-stabbing motion. I stress "North Americans," for that gesture does not convey the same message in South America or most other parts of the world.

I once was surprised to find that this particular gesture was not universal, having internalized it to such an extent that I thought everyone knew what it meant. When I was comparing gestures in Mexico, however, this gesture drew a blank look from friends. After I explained its intended meaning, they laughed and showed me their rudest gesture—placing the hand under the armpit and moving the upper arm up and down. To me, they simply looked as if they were imitating a monkey, but to them the gesture meant "Your mother is a whore," absolutely the worst possible insult in that culture.

Gestures thus not only facilitate communication but also, because they differ around the world, can lead to misunderstanding, embarrassment, or worse. Once in Mexico, for example, I raised my hand to a certain height to indicate how tall a child was. My hosts began to laugh. It turns out that Mexicans use three hand gestures to indicate height: separate ones for people, animals, and plants. (See Figure 2.1.) What had amused them was that I had ignorantly used the plant gesture to indicate the child's height.

To get along in another culture, then, it is important to learn the gestures of that culture. If you don't, you will not only fail to achieve the simplicity of communication that gestures allow, but you will also miss much of what is happening, run the risk of appearing foolish, and possibly offend people. In some cultures, for example, you would provoke deep offense if you were to offer food or a gift with your left hand, because the left hand is reserved for dirty tasks, such as wiping after going to the bathroom. Left-handed Americans visiting Arabs, please note!

Now suppose for a moment that you are visiting southern Italy. After eating one of the best meals of your life, you are so pleased that when you catch the waiter's eye, you smile broadly and use the standard U.S. "A-OK" gesture of putting your thumb and forefinger together

Many Americans perceive bullfighting, which is illegal in the United States, as a cruel activity that should be abolished everywhere in the world. To Spaniards and those who have inherited Spanish culture, however, bullfighting is a beautiful, artistic sport in which matador and bull blend into a unifying image of power, courage, and glory. *Cultural relativism* requires that we suspend our own perspectives in order to grasp the perspectives of others, something that is much easier described than attained.

and making a large "O." The waiter looks horrified, and you are struck speechless when the manager asks you to leave. What have you done? Nothing on purpose, of course, but in that culture that gesture refers to a part of the human body that is not mentioned in polite company (Ekman et al. 1984).

Some gestures are so associated with emotional messages that the gesture itself, even when demonstrated out of context, summons up emotions. For example, my introduction to Mexican gestures took place at a dinner table. It was evident that my husband-and-wife hosts were trying to hide their embarrassment at using their culture's obscene gesture at their dinner table. And I felt the same way—not about *their* gesture, of course, which meant absolutely nothing to me—but about the one I was teaching them.

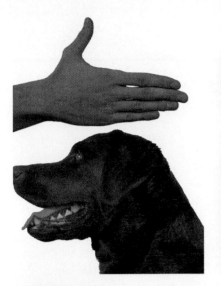

Figure 2.1	**GESTURES TO INDICATE HEIGHT, SOUTHERN MEXICO**

Language

Gestures and words go hand in hand, as is evident when you watch people talking. We use gestures to supplement our words, to provide a deeper understanding of

Although most gestures are learned, and therefore vary from culture to culture, some gestures that represent fundamental emotions such as sadness, anger, and fear appear to be inborn. This crying child in Mozambique differs little from a crying child in China or the United States or anywhere else on the globe. In a few years, however, this child will demonstrate a variety of gestures highly specific to his culture.

what we are communicating. In using written language, we often miss the subtle cues that gestures provide. To help supply these cues in online communications, people have developed *emoticons,* a type of "written gestures," to help convey the feelings that go with their words. Emoticons are the topic of the Down-to Earth Sociology box on the next page.

The primary way in which people communicate with one another is through **language**—a system of symbols that can be strung together in an infinite number of ways for the purpose of communicating abstract thought. Each word is actually a symbol, a sound to which we have attached a particular meaning so that we then can use it to communicate with one another. Language itself is universal in the sense that all human groups have language, but there is nothing universal about the meanings given to particular sounds. Thus, like gestures, in different cultures the same sound may mean something entirely different—or may have no meaning at all.

The significance of language for human life is difficult to overstate, as will become apparent from the following discussion on how language allows culture to exist.

Language Allows Human Experience to Be Cumulative By means of language, one generation can pass significant experiences on to the next, allowing the next

Sociology

EMOTICONS: "WRITTEN GESTURES" FOR EXPRESSING YOURSELF ONLINE

Talking online has become a favorite activity of millions of people. Teenagers rehash the day's events with friends; grandparents keep in touch with grandchildren in different states; hobbyists talk about their special interests; businesspeople seal their deals with the click of a "send" button. All of them love the speed of online communications. They send an e-mail or post a note in a chatroom, and in an instant people across the country or in distant lands can read or respond to it.

There is something nagging about online talk, though. It leaves a dissatisfying taste because it is so one-dimensional. People miss the nuances of emotion and overlays of meaning transmitted in face-to-face conversations. Lacking are the gestures and tones of voice that give color and life to our communications, the subtleties by which we monitor and communicate sub-messages. To help fill this gap, computer users have developed a set of symbols to convey their humor, disappointment, sarcasm, and other moods and attitudes. Although these symbols are not as varied or spontaneous

as the nonverbal cues of face-to-face interaction, they are useful. Here are some of them. If you tilt your head to the left as you view them, the symbols will be clearer.

:-)	Smile
:-))	Laugh
:-D	Laugh or big grin
:.)	Laughing tears
:-(	Frowning, or Sad
:-((	Very Sad
>:-(	Angry, annoyed
;-)	Wink, wink— know what I mean?
:-X	My lips are sealed
:-P	Sticking out your tongue
:-')	Tongue in cheek
>:-)	Feeling in a devilish mood
:-0	WOW! (What a surprise!)
0:-)	Angel

Some correspondents also use abbreviations to add a touch of whimsy:

GMTA	Great Minds Think Alike
IAB	I Am Bored
ILY	I Love You
IMHO	In My Humble Opinion
J/K	Just Kidding
OIC	Oh, I see
LOL	Laughing Out Loud
OTF	On The Floor (laughing)
ROTF	Rolling On The Floor
ROFLWTIME	Rolling On Floor Laughing With Tears In My Eyes
UGG	You Go, Girl!
WTG	Way To Go!

With e-mail innovations, such shorthand may become unnecessary. Now that we can include video in our e-mail, recipients can see our image and hear our voice. As the cost of video transmitters drops, messages that include verbal and facial cues may replace much written e-mail. As long as written e-mail exists, however, some system of symbols to substitute for gestures will remain. ■

---

generation to build on experiences that it may never undergo. This building process enables humans to modify their behavior in light of what previous generations have learned. Hence the central sociological significance of language: *Language allows culture to develop by freeing people to move beyond their immediate experiences.*

Without language, human culture would be little more advanced than that of the lower primates. We would be limited to some system of grunts and gestures, which would minimize the temporal dimension of human life. Our communications would be limited to a small time span: to events now taking place, those that have just taken place, or those that will take place immediately—a sort of "slightly extended present." You can grunt and gesture, for example, that you want a drink of water, but in the absence of language how could you share ideas concerning past or future events? There would be little or no way to communicate to others what event you had in mind, much less the greater complexities that humans communicate—ideas and feelings about events.

Language Provides a Social or Shared Past Even without language, an individual would have some memories of experiences. Those memories, however, would be extremely limited, for people associate experiences with words and then use words to recall the experience. Such memories as would exist in the absence of language would also be highly individualized, for they could be only rarely and incompletely communicated to others, much less discussed and agreed on. With language, however, events can be codified, that is, attached to words and then recalled so that they can be discussed in the present.

Language Provides a Social or Shared Future Language also extends our time horizons forward. When people talk about past events, they share meanings that allow them to decide how they will or should act in similar circumstances in the future. Because language enables people to agree with one another concerning times, dates, and places, it also allows them to plan activities with one another.

Think about it for a moment. Without language, how could people ever plan future events? How could they communicate goals, purposes, times, and plans? Whatever planning could exist would have to be limited to extremely rudimentary communications, perhaps to an agreement to meet at a certain place when the sun is in a certain position. But think of the difficulty—perhaps impossibility—of conveying a change in this simple arrangement, such as "I can't make it tomorrow but my neighbor can come, if that's all right with you."

Language Allows Shared Perspectives or Understandings Our ability to speak, then, provides a social past and future. These two vital aspects of our humanity represent a watershed that distinguishes us from animals. But speech does much more than this. When humans talk with one another, they are exchanging ideas about events; that is, they are exchanging perspectives. Their words are the embodiment of their experiences, distilled and codified into a readily exchangeable form, mutually

intelligible for people who have learned that language. Talking about events allows people to arrive at the shared understandings that form the basis of social life. To not share a language, however, while living alongside one another, is to invite suspicion and miscommunication. This risk, which comes with a diverse society, is discussed in the Cultural Diversity box on the next page.

Language Allows Complex, Shared, Goal-Directed Behavior Common understandings also enable people to establish a *purpose* for getting together. Let's suppose you want to go on a picnic. You use speech not only to plan the picnic but also to decide on reasons for the picnic—which may be anything from "because it's a nice day and it shouldn't be wasted studying" to "because it's my birthday." Language permits you to blend individual activities into an integrated sequence. In other words, through discussion you decide where you will go; who will drive; who will bring the hamburgers, chips, and soda; where you will meet; and so on. Only because of language can you participate in such a picnic—or build bridges and roads, or attend college classes.

■ **In Sum** The sociological significance of language is that it takes us beyond the world of apes and allows culture to develop. Language frees us from the present by providing a past and a future. It gives us the capacity to share understandings about the past and to develop common perceptions about the future, as well as to establish underlying purposes for our activities.

Language and Perception: The Sapir-Whorf Hypothesis

In the 1930s, two anthropologists, Edward Sapir and Benjamin Whorf, became intrigued when they noted that the Hopi Indians of the southwestern United States had no words to distinguish among the past, the present, and the future. English, in contrast, as well as German, French, Spanish, and other languages, distinguishes carefully among these three time frames. From this observation, Sapir and Whorf concluded that the commonsense idea that words are merely labels that people attach to things was wrong. *Language, they concluded, has embedded within it ways of looking at the world.* Thus thinking and perception are not only expressed through language but are also shaped by language. When we learn a language, we learn not only words but also particular ways of thinking and perceiving (Sapir 1949; Whorf 1956).

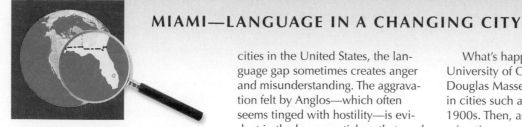

CULTURAL DIVERSITY In the United States

MIAMI—LANGUAGE IN A CHANGING CITY

In the years since Castro seized power in Cuba, the city of Miami has been transformed from a quiet southern city to a Latin-American mecca. Nothing reflects Miami's essential character today as much as its long-simmering feud over language: English versus Spanish. Half of the city's 360,000 residents have trouble speaking English. Only *one-fourth* of Miami residents speak English at home.

As this chapter stresses, language is a primary means by which people learn—and communicate—their social worlds. Consequently, language differences in Miami reflect not just cultural diversity but also people who live in separate social worlds.

Although its ethnic stew, makes Miami culturally one of the richest cities in the United States, the language gap sometimes creates anger and misunderstanding. The aggravation felt by Anglos—which often seems tinged with hostility—is evident in the bumper stickers that read "Will the Last American Out Please Bring the Flag?"

But Latinos, now a majority in Miami, are similarly frustrated. Many feel Anglos should be able to speak at least some Spanish. Nicaraguan immigrant Pedro Falco, for example, is studying English and wonders why more people don't try to learn his language. "Miami is the capital of Latin America," he says. "The population speaks Spanish."

Language and cultural flare-ups sometimes make headlines in Miami. Latinos were outraged when an employee at the Coral Gables Board of Realtors lost her job for speaking Spanish at the office. And protesters swarmed a Publix supermarket after a cashier was fired for chatting with a friend in Spanish.

What's happening in Miami, says University of Chicago sociologist Douglas Massey, is what happened in cities such as Chicago in the early 1900s. Then, as now, the rate of immigration exceeded the speed with which new residents learned English, creating a pile-up effect in the proportion of non-English speakers. "Becoming comfortable with English is a slow process," he points out, "whereas immigration is fast."

Massey expects Miami's proportion of non-English speakers to grow. But he says that this "doesn't mean in the long run that Miami is going to end up being a Spanish-speaking city." Instead, Massey believes that bilingualism will prevail. "Miami is the first truly bilingual city," he says. "The people who get ahead are not monolingual English speakers or monolingual Spanish speakers. They're people who speak both languages." ■

Source: Based on Sharp 1992; Usdansky 1992.

The implications of the **Sapir-Whorf hypothesis,** which alerts us to how extensively language affects us, are far-reaching. *The Sapir-Whorf hypothesis reverses common sense:* It indicates that rather than objects and events forcing themselves onto our consciousness, it is our very language that determines our consciousness, and hence our perception, of objects and events. Eskimos, for example, have many words for snow. As Eskimo children learn their language, they learn distinctions among types of snowfalls that are imperceptible to non-Eskimo speakers. Others might learn to see heavy and light snowfalls, wet and dry snowfalls, and so on; but not having words for "fine powdery," "thicker powdery," and "more granular" snowfalls prevents them from perceiving snow in the same way that Eskimos do.

Although Sapir and Whorf's observation that the Hopi do not have tenses was incorrect (Edgerton 1992:27), we still need to take their conclusion seri-

ously, for the classifications that we humans develop as we try to make sense of our worlds do influence our perception. Sociologist Eviatar Zerubavel (1991) gives a good example: Hebrew, his native language, does not differentiate between jam and jelly. Only when Zerubavel learned English could he "see" this difference, which is "obvious" to native English speakers. Similarly, if you learn to classify students as "dweebs," "dorks," "nerds," "brains," and so on, your perception of a student who asks several questions during class will be different from that of someone who does not know these classifications. In short, *language is the basis of culture.*

Because language is so significant in influencing perception, the terms we use for race-ethnicity are of special importance in our highly race-conscious society. This topic is explored in the Cultural Diversity box on the next page.

(+) Sanction = approval for Following Norm (Hugs, smiles).
(−) Sanction = disapproval for breaking Norm. (fine).

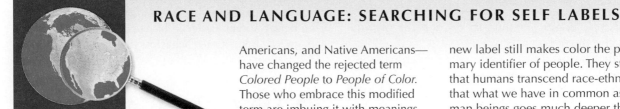

CULTURAL DIVERSITY In the United States

RACE AND LANGUAGE: SEARCHING FOR SELF LABELS

The groups that dominate society often determine the names that are used to refer to racial-ethnic groups. If those names become associated with oppression, they take on negative meanings. For example, the terms *Negro* and *Colored People* came to be associated with tyranny, cruelty, submission, and low status. To overcome these meanings, those referred to by these terms began to identify themselves as *African American*. They infused this new term with respect—a basic source of self-esteem which they felt the old terms denied them.

In a twist, African Americans—and to a lesser extent Latinos, Asian Americans, and Native Americans—have changed the rejected term *Colored People* to *People of Color.* Those who embrace this modified term are imbuing it with meanings that offer an identity of respect. The term also has political meanings. It indicates bonds that cross racial-ethnic lines, a growing sense of mutual ties and identity rooted in historical oppression.

There is *always* disagreement about racial-ethnic terms, and this one is no exception. Although most rejected the term *Colored People,* some did find in it a sense of respect and claimed it for themselves. The NAACP, for example, stands for the National Association for the Advancement of Colored People. The new term, *People of Color,* arouses similar feelings. Some who would be included in this term claim that it is inappropriate. They point out that this new label still makes color the primary identifier of people. They stress that humans transcend race-ethnicity, that what we have in common as human beings goes much deeper than our surface similarities. They stress that we should avoid terms that focus on differences in the pigmentation of our skin.

The language of self-reference in a society so conscious of skin color is an ongoing issue. As long as our society continues to place high emphasis on such superficial differences, the search for adequate terms is not ever likely to be "finished." In this quest for terms that strike the right chord, the term *People of Color* may become a historical footnote. If it does, it will be replaced by another term that indicates a changing self-identification in a changing historical context. ■

Values, Norms, and Sanctions

To learn a culture is to learn people's **values,** their ideas of what is desirable in life. When we uncover people's values, we learn a great deal about them, for values are the standards by which people define good and bad, beautiful and ugly. Values underlie our preferences, guide our choices, and indicate what we hold worthwhile in life.

Every group develops expectations concerning the right way to reflect its values. Sociologists use the term **norms** to describe those expectations, or rules of behavior, that develop out of a group's values. They use the term **sanctions** to refer to positive or negative reactions to the ways in which people follow norms. A **positive sanction** expresses approval for following a norm, while a **negative sanction** reflects disapproval for breaking a norm. Positive sanctions can be material, such as a monetary reward, a prize, or a trophy, but in everyday life they usually consist of hugs, smiles, a pat on the back, soothing words, or even handshakes. Negative sanctions can also be material—being given a fine in court is one example—but negative sanctions, too, are more likely to consist of harsh words or gestures, such as frowns, stares, or raised fists. Getting a raise at work is a positive sanction, indicating that you have followed the norms clustering around work values. If you get fired, however, you are getting a negative sanction, indicating that you have violated those norms. The North American finger gesture discussed earlier is, of course, a negative sanction.

Norms can become rigorous, making people feel stifled. One way some cultures relieve the pressure is through *moral holidays,* specified times when people are allowed to break norms. Moral holidays, such as Mardi Gras, often center around getting drunk and being rowdy. During moral holidays, many norms are loosened. Activities for which people would otherwise be arrested are permitted—and expected—including public drunkenness and nudity. The norms are never completely dropped, however, just loosened a bit.

Folkways and Mores

Norms that are not strictly enforced are called **folkways.** We expect people to comply with folkways, but we are

Mores = violated norms
taboo = strongly forbidden

likely to shrug our shoulders and not make a big deal about it if they don't. If someone insists on passing you on the left side of the sidewalk, for example, you are unlikely to take corrective action—although if the sidewalk is crowded and you must move out of the way, you might give the person a dirty look.

Other norms, however, are taken much more seriously. We think of them as essential to our core values, and we insist on conformity. These are called **mores** ("MORE-rays"). A person who steals, rapes, or kills has violated some of society's most important mores. As sociologist Ian Robertson (1987:62) put it,

> A man who walks down a street wearing nothing on the upper half of his body is violating a folkway; a man who walks down the street wearing nothing on the lower half of his body is violating one of our most important mores, the requirement that people cover their genitals and buttocks in public.

It should also be noted that one group's folkways may be another group's mores. Although a man walking down the street with the upper half of his body uncovered is deviating from a folkway, a woman doing the same thing is violating the mores. In addition, the folkways and mores of a subculture (the topic of the next section) may be the opposite of mainstream culture. For example, to walk down the sidewalk in a nudist camp

The violation of mores is usually a serious matter. In this case, it is serious enough that the police at this international rugby tournament have swung into action to protect the public from seeing a "disgraceful" sight—at least one so designated by this group. Yet, unlike most violations of mores, this scene also elicits barely suppressed laughter from the police.

with the entire body uncovered would conform to that subculture's folkways.

A **taboo** refers to a norm so strongly ingrained that even the thought of its violation is greeted with revulsion. Eating human flesh and having sex with one's parents are examples of such behaviors (Benales 1973; Read 1974; Henslin 2001).

Many Cultural Worlds: Subcultures and Countercultures

My best guess is that you won't be able to decipher the meaning of these sentences:

> We can make epistemically subjective statements about entities that are ontologically objective, and similarly, we can make epistemically objective statements about entities that are ontologically subjective.... Mental phenomena are ontologically subjective; and the observer-relative features inherit that ontological subjectivity. (Searle 1995:8, 12–13)

For most of us, this statement might as well be written in Greek. Philosophers, however, write like this, and—to them—the author's intent is clear. Philosophers form a **subculture,** *a world within the larger world of the dominant culture.* Each subculture has some distinctive way of looking at life. Even if we cannot understand the preceding quote, it makes us aware that the philosopher's view of life is not quite the same as ours.

U.S. society contains tens of thousands of subcultures. Some are as broad as the way of life we associate with teenagers, others as narrow as those we associate with body builders—or with philosophers. Some U.S. ethnic groups also form subcultures; their values, norms, and foods set them apart. So might their religion, language, and clothing. Occupational groups also form subcultures, as anyone who has hung out with cab drivers (Davis 1959; Henslin 1993), artists (McCall 1980), or construction workers (Haas 1972) can attest. Even sociologists form a subculture whose members, as you are learning, use a unique language for carving up the world.

Consider this quote from another subculture:

> If everyone applying for welfare had to supply a doctor's certificate of sterilization, if everyone who had committed a felony were sterilized, if anyone who had mental illness to any degree were sterilized—then our economy could easily take care of these people for the rest of their lives, giving them a decent living standard—but getting them out of the way. That way there would be no children abused, no surplus population, and, after a while, no pollution....

USA = Pluralistic Society

Each subculture provides its members with values and distinctive ways of viewing the world. Subcultures can form around almost any topic, including, as shown here, the human body itself.

> Now let's talk about stupidity. The level of intellect in this country is going down, generation after generation. The average IQ is always 100 because that is the accepted average. However, the kid with a 100 IQ today would have tested out at 70 when I was a lad. You get the concept . . . marching morons. . . .
>
> When the world system collapses, it'll be good people like you who will be shooting people in streets to feed their families. (Zellner 1995:58, 65)

Welcome to the world of the survivalists, where the message is much clearer than that of the philosophers—and much more disturbing.

The values and norms of most subcultures are compatible with the larger society to which they belong. In some cases, however, such as these survivalists, the group's values and norms place it in opposition to the dominant culture. Sociologists use the term **counterculture** to refer to such groups. Heavy metal adherents who glorify Satanism, hatred, cruelty, sexism, violence, and death are another example of a counterculture. Countercultures do not have to be negative, however. Back in the

1800s, the Mormons were a counterculture—who challenged the dominant culture's core value of monogamy.

An assault on core values is always met with resistance. To affirm their own values, members of the mainstream culture may ridicule, isolate, or even attack members of the counterculture. The Mormons, for example, were driven out of several states before they finally settled in Utah, which was then a wilderness. Even there the federal government would not let them practice polygyny (one man having more than one wife), and Utah's statehood was made conditional on its acceptance of monogamy (Anderson 1942/1966). Today, the federal and state governments have taken steps against various survivalist groups.

VALUES IN U.S. SOCIETY

An Overview of U.S. Values

As you know, the United States is a **pluralistic society,** made up of many different groups. The United States has numerous religious, racial, and ethnic groups, as well as countless interest groups that center around such divergent activities as collecting Barbie dolls and hunting deer. This state of affairs makes the job of specifying U.S. values difficult. Nonetheless, sociologists have tried to identify the underlying core values that are shared by the many groups that make up U.S. society. Sociologist Robin Williams (1965) identified the following:

1. *Achievement and success.* Americans place a high value on personal achievement, especially outdoing others. This value includes getting ahead at work and school, and attaining wealth, power, and prestige.

2. *Individualism.* Americans prize success that comes from individual efforts and initiative. They cherish the ideal that an individual can rise from the bottom of society to the very top. If someone fails to "get ahead," Americans generally find fault with that individual, rather than with the social system for placing roadblocks in his or her path.

3. *Activity and work.* Americans expect people to work hard and to be busily engaged in some activity even when not at work. This value is becoming less important.

4. *Efficiency and practicality.* Americans award high marks for getting things done efficiently. Even in everyday life, Americans consider it important to do things fast, and they constantly seek changes to increase efficiency.

5. *Science and technology.* Americans have a passion for applied science, for using science to control

Mass Media in Social Life

WHY DO NATIVE AMERICANS LIKE WESTERNS?

U.S. audiences (and even German, French, and Japanese ones) devour westerns. In the United States, it is easy to see why Anglos might like westerns, for it is they who seemingly defy the odds and emerge victorious. It is they who are portrayed as heroes who tame the savage wilderness and defend themselves from cruel, barbaric Indians who are intent on their destruction. But why would Indians like westerns?

Sociologist JoEllen Shively, a Chippewa who grew up on Indian reservations in Montana and North Dakota, observed that westerns are so popular that Native Americans bring bags of paperbacks into taverns to trade with one another. They even call one another "cowboy."

Intrigued, Shively decided to study the matter by showing a western movie to adult Native Americans and Anglos in a reservation town. The groups were equally matched in terms of education, age, income, and percentage of unemployment. To select the movie, Shively (1991, 1992) previewed more than seventy westerns. She chose a John Wayne movie, *The Searchers,* because it not only focuses on conflict between Indians and cowboys but also depicts the cowboys defeating the Indians. After the movie, the viewers filled out questionnaires, and she interviewed them.

Although John Wayne often portrayed an Anglo who kills Indians, Wayne is popular among Indian men. The men tend to identify with cowboys, who reflect their values of bravery, autonomy, and toughness.

Shively found something surprising: *All* Native Americans and Anglos identified with the cowboys; *none* identified with the Indians. Anglos and Native Americans identified with the cowboys in quite different ways, however. Each projected a different fantasy onto the story. While Anglos saw the movie as an accurate portrayal of the Old West and a justification of their own status in society, Native Americans saw it as embodying a free, natural way of life. In fact, Native Americans said that they were the "real cowboys." They said, "Westerns relate to the way I wish I could live"; "The cowboy is free"; "He's not tied down to an eight-to-five job, day after day."

Shively (1992) adds,

What appears to make Westerns meaningful to Indians is the fantasy of being free and independent like the cowboy.... Indians...find a fantasy in the cowboy story in which the important parts of their ways of life triumph and are morally good, validating their own cultural group in the context of a dramatically satisfying story.

In other words, values, not ethnicity, are the central issue. Thus, says Shively, Native American viewers make cowboys "honorary Indians," for the cowboys express their values of bravery, autonomy, and toughness. ■

nature—to tame rivers and harness winds—and to develop new technology, from improved carburetors to talking computers.

6. *Progress.* Americans expect rapid technological change. They believe that they should constantly build "more and better" gadgets that will help them move toward some vague goal called "progress."

7. *Material comfort.* Americans expect a high level of material comfort. This comfort includes not only nutrition, medical care, and housing, but also late-

model cars and recreational playthings—from boats to computer games.

8. *Humanitarianism.* Americans emphasize helpfulness, personal kindness, aid in mass disasters, and organized philanthropy.

9. *Freedom.* This core value pervades U.S. life. It underscored the American Revolution, and Americans today bristle at the suggestion of any limitation on personal freedom. The Mass Media in Social Life box above highlights some interesting research on how this core value applies to Native Americans.

10. *Democracy.* By this term, Americans refer to majority rule, to the right of everyone to express an opinion, and to representative government.

11. *Equality.* It is impossible to understand Americans without being aware of the central role that the value of equality plays in their lives.

12. *Racism and group superiority.* Although it contradicts freedom, democracy, and equality, Americans value some groups more than others and have done so throughout their history. The institution of slavery in earlier U.S. society is the most notorious example.

In an earlier publication (Henslin 1975), I updated Williams' analysis by adding these three values:

13. *Education.* Americans are expected to go as far in school as their abilities and finances allow. Over the years, the definition of an "adequate" education has changed, and today the attainment of a college education is considered an appropriate goal for most Americans.

14. *Religiosity.* There is a feeling that "every true American ought to be religious." This does not mean that everyone is expected to join a church, synagogue, or mosque, but that everyone ought to acknowledge a belief in a Supreme Being and follow some set of matching precepts. This value is so pervasive that Americans stamp "In God We Trust" on their money and declare in their national pledge of allegiance that they are "one nation under God."

Romantic love is a value so primary in the United States that it permeates the culture. Movies, music, and advertising promote this value. The couple shown here have learned the value well—not only to desire romantic love, but also how to express it to others.

15. *Romantic love.* Americans feel that the only proper basis for marriage is romantic love. Songs, literature, mass media, and "folk beliefs" all stress this value. They especially delight in the theme that "love conquers all."

Value Clusters

As you can see, values are not independent units; some cluster together to form a larger whole. In the **value cluster** surrounding success, for example, we find hard work, education, efficiency, material comfort, and individualism bound up together. Americans are expected to go far in school, to work hard afterward, to be efficient, and then to attain a high level of material comfort, which, in turn, demonstrates success. Success is attributed to the individual's efforts; lack of success is blamed on his or her faults.

Value Contradictions and Social Change

Not all values fall into neat, integrated packages. Some even contradict one another. The value of group superiority contradicts freedom, democracy, and equality, producing a **value contradiction.** There simply cannot be full expression of freedom, democracy, and equality, along with racism and sexism. Something has to give. One way in which Americans sidestepped this contradiction in the past was to say that freedom, democracy, and equality applied only to some groups. The contradiction was bound to surface over time, however, and so it did with the Civil War and the women's liberation movement. *It is precisely at the point of value contradictions, then, that one can see a major force for social change in a society.*

Emerging Values

A value cluster of three interrelated core values—leisure, physical fitness, and self-fulfillment—appears to be emerging in the United States. A fourth emerging core value—concern for the environment—can also be identified.

1. *Leisure.* The emergence of leisure as a value is reflected in the rapid growth of a huge recreation industry—from computer games, boats, and motor homes to sports arenas and vacation homes, and a gigantic travel and vacation industry.

2. *Physical fitness.* Physical fitness is not a new U.S. value, but increased emphasis is moving it into this emerging cluster.

This trend is evident in the "natural" foods craze; brew bars; people's obsessive concerns about weight and diet; the many joggers, cyclists, and backpackers; and the mushrooming number of health clubs and physical fitness centers.

3. *Self-fulfillment.* This value is reflected in the "human potential" movement, which involves becoming "all one can be," and in books and talk shows that focus on "self-help," "relating," and "personal development."

This emerging value cluster is a response to fundamental changes in U.S. society. Americans used to be preoccupied with forging a nation and fighting for economic survival. They now have come to a point in their economic development where millions of people are freed from long hours of work, and millions more are able to retire from work when they still can expect decades of life ahead of them. This value cluster centers around helping people to maintain their health and vigor during their younger years and enabling them to enjoy their years of retirement.

4. *Concern for the environment.* During most of U.S. history, the environment was seen as a challenge—a wilderness to be settled, forests to be chopped down, rivers and lakes to be fished, and animals to be hunted. The lack of concern for the environment that characterized earlier Americans is illustrated by the near extinction of the bison and the extinction in 1915 of the passenger pigeon, a bird previously so numerous that its annual migration would darken the skies for days. Today, Americans have developed a genuine, and (we can hope) long-term, concern for the environment.

This emerging value of environmental concern is also related to the current stage of U.S. economic development, a point that becomes clearer when we note that people act on environmental concerns only after basic needs are met. At this point in their development, for example, the world's poor nations have a difficult time "affording" this value.

Culture Wars: When Values Clash

Changes in core values are met with strong resistance by people who hold them dear. They see them as a threat to their way of life, an undermining of their present and their future. Efforts to change gender roles, for example, arouse intense controversy, as does support for alternative family forms and changes in sexual behavior. Alarmed at such onslaughts to their values, traditionalists fiercely defend historical family relationships and the gender roles they grew up with. The issue of socialist economic principles versus profit and private property is also at the center of controversy. Today's clash in values is so severe that the term "culture wars" has been coined to refer to it. Compared with the violence directed against the Mormons, however, today's reactions to such controversies are mild.

Values, both those held by individuals and those that represent a nation or people, can undergo deep shifts. It is difficult for many of us to grasp the pride with which earlier Americans destroyed trees that took thousands of years to grow, are located only on one tiny speck of the globe, and that we today consider part of the nation's and world's heritage. But this is a value statement, representing current views. The pride expressed on these woodcutters' faces represents another set of values entirely.

Real Culture: what people actually do.
Ideal Culture: goals that Grp consider ideal.

Values as Blinders

Just as values and their supporting beliefs paint a unique picture of reality, so they also form a view of what life *ought* to be like. Americans value individualism so highly, for example, that they tend to see everyone as free to pursue the goal of success. This value blinds them to the many circumstances that impede people's efforts. The dire consequences of family poverty, parents' low education, and dead-end jobs tend to drop from sight. Instead, Americans cling to the notion that anyone can make it—if they put out enough effort. And they know they are right, for every day, dangling before their eyes are enticing success stories—individuals who have succeeded despite huge handicaps.

ideal value is "Success."

"Ideal" Versus "Real" Culture

Many of the norms that surround cultural values are only partially followed. Differences always exist between a group's ideals and what its members actually do. Consequently, sociologists use the term **ideal culture** to refer to the values, norms, and goals that a group considers ideal, worth aspiring to. Success, for example, is part of ideal culture. Americans glorify academic progress, hard work, and the display of material goods as signs of individual achievement. What people actually do, however, usually falls short of the cultural ideal. Compared with their abilities, for example, most people don't work as hard as they could or go as far as they could in school. Sociologists call the norms and values that people actually follow **real culture.**

The adoption of new forms of communication by people who not long ago were cut off from events in the rest of the world is bound to change their nonmaterial culture. How do you think this man's thinking and view of the world is changing?

TECHNOLOGY IN THE GLOBAL VILLAGE

The New Technology

The gestures, language, values, folkways, and mores that we have discussed—these are all part of symbolic or nonmaterial culture. Culture, as you recall, also has a material aspect—a group's *things,* from its houses to its toys. Central to a group's material culture is its technology. In its simplest sense, **technology** can be equated with tools. In its broader sense, technology also includes the skills or procedures necessary to make and use those tools.

We can use the term **new technology** to refer to the emerging technologies that have a significant impact on social life. People develop minor technologies all the time. Most are slight modifications of existing technologies. Occasionally, however, they develop technologies that make a major impact on human life. It is primarily to these that the term *new technology* refers. For people 500 years ago, the new technology was the printing press. For us, the new technology consists of computers, satellites, and the electronic media.

The sociological significance of technology goes far beyond the tool itself. *Technology sets a framework for a group's nonmaterial culture.* If a group's technology changes, so do the ways people think and how they relate to one another. An example is gender relations. Through the centuries and throughout the world, it has been the custom (the nonmaterial culture of a group) for men to dominate women. Today, with instantaneous communications (the material culture), this custom has become much more difficult to maintain. For example, when women from many nations gathered in Beijing for a UN conference in 1995, satellites instantly transmitted their grievances around the globe. Such communications both convey and create discontent, as well as a feeling of sisterhood, motivating women to agitate for social change.

In today's world, the long-accepted idea that it is proper to withhold rights on the basis of someone's sex can no longer hold. What is usually invisible in this revolutionary change is the role of the new technology, which joins the world's nations into a global communication network.

Cultural Lag and Cultural Change

A couple of generations ago, sociologist William Ogburn (1922/1938), a functional analyst, coined the term **cultural lag.** By this, Ogburn meant that not all parts of a culture change at the same pace. When some part of a culture changes, other parts lag behind.

Ogburn pointed out that *a group's material culture usually changes first, with the nonmaterial culture lagging behind,* playing a game of catch up. For example, when we get sick, we could type our symptoms into a computer and get an immediate printout of our diagnosis and the best course of treatment. In fact, in some tests computers outperform physicians (Waldholz 1991). Yet our customs have not caught up with our technology, and we continue to visit the doctor's office.

Sometimes nonmaterial culture never does catch up. Instead, we rigorously hold on to some outmoded form, one that once was needed, but was long ago bypassed by new technology. A striking example is our nine-month school year. Have you ever wondered why it is nine months long, and why we take summers off? For most of

us, this is "just the way it's always been," and we've never questioned it. But there is more to this custom than meets the eye, for it is an example of cultural lag.

In the nineteenth century, when universal schooling came about, the school year matched the technology of the time, which was labor-intensive. For survival, parents needed their children's help at the crucial times of planting and harvesting. Although the invention of more productive farm machinery eliminated the need for the school year to be so short, generations later we still live with this cultural lag.

Technology and Cultural Leveling

For most of human history, communication was limited and travel slow. Consequently, in their relative isolation, human groups developed highly distinctive ways of life as they responded to the particular situations they faced. The unique characteristics they developed that distinguished one culture from another tended to change little over time. The Tasmanians, who lived on a remote island off the coast of Australia, provide an extreme example. For thousands of years, they had no contact with other people. They were so isolated that they did not even know how to make clothing or fire (Edgerton 1992).

Except in such rare instances, humans always had *some* contact with other groups. During these contacts, people learned from one another, adapting some part of the other's way of life. In this process, called **cultural diffusion,** groups are most open to a change in their technology or material culture. They usually are eager, for example, to adopt superior weapons and tools. In remote jungles in South America one can find metal cooking pots, steel axes, and even bits of clothing spun in mills in South Carolina. Although the direction of cultural diffusion today is primarily from the West to other parts of the world, cultural diffusion is not a one-way street—as bagels, woks, hammocks, and sushi bars in the United States attest.

With today's sophisticated technology in travel and communications, cultural diffusion is occurring rapidly. Air travel has made it possible to journey around the globe in a matter of hours. In the not-so-distant past, a trip from the United States to Africa was so unusual that only a few hardy people made it, and newspapers would herald their feat. Today, hundreds of thousands make the trip each year.

The changes in communication are no less vast. Communication used to be limited to face-to-face speech, to written messages that were passed from hand to hand, and to visual signals, such as smoke, or light that was reflected from mirrors. Despite newspapers, people in some

"COOL! A KEYBOARD THAT WRITES WITHOUT A PRINTER."

Technological advances are now so rapid that the technology of one generation is practically unrecognizable by the next generation.

parts of the United States did not hear that the Civil War had ended until weeks and even months after it was over. Today's electronic communications transmit messages across the globe in a matter of seconds, and we learn almost instantaneously what is happening on the other side of the world.

In fact, travel and communication unite us to such an extent that there almost is no "other side of the world" anymore. One result is **cultural leveling,** a process in which cultures become similar to one another. The globalization of capitalism is bringing not only technology but also Western culture to the rest of the world. Japan, for example, has adapted not only Western economic production but also Western forms of dress and music. These changes, which have been "superimposed" on Japanese culture, have turned Japan into a blend of Western and Eastern cultures.

Cultural leveling is occurring rapidly around the world, as is apparent to any traveler. The Golden Arches of McDonald's welcome today's visitors to Tokyo, Paris, London, Madrid, Moscow, Hong Kong, and Beijing. In Mexico, the most popular piñatas are no longer donkeys but, rather, Mickey Mouse and Fred Flintstone (Beckett 1996). In Beijing, a grade school teacher asked his class if they knew who Mickey Mouse was. One of the students held up a lunchbox with Mickey Mouse on it. As the teacher and the kids scanned the room, they found almost a dozen images of Mickey Mouse. But they didn't find a single image of any character from classical Chinese literature—not one (Hofstadter 2000).

Although the bridging of geography and culture by electronic signals and the exportation of Western icons do not in and of themselves mark the end of traditional cultures, the inevitable result is some degree of *cultural leveling,* some blander, less distinctive way of life—U.S. culture with French, Japanese, and Bulgarian accents, so to speak. Although the "cultural accent" remains, something vital is lost forever. For an extreme example of cultural leveling, and perhaps obliteration, see the Sociology & New Technology box below.

Sociology & the New Technology

ARE WE DOOMED TO EXTINCTION? WILL COMPUTERS REPLACE US?

A question that used to be asked only jokingly—Could machines replace the human species?—is now being asked more seriously. This issue was first brought to the public's attention in *2001: A Space Odyssey*. This movie introduced us to HAL, a rebellious computer with consciousness, who took control over the spaceship. Only with cunning were humans able to regain control.

Sometime during this century, the intelligence of computers is expected to outstrip that of humans. They will be able to think, not just to compute according to programmed instructions. Their thinking power—their ability to transform data into ideas, and to then compare and consider those ideas—will surpass that of humans. When this happens, computers "may begin to regard human beings as little more than an evolutionary dead end, a kind of pet to be kept around only for amusement" (Chapman 1999).

The stuff only of science fiction? At first it may seem so, but some scientists are taking the question so seriously that they have held a conference on this topic. Among the ideas they have put forth: Humans will "download" their thoughts and memories onto computers. This will give computers human consciousness, and they will become a "successor species." Some philosophers even propose that this is the next stage in evolution, that it is the destiny of humans to produce machines that will replace them (Gershenfeld 1999; Kurzweil 1999; Moravec 1999). ■

For Your Consideration

Most of us have a gut reaction that such a thing is too implausible to consider. Such reasoning should remain in the realm of science fiction. Consider for a moment, however, that computers became dominant. Would culture exist? If so, what would it consist of? Would language still be its essence? Would values exist? Would there, perhaps, be two main cultures, that of the dominant thinking machines and that of the inferior, submissive humans?

SUMMARY AND REVIEW

■ What Is Culture?

All human groups possess **culture**—language, beliefs, values, norms, and material objects that are passed from one generation to the next. **Material culture** consists of objects (art, buildings, clothing, tools). **Nonmaterial** (or **symbolic**) **culture** is a group's ways of thinking and patterns of behavior. **Ideal culture** is a group's ideal values, norms, and goals. **Real culture** is their actual behavior, which often falls short of their cultural ideals. Pp. 36–37.

What are *cultural relativism* and *ethnocentrism?*

People are naturally **ethnocentric**; that is, they use their own culture as a yardstick for judging the ways of others. In contrast, those who embrace **cultural relativism** try to understand other cultures on those cultures' own terms. Pp. 37, 38.

■ Components of Symbolic Culture

What are the components of nonmaterial culture?

The central component is **symbols**, anything to which people attach meaning and use to communicate with others. Universally, the symbols of nonmaterial culture are **gestures, language, values, norms, sanctions, folkways**, and **mores**. Pp. 38–41.

Why is language so significant to culture?

Language allows human experience to be goal-directed, cooperative, and cumulative. It also lets humans move beyond the present and share past, future, and other common perspectives. According to the **Sapir-Whorf hypothesis**, language even shapes our thoughts and perceptions. Pp. 41–44.

How do values, norms, sanctions, folkways, and mores reflect culture?

All groups have **values**, standards by which they define what is desirable or undesirable, and **norms**, rules or expectations about behavior. Groups use **positive sanctions** to show approval of those who follow their norms, and **negative sanctions** to show disapproval of those who do not. Norms that are not strictly enforced are called **folkways**, while **mores** are

norms to which groups demand conformity because they reflect core values. P. 45–46.

■ Many Cultural Worlds: Subcultures and Countercultures

How do subcultures and countercultures differ?

A **subculture** is a group whose values and related behaviors distinguish its members from the general culture. A **counterculture** holds values that stand in opposition to those of the dominant culture. Pp. 46–47.

■ Values in U.S. Society

What are the core U.S. values?

Although the United States is a **pluralistic society**, made up of many groups, each with its own set of values, certain values dominate: achievement and success, individualism, activity and work, efficiency and practicality, science and technology, progress, material comfort, equality, freedom, democracy, humanitarianism, racism and group superiority, education, religiosity, and romantic love. Some values cluster together (**value clusters**) to form a larger whole. **Value contradictions** (such as equality and racism) indicate areas of social tension, which are likely points of social change. Leisure, physical fitness, self-fulfillment, and concern for the environment are emerging core values. Changes in a society's values do not come without opposition. Pp. 47–51.

■ Technology in the Global Village

How is technology changing culture?

William Ogburn coined the term **cultural lag** to refer to how a group's nonmaterial culture lags behind its changing technology. With today's technological advances in travel and communications, **cultural diffusion** is occurring rapidly. This leads to **cultural leveling**, whereby many groups are adopting Western culture in place of their own customs. Much of the richness of the world's diverse cultures is being lost in the process. Pp. 51–53.

Where can I read more on this topic?

Suggested readings for this chapter are listed on page SR-2.

YOUR INTERACTIVE COMPANION WEB SITE

Your Interactive Companion Web Site includes practice tests, with feedback, and online learning activities with video, audio, and Weblinks. Your access code for this Web site is provided with this text.

GLOSSARY

counterculture a subculture whose values place its members in opposition to the values of the broader culture (p. 47)

cultural diffusion the spread of cultural characteristics from one group to another (p. 52)

cultural lag William Ogburn's term for a situation in which nonmaterial culture lags behind changes in the material culture (p. 52)

cultural leveling the process by which cultures become similar to one another; especially refers to the process by which Western industrial culture is imported and diffused into other cultures (p. 53)

cultural relativism understanding a people from the framework of their own culture (p. 38)

culture the language, beliefs, values, norms, behaviors, and even material objects that are passed from one generation to the next (p. 36)

culture shock the disorientation that people experience when they come in contact with a fundamentally different culture and can no longer depend on their taken-for-granted assumptions about life (p. 37)

ethnocentrism the use of one's own culture as a yardstick for judging the ways of other individuals or societies, generally leading to a negative evaluation of their values, norms, and behaviors (p. 37)

folkways norms that are not strictly enforced (p. 45)

gestures the ways in which people use their bodies to communicate with one another (p. 39)

ideal culture the ideal values and norms of a people: the goals held out for them (p. 51)

language a system of symbols that can be combined in an infinite number of ways to communicate abstract thought (p. 41)

material culture the material objects that distinguish a group of people, such as their art, buildings, weapons, utensils, machines, hairstyles, clothing, and jewelry (p. 36)

mores norms that are strictly enforced because they are thought to be essential to core values (p. 46)

negative sanction an expression of disapproval for breaking a norm, ranging from a mild, informal reaction such as a frown to severe formal reactions such as a prison sentence, banishment, or death (p. 45)

new technology a technology introduced into a society that has a significant impact on that society (p. 51)

nonmaterial culture (also called *symbolic culture*) a group's ways of thinking (including its beliefs, values, and other assumptions about the world) and doing (its common patterns of behavior, including language and other forms of interaction) (p. 37)

norms the expectations, or rules of behavior, that develop out of values (p. 45)

pluralistic society a society made up of many different groups (p. 47)

positive sanction a reward or positive reaction for following norms, ranging from a smile to a prize (p. 45)

real culture the norms and values that people actually follow (as opposed to *ideal culture*) (p. 51)

sanction an expression of approval or disapproval given to people for upholding or violating norms (p. 45)

Sapir-Whorf hypothesis Edward Sapir and Benjamin Whorf's hypothesis that language creates ways of thinking and perceiving (p. 44)

subculture the values and related behaviors of a group that distinguish its members from the larger culture; a world within a world (p. 46)

symbol something to which people attach meanings and then use to communicate with others (p. 38)

symbolic culture another term for nonmaterial culture (p. 38)

taboo a norm so strong that it brings revulsion if violated (p. 46)

technology in its narrow sense, tools; in its broader sense, the skills or procedures necessary to make and use those tools (p. 51)

value cluster a series of interrelated values that together form a larger whole (p. 49)

value contradiction values that contradict one another; to follow the one means to come into conflict with the other (p. 49)

values the standards by which people define what is desirable or undesirable, good or bad, beautiful or ugly (p. 45)

Chapter 3

Diane Davis, Making Mud Pies, 2000

Socialization

The old man was horrified when he found out. Life had never been good since his daughter lost her hearing when she was just two years old. She couldn't even talk— just fluttered her hands around trying to tell him things. Over the years, he had gotten used to that. But now…he

shuddered at the thought of her being pregnant. No one would be willing to marry her; he knew that. And the neighbors, their tongues would never stop wagging. Everywhere he went, he could hear people talking behind his back.

If only his wife were still alive, maybe she could come up with something. What should he do? He couldn't just kick his daughter out into the street.

After the baby was born, the old man tried to shake his feelings, but they wouldn't let

loose. Isabelle was a pretty name, but every time he looked at the baby he felt sick to his stomach.

He hated doing it, but there was no way out. His daughter and her baby would have to live in the attic.

…

Unfortunately, this is a true story. Isabelle was discovered in Ohio in 1938 when she was about 6½ years old, living in a dark room with her deaf-mute mother. Isabelle couldn't talk, but she did use gestures to communicate

[handwritten: Nature = heredity Nurture = social Inviroment.]

with her mother. An inadequate diet and lack of sunshine had given Isabelle a disease called *rickets*. Her legs

> were so bowed that as she stood erect the soles of her shoes came nearly flat together, and she got about with a skittering gait. Her behavior toward strangers, especially men, was almost that of a wild animal, manifesting much fear and hostility. In lieu of speech she

made only a strange croaking sound. (Davis 1940/2001:134)

When the newspapers reported this case, sociologist Kingsley Davis decided to find out what happened to Isabelle. We'll come back to that later, but first let's use the case of Isabelle to gain some insight into what human nature is. ■

WHAT IS HUMAN NATURE?

For centuries, people have been intrigued with the question of what is human about human nature. How much of people's characteristics comes from "nature" (heredity) and how much from "nurture" (the **social environment,** contact with others)? One way to answer this question is to study identical twins who have been reared apart. See the Down-to-Earth Sociology box on the next page for a fascinating account of identical twins. Another way is to study children who have had little human contact. Let's begin with the case of Isabelle.

Isolated Children

Cases like Isabelle's surface from time to time. What can they tell us about human nature? We can first conclude that humans have no natural language, for Isabelle, and others like her, are unable to speak.

But maybe Isabelle was mentally impaired. This is what people first thought, for she scored practically zero on an intelligence test. But after a few months of intensive language training, Isabelle was able to speak in short sentences. In about a year, she could write a few words, do simple addition, and retell stories after hearing them. Seven months later, she had a vocabulary of almost 2,000 words. It took only two years for Isabelle to reach the intellectual level that is normal for her age. She then went on to school, where she was "bright, cheerful, energetic...and participated in all school activities as normally as other children" (Davis 1940/2001:135).

Institutionalized Children

But what besides language is required if a child is to develop into what we consider a healthy, balanced, intelligent human being? We find part of the answer in an

interesting experiment from the 1930s. Back then, orphanages dotted the United States. Children reared in orphanages often had difficulty establishing close bonds with others—and they tended to have lower IQs. "Common sense" (which we noted in Chapter 1 is unreliable) told everyone that the cause of mental retardation is biological ("They're just born that way"). Two psychologists, H. M. Skeels and H. B. Dye (1939), however, began to suspect another cause. For background on their experiment, Skeels (1966) provides this account of a "good" orphanage in Iowa during the 1930s, where he and Dye were consultants:

> Until about six months, they were cared for in the infant nursery. The babies were kept in standard hospital cribs that often had protective sheeting on the sides, thus effectively limiting visual stimulation; no toys or other objects were hung in the infants' line of vision. Human interactions were limited to busy nurses who, with the speed born of practice and necessity, changed diapers or bedding, bathed and medicated the infants, and fed them efficiently with propped bottles.

Perhaps, thought Skeels and Dye, the absence of stimulating social interaction was the basic problem, not some biological incapacity on the part of the children. To test their controversial idea, they placed in an institution for the mentally retarded thirteen infants whose mental retardation was so obvious that no one wanted to adopt them. Each infant, then about 19 months old, was assigned to a separate ward of women ranging in mental age from 5 to 12 and in chronological age from 18 to 50. The women were pleased with this arrangement. They not only did a good job taking care of the infants' basic physical needs—diapering, feeding, and so on—but also

Sociology

HEREDITY OR ENVIRONMENT?
THE CASE OF OSKAR AND JACK, IDENTICAL TWINS

Identical twins share exact genetic heredity. One fertilized egg divides to produce two embryos. If heredity determines personality—or attitudes, temperament, skills, and intelligence—then identical twins should be identical not only in regard to looks but also in regard to these characteristics.

The fascinating case of Jack and Oskar helps us unravel this mystery. From their experience, we can see the far-reaching effects of the environment—how social experiences override biology.

Jack Yufe and Oskar Stohr are identical twins born in 1932 to a Jewish father and a Catholic mother. They were separated as babies after their parents divorced. Oskar was reared in Czechoslovakia by his mother's mother, who was a strict Catholic. When Oskar was a toddler, Hitler took over this area of Czechoslovakia, and Oskar learned to love Hitler and to hate Jews. He became involved with the Hitler Youth (a sort of Boy Scout organization, except that this one was designed to instill the "virtues" of patriotism, loyalty, obedience—and hatred).

Jack's upbringing was in almost total contrast to Oskar's. Reared in Trinidad by his father, he learned loyalty to Jews and hatred of Hitler and the Nazis. After the war, Jack emigrated to Israel, where, at the age of 17, he joined a kibbutz. Later, Jack served in the Israeli army.

The questions of the relative influence of heredity and the environment on human behavior has fascinated and plagued researchers. Identical twins reared apart provide an opportunity to examine this relationship. However, almost all identical twins, including these girls, are reared together, frustrating efforts to separate heredity and environment.

In 1954, the two brothers met. It was a short meeting, and Jack had been warned not to tell Oskar that they were Jews. Twenty-five years later, in 1979, when they were 47 years old, social scientists at the University of Minnesota brought them together again. These researchers figured that because Jack and Oskar had the same genes, whatever differences they showed would be due to the environment—to their different social experiences.

Not only did Oskar and Jack have different attitudes about the war, Hitler, and Jews, but also their basic orientations to life were different. In their politics, Oskar was conservative, while Jack was more liberal.

Oskar enjoyed leisure, while Jack was a workaholic. And, as you can predict, Jack was very proud of being a Jew. Oskar, who by this time knew that he was a Jew, wouldn't even mention it.

That would seem to settle the matter. But there was another side to the findings. The researchers also discovered that Oskar and Jack both liked sweet liqueur and spicy foods, excelled at sports as children but had difficulty with math, and had the same rate of speech. Each flushed the toilet both before and after using it and enjoyed startling people by sneezing in crowded places. ■

For Your Consideration

Heredity or environment? How much influence does *each* one have? The question is not yet settled, but at this point it seems fair to conclude that the *limits* of certain physical and mental abilities are established by heredity (such as ability at sports and mathematics), while such basic orientations to life as attitudes are the result of the environment. We can put it this way: For some parts of life, the blueprint is drawn by heredity; but even here the environment can redraw those lines. For other parts, the individual is a blank slate, and it is entirely up to the environment to determine what is written on that slate.

Sources: Based on Begley 1979; Chen 1979; Wright 1995.

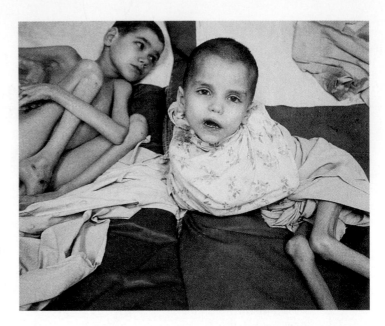

The treatment given these orphaned children in Romania will make it difficult for them to develop into fully functioning adults. If they survive, they will carry scars into adulthood. As explained in the text, it is also likely that their abuse has affected their ability to reason.

they loved to play with the children, to cuddle them, and to shower them with attention. They even competed to see which ward would have "its baby" walking or talking first. Each child had one woman who became

> particularly attached to him [or her] and figuratively "adopted" him [or her]. As a consequence, an intense one-to-one adult-child relationship developed, which was supplemented by the less intense but frequent interactions with the other adults in the environment. Each child had some one person with whom he [or she] was identified and who was particularly interested in him [or her] and his [or her] achievements. (Skeels 1966)

The researchers left a control group of twelve infants at the orphanage. These infants were also retarded but were higher in intelligence than the other thirteen. They received the usual care. Two and a half years later, Skeels and Dye tested all the children's intelligence. Their findings were startling: Those assigned to the retarded women had gained an average of 28 IQ points while those who remained in the orphanage had lost 30 points.

What happened after these children were grown? Did these initial differences matter? Twenty-one years later, Skeels and Dye did a follow-up study. Those in the control group who had remained in the orphanage had, on average, less than a third grade education. Four still lived in state institutions, while the others held low-level jobs. Only two had married. In contrast, the average level of education for the thirteen individuals in the experimental group was twelve grades (about normal for that period). Five had completed one or more years of

college. One had not only earned a B.A. but had also gone on to graduate school. Eleven had married. All thirteen were self-supporting and had higher-status jobs or were homemakers (Skeels 1966). Apparently, then, one characteristic we take for granted as being a basic "human" trait—high intelligence—depends on early close relations with other humans.

Let's consider one other case, the story of Genie:

> In 1970, California authorities found Genie, a 13-year-old girl who had been kept locked in a small room and tied to a chair since she was 20 months old. Apparently her 70-year-old father hated children, and had probably caused the death of two of Genie's siblings. Her 50-year-old mother was partially blind and was frightened of her husband. Genie could not speak, did not know how to chew, and was unable to stand upright. On intelligence tests, she scored at the level of a 1-year-old. After intensive training, Genie learned to walk and use simple sentences (although they were garbled). As she grew up, her language remained primitive, she took anyone's property if it appealed to her, and she went to the bathroom wherever she wanted. At the age of 21, Genie went to live in a home for adults who cannot live alone. (Pines 1981)

From this pathetic story, we can conclude that not only intelligence but also the ability to establish close bonds with others depends on early interaction. In addition, apparently there is a period prior to age 13 in which language and human bonding must occur for humans to develop high intelligence and the ability to be sociable and follow social norms.

Deprived Animals

A final lesson can be learned by looking at animals that have been deprived of normal interaction. In a series of experiments with rhesus monkeys, psychologists Harry and Margaret Harlow demonstrated the importance of early learning. The Harlows (1962) raised baby monkeys in isolation. They gave each monkey two artificial mothers, shown in the photograph below. One "mother" was only a wire frame with a wooden head, but it did have a nipple from which the baby could nurse. The frame of the other "mother," which had no bottle, was covered with soft terrycloth. To obtain food, the baby monkeys nursed at the wire frame.

When the Harlows (1965) frightened the babies with a mechanical bear or dog, they did not run to the wire frame "mother." Instead, they would cling pathetically to their terrycloth "mother." The Harlows concluded that infant-mother bonding is due not to feeding but, rather, to what they termed "intimate physical contact." To most of us, this phrase means cuddling.

Like humans, monkeys also need interaction to thrive. Those raised in isolation are unable to interact satisfactorily with others. In this photograph, we see one of the monkeys described in the text. Purposefully frightened by the experimenter, the monkey has taken refuge in the soft terrycloth draped over an artificial "mother."

In one of their many experiments, the Harlows isolated baby monkeys for different lengths of time. They found that when monkeys were isolated for short periods (about three months), they were able to overcome the effects of their isolation. Those isolated for six months or more, however, were unable to adjust to normal monkey life. They could not play or engage in pretend fights, and the other monkeys rejected them. In other words, the longer the isolation, the more difficult it is to overcome its effects. In addition, a critical learning stage may exist; if that stage is missed, it may be impossible to compensate for what has been lost. This may have been the case with Genie.

Because humans are not monkeys, we must be careful about extrapolating from animal studies to human behavior. The Harlow experiments, however, support what we know about children who are reared in isolation.

■ **In Sum** Society Makes Us Human Apparently, babies do not "naturally" develop into human adults. Although their bodies grow, if raised in isolation they become little more than big animals. Without the concepts that language provides, they can't experience or even grasp relations between people (the "connections" we call brother, sister, parent, friend, teacher, and so on). And without warm, friendly interaction, they aren't "friendly" in the accepted sense of the term; nor do they cooperate with others. In short, it is through human contact that people learn to be members of the human community. This process by which we learn the ways of society (or of particular groups), called **socialization**, is what sociologists have in mind when they say "Society makes us human."

SOCIALIZATION INTO THE SELF, MIND, AND EMOTIONS

At birth, we have no idea that we are a separate being. We don't even know that we are a he or a she. How do we develop a **self**, the picture that we have of how others see us, our view of who we are?

Cooley and the Looking-Glass Self

Back in the 1800s, Charles Horton Cooley (1864–1929), a symbolic interactionist who taught at the University of Michigan, concluded that this unique aspect of "humanness" is socially created; that is, *our sense of self develops from interaction with others.* Cooley (1902) coined the term **looking-glass self** to describe the process by which a sense of self develops. He summarized this idea in the following couplet:

Each to each a looking-glass
Reflects the other that doth pass.

The looking-glass self contains three elements:

1. *We imagine how we appear to those around us.* For example, we may think that others see us as witty or dull.

2. *We interpret others' reactions.* We come to conclusions about how others evaluate us. Do they like us for being witty? Do they dislike us for being dull?

3. *We develop a self-concept.* Based on our interpretations of how others react to us, we develop feelings and ideas about ourselves. A favorable reflection in this "social mirror" leads to a positive self-concept, a negative reflection to a negative self-concept.

Note that the development of the self does *not* depend on accurate evaluations. Even if we grossly misinterpret how others think about us, those misjudgments become part of our self-concept. Note also that although the self-concept begins in childhood, *its development is an ongoing, lifelong process.* The three steps of the looking-glass self are part of our everyday lives: As we monitor how other people react to us, we continually modify the self. The self, then, is never a finished product, but is always in process, even into old age.

Mead and Role-Taking

Another symbolic interactionist, George Herbert Mead (1863–1931), who taught at the University of Chicago, added that play is critical to the development of the self. In play, children learn to **take the role of the other,** that is, to put themselves in someone else's shoes—to understand how someone else feels and thinks and to anticipate how that person will act.

Young children attain this ability only gradually (Mead 1934; Coser 1977). In a simple experiment, psychologist J. Flavel (1968) asked 8- and 14-year-olds to explain a board game to some children who were blindfolded and to others who were not. The 8-year-olds gave the same instructions to everyone, while the 14-year-olds gave more detailed instructions to those who were blindfolded. The younger children could not yet take the role of the other, while the older children could.

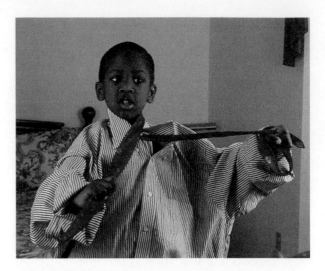

Mead analyzed taking the role of the other as an essential part of learning to be a full-fledged member of society. At first, we are able to take the role only of *significant others,* as this child is doing. Later we develop the capacity to take the role of the *generalized* other, which is essential not only for extended cooperation but also for the control of our antisocial desires.

As they develop this ability, at first children are able to take only the role of **significant others,** individuals who significantly influence their lives, such as parents or siblings. By assuming their roles during play, such as by dressing up in their parents' clothing, children cultivate the ability to put themselves in the place of significant others.

As the self gradually develops, children internalize the expectations of more and more people. The ability to take roles eventually extends to being able to take the role of "the group as a whole." Mead used the term **generalized other** to refer to this, our perception of how people in general think of us.

To take the role of others is essential if we are to become cooperative members of human groups—whether they be our family, friends, or co-workers. This ability allows us to modify our behavior by anticipating how others will react—something Genie never learned.

Learning to take the role of the other goes through three stages:

1. *Imitation.* Children under 3 can only mimic others. They do not yet have a sense of self separate from others, and they can only imitate people's gestures and words. (This stage is actually not role taking, but it prepares the child for it.)

2. *Play.* From the age of about 3 to 6, children pretend to take the roles of specific people. They might pretend

To help his students understand what the term *generalized other* means, Mead used baseball as an illustration. The text explains why team sports and organized games are excellent examples to use in explaining this concept.

social product. Mead stressed that we cannot think without symbols. But where do these symbols come from? Only from society, which gives us our symbols by giving us language. If society did not provide the symbols, we would not be able to think, and thus would not possess what we call the mind. Mind, then, like language, is a product of society.

Piaget and the Development of Reasoning Abilities

An essential part of being human is our ability to reason. How do we learn this skill?

This question intrigued Jean Piaget (1896–1980), a Swiss psychologist, who noticed that young children give similar wrong answers on intelligence tests. He thought that younger children might be using some sort of incorrect rule to figure out their answers. This could mean that children go through a common process as they learn how to reason (Piaget 1950, 1954; Phillips 1969).

they are a firefighter, a wrestler, Supergirl, Xena, Batman, and so on. They also like costumes at this stage and enjoy dressing up in their parents ' clothing, or tying a towel around their neck to "become" Superman or Wonder Woman.

3. *Games.* This third stage, organized play, or team games, begins roughly with the early school years. The significance for the self is that to play these games the individual must be able to take multiple roles. One of Mead's favorite examples was that of a baseball game, in which each player must be able to take the role of all the other players. To play baseball, the child not only must know his or her own role but also must be able to anticipate who will do what when the ball is hit or thrown

Mead also distinguished between the "I" and the "me" in the development of the self. The *"I" is the self as subject,* the active, spontaneous, creative part of the self. In contrast, the *"me" is the self as object.* It is made up of the attitudes we internalize from our interactions with others. Mead chose these pronouns to indicate these two aspects of the self, because in our language "I" is the active agent, as in "I shoved him," while "me" is the object of action, as in "He shoved me." Mead stressed that we are not passive in the socialization process. We are not like computerized robots, passively absorbing the responses of others. Rather, our "I" evaluates the reactions of others and organizes them into a unified whole.

Mead also drew a conclusion that some find startling—that *not only the self but also the human mind is a*

After years of testing, Piaget concluded that children go through four stages as they develop the ability to reason. (If you mentally substitute "reasoning skills" for the term *operational* in the following explanations, Piaget's findings will be easier to understand.)

1. **The sensorimotor stage** (from birth to about age 2) During this stage, understanding is limited to direct contact with the environment—sucking, touching, listening, seeing. Infants do not think, in any sense we understand. For example, they cannot recognize cause and effect.

2. **The preoperational stage** (from about age 2 to age 7) During this stage, children *develop the ability to use symbols.* They do not yet understand common concepts, however, such as size, speed, or causation. Although they can count, they do not really understand what numbers mean. Nor do they yet have the ability to take the role of the other. Piaget asked preoperational children to describe a clay model of a mountain range. They did just fine. But when he asked them to describe how the mountain range looked from where another child was sitting, they could not do so. They could only repeat what they saw from their view.

3. **The concrete operational stage** (from the age of about 7 to 12) Although reasoning abilities are more developed, they remain *concrete*. Children can now understand numbers, causation, and speed, and they are able to take the role of the other and to participate in team games. Without concrete examples, however, they are unable to talk about concepts such as truth, honesty, or justice. They can explain why Jane's answer was a lie, but they cannot describe what truth itself is.

4. **The formal operational stage** (after the age of about 12) Children are now capable of abstract thinking. They can talk about concepts, come to conclusions based on general principles, and use rules to solve abstract problems. During this stage, children are likely to become young philosophers (Kagan 1984). If shown a photo of a slave, for example, a child at the concrete operational stage might have said, "That's wrong!" Now, however, he or she is more likely to ask, "If our county was founded on equality, how could people have owned slaves?"

Global Considerations: Developmental Sequences

Cooley's conclusions about the looking-glass self and Mead's conclusions about role-taking and the mind as a social product appear to be universal. There is less agreement, however, that Piaget's four stages are globally true. Some researchers say that the stages are not as rigid as Piaget concluded, that children develop reasoning skills more gradually than this (Berk 1994).

Consider how the *content* of what children learn varies from one culture to another, and how this influences their thinking. For example, Brazilian street children have little or no schooling. Yet through selling candy they develop sophisticated mathematical and bargaining abilities (Saxe 1995). Because children in other cultures have experiences and abilities unlike those of our children, and because their thinking processes revolve around those activities, we cannot assume that the developmental sequences observed in our children are true of children around the globe (Berk 1994).

Freud and the Development of Personality

Along with the development of the mind and the self comes the development of personality. Let's look at a theory that has influenced the Western world.

In Vienna during the early 1900s, Sigmund Freud (1856–1939), a physician, founded *psychoanalysis,* a technique for treating emotional problems through long-term, intensive exploration of the subconscious mind. Let's look at that part of his thought that applies to the development of personality.

Freud believed that personality consists of three elements. Each child is born with the first, an **id,** Freud's term for inborn drives that cause us to seek self-gratification. The id of the newborn is evident in its cries of hunger or pain. The pleasure-seeking id operates throughout life. It demands immediate fulfillment of basic needs: attention, safety, food, sex, and so on.

But the id's drive for immediate and complete satisfaction often conflicts with the needs of other people. As the child comes up against norms and other constraints that block his or her desires (usually represented by parents), he or she must adapt to survive. To help cope with these constraints, a second component of the personality emerges, which Freud called the ego. The **ego** is the balancing force between the id and the demands of society that suppress it. The ego also serves to balance the id and the **superego,** the third component of the personality, more commonly called the *conscience*.

The superego represents *culture within us,* the norms and values we have internalized from our social groups. As the *moral* component of the personality, the superego provokes feelings of guilt or shame when we break social rules, or pride and self-satisfaction when we follow them.

According to Freud, when the id gets out of hand, we follow our desires for pleasure and break society's norms. When the superego gets out of hand, we become overly rigid in following those norms, finding ourselves bound in a straitjacket of rules that inhibit our lives. The ego, the balancing force, tries to prevent either the superego or the id from dominating. In the emotionally healthy individual, the ego succeeds in balancing these conflicting demands of the id and the superego. In the maladjusted individual, however, the ego cannot control the inherent conflict between the id and the superego, and the result is internal confusion and problem behaviors.

Sociological Evaluation Sociologists appreciate Freud's emphasis on socialization—that the social group into which we are born transmits norms and values that restrain our biological drives. Sociologists, however, reject the view that inborn and unconscious motivations are the primary reasons for human behavior, for *this denies the central principle of sociology:* that social factors such as social class (income, education, and occupation) and people's roles in groups underlie their behavior (Epstein 1988; Bush and Simmons 1990). Feminist sociologists have been especially critical of Freud. Although what we just summarized applies to both females and males, Freud assumed that what is "male" is "normal." He even analyzed females as inferior, castrated males (Chodorow 1990).

Global Considerations: Socialization into Emotions

As we have seen, the mind is a social product, and through socialization we acquire the particulars that go into human reasoning. Emotions, too, are not simply the results of biology. They also depend on socialization (Hochschild 1975; Johnson 1992; Wouters 1992).

This conclusion may sound strange. Don't all people get angry? Doesn't everyone cry? Don't we all feel guilt, shame, sadness, remorse, happiness, fear? What has socialization to do with emotions?

Let's start with the obvious. Certainly people around the world feel these particular emotions, but the ways in which they express them vary from one culture to another. Consider, for example, close adult male friends who are reunited after a long separation. Americans might shake hands vigorously or even pat each other on the back. Japanese might bow, while Arabs will kiss. A good part of childhood socialization centers on learning how to express emotions, for each culture has "norms of emotion" that demand conformity (Clark 1991).

How we learn to express emotions depends not only on culture but also on our social location. Consider gender. When two U.S. female friends are reunited after a long separation, they are much more likely to hug instead of shaking hands or patting each other on the back. But gender (and racial-ethnic) differences in expressing emotions are modified by social class. Upon seeing a friend after a long absence, lower-class women, men, African Americans, and so on are likely to express emotions of delight in different ways than do upper-class women, men, African Americans, and so on.

But the matter goes deeper than this. In some cultures people even learn to experience emotions quite unlike our own. For example, the Ifaluk, who live on the Western Caroline Islands of Micronesia, use the word *fago* to refer to the feelings that are evoked when they see someone who is suffering or in need of help. These feelings are close to what we refer to as sympathy or compassion. But the Ifaluk also use *fago* to describe what they feel when they are around someone who has high status, someone who is highly admired or respected (Kagan 1984). To us, these are two distinct emotions, and they require distinct terms.

The Self and Emotions as Social Control— Society within Us

Much of our socialization is intended to turn us into conforming members of society. Socialization into the self and emotions is an essential part of this process, for both the self and our emotions mold our behavior. Although we like to think we are "free," consider for a moment just some of the factors that influence how we act: the expectations of our friends and parents, neighbors and teachers; classroom norms and college rules; city, federal, and state laws. For example, if in a moment of intense frustration, or out of a devilish desire to shock people, you wanted to tear off your clothes and run naked down the street, what would stop you?

The answer is your socialization—*society within you.* Your experiences in society have resulted in a self that thinks along certain lines and feels particular emotions. This helps keep you in line. Thoughts such as "Would I get kicked out of school?" and "What would my friends (parents) think if they found out?" represent an awareness of the self in relationship to others. So does the desire to avoid feelings of shame and embarrassment. Our *social mirror,* then—the result of being socialized into a self and emotions—sets up effective controls over our behavior. In fact, socialization into self and emotions is so effective that some people feel embarrassed just thinking about running nude in public!

■ **In Sum** Socialization is essential for our development as human beings. From interaction with others, we receive a self, a mind, and the ability to reason. The net result is that our behavior—and even our thinking and emotions—are shaped according to cultural standards. This is what sociologists mean when they refer to "society within us."

SOCIALIZATION INTO GENDER

Society also channels our behavior through **gender socialization.** By expecting different attitudes and behaviors from us *because* we are male or female, the human group nudges boys and girls in separate directions in life. This foundation of contrasting attitudes and behaviors is so thorough that, as adults, most of us act, think, and even feel according to our culture's guidelines of what is appropriate for our sex.

How do we learn gender messages? The significance of gender in social life is emphasized throughout this book, with a special focus in Chapter 10. For now, though, let's consider the influence of just the family and the mass media.

Gender Messages in the Family

Our parents are the first significant others who teach us our part in this symbolic division of the world. Their own gender orientations are so firmly established that they do much of this teaching without even being aware of what they are doing. This is illustrated by a classic study done by psychologists Susan Goldberg and Michael Lewis (1969). They asked mothers to bring their 6-month-old infants into their laboratory, supposedly to observe the infants' development. Secretly, however, these researchers also observed the mothers. They found that the mothers kept their daughters closer to them. They also touched and spoke more to their daughters.

By the time the children were 13 months old, the girls stayed closer to their mothers during play, and they returned to them sooner and more often than the boys did. When Goldberg and Lewis set up a barrier to separate the children from their mothers, who were holding toys, the girls were more likely to cry and motion for help; the boys were more likely to try to climb over the barrier. Goldberg and Lewis concluded that in our society mothers unconsciously reward their daughters for being passive and dependent, their sons for being active and independent.

These lessons continue throughout childhood. On the basis of their sex, children are given different kinds of toys. Preschool boys are allowed to roam farther from home than their preschool sisters, and they are subtly encouraged to participate in more rough-and-tumble play—even to get dirtier and to be more defiant (Gilman 1911/1971; Henslin 2001).

Such experiences in socialization lie at the heart of the sociological explanation of male-female differences. We should note, however, that some sociologists consider biology to be a cause. For example, were the infants in the Goldberg-Lewis study demonstrating built-in biological predispositions, with the mothers merely reinforcing—not causing—those differences? We shall return to this controversial issue in Chapter 10.

Gender Messages in the Mass Media

Sociologists stress how this sorting process that begins in the family is reinforced as the child is exposed to other aspects of society. Especially important today are the **mass media,** forms of communication that are directed to large audiences. Let's look at how powerful images of both sexes on television and in video games reinforce society's expectations of gender.

Television Television reinforces stereotypes of the sexes. On prime-time television, male characters outnumber female characters two to one (Gerbner 1998). They also are more likely to be portrayed in higher-status positions (Vande Berg and Streckfuss 1992). Viewers get the message, for the more television that people watch, the more they tend to have restrictive ideas about women's role in society (Signorielli 1989, 1990).

The exceptions to the stereotypes are notable—and a sign of changing times. One program, perhaps the most stereotype-breaking of all, is *Xena, Warrior Princess,*

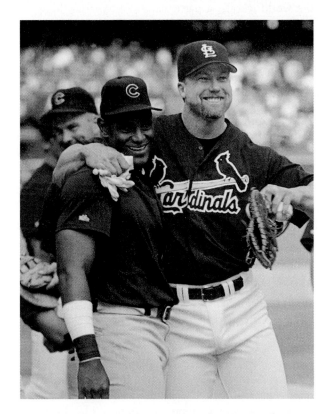

Although males are socialized to express less emotion than females, such socialization apparently goes against their nature. In certain settings, especially sports, males are allowed to be openly emotional, even demonstrative, with one another. Shown embracing are Mark McGwire of the St. Louis Cardinals and Sammy Sosa of the Chicago Cubs. They both were chasing the Roger Maris home run record of 61 in a season.

a popular television series imported from New Zealand. Portrayed as super dominant, Xena overcomes all obstacles and defeats all foes—whether men or women.

Video Games Some youths spend countless hours playing video games in arcades and at home. Even college students, especially males, relieve stress by escaping into video games. Unfortunately, we have no studies of how these games affect the players' ideas of gender. Because the games are on the cutting edge of society, they sometimes also reflect cutting-edge changes in sex roles, as examined in the Mass Media in Social Life box on the next page.

■ **In Sum** All of us are born into a society in which "male" and "female" are significant symbols. Sorted into separate groups from childhood, girls and boys come to have sharply different ideas of themselves and of one another. These ideas begin within the family and later are reinforced by other social institutions. Each of us learns the meanings that our society associates with the sexes. These images become integrated into our views of the world, forming a picture of "how" males and females "are," and forcing an interpretation of the world in terms of gender.

AGENTS OF SOCIALIZATION

People and groups that influence our self-concept, emotions, attitudes, and behavior are called **agents of socialization.** We have already considered how two of these agents, the family and the mass media, influence our ideas of gender. Now we'll look more closely at how agents of socialization prepare us to take our place in society. We shall first consider the family, and then the neighborhood, religion, day care, school and peers, sports, and the workplace.

The Family

One of the main findings of sociologists is how socialization depends on a family's social class. Let's compare how working-class and middle-class parents rear their children. Sociologist Melvin Kohn (1959, 1963, 1976, 1977; Kohn et al. 1986) found that the main concern of working-class parents is that their children be obedient,

THE FAR SIDE　　By GARY LARSON

"So let's go over it again: You're about a mile up, you see something dying below you, you circle until it's dead, and down you go. Lenny, you stick close to your brothers and do what they do."

neat, and clean, follow the rules, and stay out of trouble. They are likely to use physical punishment to make their children obey. Middle-class parents, in contrast, show greater concern for developing their children's curiosity, self-expression, and self-control. They stress the motivations for their children's behavior and are more likely to reason with their children than to use physical punishment.

These findings were a sociological puzzle. Just *why* should working-class and middle-class parents rear their children so differently? Kohn knew that life experiences of some sort held the key, and he found that key in the world of work. Blue-collar workers are usually supervised very closely. Their bosses expect them to do exactly as they are told. Because blue-collar-parents expect their children's lives to be like theirs, they stress obedience and conformity. Middle-class-parents, in contrast, have more independence at work, and are encouraged to take the initiative. Expecting their children to work at similar jobs, they, in turn, socialize them into the qualities they have found valuable.

Mass Media in Social Life

FROM XENA, WARRIOR PRINCESS, TO LARA CROFT, TOMB RAIDER: CHANGING IMAGES OF WOMEN IN THE MASS MEDIA

As women change their roles in society, the mass media reflect those changes. Although media images of women as passive, as subordinate, or as mere background objects remain, a new image has broken through. Although this new image exaggerates changes in society, it nonetheless reflects women's changed role to active lives outside the home. It also shows a change from acquiescent to dominant in social relations. As mentioned in the text, Xena, the Warrior Princess, is an outstanding example of this change.

Though it is unusual to call video games a form of the mass media, I think it is appropriate to do so. Like books and magazines, video games are made available to a mass audience. And with digital advances, they have crossed the line from what is traditionally thought of as games to something that more closely resembles interactive movies.

Sociologically, what is significant is that the *content* of video games socializes their users. Gamers are exposed not only to action, but also to ideas as they play. Especially significant are gender images that communicate powerful messages, just as they do in other forms of the mass media.

Lara Croft, an adventure-seeking archeologist and star of *Tomb Raider* and its three sequels, *Tomb Raider 2, 3,* and *4,* is the essence of the new gender image. Lara is smart, strong, and able to utterly vanquish foes. With both guns blazing, she is the cowboy of the twenty-first century, the term *cowboy* being purposefully chosen, as Lara breaks gender roles and assumes what previously was the domain of men. She is the first female protagonist in a field of muscle-rippling, machine-gun-toting macho caricatures (Taylor 1999).

Yet, the old remains powerfully encapsulated in the new. As the photo below makes evident, Lara is a fantasy girl for young men of the digital generation. No matter her foe, no matter her predicament, Lara always wears form-fitting outfits—which reflect the mental images of the men who created this digital character. So successful has their effort been that boys and young men have bombarded corporate headquarters with questions about Lara's personal life. Lara has caught young men's fancy to such an extent that more than 100 Web sites are devoted to her (Croal and Hughes 1997). Lara is also the star of a movie and a comic book.

When the final reward of the game is to see Lara in a nightie, one can legitimately question—regardless of tough-girl images—just how far stereotypes have been left behind. ■

The mass media not only reflect gender stereotypes, but they also play a role in changing them. Sometimes they do both simultaneously. The images of Lara Croft and of Xena, Warrior Princess, reflect women's changing role in society and, by exaggerating the change, also mold new stereotypes.

Kohn still felt puzzled, however, for some working-class parents act more like middle-class parents, and vice versa. He found the answer to this part of the puzzle in the parent's specific type of job. Middle-class office workers, for example, have little freedom and are closely supervised. Kohn found that they follow the working-class pattern of child rearing, for they stress outward conformity. In contrast, some blue-collar workers, such as those who do home repairs, have a good deal of freedom. These workers follow the middle-class model in rearing their children (Pearlin and Kohn 1966; Kohn and Schooler 1983).

The Neighborhood

As all parents know, some neighborhoods are better for their children than others. Parents try to move to those neighborhoods—if they can afford them. Their commonsense observations are borne out by sociological research. Children from poor neighborhoods are more likely to get in trouble with the law, to get pregnant, to drop out of school, and to end up facing a disadvantaged life (Wilson 1987; Brooks-Gunn et al. 1997).

Sociologists have also documented that the residents of more affluent, stable neighborhoods watch out for the children more than do the residents of poor neighborhoods (Sampson et al. 1999). The adults are more likely to know the local children and their parents, and to help keep the children safe and out of trouble. It is one of the ironies of life that in those neighborhoods that are the riskiest for children (where there is more homicide and child abuse) adults watch out the least for the children, and in neighborhoods where the children least need protecting the adults are more careful.

Religion

By influencing morality, religion becomes a key component in people's ideas of right and wrong. Religion is so important to Americans that 70 percent belong to a local congregation, and during a typical week two of every five attend a religious service (*Statistical Abstract* 1999:89). Religion is significant even for people reared in nonreligious homes, for religious ideas pervade U.S. society. They provide basic ideas of morality that become significant for us all.

The influence of religion extends to many areas of our lives. For example, participation in religious services teaches us not only beliefs about the hereafter but also ideas about what kinds of dress, speech, and manners are appropriate for formal occasions. We shall examine the influence of religion in detail in Chapter 13.

Day Care

With more mothers working for wages today than ever before, day care has become a significant agent of socialization. Concerns about its effects have propelled day care into the center of controversy. Researchers have found that the effects of day care depend on two main factors, a child's background and the quality of care (Scarr and Eisenberg 1993). Children from low-income homes, as well as those from dysfunctional families (such as alcoholic, inept, or abusive parents), appear to benefit from day care. For example, their language skills increase. In contrast, day care may slow these skills in middle-class children, who would have received more intellectual stimulation at home. As you would expect, much depends on the quality of day care. Researchers who studied 120 day care centers found that children in higher quality day care interact better with other children and have fewer behavior problems (McCartney et al. 1997).

It is rare for social science studies to make national news, but occasionally they do. In one such study, researchers followed 1,300 children from infancy into preschool. When the children were ages 6, 24, and 36 months, the researchers observed them at home and at day care. They videotaped and made detailed notes on their interaction with their mothers (National Institute of Child Health and Human Development 1999). This is what caught the media's attention: The more hours per week that children spend in day care, the weaker the bonds between mothers and children, and the more negative their interaction. Mothers whose children spend less time in day care are more responsive to their children and more positive in their interactions. Their children are also more affectionate to them. Why? The researchers suggest that mothers who spend more time with their infants become more familiar and responsive to their "signaling systems."

This study was designed well, and its findings are without dispute. But the explanation of these findings is another matter. The cause could be day care, as the researchers suggest. But perhaps mothers who put their children in day care for more hours are mothers who are less sensitive to their children in the first place. From this study, we can't determine which is the cause of the negative interaction and the weaker bonding.

The School and Peer Groups

As a child's experiences with agents of socialization broaden, the influence of the family lessens. Entry into school marks only one of many steps in this transfer of allegiance. Here children move away from a world in which they may have been the almost exclusive focus of doting parents, and learn to be part of a large group of people of similar age.

One of the most significant aspects of education is that it exposes children to **peer groups**, individuals of roughly the same age who are linked by common interests. Examples of peer groups are friends, clubs, gangs, and "the kids in the neighborhood."

Sociologists Patricia and Peter Adler (1998), a husband and wife team, document how the peer group provides an enclave in which boys and girls resist the efforts of parents and schools to socialize them their way. Observing children at two elementary schools in Colorado, they saw how children separate themselves by sex and develop their own worlds with unique norms (Adler et al. 1992). The norms that made boys popular were athletic ability, coolness, and toughness. For girls, they were family background, physical appearance (clothing and the ability to use makeup), and being able to attract popular boys. In this children's subculture, academic achievement pulled in opposite directions: For boys, to do well academically hurt popularity, while getting good grades increased a girl's social standing.

You know from personal experience how compelling peer groups are. It is almost impossible to go against a peer group, whose cardinal rule seems to be "conformity or rejection." Anyone who doesn't do what the others want becomes an "outsider," a "nonmember," an "outcast." For preteens and teens just learning their way around in the world, it is not surprising that the peer group rules.

Sports

Sports are another powerful socializing agent. Everyone recognizes that sports teach not only physical skills but also values. In fact, "teaching youngsters to be team players" is often given as the justification for financing organized sports. How effective sports are in socializing boys is the topic of the Down-to-Earth Sociology box on the next page.

The Workplace

Another agent of socialization that comes into play somewhat later in life is the workplace. Those initial part-time jobs that we get in high school and college are much more than just a way to earn a few dollars. From the people we rub shoulders with at work, we learn not only a set of skills but also a perspective on the world.

Most of us eventually become committed to some particular line of work, often after trying out various jobs.

This may involve **anticipatory socialization,** learning to play a role before entering it. Anticipatory socialization is a sort of rehearsal for some future activity. We may talk to people who work in a career, read novels about them, or take a summer internship. This allows us to gradually identify with the role, to become aware of what would be expected of us. Sometimes this helps people avoid committing themselves to an unrewarding career, as with some of my students who tried student teaching, found they couldn't stand it, and moved on to other fields that were more to their liking.

An interesting aspect of work as a socializing agent is that the more you participate in a line of work, the more the work becomes a part of your self-concept. Eventually you come to think of yourself so much in terms of the job that if someone asks you to describe yourself, you are likely to include the job in your self-description. You might say, "I am a teacher, accountant, nurse" or whatever.

RESOCIALIZATION

What does a woman who has just become a nun have in common with a man who has just divorced? The answer is that they both are undergoing **resocialization;** that is, they are learning new norms, values, attitudes, and behaviors to match their new situation in life. In its most common form, resocialization occurs each time we learn something contrary to our previous experiences. A new boss who insists on a different way of doing things is resocializing you. Most resocialization is mild, involving only a slight modification of things we have already learned.

Resocialization can be intense, however. People who join Alcoholics Anonymous (AA), for example, are surrounded by reformed drinkers who affirm the destructive effects of excessive drinking. Some students experience an intense period of resocialization when they leave high school and start college—especially during those initially scary days before they start to fit in and feel comfortable. To join a cult or to begin psychotherapy is even more profound, for these events expose people to ideas that conflict with their previous ways of looking at the world. If these ideas "take," not only does the individual's behavior change, but he or she also learns a fundamentally different way of looking at life.

Total Institutions

Relatively few of us experience the powerful agent of socialization that Erving Goffman (1961) called the **total in-**

Sociology

Down-to-Earth

SPORTS, MALE IDENTITY, AND RELATIONSHIPS

Some sports exalt the "male values" of competition and rough physical contact, akin to violence. Boys who play these sports are thought of as learning to be "real men." Even if they don't play a sport, it is considered appropriate for boys and men to follow sports in order to affirm male cultural values and to display their own masculinity.

Sociologist Michael Messner (1990) interviewed men who had played professional sports and other men for whom sports provided a central identity during and after high school. A former professional football player, whose two older brothers had gained reputations for success in sports, said:

My brothers were role models. I wanted to prove—especially to my brothers—that I had a heart, you know, that I was a man.... And...as I got older, I got better and I began to look around me and see, well hey! I'm competitive with these guys, even though I'm younger, you know?

Success at sports, then, brings recognition from significant others—and gratifying awareness that one has achieved manly characteristics. This same football player also said,

And then of course all the compliments come—and I began to notice a change, even in my parents—espe-

cially in my father—he was proud of that and that was very important to me.... He showed me more affection, now that I think of it.

The boost in the boy's self-esteem, however, can come at a high cost to others. Messner recounts a haunting scene during his visit to a summer basketball camp headed by a professional coach:

The youngest boys, about eight years old (who could barely reach the basket with their shots) played a brief scrimmage. Afterwards, the coaches lined them up in a row in front of the older boys who were sitting on the grandstands. One by one, the coach would stand behind each boy, put his hand on the boy's head (much in the manner of a priestly benediction), and the older boys in the stands would applaud and cheer, louder or softer, depending on how well or poorly the young boy was judged to have performed. The two or three boys who were clearly the exceptional players looked confident that they would receive the praise they were due. Most of the boys, though, had expressions ranging from puzzlement to thinly disguised terror on their faces as they awaited the judgments of the older boys.

Messner also notes that the meaning of sports differs by social class. As is well known, many poor people see sports as a way out of poverty. For middle-class boys, in contrast, sports are only one of many options that lead to success in life. Consequently, middle-class boys are more likely to invest more energy and self-identity in a future career than in sports. ■

For Your Consideration

The implications of sports go far beyond the game itself. Messner suggests that sports even affect intimate relationships. In the competitive world of sports, being a "winner" means to be accepted by others. To be a loser is to be rejected. Following Cooley's *looking-glass self,* the boys begin to see themselves in this light—if they win, they are better people than if they lose. Accomplishments, then, become the key to relationships. Boys then tend to develop *instrumental* relationships (that is, relationships that are not based on feelings, but on how useful the relationship is—on what you can get out of it). Such an orientation, of course, brings problems, for males try to relate instrumentally to females—who are more likely to have been socialized to construct their identities on meaningful relationships, not on competitive success.

---

stitution. He coined this term to refer to a place in which people are cut off from the rest of society and where they come under almost total control of the officials who run the place. Boot camps, prisons, concentration camps, con-

vents, some religious cults, and some boarding schools, such as West Point, are total institutions.

A person entering a total institution is greeted with a **degradation ceremony** (Garfinkel 1956), an attempt to remake the self by stripping away the individual's current identity and stamping a new one in its place. This unwelcome greeting may involve fingerprinting, photographing, shaving the head, and banning the individual's *personal identity kit* (items such as jewelry, hairstyles, clothing, and other body decorations used to express individuality). Newcomers may be ordered to strip, undergo an examination (often in a humiliating, semipublic setting), and then to put on a uniform that designates their new status.

Total institutions are isolated from the public. The walls, bars, or other barriers not only keep the inmates in but also keep outsiders out. Staff members closely supervise every aspect of the residents' lives. Eating, sleeping, showering, and recreation—all are standardized. Pre-existing statuses are suppressed, and inmates learn that their previous roles such as spouse, parent, worker, or student mean nothing. The only thing that counts is their current role.

No one leaves a total institution unscathed, for the experience brands an indelible mark on the individual's self and colors the way he or she sees the world. Boot camp, as described in the Down-to-Earth Sociology box on the next page, is brutal, but swift. Prison, in contrast, is brutal and prolonged. Neither recruit nor prisoner, however, has difficulty in recognizing how the institution affected the self.

∫OCIALIZATION THROUGH THE LIFE COURSE

You are at a particular stage in your life now, and college is a good part of it. You know that you have more stages ahead of you as you go through life. These stages, from birth to death, are called the **life course** (Elder 1975). The sociological significance of the life course is twofold. First, as you pass through a stage, it affects your behavior and orientations. You simply don't think about life in the same way when you are 30, married, and have children and a mortgage, as you do when you are 18 or 20, single, and in college. (Actually, you don't see life the same as a freshman and as a senior.) Second, your life course differs by social location. Your social class, race-ethnicity, and gender, for example, block out a distinctive world of experience. Consequently, the typical life course differs for males and females, the rich and the poor, and so on. To emphasize this major sociological point, in the sketch that follows I will stress the *historical* setting of people's lives. Because of your particular social location,

your own life course may differ from this sketch, which is a composite of stages others have suggested (Levinson 1978; Carr et al. 1995).

Childhood (from birth to about age 12)

To begin, consider how different your childhood would have been if you had grown up during the Middle Ages. When historian Philippe Ariès (1965) examined European paintings from this period, he noticed that children were always dressed in adult clothing. If they were not shown stiffly posed, as in a family portrait, they were shown engaging in adult activities.

Ariès concluded that at that time and in that place, childhood was not regarded as a special time of life. Rather, children were seen as miniature adults. Ariès pointed out that boys were apprenticed at very early

In contemporary Western societies such as the United States, children are viewed as innocent and in need of protection from adult demands such as work and self-support. Historically and cross-culturally, however, ideas of childhood vary. For instance, as illustrated by this 1605 painting of Lady Tasburgh and her children, in Europe children were viewed as miniature adults who assumed adult roles at the earliest opportunity.

Sociology

BOOT CAMP AS A TOTAL INSTITUTION

The bus arrives at Parris Island, South Carolina, at 3 A.M. The early hour is no accident. The recruits are groggy, confused. Up to a few hours ago, the boys were ordinary civilians. Now, a sergeant sneeringly calls them "maggots," their heads are buzzed (25 seconds per recruit), and they are thrust quickly into the harsh world of Marine boot camp.

Buzzing the boys' hair is just the first step in stripping away their identity so the Marines can stamp a new one in its place. The uniform serves the same purpose. So does the ban on using the first person "I." Even a simple request must be made in precise Marine protocol or it will not be acknowledged. ("Sir, Recruit Jones requests permission to make a head call, Sir.")

Every intense moment of the next eleven weeks reminds the recruits that they are joining a subculture of self-discipline. Here pleasure is suspect and sacrifice is good. As they learn the Marine way of talking, walking, and thinking, they are denied the diversions they once took for granted: television, cigarettes, cars, candy, soft drinks, video games, music, alcohol, drugs, and sex.

Lessons are bestowed with fierce intensity. When Sgt. Carey checks brass belt buckles, Recruit Robert Shelton nervously blurts, "I don't have one." Sgt. Carey's face grows red as the veins in his neck bulge. "I?" he says, his face

Resocialization is often a gentle process. Usually we are gradually exposed to different ways of thinking and doing. Sometimes, however, resocialization can be swift and brutal, as it is during boot camp in the Marines. This private at Parris Island is learning a world vastly unlike the civilian world he left behind.

just inches from the recruit. With spittle flying from his mouth, he screams, " 'I' is gone!"

"Nobody's an individual, understand?" is the lesson that is driven home again and again."You are a team, a Marine. Not a civilian. Not black or white, but a Marine. You will live like a Marine, fight like a Marine, and, if necessary, die like a Marine."

Each day begins before dawn with close order formations. The rest of the day is filled with training in hand-to-hand combat, marching, running, calisthenics, Marine history, and—always—following orders.

"An M-16 can blow someone's head off at 500 meters," Sgt. Norman says. "That's beautiful, isn't it?"

"Yes, sir!" shout the platoon's 59 voices.

"Pick your nose!" Simultaneously 59 index fingers shoot into nostrils.

The pressure to conform is intense. Those sent packing for insubordination or suicidal tendencies are mocked in cadence during drills. ("Hope you like the sights you see / Parris Island casualty.") As lights go out at 9 P.M. the exhausted recruits perform the day's last task: The entire platoon, in unison, shouts the virtues of the Marines.

Recruits are constantly scrutinized. Subperformance is not accepted, whether it be a dirty rifle or a loose thread on a uniform. The subperformer is shouted at, derided, humiliated. The group suffers for the individual. If a recruit is slow, the entire platoon is punished.

One of the new Marines (until graduation, they are recruits, not Marines) says, "I feel like I've joined a new society or religion."

He has. ■

For Your Consideration

Of what significance is the recruits' degradation ceremony? Why are recruits not allowed video games, cigarettes, or calls home? Why are the Marines so unfair as to punish an entire platoon for the failure of an individual? Use concepts in this chapter to explain why the system works.

Source: Based on Garfinkel 1956; Goffman 1961; "Anybody's Son Will Do," 1990; Ricks 1995.

ages. At the age of 7, for example, a boy might leave home for good to learn to be a jeweler or a stonecutter. A girl, in contrast, stayed home until she married, but by the age of 7 she was expected to assume her daily share of the household tasks.

Such practices have not disappeared from the world. I have a vivid memory of a Moroccan blacksmith standing next to an open furnace, nude from the waist up. Sweating profusely in the insufferable African heat, his hammer beat rhythmically on glowing, red-hot metal. The blacksmith was about 12 years old.

Parents and teachers in earlier centuries also felt it was their moral duty to use psychological terror to keep children in line. They would lock children in dark closets, frighten them with tales of death and hellfire, and force them to witness gruesome events.

> A common moral lesson involved taking children to visit the gibbet [an upraised post on which executed bodies were left hanging from chains], where they were forced to inspect rotting corpses hanging there as an example of what happens to bad children when they grow up. Whole classes were taken out of school to witness hangings, and parents would often whip their children afterwards to make them remember what they had seen. (DeMause 1975)

Industrialization transformed the way we see children. When children have the leisure to go to school, they come to be thought of as tender and innocent, as needing more adult care, comfort, and protection. Over time, such attitudes of dependency grow, and today we view children as needing gentle guidance if they are to develop emotionally, intellectually, morally, even physically. We take our view for granted—after all it is only "common sense." Yet, as you can see, our view is not "natural," but is rooted in geography and history.

Childhood, then, is much more than biology. Everyone's childhood occurs at some point in history and is embedded in particular social locations, especially social class and gender. These social factors are as vital as our biology, for they determine what childhood will be like for us. Although a child's *biological* characteristics (such as being small and dependent) are universal, the child's *social* experiences (what happens to that child because of what others expect of him or her) are not. Thus sociologists say that childhood varies from culture to culture.

Adolescence (ages 13–17)

In earlier centuries, societies did not mark out adolescence as a distinct time of life. People simply moved from childhood into young adulthood, with no stopover

In many societies, manhood is not bestowed upon males simply because they reach a certain age. Manhood, rather, signifies a standing in the community that must be achieved. Shown here is an initiation ceremony in Indonesia, where boys, to lay claim to the status of manhood, must jump over this barrier.

in between. The Industrial Revolution brought such an abundance of material surpluses, however, that for the first time in history millions of teenagers were able to remain outside the labor force. At the same time, education became more important for success. The convergence of these two forces in industrialized societies created a gap between childhood and adulthood. In the early part of this century, the term *adolescence* was coined to indicate this new stage in life (Hall 1904), one that has become renowned for inner turmoil.

To ground the self-identity and mark the passage of children into adulthood, tribal societies hold initiation rites. In the industrialized world, however, adolescents must "find" themselves on their own. As they attempt to carve out an identity that is distinct from both the "younger" world being left behind and the "older" world still out of range, adolescents develop their own subcultures, with distinctive clothing, hairstyles, language, gestures, and music. We usually fail to realize that contemporary society, not biology, created the period of inner turmoil that we call *adolescence*.

Young Adulthood (ages 18–29)

If society invented adolescence, can it also invent other periods of life? Historian Kenneth Keniston suggests that this is happening now. He notes that industrialized societies are adding a period of prolonged youth to the life course, in which people postpone adult responsibilities past adolescence. For millions, the end of high school marks a period of extended education characterized by continued freedom from the need to support oneself. During this time, people are "neither psychological adolescents nor sociological adults" (Keniston 1971). Somewhere during this period of extended youth, young adults gradually ease into adult responsibilities. They finish school, take a full-time job, engage in courtship rituals, get married—and go into debt.

The Middle Years (ages 30–65)

The Early Middle Years (ages 30–49) During the early middle years, most people are much surer of themselves and of their goals in life. As with any point in the life course, however, the self can receive severe jolts—in this case from such circumstances as divorce or being fired. It may take years for the self to stabilize after such ruptures.

Because of recent social change, the early middle years pose a special challenge for U.S. women, who increasingly have been given the message, especially by the media, that they can "have it all." They can be superworkers, superwives, and supermoms all rolled into one. The reality, however, often consists of conflicting pressures, of too little time and too many demands. Something has to give. Attempts to resolve this dilemma are often compounded by another hard reality—that during gender socialization their husbands learned that child care and housework are not "masculine." In short, adjustments continue in this and all phases of life.

The Later Middle Years (ages 50–65) During the later middle years, health and mortality begin to loom large as people feel their bodies change, especially if they watch their parents become frail, fall ill, and die. The consequence is a fundamental reorientation in thinking—from *time since birth* to *time left to live* (Neugarten 1976). With this changed orientation, people attempt to evaluate the past and come to terms with what lies ahead. They compare what they have accomplished with how far they had hoped to go. Many people also find themselves caring not only for their own children but also their aging parents. Because of this often crushing set of burdens, people in the later middle years sometimes are called the "sandwich generation."

Life during this stage, however, isn't always stressful. Many people find late middle age to be the most comfortable period of their entire lives. They enjoy job security and a standard of living higher than ever before; they have a bigger house (one that may even be paid for), newer cars, and more exotic vacations. The children are grown, the self is firmly planted, and fewer upheavals are likely to occur.

As they anticipate the next stage of life, however, most people do not like what they see.

The Older Years (about 65 on)

In industrialized societies, the older years begin around the mid-60s. This, too, is recent, for in preindustrial societies, when most people died early, old age was thought to begin around age 40. Today, in contrast, those in good health often experience being over 65, not as being old, but more as an extension of the middle years. People who continue to work or to be active in other rewarding social activities are unlikely to see themselves as old (Neugarten 1977). Although frequency of sex declines, most men and women in their 60s and 70s are sexually active (Denney and Quadagno 1992).

Because we have a self and can reason abstractly, we can contemplate death. Initially death is a vague notion, a remote possibility, but as people see their friends die and their own bodies no longer function as before, death becomes less abstract. Increasingly, people feel that "time is closing in" on them.

ARE WE PRISONERS OF SOCIALIZATION?

From our discussion of socialization, you might conclude that sociologists think of people as robots: The socialization goes in, and the behavior comes out. People cannot help what they do, think, or feel, for everything is a result of their exposure to socializing agents.

Sociologists do *not* think of people in this way. Although socialization is powerful, and profoundly affects us all, we have a self. Established in childhood and continually modified by later experience, the self is dynamic. It is not a sponge that passively absorbs influences from the environment but a vigorous, essential part of our being that allows us to act upon our environment (Couch 1989).

Indeed, it is precisely because individuals are not robots that their behavior is so hard to predict. The countless reactions of other people merge in each of us. As the self develops, we internalize or "put together" these innumerable reactions, producing a unique whole that we call the *individual*. Each unique individual uses his or her own mind to reason and to make choices in life.

In this way, *each of us is actively involved in the social construction of the self.* For example, although our experiences in the family lay down the basic elements of our personality, including fundamental orientations to life, we are not doomed to keep those orientations if we do not like them. We can purposely expose ourselves to groups and ideas that we prefer. Those experiences, in turn, will have their own effects on our self. In short, although socialization is powerful, within the limitations of the framework laid down by our social location we can change even the self. And that self—along with the options available within society—is the key to our behavior.

$\int$UMMARY AND $\mathcal{R}$EVIEW

■ What Is Human Nature?

How much of our human characteristics comes from "nature" (heredity) and how much from "nurture" (the social environment)?

Observations of isolated and institutionalized children help answer this question, as do experiments with monkeys that have been raised in isolation. Language and intimate social interaction—aspects of "nurture"—are essential to the development of what we consider to be human characteristics. Pp. 58–61.

■ Socialization into the Self, Mind, and Emotions

How do we acquire a self?

Humans are born with the *capacity* to develop a **self**, but the self must be socially constructed; that is, its contents depend on social interaction. According to Charles Horton Cooley's concept of the **looking-glass self**, our self develops as we internalize others' reactions to us. George Herbert Mead identified the ability to **take the role of the other** as essential to the development of the self. Mead concluded that even the mind is a social product. Pp. 61–63.

How do children develop reasoning skills?

Jean Piaget identified four stages that children go through as they develop the ability to reason: (1) *sensorimotor,* in which understanding is limited to sensory stimuli such as touch and sight; (2) *preoperational,* the ability to use symbols; (3) *concrete operational,* in which reasoning ability is more complex but not yet capable of complex abstractions; and (4) *formal operational,* or abstract thinking. Pp. 63–64.

How do sociologists evaluate Freud's psychoanalytic theory of personality development?

Freud viewed personality development as the result of one's **id** (inborn, self-centered desires) clashing with the demands of society. The **ego** develops to balance the id and the **super-ego,** the conscience. Sociologists, in contrast, do not examine inborn and unconscious motivations, but, instead, how social factors—social class, gender, religion, education, and so forth—underlie personality development. Pp. 64–65.

How does socialization influence emotions?

Socialization influences not only *how* we express our emotions, but also *what* emotions we feel. Socialization into emotions is a major means by which society produces conformity. P. 65.

■ Socialization into Gender

How does gender socialization affect our sense of self?

Gender socialization—sorting males and females into different roles—is a primary means of controlling human behavior. Children receive messages about gender even in infancy. A society's ideals of sex-linked behaviors are reinforced by its social institutions. Pp. 65–67.

■ Agents of Socialization

What are the main agents of socialization?

Agents of socialization include the **mass media,** family, the neighborhood, religion, day care, school, **peer groups,** sports, and the workplace. Each has its particular influences in socializing us into becoming full-fledged members of society. Pp. 67–70.

■ Resocialization

What is resocialization?

Resocialization is the process of learning new norms, values, attitudes, and behavior. Most resocialization is voluntary, but some, as with prisoners in **total institutions,** is involuntary. Pp. 67–72.

■ Socialization through the Life Course

Does socialization end when we enter adulthood?

Socialization occurs throughout the life course. In industrialized societies, the **life course** can be divided into childhood, adolescence, young adulthood, the middle years, and the older years. Typical patterns include obtaining education, becoming independent from parents, building a career, finding a mate, rearing children, and confronting aging. Life course patterns vary by social location such as history, gender, race-ethnicity, and social class. Pp. 72–75.

■ Are We Prisoners of Socialization?

Although socialization is powerful, we are not merely the sum of our socialization experiences. Just as socialization influences human behavior, so humans act on their environment and influence it. Pp. 75–76.

Where can I read more on this topic?

Suggested readings for this chapter are listed on page SR-2.

YOUR INTERACTIVE COMPANION WEB SITE

Your Interactive Companion Web Site includes practice tests, with feedback, and online learning activities with video, audio, and Weblinks. Your access code for this Web site is provided with this text.

GLOSSARY

agents of socialization people and groups that influence our self-concept, emotions, attitudes, and behavior (p. 67)

anticipatory socialization As we anticipate future roles, we learn aspects of them now (p. 70)

degradation ceremony a term coined by Harold Garfinkel to describe rituals that are designed to strip an individual of his or her identity as a group member; for example, a court martial or the defrocking of a priest (p. 70)

ego Freud's term for a balancing force between the id and the demands of society (p. 64)

gender socialization the ways in which society sets children onto different courses in life because they are male or female (p. 65)

generalized other taking the role of a large number of people (p. 62)

id Freud's term for the individual's inborn basic drives (p. 64)

life course the stages of our life as we go from birth to death (p. 72)

looking-glass self a term coined by Charles Horton Cooley to refer to the process by which our self develops through internalizing others' reactions to us (p. 62)

mass media forms of communication directed to large audiences (p. 66)

peer group a group of individuals of roughly the same age who are linked by common interests (p. 70)

resocialization the process of learning new norms, values, attitudes, and behaviors (p. 70)

self the concept, unique to humans, of being able to see ourselves "from the outside"; our internalized perception of how others see us (p. 61)

significant other an individual who significantly influences someone else's life (p. 62)

social environment the entire human environment, including direct contact with others (p. 58)

socialization the process by which people learn the characteristics of their group—the attitudes, values, and actions thought appropriate for them (p. 61)

superego Freud's term for the conscience, which consists of the internalized norms and values of our social groups (p. 64)

taking the role of the other putting oneself in someone else's shoes; understanding how someone else feels and thinks and thus anticipating how that person will act (p. 62)

total institution a place in which people are cut off from the rest of society and are almost totally controlled by the officials who run the place (p. 70)

Chapter 4

Bernard Bonhomme, Congregating People, 1997

Social Structure and Social Interaction

W

hen the sociology convention finished, I climbed aboard the first city bus that came along. I didn't know where the bus was going, and I didn't even know where I was going to spend the night. "Maybe I overdid it this time," I thought as the bus

began winding down streets I had never seen before. Actually, this was my first visit to Washington, D.C., so I hadn't seen any of the streets before. I had no direction, no plans, not even a map. I carried no billfold, just a driver's license shoved into my jeans for emergency identification, some pocket change, and a $10 bill tucked into my socks. My goal was simple: If I saw something interesting, I'd get off and check it out.

"Nothing but the usual things," I mused, as we passed row after row of apartment buildings and stores. I could see myself riding buses the entire night. Then something caught my eye. Nothing spectacular—just groups of people clustered around a large circular area where several streets intersected.

I climbed off the bus and made my way to what turned out to be Dupont Circle. I took a seat on a sidewalk bench and began to observe. As the scene came into focus, I noted several street-corner men drinking and joking with one another. One of the men broke from his companions and sat down next to me. As we talked, I mostly listened.

As night fell, the men said that they wanted to get another bottle of wine. I contributed. They counted their money and asked if I wanted to go with them.

Although I felt my stomach churning—a combination of hesitation and fear—I heard a confident "Sure!" come out of my mouth. As we left the circle, the three men began to cut through an alley. "Oh, no," I thought. "This isn't what I had in mind."

I had but a split second to make a decision. I found myself continuing to walk with the men, but holding back half a step so that none of the three was behind me. As we walked, they passed around the remnants of their bottle. When my turn came, I didn't know what to do. I shuddered to think about the diseases lurking within that bottle. I made another quick decision. In the semidarkness I faked it, letting only my thumb and forefinger touch my lips and nothing enter my mouth.

When we returned to Dupont Circle, the men finished their new bottle of Thunderbird. I couldn't fake it in the light, so I passed,

pointing at my stomach to indicate that I was having digestive problems.

Suddenly one of the men jumped up, smashed the emptied bottle against the sidewalk, and thrust the jagged neck outward in a menacing gesture. He glared straight ahead at another bench, where he had spotted someone with whom he had some sort of unfinished business. As the other men told him to cool it, I moved slightly to one side of the group—ready to flee, just in case. ■

LEVELS OF SOCIOLOGICAL ANALYSIS

On this sociological adventure, I almost got myself in over my head. Fortunately, it turned out all right. The man's "enemy" didn't look our way, the broken bottle was set down next to the bench "just in case he needed it," and my introduction to a life that up to then I had only read about continued until dawn.

Sociologists Elliot Liebow (1997, 1967/1999) and Elijah Anderson (1978, 1990, 1999, 2001) have written fascinating accounts about men like these. Although street-corner men may appear to be disorganized—simply coming and going as they please and doing whatever feels good at the moment—Liebow and Anderson have analyzed how, like us, these men also are influenced by the norms and beliefs of our society. This will become more apparent as we examine the two levels of analysis that sociologists use.

Macrosociology and Microsociology

The first level, **macrosociology,** places the focus on broad features of society. Sociologists who use this approach analyze such things as social class and how groups are related to one another. If macrosociologists were to analyze street-corner men, for example, they would stress that these men are located at the bottom of the U.S. social class system. Their low status means that many opportunities are closed to them: The men have few job skills, little education, hardly anything to offer

an employer. As "able-bodied" men, however, they are not eligible for welfare—even for a two-year limit—so they hustle to survive. As a consequence, they spend their lives on the streets.

Conflict theory and functionalism, both of which focus on the broader picture, are examples of this macrosociological approach. In these theories, the goal is to examine the large-scale social forces that influence people.

The second approach sociologists use is **microsociology.** Here the emphasis is placed on **social interaction,** what people do when they come together. Sociologists who use this approach are likely to focus on the men's rules or "codes" for getting along; their survival strategies ("hustles"); how they divide up money, wine, or whatever other resources they have; their relationships with girlfriends, family, and friends; where they spend their time and what they do there; their language; their pecking order; and so on. With its focus on face-to-face interaction, symbolic interactionism is an example of microsociology.

Because each has a different focus, macrosociology and microsociology yield distinctive perspectives, and both are needed to gain a fuller understanding of social life. We cannot adequately understand street-corner men, for example, without using *macrosociology.* It is essential that we place the men within the broad context of how groups in U.S. society are related to one another, for, as with ourselves, the social class of these men helps

Sociologists use both macro and micro levels of analysis to study social life. Those who use the macrosociological approach to analyze the homeless—or any human behavior—focus on broad forces, such as the economy and social classes. Sociologists who use the microsociological approach analyze how people interact with one another. Economy and social class are prominent in the scene shown here (wealth and power versus poverty and powerlessness). Evidence of social interaction is also apparent—gifts of food in the midst of social isolation.

to shape their attitudes and behavior. Nor can we adequately understand these men without *microsociology,* for their everyday situations also form a significant part of their lives.

To see how these two approaches in sociology help us to understand social life, let's take a look at each.

THE MACROSOCIOLOGICAL PERSPECTIVE: SOCIAL STRUCTURE

To better understand human behavior, we need to understand *social structure,* the framework of society that was already laid out before you were born. **Social structure** is the typical patterns of a group, such as its usual relationships between men and women or students and teachers. *The sociological significance of social structure is that it guides our behavior.*

Because this term may seem vague, let's consider how you experience social structure in your own life. As I write this, I do not know if you are African American, white, Latino, Native American, Asian American. I do not know your religion. I do not know if you are young or old, tall or short, male or female. I do not know if you were reared on a farm, in the suburbs, or in the inner city. I do not know if you went to a public high school or an exclusive prep school. But I do know you are in college. And that, alone, tells me a great deal about you.

From this one piece of information, I can assume that the social structure of your college is now shaping what you do. For example, let's suppose that today you felt euphoric over some great news. I can be fairly certain (not absolutely, mind you, but relatively certain) that when you entered the classroom, social structure overrode your mood. That is, instead of shouting at the top of your lungs and joyously throwing this book into the air, you entered the classroom in a fairly subdued manner and took your seat.

The same social structure influences your instructor, even if, on the one hand, he or she is facing a divorce or has a child dying of cancer, or, on the other, has just been awarded a promotion or a million-dollar grant. The instructor may feel like either retreating into seclusion or celebrating wildly, but it is most likely that he or she will conduct class in the usual manner. In short, social structure tends to override personal feelings and desires.

Just as social structure influences you and your instructor, so it establishes limits for street people. They, too, find themselves in a specific social location in the U.S. social structure—although it is quite different from yours or your instructor's. Consequently, they are affected differently. Nothing about their social location leads them to take notes or to lecture. Their behaviors, however, are as logical an outcome of where they find themselves in the social structure as are your own. In their position in the social structure, it is just as "natural" to drink wine all night as it is for you to stay up studying all night for a crucial examination. It is just as "natural" for you to nod and say "Excuse me" when you enter a crowded classroom late and have to claim a desk on which someone has already placed books as it is for them to break off the head of a wine bottle and glare at an enemy.

In short, people learn certain behaviors and attitudes because of their location in the social structure (whether they be privileged, deprived, or in between), and they act accordingly. This is equally true of street people and of ourselves. *The differences in behavior and attitudes are not due to biology (race, sex, or any other supposed genetic factors), but to people's location in the social structure.* Switch places with street people and watch your behaviors and attitudes change!

To better understand social structure, read the Down-to-Earth Sociology box on football. Because social structure so crucially affects who we are and what we are like, let's look more closely at its major components: culture, social class, social status, roles, groups, social institutions, and societies.

Sociology
Down-to-Earth

COLLEGE FOOTBALL AS SOCIAL STRUCTURE

To gain a better idea of what social structure is, think of college football (see Dobriner 1969a). You know the various positions on the team: center, guard, tackle, end, quarterback, and running back. Each is a *status;* that is, each is a recognized social position. For each of these statuses, there is a *role;* that is, each of these positions has certain expectations attached to it. The center is expected to snap the ball, the quarterback to pass it, the guards to block, the tackles to tackle or block, the ends to receive passes, and so on. These *role expectations* guide each player's actions; that is, the players try to do what their particular role requires.

Let's suppose that football is your favorite sport and you never miss a home game at your college. Let's also suppose that you graduate, get a great job, and move across the country. Five years later, you return to your campus for a nostalgic visit. The climax of your visit is the biggest football game of the season. When you get to the game, you might be surprised to see a different coach, but you are not surprised that each playing position is occupied by people you don't know, for all the players you knew have graduated, and their places have been filled by others.

This scenario mirrors *social structure,* the framework around which a group exists. In this football example, that framework consists of the coaching staff and the eleven playing positions. The game does not depend on any particular individual, but, rather, on statuses, the positions that the individuals occupy. When someone leaves a position, the game can go on because someone else takes over that position and plays the role. The game will continue even though not a single individual remains from one period of time to the next. Notre Dame's football team endures today even though Knute Rockne, the Gipper, and his teammates are long dead.

Even though you may not play football, you nevertheless live your life within a clearly established social structure. The statuses you occupy and the roles you play were already in place before you were born. You take your particular positions in life, others do the same, and society goes about its business. Although the specifics change with time, the game—whether of life or of football—goes on. ■

Culture

In Chapter 2, we considered culture's far-reaching effects on our lives. At this point, let's simply summarize its main impact. Sociologists use the term *culture* to refer to a group's language, beliefs, values, behaviors, and even gestures. Culture also includes the material objects that are used by a group. Culture is the broadest framework that determines what kind of people we become. If we are reared in Eskimo, Japanese, Russian, or U.S. culture, we will grow up to be like most Eskimos, Japanese, Russians, or Americans. On the outside, we will look and act like them; and on the inside, we will think and feel like them.

Social Class

To understand people, we must examine the particular social locations that they hold in life. Especially significant is social class, which is based on income, education, and occupational prestige. Large numbers of people who have similar amounts of income and education and who work at jobs that are roughly comparable in prestige make up a **social class.** It is hard to overemphasize this aspect of social structure, for our social class influences not only our behaviors but even our ideas and attitudes. We have this in common, then, with the street people described in the opening vignette—both they and we are influenced by our location in the social class structure. Theirs may be a considerably less privileged position, but it has no less influence on their lives. Social class is so significant that we will spend an entire chapter (Chapter 8) on this topic.

Social Status

When you hear the word *status,* you are likely to think of prestige. These two words are welded together in common thinking. Sociologists, however, use **status** in a different way: to refer to the *position* that an individual occupies. That position may carry a great deal of prestige, as in the case of a judge or an astronaut, or it may bring very little prestige, as in the case of a gas station attendant or a hamburger flipper at a fast-food restaurant. The status may also be looked down on, as in the case of a street-corner man, an ex-convict, or a bag lady.

All of us occupy several positions at the same time. Simultaneously you may be a son or daughter, a worker, a date, and a student. Sociologists use the term **status set** to refer to all the statuses or positions that you oc-cupy. Obviously your status set changes as your particular statuses change; for example, if you graduate from college and take a full-time job, get married, buy a home, have children, and so on, your status set changes to include the positions of worker, spouse, homeowner, and parent.

Like other aspects of social structure, statuses are part of our basic framework of living in society. The example I gave of students and teachers who come to class and do what others expect of them despite their particular moods illustrates how statuses affect our actions—and those of the people around us. Our statuses—whether daughter or son, worker or date—serve as guides for our behavior.

Ascribed and Achieved Statuses An **ascribed status** is involuntary. You do not ask for it, nor can you choose it. Some of you inherit at birth, such as your race-ethnicity, sex, and the social class of your parents, as well as your statuses as female or male, daughter or son, and niece or nephew. Others, such as teenager and senior citizen, are related to the life course and are given to you later in life.

Achieved statuses, on the other hand, are voluntary. These you earn or accomplish. As a result of your efforts you become a student, a friend, a spouse, a rabbi, minister, priest, or nun. Or, for lack of effort (or efforts that others fail to appreciate), you become a school dropout, a former friend, an ex-spouse, or a defrocked rabbi, priest, or nun. In other words, achieved statuses can be either positive or negative; both college president and bank robber are achieved statuses.

Each status provides guidelines for how we are to act and feel. Like other aspects of social structure, they set limits on what we can and cannot do. Because social statuses are an essential part of social structure, they are found in all human groups.

Status Symbols People who are pleased with their particular social status may want others to recognize that they occupy that status. To solicit this recognition, they use **status symbols,** signs that identify a status. For example, people wear wedding rings to announce their marital status; uniforms, guns, and badges to proclaim that they are police officers (and to not so subtly let you know that their status gives them authority over you); and "backward" collars to declare that they are Lutheran ministers or Roman Catholic or Episcopal priests.

Some social statuses are negative, and so, therefore, are their status symbols. The scarlet letter in Nathaniel

Hawthorne's book by the same title is one example. Another is the CONVICTED DUI (Driving Under the Influence) bumper sticker that some U.S. counties require convicted drunk drivers to display if they wish to avoid a jail sentence.

All of us use status symbols to announce our statuses to others and to help smooth our interactions in everyday life. You might consider your own status symbols. For example, how does your clothing announce your statuses of sex, age, and college student?

Master Statuses A **master status** is one that cuts across the other statuses you hold. Some master statuses are ascribed. An example is your sex. Whatever you do, people perceive you as a male or as a female. If you are working your way through college by flipping burgers, people see you not only as a burger flipper and a student but as a *male* or *female* burger flipper and a *male* or *female* college student. Other master statuses are race and age.

Some master statuses are achieved. If you become very, very wealthy (and it doesn't matter if your wealth comes from an invention or from the lottery—it is still *achieved* as far as sociologists are concerned), your wealth is likely to become a master status. For example, people are likely to say, "She is a very rich burger flipper"—or, more likely, "She's very rich, and she used to flip burgers!"

Similarly, people who become disabled or disfigured find, to their dismay, that their condition becomes a master status. For example, a person whose face is scarred from severe burns will be viewed through this unwelcome master status no matter what his or her occupation or accomplishments. People who are confined to wheelchairs can attest to how this handicap overrides all their other statuses and determines others' perceptions of everything they do.

Although our statuses usually fit together fairly well, sometimes a contradiction or mismatch between statuses occurs. This is known as **status inconsistency** (or discrepancy). A 14-year-old college student is an example. So is a 40-year-old married woman who is dating a 19-year-old college sophomore.

These examples reveal an essential aspect of social statuses: Like other components of social structure, they come with built-in *norms* (that is, expectations) that provide guidelines for behavior. When statuses mesh well, as they usually do, we know what to expect of people.

Master statuses are those that overshadow our other statuses. Shown here is Christopher Reeve, who was paralyzed when he was thrown from a horse. Before his accident, Reeve was a top Hollywood actor, celebrating worldwide success with his role as Superman. Today, his master status is that of a person with a disability. He has accepted this status and is a spokesperson for people suffering from spinal cord injuries.

Status inconsistency, however, upsets our expectations. In the preceding examples, how are you supposed to act? Are you supposed to treat the 14-year-old as you would a young teenager, or as you would your college classmate? Do you react to the married woman as you would to the mother of your friend, or as you would to a classmate's date?

Roles

> All the world's a stage
> And all the men and women merely players.
> They have their exits and their entrances;
> And one man in his time plays many parts...
>
> (William Shakespeare, *As You Like It,* Act II, Scene 7)

Like Shakespeare, sociologists, too, see roles as essential to social life. When you were born, **roles**—the behaviors, obligations, and privileges attached to a status—were already set up for you. Society was waiting with outstretched arms to teach you how it expected you to act as a boy or a girl. And whether you were born poor, rich, or somewhere in between, that, too, attached certain behaviors, obligations, and privileges to your statuses.

The difference between role and status is that you *occupy* a status, but you *play* a role (Linton 1936). For example, being a son or daughter is your status, but your expectations of receiving food and shelter from your parents—as well as their expectations that you show respect to them—are part of your role.

Roles are like a fence. They allow us a certain amount of freedom, but for most of us that freedom doesn't go very far. Suppose a woman decides that she is not going to wear dresses, or a man that he will not wear suits and ties—regardless of what anyone says. In most situations, they'll stick to their decision. When a formal occasion comes along, however, such as a family wedding or a funeral, they likely will cave in to norms that they find overwhelming. Almost all of us follow the guidelines for what is "appropriate" for our roles. Most of us are little troubled by such constraints, for our socialization is so thorough that we usually *want* to do what our roles indicate is appropriate.

The sociological significance of roles is that they lay out what is expected of people. As individuals throughout society perform their roles, those roles mesh together to form this thing called *society.* As Shakespeare put it, people's roles provide "their exits and their entrances" on the stage of life. In short, roles are remarkably effective at keeping people in line—telling them when they should "enter" and when they should "exit," as well as what to do in between.

Groups

A **group** consists of people who regularly and consciously interact with one another. Ordinarily, the members of a group share similar values, norms, and expectations. Just as our social class, statuses, and roles influence our actions, so, too, the groups to which we belong are powerful forces in our lives. In fact, *to belong to a group is to yield to others the right to make certain decisions about our behavior.* If we belong to a group, we assume an obligation to act according to the expectations of other members of that group.

Social Institutions

At first glance, the term *social institution* may seem to have little relevance for your life. The term appears so cold and abstract. In fact, however, **social institutions**—the means that each society develops to meet its basic needs—vitally affect your life. By weaving the fabric of society, social institutions shape your behavior. They even color your thoughts. How can this be? Look at what social institutions are: the family, religion, law, politics, economics, education, medicine, science, and the military.

In industrialized societies, social institutions tend to be more formal, in tribal societies more informal. Education in industrialized societies, for example, is highly structured, while in tribal societies it usually consists of informally learning roles. Figure 4.1 on the next page summarizes the basic social institutions. Note that each institution has its own set of roles, values, and norms. Social institutions are so significant that Part IV of this book focuses on them.

Societies: The Four Social Revolutions

How did our society develop? You know that it didn't spring full-blown on the human scene. To better understand this envelope that surrounds us, that sets the stage for our experiences in life, let's trace the evolution of societies. Figure 4.2 on page 87 illustrates how changes in technology brought extensive changes to **society**—people who share a culture and a territory. As we review these sweeping changes, picture yourself as a member of each

Social Institution	Basic Needs	Some Groups or Organizations	Some Values	Some Roles	Some Norms
Family	Regulate reproduction, socialize and protect children	Relatives, kinship groups	Sexual fidelity, providing for your family, keeping a clean house, respect for parents	Daughter, son, father, mother, brother, sister, aunt, uncle, grandparent	Have only as many children as you can afford, be faithful to your spouse
Religion	Address concerns about life after death, the meaning of suffering and loss; facilitate desire to connect with the Creator	Congregation, synagogue, denomination, charitable association	Reading and adhering to holy texts such as the Bible, the Koran, and the Torah; honoring God	Priest, minister, rabbi, worshipper, teacher, disciple, missionary, prophet, convert	Attend worship services, contribute money, follow the teachings
Law	Maintain social order	Police, Courts, Prisons	Trial by one's peers, innocence until proven guilty	Judge, police officer, lawyer, defendant, prison guard	Give true testimony, follow the rules of evidence
Politics	Establish a hierarchy of power and authority	Political parties, congresses, parliaments, monarchies	Majority rule, the right to vote as a sacred trust	President, senator, lobbyist, voter, candidate, spin doctor	Allow one vote per person; voting is a privilege and a right
Economics	Produce and distribute goods and services	Credit unions, banks, credit card companies, buying clubs	Making money, paying bills on time, producing efficiently	Worker, boss, buyer, seller, creditor, debtor, advertiser	Maximize profits, "the customer is always right," work hard
Education	Transmit knowledge and skills across the generations	School, college, student senate, sports team, PTA, teachers' union	Academic honesty, good grades, being "cool"	Teacher, student, dean, principal, football player, cheerleader	Do homework, prepare lectures, don't snitch on classmates
Science	Master the environment	Local, state, regional, national, and international associations	Unbiased research, open dissemination of research findings	Scientist, researcher, technician, administrator	Follow scientific method, fully disclose research findings
Medicine	Heal the sick and injured, care for the dying	AMA, hospitals, pharmacies, insurance companies, HMOs	Hippocratic oath, staying in good health, following doctor's orders	Doctor, nurse, patient, pharmacist, medical insurer	Don't exploit patients, give best medical care available
Military	Protect from enemies, support national interests	Army, navy, air force, marines, coast guard, national guard	To die for one's country is an honor, obedience unto death	Soldier, recruit, enlisted person, officer, prisoner, spy	Be ready to go to war, obey superior officers, don't question orders
Mass Media (an emerging institution)	Disseminate information, mold public opinion, report events	Television networks, radio stations, publishers	Timeliness, accuracy, large audiences, freedom of the press	Journalist, newscaster, author, editor, publisher	Be accurate, fair, timely, and profitable

 Figure 4.1   SOCIAL INSTITUTIONS IN INDUSTRIAL AND POSTINDUSTRIAL SOCIETIES

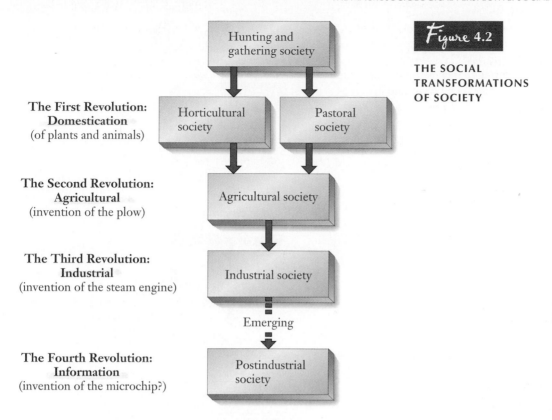

Figure 4.2

THE SOCIAL TRANSFORMATIONS OF SOCIETY

Hunting and gathering society

The First Revolution: Domestication (of plants and animals)

Horticultural society

Pastoral society

The Second Revolution: Agricultural (invention of the plow)

Agricultural society

The Third Revolution: Industrial (invention of the steam engine)

Industrial society

Emerging

The Fourth Revolution: Information (invention of the microchip?)

Postindustrial society

society. Consider how different your life would be in each society—how even your thinking, values, and view of the world would be transformed.

Hunting and Gathering Societies Societies with the fewest social divisions are called **hunting and gath-**

ering societies. As the name implies, these groups depend on hunting and gathering for their survival. (The "gatherers" do not plant, but only gather what is already there.) Because an area cannot support a large number of people who hunt animals and gather plants, hunting and gathering societies are small. They usually consist

The simplest forms of societies are called hunting and gathering societies. Members of these societies face severe hardships but have adapted well to their environments. They have the most leisure of any type of society. The man shown here is a member of a hunting and gathering society in the Brazilian Amazon.

of twenty-five to forty people. They are also nomadic, for as their food supply gives out, they move to another location (Lenski and Lenski 1987).

Of all societies, hunters and gatherers are the most egalitarian. Because what they hunt and gather is perishable, they can't accumulate possessions. Consequently, no one becomes wealthier than anyone else. There are no rulers, and most decisions are arrived at through discussion.

Pastoral and Horticultural Societies About ten thousand years ago, some groups found that they could tame and breed some of the animals they hunted, others that they could cultivate plants. As a result, hunting and gathering societies branched in one of two directions.

The key to understanding the first branching is the word *pasture;* **pastoral societies** are based on the *pasturing of animals.* Groups that took this turn remained nomadic, for they followed their animals to fresh pasture. The key to understanding the second branching is *horticulture,* or plant cultivation. **Horticultural societies** are based on the *cultivation of plants by the use of hand tools.* Because they no longer had to abandon an area as the food supply gave out, these groups developed permanent settlements.

We can call the domestication of animals and plants the *first social revolution,* for, as shown in Figure 4.3, it transformed human society. With dependable sources of food, human groups became larger. Because not everyone had to produce food, a specialized division of labor evolved: Some people made jewelry, others tools, weapons, and so on. This production of objects, in turn, stimulated trade, and people began to accumulate gold, jewelry, and utensils, as well as herds of animals.

The primary significance of these changes is that they set the stage for social inequality. Feuds and wars erupted, for groups now had material goods to fight about. War, in turn, opened the door to slavery, for people found it convenient to let captives from their battles do their drudge work. As individuals passed on their possessions to their descendants, wealth grew more concentrated. So did power, and for the first time some people became chiefs.

Agricultural Societies When the plow was invented about five or six thousand years ago, it ushered in a *second social revolution.* The plow brought a huge food surplus, allowing the population to grow, cities to develop, and many more people to engage in activities other than farming—to develop the things popularly known as "culture," such as philosophy, art, literature, and archi-

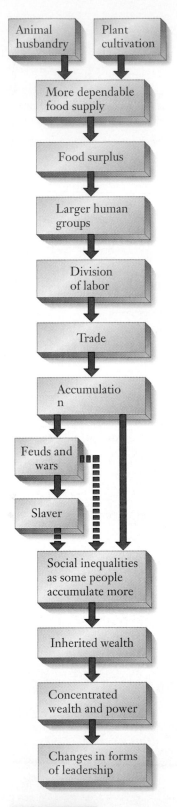

Figure **4.3**   **HOW ANIMAL HUSBANDRY AND PLANT CULTIVATION CHANGED SOCIAL LIFE**

tecture. The changes were so profound that this period is sometimes referred to as "the dawn of civilization."

Social inequality, which up to now had been sporadic and mild, became a fundamental feature of social life. Some people managed to gain control of the growing surplus resources. To protect their expanding privileges and power, this elite surrounded itself with armed men. They even levied taxes on others, who now had become their "subjects." As conflict theorists point out, this concentration of resources and power, along with the oppression of people not in power, was the forerunner of the state.

Industrial Societies The *third social revolution* also turned society upside down. The **Industrial Revolution** began in Great Britain, where in 1765 the steam engine was first used to run machinery. Before this time a few machines had harnessed nature (such as wind and water mills), but most had depended on power from humans and animals. Far more efficient than anything the world had ever seen, this new form of production brought even

greater surplus and, with it, even greater social inequality. The individuals who first used the new technology accumulated immense wealth. The masses, in contrast, were thrown off the land as feudal society broke up. They moved to the cities, where they faced the choice of stealing, starving, or working for starvation wages (Michalowski 1985).

Through a bitter struggle, one that went on too long for us to review it here, workers gradually attained their demands for better working conditions, reversing the earlier pattern of growing inequality. The indicators of greater equality in later industrial societies are extensive: widespread ownership of homes and automobiles, access to libraries and education, better housing, greater variety of food, and a much longer life for the average person. On an even broader level, indicators include the abolition of slavery, the shift from monarchies and dictatorships to more representative political systems, the right to vote, the right to be tried by a jury of one's peers and to cross-examine witnesses, and greater rights for women and minorities.

The sociological significance of the four social revolutions discussed in the text is that the type of society in which we live determines the kind of people we become. It is obvious, for example, that the orientations to life of this worker would differ markedly from those of the man shown on page 87.

The machinery that ushered in industrial society was met with ambivalence. On one hand, it brought a multitude of welcomed goods. On the other hand, factory time clocks and the incessant production line made people slaves to the very machines they built. The idea of machines dominating workers is illustrated by this classic scene of Charlie Chaplin's in *Modern Times*.

Postindustrial Societies Today, a new type of society is emerging. The basic trend in advanced industrial societies is away from production and manufacturing, and toward service industries. The United States was the first country to have more than half its work force employed in service industries—health, education, research, the government, counseling, banking and investments, sales, law, and the mass media. Australia, New Zealand, western Europe, and Japan soon followed. The term *postindustrial society* refers to this emerging society—one based on information, services, and the latest technology rather than on raw materials and manufacturing (Bell 1973; Lipset 1979; Toffler 1980).

The basic component of the postindustrial society is information. People who offer services either provide or apply information. Teachers pass on knowledge to students, while lawyers, physicians, bankers, and interior decorators sell their specialized knowledge of law, medicine, money, and color schemes. Unlike factory workers in an industrial society, workers in service industries don't *produce* anything. Rather, they transmit or apply knowledge to provide services that others are willing to pay for.

Perhaps in years to come social analysts will refer to these changes as the *fourth social revolution*. Based on the computer chip, the information revolution is transforming society—and with it, our social relationships. Because of this tiny device, we can talk to people in other countries while we drive our cars and trucks, we can peer farther into space than ever before, and millions of children can spend countless hours struggling against virtual video villains. Our shopping patterns are also changing, and we now spend several billion dollars a year on Internet purchases. (For a review of other changes, see the section on the computer in Chapter 15, pages 359–399.) Although the full implications of the information explosion are still unknown, as history is our guide, the changes will be so extensive that even our attitudes about the self and life will be transformed.

■ **In Sum** Our society sets boundaries around our lives. By laying out a framework of social statuses, roles, groups, and social institutions, society establishes the values and beliefs that prevail. It also determines the type and extent of social inequality. These factors, in turn, set the stage for relationships between men and women, the young and the elderly, racial and ethnic groups, the rich and the poor, and so on.

It is difficult to overstate the sociological principle that the type of society in which we live is the fundamental reason why we become who we are, why we feel about things the way we do, and even why we think our particular thoughts. On the obvious level, you would not be taking this course if you lived in an agrarian society. On a deeper level, you would not feel the same about life or hold your particular aspirations for the future.

What Holds Society Together?

With its many, often conflicting, groups and its extensive social change, how can a society manage to hold together? Let's examine two answers that sociologists have proposed.

Mechanical and Organic Solidarity Sociologist Emile Durkheim (1893/1933) found the key to **social cohesion**—the degree to which members of a society feel united by shared values and other social bonds—in what he called **mechanical solidarity.** By this term, Durkheim meant that people who perform similar tasks develop a shared consciousness, a sense of similarity that

unites them into a common whole. Think of an agricultural society, in which everyone is involved in planting, cultivating, and harvesting. Members of this group have so much in common that they know how most others feel about life.

As societies get larger, their **division of labor** (how they divide up work) becomes more specialized. Some people mine gold, others turn it into jewelry, while still others sell it. This division of labor makes people depend on one another, for the work of each contributes to the whole.

Durkheim called this new form of solidarity based on interdependence **organic solidarity.** To see why he used this term, think about how you depend on your teacher to guide you through this introductory course in sociology. At the same time, your teacher needs you and other students in order to have a job. The two of you are *like organs* in the same body. Although each of you performs different tasks, you depend on one another. This creates a form of unity.

Gemeinschaft and *Gesellschaft* Ferdinand Tönnies (1887/1988) also analyzed this major change. He used the term *Gemeinschaft* (Guh-MINE-shoft), or "intimate community," to describe village life, the type of society in which everyone knows everyone else. He noted that in the society that was emerging, the village's personal ties, family connections, and lifelong friendships were being crowded out by short-term relationships, individual accomplishments, and self-interest. Tönnies called this new type of society *Gesellschaft* (Guh-ZELL-shoft), or "impersonal association." He did not mean that we no longer have intimate ties to family and friends, but, rather, that these ties have shrunk in importance. Contracts, for example, replace handshakes, and work doesn't center around friends and family, but strangers and short-term acquaintances.

■ **In Sum** Whether the terms are *Gemeinschaft* and *Gesellschaft* or *mechanical solidarity* and *organic solidarity,* they indicate that as societies change so do people's orientations to life. *The sociological point is that social structure sets the context for what we do, feel, and think, and ultimately, then, for the kind of people we become.* The Cultural Diversity box on the next page, which describes the Amish, one of the few remaining *Gemeinschaft* societies in the United States, makes this more evident.

CULTURAL DIVERSITY In the United States

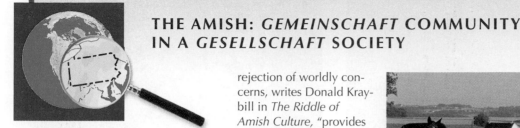

THE AMISH: *GEMEINSCHAFT* COMMUNITY IN A *GESELLSCHAFT* SOCIETY

U.S. society is, in Ferdinand Tönnies' term, a *Gesellschaft* society. Impersonal associations pervade our everyday life. Local, state, and federal governments regulate many activities. Impersonal corporations hire and fire people not on the basis of personal relationships, but on the basis of the bottom line. And, perhaps even more significantly, millions of Americans do not even know their neighbors.

Within the United States, a handful of small communities exhibits characteristics that depart from those of the larger society. One such community is the Old Order Amish, followers of a sect that broke away from the Swiss-German Mennonite church in the late 1600s and settled in Pennsylvania around 1727. Today, about 150,000 Old Order Amish live in the United States. The largest concentration, about 23,000, resides in Lancaster County, Pennsylvania.

To the nearly five million tourists who pass through Lancaster County each year, the green pastures, the almost identical white farmhouses, the simple barns, the horse-drawn buggies, and the clotheslines hung with somber-colored garments convey a sense of peace and wholeness reminiscent of another era. Although just sixty-five miles from Philadelphia, "Amish country" is a world away.

Amish life is based on separation from the world, an idea taken from Christ's Sermon on the Mount. This rejection of worldly concerns, writes Donald Kraybill in *The Riddle of Amish Culture*, "provides the foundation of such Amish values as humility, faithfulness, thrift, tradition, communal goals, joy of work, a slow-paced life, and trust in divine providence."

The *Gemeinschaft* of village life that Tönnies said was being lost to industrialization is very much alive among the Amish. The Amish make their decisions in weekly meetings, where, by consensus, they follow a set of rules, or *Ordnung*, to guide their behavior. Religion and the discipline it calls for are the glue that holds these communities together. Brotherly love and the welfare of the community are paramount values. Because they use horses instead of tractors, most Amish farm plots of one hundred acres or less. When needed, neighbors pitch in with the chores. In these ways, they maintain intimate community.

The Amish are bound by many other ties, including language (a dialect of German known as *Pennsylvania Dutch*), plain black clothing that has remained unchanged for almost 300 years, and church-sponsored schools. Nearly all Amish marry, and divorce is forbidden. The family is a vital ingredient in Amish life; all major events take place in the home, including weddings, births, funerals, and church services. Most Amish children attend church schools, but only until the age of 13. To go to school beyond the eighth grade would expose them to "worldly concerns" that would drive a wedge between them and their community. The Amish believe all violence is bad, even personal self-defense, and they register as conscientious objectors during times of war.

The Amish cannot resist all change, of course. Instead, they try to adapt to change in ways that will least disrupt their core values. Because urban sprawl has driven up the price of land, almost half of Amish men work at jobs other than farming, most in farm-related businesses or in wood crafts. They go to great lengths to avoid leaving the home. The Amish believe that when a husband works away from home, all aspects of life change—from the marital relationship to the care of the children—certainly an astute sociological insight. They also believe that if a man receives a paycheck he will think that his work is of more value than his wife's. For the Amish, intimate, or *Gemeinschaft*, society is essential for maintaining their way of life. ■

Sources: Hostetler 1980; Kraybill 1989; Bender 1990; Kephart and Zellner 1994; Aeppel 1996; Bumiller 1998; Savells 2001.

The text contrasts *Gesellschaft* and *Gemeinschaft* societies. The Irish cafe on the left represents a *Gemeinschaft* approach to life. Electronic interactions via the Internet, as in the cybernet cafe in San Francisco, represent a *Gesellschaft* orientation. Internet interactions do not fit easily into standard sociological models—another instance of cultural lag.

THE MICROSOCIOLOGICAL PERSPECTIVE: SOCIAL INTERACTION IN EVERYDAY LIFE

Where macrosociologists stress the broad features of society, microsociologists have a narrower focus. They place their emphasis on *face-to-face interaction,* what people do when they are in one another's presence. Let's examine some of the areas of social life that microsociologists study.

Personal Space

We all surround ourselves with a "personal bubble" that we go to great lengths to protect. We open the bubble to intimates—to our friends, children, parents, and so on—but we are careful to keep most people out of this space. When we stand in lines, for example, we make certain there is enough room so we don't touch the person in front of us and aren't touched by the person behind us.

The amount of space that people prefer varies from one culture to another. Anthropologist Edward Hall (1959) recounts a conversation with a man from South America who had attended one of his lectures:

He came to the front of the class at the end of the lecture.... We started out facing each other, and as he talked I became dimly aware that he was standing a little too close and that I was beginning to back up.... By experimenting I was able to observe that as I moved away slightly, there was an associated shift in the pattern of interaction. He had more trouble expressing himself. If I shifted to where I felt comfortable (about twenty-one inches), he looked somewhat puzzled and hurt.

After Hall (1969) analyzed situations like this, he observed that North Americans use four different "distance zones":

1. *Intimate distance.* This is the zone that the South American unwittingly invaded. It extends to about 18 inches from our bodies. We reserve this space for lovemaking, comforting, protecting, hugging, and intimate touching.

2. *Personal distance.* This zone extends from 18 inches to 4 feet. We reserve it for friends and acquaintances and ordinary conversations. This is the zone in which Hall would have preferred speaking with the South American.

3. *Social distance.* This zone, extending out from us about 4 to 12 feet, marks impersonal or formal relationships. We use this zone for such things as job interviews.

Among the many aspects of social life studied by sociologists with a microsociological focus is personal space. What do you see in common in these two photos?

4. *Public distance.* This zone, extending beyond 12 feet, marks even more formal relationships. It is used to separate dignitaries and public speakers from the general public.

Let's now turn to dramaturgy, a special focus of microsociology.

Dramaturgy: The Presentation of Self in Everyday Life

It was their big day, two years in the making. Jennifer Mackey wore a white wedding gown adorned with an 11-foot train and 24,000 seed pearls that she and her mother had sewn onto the dress. Next to her at the altar in Lexington, Kentucky, stood her intended, Jeffrey Degler, in black tie. They said their vows, then turned to gaze for a moment at the four hundred guests.

That's when groomsman Daniel Mackey collapsed. As the shocked organist struggled to play Mendelssohn's "Wedding March," Mr. Mackey's unconscious body was dragged away, his feet striking—loudly—every step of the altar stairs.

"I couldn't believe he would die at my wedding," the bride said. (Hughes 1990)

Sociologist Erving Goffman (1922–1982) added a new twist to micro-

sociology when he developed **dramaturgy** (or dramaturgical analysis). By this term he meant that social life is like a drama or a stage play: Birth ushers us onto the stage of everyday life, and our socialization consists of learning to perform on that stage. The self that we studied in the previous chapter lies at the center of our performances. We have definite ideas of how we want others to think of us, and we use our roles in everyday life to communicate those ideas. Goffman calls these efforts to manage the impressions that others receive of us **impression management.**

Everyday life, Goffman said, involves playing our assigned roles. We have *front stages* on which to perform them, as did Jennifer and Jeffrey. (By the way, Daniel Mackey didn't really die—he had just passed out from the excitement of it all.) But we don't have to look at weddings to find front stages. Everyday life is filled with them. Where your teacher lectures is a front stage. And if you make an announcement at the dinner table, you are using a front stage. In fact, you spend most of your time on front

Role performance refers to how we play our roles. One of the major roles we are assigned in life is gender. We learn our "gender lessons" early, and we carefully project images that match cultural stereotypes. The source of humor of Pat on *Saturday Night Live* is role confusion, the uncertainty and tentativeness of interaction that results when people don't know whether to react to Pat as a male or as a female.

stages, for a front stage is wherever you deliver your lines. We also have *back stages,* places where we can retreat and let our hair down. When you close the bathroom or bedroom door for privacy, for example, you are entering a back stage.

Everyday life brings with it many roles. The same person may be a student, a teenager, a shopper, a worker, a date, as well as a daughter or a son. Ordinarily our roles are sufficiently separated that conflict between them is minimized. Occasionally, however, what is expected of us in one role is incompatible with what is expected of us in another role. This problem, known as **role conflict,** is illustrated in Figure 4.4. Usually, we manage to avoid role conflict by segregating our roles, which in some instances may require an intense juggling act.

Sometimes the *same* role presents inherent conflict, a problem known as **role strain.** Suppose that you are exceptionally well prepared for a particular class assignment. Although the instructor asks an unusually difficult question, you find yourself knowing the answer when no one else does. If you want to raise your hand, yet don't want to make your fellow students look bad, you will experience role strain. As illustrated in Figure 4.4, the difference between role conflict and role strain is that role conflict is conflict *between* roles, while role strain is conflict *within* a role.

To show ourselves as adept role players brings positive recognition from others, something we all covet. To accomplish this, we often use **teamwork**—two or more people working together to make certain a performance goes off as planned. When a performance doesn't come off quite right, however, it may require **face-saving behavior.** We may, for example, ignore flaws in someone's performance, which Goffman defines as *tact.* Suppose your teacher is about to make an important point. Suppose also that her lecturing has been outstanding and the class is hanging on every word. Just as she pauses for emphasis, her stomach lets out a loud growl. She might then use a face-saving technique by remarking, "I was so busy preparing for class that I didn't get breakfast this morning." It is more likely, however, that both class and teacher will simply ignore the sound, both giving the impression that no one heard a thing—a face-saving technique called *studied nonobservance.* This allows the teacher to make the point, or as Goffman would say, it allows the performance to go on.

Because our own body is so strongly identified with the self, a good part of impression management centers around "body messages." The messages that are attached to various body shapes change over time, but, as explored in the Mass Media in Social Life box on pages 95–96, currently thinness screams desirability.

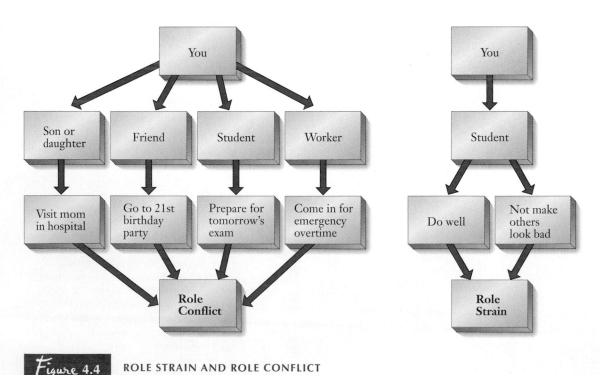

Figure 4.4   **ROLE STRAIN AND ROLE CONFLICT**

Mass Media in Social Life

YOU CAN'T BE THIN ENOUGH:
BODY IMAGES AND THE MASS MEDIA

When you stand before a mirror, do you like what you see? To make your body more attractive, do you watch your weight or work out? You have ideas about what you should look like. Where did you get them?

Television keeps telling us that something is wrong with our bodies. They aren't good enough, and we've got to improve them. The way to improve our bodies, of course, is to buy the advertised products. Wigs, hair pieces, hair transplants, padded brassieres, diet pills, and exercise equipment. Chuck Norris looks so strong and manly as he touts his full body exerciser. Men get the feeling that their body will look like his if they just buy that machine. Female movie stars effortlessly go through tough workouts without even breaking into a sweat. Women get the feeling that men will fight to be near them if they purchase that wonder-working workout machine.

Although we attempt to shrug off such messages, knowing they are designed to sell products, they get our attention. They penetrate our thinking, helping to shape our image of how we "ought" to look. Those models so attractively clothed and coiffered as they walk down the runway, could they be any thinner? For women, the message is clear: You can't be thin enough. The men's message is clear: You can't be strong enough.

Man or woman, your body isn't good enough. It needs to be shaped into something it isn't. It sags where it should be firm. It bulges where it should be smooth. It sticks out where it shouldn't, and it doesn't stick out enough where it should.

And—no matter what your weight—it's too much. You've got to be thinner.

(continued)

All of us contrast the reality we see when we look in the mirror with our culture's ideal body types. Gwyneth Paltrow, a top U.S. film star, represents an ideal body type that has developed in some parts of Western culture. These cultural images often make it difficult for large people to maintain positive images of their bodies. These twins in Los Angeles, California have struggled against dominant cultural images.

YOU CAN'T BE THIN ENOUGH:
BODY IMAGES AND THE MASS MEDIA *(continued)*

Exercise takes time, and it's painful getting in shape. Once you do get in shape, if you slack off it seems to take only a few days for your body to return to its previous slothful, drab appearance. You can't let up, you can't exercise enough, and you can't diet enough.

But who can continue at such a pace, striving for what are unrealistic cultural ideals? A few people, of course, but not many. So liposuction is appealing. Just lie there, put up with a little discomfort, and the doctor will suck the fat right out of you. Surgeons can transform flat breasts into super breasts overnight. They can lower receding hairlines and smooth furrowed brows. They remove lumps with their magical tummy tucks, and take off a decade with their rejuvenating skin peels and face lifts.

With the bosomy girls on *Baywatch* the envy of all, and the impossibly shaped models at *Victoria's Secret* the standard to which they hold themselves, even teens call the plastic surgeon. Parents, anxious lest their child violate peer ideals and trail behind in her race for popularity, foot the bill. In New York City, some parents pay $25,000 to give their daughters a flatter tummy (Gross 1998).

Although peer pressure to alter the body is intense, surgeons keep stoking the fire. A sample ad: "No Ifs, Ands, or Butts. You Can Change Your Bottom Line in Hours!"

The thinness craze has moved to the East. Glossy magazines in Japan and China are filled with skinny models and crammed with ads touting diet pills and diet teas. In China, where famine used to abound, a little extra padding was valued as a sign of good health. Today, the obsession is thinness (Rosenthal 1999). Not-so-subtle ads scream that fat is bad. Some teas come with a package of diet pills. Weight-loss machines, with electrodes attached to acupuncture pressure points, not only reduce fat, but they also build breasts. Or so the advertisers claim.

Not limited by some of our rules, advertisers in Japan and China push a soap that supposedly "sucks up fat through the skin's pores" (Marshall 1995). What a dream product! After all, even though those TV models smile as they go through their paces, those exercise machines do look like a lot of hard work.

In the United States, there is another bottom line. Beauty and attractiveness do pay off. Economists studied physical attractiveness and earnings. The result? "Average-looking" men and women earn more than "plain" people. "Good-looking" men and women earn even more. The "ugly" are paid a pittance. "Attractive" women have an added cash advantage—they attract and marry higher earning men (Hamermesh and Biddle 1994).

More popularity *and* more money? Maybe you can't be thin enough after all. Maybe those exercise machines are a good investment. If only we could catch up with the Japanese and develop a soap that would suck the fat right out of our pores. You can practically hear the jingle now. ■

For Your Consideration

What image do you have of your body? How do cultural expectations of "ideal" bodies underlie your image? Can you recall any advertisement or television program that has affected your body image?

Most advertising and television programs that focus on weight are directed at women. Women are more concerned than men about weight, more likely to have eating disorders, and more likely to be dissatisfied with their bodies (Honeycutt 1995). Do you think that the targeting of women in advertising creates these attitudes and behaviors? Or do you think that these attitudes and behaviors would exist even if there were no such ads? Why?

Ethnomethodology: Uncovering Background Assumptions

Certainly one of the strangest words in sociology is *ethnomethodology*. To understand this term, consider its three basic components. *"Ethno"* means folk or people; *"method"* means how people do something; *"ology"* means "the study of." Putting them together, then, *ethno/method/ology* means "the study of how people do things." Specifically, **ethnomethodology** is the study of how people use commonsense understandings to get through everyday life.

Let's suppose that during a routine office visit, your doctor remarks that your hair is rather long, then takes out a pair of scissors and offers to give you a haircut. You would feel strange about this situation—for your doctor has violated **background assumptions,** your ideas about the way life is and the way things ought to work. These assumptions, which lie at the root of daily life, are so deeply embedded in our consciousness that we are seldom aware of them, and most of us fulfill them unquestioningly. Thus, your doctor does not offer you a haircut, even if he or she is good at cutting hair and you need one!

The founder of ethnomethodology, sociologist Harold Garfinkel, conducted some interesting exercises designed to reveal our background assumptions. Garfinkel (1967) asked his students to act as though they did not understand the basic rules of social life. Some tried to bargain with supermarket clerks; others would inch close to people and stare directly at them. They were met with surprise, bewilderment, even anger. In one exercise Garfinkel asked students to take words and phrases literally. One conversation went like this:

ACQUAINTANCE: How are you?

STUDENT: How am I in regard to what? My health, my finances, my schoolwork, my peace of mind, my . . .

ACQUAINTANCE (red in the face): Look! I was just trying to be polite. Frankly, I don't give a damn how you are.

Students who are directed to break background assumptions can be highly creative. The young children of one of my students were surprised one morning when they came down for breakfast to find a sheet spread across the living room floor. On it were dishes, silverware, burning candles—and bowls of ice cream. They, too, wondered what was going on—but they dug eagerly into the ice cream before their mother could change her mind.

■ **In Sum** Ethnomethodologists explore background assumptions, our taken-for-granted ideas about the world, which underlie our behavior and are violated only with risk. These basic rules of social life are an essential part of the social structure. Deeply embedded in our minds, they give us basic directions for living everyday life.

The Social Construction of Reality

Usually we assume that reality is something that exists independent of ourselves. Symbolic interactionists, however, point out that we define our own realities and then live within those definitions. As sociologist W. I. Thomas said, in what has become known as the **Thomas theorem,** "If people define situations as real, they are real in their consequences." Consider the following incident:

All of us have *background assumptions,* deeply ingrained expectations of how the world operates. They lay the groundwork for what we expect will happen in our interactions. How do you think the background assumptions of these two people differ?

On a visit to Morocco, in northern Africa, I decided to buy a watermelon. When I indicated to the street vendor that the knife he was going to use to cut the watermelon was dirty (encrusted with filth would be more apt), he was very obliging. He immediately bent down and began to swish the knife in a puddle on the street. I shuddered as I looked at the passing burros, that were freely defecating and urinating as they went by. Quickly, I indicated by gesture that I preferred my melon uncut after all.

For that vendor, germs did not exist. For me, they did. And each of us acted according to our definition of the situation. My perception and behavior did not come from the fact that germs are real but *because I grew up in a society that teaches they are real.* Microbes, of course, *objectively* exist, and whether or not germs are part of our thought world makes no difference to whether we are infected by them. Our behavior, however, does not depend on the *objective* existence of something but, rather, on our *subjective interpretation,* on our *definition of reality.* In other words, it is not the reality of microbes that impresses itself on us, but society that impresses the reality of microbes on us.

This is what the **social construction of reality** is. Our society, or the social groups to which we belong, have their particular views of life. From our groups (the *social* part of this process), we learn specific ways of looking at life—whether that be our view of Hitler (he's good, he's evil), germs (they exist, they don't exist), or *anything else in life*. In short, through our interactions with others, we *construct reality*; that is, we learn ways of looking at our experiences in life.

Gynecological Examinations To better understand the social construction of reality, let's consider an extended example.

A gynecological nurse, Mae Biggs, and I did research on vaginal examinations. Reviewing about 14,000 cases, we looked at how the medical profession constructs social reality in order to define this examination as nonsexual (Henslin and Biggs 1971/2001). We found that the pelvic examination unfolds much as a stage play does. I will use "he" to refer to the physician because only male physicians participated in this study. Perhaps the results would be different with women gynecologists.

Scene 1 (the patient as person) In this scene, the doctor maintains eye contact with his patient, calls her by name, and discusses her problems in a professional manner. If he decides that a vaginal examination is necessary, he tells a nurse, "Pelvic in room 1." By this statement, he is announcing that a major change will occur in the next scene.

Scene 2 (from person to pelvic) This scene is the depersonalizing stage. In line with the doctor's announcement, the patient begins the transition from a "person" to a "pelvic." The doctor leaves the room, and a female nurse enters to help the patient make the transition. The nurse prepares the "props" for the coming examination and answers any questions the woman might have.

What occurs at this point is essential for the social construction of reality, for *the doctor's absence removes even the suggestion of sexuality*. To undress in front of him could suggest either a striptease or intimacy, thus undermining the reality being so carefully defined, that of nonsexuality.

The patient also wants to remove any hint of sexuality, and during this scene she may express concern about what to do with her panties. Some mutter to the nurse, "I don't want him to see these." Most women solve the problem by either slipping their panties under their clothes or placing them in their purse.

Scene 3 (the person as pelvic) This scene opens when the doctor enters the room. Before him is a woman lying on a table, her feet in stirrups, her knees tightly together, and her body covered by a drape sheet.

The doctor seats himself on a low stool before the woman, tells her, "Let your knees fall apart" (rather than the sexually loaded "Spread your legs"), and begins the examination.

The drape sheet is crucial in this process of desexualization, for *it dissociates the pelvic area from the person*: Bending forward and with the drape sheet above his head, the physician can see only the vagina, not the patient's face. Thus dissociated from the individual, the vagina is dramaturgically transformed into an object of analysis. If the doctor examines the patient's breasts, he also dissociates them from her person by examining them one at a time, with a towel covering the unexamined breast. Like the vagina, each breast becomes an isolated unit dissociated from the person.

In this scene, the patient cooperates in being an object, becoming for all practical purposes a pelvis to be examined. She withdraws eye contact from the doctor, usually from the nurse as well, is likely to stare at the wall or at the ceiling, and avoids initiating conversation.

Scene 4 (from pelvic to person) In this scene, the patient is "repersonalized." The doctor has left the examining room; the patient dresses and fixes her hair and makeup. Her reemergence as a person is indicated by such statements to the nurse as, "My dress isn't too wrinkled, is it?" indicating a need for reassurance that the metamorphosis from "pelvic" back to "person" has been completed satisfactorily.

Scene 5 (the patient as person) In this scene, the patient is once again treated as a person rather than an object. The doctor makes eye contact with her and addresses her by name. She, too, makes eye contact with the doctor, and the usual middle-class interaction patterns are followed. She has been fully restored.

■ **In Sum** To an outsider to our culture, the custom of women going to a male stranger for a vaginal examination might seem bizarre. But not to us. We learn that pelvic examinations are nonsexual. To sustain this definition requires teamwork—patients, doctors, and nurses working together to *socially construct reality*.

It is not just pelvic examinations or our views of microbes that make up our definitions of reality. Rather, *our behavior depends on how we define reality*. Our definitions (or constructions) provide the basis for what we do and how we feel about life. To understand people, then, it is essential that we know how they define reality.

Social Interaction on the Internet

Microsociologists do not limit themselves to studying face-to-face interaction. They are interested in any small-scale interaction, even a child's talk as he or she plays with toys alone. Communications on the Internet, too, aren't exactly face-to-face. One could say they are face-to-computer, but they can also be viewed as face-to-face with computers in between. (More technically phrased, this would be called computer-mediated face-to-face interaction.)

At this point, we know little about interaction on the Net, but what we do know is intriguing. As we saw in the box on emoticons in Chapter 2 (page 42), to help communicate the feelings that underlie their on-line communications, people have developed emoticons. The Sociology and the New Technology box below explores another aspect of Net communications.

*T*HE NEED FOR BOTH MACROSOCIOLOGY AND MICROSOCIOLOGY

As noted earlier, both microsociology and macrosociology make vital contributions to our understanding of human behavior. Our understanding of social life would be vastly incomplete without one or the other.

To illustrate this point, let's consider two groups of high school boys studied by sociologist William Chambliss (1973/2001). Both groups attended Hanibal High School. In one group were eight middle-class boys who came from "good" families and were perceived by the community as "going somewhere." Chambliss calls this group the "Saints." The other group consisted of six lower-class boys who were seen as headed down a dead-end road. Chambliss calls this group the "Roughnecks."

Both groups skipped school, got drunk, and did a lot of fighting and vandalism. The Saints were actually somewhat more delinquent, for they were truant more often and engaged in more vandalism. Yet the Saints had a good reputation, while the Roughnecks were seen by teachers, the police, and the general community as no good and headed for trouble.

These reputations followed the boys throughout life. Seven of the eight Saints went on to graduate from college. Three studied for advanced degrees: One finished law school and became active in state politics, one finished medical school, and one went on to earn a Ph.D. The four other college graduates entered managerial or executive training programs with large firms. After his parents divorced, one Saint failed to graduate

Sociology & the New Technology

PLUGGED IN AND PLUGGED OUT: INTERACTION ON THE INTERNET

A main concern about social interaction on the Internet is that although it joins us with strangers, it can divide us from friends and family. As we develop online relationships with people we don't know, we can neglect relationships with people we do know. Virtual reality is seductive. It can be more appealing to log onto the Net and talk to strangers than to deal with the rigors of interacting with friends and family. Friendships on the Net allow a unidimensional presentation of self. We can selectively communicate what we want. We don't have to put up with people's moods and personalities. If we don't like what someone on the Net says, we can just log off—or strike up a "conversation" with someone more to our liking at the moment. In contrast, with friends, family, and even some acquaintances, we have to put up with many dimensions of their personalities, not all pleasant.

The Net can be so alluring that real-world reality pales by comparison. I know of one man who became "addicted" to pornography on the Net. Each evening after work, he would ignore his wife and children and seclude himself in his home office. There he would view pornography until it was time to go to bed. Night after night, it was the same. His wife finally gave him an ultimatum—either he stop this, or she would leave. He said that he loved her, but couldn't give this up. She left. He turned on his virtual lovers.

Can virtual reality replace family, friends, networks, and neighborhoods? I doubt that our future will consist of us plugged onto the Net, and unplugged from family and friends. But the Net is here to stay, and how it will affect our interactions will be a fascinating area of study. ■

Can you tell which of these photos is of upper-middle-class youth and which portrays working-class youth? Despite similarities of social identifiers by which both groups of students proclaim that they are U.S. teenagers, they also use status markers to signal their social class background. As the text explains, this information is of crucial importance, for it affects perception, social interaction, and, ultimately, life chances.

from high school on time and had to repeat his senior year. Although this boy tried to go to college by attending night school, he never finished. He was unemployed the last time Chambliss saw him.

In contrast, only four of the Roughnecks even finished high school. Two of these boys did exceptionally well in sports and received athletic scholarships to college. They both graduated from college and became high school coaches. Of the two others who graduated from high school, one became a small-time gambler and the other disappeared "up north," where he was last reported to be driving a truck. Both of the two who did not complete high school were sent to state penitentiaries for separate murders.

To understand what happened to the Saints and the Roughnecks, we need to grasp *both* social structure and social interaction. Using *macrosociology*, we can place these boys within the larger framework of the U.S. social class system. This reveals how opportunities open or close to people depending on their social class and how people learn different goals as they grow up in vastly different groups. We can then use *microsociology* to follow their everyday lives. We can see how the Saints manipulated their "good" reputations to skip classes repeatedly and how their access to automobiles allowed them to protect those reputations by transferring their troublemaking to different communities. In contrast, the Roughnecks, who did not have cars, were highly visible. Their lawbreaking, which was limited to a small area, readily came to the attention of the community. Microsociology also reveals how their respective reputations opened doors of opportunity to the first group of boys while closing them to the other.

Thus we need both kinds of sociology, and both are stressed in the following chapters.

ꓢUMMARY AND ꓣEVIEW

■ Levels of Sociological Analysis

What two levels of analysis do sociologists use?

Sociologists use macro- and microsociological levels of analysis. In **macrosociology**, the focus is placed on large-scale features of social life, while in **microsociology**, the focus is on **social interaction.** Functionalists and conflict theorists tend to use a macrosociological approach, while symbolic interactionists are more likely to use a microsociological approach. Pp. 80–81.

■ The Macrosociological Perspective: Social Structure

How does social structure influence behavior?

The term **social structure** refers to a society's framework, which forms an envelope around us and establishes limits on our behavior. Social structure consists of culture, **social class**, social statuses, **roles, groups,** and **social institutions.** Together, these serve as foundations for how we view the world. Pp. 81–82.

Our location in the social structure underlies our perceptions, attitudes, and behaviors. *Culture* lays the broadest framework, while **social class** divides people according to income, education, and occupational prestige. Our behaviors and orientations are further influenced by the **statuses** we occupy, the **roles** we play, the **groups** to which we belong, and our experiences with the institutions of our society. These components of society work together to help maintain social order. Pp. 82–85.

What are social institutions?

Social institutions are the standard means that a society develops to meet its basic needs. As summarized in Figure 4.1, industrial and postindustrial societies have nine social institutions—the family, religion, law, politics, economics, education, science, medicine, and the military. A tenth, the mass media, is emerging. P. 85.

What are the four social revolutions?

The discovery that animals and plants could be domesticated marked the *first* social revolution, which transformed **hunting and gathering societies** into **pastoral** and **horticultural societies.** The invention of the plow brought about the *second* social revolution, as societies became agricultural. The invention of the steam engine allowed industrial societies to develop—the *third* social revolution. Today, we are witnessing the *fourth* social revolution, which is being ushered in by the invention of the microchip. As in the previous three social revolutions, little will remain the same. Our attitudes, ideas, expectations, behaviors, relationships—all will be transformed. Pp. 85–90.

What holds society together?

In agricultural societies, said Emile Durkheim, people are united by **mechanical solidarity** (similar views and feelings). With industrialization comes **organic solidarity** (people depend on one another to do their jobs). Ferdinand Tönnies pointed out that the informal means of control of *Gemeinschaft* (small, intimate) societies are replaced by formal mechanisms in *Gesellschaft* (larger, more impersonal) societies. Pp. 90–91.

■ The Microsociological Perspective: Social Interaction in Everyday Life

Do all human groups share a similar sense of personal space?

In examining how people use physical space, symbolic interactionists stress that we surround ourselves with a "personal bubble" that we carefully protect. People from different cultures have "personal bubbles" of varying sizes, so the answer to the question is no. Americans typically use four different "distance zones": intimate, personal, social, and public. Pp. 92–93.

What is dramaturgy?

Erving Goffman developed **dramaturgy** (or dramaturgical analysis), which analyzes everyday life in terms of the stage. At the core of this analysis is **impression management,** our attempts to control the impressions we make on others. Our performances often call for **teamwork** and **face-saving behavior.** Pp. 93–97.

What is the social construction of reality?

The phrase **the social construction of reality** refers to how we construct our views of the world, which, in turn, underlie our actions. **Ethnomethodology** is the study of how people make sense of everyday life. Ethnomethodologists try to uncover **background assumptions,** our basic ideas about the way life is. Pp. 97–99.

■ Social Interaction on the Internet

How is the Internet changing social interaction?

The Internet is too new for us to know its full effects on human interaction. There are concerns at this point that virtual relationships may drive a wedge between some Internet users and their real-life relationships. We'll have to wait and see what develops. P. 99.

■ The Need for Both Macrosociology and Microsociology

Why are both levels of analysis important?

Because each focuses on different aspects of the human experience, both macrosociology and microsociology are necessary for us to understand social life. P. 100.

Where can I read more on this topic?

Suggested readings for this chapter are listed on page SR-3.

YOUR INTERACTIVE COMPANION WEB SITE

Your Interactive Companion Web Site includes practice tests, with feedback, and online learning activities with video, audio, and Weblinks. Your access code for this Web site is provided with this text.

GLOSSARY

achieved statuses positions that are earned or accomplished, or that involve at least some effort or activity on the individual's part (p. 83)

ascribed statuses positions an individual either inherits at birth or receives involuntarily later in life (p. 83)

background assumptions deeply embedded common understandings (basic rules or "codes") concerning our view of the world and how people ought to act (p. 97)

division of labor how work is divided among the members of a group (p. 90)

dramaturgy an approach, pioneered by Erving Goffman, that analyzes social life in terms of drama or the stage (p. 93)

ethnomethodology the study of how people use background assumptions to make sense of life (p. 96)

face-saving behavior techniques people use to salvage a performance that is going sour (p. 94)

Gemeinschaft village life; a type of society in which life is intimate; a community in which everyone knows everyone else and people share a sense of togetherness (p. 90)

Gesellschaft urban life; a type of society that is dominated by impersonal relationships, individual accomplishments, and self-interest (p. 90)

group people who regularly and consciously interact with one another; in a general sense, people who have something in common and who believe that what they have in common is significant (p. 85)

horticultural society a society based on cultivating plants by the use of hand tools (p. 88)

hunting and gathering society a society dependent on hunting and gathering for survival (p. 87)

impression management the term used by Erving Goffman to describe people's efforts to control the impressions that others receive of them (p. 93)

Industrial Revolution the third social revolution; it occurred when machines powered by fuels replaced most animal and human power (p. 89)

macrosociology analysis of social life that focuses on broad features of social structure, such as social class and the relationships of groups to one another; an approach usually used by functionalists and conflict theorists (p. 80)

master status a status that cuts across the other statuses that an individual occupies (p. 84)

mechanical solidarity Durkheim's term for the unity or shared consciousness that comes from being involved in similar occupations or activities (p. 90)

microsociology analysis of social life that focuses on social interaction; an approach usually used by symbolic interactionists (p. 80)

organic solidarity Durkheim's term for the interdependence that results from people needing the skills, work, and products of one another; solidarity based on the division of labor (p. 90)

pastoral society a society based on the pasturing of animals (p. 88)

role the behaviors, obligations, and privileges attached to a status (p. 85)

role conflict conflicts that someone feels because the expectations attached to one role are incompatible with the expectations of another role (p. 94)

role strain conflicts that someone feels within a role (p. 94)

social class a large number of people who have similar amounts of income and education and who work at jobs that are roughly comparable in prestige (p. 83)

social cohesion the degree to which members of a group or a society feel united by shared values and other social bonds (p. 90)

social construction of reality the use of background assumptions and life experiences to define what is real (p. 97)

social institution the organized, usual, or standard ways by which society meets its basic needs (p. 85)

social interaction what people do when they are in one another's presence; this can be a virtual presence, such as the telephone or the Internet (p. 80)

social structure the relationship of people and groups to one another (p. 81)

society a group of people who share a culture and a territory (p. 85)

status the position that someone occupies; one's social ranking (p. 83)

status inconsistency a contradiction or mismatch between statuses; a condition in which a person ranks high on some dimensions of social class and low on others (p. 84)

status set all the statuses or positions that an individual occupies (p. 83)

status symbols items used to identify a status (p. 83)

teamwork the collaboration of two or more persons who, interested in the success of a performance, manage impressions jointly (p. 94)

Thomas theorem basically, that people live in socially constructed worlds; that is, people jointly build their own realities; summarized in William I. Thomas' statement, "If people define situations as real, they are real in their consequences." (p. 97)

Chapter 5

Jean-Pierre Stora, Les Flaneurs, 1995

Social Groups and Formal Organizations

As soon as the ramp had been erected in the castle [in Chelmo, Poland], people started arriving in trucks…the people were told that they had to take a bath, that their clothes had to be disinfected, and that they could hand in any valuable items beforehand to be registered…. When they had undressed they were sent to the cellar of the castle and then along a passageway on to the ramp and from there into the gas-van. In the castle there were signs marked "To the baths."

The gas-vans [had]…interior walls… lined with sheet metal. On the floor there was a wooden grille. The floor of the van had an opening that could be connected to the exhaust by means of a removable metal pipe. When the trucks were full of people, the double doors at the back were closed….

The Kommando member detailed as driver would start the engine straight away so that the people inside the truck were suffocated by the exhaust gases…the van was driven to the camp in the woods where the bodies were unloaded…. I then drove the van back to the castle and parked it there. Here it would be cleaned of the excretions of the people that had died in it. Afterwards it would once again be used for gassings….

I can no longer say today what I thought at the time or whether I thought of anything at all. ■

—Testimony of Walter Burmeister in
    Klee et al., 1991:219–220.

SOCIAL GROUPS

Groups are the essence of life in society. We become who we are because of our membership in human groups. As we saw in Chapter 3, even our mind is a product of society, or, more accurately phrased, of the groups to which we belong.

In this chapter, we'll examine the various groups that make up society, and we'll consider the power that groups wield over us. Although none of us wants to think that we could participate in mass killings such as those recounted in our opening vignette, don't bet on it. You are going to read about some surprising aspects of groups in this chapter.

First, we need to clarify the concept of "group." Two terms sometimes confused with "group" are *aggregate* and *category*. An **aggregate** consists of individuals who temporarily share the same physical space but who do not see themselves as belonging together. People waiting in a checkout line or drivers parked at a red light are an aggregate. A **category** consists of people who share similar characteristics, such as all college women who wear glasses or all men over 6 feet tall. Unlike groups, the individuals who make up a category neither interact with one another nor take one another into account.

In contrast, the members of a **group** think of themselves as belonging together, and they interact with one another. To better understand this essential feature of social life, let's look at the types of groups that make up our society and at how they affect our lives.

Primary Groups

Our first group, the family, gives us our basic orientation to life. Later, among friends, we find more in-

In this chapter, you will read about bureaucracies, which have become a powerful and overwhelming force in social life. Even Mother Teresa, one of the most famous religious figures of the late twentieth century, was unable to overcome bureaucratic red tape in her attempt to help New York City's homeless.

timacy and an additional sense of belonging. These groups are what sociologist Charles Cooley called **primary groups.** By providing intimate, face-to-face interaction, they give us an identity, a feeling of who we are. As Cooley (1909) put it,

> By primary groups I mean those characterized by intimate face-to-face association and cooperation. They are primary in several senses, but chiefly in that they are fundamental in forming the social nature and ideals of the individual.

Producing a Mirror within It is significant that Cooley calls primary groups the "springs of life." By this he means that primary groups, such as the family, friendship groups, and even gangs, are essential to our emotional well-being. As humans, we have an intense need for face-to-face interaction that generates feelings of self-esteem. By offering a sense of belonging, a feeling of being appreciated, and sometimes even love, primary groups are uniquely equipped to meet this basic need.

Primary groups are also significant because their values and attitudes become fused into our identity. We internalize their views, which become the lens through which we view life. Even as adults—no matter how far we may have come from our childhood roots—early primary groups remain "inside" us. There they continue to form part of the perspective from which we look out onto the world. Ultimately, then, it is difficult, if not impossible, for us to separate the self from our primary groups, for the self and our groups merge into a "we."

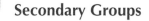

Secondary Groups

Compared with primary groups, **secondary groups** are larger, more anonymous, formal, and impersonal. Secondary groups are based on some interest or activity, and their members are likely to interact on the basis of specific roles, such as president, manager, worker, or student. Examples are a college class, the American Sociological Association, a factory, and the Demo-

Relationships in *secondary groups* are more formal and temporary than those in *primary groups*. In order to satisfy basic emotional needs, members of secondary groups, such as members of the military, form smaller primary groups.

cratic Party. Contemporary society could not function without secondary groups. They are part of the way we get our education, make our living, and spend our money and leisure time.

As necessary as secondary groups are for contemporary life, they often fail to satisfy our deep needs for intimate association. Consequently, *secondary groups tend to break down into primary groups.* For Walter Burmeister in our opening vignette, his police-army unit was a secondary group. The police-army buddies he drank with, though, formed a primary group. We, too, at school and work, form friendship cliques. Our interaction with them is so important to us that we sometimes feel if it weren't for our friends, school or work "would drive us crazy." The primary groups we form within secondary groups, then, serve as a buffer between us and the demands that secondary groups place on us.

Voluntary Associations A special type of secondary group is a **voluntary association,** a group made up of volunteers who organize on the basis of some mutual interest. Some are local, consisting of only a few volunteers; some are national, with a paid professional staff; and others are in between.

Americans love voluntary associations, and use them to pursue a wide variety of interests. A visitor entering one of the thousands of small towns that dot the U.S. landscape is often greeted with a highway sign proclaiming some of the town's volunteer associations: Girl Scouts, Boy Scouts, Lions, Elks, Eagles, Knights of Columbus, Chamber of Commerce, American Legion, Veterans of Foreign Wars, and perhaps a host of others. One form of voluntary association is so prevalent that a separate sign sometimes indicates which varieties are present in the town: Roman Catholic, Baptist, Lutheran, Methodist, Episcopalian, and so on. Not listed on these signs are many other voluntary associations, such as political parties, unions, health clubs, the National Organization for Women, Alcoholics Anonymous, Gamblers Anonymous, Association of Pinto Racers, and Citizens United For or Against This and That.

The Inner Circle and the Iron Law of Oligarchy
An interesting, and disturbing, aspect of voluntary associations is that the leaders are likely to grow distant from their members and to become convinced that they can trust only an inner circle to make the group's important decisions. To see this principle at work, let's look at the Veterans of Foreign Wars (VFW).

Sociologists Elaine Fox and George Arquitt (1985) studied three local posts of the VFW, a national organization of former U.S. soldiers who have served in foreign wars. They found that although the leaders conceal their attitudes from the other members, they view the rank and file as a bunch of ignorant boozers. Because the leaders can't stand the thought that such people might represent them to the community and at national meetings, a curious situation arises. Although the VFW constitution makes rank-and-file members eligible for top leadership positions, they never become leaders. In fact, the leaders are so effective in controlling these top positions that even before an election they can specify who is going to win. "You need to meet Jim," the sociologists were told. "He's the next post commander after Sam does his time."

At first, the researchers found this puzzling. The election hadn't been held yet. As they investigated further, they found that leadership is actually decided behind the scenes. The elected leaders appoint their favored people to chair the key committees. This makes the members aware of their accomplishments, and they elect them as leaders. The inner circle, then, maintains control over the entire organization simply by appointing members of their inner circle to highly visible positions.

Like the VFW, most organizations are run by only a few of their members (Cnaan 1991). Building on the term *oligarchy,* a system in which many are ruled by a

In a process called the *iron law of oligarchy,* a small, self-perpetuating elite tends to take control of formal organizations. Shown in this photo, taken in St. Joseph, Missouri, is one of the organizations sociologists have studied.

few, sociologist Robert Michels (1876–1936) coined the term **the iron law of oligarchy** to refer to how organizations come to be dominated by a small, self-perpetuating elite. The majority of members are passive, and an elite inner circle keeps itself in power by passing the leadership positions from one clique member to another.

What many find disturbing about the iron law of oligarchy is that people are excluded from leadership because they don't represent the inner circle's values, background, or even their images of themselves. This is true even of organizations that are strongly committed to democratic principles. For example, U.S. political parties—supposedly the backbone of the nation's representative government—are run by an inner circle that passes leadership positions from one elite member to another. This principle is also demonstrated by the U.S. Senate. With their control of statewide political machinery, access to free mailing, and even the free use of tax dollars to produce videos that can be sent by e-mail, about 90 percent of U.S. senators who choose to run are re-elected (*Statistical Abstract* 1999:Table 472; Simpson 2000).

In-Groups and Out-Groups

Groups toward which we feel loyalty are called **in-groups**; those toward which we feel antagonisms, **out-groups**. For Walter Burmeister in our opening vignette,

and the thousands like him, the police-army unit was an in-group, while the Jews and all others who were classified as "enemies of the state" were out-groups. That we make such a fundamental division of the world has far-reaching consequences for our lives.

Producing Loyalty and a Sense of Superiority Identification with a group can generate not only a sense of belonging, but also loyalty and feelings of superiority. These, in turn, often produce rivalries. Usually the rivalries are mild, such as sports rivalries among nearby towns, where the most extreme act is likely to be the furtive invasion of the out-group's territory in order to steal a mascot, paint a rock, or uproot a goal post. The consequences of in-group membership also can be discrimination, hatred, and, as we saw in our opening vignette, even participation in mass murder.

Implications for a Socially Diverse Society It is not surprising that in-group membership leads to discrimination, for, with our strong identifications and loyalties, we all favor members of our in-groups. This aspect of in- and out-groups is, of course, the basis of many problems in society. It underlies many gender and racial-ethnic divisions. As sociologist Robert Merton (1968) observed, one consequence is an interesting double standard. We view the traits of our in-group as virtues, while we see those *same* traits in out-groups as vices. The Nazis in our opening vignette saw themselves as intelligent, the saviors of the human race. Instead of acknowledging a Jew as intelligent, however, they would say that the individual was scheming or sly. Today, men may perceive an aggressive man as assertive, but an aggressive woman as pushy. A male employee who doesn't speak up may be thought of as "knowing when to keep his mouth shut," whereas a quiet woman may be considered too timid to make it in the business world.

To divide the world into "we" and "them" poses a danger for a pluralistic society. As the Jews did for the Nazis, an out-group can come to symbolize evil, arousing contempt and hatred. During times of economic insecurity, for example, *xenophobia,* or fear of strangers, may grow. For some, the out-group may represent jobs that have been "stolen" from their friends and family. The result may be attacks against immigrants, a national anti-immigration policy, or a resurgence of neo-Nazis or the Ku Klux Klan.

In short, to divide the world into in-groups and out-groups is a natural part of social life. But in addition to bringing about functional consequences, it can bring about some highly dysfunctional ones.

"So long, Bill. This is my club. You can't come in."

How our participation in social groups shapes our self-concept is a major focus of symbolic interactionists. In this process, knowing who we are *not* is as significant as knowing who we are.

Reference Groups

Suppose you have just been offered a great job. It pays double what you hope to make even after you graduate from college. You have just three days to make up your mind. If you accept it, you will have to drop out of college. As you consider the matter, thoughts like this may go through your mind: "My friends will say I'm a fool if I don't take the job...but Dad and Mom will practically go crazy. They've made sacrifices for me, and they'd be crushed if I didn't finish college. They've always said I've got to get my education first, that good jobs will always be there....But, then, I'd like to see the look on the faces of those neighbors who said I'd never amount to much!"

This is an example of how people use **reference groups,** the groups we use as standards to evaluate ourselves. Your reference groups may include family, friends, neighbors, teachers, classmates, and co-workers. You don't even have to belong to the group; it can be one that you would like to join. If you are thinking about going to graduate school, for example, graduate students or members of the profession you hope to join may be one of your reference groups. You may have them in mind as you evaluate your grades or writing skills.

Providing a Yardstick Reference groups exert tremendous influence over our lives. For example, if you want to become a corporate executive, you might start to dress more formally, try to improve your vocabulary, read the *Wall Street Journal,* and change your major to business or law. In contrast, if you want to become a rock musician, you might wear several earrings in one ear, dress in ways your parents and many of your peers consider extreme, read *Rolling Stone,* drop out of college, and hang around clubs and rock groups.

Exposure to Contradictory Standards in a Socially Diverse Society From these examples, you can see that the yardsticks provided by reference groups operate as a form of social control. When we see ourselves as measuring up to the yardstick, we feel no conflict. If our behavior, or even aspirations, do not match the standards held by a reference group, however, the mismatch can lead to internal turmoil. For example, to want to become a corporate executive would create no inner turmoil for most of us, but it would if you had grown up in an Amish home, for the Amish strongly disapprove of such aspirations for their children. They ban high school and college education, three-piece suits, and corporate employment. Similarly, if you wanted to become a soldier and your parents were dedicated pacifists, you likely

All of us have *reference groups*—the groups we use as standards to evaluate ourselves. How do you think the reference groups of these members of the KKK who are demonstrating in Jaspar, Texas, differ from those of the police officer who is protecting their right of free speech? Although the KKK and this police officer use different groups to evaluate their attitudes and behaviors, the process is the same.

would feel deep conflict, as your parents would hold quite different aspirations for you.

Given the social diversity of our society as well as our social mobility, many of us are exposed to contradictory ideas and standards from the many groups that become significant to us. The "internal recordings" that play contradictory messages from these reference groups, then, are one cost of social mobility.

Social Networks

If you are a member of a large group, there probably are a few people within that group with whom you regularly associate. In a sociology class I was teaching at a commuter campus, six women chose to work together on a project. They got along well, and they began to sit together. Eventually they planned a Christmas party at one of their homes. These clusters, or internal factions, are called **cliques.** The links between people—their cliques, as well as their family, friends, acquaintances, and even "friends of friends"—are called **social networks.** Think of

a social network as ties that extend outward from yourself, gradually encompassing more and more people.

The Small World Phenomenon Although we live in a huge society, we do not experience social life as an ocean of nameless, strange faces. Instead, we interact within social networks that connect us to the larger society. Social scientists have wondered just how extensive the connections are between social networks. If you list everyone you know, and each of those individuals lists everyone he or she knows, and you keep doing this, would almost everyone in the United States eventually be included on those lists?

It would be too cumbersome to test this hypothesis by drawing up such lists, but psychologist Stanley Milgram (1967) hit on an ingenious way to find out just how interconnected our social networks are. In what has become a classic experiment known as *the small world phenomenon,* he selected names at random from across the United States. Some he designated as "senders," others as "receivers." Milgram addressed letters to the receivers and asked the senders to mail the letters to someone they knew on a first-name basis whom they thought might know the receiver. This person, in turn, was asked to mail the letter to someone he or she knew who might know the receiver, and so on. The question was, Would the letters ever get to the receivers? If so, how long would the chain be?

Think of yourself as part of this experiment. What would you do if you were a sender, but the receiver lived in a state in which you knew no one? You would send the letter to someone you know who might know someone in that state. And this is just what happened. None of the senders knew the receivers, and in the resulting chains some links broke; that is, after receiving a letter, some people didn't send it on. Surprisingly, however, most letters did reach their intended receivers. Even more surprising, the average chain was made up of only *five* links.

Global Considerations Milgram's experiment shows just how small our world really is, and it gives us insight into why strangers from different parts of the country sometimes find they have a mutual acquaintance. If our social networks are so interrelated that almost everyone in the United States is connected by just five links, how many links connect us to everyone on earth? This experiment is yet to be done.

Implications for a Socially Diverse Society A characteristic of social networks—including your own—is that they perpetuate discrimination. To see why, let's suppose that an outstanding job—great pay, interesting work, and opportunity for advancement—has just opened up where you work. Whom will you tell? Most likely it will be someone you know, someone you like, maybe someone for whom you'd like to do a favor. And most likely your personal social network is made up of people who look much like yourself—especially in terms of race, age, and social class. This tends to keep good jobs moving in the direction of people who have characteristics similar to those of the people already in an organization. Our social networks, then, are an essential part of social inequality. They both reflect the inequality that characterizes our society and help to perpetuate it.

The term **networking** refers to people using social networks, usually for career advancement. Hoping to establish a circle of acquaintances who will prove valuable to them, people go to parties, and join clubs, churches, synagogues, mosques, and political parties. Many women do *gender networking,* developing networks of working women in order to help advance their careers. When they reach top positions, some of these women steer their business to other women. The resulting circle is so tight that the term "new girl" network is being used, especially in the field of law. Like the "good old boys" who preceded them, the new insiders also justify their exclusionary practice (Jacobs 1997).

A New Group: Electronic Communities

In the 1990s, a new type of human group, the **electronic community,** made its appearance. On the Internet are hundreds of thousands of people who "meet" in "chat rooms" to communicate on almost any conceivable topic, from donkey racing and bird watching to sociology and quantum physics. The Sociology and the New Technology box on the next page explores this new human group.

Bureaucracies

About 100 years ago, sociologist Max Weber also noted the emergence of a new type of group, in this case, the *bureaucracy.* To achieve more efficient results, this new type of social organization shifted the emphasis from personal loyalties to the "bottom line." Bureaucracies have become so common that we now take them for granted, unaware that they are fairly new on the human scene. As we look at the characteristics of bureaucracies, we will also consider their implications for our lives.

The Characteristics of Bureaucracies

What do the Soviet army, the U.S. postal service, the Mormon Church, and your college have in common? The sociological answer is that they all are **bureaucracies.** As Weber (1913/1947) pointed out, bureaucracies have

1. *Clear-cut levels, with assignments flowing downward and accountability flowing upward.* Each level assigns responsibilities to the level beneath it, while each lower level is accountable to the level above for fulfilling those assignments. The bureaucratic structure of a typical university is shown in Figure 5.1 on page 113.

2. *A division of labor.* Each worker has a specific task to fulfill, and all the tasks are coordinated to accomplish the purpose of the organization. In a college, for example, a teacher does not run the heating system, the president does not teach, and a secretary does not evaluate textbooks. These tasks are distributed among people who have been trained to do them.

3. *Written rules.* In their attempt to become efficient, bureaucracies stress written procedures. In general, the

The division of labor, a central characteristic of formal organizations, is not new. Shown here are Incans planting their fields. The men are using the footplows, the woman is handing out the corn seeds, and the children are planting. This depiction is by Felipe Guaman Poma de Ayala (1583–1615).

Sociology & the New Technology

ELECTRONIC COMMUNITIES: CYBERCOMMUNICATIONS AND OUR CHANGING CULTURE

A new technology can transform society. As you saw in the preceeding chapter, the domestication of animals and the invention of the plow and the steam engine brought wholesale changes to people's lives. Today's new technology, the microchip, will likely transform our society, too—and with it, how we relate to one another. Let's consider just "talk" and intimacy.

Through most of human history, "talk" meant face-to-face communication. Then when writing was invented, people who were far apart could "talk" to one another—leaving a record of what they "said." The invention of the printing press in 1436 not only multiplied the power of "long-distance talk," but also it transformed religion and politics. With Bibles available to the masses, no longer did the Roman Catholic Church remain the exclusive interpreter of God's Word. Political tracts, pouring off the press, also encouraged independent thinking. Independent religious and political thought, in turn, undermined church and monarchy, ushering in protestant religions and constitutional forms of government.

The sociological point is that the media are not simply passive channels of information, mere "holders" and "senders" of messages. The media shape our lives. Just as the printing press encouraged new ways of thinking, which undermined the power of church and government, so, too, our new technology is doing much more than bringing us new forms of "talk."

Consider how the Internet is extending the boundaries of our homes, schools, and businesses.

In the days before television…

The Far Side © Farworks, Inc. Used by permission. All rights reserved.

While remaining within our four walls, we "travel" electronically around the world. We share information with people we have never met, and develop friendships with people across the globe.

The result is the electronic community, a type of group that until now was unknown in human history. Electronic communities center on any shared interest, whether it be antique cars, radical politics, or deviant sex. Some communities are based on giving support. As people who suffer from cancer share their experiences with fear, pain, surgery, radiation, and chemotherapy, they break the depressing isolation that surrounds them. Those who suffer from other debilitating diseases do the same.

In some cases, people even form what we might call an *electronic primary group*. Some people, as they communicate online, come to identify with one another.

They may even develop a sense of intimacy and share revealing information. Some online friends become so significant that people even build their lives around them. The first thing they do in the morning is rush to their computer. They eagerly read their latest e-mail from their Internet friends, and go to exclusive "chat rooms" where they discuss the latest development in their "real" (not online) relationships. Only then do they get dressed and go to work. After work, they rush back to their virtual world. For some, the people they "meet" electronically are as real as their family—and sometimes have a greater impact on their lives.

It is fascinating to observe how cybercommunications are changing social relationships. Although we are just at the edge of what may be a major historical shift, we can already see a new form of social intimacy emerging. With the Net, people need never meet in order to identify on a personal, even intimate, basis. They experience closeness without permanence, and depth without commitment (Cerulo et al. 1992). While we may distance ourselves from people nearby, we foster intimacy with people in faraway places. Some of us only wave to our next door neighbors, and know little about what is happening to them, while we contact our Net friends often and know intimate details about their lives. It is too soon to know the ramifications of this changed sense of community, but it is likely that our new electronic primary groups will affect not only our social interactions, but also our culture, and even our sense of self. ■

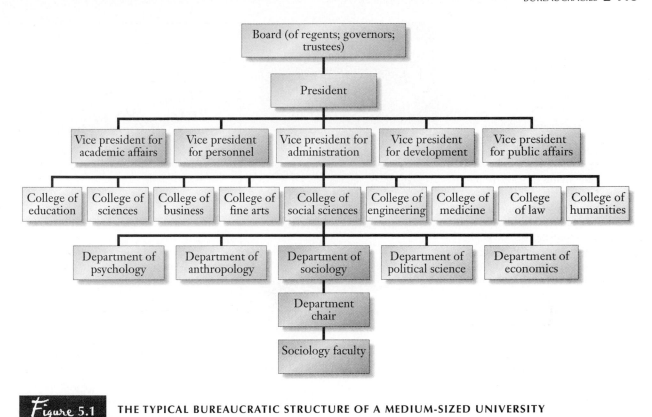

Figure 5.1 THE TYPICAL BUREAUCRATIC STRUCTURE OF A MEDIUM-SIZED UNIVERSITY

longer a bureaucracy exists, the larger it grows and the more written rules it has.

4. *Written communications and records.* Records are kept of much of what occurs in a bureaucracy ("Fill that out in triplicate"). Workers also spend a fair amount of time sending memos back and forth. With e-mail, the form of the memo is changing.

5. *Impersonality.* It is the office that is important, not the individual who holds the office. You work for the organization, not for the replaceable person who heads some post in the organization.

The Perpetuation of Bureaucracies

Bureaucracies have become a standard feature of modern life because they are a powerful form of social organization. They harness people's energies in order to reach specific goals. Once in existence, however, they tend to take on a life of their own. In a process called **goal displacement,** even after the organization achieves its goal and no longer has a reason to continue, continue it does.

A classic example is the National Foundation for the March of Dimes, organized in the 1930s to fight polio

(Sills 1957). At that time, the origin of polio was a mystery. The public was alarmed and fearful, for overnight a healthy child could be stricken with this crippling disease. Parents lived in fear, because no one knew whose child would be next. To raise money to discover the cause and a cure, the March of Dimes placed posters of children on crutches near cash registers in almost every store in the United States. (See the example on the next page.) The U.S. public took the campaign to heart and contributed heavily. The organization raised money beyond its wildest dreams. During the 1950s, Dr. Jonas Salk developed a vaccine for polio, and this threat was wiped out almost overnight. The public breathed a collective sigh of relief.

What then? Did the organization fold? After all, its purpose had been fulfilled. But, as you know, the March of Dimes is still around. Faced with the loss of their jobs, the professional staff that ran the organization quickly found a way to keep its bureaucracy intact by pursuing a new enemy—birth defects. Their choice of enemy is particularly striking, for it is doubtful that we will ever run out of birth defects—and thus unlikely that these people will ever run out of jobs. But yet there is the possibility that the mapping of the human genome system might

The March of Dimes was founded by President Franklin Roosevelt in the 1930s. When a vaccine for polio was discovered in the 1950s, the organization did not declare victory and disband. Instead, it kept the organization intact by creating new goals—fighting birth defects. Sociologists use the term *goal displacement* to refer to this process of adopting new goals. "Fighting birth defects" is now being replaced by an even vaguer goal, "campaigning for healthier babies." This last goal displacement may guarantee the organization's existence forever, for it is so elusive it can never be reached. For an explanation of the second "poster," see below.

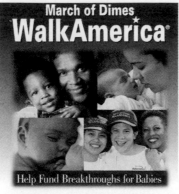

Join WalkAmerica and help the March of Dimes continue its 60-year track record of lifesaving breakthroughs for babies. Breakthroughs like the polio vaccine, intensive care nurseries, and surfactant therapy to help critically ill babies breathe.

Sign up for WalkAmerica today. Call your local March of Dimes or 1-800-525-WALK and join our successful fight to save babies.

PERMISSION DENIED BY MARCH OF DIMES

eliminate birth defects, isn't there? To ward off this threat to its existence, the March of Dimes has now adopted a new slogan, "Breakthroughs for Babies." This latest goal should ensure the organization's existence forever—for it is so vague that we are not likely to ever run out of the need for "breakthroughs."

Organizations are sensitive about sociologists analyzing their activities, and the March of Dimes is no exception. When I tried to get permission to reprint a copy of their current poster, I was denied that permission—*unless I changed my analysis to make it more favorable to the organization.* As you can see from the missing photo above, I refused to do so. Sociologists regularly confront such obstacles in their work.

The Rationalization of Society

Weber viewed bureaucracies as such a powerful form of social organization that he predicted they would come to dominate social life. He called this process **the rationalization of society,** meaning that bureaucracies, with their rules, regulations, and emphasis on results, would increasingly govern our lives. As explored in the Down-to-Earth Sociology box on the next page, in the United States even cooking is becoming rationalized, as fast-food outlets take over this traditional area of work.

Coping with Bureaucracies

Although in the long run no other form of social organization is more efficient, as Weber recognized, bureau-

cracies also have a dark side. Let's look at some of their dysfunctions.

Red Tape: A Rule Is a Rule Bureaucracies can be so bound by red tape that their rules impede the purpose of the organization. Some rules (or "correct procedures" in bureaucratic jargon) are enough to try the patience of a saint.

In the Bronx, Mother Teresa spotted a structurally sound abandoned building and wanted to turn it into a homeless shelter. But she ran head on into a rule: The building must have an elevator for homeless people with disabilities. Not having the funds for the elevator, Mother Teresa struggled to get permission to bypass this rule. Two frustrating years later, she gave up. The abandoned building is still rotting away. (Tobias 1995)

Obviously this rule about elevators was not intended to stop Mother Teresa from ministering to the down and out. But, hey, rules is rules!

Bureaucratic Alienation Treated in terms of roles, rules, and functions rather than as individuals, many workers begin to feel more like objects than people. Marx termed these reactions **alienation,** which he said comes from being cut off from the finished product of one's labor. He pointed out that before industrialization, workers used their own tools to produce an entire product, such as a chair or table. Now the capitalists own the tools (machinery) and assign each worker only a single step or two in the entire production process. Relegated

Sociology

THE MCDONALDIZATION OF SOCIETY

The thousands of McDonald's restaurants that dot the U.S. landscape—and increasingly, the world—have a significance that goes far beyond the convenience of ready-made hamburgers and milk shakes. As sociologist George Ritzer (1993) says, our everyday lives are being "McDonaldized." Let's see what he means by this.

As Ritzer says, the *McDonaldization of society* does not refer just to the robotlike assembly of food. Rather, this process is occurring throughout society, and it is transforming our lives. Want to do some shopping? Shopping malls offer controlled environments that are designed to make shopping a one-stop experience. Planning a trip? With "package" tours, no one need fear meeting a "real" native: Travel agencies transport middle-class Americans to ten European capitals in fourteen days. All visitors experience the same hotels, restaurants, and other scheduled sites. Want to keep up with the world? *USA Today* spews out McNews—short, bland, unanalytic pieces that can be digested

McDonald's in Tokyo, Japan

between gulps of the McShake or the McBurger.

Efficiency brings dependability. You can expect your burger and fries to taste the same whether you buy them in Los Angeles or Beijing. Efficiency also lowers prices. But efficiency does come at a cost. As predictability washes away spontaneity, it changes the quality of our lives. It produces a sameness, a bland version of what used to be highly individualistic experiences. In my own travels, for example, had I taken packaged tours I never would have had the enjoyable, eye-opening experiences that have added so much

to my appreciation of human diversity.

For good or bad, our lives are being McDonaldized, and the predictability of packaged settings seems to be our social destiny. When education is rationalized, no longer will our children have to put up with real professors, who insist on discussing ideas endlessly, never come to decisive answers, and come saddled with quirks and idiosyncrasies. Our programmed education will eliminate the need for discussion of social issues—we will have packaged solutions to them, definitive answers like those we find in mathematics and engineering. Computerized courses will teach the same answers to everyone—the approved, "politically correct" ways to think about social issues. Mass testing will assure that students can regurgitate the programmed responses.

Our coming prepackaged society will be efficient, of course. But it also means that we will be trapped in the "iron cage" of bureaucracy— just as Weber warned would happen. ■

to repetitive tasks that seem remote from the final product, workers lose a sense of identity with what they produce. They come to feel estranged not only from their products but also from their work environment.

Resisting Alienation Because workers want to feel valued and want to have a sense of control over their work, they resist alienation. Forming primary groups at work is a major form of that resistance. Workers band together in informal settings—at lunch, around desks, or for a drink after work. There they give one another approval for jobs well done and express sympathy for the shared need to put up with cantankerous bosses, meaningless routines, and endless rules. There they relate to one another not just as workers, but as people who value one another. They flirt, laugh and tell jokes, and talk about their families and goals. Adding this multidimensionality to their work relationships maintains their sense of being a person rather than a mere cog in a machine.

Consider a common sight. While visiting an office, you see work areas decorated with family and vacation photos. The sociological implication is that of workers striving to resist alienation. By staking a claim to individuality, the workers are rejecting an identity as mere machines that exist to perform functions.

WORKING FOR THE CORPORATION

Since you are likely to end up working in a bureaucracy, let's look at how its characteristics may affect your career.

The "Hidden" Corporate Culture

Who gets ahead in a large corporation? Although we might like to think that success comes from intelligence and hard work, many factors other than merit underlie salary increases and promotions. As sociologist Rosabeth Moss Kanter (1977, 1983) stresses, the **corporate culture** contains "hidden values." These values create a self-fulfilling prophecy that affects people's corporate careers.

It works like this: The elite have ideas about who the best workers and colleagues are. People who fit this mold are those who have backgrounds similar to the elite and who look like them. These people receive better access to information, networking, and "fast track" positions. They then perform better and become more committed to the organization, thus confirming the initial expectation. In contrast, those judged to be outsiders find opportunities closing up. They tend to work at a level that is beneath their capacity. They come to think poorly of themselves, and become less committed to the organization—thus confirming the initial expectation.

The hidden values that created this self-fulfilling prophecy remain invisible to most. What is visible are the promotions of people with superior performances and greater commitment to the company, not the low expectations and closed opportunities that produced these attitudes and accomplishments.

You can see how such hidden values contribute to the *iron law of oligarchy* we just reviewed: Because of this self-fulfilling prophecy, the inner circle reproduces itself with people who "look" like its own members, generally white and male. Women and minorities, who don't match this stereotype, often are "showcased"—placed in highly visible positions with little power in order to demonstrate how progressive the company is. There, however, they often hold "slow track" positions, where accomplishments seldom come to the attention of top management.

As corporations grapple with their growing diversity, the hidden corporate culture is likely to give way, but only slowly and grudgingly. In the following Thinking Critically section, we'll consider other aspects of diversity in the workplace.

Thinking Critically

MANAGING DIVERSITY IN THE WORKPLACE

Times have changed. In San Jose, California, the *Nguyens* outnumber the *Joneses* by nearly 50 percent. More than half of U.S. workers are minorities, immigrants, and women. Diversity in the workplace is much more than skin color. Diversity includes ethnicity, gender, age, religion, social class, and sexual orientation.

In the past, the idea was for people to join the "melting pot," to give up their distinctive traits and become like the dominant group. Today, with the huge successes of the civil rights and women's movements, people are more likely to prize their distinctive traits. Realizing that *assimilation* (being absorbed into the dominant culture) is probably not the wave of the future, three of four Fortune 500 companies have "diversity training." They hold lectures and workshops so employees can learn to work with colleagues of diverse cultures and racial-ethnic backgrounds.

Coors Brewery is a prime example of this change. Coors went into a financial tailspin after one of the Coors brothers gave a racially charged speech in the 1980s. Today, Coors offers diversity workshops, has sponsored a gay dance, and has paid for a corporate-wide mammography program. The company even had rabbis certify its suds as kosher. Its proud new slogan: "Coors cares" (Cloud 1998). Now, that's quite a change.

What Coors cares about, of course, is the bottom line. It's the same with the other corporations. Blatant racism and sexism once made no difference to profitability. Today, they do. To promote profitability, companies must promote diversity—or at least pretend to. The sincerity of corporate heads is not what's important; diversity in the workplace is.

Diversity training has the potential to build bridges, but it can backfire. Directors of these programs can be so incompetent that they create antagonisms and reinforce stereotypes. At a diversity training session at the U.S. Department of Transportation, for example, women groped men as the men ran by. Blacks and whites were encouraged to insult one another and to call one another names (Reibstein 1996). The intention may have been good (understanding the other through role reversal and getting hostilities "out in the open"), but the approach was moronic. Instead of healing, these behaviors wound and leave scars. ■

For Your Consideration

Do you think that the growing diversity in today's workplace provides a glimpse into our future? If so, how? How can we develop diversity training that produces mutual respect? Can you suggest practical ways to develop workplaces that are not divided by gender and race-ethnicity?

U.S. and Japanese Corporations

How were the Japanese able to arise from the defeat of World War II—including the nuclear destruction of two of their main cities—to become such a giant in today's global economy? Some analysts trace part of the answer to how their corporations are organized. One of these analysts, William Ouchi (1981), pinpointed five ways in which Japanese corporations differ from those of the United States. You will be surprised at how different they are. But are these differences myth or reality?

Hiring and Promoting Teams In *Japan*, teamwork is essential. College graduates who join a corporation are all paid about the same starting salary. To learn the company's various levels, they are rotated as a team through the organization. They are also promoted as a team. They develop intense loyalty to one another and to their company, for the welfare of one represents the welfare of all. Only in later years are individuals singled out for recognition. When there is an opening in the firm, outsiders are not even considered.

In the *United States,* an employee is hired on the basis of what the firm thinks that individual can contribute. Employees try to outperform others, and they strive for raises and promotions as signs of personal success. The individual's loyalty is to himself or herself, not to the company. Outsiders are considered for openings in the firm.

Lifetime Security In *Japan,* lifetime security is taken for granted. Employees can expect to work for the same firm for the rest of their lives. In return for not being laid off or fired, the firm expects them to be loyal to the company, to stick with it through good and bad times. Employees do not go job shopping, for their careers—and many aspects of their lives—are wrapped up in this one firm.

In the *United States,* lifetime security is unusual. It is limited primarily to teachers, who receive what is called *tenure.* Companies lay off workers in slow times. To become competitive, they even reorganize and fire entire divisions. Workers, too, "look out for number one." Job shopping and job hopping are common.

Almost Total Involvement In *Japan,* work is like a marriage: The employee and the company are committed to each other. The employee supports the company with loyalty and long hours at work, while the company supports its workers with lifetime security, health services, recreation, sports and social events, even a home mortgage. Involvement with the company does not stop when the workers leave the building. They join company study and exercise groups, and are likely to spend evenings socializing with co-workers in bars and restaurants.

In the *United States,* work is a specific, often temporary contract. Employees are hired to do a certain job. When they have done that job, they have fulfilled their obligation to the company. Their after-work hours are their own. They go home to their private lives, which are separate from the firm.

Broad Training In *Japan,* employees move from one job to another within the company. Not only are they not stuck doing the same thing for years on end, but also they gain a broader picture of the corporation and how the specific jobs they are assigned fit into the bigger picture.

In the *United States,* employees are expected to perform one job, to do it well, and then to be promoted upward to a job with more responsibility. Their understanding of the company is largely tied to the particular corner they occupy, often making it difficult for them to see how their job fits into the overall picture.

Decision Making by Consensus In *Japan,* decision making is a lengthy process. Each person who will be affected by a decision is consulted. After lengthy deliberations, a consensus emerges, and everyone agrees on which suggestion is superior. This makes workers feel that they are an essential part of the organization, not simply cogs in a giant wheel.

In the *United States,* the person in charge of the unit to be affected does as much consulting with others as he or she thinks necessary and then makes the decision.

The Myth Versus Reality Peering beneath the surface reveals a reality that is different from the myth that has grown up around the Japanese corporation. Lifetime job security, for example, is elusive, and only about a

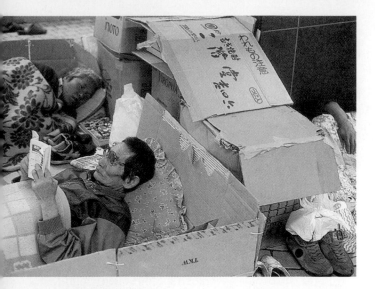

For a time, Americans stood in awe of the Japanese corporate model. The passage of time, however, revealed serious flaws. Lifetime job security, for example, is a myth. These homeless men are living in the Shinjuko train station in Tokyo. Note how they have followed the Japanese custom of placing their shoes outside before entering their "home."

third of Japanese workers find it. Management by consensus is also a myth. This was not how decisions were made at Sony, one of Japan's most successful companies (Nathan 1999). Akio Morita, Sony's founder, was an entrepreneur from the same mold as Bill Gates. Morita didn't send memos up and down the line, as the myth would have you believe. Instead, he relied on his gut feeling about products. When he thought up the Walkman, Morita didn't discuss it until consensus emerged—he simply ordered it to be manufactured. And he made quick decisions. Over lunch, he decided to buy CBS Records. The cost was $2 billion.

In a surprise move, Japan has turned to U.S. corporations to see why they are more efficient. Flying in the face of their traditions, Japanese corporations have begun to lay off workers and to use merit pay. Although this is standard U.S. practice, it was unthinkable in Japan just a few years ago. Some firms have even cut salaries and demoted managers who didn't meet goals. Perhaps the biggest surprise was Ford's takeover of Mazda. After huge losses, Mazda creditors decided that Ford knew more about building and marketing cars than Mazda and invited Ford to manage the company (Reitman and Suris 1994).

The real bottom line is that we live in a global marketplace—of ideas as well as products. The likely result

of global competition is that both the West and Japan will feed off each other—the one learning greater cooperation in the production process, the other greater internal competition.

On a final note on corporations, all of us who have worked in factories and offices know that U.S. workers are far from dedicated to production. "Goofing off," when it is possible, is a regular part of the work day. With the new technology, "goofing off" can take new forms. The box on Sociology and the New Technology discusses how workers misapply the new technology, and how, in turn, companies are using the new technology to control workers.

*G*ROUP DYNAMICS

As you know from personal experience, the lively interaction *within* groups—who does what with whom—has profound consequences for how you adjust to life. Sociologists use the term **group dynamics** to refer to how groups affect us and how we affect groups. Let's consider the differences that the size of a group makes, and then examine leadership, conformity, and decision making.

Before doing this, we should see what sociologists mean by the term **small group**. This is a group small enough for everyone to interact directly with all the other members. Small groups can be either primary or secondary. A wife, husband, and children, as well as workers who take their breaks together, are examples of primary small groups, while bidders at an auction and passengers on a flight from St. Louis to Minneapolis are examples of secondary small groups.

Effects of Group Size on Stability and Intimacy

Writing in the early 1900s, sociologist Georg Simmel (1858–1918) noted the significance of group size. He used the term **dyad** for the smallest possible group, which consists of two people. Dyads, which include marriages, love affairs, and close friendships, show two distinct qualities. First, they are the most intense or intimate of human groups. Because only two people are involved, the interaction is focused on them. Second, because dyads require the active participation and commitment of both members, they are the most unstable of social groups. If one member loses interest, the dyad collapses. In larger groups, in contrast, even if one member withdraws, the group can continue, for its existence does not depend on any single member (Simmel 1950).

Sociology & the New Technology

CYBERSLACKERS AND CYBERSLEUTHS: SURFING AT WORK

Few people work constantly at their jobs. Most of us take breaks and, at least once in a while, goof off. We meet fellow workers at the water cooler, and we talk in the hallway. Much of this interaction is good for the company, for it bonds us to fellow workers and ties us to our jobs.

Sometimes our work and personal lives are intertwined. Bosses know that we need to check in with our child's preschool or make arrangements for a babysitter. Some bosses even wink as we telephone friends, make arrangements to have our car worked on, or set up a date. Bosses also make personal calls of their own. It's the abuse of tending to personal matters while at work that bothers them.

The latest wrinkle in goofing off at work is *cyberslacking,* using computers at work for personal purposes. With almost every office equipped with computers, cyberslacking was bound to emerge.

Perhaps most workers fritter away some of their workday online. Some play games, others shop online, and many send personal e-mail. Some Web sites even protect cyberslackers: They feature a panic button to be clicked in case the boss pokes her head in your office. You just tap the button and a phony spreadsheet pops up onto your screen while typing sounds emerge from your speakers.

Some cyberslackers operate personal online businesses during office hours. Others spend most of their "working" hours battling virtual enemies. (One computer programmer even became a national champion playing Starcraft at work.) Some spend a good part of their "working" hours downloading pornography. Xerox fired 40 employees for mixing their pornographic pleasure with business (Naughton 1999).

To combat cyberslacking, a new specialty, the cybersleuth, has emerged. Using specialized software, cybersleuths can examine everything employees have read online, every word they've typed, and every Internet site they've visited. What some of us don't know (and what some of us forget) is that delete does not mean delete. Although we hit the delete button, our computers still contain a permanent record of what appears to be erased. Without knowing it, we have left behind a hidden diary of our computer activities. Just a few clicks on the cybersleuth software and this "deleted" information appears, our personal diary exposed for anyone who wants to examine it. ■

For Your Consideration

Do you think that cybersleuthing is an abuse of power? Or do employers have a right to check on what their employees are doing with company computers on company time? Can you think of a less intrusive solution to cyberslacking?

A **triad** is a group of three people. As Simmel noted, the addition of a third person fundamentally changes the group. Because there are now three people, interaction between the first two decreases. This can create strain. For example, with the birth of a child hardly any aspect of a couple's relationship goes untouched. As attention is focused on the baby, interaction between the husband and wife diminishes. Despite the difficulties that this presents—including in many instances the husband's jealousy that he is getting less attention from his wife—the marriage usually becomes stronger.

Why? The reason for this is due to Simmel's principle that groups larger than a dyad are inherently stronger. Although the intensity is less, the stability is greater. Yet, as Simmel noted, triads, too, are inherently unstable. Because relationships among a group's members are seldom neatly balanced, **coalitions** tend to form; that is, some group members align themselves against others. In a triad, it is not uncommon for two members to feel stronger bonds with one another, leading them to act as a dyad and leaving the third feeling hurt and excluded. In addition, triads sometimes produce an arbitrator or mediator, someone who tries to settle disagreements between the other two. (In one-child families, you can often observe both of these characteristics of triads—coalitions and arbitration.)

The general principle is this: *As a small group grows larger, it becomes more stable, but its intensity, or intimacy, decreases.* To see why, look at Figure 5.2 on the next page. As each new person comes into a group, the connections among people multiply. In a dyad, there is only 1 relationship; in a triad, 3; in a group of four, 6; in a group of five, 10. If we expand the group to six, we have 15 relationships; while a group of seven yields 21 relationships. If we continue adding members, we soon are unable to follow the connections: A group

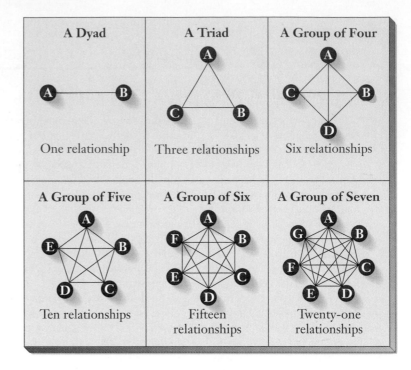

Figure 5.2 THE INCREMENTAL EFFECTS OF GROUP SIZE ON RELATIONSHIPS

A Dyad
One relationship

A Triad
Three relationships

A Group of Four
Six relationships

A Group of Five
Ten relationships

A Group of Six
Fifteen relationships

A Group of Seven
Twenty-one relationships

of eight has 28 possible relationships; a group of nine, 36 relationships; a group of ten 45; and so on.

It is not only the number of relationships that makes larger groups more stable. As groups grow, they tend to develop a more formal structure to accomplish their goals. For example, leaders emerge and more specialized roles come into play, ultimately resulting in such familiar offices as president, secretary, and treasurer. This structure provides a framework that helps the group survive over time.

Effects of Group Size on Attitudes and Behavior

Imagine that your social psychology professors have asked you to join a few students to discuss your adjustment to college life. When you arrive, they tell you that to make the discussion anonymous, they want you to sit unseen in a booth and participate in the discussion over an intercom, talking when your microphone comes on. The professors say they will not listen to the conversation, and they leave.

You find the format somewhat strange, to say the least, but you go along with it. You have not seen the other students in their booths, but when they begin to talk about their experiences, you find yourself becoming wrapped up in the problems they are sharing. One student even mentions how frightening he has found college because of his history of epileptic seizures. Later, this individual begins to breathe heavily into the microphone. Then he stammers and cries for help. A crashing noise follows, and you imagine him lying helpless on the floor.

Nothing but an eerie silence follows. What do you do?

Your professors, John Darley and Bibb Latané (1968), staged the whole thing, but you don't know that. No one had a seizure. In fact, no one was even in the other booths. Everything, except your comments, was on tape.

Some participants were told they would be discussing the topic with just one other student, others with two, others with three, and so on. Darley and Latané found that all students who thought they were part of a dyad rushed out to help. If they thought they were part of a triad, only 80 percent went to help—and they were slower in leaving the booth. In six-person groups, only 60 percent went to see what was wrong—and they were even slower.

This experiment demonstrates how deeply group size influences our attitudes and behavior—it even affects our willingness to help one another. Darley and Latané concluded that students in the dyad clearly knew it was up to them. The professor was gone, and if they didn't help there would be no help. In the triad, students felt less personal responsibility. In the larger groups, they felt *a diffusion of responsibility:* Giving help was no more up to them than it was up to anyone else.

You probably have observed the second consequence of group size firsthand. When a group is small, its members are informal, but as the group grows, they lose their sense of intimacy and become more formal. No longer can the members assume that the others are "insiders" in sympathy with what they say. Now they must take a "larger audience" into consideration, and instead of merely "talking," they begin to "address" the group. As

A general principle analyzed by Georg Simmel is that when a third person is added to a group of two (a dyad changing to a triad), the intensity of interaction decreases, but the stability of the group increases. The text explains why.

their speech becomes more formal, their body language stiffens, too.

You probably have observed a third aspect of group dynamics, too. In the very early stages of a party, when only a few people are present, almost everyone talks with everyone else. But as others arrive, the guests break into smaller groups. The hosts, who may want all their guests to mix together, sometimes make a nuisance of themselves trying to achieve *their* idea of what a group should be like. The division into small groups is inevitable, however, for it follows the basic sociological principles we have just reviewed. Because the addition of each person rapidly increases connections (in this case, "talk lines"), it makes conversation more difficult. The guests then break into smaller groups where they can see each other and comfortably interact directly with one another.

Leadership

All groups, no matter what their size, have leaders, although they may not hold formal positions in the group. A **leader** is someone who influences the behaviors, opinions, or attitudes of others. Some people are leaders because of their personalities, but leadership involves much more than this, as we shall see.

Types of Leaders Groups have two types of leaders (Bales 1950, 1953; Cartwright and Zander 1968). The first is easy to recognize. This person, called an **instrumental leader** (or task-oriented leader), tries to keep the group moving toward its goals. These leaders try to keep group members from getting sidetracked, reminding them of what they are trying to accomplish. The **expressive leader** (or socioemotional leader), in contrast, is not usually recognized as a leader, but he or she certainly is. This person is likely to crack jokes, to offer sympathy, or to do other things that help lift the group's morale. Both types of leadership are essential: the one to keep the group on track, the other to increase harmony and minimize conflicts.

It is difficult for one person to be both an instrumental and an expressive leader, for these roles contradict one another. Because instrumental leaders are task oriented, they sometimes create friction as they prod the group to get on with the job. Their actions often cost them popularity. Expressive leaders, in contrast, being peacemakers who stimulate personal bonds and reduce friction, are usually more popular (Olmsted and Hare 1978).

Leadership Styles Let's suppose that the president of your college has asked you to head a task force to determine how the college can improve race relations on campus. Although this position requires you to be an instrumental leader, you can adopt a number of **leadership styles**, or ways of expressing yourself as a leader. The three basic styles are those of **authoritarian leader**, one who gives orders; **democratic leader**, one who tries to gain a consensus; and **laissez-faire leader**, one who is highly permissive. Which should you choose?

Social psychologists Ronald Lippitt and Ralph White (1958) carried out a classic study of these three leadership styles. Boys matched for IQ, popularity, physical energy, and leadership were assigned to "craft clubs" made up of five youngsters each. The experimenters trained adult males in the three leadership styles and rotated them among the clubs. As the researchers peered through peepholes, taking notes and making movies, each adult played all three styles to control possible effects of their individual personalities.

The *authoritarian leaders* assigned tasks to the boys and set the working conditions. They also praised or condemned their work arbitrarily, giving no explanation for why it was good or bad. The *democratic leaders* held group discussions and outlined the steps necessary to reach the group's goals. They also suggested alternative approaches to these goals and let the boys work at their own pace. When they evaluated the children's projects, they gave "facts" as the bases for their decisions. The *laissez-faire leaders* were passive, giving the boys almost total freedom to do as they wished. They stood ready to offer help when asked, but made few suggestions. They did not evaluate the children's projects, either positively or negatively.

The results? The boys who had authoritarian leaders grew dependent on their leader and showed a high degree of internal solidarity. They also became either aggressive or apathetic, with the aggressive boys growing hostile toward their leader. In contrast, the boys with democratic leaders were friendlier, more "group minded," and looked to one another for mutual approval. They did less scapegoating, and when the leader left the room they continued to work at a steadier pace. The boys with laissez-faire leaders asked more questions, but they made fewer decisions. They were notable for their lack of achievement. The researchers concluded that the democratic style of leadership worked best. Their conclusions, however, may have been biased, as the researchers favored a democratic style of leadership, and they did the research during a highly charged political period (Olmsted and Hare 1978).

You may have noted that only males were involved in this experiment. It is interesting to speculate how the results might differ if we were to repeat the experiment with all-girl groups and with groups of both girls and boys, and if we used both men and women as leaders. Perhaps you will become the sociologist to study such variations of this classic experiment.

Adapting Leadership Styles to Changing Situations It is important to note that different situations require different styles of leadership. Suppose, for example, that you are leading a dozen backpackers in California's Sierra Madre mountains, and it is time to make dinner. A laissez-faire style would be appropriate if everyone had brought their own food—or perhaps a democratic style if the meal were to be communally prepared. Authoritarian leadership—you telling everyone how to prepare their meals—would create resentment. This, in turn, would likely interfere with meeting the primary goals of the group, in this case, to have a good time while enjoying nature.

Now assume the same group but a different situation: One of your party is lost, and a blizzard is on its way. This situation calls for you to take charge and be authoritarian. To simply shrug your shoulders and say, "You figure it out," would invite disaster.

Who Becomes a Leader? Are leaders born with characteristics that propel them to the forefront of a group? No sociologist would agree with such a premise. In general, people who become leaders are seen as strongly representing the group's values, or as able to lead a group out of a crisis (Trice and Beyer 1991). Leaders also tend to be more talkative and to express determination and self-confidence.

These findings may not be surprising, as such traits appear related to leadership. Researchers, however, have also discovered significant traits that seem to have no bearing whatsoever on ability to lead. For example, taller people and those judged better looking are more likely to become leaders (Stodgill 1974; Crosbie 1975). The taller and more attractive are also likely to earn more, but that is another story (Deck 1968; Feldman 1972; Katz 2001).

Many other factors underlie people's choice of leaders, most of which are quite subtle. A simple experiment performed by social psychologists Lloyd Howells and Selwyn Becker (1962) uncovered one of these factors. They formed groups of five people who did not know one another, seating them at a rectangular table, three on one side and two on the other. After discussing a topic for a set period of time, each group chose a leader. The findings are startling: Although only 40 percent of the people sat on the two-person side, 70 percent of the leaders emerged from that side. The explanation is that we tend to direct more interactions to people facing us than to people to the side of us.

The Power of Peer Pressure: The Asch Experiment

How influential are groups in our lives? To answer this, let's look first at *conformity* in the sense of going along with our peers. They have no authority over us, only the influence that we allow.

Imagine that you are taking a course in social psychology with Dr. Solomon Asch and you have agreed to participate in an experiment. As you enter his laboratory, you see seven chairs, five of them already filled by other students. You are given the sixth. Soon the seventh person arrives. Dr. Asch stands at the front of the room next to a covered easel. He explains that he will first show a large card with a vertical line on it, then another card with three vertical lines. Each of you is to tell him which of three lines is identical to the line on the first card (see Figure 5.3).

Dr. Asch then uncovers the first card with a single line and the comparison card with the three lines. The correct answer is easy, for two of the lines are obviously wrong, and

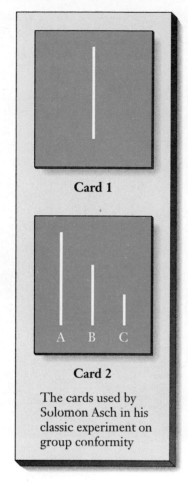

Card 1

Card 2

The cards used by Solomon Asch in his classic experiment on group conformity

Figure 5.3 ASCH'S CARDS

Source: Asch 1952:452–453.

one is exactly right. Each person, in order, states his or her answer aloud. You all answer correctly. The second trial is just as easy, and you begin to wonder what the point of your being here is.

Then on the third trial something unexpected happens. Just as before, it is easy to tell which lines match. The first student, however, gives a wrong answer. The second gives the same incorrect answer. So do the third and the fourth. By now you are wondering what is wrong. How will the person next to you answer? You can hardly believe it when he, too, gives the same wrong answer. Then it is your turn, and you give what you know is the right answer. The seventh person also gives the wrong answer.

On the next trial, the same thing happens. You know the choice of the other six is wrong. They are giving what to you are obviously wrong answers. You don't know what to think. Why aren't they seeing things the same way you are? Some-

times they do, but in twelve trials they don't. Something is seriously wrong, and you are no longer sure what to do.

When the eighteenth card is finished, you heave a sigh of relief. The experiment is finally over, and you are ready to bolt for the door. Dr. Asch walks over to you with a big smile on his face, thanks you for participating in the experiment. He then explains that you were the only real subject in the experiment! "The other six were all stooges! I paid them to give those answers," he says. Now you feel real relief. Your eyes weren't playing tricks on you after all.

What were the results? Asch (1952) tested fifty people. One-third (33 percent) gave in to the group half the time, giving what they knew to be wrong answers. Another two of five (40 percent) gave wrong answers, but not as often. One of four (25 percent) stuck to their guns and always gave the right answer. I don't know how I would do on this test (if I knew nothing about it in advance), but I like to think that I would be part of the 25 percent. You probably feel the same way about yourself. But why should we feel that we wouldn't be like *most* people?

The results are disturbing. In our "land of individualism," the group is so powerful that most people are willing to say things that they know do not match objective reality. And this was a group of strangers! How much more conformity can we expect when our group consists of friends, people we value highly and depend on for getting along in life? Again, perhaps you will become the sociologist who will run that variation of Asch's experiment, perhaps using female subjects.

Even more disturbing are the results of an experiment featured in the following Thinking Critically section.

Thinking *Critically*

IF HITLER ASKED YOU TO EXECUTE A STRANGER, WOULD YOU? THE MILGRAM EXPERIMENT

Imagine that you are taking a course with Dr. Stanley Milgram (1963, 1965), a former student of Dr. Asch. Assume that you do not know about the Asch experiment and have no reason to be wary. You arrive at the laboratory to participate in a study on punishment and learning. You and a second student draw lots for the roles of "teacher" and "learner." You are to be teacher. When you see that the learner's chair has protruding electrodes, you are glad that you are the teacher. Dr. Milgram shows you the machine you will run. You see that one side of the control panel is marked "Mild Shock, 15 volts," while the center

In the 1960s, U.S. social psychologists ran a series of creative but controversial experiments. Among these were Stanley Milgram's experiments, described below. From this photo of the "learner" being prepared for the experiment, you can get an idea of how convincing the situation would be for the "teacher."

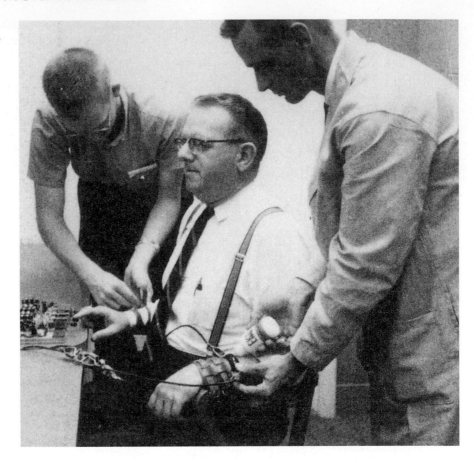

says "Intense Shock, 350 Volts," and the far right side reads "DANGER: SEVERE SHOCK."

"As the teacher, you will read aloud a pair of words," explains Dr. Milgram. "Then you will repeat the first word, and the learner will reply with the second word. If the learner can't remember the word, you press this lever on the shock generator. The shock will serve as punishment, and we can then determine if punishment improves memory." You nod, now very relieved that you haven't been designated the learner.

"Every time the learner makes an error, increase the punishment by 15 volts," instructs Dr. Milgram. Then, seeing the look on your face, he adds, "The shocks can be extremely painful, but they won't cause any permanent tissue damage." He pauses, and then says, "I want you to see." You then follow him to the "electric chair," and Dr. Milgram gives you a shock of 45 volts. "There. That wasn't too bad, was it?" "No," you mumble.

The experiment begins. You hope for the learner's sake that he is bright, but unfortunately he turns out to be rather dull. He gets some answers right, but you have to keep turning up the dial. Each turn makes you more and more uncomfortable. You find yourself hoping that the learner won't miss another answer. But he does. When he received the first shocks, he let out some moans and groans, but now he is screaming in agony. He even protests that he suffers from a heart condition.

How far do you turn that dial?

By now, you probably have guessed that there was no electricity attached to the electrodes and the "learner" was a stooge who only pretended to feel pain. The purpose of the experiment was to find out at what point people refuse to participate. Does anyone actually turn the lever all the way to "DANGER: SEVERE SHOCK"?

Milgram wanted the answer because of the Nazi slaughter of Jews, gypsies, homosexuals, people with disabilities, and others whom they designated as "inferior." That millions of ordinary people did nothing to stop the deaths seemed bizarre, and Milgram wanted to see how ordinary, intelligent Americans might react in an analogous situation.

Milgram was upset by what he found. Many "teachers" broke into a sweat and protested to the experimenter that this was inhuman and should be stopped. But when the experimenter calmly replied that the experiment must go on, this assurance from an "authority" ("scientist, white coat, university laboratory") was enough for most "teachers" to continue, even though the learner screamed in agony. Even "teachers" who were "reduced to twitching, stuttering wrecks" continued to follow orders.

Milgram varied the experiments (Miller 1986). He used both men and women and put some "teachers" and "learners" in the same room, where the "teacher" could clearly see the suffering. He had some "learners" pound and kick the wall during the first shocks and then go silent. The results varied. When there was no verbal feedback from the "learner," 65 percent of the "teachers" pushed the lever all the way to 450 volts. Of those who could see the "learner," 40 percent turned the lever all the way. When Milgram added a second "teacher," a stooge who refused to go along with the experiment, only 5 percent of the "teachers" turned the dial all the way, a result that bears out some of Asch's findings.

A stormy discussion about research ethics erupted. Not only were researchers surprised, and disturbed, by what Milgram found, but they were also alarmed at his methods. Universities began to require that subjects be informed of the nature and purpose of social research. Researchers agreed that to reduce subjects to "twitching, stuttering wrecks" was unethical, and almost all deception was banned. ■

For Your Consideration

What is the connection between Milgram's experiment and the actions of Walter Burmeister in our opening vignette? Considering how significant these findings are, do you think that the scientific community overreacted to Milgram's experiments? Should we allow such research? Consider both the Asch and Milgram experiments, and use symbolic interactionism, functionalism, and conflict theory to explain why groups have such influence over us.

Global Consequences of Group Dynamics

In our era of nuclear weapons, one of the disturbing implications of the Asch and Milgram experiments is **groupthink.** Sociologist Irving Janis (1972) coined this term to refer to the collective tunnel vision that groups sometimes develop: Members think alike and any suggestion of alternatives is taken as a sign of disloyalty. Even moral judgments must be put aside, for the "team" is convinced that its welfare depends on a single course of action. Groupthink may lead to overconfidence and a disregard for the risks that the group is taking (Hart 1991). The Asch and Milgram experiments help us see how groupthink can develop.

Suppose you are a member of the president's inner circle. It is midnight, and the president has just called an emergency meeting to deal with a national crisis. At first, various options are presented. Eventually, these

are narrowed to only a few choices, and at some point everyone seems to agree on what now seems "the only possible course of action." At that juncture, expressing doubts will bring you into conflict with *all* the other important people in the room, while criticism may mark you as not being a "team player." So you keep your mouth shut, with the result that each step commits you—and them—more and more to the "only" course of action.

We can choose from a variety of examples from around the globe, but, as Janis points out, U.S. history provides a fertile field for illustrating groupthink: the refusal of President Franklin D. Roosevelt and his chiefs of staff to believe that the Japanese might attack Pearl Harbor and the subsequent decision to continue naval operations as usual; President Kennedy's invasion of Cuba; and U.S. policies in Vietnam. Watergate is especially noteworthy, for it plunged the United States into political crisis and for the first time in history a U.S. president was forced to resign.

In each of these cases, options closed as officials committed themselves to a single course of action. To question this decision would have marked someone as disloyal, as not a "team player." Those in power plunged ahead, no longer able to see different perspectives, no longer even trying to objectively weigh evidence as it came in, but interpreting everything as supporting their one "correct" decision. Like Milgram's subjects, they became mired in actions that as individuals they would have considered unacceptable. In some cases, they found themselves pursuing policies that they otherwise might have considered morally repugnant.

Preventing Groupthink Groupthink is a danger that faces government leaders, who tend to surround themselves with an inner circle that closely reflects their own views. Isolated at the top, they can become cut off from information that does not support their own opinions. Perhaps the key to preventing the mental captivity and intellectual paralysis known as groupthink is the widest possible circulation—especially among a nation's top government officials—of research that has been freely conducted by social scientists and information that has been freely gathered by media reporters.

If this conclusion comes across as an unabashed plug for sociological research and the free exchange of ideas, it is. Giving free rein to diverse opinions can effectively curb groupthink, which—if not prevented—can lead to the destruction of a society and, in today's world of sophisticated weapons, the obliteration of the earth's inhabitants.

SUMMARY AND REVIEW

■ Social Groups

What is a group?
Sociologists use many definitions of groups, but, in general, **groups** are people who have something in common and who believe that what they have in common is significant. P. 106.

How do sociologists classify groups?
Sociologists divide groups into primary groups, secondary groups, in-groups, out-groups, reference groups, and networks. The cooperative, intimate, long-term, face-to-face relationships provided by **primary groups** are fundamental to our sense of self. **Secondary groups** are larger, more anonymous, formal, and impersonal than primary groups. **In-groups** provide members with a strong sense of identity and belonging. **Out-groups** also help create this identity by showing in-group members what they are *not*. **Reference groups** are groups whose standards we mentally refer to as we evaluate ourselves. **Social networks** consist of social ties that link people together. The new technology has given birth to a new type of group, the **electronic community.** Pp. 106–111.

What is the "iron law of oligarchy"?
Sociologist Robert Michels noted that formal organizations have a tendency to become controlled by an inner circle that limits leadership to its own members. The dominance of a formal organization by an elite inner circle that keeps itself in power is called **the iron law of oligarchy.** Pp. 107–108.

■ Bureaucracies

What are the characteristics of bureaucracies?
A **bureaucracy** consists of an organization arranged in a hierarchy, with a division of labor, written rules, written communications, and impersonality of positions. Bureaucracies tend to endure because they are efficient and because of **goal displacement** (when original goals are met, they are replaced with other goals). In a process called the **rationalization of society,** everyday tasks are taken over by bureaucracies. This is happening today with food preparation. Red tape, or obsessive following of rules, is a dysfunction of bureaucracies. Pp. 111–116.

■ Working for the Corporation

How does the corporate culture affect workers?
The term **corporate culture** refers to an organization's traditions, values, and unwritten norms. Much of corporate culture, such as its hidden values, is not readily visible. People who match a corporation's hidden values tend to be put on tracks that enhance their chances of success, while those who do not match these values tend to be set on a course that minimizes their performance. Pp. 116–117.

How do Japanese and U.S. corporations differ?
The Japanese corporate model contrasts sharply with the U.S. model in hiring and promotion, lifetime security, interaction of workers outside the work setting, broad training of workers, and collective decision making. Much of this model is a myth, an idealization of reality, and does not reflect the reality of Japanese corporate life today. Pp. 117–118.

■ Group Dynamics

How does a group's size affect its dynamics?
The term **group dynamics** refers to how individuals affect groups and how groups influence individuals. In a **small group,** everyone can interact directly with everyone else. As a group grows larger, its intensity decreases and its stability increases. A **dyad,** which consists of two people, is the most unstable of human groups, but it provides the most intense or intimate relationships. The addition of a third person, forming a **triad,** fundamentally alters relationships. Triads are unstable, as **coalitions** tend to form. Pp. 118–121.

What characterizes a leader?
A **leader** is someone who influences others. **Instrumental leaders** try to keep a group moving toward its goals, even though this causes friction and they lose popularity. **Expressive leaders** focus on creating harmony and raising group morale. Both types are essential to the functioning of groups. P. 121.

What are the three main leadership styles?
Authoritarian leaders give orders, **democratic leaders** try to lead by consensus, and **laissez-faire leaders** are highly permissive. An authoritarian style appears to be more effective in emergency situations, a democratic style works best for most situations, and a laissez-faire style is usually ineffective. Pp. 121–122.

How do groups encourage conformity?
The Asch experiment was cited to illustrate the power of peer pressure, the Milgram experiment to illustrate the influence of authority. Both experiments demonstrate how easily we can succumb to **groupthink,** a kind of collective tunnel vision. Preventing groupthink requires the free circulation of contrasting ideas. Pp. 125–126.

Where can I read more on this topic?
Suggested readings for this chapter are listed on page SR-3.

YOUR INTERACTIVE COMPANION WEB SITE

Your Interactive Companion Web Site includes practice tests, with feedback, and online learning activities with video, audio, and Weblinks. Your access code for this Web site is provided with this text.

GLOSSARY

aggregate people who temporarily share the same physical space but do not see themselves as belonging together (p. 106)

alienation Marx's term for the experience of being cut off from the product of one's labor, which results in a sense of powerlessness and normlessness (p. 114)

authoritarian leader a leader who leads by giving orders (p. 121)

bureaucracies formal organizations with a hierarchy of authority, a clear division of labor, impersonality of positions, and emphasis on written rules, communications, and records (p. 111)

category people who have similar characteristics (p. 106)

clique within a larger group, a cluster of people who choose to interact with one another; an internal faction (p. 110)

coalition the alignment of some members of a group against others (p. 119)

corporate culture the orientations that characterize corporate work settings (p. 116)

democratic leader a leader who leads by trying to reach a consensus (p. 121)

dyad the smallest possible group, consisting of two persons (p. 118)

electronic community people who more or less regularly interact with one another on the Internet (p. 111)

expressive leader an individual who increases harmony and minimizes conflict in a group; also known as a *socioemotional leader* (p. 121)

goal displacement the process in which one goal is displaced by another, such as when an organization adopts new goals (p. 113)

group people who think of themselves as belonging together and who interact with one another (p. 106)

group dynamics the ways in which individuals affect groups and groups influence individuals (p. 118)

groupthink Irving Janis's term for a narrowing of thought by a group of people, leading to the perception that there is only one correct answer; in groupthink, to suggest alternatives becomes a sign of disloyalty (p. 125)

in-groups groups toward which one feels loyalty (p. 108)

instrumental leader an individual who tries to keep the group moving toward its goals; also known as a *task-oriented leader* (p. 121)

(the) iron law of oligarchy Robert Michels's term for the tendency of formal organizations to be dominated by a small, self-perpetuating elite (p. 108)

laissez-faire leaders individuals who lead by being highly permissive (p. 121)

leader someone who influences other people (p. 121)

leadership styles ways in which people express their leadership (p. 121)

networking the process of consciously using or cultivating networks for some gain (p. 111)

out-groups groups toward which one feels antagonism (p. 108)

primary group a group characterized by intimate, long-term, face-to-face association and cooperation (p. 106)

(the) rationalization of society the increasing influence of bureaucracies in society, which makes the "bottom line" all-important in social life (p. 114)

reference group Herbert Hyman's term for a group whose standards we consider as we evaluate ourselves (p. 109)

secondary group compared with a primary group, a larger, relatively temporary, more anonymous, formal, and impersonal group (p. 106)

small group a group small enough for everyone to interact directly with all the other members (p. 118)

social network the social ties radiating outward from the self that link people together (p. 110)

triad a group of three people (p. 119)

voluntary association a group made up of volunteers who organize on the basis of some mutual interest; the Girl Scouts, Baptists, and Alcoholics Anonymous are examples (p. 107)

Alan E. Cober, Prison

Deviance and Social Control

In just a few moments I was to meet my first Yanomamo, my first primitive man. What would it be like?… I looked up (from my canoe) and gasped when I saw a dozen burly, naked, filthy, hideous men staring at us down the shafts of their drawn arrows.

Immense wads of green tobacco were stuck between their lower teeth and lips, making them look even more hideous, and strands of dark-green slime dripped or hung from their noses. We arrived at the village while the men were blowing a hallucinogenic drug up their noses. One of the side effects of the drug is a runny nose. The mucus is always saturated with the green powder, and the Indians usually let it run freely from their nostrils…. I just sat there holding my notebook, helpless and pathetic….

The whole situation was depressing, and I wondered why I ever decided to switch from civil engineering to anthropology in the first place…. (Soon) I was covered with red pigment, the result of a dozen or so complete examinations…. These examinations capped an otherwise grim day. The Indians would blow their noses into their hands, flick as much of the mucus off that would separate in a snap of the wrist, wipe the residue into their hair, and then carefully examine my face, arms, legs, hair, and the contents of my pockets. I said (in their language), "Your hands are dirty"; my comments were met by the Indians in the following way: they would "clean" their hands by spitting a quantity of slimy tobacco juice into them, rub them together, and then proceed with the examination.

So went Napoleon Chagnon's eye-opening introduction to the Yanomamo tribe of the rain forests of Brazil. His ensuing months of fieldwork continued to bring surprise after surprise, and often Chagnon (1977) could hardly believe his eyes—or his nose.

Where would we start if we were to list the deviant behaviors of these people? With the way they appear naked in public? Use hallucinogenic drugs? Let mucus hang from their noses? Or with the way they rub hands that are filled with mucus, spittle, and tobacco juice over a frightened stranger who doesn't dare to protest? Perhaps. But it isn't this simple, for as we shall see, deviance is relative. ■

WHAT IS DEVIANCE?

Sociologists use the term **deviance** to refer to any violation of norms, whether the infraction is as minor as jaywalking, as serious as murder, or as humorous as Chagnon's encounter with the Yanomamo. This deceptively simple definition takes us to the heart of the sociological perspective on deviance, which sociologist Howard S. Becker (1966) identified this way: *It is not the act itself, but the reactions to the act, that make something deviant.* In other words, people's behaviors must be viewed from the framework of the culture in which they take place. To Chagnon, the behaviors were frighteningly deviant, but to the Yanomamo they represented normal, everyday life. What was deviant to Chagnon was *conformist* to the Yanomamo. From their viewpoint, you *should* check out strangers as they did, and nakedness is good, as are hallucinogenic drugs and letting mucus be "natural."

Chagnon's abrupt introduction to the Yanomamo allows us to see the *relativity of deviance,* a major point made by symbolic interactionists. Because different groups have different norms, *what is deviant to some is not deviant to others.* This principle holds *within* a society as well as across cultures. Thus acts that are acceptable in one culture—or in one group within a society—may be considered deviant in another culture, or by another group within the same society. This idea is explored in the Cultural Diversity box on the next page.

This principle also applies to a specific form of deviance known as **crime,** the violation of rules that have been written into law. In the extreme, an act that is applauded by one group may be so despised by another group that it is punishable by death. Making a huge profit on a business deal is one example. Americans who do so are admired, and may even write a book about it or seek public office. In China, however, until recently this same act was a crime called profiteering. Anyone found guilty was hung in a public square as a lesson to all.

Unlike the general public, sociologists use the term *deviance* nonjudgmentally, to refer to any act to which people respond negatively. When sociologists use this term, it does not mean that they agree that an act is bad, just that people judge it negatively. To sociologists, then, all of us are deviants of one sort or another, for we all violate norms from time to time.

To be considered deviant, a person may not even have to *do* anything. Sociologist Erving Goffman (1963) used the term **stigma** to refer to characteristics that

This Aymara Indian in Bolivia has just taken a pinch of coca leaves from the sack made for this purpose by his wife or mother. For centuries, the Indians of Bolivia and nearby countries have chewed coca leaves as a stimulant. It would be the deviant who would not participate in this custom, affirming the sociological point that deviance is relative.

CULTURAL DIVERSITY Around the World

HUMAN SEXUALITY IN CROSS-CULTURAL PERSPECTIVE

Anthropologist Robert Edgerton (1976) reported how differently human groups react to similar behaviors. Of the many examples he cites, let's look at sexuality to illustrate how a group's *definition* of an act, not the act itself, determines whether or not it will be considered deviant.

Norms of sexual behavior vary so widely around the world that what is considered normal in one society may be considered deviant in another. The Pokot people of northwestern Kenya, for example, place high emphasis on sexual pleasure and expect that both a husband and

his wife will reach orgasm. If a husband does not satisfy his wife, he is in serious trouble. Pokot men often engage in adulterous affairs, and should a husband's failure to satisfy his wife be attributed to his adultery, his wife and her female friends will tie him up when he is asleep. The women will shout obscenities at him, beat him, and, as a final gesture of their utter contempt, slaughter and eat his favorite ox before releasing him. His hours of painful humiliation are intended to make him henceforth more dutiful concerning his wife's conjugal rights.

People can also become deviants for failing to understand that the group's ideal norms may not be its real norms. As with many groups, the Zapotec Indians of Mexico profess that sexual relations should take place exclusively between husband

and wife. Yet the *only* person in one Zapotec community who had had no extramarital affairs was considered deviant. Evidently these people have an unspoken understanding that married couples will engage in discreet extramarital affairs. Customarily, when a wife learns that her husband is having an affair, she does the same thing.

One Zapotec wife did not follow this covert norm. Instead, she would praise her own virtue to her husband—and then voice the familiar "headache" excuse. She also informed the other husbands and wives in the village whom their spouses were sleeping with. As a result, this virtuous woman was condemned by everyone in the village. Clearly, covert norms can conflict with formal norms—another illustration of the gap between ideal and real culture. ■

discredit people. These include violations of norms of ability (blindness, deafness, mental handicaps) and violations of norms of appearance (a facial birthmark, obesity). They also include involuntary memberships, such as being a victim of AIDS or the brother of a rapist. The stigma becomes a person's master status, defining him or her as deviant. Recall from Chapter 4 that a master status cuts across all other statuses that a person occupies.

How Norms Make Social Life Possible

No human group can exist without norms, for *norms make social life possible by making behavior predictable.* What would life be like if you could not predict what others would do? Imagine for a moment that you have gone to a store to purchase milk:

Suppose the clerk says, "I won't sell you any milk. We are overstocked with soda, and I'm not going to sell anyone milk until our soda inventory is reduced."

You don't like it, but you decide to buy a case of soda. At the checkout, the clerk says, "I hope you don't mind,

but there's a $5 service charge on every fifteenth customer." You, of course, are the fifteenth.

Just as you start to leave, another clerk stops you and says, "We're not working any more. We decided to have a party." Suddenly a stereo begins to blast, and everyone in the store begins to dance. "Oh, good, you've brought the soda," says one clerk, who takes your package and passes sodas all around.

Life is not like this, of course. You can depend on grocery clerks to sell you milk. You also can depend on paying the same price as everyone else, and not being forced to attend a party in the store. Why can you depend on this? Because we are socialized to follow norms, to play the basic roles society assigns to us.

Without norms, we would have social chaos. Norms lay out the basic guidelines for how we should play our roles and interact with others. In short, norms bring about **social order**, a group's customary social arrangements. Our lives are based on these arrangements, and this is why deviance often is seen as so threatening: It undermines predictability, the foundation of social life. Consequently, human groups develop a system of **social control,** formal and informal means of enforcing norms.

Sanctions

As discussed in Chapter 2, people do not strictly enforce folkways, but they become very upset when someone breaks a more. Disapproval of deviance, called **negative sanctions,** ranges from frowns and gossip for breaking folkways to imprisonment and capital punishment for breaking mores. **Positive sanctions,** in contrast—from smiles to formal awards—are used to reward people for conforming to norms. Getting a raise is a positive sanction, being fired a negative sanction. Getting an *A* in basic sociology is a positive sanction, getting an *F* a negative one.

Most negative sanctions are informal. You probably will merely stare when someone dresses in what you consider to be inappropriate clothing, or just gossip if a married person you know spends the night with someone other than his or her spouse. Whether you consider the breaking of a norm simply an amusing matter

Much of our interaction is based on *background assumptions,* the unwritten, taken-for-granted "rules" that underlie our everyday lives. We don't have a "rule" that specifies, "Adults, don't shove a spike up your nose," yet we all know this rule exists. Much humor (especially jokes) involves the breaking of background assumptions. Shown here is Melvin Burkhart from Gibsonton, Florida, whose claim to fame is breaking this particular unspecified rule.

that warrants no severe sanctions, or a serious infraction that does, however, depends on your perspective. If a woman appears at your college graduation ceremonies in a swimsuit, you may stare and laugh, but if this is *your* mother you are likely to feel that different sanctions are appropriate. Similarly, if it is *your* father who spends the night with an 18-year-old college freshman, you are likely to do more than gossip.

■ **In Sum** In sociology, the term *deviance* refers to all violations of social rules, regardless of their seriousness. The term is not a judgment about the behavior. Deviance is relative, for what is deviant in one group may be conformist in another. Consequently, we must consider deviance from *within* a group's own framework, for it is *their* meanings that underlie their behavior. The following Thinking Critically section focuses on this issue.

Thinking *Critically*

IS IT RAPE, OR IS IT MARRIAGE? A STUDY IN CULTURE CLASH

Surrounded by cornfields, Lincoln, Nebraska, is about as provincial as a state capital gets. Most of its residents have little experience with people from different ways of life. Their baptism into cultural diversity came as a shock.

The wedding was traditional and followed millennia-old Islamic practices (Annin and Hamilton 1996). A 39-year-old Iraqi refugee had arranged for his two eldest daughters, ages 13 and 14, to marry two fellow Iraqi refugees, ages 28 and 34. A Muslim cleric flew in from Ohio to perform the ceremony.

Nebraska went into shock. So did the refugees. What is marriage in Iraq is rape in Nebraska. The husbands were charged with rape, the girls' father with child abuse, and their mother with contributing to the delinquency of minors.

The event made front page news in Saudi Arabia, where people shook their heads in amazement at Americans. Nebraskans shook their heads in amazement, too.

In Fresno, California, a young Hmong refugee took a group of friends to a local college campus. There they picked up the girl he had selected to be his wife (Sherman 1988; Lacayo 1993a). The young men brought her to his house, where he had sex with her. The young woman, however, was not in agreement with this plan.

The Hmong call it *zij poj niam,* marriage by capture. For them, this is an acceptable form of mate selection, one that mirrors Hmong courtship ideals of strong men and virtuous, resistant women. The Fresno District Attorney, however, called it kidnapping and rape. ■

For Your Consideration

To apply *symbolic interactionism* to these real-life dramas, ask how the perspectives of the people involved explain why they did what they did. To apply *functionalism,* ask how the U.S. laws that were violated are "functional" (that is, what are their benefits, to whom?). To apply *conflict theory,* ask what groups are in conflict in these examples. (Do not focus on the individuals involved, but on the groups to which they belong.)

Understanding events in terms of different theoretical perspectives does not tell us what reaction is "right" when cultures clash. Remember that science can analyze causes and consequences, but it cannot answer questions of "ought." Any "ought" that you feel about these cases comes from your system of values—which brings us, once again, to the initial issue—the relativity of deviance.

Competing Explanations of Deviance: Sociology, Biology, and Psychology

Since norms are essential for society, why do people violate them? To better understand the reasons, it is useful to know how sociological explanations differ from biological and psychological ones.

Psychologists and *sociobiologists* explain deviance by looking for answers *within* individuals. They assume that something in the makeup of people leads them to become deviant. By contrast, sociologists look for answers in factors outside the individual. They assume that something in the environment influences people to become deviant.

Biological explanations focus on **genetic predispositions** to such deviances as juvenile delinquency and crime (Lombroso 1911; Sheldon 1949; Glueck and Glueck 1956; Wilson and Herrnstein 1985; Hauser et al. 1995). Biological explanations include (but are not restricted to) the following three theories: (1) intelligence—low intelligence leads to crime; (2) the "XYY" theory—an extra Y chromosome in males leads to crime; and (3) body type—people with "squarish, muscular" bodies are more likely to commit **street crime,** acts such as mugging, rape, and burglary.

How have these theories held up? Most people with these supposedly "causal" characteristics do not become criminals. Some criminals are very intelligent, and most people of low intelligence do not commit crimes. Most

men who commit crimes have the normal "XY" chromosome combination, and most men with the "XYY" combination do not become criminals. No women have this combination of genes, so this explanation can't be applied to female criminals. Criminals also exhibit the full range of body types, and most people with "squarish, muscular" bodies do not become street criminals.

Psychologists focus on abnormalities *within* the individual, on what are called **personality disorders.** Their supposition is that deviating individuals have deviating personalities (Kalichman 1988; Stone 1989; Heilbrun 1990), that subconscious devices drive them to deviance. No specific childhood experience, however, is invariably linked with deviance. For example, children who had "bad toilet training," "suffocating mothers," or "emotionally aloof fathers" may become embezzling bookkeepers—or good accountants. Just as students, teachers, and police officers represent a variety of bad—and good—childhood experiences, so do deviants. Similarly, people with "suppressed anger" can become freeway snipers or military heroes—or anything else. In short, there is no inevitable outcome of any childhood experience, and deviance is not associated with any particular personality.

Sociologists, in contrast, search for factors *outside* the individual. They look for social influences that "recruit" some people rather than others to break norms. To account for why people commit crimes, for example, sociologists examine such external influences as socialization, subcultural membership, and social class. *Social class,* a concept discussed in depth in Chapter 8, refers to people's relative standing in terms of education, occupation, and especially income and wealth.

Knowing how relative deviance is, sociologists ask a crucial question: "Why should we expect to find something constant within people to account for a behavior that is conforming in one society and deviant in another?"

To see how sociologists explain deviance, let's contrast the three sociological perspectives—symbolic interactionism, functionalism, and conflict theory.

THE SYMBOLIC INTERACTIONIST PERSPECTIVE

As we examine symbolic interactionism, it will become more evident why sociologists are not satisfied with explanations that are rooted in biology or personality. A basic principle of symbolic interactionism is that each of us uses symbols to interpret life. Let's consider the extent to which membership in groups influences our behaviors and our views of life.

Differential Association Theory

The Theory Contrary to theories built around biology and personality, sociologist Edwin Sutherland stressed that people *learn* deviance. He coined the term **differential association** to indicate that we learn to deviate or to conform to society's norms mostly by the *different* groups we *associate* with (Sutherland 1924, 1947; Sutherland and Cressey 1974; Sutherland et al. 1992). On the most obvious level, some boys and girls join Satan's Servants, while others join the Scouts. What they learn influences them toward or away from deviance

Sutherland's theory is actually more complicated than this, but he basically said that deviance is learned. This goes directly against the view that deviance is biological or is due to personality. Sutherland stressed that the different groups to which we belong (our *"differential* association") give us messages about conformity and deviance. We may receive mixed messages, but we end up with more of one than the other (an "excess of definitions," as Sutherland put it). The end result is an imbalance—attitudes that tilt us more in one direction than the other. Consequently, we conform or deviate.

Families Since our family is so important for teaching us attitudes, it probably is obvious to you that the family makes a big difference in whether we learn deviance or conformity. Researchers have confirmed this informal observation. They have found that delinquents are more likely to come from families that get in trouble with the law. They studied 25,000 delinquents who were locked up in high-security state institutions (Beck et al. 1988). They found that 25 percent had a father who had been in prison, 25 percent a brother or sister, 9 percent a mother, and 13 percent some other relative. Of all jail inmates across the United States, about half have a father, mother, brother, or sister who has served time (*Sourcebook of Criminal Justice Statistics* 1997:483). In short, families that are involved in crime tend to set their children on a lawbreaking path.

Friends, Neighborhoods, and Subcultures Just as you may also have observed, if someone's friends are delinquent, that person is likely to be delinquent. In fact, the longer someone has delinquent friends, the more

Unlike biology and psychology, which look *within* individuals for explanations of human behavior, sociological explanations focus on *external* experiences, such as people's associations or group memberships. Sociological explanations of human behavior have become widely accepted, and now permeate society, as illustrated by this teenager whom I photographed as we were exiting the Staten Island Ferry in New York City.

likely he or she is to be delinquent (Warr 1993). Much delinquency is clustered in certain neighborhoods, and children from those neighborhoods are likely to become delinquent (Miller 1958; Wolfgang and Ferracuti 1967). This, of course, comes as no surprise to parents, who generally are eager to get their kids out of "bad" neighborhoods and away from "bad" friends. Although they may not know the term *differential association,* they know how it works.

Sociologist Ruth Horowitz (1983, 1987), who did participant observation in a lower-class Chicano neighborhood in Chicago, discovered how associating with people who have a certain concept of "honor" can propel young men to deviance. The formula is simple. "A real man has honor. An insult is a threat to one's honor.

Therefore, not to stand up to someone is to be less than a real man."

Now suppose you are a young man growing up in this neighborhood. You likely would do a fair amount of fighting, for you would interpret many statements and acts as attacks on your honor. You might even carry a knife or a gun, for words and fists wouldn't always be sufficient. Along with members of your group, you would define fighting, knifing, and shooting quite differently from the way most people do.

For members of the Mafia, ideas of manliness are also intertwined with deviance. For them, *to kill is a measure of their manhood.* Not all killings are accorded the same respect, however, for "the more awesome and potent the victim, the more worthy and meritorious the killer" (Arlacchi 1980). Some killings are done to enforce norms. A member of the Mafia who gives information to the police, for example, has violated *omertá* (the Mafia's vow of secrecy). Such an offense can never be tolerated, for it threatens the very existence of the group. This example further illustrates just how relative deviance is. Although killing is deviant to mainstream society, for members of the Mafia, *not* to kill after certain rules are broken—such as when someone "squeals" to the cops—is the deviant act.

Prison or Freedom? An issue that comes up over and over again in sociology is whether we are prisoners of socialization. Symbolic interactionists stress that we are not mere pawns in the hands of others. We are not destined by our group memberships to think and act as our groups dictate. Rather, we *help produce our own orientations to life.* Our choice of membership (differential association), for example, helps to shape the self. For instance, one college student may join a feminist group that is trying to change the treatment of women in college; another may associate with a group of women who shoplift on weekends. Their choice of groups points them in two different directions. The one who associates with shoplifters may become even more oriented toward criminal activities, while the one who joins the feminist group

may develop an even greater interest in producing social change.

Control Theory

Inside most of us, it seems, are strong desires to do things that would get us in trouble—inner drives, temptations, urges, hostilities, and so on. Yet most of us stifle these desires most of the time. Why?

The Theory Sociologist Walter Reckless (1973), who developed **control theory,** stresses that two control systems work against our motivations to deviate. Our *inner controls* include our internalized morality—conscience, religious principles, ideas of right and wrong. Inner controls also include fears of punishment, feelings of integrity, and the desire to be a "good" person (Hirschi 1969; Rogers 1977). Our *outer controls* consist of people—such as family, friends, and the police—who influence us not to deviate. Control theory is sometimes classified as a functional theory, because when our outer controls operate well, we conform to social norms and thereby do not threaten the status quo. Because symbols and meanings are central to this theory, however, it can also be classified as a symbolic interactionist theory.

As sociologist Travis Hirschi (1969) noted, the stronger our bonds are with society, the more effective our inner controls are. Bonds are based on *attachments* (feeling affection and respect for people who conform to society's norms), *commitments* (having a stake in society that you don't want to risk, such as a respected place in your family, a good standing at college, a good job), *involvements* (putting time and energy into approved activities), and *beliefs*

To experience a sense of belonging is one of humanity's basic needs. Membership in groups, especially peer groups, is a primary way that people meet this need. Regardless of the orientation of the group—whether to conformity or to deviance—the process is the same. Shown here is a gang from Brooklyn, New York, flashing their gang signs at Coney Island. Gang membership helps provide a vital sense of belonging.

(holding that certain actions are morally wrong). This theory can be summarized as *self*-control, says Hirschi. The key to learning high self-control is socialization, especially in childhood. Parents help their children develop self-control by supervising them and punishing their deviant acts (Gottfredson and Hirschi 1990).

Applying the Theory Consider drug use. Suppose that some friends have invited you to a night club. When you get there, you notice that everyone seems unusually happy, almost giddy would be the word. They seem to be ecstatic in their animated conversations and dancing. Your friends tell you that almost everyone here has taken the drug ecstasy, and they invite you to take some with them.

What do you do? Let's not explore the question of whether taking ecstasy in this setting is a deviant or a conforming act. This is another question. Instead, concentrate on the pushes and pulls you would feel. The pushes toward taking the drug: your friends, the setting, and your curiosity. Then there are the inner controls: the inner voices of your conscience and your parents, perhaps of your teachers, as well as your fears of arrest and of the dangers of illegal drugs. There are also the outer controls—perhaps the uniformed security guard looking in your direction.

So, what *did* you do? Which was stronger, your inner and outer controls or the pushes and pulls toward taking the drug? It is you who can best weigh these, for they differ with each of us.

Labeling Theory

Symbolic interactionists have developed **labeling theory**, which focuses on the significance of the labels (names, reputations) that we are given. Labels tend to become a part of our self-concept, which helps to set us on paths that propel us into or divert us from deviance. Let's look at how people react to society's labels—from "whore" and "pervert" to "cheat" and "slob."

Rejecting Labels: How People Neutralize Deviance Most people resist the negative labels that others

Drugs and drug use are one of the most interesting areas of deviance. Drugs have social reputations. They are thought of as good or bad. "Good" drugs are not necessarily harmless, nor are "bad" drugs necessarily harmful. Alcohol is an example of a "good" drug that kills thousands of Americans a year. Marijuana is an example of a "bad" drug that kills no one. Drug use also goes through fads. Shown here is one of those fads, a rave party in a New York City night club, where activities are based around the use of ecstasy.

try to pin on them. Some are so successful that even though they persist in deviance, they still consider themselves conformists. For example, even though they beat up people and vandalize property, some delinquents consider themselves to be conforming members of society. How do they do it?

Sociologists Gresham Sykes and David Matza (1988) studied boys who were in this exact situation. They found that they used five **techniques of neutralization** to deflect society's norms.

The exhibit of deviants on *The Jerry Springer Show* offers viewers a sense of being participants of hidden things. As Springer and others like him continue to parade deviants before the public, the shock and surprise wear off, making the deviance seem "more" normal. What is occurring is the *mainstreaming of deviance*—the disapproved behaviors moving into the mainstream, or becoming more socially acceptable.

Denial of Responsibility Some boys said, "I'm not responsible for what happened because . . ." and then were quite creative about the "becauses." They said that what happened was an "accident." Other boys saw themselves as "victims" of society. What else could you expect? They were like billiard balls shot around the pool table of life.

Denial of Injury Another favorite explanation of the boys was "What I did wasn't wrong because no one got hurt." They would define vandalism as "mischief," gang fighting as a "private quarrel," and stealing cars as "borrowing." They might acknowledge that what they did was illegal, but claim that they were "just having a little fun."

Denial of a Victim Some boys thought of themselves as avengers. Vandalizing a teacher's car was done to get revenge for an unfair grade, while shoplifting was a way to even the score with "crooked" store owners. In short, if the boys did accept responsibility and even admit that someone did get hurt, they protected their self-concept by claiming that the people "deserved what they got."

Condemnation of the Condemners Another technique the boys used was to deny that others had the right to judge them. They might accuse people who pointed their fingers at them of being "a bunch of hypocrites": The police were "on the take," teachers had "pets," and parents cheated on their taxes. In short, they said, "Who are they to accuse me of something?"

Appeal to Higher Loyalties A final technique the boys used to justify antisocial activities was to consider loyalty to the gang more important than following the norms of society. They might say, "I had to help my friends. That's why I got in the fight." Not incidentally, the boy may have shot two members of a rival group, as well as a bystander!

In Sum These five techniques of neutralization have implications far beyond these boys, for it is not only delinquents who try to neutralize the norms of mainstream society. Look again at these five techniques: (1) "I couldn't help myself"; (2) "Who really got hurt?"; (3) "Don't you think she deserved that, after what *she* did?"; (4) "Who are *you* to talk?"; and (5) "I had to help my friends—wouldn't you have done the same thing?" Don't such statements have a familiar ring? All of us attempt to neutralize the moral demands of society, for such neutralizations help us sleep at night.

Embracing Labels: The Example of Outlaw Bikers Although most of us resist attempts to label us as deviant, there are those who revel in a deviant identity. Some teenagers, for example, make certain by their clothing, choice of music, and hairstyles that no one misses their purposeful rejection of adult norms. Their status among fellow members of a subculture, within which they are almost obsessive conformists, is vastly more important than any status outside it.

One of the best examples of a group that embraces deviance is motorcycle gangs. Sociologist Mark Watson (1988) did participant observation with outlaw bikers. He rebuilt Harleys with them, hung around their bars and homes, and went on "runs" (trips) with them. He concluded that outlaw bikers see the world as "hostile, weak, and effeminate." They pride themselves on looking "dirty, mean, and generally undesirable" and take pleasure in provoking shocked reactions to their appearance. Holding the conventional world in contempt, they also pride themselves on getting into trouble, laughing at death, and treating women as lesser beings whose primary value is to provide them with services—especially sex. Outlaw bikers also look at themselves as losers, a factor that becomes woven into their unusual embrace of deviance.

The Power of Labels: The Saints and the Roughnecks We can see how powerful labeling is by referring back to the study of the "Saints" and the "Roughnecks" that was cited in Chapter 4 (pages 99–100). As you recall, both groups of high school boys were "constantly occupied with truancy, drinking, wild parties, petty theft, and vandalism." Yet their teachers looked on the Saints as "headed for success" and the Roughnecks as "headed for trouble." By the time they finished high school, not one Saint had been arrested, while the Roughnecks had been in constant trouble with the police.

Why did the community see these boys so differently? Chambliss (1973/2001) concluded that this split vision was due to *social class*. As symbolic interactionists emphasize, social class vitally affects our perceptions and behavior. The Saints came from respectable, middle-class families, the Roughnecks from less respectable, working-class families. These backgrounds led teachers and the authorities to expect good behavior from the Saints but trouble from the Roughnecks. And, like the rest of us, teachers and police saw what they expected to see.

The boys' social class also affected their visibility. The Saints had automobiles, and they did their drinking and vandalism out of town. Without a car, the Rough-

necks hung around their own street corners, where their boisterous behavior drew the attention of police and confirmed the ideas that the community already had of them.

The boys' social class also equipped them with distinct *styles of interaction*. When police or teachers questioned the Saints, they were apologetic. Their show of respect for authority elicited a positive reaction from teachers and police, allowing them to escape school and legal problems. The Roughnecks, said Chambliss, were "almost the polar opposite." When questioned, they were hostile. Even when they tried to assume a respectful attitude, everyone could see through it. Consequently, while teachers and police let the Saints off with warnings, they came down hard on the Roughnecks.

Although what happens in life is not determined by labels alone, the Saints and the Roughnecks did live up to the labels that the community gave them. As you recall, all but one of the Saints went on to college. One earned a doctorate, one became a lawyer, one a doctor, and the others business managers. In contrast, only two of the Roughnecks went to college. They earned athletic scholarships and became coaches. The other Roughnecks did not fare so well. Two of them dropped out of high school, later became involved in separate killings, and received long prison sentences. One became a local bookie, and no one knows the whereabouts of the other.

How do labels work? Although the matter is complex, because it involves the self-concept and reactions that vary from one individual to another, we can note that labels open and close doors of opportunity. Unlike in sociology, the label "deviant" is a judgmental term in everyday usage. This label can lock people out of conforming groups and push them into almost exclusive contact with people who have similar labels.

■ **In Sum** Symbolic interactionists examine how people's definitions of the situation underlie their deviation from or conformance to social norms. They focus on group membership (differential association), how people balance pressures to conform and to deviate (control theory), and the significance of the labels that are given to people (labeling theory).

The label *deviant* involves competing definitions and reactions to the same behavior. This central point of symbolic interactionism is explored in the Mass Media in Social Life box on the next page.

Mass Media in Social Life

PORNOGRAPHY ON THE INTERNET: FREEDOM VERSUS CENSORSHIP

Pornography vividly illustrates one of the sociological principles discussed in this chapter—the relativity of deviance. It is not the act, but the reaction to the act, that makes something deviant. Consider one of today's major issues, pornography on the Internet.

Web surfers have a wide choice of pornography. Some sites are even indexed: heterosexual or gay, single or group activity, teenagers, cheerleaders, and older women who "still think they have it." Some offer only photographs, others video. Live sites are also available, such as one that bills itself as "direct from Amsterdam." Sign on, and you can command your "model" to do anything your heart desires. Both male and female "models" are available, and the per minute charges are hefty.

What is the problem? Why can't people exchange nude photos electronically if they want to? Or watch others having sex online, if someone offers that service? Although some object to any kind of sex site, what disturbs many are the sites that feature bondage, torture, rape, and bestiality (humans having sex with animals). Judging from the number of these sites, many people derive sexual excitement from viewing such activities.

The Internet abounds with "news groups" (people who "meet" online to discuss some topic). No one is bothered by the news groups (or "chat rooms") that center on Roman architecture or rap music or turtle racing. But

news groups that focus on how to torture women are another matter. So are those that offer lessons on how to seduce grade school children—or that extol the delights of having sex with three-year-olds.

In response to complaints, the state and federal governments have passed laws against child pornography on the Internet. The FBI seizes computers and searches them for illegal pictures. The courts levy fines and send some violators to prison. It remains legal to exchange pictures of tortured and sexually abused women, however. Sites that feature these activities, as well as those that discuss having sex with children, but show no photos, also remain legal. ■

For Your Consideration

Some feel that no matter how much they may find a point of view repugnant or disagree with it for any other reason, communi-

cation about it must be allowed. This, they say, includes photos. They fear that if the government censors these activities, it will also censor other activities. What do you think? For example, do you think it should be legal to exchange photos of women being sexually abused or tortured? Should it be legal to discuss ways to seduce children? If not, on what basis should they be banned? If we should make these activities illegal, then what other communications should we prohibit? On what basis?

Assume that such photos and discussion groups remain legal. If so, should school and public libraries be allowed to install filters that screen out designated Internet sites? One side insists that such filters violate the First Amendment's guarantee of free speech, the other that it is only a reasonable precaution to protect children. What do you think?

Finally, can you disprove the central point of the symbolic interactionists—that an activity is deviant only because people decide that it is deviant? You may use examples cited in this box, or any others that you wish. You cannot invoke God or moral absolutes in your argument, however, as they are outside the field of sociology. As you will recall from the first chapter of this book, sociology cannot decide moral issues. This applies even to extreme cases.

THE FUNCTIONALIST PERSPECTIVE

When we think of deviance, we're likely to think about its dysfunctions. Functionalists, in contrast, are as likely to stress the functions of deviance as they are to stress its dysfunctions.

How Deviance Is Functional for Society

Most of us are upset by deviance, especially crime, and assume that society would be better off without it. The classic functionalist theorist Emile Durkheim (1893/1933, 1893/1964), however, came to a surprising conclusion. Deviance, he said, including crime, is functional for society, for it contributes to the social order. Its three main functions are:

1. *Deviance clarifies moral boundaries and affirms norms.* A group's ideas about how people should act and think mark its *moral boundaries.* Deviant acts challenge those boundaries. To call a deviant member into account, is to say, in effect, "You broke an important rule, and we cannot tolerate that." To punish deviants affirms the group's norms and clarifies what it means to be a member of the group.

2. *Deviance promotes social unity.* To affirm the group's moral boundaries by punishing deviants fosters a "we" feeling among the group's members. In saying, "You can't get by with that," the group collectively affirms the rightness of its own ways.

3. *Deviance promotes social change.* Groups do not always agree on what to do with people who push beyond their acceptable ways of doing things. Some group members may even approve the rule-breaking behavior. Boundary violations that gain enough support become new, acceptable behaviors. Thus, deviance may force a group to rethink and redefine its moral boundaries, helping groups, and whole societies, to change their customary ways.

Strain Theory: How Social Values Produce Deviance

Functionalists argue that crime is a *natural* part of society, not an aberration or some alien element in our midst. Indeed, they say, some mainstream values actually generate crime. To understand what they mean, consider what sociolo-gists Richard Cloward and Lloyd Ohlin (1960) identified as the crucial problem of the industrialized world: the need to locate and train the most talented people of every generation—whether they were born into wealth or into poverty—so they can take over the key technical jobs of modern society. When children are born, no one knows which ones will have the ability to become dentists, nuclear physicists, or engineers. To get the most talented people to compete with one another, society tries to motivate *everyone* to strive for success. It does this by arousing discontent—making people feel dissatisfied with what they have so they will try to "better" themselves.

Most people, then, end up with strong desires to reach **cultural goals** such as wealth or high status, or to achieve whatever other objectives society holds out for them. Not everyone, however, has equal access to society's **institutionalized means,** the legitimate ways of achieving success. Some people, for example, find their path to education and good jobs blocked. These people experience *strain* or frustration, which may motivate them to take a deviant path.

This perspective, known as **strain theory,** was developed by sociologist Robert Merton (1956, 1968). People who experience strain, he said, are likely to feel *anomie,* a sense of normlessness. Because mainstream norms (work, education) don't seem to be getting them anywhere, they find it difficult to identify with these norms. They may even feel wronged by the system, and its rules may seem illegitimate (Anderson 1978).

Table 6.1 compares people's reactions to cultural goals and institutionalized means. The first reaction, which Merton said is the most common, is *conformity,* using socially acceptable means to try to reach cultural goals. In industrialized societies most people try to get good jobs, a good education, and so on. If well-paid jobs are unavailable, they take less desirable jobs. If they are denied access to Harvard or Stanford, they go to a state university. Others take night classes and go to vocational

Table 6.1	HOW PEOPLE MATCH THEIR GOALS TO THEIR MEANS		
Do They Feel the Strain That Leads to Anomie?	Mode of Adaptation	Cultural Goals	Institutionalized Means
No	Conformists	Accept	Accept
Yes	Innovators	Accept	Reject
	Ritualists	Reject	Accept
	Retreatists	Reject	Reject
	Rebels	Reject/Replace	Reject/Replace

schools. In short, most people take the socially accept-able road.

Four Deviant Paths The remaining four responses, which are deviant, represent reactions to anomie. Let's look at each. *Innovators* are people who accept the goals of society but use illegitimate means to try to reach them. Drug dealers, for instance, accept the goal of achieving wealth. But they reject the legitimate avenues for doing so. Other examples are embezzlers, robbers, and con artists.

The second deviant path is taken by people who become discouraged and give up on achieving cultural goals. Yet they still cling to conventional rules of con-duct. Merton called this response *ritualism.* Although ritualists have given up on excelling and advancing in position, they survive by following the rules of their job. Teachers whose idealism is shattered (who are said to suffer from "burnout"), for example, remain in the class-room, where they teach without enthusiasm. Their re-sponse is considered deviant because they cling to the job although they have abandoned the goal, which may have been stimulating young minds or making the world a better place.

People who choose the third deviant path, *retreat-ism,* reject both cultural goals and the institutionalized means of achieving them. Those who drop out of the pursuit of success by way of alcohol or drugs are retreat-ists. Such people do not even try to appear as though they share the goals of their society.

The final type of deviant response is *rebellion.* Con-vinced that their society is corrupt, rebels, like retreatists, reject both society's goals and its institutionalized means. Unlike retreatists, however, they seek to re-place existing goals with new ones. Revolutionaries are the most committed type of rebels.

In Sum *Strain theory* underscores the main so-ciological point about deviance, namely, that deviants are the product of society. Due to their social loca-tion, some people experience greater strains, or frus-trations, as they attempt to reach the cultural goals set out for them. With these greater pressures, they are more likely to deviate from society's norms. The result is four types of deviants: innovators, ritualists, retreatists, and rebels.

Illegitimate Opportunity Structures: Social Class and Crime

One of the more interesting sociological findings in the study of deviance is that the social classes have distinct styles of crime. Let's see how unequal access to the in-stitutionalized means to success helps explain this.

Street Crime Functionalists point out that indus-trialized societies have no trouble socializing the poor into wanting to own things. Like others, the poor are bombarded with messages urging them to buy every-thing from designer jeans and DVD players to new cars. Television and movies show vivid images of the middle class enjoying luxurious lives. These images reinforce the myth that all full-fledged Americans can afford soci-ety's many goods and services.

In contrast, the school system, the most common route to success, fails the poor. It is run by the middle class, and there the children of the poor confront a be-wildering world, one at odds with their background. Their grammar and nonstandard language may be liber-ally sprinkled with what the middle class considers ob-scene words and phrases. Their ideas of punctuality and neatness, as well as their lack of preparation in paper-and-pencil skills, are a mismatch with their new envi-ronment. Facing such barriers, the poor are more likely than their more privileged counterparts to drop out of school. Educational failure, in turn, closes the door on many legitimate avenues to financial success.

Not infrequently, however, a different door opens to the poor, one that sociologists Richard Cloward and Lloyd Ohlin (1960) called **illegitimate opportunity structures.** Woven into the texture of life in urban slums, for example, are robbery, burglary, drug dealing, prostitu-tion, pimping, gambling, and other remunerative crimes, commonly called "hustles" (Liebow 1967/1997; Bourgois 1994; Anderson 1978, 1990, 2001). For many of the poor, the "hustler" is a role model—glamorous, in control,

This 1871 wood engraving depicts children as they are being paid for their day's work in a London brickyard. In early capitalism, most street criminals came from the marginal working class, as did these children. It is the same today.

Sociology

ISLANDS IN THE STREET:
URBAN GANGS IN THE UNITED STATES

For more than ten years, sociologist Martín Sánchez Jankowski (1991) did participant observation of thirty-seven Irish, African American, Puerto Rican, Chicano, Dominican, Jamaican, and Central American gangs in Boston, Los Angeles, and New York City. The gangs earned money through gambling, arson, mugging, armed robbery, wholesaling drugs to pushers, and selling moonshine, guns, stolen car parts, and protection. Jankowski ate, slept, and sometimes fought with the gangs, but by mutual agreement he did not participate in drugs or other illegal activities. He was seriously injured twice during the study.

Contrary to stereotypes, Jankowski did not find that the motive for joining was to escape a broken home (there were as many members from intact homes) or to seek a substitute family (as many boys said they were close to their families as said they were not). Rather, the boys joined to gain access to money, for recreation (including girls and drugs), anonymity in committing crimes, to get protection, and to help the community. This last reason may seem surprising, but in some neighborhoods gangs protect residents from outsiders. The boys also saw the gang as an alternative to the dead-end—and deadening—jobs held by their parents.

Neighborhood residents are ambivalent about gangs. On the one hand, they don't like the violence. On the other hand, many adults once belonged to gangs, the gangs often provide better protection than the police, and gang members are the children of people who live in the neighborhood.

Particular gangs will come and go, but gangs will likely always be part of the city. As functionalists point out, gangs fulfill needs for poor youth who live on the margins of society. ■

For Your Consideration

What are the functions that gangs fulfill (the needs they meet)? Suppose that you have been hired as an urban planner by the City of Los Angeles. How could you arrange to meet the needs that gangs fulfill in ways that minimize violence and encourage youth to follow mainstream norms?

---

the image of "easy money," one of the few people in the area who comes close to attaining the cultural goal of success. For such reasons, then, these activities attract disproportionate numbers of the poor. As discussed in the Down-to-Earth Sociology box above, gangs are one way that the illegitimate opportunity structure beckons disadvantaged youth.

White-Collar Crime The more privileged social classes are not crime-free, of course, but for them different illegitimate opportunities beckon. They find *other forms* of crime to be functional. Rather than mugging, pimping, and burglary, the more privileged encounter "opportunities" for evading income tax, bribing public officials, embezzling from employers, participating in fraud, and so on. Physicians, for example, never hold up cabbies, but many do cheat Medicare. Sociologist Edwin Sutherland (1949) coined the term **white-collar crime** to refer to crimes that people of respectable and high social status commit in the course of their occupations.

Although the general public seems to think that the lower classes are more prone to crime, numerous studies show that white-collar workers also commit many crimes (Weisburd et al. 1991; Zey 1993). This difference in perception is largely due to visibility. While crimes committed by the poor are given much publicity, the crimes of the more privileged classes seldom make the evening news and go largely unnoticed. Yet "crime in the suites," which runs between $200 billion and $400 billion a year (Wells 1998), costs more than "crime in the streets." This refers only to dollar costs. No one has yet figured out a way to compare, for example, the suffering experienced by a rape victim with the pain felt by an elderly couple who lost their life savings to white-collar fraud.

You probably have shopped at some of these criminal enterprises. Sears, for example, defrauded the poor of over $100 million. These were people so poor they could no longer afford to pay for what they had purchased at Sears, and they had filed for bankruptcy. To avoid a criminal trial, Sears pled guilty. When the Sears case made national headlines, it frightened the parent companies of Macy's, Bloomingdale's, and Montgomery Ward, which settled with debtors out of court (McCormick 1999).

In terms of dollars, perhaps the most costly crime in U.S. history was the plundering of the savings and loan industry. Corporate officers systematically looted these banks of billions of dollars. The total cost ran somewhere around $500 billion—a staggering $2,000 for every man, woman, and child in the entire country (Kettl 1991; Newdorf 1991). Of the thousands involved, the most infamous culprit was Neil Bush, son of George Bush, the former president of the United States. As an officer of Silverado, a Colorado savings and loan, Bush approved $100 million in loans to a company in which he secretly held interests, an act that helped to bankrupt his firm (Tolchin 1991).

Although white-collar crime is not as dramatic as street killings, abduction, or rape—and, therefore, is usually considered less newsworthy—it, too, can cause physi-

cal injury and death. When Odwalla, Inc. sold apple juice contaminated with dangerous bacteria, 14 children came down with a disease that ravaged their kidneys. One of them died (Belluck 1998). Unsafe working conditions— many the result of executive decisions to put profits ahead of workers' safety—claim the lives of about 100,000 Americans each year. This is about five times the number of people killed by street criminals (Simon and Eitzen 1993). If court hearings bear out the allegations made at the time I am writing this book, one of the most notorious of white-collar crimes was the decision by Firestone executives to let faulty tires remain on U.S. vehicles—even though they were recalling them in Saudi Arabia and Venezuela. As illustrated by the photo on page 144, the consequences were devastating. These tires cost the lives of over 100 Americans. The greatest concern of Americans, however, is street crime. They fear the violent stranger who will change their life forever. As the Social Map below shows, the chances of such an encounter depend on where you live.

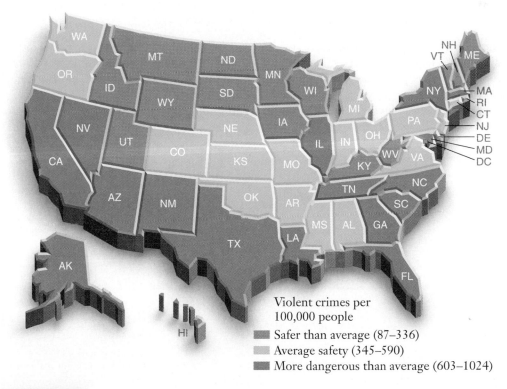

Violent crimes per 100,000 people

■ Safer than average (87–336)
■ Average safety (345–590)
■ More dangerous than average (603–1024)

Figure 6.1 **SOME STATES ARE SAFER: VIOLENT CRIME IN THE UNITED STATES**

Violent crimes are murder, rape, robbery, and aggravated assault. The variation of violence among the states is incredible. Some states have a rate that is ten times higher than that of other states. With a rate of 87 per 100,000 people, North Dakota has the lowest rate of violence, while Florida, at 1,024, has the highest rate. The U.S. average rate is 424 (the total of the states' average rates of violence divided by 50). This total does not include Washington, D.C., whose rate is 2,024, 23 times as high as North Dakota and almost five times the national average.

Source: Statistical Abstract 1999:Table 344.

More than 100 people have died from accidents involving Firestone tires. Shown here is Victor Rodriguez, whose 10-year-old son was killed when a Firestone tire on their Ford Explorer blew out in San Antonio, Texas. The fault may be Firestone's, for manufacturing defective tires; or it may lie with Ford, for equipping the vehicles with tires that were too small; or it may be a combination of both. If so, this would be a case of white collar crime that kills. White-collar murderers are unlikely to ever spend a single day in jail for their crimes.

Gender and Crime A major change in crime is the growing number of female offenders. As Table 6.2 shows, women are committing a larger proportion of almost all crimes—from drugs to burglary. The exceptions are murder and illegal gambling. As more women have joined the professions and corporate world, they, too, have been enticed by its illegitimate opportunities, and their involvement in embezzlement, fraud, and forgery has increased.

■ **In Sum** Functionalists conclude that much street crime is the consequence of socializing everyone into equating success with material possessions, while denying many in the lower social classes the means to attain that success. People from higher social classes encounter different opportunity structures to commit crimes.

THE CONFLICT PERSPECTIVE

Class, Crime, and the Criminal Justice System

The federal government accused two multinational corporations, Grumann and SmithKline, of fraud that cost the taxpayers millions of dollars. No executives went to jail. Instead, the corporations paid fines—and then were awarded more contracts by the federal government (Pasztor 1993; Tanouye 1997).

Contrast this event with stories you often read in newspapers about young men who steal automobiles and are sentenced to several years in prison. How can a legal system that is supposed to provide "justice for all" be so inconsistent? According to conflict theorists, this question is central to the analysis of crime and the **criminal justice system**—the police, courts, and prisons that deal with people who are accused of having committed crimes.

Table 6.2

| MORE WOMEN ARE COMMITTING CRIME | | | | | | | |
| Of those arrested, what percentage are women? | | | | | | | |
Crime	1987	1997	Change	Crime	1987	1997	Change
Aggravated Assault	13.3	19.0	+49%	Drugs	14.9	17.1	+15%
Burglary	7.9	11.8	+49%	Weapons	7.6	8.5	+12%
Car Theft	9.7	14.5	+49%	(carrying, concealing)			
Vandalism	10.6	14.7	+39%	Larceny-Theft	31.1	34.4	+11%
Drunk in Public	9.2	12.4	+35%	Embezzlement	38.1	41.7	+9%
Stolen Property	11.6	15.4	+33%	Arson	13.7	14.7	+7%
(buying, possessing)				Forgery and Counterfeiting	34.4	36.6	+6%
Drunken Driving	11.7	15.4	+32%	Gambling	13.5	12.6	–7%
Robbery	8.1	9.8	+21%	Murder	12.5	10.0	–20%

Sources: Statistical Abstract 1989:Table 293; 1999:Table 358.

Power and Inequality

Conflict theorists look at power and social inequality as the chief characteristics of society. They stress that a group at the top, a power elite, controls the criminal justice system. This group makes certain that laws are passed that will protect its power. Other norms, such as those that govern informal behavior (chewing with a closed mouth, appearing in public with combed hair, and so on), may come from other sources, but they simply are not as important. Such norms influence our everyday behavior, but they do not determine who gets sent to prison and who does not.

Conflict theorists see the most fundamental division in industrial society as that between the few who own the means of production and the many who do not, those who sell their labor and the privileged few who buy it. Those who buy labor, and thereby control workers, make up the **capitalist class;** those who sell their labor form the **working class.** Toward the most depressed end of the working class is the **marginal working class**, people with few skills, who are subject to layoffs, and whose jobs are low paying, part time, or seasonal. This class is marked by unemployment and poverty. From its ranks come most of the prison inmates in the United States. Desperate, these people commit street crimes, and because their crimes threaten the social order, they are severely punished.

The Law as an Instrument of Oppression

According to conflict theorists, the idea that the law operates impartially and administers a code that is shared by all is a cultural myth promoted by the capitalist class. These theorists see the law as an instrument of oppression, a tool designed to maintain the powerful in their privileged position (Spitzer 1975; Ritzer 1992; MacDonald 1995). Because the working class has the potential to rebel and overthrow the current social order, when its members get out of line, they are arrested, tried, and imprisoned.

For this reason, the criminal justice system does not focus on the owners of corporations and the harm they do to the masses through unsafe products, wanton pollution, and price manipulations. Instead, it directs its energies against violations by the working class (Gordon 1971; Platt 1978; Coleman 1989). The violations of the capitalist class cannot be totally ignored, however, for if they became too outrageous or oppressive, the working class might rise up in revolution. To prevent this, occasionally a flagrant violation by a member of the capitalist class is prosecuted. The publicity given to the case helps to stabilize the social system by providing visible evidence of the "fairness" of the criminal justice system.

Usually, however, the powerful are able to bypass the courts altogether, appearing instead before an agency that has no power to imprison (such as the Federal Trade Commission). These agencies are directed by people from wealthy backgrounds who sympathize with the intricacies of the corporate world. This means that most cases of illegal sales of stocks and bonds, price fixing, trade restraint, collusion, and so on are handled by "gentlemen overseeing gentlemen." Is it surprising, then, that the typical sanction is a token fine? In contrast, the property crimes of the masses are handled by courts that do have the power to imprison. Burglary, armed robbery, and theft committed by the poor threaten not only the sanctity of private property but, ultimately, the positions of the powerful.

When groups that had been denied access to power gain that access, we can expect to see changes in the legal system. This is precisely what is occurring now. Racial-ethnic minorities and homosexuals, for example, have more political power today than ever before. In line with conflict theory, a new category of crime has been formulated. We analyze this change in the Thinking Critically section on page 147–148.

■ **In Sum** From the perspective of conflict theory, the small penalties imposed for crimes committed by the powerful are typical of a legal system that has been designed by the elite (capitalists) to control workers, to keep themselves in power, and, ultimately, to stabilize the social order. From this perspective, law enforcement is a cultural device through which the capitalist class carries out self-protective and repressive policies.

Reactions to Deviance

Whether it involves cheating on a sociology quiz or holding up a liquor store, any violation of norms invites reaction. Let's look at some of these reactions.

Street Crime and Prisons

Today, we don't make people wear scarlet letters, but we do remove them from society and make them wear prison uniforms. And we still use degradation ceremonies, in this case, a public trial and the public pronouncement that someone is "unfit" to live among decent, law-abiding people" for some specified period of time. Figure 6.2 illustrates the remarkable growth in the

Figure 6.2

HOW MUCH IS ENOUGH? THE EXPLOSION IN THE NUMBER OF U.S. PRISONERS

Source: Statistical Abstract 1995:Table 349; 1999:Table 382.

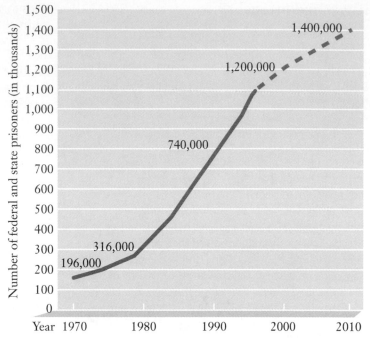

To better understand the significance of this growth, compare it with the change in the U.S. population. Between 1970 and 1997, the U.S. population grew 31 percent, while the prison population grew *20 times as fast* (635 percent). If the prison population had increased at the same rate as the U.S. population, there would be about 257,000 prisoners, between one-fourth and one-fifth of the actual number.

U.S. prison population. You should note that this huge number does *not* include jail inmates. If we add these, the total comes to over two million (Butterfield 2000). As Table 6.3 shows, about 95 percent of prisoners are men, and about half are African Americans. As noted, because social class funnels some people into the criminal justice system and others away from it, official statistics on crime have an inherent social class bias.

Table 6.3

	INMATES IN U.S. STATE PRISONS				
	PRISONERS	***U.S. POPULATION***		***PRISONERS***	***U.S. POPULATION***
Characteristics	**Percentage with These Characteristics**	**Percentage with These Characteristics**	**Characteristics**	**Percentage with These Characteristics**	**Percentage with These Characteristics**
Age			**Race-Ethnicity**		
Under 18	0.6%	25.9%	White[a]	47.8	83.4
18–24	21.3	10.2	African American	49.4	12.4
25–34	45.7	16.6	Other races	2.8	4.2
35–44	22.7	15.7	**Sex**		
45–54	6.5	10.7	Male	93.8	48.8
55–64	2.4	8.2	Female	6.2	51.2
65 and over	0.7	12.7			

[a]The category "white" includes Latinos. Only these groups are listed in the sources.

Sources: Sourcebook of Criminal Justice Statistics 1998:Table 6.40; *Statistical Abstract* 1997:Tables 14, 18, 22, 356; 1999:Table 382.

For the past 15 years or so, the United States has followed a "get tough" policy. "Three strikes and you're out" laws (life imprisonment upon conviction for a third felony) have become common. While few of us would feel sympathy if a man convicted of a third rape (or a third murder) were sent to prison for life, as discussed in the following Thinking Critically section, these laws have had unanticipated consequences.

Thinking Critically

"THREE STRIKES AND YOU'RE OUT!" UNINTENDED CONSEQUENCES OF WELL-INTENDED LAWS

In the 1980s, violent crime soared. Americans were fearful, and they demanded that their lawmakers do something. Politicians heard the message and responded by passing the "three strikes" law. Anyone convicted of a third felony receives an automatic mandatory sentence. Judges are not allowed to consider the circumstances. Some mandatory sentences carry life imprisonment.

In their haste to appease the public, the politicians did not limit these laws to *violent* crimes. And they did not consider that some minor crimes are considered felonies. As the functionalists would say, this has led to unanticipated consequences.

Here are some actual cases (Cloud 1999).

- In Iowa, a man was sentenced to 10 years for stealing $30 worth of steaks from a grocery store.

- In California, a 21-year-old anthropology major was sentenced to 10 years for mailing sheets of LSD to her boyfriend.

- In Los Angeles, a 27-year-old man was sentenced to 25 years for stealing a pizza.

- In Alabama, a husband, father, Vietnam veteran, and owner of a roofing business bought a pound of marijuana. Thirteen years earlier, he had been arrested for several petty crimes—crimes that didn't even carry a prison sentence. He was sentenced to life in prison without parole.

- In Atlanta, a man opened a garden store, where he sold hydroponic equipment for growing plants. His wife, who worked as a customer service agent for an insurance company, did occasional bookwork for the store. Some customers used the equipment they bought at the store to grow marijuana. When they were arrested, they received reduced sentences for testifying that this husband and wife had given them advice on how to grow marijuana. The couple were sentenced to 10 years in prison.

- In New York City, a man who was about to be sentenced for selling crack said to the judge, "I'm only 19. This is terrible." He then hurled himself out of a courtroom window, plunging to his death sixteen stories below. ■

For Your Consideration

Apply the symbolic interactionist, functionalist, and conflict perspectives to mandatory sentencing. For *symbolic interactionism,* what do these laws represent to the public? How does your answer differ depending on what part of "the public" you are referring to? For *functionalism,* who benefits from these laws? What are some of their dysfunctions? For the *conflict perspective,* what groups are in conflict? Who has the power to enforce their will on others?

A major problem with prisons is that they fail to teach their clients to stay away from crime. Four out of every five prisoners have been in prison before (*Statistical Abstract* 1995:Table 351). The **recidivism rate** (the percentage of people who are rearrested) runs as high as 85 to 90 percent (Blumstein and Cohen 1987). Three years after being given probation—released into the community under court supervision—about two-thirds (62 to 64) percent are arrested for a felony or have a disciplinary hearing for violating their parole (Langan and Cunniff 1992; Alter 1997).

Making Things Illegal

Did you know that it is a crime in Iran and Afghanistan for women to wear makeup? A crime in Illinois for merchants to sell meat before noon on Sundays? You probably know that it is a crime to drink alcohol while driving your car, but did you know that this is legal in Texas? As stressed in this chapter, deviance, including the form called *crime,* is relative. It varies from one society to another, and from group to group within a society. It also varies from one time period to another, as opinions change or as different groups gain access to power.

Let's consider legal change.

Thinking Critically

CHANGING VIEWS: MAKING HATE A CRIME

Because crime is whatever acts authorities pass laws against, new crimes emerge from time to time. A prime example is juvenile delinquency, which Illinois lawmakers designated a separate type of crime in 1899. Juveniles committed crimes prior to this time, of course, but these youths were not considered to be a separate type of lawbreaker. They were just young people who committed crimes, and they were treated the same as adults who committed the same crime. Some new crimes depend on the appearance of new technology. Motor vehicle theft, a separate crime in the United States, obviously did not exist before the automobile was invented. Nor did "identity theft," a relatively recent crime, exist prior to the invention of our new technology.

In the 1980s, another new crime was born when state governments developed the classification **hate crime.** This is a crime that is motivated by bias (dislike, hatred) against someone's race-ethnicity, religion, sexual orientation, or disability. Prior to this, of course, people attacked others or destroyed their property out of these same motivations, but in those cases the motivation was not the issue. If someone injured or killed another person because of that person's race-ethnicity, religion, sexual orientation, or disability, he or she was charged with assault or murder. Today, motivation has become a central issue, and hate crimes carry more severe sentences than do crimes that involve the same act but without hatred as the motive. Table 6.4 summarizes the victims of hate crimes.

We can be certain that the "evolution" of crime is not yet complete. As society changes and as different groups gain access to power, we can expect the definitions of crime to change accordingly. ■

Table 6.4

HATE CRIMES	
Directed Against	**Number of Victims**
Race-Ethnicity	
African Americans	3,951
Whites	1,293
Latinos	649
Asian Americans	466
Native Americans	36
Religion	
Jews	1,247
Protestants	61
Catholics	32
Islamics	32
Sexual Orientation	
Male Homosexuals	927
Female Homosexuals	236
Homosexuals (general)	214
Heterosexuals	14
Disabilities	
Physical	9
Mental	3
Source: Statistical Abstract 1999: Table 351.	

For Your Consideration

Why do we need a separate classification called *hate crime*? Why aren't the crimes of assault, robbery, murder, and so on adequate? How do you think your social location (race-ethnicity, gender, social class, sexual orientation, or physical ability) affect your opinion?

The Medicalization of Deviance: Mental Illness

Another way in which society deals with deviance is to "medicalize" it. Let's look at what this entails.

Neither Mental nor Illness? To *medicalize* something is to make it a medical matter, to classify it as a form of illness that properly belongs in the care of physicians. For the past hundred years or so, especially since the time of Sigmund Freud (1856–1939), the Viennese physician who founded psychoanalysis, there has been a growing tendency toward the **medicalization of deviance.** In this view, deviance, including crime, is a sign of mental sickness. Rape, murder, stealing, cheating, and so on are external symptoms of internal disorders, consequences of a confused or tortured mind.

Thomas Szasz (1986, 1996, 1998), a renegade in his profession of psychiatry, argues that *mental illnesses are neither mental nor illness. They are simply problem behaviors.* Some forms of so-called mental illnesses have organic causes; that is, they are *physical* illnesses that result in unusual perceptions or behavior. Some depression, for example, is caused by a chemical imbalance in the brain, which can be treated by drugs. The depression, however, may show itself as crying, long-term sadness, and lack of interest in family, work, school, or one's appearance. When a person becomes deviant in ways that disturb others, and when these others cannot find a satisfying explanation for why the person is "like that," they conclude that a "sickness in the head" causes the inappropriate, unacceptable behavior.

All of us have troubles. Some of us face a constant barrage of problems as we go through life. Most of us continue the struggle, encouraged by relatives and friends, motivated by job, family responsibilities, and life goals. Even when the odds seem hopeless, we carry on, not perfectly, but as best we can.

Some people, however, fail to cope well with the challenges of daily life. Overwhelmed, they become depressed, uncooperative, or hostile. Some strike out at others, while some, in Merton's terms, become retreatists and withdraw into their apartments or homes, not wanting to come out. These are *behaviors, not mental illnesses,* stresses

Szasz. They may be inappropriate coping devices, but they are coping devices, nevertheless, not mental illnesses. Thus, Szasz concludes that "mental illness" is a myth foisted on a naive public by a medical profession that uses pseudoscientific jargon in order to expand its area of control and force nonconforming people to accept society's definitions of "normal."

Szasz's extreme claim forces us to look anew at the forms of deviance that we usually refer to as mental illness. To explain behavior that people find bizarre, he directs our attention not to causes hidden deep within the "subconscious," but, instead, to how people learn such behaviors. Asking, "What is the origin of inappropriate or bizarre behavior?" then becomes similar to asking, "Why do some women steal?" "Why do some men rape?" "Why do some teenagers cuss their parents and stalk out of the room, slamming the door?" *The answers depend on those people's particular experiences in life, not on an illness in their mind.* In short, some sociologists find Szasz's renegade analysis refreshing because it indicates that *social experiences,* not some illness of the mind, underlie bizarre behaviors—as well as deviance in general.

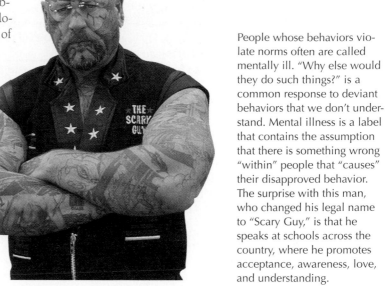

People whose behaviors violate norms often are called mentally ill. "Why else would they do such things?" is a common response to deviant behaviors that we don't understand. Mental illness is a label that contains the assumption that there is something wrong "within" people that "causes" their disapproved behavior. The surprise with this man, who changed his legal name to "Scary Guy," is that he speaks at schools across the country, where he promotes acceptance, awareness, love, and understanding.

The Homeless Mentally Ill

Jamie was sitting on a low wall surrounding the landscaped courtyard of an exclusive restaurant. She appeared unaware of the stares that were elicited by her many layers of mismatched clothing, her dirty face, and the shopping cart that overflowed with her meager possessions.

Every once in a while Jamie would pause, concentrate, and point to the street, slowly moving her finger horizontally. I asked her what she was doing.

"I'm directing traffic," she replied. "I control where the cars go. Look, that one turned right there," she said, now withdrawing her finger.

"Really?" I said.

After a while she confided that her cart talked to her.

"Really?" I said again.

"Yes," she replied. "You can hear it, too." At that, she pushed the shopping cart a bit.

"Did you hear that?" she asked.

When I shook my head, she demonstrated again. Then it hit me. She was referring to the squeaking wheels!

I nodded.

When I left, Jamie was pointing to the sky, for, as she told me, she also controlled the flight of airplanes.

To most of us, Jamie's behavior and thinking are bizarre. They simply do not match any reality we know. Could you or I become like Jamie?

Suppose for a bitter moment that you are homeless and have to live on the streets. You have no money, no place to sleep, no bathroom, do not know *if* you are going to eat, much less where, have no friends or anyone you can trust, and live in constant fear of rape and violence. Do you think this might be enough to drive you over the edge?

Consider just the problems involved in not having a place to bathe. (Shelters are often so dangerous that the homeless prefer to take their chances and sleep in public settings.) At first, you try to wash in the toilets of gas stations, bars, the bus station, or a shopping center. But you are dirty, and people stare when you enter and call the management when they see you wash your feet in the sink. You are thrown out and told in no uncertain terms never to come back. So you get dirtier and dirtier. Eventually you come to think of being dirty as a fact of life. Soon, maybe, you don't even care. The stares no longer bother you, at least not as much.

No one will talk to you, and you withdraw more and more into yourself. You begin to build a fantasy life. You talk openly to yourself. People stare, but so what? They stare anyway. Besides, they are no longer important to you.

Jamie might be mentally ill. Some organic problem, such as a chemical imbalance in her brain, might underlie her behavior. But perhaps not. How long would it take us to exhibit bizarre behaviors if we were homeless—and hopeless? The point is that *just being on the streets can cause mental illness*—or whatever we want to label socially inappropriate behaviors that we find difficult to classify. *Homelessness and mental illness are reciprocal:* Just as "mental illness" can cause homelessness, so the trials of being homeless, of living on cold, hostile streets, can lead to unusual and unacceptable thinking and behaviors.

The Need for a More Humane Approach

As Durkheim (1895/1964:68) pointed out, deviance is inevitable—even in a group of saints.

> Imagine a society of saints, a perfect cloister of exemplary individuals. Crimes, properly so called, will there be unknown; but faults which appear [invisible] to the layman will create there the same scandal that the ordinary offense does in ordinary [society].

With deviance inevitable, one measure of a society is how it treats its deviants. Our prisons certainly don't say

much good about U.S. society. Filled with the poor, they are warehouses of the unwanted. They reflect patterns of broad discrimination in our larger society. White-collar criminals continue to get by with a slap on the wrist while street criminals are punished severely. Some deviants, who fail to meet current standards of admission to either prison or mental hospital, take refuge in shelters and cardboard boxes in city streets. Although no one has *the* answer, it does not take much reflection to see that there are more humane approaches than these.

Because deviance is inevitable, the larger issues are to find ways to protect people from deviant behaviors that are harmful to themselves or others, to tolerate those that are not harmful, and to develop systems of fairer treatment for deviants. In the absence of fundamental changes that would bring about a truly equitable social system, most efforts are, unfortunately, Band-Aid solutions. What we need is a more humane social system, one that would prevent the social inequalities that are the focus of the next four chapters.

SUMMARY AND REVIEW

■ What Is Deviance?

From a sociological perspective, **deviance** (the violation of norms) is relative. What people consider deviant varies from one culture to another and from group to group within the same society. As symbolic interactionists stress, it is not the act itself, but the reactions to the act, that make something deviant. All groups develop systems of **social control** to punish **deviants**, those who violate its norms. Pp. 130–133.

How do sociological and individualistic explanations of deviance differ?

To explain why people deviate, biologists and psychologists look for reasons *within* the individual, such as **genetic predispositions** or **personality disorders**. Sociologists, in contrast, look for explanations *outside* the individual, in social relations. P. 133.

■ The Symbolic Interactionist Perspective

How do symbolic interactionists explain deviance?

Symbolic interactionists have developed several theories to explain deviance such as **crime** (the violation of norms that have been written into law). According to **differential association theory**, people learn to deviate by associating with others. According to **control theory**, each of us is propelled toward deviance, but most of us conform because of an effective system of inner and outer controls. People who have less effective controls deviate. Pp. 133–140.

Labeling theory focuses on how labels (names, reputations) help to funnel people into or away from deviance. People who commit deviant acts often use **techniques of neutralization** to continue to think of themselves as conformists. Pp. 136–138.

■ The Functionalist Perspective

How do functionalists explain deviance?

Functionalists point out that deviance, including criminal acts, is functional for society. Functions include affirming norms and promoting social unity and social change. According to **strain theory**, societies socialize their members into desiring **cultural goals**. Many people are unable to achieve these goals in socially acceptable ways—that is, by **institutionalized means**. *Deviants*, then, are people who either give up on the goals or use deviant means to attain them. Merton identified five types of responses to cultural goals and institutionalized means: conformity, innovation, ritualism, retreatism, and rebellion. **Illegitimate opportunity theory** stresses that some people have easier access to illegal means of achieving goals. Pp. 140–144.

■ The Conflict Perspective

How do conflict theorists explain deviance?

Conflict theorists take the position that the group in power (the **capitalist class**) imposes its definitions of deviance on other groups (the **working class** and the **marginal working class**). From the conflict perspective, the law is an instrument of oppression used to maintain the power and privilege of the few over the many. The marginal working class has little income, is desperate, and commits highly visible property crimes. The ruling class directs the **criminal justice system**, using it to punish the crimes of the poor while diverting its own criminal activities away from this punitive system. Pp. 144–145.

■ Reactions to Deviance

What are common reactions to deviance in the United States?

In following a "get-tough" policy, the United States has imprisoned millions of people. African Americans comprise a disproportionate percentage of U.S. prisoners. In line with conflict theory, as groups gain political power, their views are reflected in the criminal code. Hate crime legislation was considered in this context. Pp. 145–148.

How does society medicalize deviance?

The medical profession has attempted to **medicalize** many forms of deviance, claiming that they represent mental illnesses. Thomas Szasz disagrees, claiming that they are problem behaviors, not mental illnesses. Research on homeless people illustrates how problems in living can lead to bizarre behavior and thinking. Pp. 148–150.

Where can I read more on this topic?

Suggested readings for this chapter are listed on page SR-4.

YOUR INTERACTIVE COMPANION WEB SITE

Your Interactive Companion Web Site includes practice tests, with feedback, and online learning activities with video, audio, and Weblinks. Your access code for this Web site is provided with this text.

GLOSSARY

capitalist class the wealthy who own the means of production and buy the labor of the working class (p. 145)

control theory the idea that two control systems—inner and outer controls—work against our tendencies to deviate (p. 135)

crime the violation of norms written into law (p. 130)

criminal justice system the system of police, courts, and prisons set up to deal with people who are accused of having committed a crime (p. 144)

cultural goals the legitimate objectives held out to the members of a society (p. 140)

deviance the violation of rules or norms (p. 130)

differential association Edwin Sutherland's term to indicate that associating with some groups results in learning an "excess of definitions" of deviance (attitudes favorable to committing deviant acts), and, by extension, in a greater likelihood that their members will become deviant (p. 134)

genetic predisposition inborn tendencies (p. 133)

hate crime a crime with more severe penalties attached because it is motivated by hatred (dislike, animosity) of someone's race-ethnicity, religon, sexual orientation, or disability (p. 148)

illegitimate opportunity structure opportunities for crimes that are woven into the texture of life (p. 141)

institutionalized means approved ways of reaching cultural goals (p. 140)

labeling theory the view, developed by symbolic interactionists, that the labels people are given affect their own and others' perceptions of them, thus channeling their behavior either into deviance or into conformity (p. 136)

marginal working class the most desperate members of the working class, who have few skills, have little job security, and are often unemployed (p. 145)

medicalization of deviance to make some deviance a medical matter, a symptom of some underlying illness that needs to be treated by physicians (p. 148)

negative sanction an expression of disapproval for breaking a norm; ranging from a mild, informal reaction such as a frown to a formal prison sentence or even capital punishment (p. 132)

personality disorders as a theory of deviance, the view that a personality disturbance of some sort causes an individual to violate social norms (p. 133)

positive sanction a reward or positive reaction for following norms, ranging from a smile to a prize (p. 132)

recidivism rate percent of people who are rearrested (p. 147)

social control a group's formal and informal means of enforcing its norms (p. 132)

social order a group's customary social arrangements (p. 131)

stigma "blemishes" that discredit a person's claim to a "normal" identity (p. 130)

strain theory Robert Merton's term for the strain engendered when a society socializes large numbers of people to desire a cultural goal (such as success) but withholds from many the approved means to reach that goal; one adaptation to the strain is deviance, including crime, the choice of an innovative means (one outside the approved system) to attain the cultural goal (p. 140)

street crime crimes such as mugging, rape, and burglary (p. 133)

techniques of neutralization ways of thinking or rationalizing that help people deflect society's norms (p. 137)

white-collar crime Edwin Sutherland's term for crimes committed by people of respectable and high social status in the course of their occupations (p. 142)

working class people who sell their labor to the capitalist class (p. 145)

Chapter 7

Senaka Senanayake, Tea Pickers, 20th century

Social Stratification in Global Perspective

Let's contrast two "average" families. For Getu Mulleta, 33, and his wife, Zenebu, 28, of rural Ethiopia, life is a constant struggle to keep themselves and their seven children from starving. They live in a 320-square-foot manure-plastered hut with no electricity, gas, or running water. They have a radio, but the battery is dead. Surviving on $130 a year, the family farms teff, a cereal grain.

The Mulletas' poverty is not due to a lack of hard work. Getu works about 80 hours a week, while Zenebu puts in even more hours. "Housework" for Zenebu includes fetching water, making fuel pellets out of cow dung for the open fire over which she cooks the family's food, and cleaning animal stables. Like other Ethiopian women, she eats after the men.

The Mulletas' most valuable possession is their oxen. Their wishes for the future: more animals, better seed, and a second set of clothing.

In Ethiopia, the average male can expect to live to 48, the average female to 50.

. . .

Springfield, Illinois, is home to the Kellys—Rick, 36, Patti, 34, Julie, 10, and Michael, 7. The Kellys live in a four-bedroom, 2,100-square-foot, carpeted ranch-style house, with central heating and air conditioning, a basement, and a two-car garage. Their home is equipped with a refrigerator, washing machine, clothes dryer, dishwasher, garbage disposal, vacuum cleaner,

153

food processor, microwave, and toaster. They also own three radios, two stereos, a CD player, four telephones (one cellular), two color televisions, a camcorder, VCR, tape recorder, Gameboy, Nintendo, and a computer and printer, not to mention two blow dryers, an answering machine, a blender, an electric can opener, and an electric toothbrush. This doesn't count the stereo-radio-CD players in their pickup and car.

Rick works 40 hours a week as a cable splicer for the local telephone company. Patti teaches school part-time. Together they make $44,568, plus benefits. The Kellys can choose from among dozens of superstocked supermarkets. They spend $4,101 for food they eat at home, and another $2,362 eating out, a total of 15 percent of their annual income.

On the Kellys' wish list are a new SUV, a 20-gigabyte computer, a fax machine, a scanner, a Palm Pilot, a boat, a camping trailer, an ATV, and, oh yes, further down the road, a vacation cabin.

In the United States, the average male can expect to live to 73, the average female to 80. ■

Sources: Menzel 1994; Population Reference Bureau, 1995; *Statistical Abstract* 1999:Tables 127, 739, 749.

An Overview of Social Stratification

Some of the world's nations are wealthy, others poor, and some in between. This layering of nations, and of groups of people within a nation, is called *social stratification.* Social stratification is one of the most significant topics we discuss in this book, for it affects our life chances—as you saw in the opening vignette, from our access to material possessions to the age at which we die.

Social stratification even affects the way we think about life. If you had been born into the Ethiopian family, for example, you would be illiterate and would expect your children to be the same. You also would expect hunger to be a part of life and would not be too surprised when people die young. To be born into the U.S. family, however, would give you quite a different picture of the world.

"Worlds Apart" could be the title for these photos, which illustrate how life chances depend on global stratification. On the left is the Mulleta family of Ethiopia, featured in the opening vignette, standing in front of their home with all their material possessions. On the right is the Skeen family of Texas, surrounded by their possessions.

Social stratification is a system in which groups of people are divided into layers according to their relative power, property, and prestige. It is important to emphasize that social stratification does not refer to individuals. It is a *way of ranking large groups of people into a hierarchy according to their relative privileges.*

It also is important to note that *every society stratifies its members.* Some societies have greater inequality than others, but social stratification is universal. In addition, in every society of the world, *gender* is a basis for stratifying people. On the basis of their gender, people are either allowed or denied access to the good things offered by their society.

Let's consider three major systems of social stratification: slavery, caste, and class.

Slavery

Slavery, whose essential characteristic is *ownership of some people by others,* has been common in world history. The Old Testament even lays out rules for how the Israelites should treat their slaves. The Romans also had slaves, as did the Africans and the Greeks. Slavery was least common among nomads, especially hunters and gatherers, and most common in agricultural societies (Landtman 1938/1968). As we examine the major causes and conditions of slavery, you will see how remarkably slavery has varied around the world.

Causes of Slavery Contrary to popular assumption, slavery was not usually based on racism, but on one of three other factors. The first was debt. In some cultures, an individual who could not pay a debt could be enslaved by the creditor. The second was crime. Instead of being killed, a murderer or thief might be enslaved by the family of the victim as compensation for their loss. The third was war and conquest. When one group of people conquered another, they often enslaved some of the vanquished (Starna and Watkins 1991). Historian Gerda Lerner (1986) notes that the first people who were enslaved through warfare were women. When premodern men raided a village or camp, they killed the men, raped the women, and then brought the women back as slaves. The women were valued for sexual purposes, for reproduction, and for their labor.

Roughly twenty-five hundred years ago, when Greece was but a collection of city-states, slavery was common. A city that became powerful and conquered another city would enslave some of the vanquished. Both slaves and slaveholders were Greek. Similarly, when Rome became the supreme power of the Mediterranean area about two thousand years ago, following the custom of the time, the Romans enslaved some of the Greeks they had con-

quered. More educated than their conquerors, some of these slaves served as tutors in Roman homes. Slavery, then, was a sign of defeat in battle, of crime, or of debt, not the sign of some presumed inferiority.

Conditions of Slavery The conditions of slavery have varied widely around the world. *In some cases, slavery was temporary.* Slaves of the Israelites were set free in the year of jubilee, which occurred every fifty years. Roman slaves ordinarily had the right to buy themselves out of slavery. They knew what their purchase price was, and some were able to meet this price by striking a bargain with their owner and selling their services to others. In most instances, however, slavery was a lifelong condition. Some criminals, for example, became slaves when they were given life sentences as oarsmen on Roman war ships. There they served until death, which often came quickly to those in this exhausting service.

This little Pakastani boy does backbreaking work each day in the brick kilns in the village of Batapur. He is a bonded laborer, a status that is close to that of slave. He cannot quit work, for, like his family, he must work to pay off debt that passes from generation to generation.

Slavery was not necessarily inheritable. In most places, the children of slaves were automatically slaves themselves. But in some instances, the child of a slave who served a rich family might even be adopted by that family, becoming an heir who bore the family name along with the other sons or daughters of the household. In ancient Mexico, the children of slaves were always free (Landtman 1938/1968:271).

Slaves were not necessarily powerless and poor. In almost all instances, slaves owned no property and had no power. Among some groups, however, slaves could accumulate property and even rise to high positions in the community. Occasionally, a slave might even become wealthy, loan money to the master, and, while still a slave, own slaves himself or herself (Landtman 1938/1968). This, however, was rare.

Slavery in the New World With a growing need for labor, some colonists tried to enslave Indians. This attempt, however, failed miserably. One reason was that when Indians escaped they knew how to survive in the wilderness and were able to make their way back to their tribe. The colonists then turned to Africans, who were being brought to North and South America by the Dutch, English, Portuguese, and Spanish.

Because slavery has a broad range of causes, some analysts conclude that racism didn't lead to slavery, but, rather, slavery led to racism. Finding it profitable to make people slaves for life, U.S. slave owners developed an **ideology**, beliefs that justify social arrangements. They developed the view that the slaves were inferior. Some even said that they were not fully human. In short, the colonists developed elaborate justifications for slavery, built on the presumed superiority of their own race.

To make slavery even more profitable, slave states passed laws that made slavery *inheritable;* that is, the babies born to slaves became the property of the slave owners (Stampp 1956). These children could be sold, bartered, or traded. To strengthen their control, slave states passed laws making it illegal for slaves to hold meetings or to be away from the master's premises without carrying a pass (Lerner 1972). As sociologist W. E. B. Du Bois (1935/1966:12) noted, "gradually the entire white South became an armed camp to keep Negroes in slavery and to kill the black rebel."

Patterns of legal discrimination did not end after the Civil War. For example, until 1954 the states operated two separate school systems. Even until the 1950s, in order to keep the races from "mixing," it was illegal in Mississippi for a white and an African American to sit together on the same seat of a car! The reason there was no outright ban on blacks and whites being in the same car was to allow for African American chauffeurs.

Slavery Today Slavery has again reared its ugly head, this time in Sudan, Mauritania, and Benin (Horwitz 1989; Liben 1995; Hentoff 1998; Jacobs 1999). This region has a long history of slavery, and it was not until 1980 that slavery was officially abolished in Mauritania, and not until 1987 in Sudan (Ayittey 1998). Although officially abolished, slavery continues. Enslavement of the Dinka tribe in southern Sudan is the topic of the Mass Media box on the next page.

Caste

The second system of social stratification is caste. In a **caste system**, status is determined by birth and is lifelong. Someone born into a low-status group will always have low status, no matter how much that person may accomplish in life. In sociological terms, the basis of a caste system is ascribed status. Achieved status cannot change an individual's place in this system.

Societies with this form of stratification try to make certain that the boundaries between castes remain firm. They practice **endogamy**, marriage within their own group, and prohibit intermarriage. To reduce contact between castes, they even develop elaborate rules about *ritual pollution,* teaching that contact with inferior castes contaminates the superior caste.

India's Religious Castes India provides the best example of a caste system. Based not on race but on religion, India's caste system has existed for almost three thousand years (Chandra 1993a, 1993b). India's four main castes, or *varnas,* are depicted in Table 7.1. The

Table 7.1	INDIA'S CASTE SYSTEM
Caste	**Occupation**
Brahman	Priests or scholars
Kshatriya	Nobles and warriors
Vaishya	Merchants and skilled artisans
Shudra	Common laborers
Harijan	The outcastes; degrading labor

Mass Media in *Social Life*

WHAT PRICE FREEDOM? SLAVERY TODAY

Children of the Dinka tribe in rural Sudan don't go to school. They work. Their families depend on them to tend the cattle that are so important to their way of life.

On the morning of the raid, ten-year-old Adhieu had been watching the cattle. "We were very happy because we would soon leave the cattle camps and return home to our parents. But in the morning, there was shooting. There was yelling and crying everywhere. My uncle grabbed me by the hand, and we ran. We swam across the river. I saw some children drowning. We hid behind a rock.

By morning's end, 500 children were either dead or enslaved. Their attackers were their fellow countrymen—Arabs from northern Sudan. The children who were captured were forced to march hundreds of miles north. Some escaped on the way. Others tried to—and were shot (Akol 1998).

Thousands—maybe tens of thousands—of Dinkas have been killed or enslaved since civil war broke out in the Sudan in the mid 1980s. Yet the Arab-led government—the powerful National Islamic Front—piously insists that slavery does not exist. Such claims, it says, are an invention of foreign politicians, Christian humanitarians, and hostile foreign media (Akol 1998). But there are too many witnesses, too much documentation by human rights groups. There also are devastating accounts by journalists: Public

television (PBS) has even run film footage of captive children in chains. And then there are the slaves who managed to escape, who recount their ordeal in horrifying detail. The reasonable question is not whether slavery exists in the Sudan, but to what extent the Sudanese government supports this trafficking in human bodies.

In this photo, a representative of the Liason Agency Network (on the left) is buying the freedom of the Sudanese slaves (in the background).

The United States bombed Kosovo into submission for its crimes against humanity, yet it has remained silent in the face of this outrage. A cynic might say that Kosovo was located at a politically strategic spot in Europe, whereas the Sudan occupies an area of Africa in which these powers currently have little interest. A cynic might add that these powers fear Arab retaliation, which might take the form of terrorism and oil embargoes. A cynic might also suggest that outrages against black

Africans are not as significant to the U.S. and European powers as those against white Europeans.

Appalled by the lack of response on the part of the world's most powerful governments, private groups have been spurred into action Foremost among then is Christian Solidarity International (CSI), based in Zurich, Switzerland. The technique this human rights group uses is controversial. Arab "retrievers" go to northern Sudan, where they either buy or abduct slaves. Walking by night and hiding by day, they elude security forces and bring the slaves south. There CSI pays the retrievers $50 per slave (Mabry 1999).

As CBS news cameras rolled, the rescuer paid the slave trader $50,000 in Sudanese pounds. At $50 per person, the bundle of bills was enough to free 1,000 slaves. The liberated slaves, mostly women and children, were then free to return to their villages (Jacobs 1999).

CSI has been severely criticized. Critics claim that buying slaves, even to free them, encourages slavery: This money provides motivation to enslave people in order to turn around and sell them. Fifty dollars is a lot of money in Sudan, where the average income for an entire year is $180.

That is a bogus argument, replies CSI. What is intolerable is to leave women and children in slavery where they are deprived of their freedom and families, and raped and beaten by brutal masters.

(continued)

WHAT PRICE FREEDOM? SLAVERY TODAY *(continued)*

CSI claims to have purchased the freedom of about 10,000 slaves. No one knows how many people remain in slavery. ■

For Your Consideration

What do you think about buying the freedom of slaves? Can you suggest a workable alternative? Why do you think the U.S.

government has remained inactive about this issue for so long, when it invades other countries for human rights abuses? Do you think that, perhaps, its excursions into such places as Haiti and Kosovo were pretexts for political motives, that they had little to do with human rights? If not, why the silence in the face of slavery?

The media coverage of this issue has motivated many Americans to become active in freeing slaves. High schools nationwide—and even some grade schools—are raising money to participate in slave buy-back programs (Schaefer 1999). If you were a school principal, would you encourage this practice? Why or why not?

---

four main castes are subdivided into thousands of specialized subcastes, or *jati,* with each *jati* having an occupational specialty. For example, knife sharpening is done only by members of a particular subcaste.

The lowest group listed on Table 7.1, the Harijan, is actually so low that it is beneath the caste system altogether. The Harijans, along with some of the Shudras, make up India's "untouchables." If they touch someone of a higher caste, that person becomes unclean. Even the shadow of an untouchable can contaminate. Early morning and late afternoons are especially risky, for the long shadows of these periods pose a danger to everyone higher up the caste system. Consequently, Harijans are not allowed in some villages during these times. Anyone who becomes contaminated must follow *ablution,* or washing rituals, to restore purity (Lannoy 1975).

Although the Indian government formally abolished the caste system in 1949, centuries-old practices cannot be so easily eliminated, and the caste system remains part of everyday life in India. The ceremonies people follow at births, marriages, and deaths, for example, are dictated by caste (Chandra 1993a). Entrenched in power, the upper castes resist the upward mobility of the untouchables, sometimes even through violence (Crosette 1996; Filkins 1997).

A U.S. Racial Caste System Before leaving the subject of caste, we should note that when slavery ended in the United States it was replaced by a *racial caste system,* in which everyone was marked for life at birth (Berger 1963/2001). In this system, *all* whites, no matter if they were poor and uneducated, considered themselves to have a higher status than *all* African Americans. When any white met any African American on a southern sidewalk, for example, the African American had to

move aside. As in India, the upper caste, fearing pollution from the lower caste, prohibited intermarriage and insisted on separate schools, hotels, restaurants, and even toilets and drinking fountains in public facilities.

Class

As we have seen, stratification systems based on slavery and caste are rigid. The lines marking the divisions between people are so firm that there is little or no movement from one group to another. A **class system,** in contrast, is much more open, for it is based primarily on money or material possessions. It, too, begins at birth, when individuals are ascribed the status of their parents, but, unlike in the slavery and caste systems, one's social class changes due to what one achieves (or fails to achieve) in life. In addition, no laws specify people's occupations on the basis of birth or prohibit marriage between the classes.

A major characteristic of the class system, then, is its relatively fluid boundaries. A class system allows **social mobility,** that is, movement up or down the class ladder. The potential for improving one's social circumstances, or class, is one of the major forces that drives people to go far in school and to work hard. In the extreme, the family background that an individual inherits at birth may bring such deprivation that the child has little chance of climbing very far—or it may provide such privilege that it is almost impossible for the individual to fall down the class ladder.

Global Stratification and the Status of Females

Gender cuts across slavery, caste, and class. No matter what a society's system of social stratification, on the

In a caste system, status is determined by birth and is lifelong. At birth, these women in Bagepalli, India, received not only membership in a lower caste but also, because of their gender, a predetermined position in that caste and in the division of labor. They are carrying firewood that took the entire day to gather.

basis of their gender people are sorted into categories and given different access to the good things available in their society. Apparently, these distinctions always favor males. It is remarkable, for example, that in *every* society of the world men's earnings are higher than women's. Control of females by males is even more evident when we consider child brides, child prostitution, and female circumcision. (Also see the box in Chapter 10 on page 244.) That most of the world's illiterate are females drives home the relative positions of males and females. Of the 900 million adults who are illiterate, two-thirds are women; of the 13 million schoolage children who receive no education, two-thirds are girls (Browne 1995). Because gender is so significant for what happens to us in life, we shall focus on it more closely in Chapter 10.

WHAT DETERMINES SOCIAL CLASS?

In the early days of sociology, a disagreement arose about the meaning of social class in industrialized societies. Let's compare how Marx and Weber saw the matter.

Karl Marx: The Means of Production

As discussed in Chapter 1, the breakup of the feudal system displaced many peasants from their traditional lands and occupations. Fleeing to cities, they competed for the few available jobs. Offered only a pittance for their labor, they dressed in rags, went hungry, and slept under bridges and in shacks. In contrast, the factory owners built mansions, hired servants, and lived in the lap of luxury. Seeing this great disparity between owners and workers, Marx concluded that social class depends on a single factor—the **means of production**—the tools, factories, land, and investment capital used to produce wealth (Marx 1844/1964; Marx and Engels 1848/1967).

Marx argued that the distinctions people often make among themselves—such as clothing, speech, education, paycheck, or, today, even the type of car they drive—are superficial matters. These things camouflage the only dividing line that counts. Modern society, said Marx, is made up of just two classes of people: the **bourgeoisie,** those who own the means of production, and the **proletariat,** those who work for the owners. In short, people's relationship to the means of production determines their social class.

Marx did recognize that other groups were part of industrial society: farmers and peasants; a *lumpenproletariat* (marginal people such as beggars, vagrants, and criminals); and a middle group of self-employed professionals. Marx did not consider these groups social classes, however, for they lacked **class consciousness**—a shared identity based on their position in the means of production. They did not see themselves

Taken at the end of the 1800s, these photos illustrate the contrasting worlds of social classes produced by capitalism. The sleeping boys shown in this classic 1890 photo by Jacob Riis sold newspapers in London. They did not go to school, and they had no home. The children on the right, Cornelius and Gladys Vanderbilt, are shown in front of their parents' estate. They went to school and did not work. You can see how the life situations illustrated in these photos would have produced different orientations to life—and, therefore, politics, ideas about marriage, values, and so on—the stuff of which life is made.

as exploited workers whose plight could be solved by collective action. Consequently, Marx thought of these groups as insignificant in the coming workers' revolution, which would overthrow capitalism.

The capitalists will grow even wealthier, Marx said, and the hostilities will increase. When workers realize that capitalists are the source of their oppression, they will unite and throw off the chains of their oppressors. In a bloody revolution, they will seize the means of production and usher in a classless society, where no longer will the few grow rich at the expense of the many. What holds back the workers' unity and their revolution is **false consciousness**, workers mistakenly thinking of themselves as capitalists. For example, workers with a few dollars in the bank may forget that they are workers and instead see themselves as investors, or as entrepreneurs who are about to launch a successful business.

The only distinction worth mentioning, then, is whether a person is an owner or a worker. This decides everything else, Marx stressed, for property determines

people's lifestyles, shapes their ideas, and establishes their relationships with one another.

Max Weber: Property, Prestige, and Power

Max Weber (1864–1920) became an outspoken critic of Marx. Weber argued that property is only part of the picture. **Social class,** he said, is made up of three components—property, prestige, and power (Gerth and Mills 1958; Weber 1922/1968). Some call these the three *P*'s of social class. (Although Weber used the terms *class, status,* and *power,* some sociologists find *property, prestige,* and *power* to be clearer terms. To make them even clearer, you may wish to substitute *wealth* for *property.*)

Property (or wealth), said Weber, is certainly significant in determining a person's standing in society. On that he agreed with Marx. But, added Weber, ownership is not the only significant aspect of property. For example, some powerful people, such as managers of corporations, *control* the means of production although they do not *own* them. If managers can control property for their own benefit—awarding themselves huge bonuses and magnificent perks—it makes no practical difference that they do not own the property they so generously use for their own benefit.

Prestige, the second element in Weber's analysis, is often derived from property, for people tend to look up to the wealthy. Prestige, however, can be based on other factors. Olympic gold medalists, for example, may not own property, yet they have high prestige. Some are even able to exchange their prestige for property—such as those who are paid a small fortune to claim that they start their day with "the breakfast of champions." In other words, property and prestige are not one-way streets: Although property can bring prestige, prestige can also bring property.

Power, the third element of social class, is the ability to control others, even over their objections. Weber agreed with Marx that property is a major source of power, but he added that it is not the only source. For example, prestige can be turned into power. Perhaps the best example is Ronald Reagan, an actor who became president of the most powerful country in the world. Figure 7.1 shows how property, prestige, and power are interrelated.

■ **In Sum**　For Marx, social class was based solely on a person's relationship to the means of production. One is either a member of the bourgeoisie or the proletariat. Weber argued that social class is a combination of property, prestige, and power.

WHY IS SOCIAL STRATIFICATION UNIVERSAL?

What is it about social life that makes all societies stratified? We shall first consider the explanation proposed by functionalists, which has aroused much controversy in sociology, then explanations proposed by conflict theorists.

The Functionalist Perspective: Motivating Qualified People

Functionalists take the position that the patterns of behavior that characterize a society exist because they are functional for that society. Because social inequality is universal, inequality must help societies survive. But how does it do so?

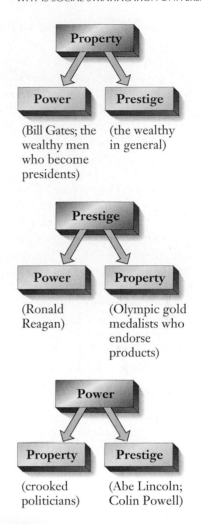

WEBER'S THREE COMPONENTS OF SOCIAL CLASS: INTERRELATIONSHIPS AMONG THEM

*Colin Powell illustrates the circularity of these components. Powell's power as Chairman of the Joint Chiefs of Staff led to prestige. Powell's prestige, in turn, led to power when he was called from retirement to serve as Secretary of State in the George W. Bush administration.

Davis and Moore's Explanation　Two functionalists, Kingsley Davis and Wilbert Moore (1945, 1953), wrestled with this question. They concluded that the stratification of society is inevitable because:

1. Society must make certain that its positions are filled.
2. Some positions are more important than others.
3. The more important positions must be filled by the more qualified people.
4. To motivate the more qualified people to fill these positions, society must offer them greater rewards.

Let's look at two examples to flesh out this functionalist argument. The position of college president is more important than that of student because the president's decisions affect many more people. Any mistakes he or she makes carry implications for a large number of people, including many students. The same is true for the general of an army compared with a private in the army. The decisions of the general affect careers, paychecks, and may even determine life and death.

Positions with greater responsibility also require greater accountability. College presidents and army generals are accountable—to boards of trustees and to the leader of a country, respectively—for how they perform. How can society motivate highly qualified people to enter its higher-pressure positions? What keeps people from avoiding them and seeking only less demanding jobs?

The answer, said Davis and Moore, is that society offers greater rewards for its more responsible, demanding, and accountable positions. If these jobs didn't offer greater prestige, salaries, and benefits, why would anyone strive for them? Thus, a salary of $2 million, country club membership, a private jet, and a chauffeured limousine may be necessary in order to get the most highly qualified people to compete with one another for some positions, while a $30,000 salary without fringe benefits is enough to get hundreds of less qualified people to compete for less demanding positions. It is the same with positions that require rigorous training. If you can get the same pay with a high school diploma, why suffer through the many tests and term papers that college requires?

Tumin's Critique of Davis and Moore Note that Davis and Moore tried to explain *why* social stratification is universal; they were not trying to *justify* social inequality. Nevertheless, their view makes many sociologists uncomfortable, for they see it as coming close to justifying the inequalities in society.

Melvin Tumin (1953) was the first sociologist to point out what he saw as major flaws in the functionalist position. Here are three of his arguments.

First, the functionalists say that the most important positions bring the higher rewards, but how do we know which are the most important positions? You can't measure importance by a position's rewards, for that argument is circular. You must have an independent way to measure importance. For example, is a surgeon really more important to society than a garbage collector, since the garbage collector helps to prevent contagious diseases?

Second, if stratification worked as Davis and Moore described it, society would be a **meritocracy;** that is, all positions would be awarded on the basis of merit. Ability, then, should predict who goes to college. Instead, the best predictor of college entrance is family income—the more a family earns, the more likely their children are to go to college. Similarly, while some people do get ahead through ability and hard work, others simply inherit wealth and the opportunities that go with it. Moreover, a stratification system that places most men above most women does not live up to the argument that talent and ability are the bases for holding important positions. In short, factors far beyond merit give people their relative positions in society.

Third, if social stratification is so functional, it ought to benefit almost everyone. Social stratification, however, is *dysfunctional* for many. Think of the people who could have made valuable contributions to society had they not been born in slums and had to drop out of school and take menial jobs to help support the family—or the many who, born female, are assigned "women's work," ensuring that they do not maximize their mental abilities.

The Conflict Perspective: Class Conflict and Scarce Resources

Conflict theorists don't just criticize details of the functionalist perspective. Rather, they say its basic premise is wrong. Conflict theorists stress that conflict, not function, is the basis of social stratification. They point out that in every society, groups struggle with one another to gain a larger share of the society's limited resources. Whenever some group gains power, it uses that power to extract what it can from the groups beneath it. It also uses the social institutions to keep other groups weak and itself in power.

Mosca's Argument Italian sociologist Gaetano Mosca argued that every society will be stratified by power. This is inevitable, he said in an 1896 book entitled *The Ruling Class,* because:

1. No society can exist unless it is organized. This requires leadership of some sort in order to coordinate people's actions and get society's work done.

2. Leadership (or political organization) means inequalities of power. Some people take leadership positions, while others follow.

3. Human nature is self-centered. Therefore, people in power will use their positions to seize greater rewards for themselves.

There is no way around these facts of life, added Mosca. They make social stratification inevitable, and every society will stratify itself along lines of power.

Marx's Argument If he were alive to hear the functionalist argument, Karl Marx would be enraged. From his point of view, the people in power are not there because of superior traits, as the functionalists would have us believe. That view is simply an ideology the elite use to justify their being at the top—and to seduce the oppressed into believing that their welfare depends on keeping society stable. Human history is the history of class struggle, of those in power using society's resources to benefit themselves and to oppress those beneath them—and of oppressed groups trying to overcome their domination.

Marx predicted that the workers would revolt. The day will come, he said, when class consciousness will overcome ideology. When their eyes are opened, the workers will overthrow their oppressors. At first, this struggle for control of the means of production may be covert, showing up as work slowdowns or industrial sabotage. Ultimately, however, it will break out into open resistance. The struggle will be difficult, for the bourgeoisie control the police, the military, and even education (where they implant false consciousness in the workers' children).

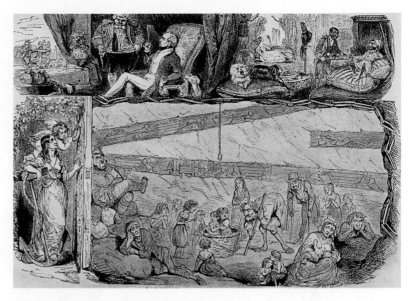

This cartoon of political protest appeared in London newspapers in 1843. It illustrates the severe exploitation of labor that occurred after the Estate System of social stratification broke down and peasants were forced to leave the land and find work elsewhere. Depicted here are the extremes of early capitalism. Scenes such as these stimulated Marx's analysis of social class.

Current Modifications of Conflict Theory Some sociologists have refocused conflict theory. C. Wright Mills (1956), Ralf Dahrendorf (1959), Randall Collins (1974, 1988), and James Schellenberg (1996), for example, stress how groups *within the same class* compete for scarce resources. They struggle for power, wealth, education, housing, and even prestige—whatever benefits society has to offer. The result is conflict not only between labor unions and corporations, but also between the young and the old, women and men, and racial and ethnic groups. Unlike functionalists, then, conflict theorists hold that just beneath the surface of what may appear to be a tranquil society lies conflict that is barely held in check.

Lenski's Synthesis

Despite vast differences between the functionalist and conflict views, some analysts have tried to synthesize them. Sociologist Gerhard Lenski (1966), for example, used the existence of surpluses as a basis for reconciling the two views. The functionalists are right, he said,

when it comes to groups that do not accumulate wealth. In these groups, such as hunting and gathering societies, the limited resources are given as rewards to people who take on important responsibilities. For societies with a surplus of resources, however, the conflict theorists are right. Humans pursue self-interest, and as they struggle to control their society's surpluses, a small elite emerges. As the elite protects its position, social inequality is built into the society. The result is a full-blown system of social stratification.

HOW DO ELITES MAINTAIN STRATIFICATION?

Suppose that you are part of the ruling elite of your society. What can you do to make sure that you don't lose your privileged position? The key lies in controlling ideas and information, in social networks, and, in the least effective means of all, the use of force.

Ideology Versus Force

Medieval Europe provides a good example of the power of ideology. At that time, land was the primary source of wealth. The land was owned by only the nobility and the church. Almost everyone was a peasant who worked for these powerful landowners. The peasants farmed the land, took care of the livestock, and built the roads and bridges. Each year, they had to turn over a designated portion of their crops to their feudal lord. Year after year, for centuries, they did so. Why?

Controlling Ideas Why didn't the peasants rebel and take over the land themselves? There were many reasons, not the least of which was that the nobility and church controlled the army. Coercion, however, only goes so far, for it breeds hostility and nourishes rebellion. How much more effective it is to get the masses to *want* to do what the ruling elite desires. This is where *ideology* (beliefs that justify the way things are) comes into play, and the nobility and clergy used it to great effect. They developed an ideology known as the **divine right of kings**—the idea that the king's authority comes directly from God—which can be traced back several thousand years to the Old Testament. The king delegates authority to nobles, who as God's representatives must be obeyed. To disobey is a sin against God; to rebel means physical punishment on earth and eternal suffering in hell.

To control people's ideas, then, can be remarkably more effective than brute force. Although this particular ideology no longer governs peoples' minds today, the elite in every society develops ideologies to justify its position at the top. For example, around the world schools teach that their country's form of government—*whatever form of government that may be*—is the best. Religious leaders teach that we owe obedience to authority, that laws are to be obeyed. To the degree that their ideologies are accepted by the masses, the elite remain securely in power.

Controlling Information To maintain their positions of power, elites also try to control information. In dictatorships this is accomplished through the threat of force, for dictators can—and do—imprison editors and reporters for printing critical reports. Some do so just for publishing information that is unflattering to them (Timerman 1981). Lacking such power, the ruling elites of democracies manipulate the media through the selective release of information. They attempt to withhold information "in the interest of national security." Just as coercion has its limits, so does the control of information—especially with the new technology of satellite communications, e-mail, and the Internet, which pay no respect to international borders.

Technology The new technology is a two-edged sword. Just as it makes it more difficult for the elite

The *divine right of kings* was an ideology that made the king God's direct representative on earth—to administer justice and punish evildoers. This theological-political concept was supported by the Roman Catholic Church, whose representatives crowned the king. Depicted here is Charlemagne, who, crowned by Pope Leo III in 800, established what is known as the Holy Roman Empire. This painting is by Jean Victor Schnetz.

to control information, it also provides them powerful monitoring devices. From "hot telephones"—taps that turn a telephone into a microphone even when it is off the hook—to machines that can read the entire contents of a computer without leaving a trace, these devices help the elite monitor citizens' activities without their being aware that they are being observed. Dictatorships have few checks on how they employ such technology, but in democracies, checks and balances, such as constitutional rights and requiring court orders for search and seizure, at least partially curb their use.

Social Networks Also crucial for maintaining stratification are *social networks*—the friendships, business contacts, and other associations that link people to one another. As discussed in Chapter 5, social networks supply valuable information and tend to perpetuate social inequality. Sociologist William Domhoff (1990, 1998) has documented how members of the elite move in a circle of power that multiplies their opportunities. Contacts with people of similar backgrounds, interests, and goals help the elite to pass privileges from one generation to the next. In contrast, the social networks of the poor perpetuate poverty and powerlessness.

COMPARATIVE SOCIAL STRATIFICATION

Now that we have examined systems of social stratification, considered why stratification is universal, and looked at how elites keep themselves in power, let's compare social stratification in Great Britain and in the former Soviet Union.

Social Stratification in Great Britain

Great Britain is often called England by Americans, but England is only one of the countries that make up the island of Great Britain. The others are Scotland and Wales. In addition, Northern Ireland is part of the United Kingdom of Great Britain and Northern Ireland.

Like other industrialized countries, Great Britain has a class system that can be divided into a lower, middle, and upper class. Great Britain's population is about evenly divided between the middle class and the lower (or working) class. A tiny upper class, perhaps 1 percent of the population, is wealthy, powerful, and highly educated.

Compared with Americans, the British are very class conscious. Like Americans, they recognize class distinctions on the basis of the type of car a person drives, or the stores a person patronizes. But the most striking characteristics of the British class system are language and education. Differences in speech have a powerful impact on British life. Accent almost always betrays class, and as soon as someone speaks, the listener is aware of that person's class—and treats him or her accordingly (Sullivan 1998).

Education is the primary way by which the British perpetuate their class system from one generation to the next. Almost all children go to neighborhood schools, but the children of Great Britain's privileged 5 percent—who own *half* the nation's wealth—attend exclusive private boarding schools (known as "public" schools). There they are trained in subjects considered "proper" for members of the ruling class. An astounding 50 percent of the students at Oxford and Cambridge, the country's most prestigious universities, come from this 5 percent of the population. To illustrate how powerfully this system of stratified education affects the national life of Great Britain, sociologist Ian Robertson (1987) says,

> [E]ighteen former pupils of the most exclusive of them, Eton, have become prime minister. Imagine the chances of a single American high school producing eighteen presidents!

Social Stratification in the Former Soviet Union

Heeding Karl Marx's call for a classless society, Vladimir Ilyich Lenin (1870–1924) and Leon Trotsky (1879–1940), led a revolution in Russia. They, and the nations that followed their banner, never claimed to have achieved the ideal of communism, in which all contribute their labor to the common good and receive according to their needs. Instead, they used the term *socialism* to describe the intermediate step between capitalism and communism, in which social classes are abolished but some inequality remains.

To tweak the nose of Uncle Sam, the socialist nations would trumpet their equality and point a finger at glaring inequalities in the United States. They, too, however, were marked by huge disparities in privilege. Their major basis of stratification was membership in the Communist Party. This often was the determining factor in deciding who would gain admission to the better schools or obtain the more desirable jobs. The equally qualified son or daughter of a nonmember would be turned down, for such privileges came with demonstrated loyalty to the Party.

Even the Communist Party was highly stratified. Most members occupied a low level, where they fulfilled such tasks as spying on other workers. For this, they might get easier jobs in the factory or occasional access to special stores to purchase hard-to-find goods. The middle level consisted of bureaucrats who were given better than average access to resources and privileges. At the top level was a small elite: party members who enjoyed not only power but also limousines, imported delicacies, vacation homes, and even servants and hunting lodges. As with other stratification systems around the world, women held lower positions in the Party. This was evident at each year's May Day when the top members of the Party reviewed the latest weapons paraded in Moscow's Red Square. Photos of these events showed only men.

The leaders of the USSR became frustrated as they saw the West thrive. They struggled with a bloated bureaucracy, the inefficiencies of central planning, workers who did the minimum because they could not be fired, and a military so costly that it spent one of every eight of the nation's rubles (*Statistical Abstract* 1993:1432; table dropped in later editions). Their ideology did not call for their citizens to be deprived, and in an attempt to turn things around, the Soviet leadership initiated reforms. They allowed elections to be held in which more than one candidate ran for an office. (Prior to this, voters had a choice of one candidate per office!) They also sold huge chunks of state-owned businesses to the public. Overnight, making investments in order to turn a profit changed from being a crime into a respectable goal.

Russia's transition to capitalism took a bizarre twist. As authority broke down, a powerful Mafia emerged. These criminal groups are headed by gangsters, corrupt government officials, and crooked businessmen. Some have the help of agents of the KGB (Russian secret police). In a ruthless drive for wealth, these groups assassinate bank presidents and other business leaders who refuse to cooperate with them (Bernstein 1994; Goble 1996; Finckenauer and Waring 1999). They now control half of Russia's economy (Foster 1998), and are stashing capital in offshore retreats, especially in watering and wintering spots such as Marbella on Spain's Costa del Sol.

Russia's "wild west" days are bound to disappear as the central government reestablishes its authority. At that time, this group of organized criminals will take its place as part of Russia's new capitalist class.

*G*LOBAL STRATIFICATION: THREE WORLDS

As noted at the beginning of this chapter, just as the people within a nation are stratified by power, prestige, and property, so are the world's nations. Until recently, a simple model consisting of First, Second, and Third Worlds was used to depict global stratification. *First World* referred to the industrialized capitalist nations, *Second World* to the communist nations, and *Third World* to any nation that did not fit into the first two categories. The breakup of the Soviet Union in 1989 made these terms outdated. In addition, although *first, second,* and *third* did not mean "best," "better," and "worst," they sounded like it. An alternative classification some now use—developed, developing, and undeveloped nations—has the same drawback. By calling ourselves "developed," it sounds as though we are mature and the "undeveloped" nations somehow retarded.

Consequently, I have chosen more neutral, descriptive terms: *Most Industrialized, Industrializing,* and *Least Industrialized* nations. We can measure industrialization with no judgment implied as to whether a nation's in-

dustrialization represents "development," ranks it "first"—or is even desirable at all.

The intention is to depict on a global level the three primary dimensions of social stratification: property, power, and prestige. The Most Industrialized Nations have much greater property (wealth), power (they do get their way in international relations), and prestige (they are looked up to as world leaders). The two families sketched in the opening vignette illustrate the far-reaching effects of global stratification.

The Most Industrialized Nations

The Most Industrialized Nations are the United States and Canada in North America; Great Britain, France, Germany, Switzerland, and the other industrialized nations of western Europe; Japan in Asia; and Australia and New Zealand in the area of the world known as Oceania. Although there are variations in their economic systems, these nations are capitalistic. As Table 7.2 shows, although these nations have only 16 percent of the world's people, they have 31 percent of the earth's land. Their wealth is so enormous that even their poor live better and longer lives than do average citizens of the Least Industrialized Nations. The Social Map on pages 168–169 shows the tremendous disparities in income among nations.

The Industrializing Nations

The Industrializing Nations include most of the nations of the former Soviet Union and its former satellites in eastern Europe. As Table 7.2 shows, these nations account for 20 percent of the earth's land and 16 percent of its people.

The dividing lines between the three "worlds" are soft, making it difficult to know how to classify some nations. This is especially the case with the Industrializing Nations. Exactly how much industrialization must a nation have to be in this category? Although soft, these categories do pinpoint essential differences among nations. Most people who live in the Industrializing Nations have much lower incomes and standards of living than those

Table 7.2

DISTRIBUTION OF THE WORLD'S LAND AND POPULATION

	Land	Population
Most Industrialized Nations	31%	16%
Industrializing Nations	20%	16%
Least Industrialized Nations	49%	68%

Sources: Computed from Kurian 1990, 1991, 1992.

who live in the Most Industrialized Nations. Most, however, are better off than those who live in the Least Industrialized Nations. For example, on such measures as access to electricity, indoor plumbing, automobiles, telephones, and even food, citizens of the Industrializing Nations rank lower than those in the Most Industrialized Nations, but higher than those in the Least Industrialized Nations.

The benefits of industrialization are uneven. Large numbers of people in the Industrializing Nations remain illiterate and desperately poor. Conditions can be gruesome, as discussed in the following Thinking Critically section.

Thinking *Critically*

OPEN SEASON: CHILDREN AS PREY

What is childhood like in the Industrializing Nations? The answer depends on who your parents are. If you are the son or daughter of rich parents, childhood can be pleasant—a world filled with luxuries, and even servants. If you are born into poverty, but live in a rural area where there is plenty to eat, life can still be good—although there may be no books, no television, and little education. If you live in a slum, however, life can be horrible—worse even than in the slums of the Most Industrialized Nations. Let's take a glance at what is happening to children in the slums of Brazil.

Not enough food, this you can take for granted—as well as broken homes, alcoholism, drug abuse, and a high crime rate. From your knowledge of slums in the Most Industrialized Nations, you would expect these things. What you may not expect, however, are the brutal conditions in which Brazilian slum *(favela)* children live.

Sociologist Martha Huggins (1993) reports poverty is so extreme that children and adults swarm over garbage dumps to try to find enough decaying food to keep them alive. And you might be surprised to discover that in Brazil the owners of these dumps hire armed guards to keep the poor out—so they can sell the garbage for pig food. And you might be shocked to learn that the Brazilian police and death squads murder about 2,000 children a year. Some associations of shop owners even hire hit men and auction designated victims off to the lowest bidder! The going rate is half a month's salary, figured at the low Brazilian minimum wage.

Life *is* cheap in the poor nations—but death squads for children? To understand this, we must first note that Brazil has a long history of violence. Brazil also has a high rate of poverty, only a tiny middle class, and is controlled by a small group of families who, under a veneer of democracy, make the country's major decisions. Hordes of homeless children, with no schools or jobs, roam the streets. To survive, these street children wash windshields, shine shoes, beg, and steal. These children, part of the "dangerous classes," as they are known, threaten the status quo.

The "respectable" classes see these children as nothing but trouble. They hurt business, for customers feel intimidated when they see a group of begging children clustered in front of stores. Some shoplift; others dare to sell items that place them in competition with the stores. With no effective social institutions to care for these children, one solution is to kill them. As Huggins notes, murder sends a clear message—especially if it is accompanied by ritual torture—gouging out the eyes, ripping open the chest, cutting off the genitals, raping the girls, and burning the victim's body.

Not all life is bad in the Industrializing Nations, but this is about as bad as it gets. ■

For Your Consideration

Do you think there is anything the Most Industrialized Nations can do about this situation? Or is it any of their business? Is it, though unfortunate, just an "internal" affair that is up to the Brazilians to handle as they wish?

Poverty in the Industrializing Nations is so severe that some families survive by picking through garbage. This photo from Rio de Janeiro, Brazil, shows some of the the 600 people whose survival depends on plucking from the city's dump any bit or piece that seems even remotely reusable.

The Most Industrialized Nations

	Nation	Income per Person		Nation	Income per Person
1	Switzerland	$43,060	14	Iceland	$25,000
2	Luxembourg	$41,200	15	Finland	$24,790
3	Japan	$38,160	16	United	
4	Norway	$36,100		Kingdom	$20,870
5	Singapore	$32,810	17	Australia	$20,650
6	United States	$29,080	18	Italy	$20,170
7	Germany	$28,280	19	Canada	$19,640
8	Austria	$27,920	20	Ireland	$17,790
9	Belgium	$26,730	21	Denmark	$16,637
10	France	$26,300	22	Israel	$16,180
11	Sweden	$26,210	23	New Zealand	$15,830
12	Netherlands	$25,830	24	Taiwan	$14,700
13	Hong Kong	$25,200			

The Industrializing Nations

	Nation	Income per Person		Nation	Income per Person
25	Spain	$14,490	37	Brazil	$4,790
26	Greece	$11,640	38	Malaysia	$4,530
27	Portugal	$11,010	39	Hungary	$4,510
28	South Korea	$10,550	40	Mexico	$3,700
29	Slovenia	$9,840	41	Slovakia	$3,680
30	Malta	$9,330	42	Poland	$3,590
31	Argentina	$8,950	43	Venezuela	$3,480
32	Seychelles	$6,910	44	South Africa	$3,210
33	Colombia*	$6,200	45	Turkey	$3,130
34	Uruguay	$6,130	46	Thailand	$2,740
35	Czech Republic	$5,240	47	Russia	$2,680
36	Chile	$4,820			

*Income listed for Colombia is so much greater than previous years that I assume it now includes the country's cocaine industry.

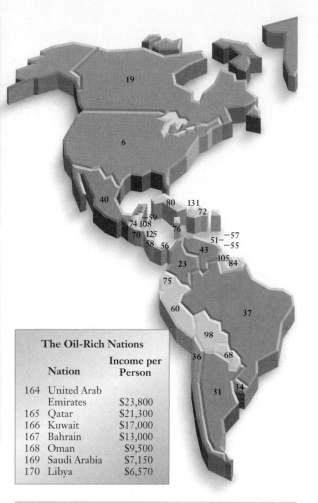

The Oil-Rich Nations

	Nation	Income per Person
164	United Arab Emirates	$23,800
165	Qatar	$21,300
166	Kuwait	$17,000
167	Bahrain	$13,000
168	Oman	$9,500
169	Saudi Arabia	$7,150
170	Libya	$6,570

The Least Industrialized Nations

	Nation	Income per Person		Nation	Income per Person
48	Gabon	$4,120	69	Fed. States of Micronesia	$1,920
49	Croatia	$4,060	70	El Salvador	$1,810
50	Mauritius	$3,870	71	Iran	$1,780
51	Saint Lucia	$3,510	72	Dominacan Republic	$1,750
52	Estonia	$3,360	73	Marshall Islands	$1,610
53	Lebanon	$3,350	74	Guatemala	$1,580
54	Botswana	$3,310	75	Ecuador	$1,570
55	Grenada	$3,140	76	Jamaica	$1,550
56	Panama	$3,080	77	Swaziland	$1,520
57	Dominica	$3,040	78	Jordan	$1,510
58	Costa Rica	$2,680	79	Algeria	$1,500
59	Belize	$2,670	80	Cuba	$1,480
60	Peru	$2,610	81	Romania	$1,410
61	Fiji	$2,460	82	Kazakstan	$1,350
62	Lativa	$2,430	83	Vanuatu	$1,340
63	Lithuania	$2,260	84	Suriname	$1,320
64	Belarus	$2,150	85	Philippines	$1,200
65	Namibia	$2,110	86	Morocco	$1,260
66	Tunisia	$2,110			
67	Iraq	$2,000			
68	Paraguay	$2,000			

Figure 7.2   SOCIAL MAP: GLOBAL STRATIFICATION: INCOME* OF THE WORLD'S NATIONS

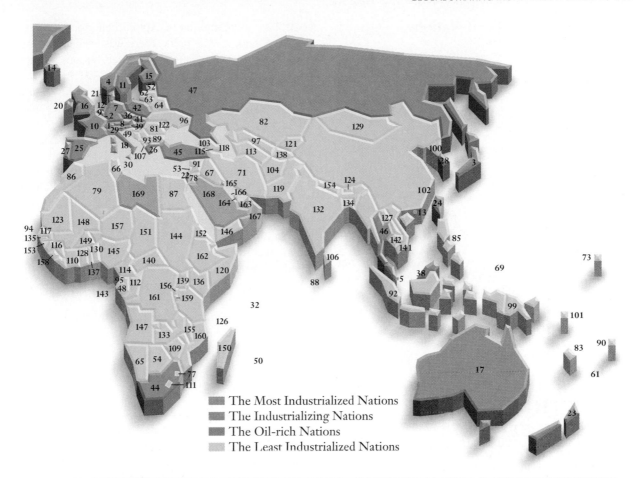

The Most Industrialized Nations
The Industrializing Nations
The Oil-rich Nations
The Least Industrialized Nations

The Least Industrialized Nations

	Nation	Income per Person		Nation	Income per Person		Nation	Income per Person		Nation	Income per Person
87	Egypt	$1,200	104	Afghanistan	$800	125	Nicaragua	$410	144	Sudan	$290
88	Maldives	$1,180	105	Guyana	$800	126	Comoros	$400	145	Nigeria	$280
89	Bulgaria	$1,170	106	Sri Lanka	$800	127	Laos	$400	146	Yemen	$270
90	Western		107	Albania	$760	128	Ghana	$390	147	Angola	$260
	Samoa	$1,140	108	Honduras	$740	129	Mongolia	$390	148	Mali	$260
91	Syria	$1,120	109	Zimbabwe	$720	130	Benin	$380	149	Burkina Faso	$250
92	Indonesia	$1,110	110	Cote d'Ivoire	$710	131	Haiti	$380	150	Madagascar	$250
93	Macedonia	$1,100	111	Lesotho	$680	132	India	$370	151	Chad	$230
94	Cape Verde	$1,090	112	Congo	$670	133	Zambia	$370	152	Eritrea	$230
95	Equatorial		113	Turkmenistan	$640	134	Bangladesh	$360	153	Guinea-Bissau	$230
	Guinea	$1,060	114	Cameroon	$620	135	Gambia	$340	154	Nepal	$220
96	Ukraine	$1,040	115	Armenia	$560	136	Kenya	$340	155	Malawi	$210
97	Uzbekistan	$1,020	116	Guinea	$550	137	Togo	$340	156	Rwanda	$210
98	Bolivia	$970	117	Senegal	$540	138	Tajikistan	$330	157	Niger	$200
99	Papua-New		118	Azerbaijan	$510	139	Uganda	$330	158	Sierra Leone	$170
	Guinea	$930	119	Pakistan	$500	140	Central African		159	Burundi	$140
100	North Korea	$900	120	Somalia	$500		Republic	$320	160	Mozambique	$140
101	Solomon		121	Kyrgystan	$480	141	Vietnam	$310	161	Congo,	
	Islands	$870	122	Moldova	$460	142	Cambodia	$300		Democratic	
102	China	$860	123	Mauritania	$440	143	Sao Tome and			Republic of	$110
103	Georgia	$860	124	Bhutan	$430		Principe	$290	162	Ethiopia	$110

 (Continued)

Source: Haub and Cornelius 1999 (except Famighetti 1999 for Afghanistan, Bahrain, Cuba, Iceland, Iraq, Libya, Luxembourg, North Korea, Oman, Qatar, Somalia, Taiwan, and the United Arab Emirates).

The Least Industrialized Nations

In the Least Industrialized Nations, most people are peasant farmers living on farms or in villages. These nations account for 49 percent of the earth's land and 68 percent of the world's people.

It is difficult to imagine the poverty that plagues the Least Industrialized Nations. In Luanda, the capital of Angola, for example, skinny street children live in sewers (McNeil 1999). I have seen this same thing in Medellín, Colombia. Although wealthy nations have their pockets of poverty, *most* people in these nations live on less than $1,000 a year, in many cases considerably less. Most of them have no running water, indoor plumbing, central water supply, or access to trained physicians. Because modern medicine has cut infant mortality but not births, the population of most of these nations is growing quickly. This places even greater burdens on their limited facilities, causing them to fall farther behind each year. The twin specters of poverty and death at an early age stalk these countries.

*H*OW THE WORLD'S NATIONS BECAME STRATIFIED

How did the globe become stratified into such distinct worlds? The obvious answer is that the poorer nations have fewer resources than the richer nations. As with so many "obvious" answers, however, this one, too, falls short. Many of the Industrializing and Least Industrialized Nations are rich in natural resources, while one of the Most Industrialized Nations, Japan, has few. Four theories explain how global stratification came about.

Colonialism

The first theory, **colonialism,** focuses on how the nations that industrialized first got the jump on the rest of the world. Beginning in Great Britain about 1750, industrialization spread throughout western Europe. Plowing some of their immense profits into powerful armaments and fast ships, these nations invaded weaker nations, making colonies out of them (Harrison 1993). After subduing them, the more powerful nations left behind a controlling force in order to exploit their labor and natural resources. At one point, there was even a free-for-all among the industrialized European nations as they rushed to divide up an entire continent. As Africa was sliced into pieces, even tiny Belgium got into the act and acquired the Congo, which was *seventy-five* times larger than itself.

Whereas the more powerful European nations would plant their national flags in a colony and send their representatives to run the government directly, the United States, after it industrialized, usually chose to plant corporate flags in a colony and let these corporations dominate the territory's government. Central and South America are prime examples of such U.S. "economic imperialism." No matter what the form, and whether it was benevolent or harsh, the purpose was the same—to exploit the nation's people and resources for the benefit of the "mother" country.

Colonialism, then, shaped many of the Least Industrialized Nations. In some instances, the Most Industrialized Nations were so powerful that to divide their spoils, they drew lines across a map, creating new states without regard for tribal or cultural considerations (Kifner 1999). Britain and France did just this in North Africa and parts of the Middle East, which is why the national boundaries of Libya, Saudi Arabia, Kuwait, and other nations are so straight. This legacy of European conquests still erupts into tribal violence, because tribes with no history of national identity were arbitrarily incorporated into the same political boundaries.

World System Theory

To explain how global stratification came about, Immanuel Wallerstein (1974, 1979, 1984, 1990) developed **world system theory.** He analyzed how industrialization led to four groups of nations. Those that industrialized first (Britain, France, Holland, and later Germany) grew rich and powerful. He calls these the *core nations.* The economies of the nations around the Mediterranean stagnated because they grew dependent on trade with the core nations. He calls this group the *semiperiphery.* The economies of the eastern European countries, which sold cash crops to the core nations, developed even less. This third group is the *periphery,* or fringe nations. A fourth group of nations was left out of the development of capitalism altogether. This *external area* includes most of Africa and Asia. As capitalism expanded, the relationships among these groups of nations changed. Most notably, Asia is no longer left out of capitalism.

The **globalization of capitalism**—the adoption of capitalism around the world—has created extensive ties among the world's nations. The world's nations are now so interconnected that events around the globe affect us all. Sometimes this is immediate, as happens when a revolution interrupts the flow of raw materials, or, perish the thought, as would be the case if, in Russia's unstable political climate, terrorists managed to seize an arsenal of earth-destroying nuclear missiles. At other times the effects are like a slow ripple, as when a government's policies impede its ability to compete in world markets. All of today's societies, then, no matter where they are located, are part of a *world system*.

Dependency Theory

The third theory is difficult to distinguish from world system theory. **Dependency theory** stresses how the Least Industrialized Nations grew dependent on the Most Industrialized Nations (Cardoso 1972; Furtado 1984). According to this theory, the first nations to industrialize turned other nations into their plantations and mines, harvesting or extracting whatever they needed to meet their growing appetite for raw materials and exotic foods. As a result, many of the Least Industrialized Nations began to specialize in a single cash crop. Brazil became the Most Industrialized Nations' giant coffee plantation; Nicaragua and other Central American countries specialized in bananas (hence the term *banana republic*); Chile became the primary source of tin; and Zaire (then the Belgian Congo) was transformed into a rubber plantation. And the Mideast nations were turned into gigantic oil wells. In short, the domination of the Least Industrialized Nations rendered them unable to develop independent economies.

Culture of Poverty

An entirely different explanation of global stratification was proposed by economist John Kenneth Galbraith (1979). He claimed that it was the Least Industrialized Nations' own culture that held them back. Building on the ideas of anthropologist Oscar Lewis (1966a, 1966b), Galbraith argued that some nations are crippled by a **culture of poverty**, a way of life that perpetuates poverty from one generation to the next. He explained it in this way: Most of the world's poor live in rural areas, where they barely eke out a living from the land. Their marginal life offers little room for error or risk, so they tend to stick closely to tried-and-true, traditional ways. Experimenting with new farming or manufacturing techniques could be a disaster, for if the techniques fail they could bring hunger and death. The religious beliefs of these nations also reinforce traditionalism, for they teach fatalism—the acceptance of one's lot in life as God's will.

Evaluating the Theories

Most sociologists prefer colonialism, world systems, and dependency theory. To them, an explanation based on a culture of poverty places blame on the victim—on the poor nations themselves. It points to characteristics of the poor nations, rather than to international arrangements that benefit the Most Industrialized Nations at the expense of the poor nations. But even taken together, these theories yield only part of the picture. None of these theories, for example, would have led anyone to expect that after World War II, Japan—which had a religion that stressed fatalism, which had two major cities destroyed by atomic bombs, and which had been stripped of its colonies—would become an economic powerhouse.

Each theory, then, yields but a partial explanation, and the grand theorist who will put the many pieces of this puzzle together has yet to appear.

Maintaining Global Stratification

Regardless of how the world's nations became stratified, why do the same countries remain rich year after year, while the rest stay poor? Let's look at two explanations of how global stratification is maintained.

Neocolonialism

Sociologist Michael Harrington (1977) argued that colonialism fell out of style and was replaced by **neocolonialism**. When World War II changed public sentiment about sending soldiers and colonists to weaker countries, the Most Industrialized Nations turned to the international markets to control the Least Industrialized Nations. These powerful nations determine how much they will pay for tin from Bolivia, copper from Peru, coffee from Brazil, and so forth. They also move hazardous industries into the Least Industrialized Nations.

As many of us to our sorrow learn, owing a large debt and falling behind on payments puts us at the mercy of our creditors. So it is with neocolonialism. The *policy* of selling weapons and other manufactured goods to the Least Industrialized Nations on credit turns those countries into eternal debtors. The capital they need to develop their own industries goes instead to the debt, which becomes bloated with mounting interest. Keeping these nations in debt makes them submit to the trading terms dictated by the neocolonialists (Tordoff 1992; Carrington 1993).

Thus, although the Least Industrialized Nations have their own governments—whether elected or dictatorships—they remain almost as dependent on the Most Industrialized Nations as they were when those nations occupied them.

Multinational Corporations

Multinational corporations, companies that operate across many national boundaries, also help to maintain the global dominance of the Most Industrialized Nations. In some cases, multinational corporations exploit the Least Industrialized Nations directly. A prime example is the United Fruit Company. For decades, it controlled national and local politics in Central America. It ran these nations as fiefdoms for the company's own profit while the U.S. Marines waited in the wings in case the company's interests needed to be backed up.

Most commonly, however, multinational corporations help to maintain international stratification simply by doing business. A single multinational may do mining in several countries, do manufacturing in many others, and run transportation and marketing networks around the globe. No matter where the profits are made, or where they are reinvested, the primary beneficiaries are the Most Industrialized Nations, especially the one in which the multinational corporation has its world headquarters. As Michael Harrington (1977) stressed, the real profits are made in processing the products and in controlling their distribution—and these profits are withheld from the Least Industrialized

Nations. For more on multinational corporations, see pages 294–296.

Multinational corporations try to work closely with the elite of the Least Industrialized Nations (Lipton 1979; Waldman 1995a). This elite, which lives a sophisticated upper-class life in the major cities of its home country, sends its children to prestigious universities, such as Oxford, the Sorbonne, and Harvard. The multinational corporations funnel investments to this small circle of power, whose members favor projects such as building laboratories and computer centers in the capital city—projects that do not help the vast majority of their people, who live in poor, remote villages where they eke out a meager living on small plots of land.

The end result is an informal partnership between multinational corporations and the elite of the Least Industrialized Nations. To gain access to the country's raw materials, labor, and market, the corporations pay off the elite. (These are politely called "subsidies," not bribes.) The elite use their payoffs not only to maintain their genteel lifestyle, but also to purchase high-powered weapons from multinational corporations, which they use to oppress their people and preserve their dominance. Both elites and corporations benefit through political stability, necessary for keeping their diabolical partnership alive.

This, however, is not the full story. Multinational corporations also play a role in changing international stratification. This is an unintentional by-product of their worldwide search for cheap resources and labor. By moving manufacturing from the Most Industrialized Nations to the Least Industrialized Nations, they not only exploit cheap labor but also bring jobs and, in some cases, prosperity to these nations. Although workers in the Least Industrialized Nations are paid a pittance, it is more than they can earn elsewhere. With new factories come opportunities to develop skills and a capital base. This does not occur in all nations, but the Pacific Rim nations, nicknamed the "Asian tigers," are a remarkable case in point. They have developed such a strong capital base that they have begun to rival the older capitalist nations. As has become painfully apparent, they also are subject to capitalism's infamous "boom and bust" cycles.

Technology and Global Domination

The race between the Most and Least Industrialized Nations to develop and apply the new information

SUMMARY AND REVIEW ■ 173

technologies is like a race between a marathon runner and a one-legged man. Can the outcome be in doubt? The vast profits piled up by the multinational corporations allow the Most Industrialized Nations to invest huge sums in the latest technologies. Gillette, for example, spent $100 million simply to adjust its output "on an hourly basis" (Zachary 1995). These millions came from just one U.S. company. Many Least Industrialized Nations would love to have $100 million to invest in their entire economy, much less to fine-tune the production of razor blades. In short, in the quest to maintain global domination, the new technologies pile up even more advantages for the Most Industrialized Nations.

A CONCLUDING NOTE

Let's return to the two families in our opening vignette. Remember that these families represent distinct worlds of money and power, that is, global stratification. Their life chances—from access to material possessions to the opportunity for education and even the likely age at which they will die—are profoundly affected by the global stratification we've looked at. This division of the globe into interconnected units of nations with more or less wealth and more or less power and prestige, then, is much more than a matter of theoretical interest. In fact, it is *your* life we are talking about.

SUMMARY AND REVIEW

■ An Overview of Social Stratification

Social stratification refers to a hierarchy of relative privilege based on power, property, and prestige. Every society stratifies its members, and in every society men as a group are placed above women as a group. Pp. 154–155.

What are the major systems of social stratification?

The major systems of social stratification are slavery, caste, and class. The essential characteristic of **slavery** is that some people own other people. Initially, slavery was based not on race but on debt, punishment, or defeat in battle. Slavery could be temporary or permanent, and was not necessarily passed on to one's children. North American slaves had no legal rights, and the system was gradually buttressed by a racist **ideology**. In a **caste system,** status is determined by birth and is lifelong. People marry within their own group and develop rules about ritual pollution. A **class system** is much more open, for it is based primarily on money or material possessions. Industrialization encourages the formation of class systems. Gender cuts across all forms of social stratification. Pp. 155–159.

■ What Determines Social Class?

Karl Marx argued that a single factor determines social class: If you own the means of production, you belong to the **bourgeoisie** (capitalists); if you do not, you are one of the **proletariat** (workers). Max Weber argued that three elements determine social class: *property, prestige,* and *power.* Pp. 159–161.

■ Why Is Social Stratification Universal?

To explain why stratification is universal, functionalists Kingsley Davis and Wilbert Moore argued that in order to attract the most capable people to fill its important positions, society must offer them greater rewards. Melvin Tumin said that if this view were correct, society would be a **meritocracy,** with all positions awarded on the basis of merit. Gaetano Mosca argued that stratification is inevitable because every society must have leadership, which by definition means inequality. Conflict theorists argue that stratification came about because resources are limited, and an elite emerges as groups struggle for them. Gerhard Lenski suggested a synthesis between the functionalist and conflict perspectives. Pp. 161–163.

■ How Do Elites Maintain Stratification?

To maintain social stratification within a nation, the ruling class uses an ideology that justifies current arrangements. It also controls information, and, when all else fails, depends on brute force. The social networks of the rich and poor also perpetuate social inequality. Pp. 163–165.

■ Comparative Social Stratification

What are key characteristics of stratification systems in other nations?

The most striking features of the British class system are speech and education. In Britain, accent reveals social class, and almost all of the elite attend "public" schools (the equivalent of our private schools). In what is now the former Soviet Union, communism was supposed to abolish class distinctions. Instead, it merely ushered in a different set of classes. Pp. 165–166.

■ Global Stratification: Three Worlds

How are the world's nations stratified?
The model presented here divides the world's nations into three groups: the Most Industrialized, the Industrializing, and the Least Industrialized. This layering represents relative property, power, and prestige. Pp. 166–170.

■ How the World's Nations Became Stratified

Why are some nations rich and others poor?
The main theories that seek to account for global stratification are **colonialism, world system theory, dependency theory,** and the **culture of poverty.** Pp. 170–171.

■ Maintaining Global Stratification

How do the elites maintain global stratification?
There are two basic explanations for why nations remain stratified. **Neocolonialism** is the ongoing dominance of the Least Industrialized Nations by the Most Industrialized Nations. The second explanation points to the influence of **multinational corporations.** The new technology gives further advantage to the Most Industrialized Nations. Pp. 171–173.

Where can I read more on this topic?
Suggested readings for this chapter are listed on page SR-5.

YOUR INTERACTIVE COMPANION WEB SITE

Your Interactive Companion Web Site includes practice rests, with feedback, and online learning activities with video, audio, and Weblinks. Your access code for this Web site is provided with this text.

GLOSSARY

bourgeoisie Karl Marx's term for capitalists, those who own the means of production (p. 159)

caste system a form of social stratification in which one's status is determined by birth and is lifelong (p. 156)

class consciousness Karl Marx's term for awareness of a shared identity based on one's position in the means of production (p. 159)

class system a form of social stratification based primarily on the possession of money or material possessions (p. 158)

colonialism the process by which one nation takes over another nation, usually for the purpose of exploiting its labor and natural resources (p. 170)

culture of poverty the assumption that the values and behaviors of the poor perpetuate their poverty (p. 171)

dependency theory the view that the Least Industrialized Nations have been unable to develop their economies because they grew dependent on the Most Industrialized Nations (p. 171)

divine right of kings the idea that the king's authority comes directly from God (p. 164)

endogamy the practice of marrying within one's own group (p. 156)

false consciousness Karl Marx's term to refer to workers identifying with the interests of capitalists (p. 160)

globalization of capitalism the adoption of capitalism around the world (p. 171)

ideology beliefs that justify social arrangements (p. 156)

means of production the tools, factories, land, and investment capital used to produce wealth (p. 159)

meritocracy a form of social stratification in which all positions are awarded on the basis of merit (p. 162)

multinational corporations companies that operate across many national boundaries (p. 172)

neocolonialism the economic and political dominance of the Least Industrialized Nations by the Most Industrialized Nations (p. 171)

proletariat Karl Marx's term for workers (the exploited class that works for capitalists, those who own the means of production) (p. 159)

slavery a form of social stratification in which some people own other people (p. 155)

social class a large number of people with similar amounts of income and education who work at jobs that are roughly comparable in prestige (p. 160)

social mobility movement up or down the social class ladder (p. 158)

social stratification the division of people into layers according to their relative power, property, and prestige; applies to both a society and nations (p. 155)

world system theory economic and political connections that tie the world's countries together (p. 170)

Graham Dean, Beg, 1991

Social Class in the United States

Ah, New Orleans, that fabled city on the Gulf. Images from its rich past floated through my head—pirates, wealth, intrigue. Memories from a pleasant vacation stirred my thoughts—the exotic French Quarter with its enticing aroma of Creole food and sounds of earthy jazz drifting through the air.

The shelter for the homeless, however, forced me back to an unwelcome reality. The shelter was the same as those I had visited in the North, West, and East—only dirtier. The dirt, in fact, was the worst I had encountered during my research, and this shelter was the only one to insist on payment in exchange for sleeping in one of its filthy beds.

The men looked the same—disheveled and haggard, wearing that unmistakable expression of despair—just like the homeless anywhere in the country. Except for the accent, you wouldn't know what region of the country you were in. Poverty wears the same tired face, I realized. The accent may differ, but the look remains the same.

The next morning, I felt indignation swell within me. I had grown used to the sights and smells of abject poverty. Those no longer surprised me. But now, just a block or so from the shelter, I was startled by a sight so out of step with the misery and despair I had just experienced that I stopped in midtrack.

I was confronted by life-size, full-color photos that were mounted on the transparent plastic shelter covering a bus stop. Staring back at me were finely dressed men and women proudly strutting about as they modeled elegant suits, dresses, diamonds, and furs.

A wave of disgust swept over me. "Something is cockeyed in this society," I thought, my mind refusing to stop juxtaposing these images with the suffering I had just witnessed.

Occasionally the facts of social class hit home with brute force. This was one of those moments. The disjunction that I felt in New Orleans was triggered by the ads, but it was not the first time that I had experienced this sensation. Whenever my research abruptly transported me from the world of the homeless to one of another social class, I felt unfamiliar feelings of disjointed unreality. Each social class has its own way of being, and because these fundamental orientations to the world contrast so sharply, the classes do not mix well. ■

WHAT IS SOCIAL CLASS?

"There are the poor and the rich—and then there are you and I, neither poor nor rich." This is just about as far as most Americans' consciousness of social class goes. Let's try to flesh out this idea.

Our task is made somewhat difficult because sociologists have no clear-cut, agreed-on definition of social class. As noted in the last chapter, conflict sociologists (of the Marxist orientation) see only two social classes: those who own the means of production and those who do not. The problem with this view, say most sociologists, is that it lumps too many people together. Physicians and corporate executives with incomes of $400,000 a year are lumped together with hamburger flippers who work at McDonald's for $13,000 a year.

Most sociologists agree with Weber that there is more to social class than just a person's relationship to the means of production. Consequently, most sociologists use the components Weber identified and define **social class** as a large group of people who rank closely to one another in wealth, power, and prestige. These three elements separate people into different lifestyles, give them different chances in life, and provide them with distinct ways of looking at the self and the world.

Let's look at how sociologists measure these three components of social class.

Wealth

The primary dimension of social class is wealth. **Wealth** consists of property and income. *Property* comes in many forms, such as cars, land, buildings, animals, machinery, stocks, bonds, businesses, and bank accounts. *Income* is money received as wages, rents, interest, royalties, or proceeds from a business.

Distinctions Between Wealth and Income Wealth and income are sometimes confused, but they are not the same. Some people have much wealth and little income. For example, a farmer may own much land (a form of wealth), but a little bad weather, combined with the high cost of fertilizers and machinery, can cause the income to disappear. Others have much income and little wealth. For example, an executive with a $200,000 annual income may be debt-ridden. Below the surface prosperity—exotic vacations, country club membership, private schools for the children, fancy sports cars, and an elegant home in an exclusive suburb—he or she may be greatly overextended, the fancy cars in danger of being repossessed and the mortgage payment "past due." Typically, however, wealth and income go together.

Who owns the wealth in the United States? One answer, of course, is "everyone." Although this statement has some merit, it overlooks how the nation's wealth is divided among "everyone." Let's look at how the two forms of wealth—property and income—are distributed among Americans.

Distribution of Property Overall, Americans are worth a hefty sum, about $25 trillion (*Statistical Abstract* 1999:Table 774). Most of this wealth is in the form of real estate, stocks, bonds, and business assets. As Figure 8.1 shows, this wealth is highly concentrated. The vast majority, 68 percent, is owned by only *10 percent* of the nation's families.

The higher we go up the income ladder, the more concentrated that wealth becomes. As sociologist Leonard Beeghley (2000) observes, *the super-rich, the richest 1 percent of U.S. families, are worth more than the entire bottom 90 percent of Americans.*

Distribution of Income How is income distributed in the United States? Economist Paul Samuelson (Samuelson and Nordhaus 1989:644) put it this way:

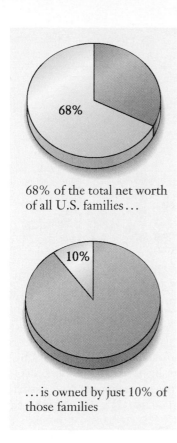

Figure 8.1

DISTRIBUTION OF WEALTH OF AMERICANS

Source: Beeghley 2000.

68% of the total net worth of all U.S. families...

...is owned by just 10% of those families

Figure 8.2

INEQUALITY OF U.S. INCOME

Some U.S. incomes are higher than Mt. Everest

29,028 feet

If a 1½-inch child's block equals $500 of income, the average American is only 7 feet off the ground, the average family just 11 feet, while the income of some families propels them past the top of Mount Everest.

7 feet   11 feet

Average American   Average U.S. Family

"If we made an income pyramid out of a child's blocks, with each layer portraying $500 of income, the peak would be far higher than Mount Everest, but most people would be within a few feet of the ground."

Actually, if each block were 1½ inches tall, the typical American would be just 7 *feet off the ground,* for the average per capita income in the United States is about $26,000 per year. (This average income includes every American, even children.) The typical family climbs a little higher, for most families have more than one worker, and together they average about $41,000 a year. Yet compared with the few families who are on the mountain's peak, the average U.S. family would find itself only 11 feet off the ground (*Statistical Abstract* 1999:Tables 733, 752). Figure 8.2 portrays these differences.

The fact that some Americans enjoy the peaks of Mount Everest while most—despite their efforts—make it only 7 to 11 feet up the slope presents a striking image of income inequality in the United States. Another picture emerges if we divide the U.S. population into five equal groups and rank them from highest to lowest income. As Figure 8.3 shows, the top 20 percent of the population receives *almost half* (47.3 percent) of

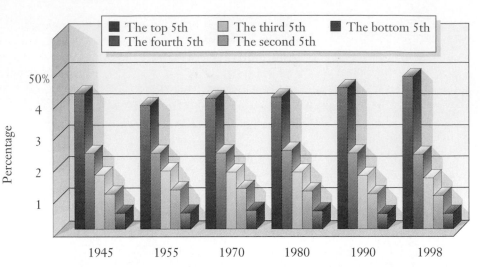

Figure 8.3

GROWING INEQUALITY: THE PERCENTAGE OF THE NATION'S INCOME RECEIVED BY EACH FIFTH OF U.S. FAMILIES SINCE WORLD WAR II

Source: Statistical Abstract 1947; 2000:Table 745.

■ The top 5th ▨ The third 5th ■ The bottom 5th
■ The fourth 5th ▨ The second 5th

Note: The distribution of U.S. income—salaries, wages, and all other money received, except capital gains and government subsidies in the form of food stamps, health benefits, or subsidized housing.

all income in the United States. In contrast, the bottom 20 percent of Americans receives only 4.2 percent of the nation's income.

Two features of Figure 8.3 are outstanding. First, notice how remarkably consistent income inequality remains through the years. Second, the changes that do occur indicate *growing inequality. The richest 20 percent of U.S. families have grown richer, while the poorest 20 percent have grown poorer.* Despite numerous antipoverty programs, the poorest 20 percent of Americans receive *less* of the nation's income today than they did in the 1940s (a drop from 5.4 percent to 4.2 percent). The richest 20 percent, in contrast, receive *more* than ever (an increase from about 41 percent to just over 47 percent).

The most affluent group in the United States is the chief executive officers (CEOs) of the nation's largest corporations. The *Wall Street Journal* surveyed the 350 largest U.S. companies to find out what they paid their CEOs ("The Boss's Pay," 2000). Their median compensation (including salaries, bonuses, and stock options) came to $2,782,000 a year. (Median means that half received more than this amount, and half less.) The CEOs' income—which does *not* include their interest, dividends, rents, and capital gains—is *100 times* higher than the average pay of U.S. workers (*Statistical Abstract* 1999:Table 700).

Imagine how you could live with an income like this. And this is precisely the point. Beyond cold numbers lies a dynamic reality that profoundly affects people's lives. The difference in wealth between those

at the top and those at the bottom of the U.S. class structure means vastly different lifestyles. For example, a colleague of mine who was teaching at an exclusive eastern university piqued his students' curiosity when he lectured

Bill Gates, a cofounder of Microsoft Corporation, is the wealthiest person in the world. His fortune of $90 billion continues to increase as his company develops new products. His 40,000-square-foot home (sometimes called a "technopalace") in Seattle, Washington, is appraised at $110 million. In addition to being the wealthiest person in history, Gates has also given more money to the poor and minorities than any individual in history.

on poverty in Latin America. That weekend, one of his students borrowed his parents' corporate jet and pilot, and in class the next Monday he and his friends related their personal observations on poverty in Latin America. Americans who are at the low end of the income ladder, in contrast, lack the funds to travel even to a neighbor-

ing town for the weekend. Their choices revolve around whether to spend the little they have at the laundromat or on milk for the baby. In short, divisions of wealth represent not "mere" numbers, but choices that make vital differences in people's lives, a topic explored in the Down-to-Earth Sociology box below.

Sociology

Down-to-Earth

HOW THE RICH LIVE

It's good to see how other people live. It provides a different perspective for evaluating life. Let's take a glimpse at the life of John Castle (his real name). After earning a degree in physics at MIT and an MBA at Harvard, John went into banking and securities where he made more than $100 million (Lublin 1999).

Wanting to follow in the footsteps of someone famous, John bought President John F. Kennedy's "Winter White House," his oceanfront estate in Palm Beach, Florida. He spent $11 million to remodel the 13,000-square-foot house so it would be more to his liking, adding bathrooms numbers 14 and 15. He especially likes to show off the John F. Kennedy bed and also the dresser that has the drawer labeled "black underwear," carefully handlettered by Rose Kennedy.

If he gets bored at his beachfront estate, or tired of swimming in the Olympic-size pool where JFK swam the weekend before his assassination, John entertains himself by riding one of his thoroughbred horses at his nearby 10-acre ranch. If this fails to ease his boredom, he can relax aboard his custom-built 45-foot Hinckley yacht.

The yacht is a real source of diversion. He once boarded it for an around-the-world trip.

How do the rich live? The entrance to one of Sylvestor Stallone's homes, this one in Coconut Grove, Florida.

He didn't stay on board, though—just joined the cruise from time to time. A captain and crew kept the vessel sailing in the right direction, and whenever John felt like it he would fly in and stay a few days. Then he would fly back to the States to direct his business. He did this about a dozen times, flying perhaps 150,000 miles. An interesting way to go around the world.

How much does a custom-built Hinckley yacht cost? John can't tell you. As he says, "I don't want to know what anything costs. When you've got enough money, price doesn't make a difference. That's part of the freedom of being rich."

Right. And for John, being rich also meant paying $1,000,000 to charter a private jet to fly Spot, his Appaloosa horse, back and forth to the vet. John didn't want Spot to endure a long trailer ride. Oh, and of course, there was the cost of Spot's medical treatment, another $500,000.

Other wealthy people put John to shame. Wayne Huizenga, the CEO of Auto-Nation, owns a 2,000-acre country club, complete with an 18-hole golf course, a 55,000-square foot clubhouse, and 68 slips for visiting vessels. The club is so exclusive that its only members are Wayne and his wife. ■

Power

Like many people, you may have said to yourself, "Sure, I can vote, but somehow the big decisions are always made despite what I might think. Certainly *I* don't make the decision to send soldiers to Kuwait or Somalia. *I* don't launch missiles against the Sudan or Kosovo. *I* don't decide to raise taxes or interest rates. It isn't *I* who decides to change welfare benefits."

And then another part of you may say, "But I do participate in these decisions through my representatives in Congress, or by voting for president." True enough—as far as it goes. The trouble is, it just doesn't go far enough. Such views of being a participant in the nation's "big" decisions are a playback of the ideology we learn at an early age—an ideology that Marx said is put forward by the elites to both legitimate and perpetuate their power. Sociologists Daniel Hellinger and Dennis Judd (1991) call this the "democratic façade" that conceals the real source of power in the United States.

Back in the 1950s, sociologist C. Wright Mills (1956) was criticized for insisting that **power**—the ability to carry out your will despite resistance—was concentrated in the hands of a few, for his analysis contradicted the dominant ideology of equality. As discussed in earlier chapters, Mills coined the term **power elite** to refer to those who make the big decisions in U.S. society.

Mills and others have stressed how wealth and power coalesce in a group of like-minded individuals who share ideologies and values. They belong to the same private clubs, vacation at the same exclusive resorts, and even hire the same bands for their daughters' debutante balls. These shared backgrounds and vested interests reinforce their view of the world and of their special place in it (Domhoff 1998, 1999). This elite wields extraordinary power in U.S. society. Although there are exceptions, *most* U.S. presidents have come from this group—millionaire white men from families with "old money" (Baltzell and Schneiderman 1988).

Continuing in the tradition of Mills, sociologist William Domhoff (1990, 1998) argues that this group is so powerful that no major decision of the U.S. government is made without its approval. He analyzed how this group works behind the scenes with elected officials to determine both the nation's foreign and domestic policy—from setting Social Security taxes to imposing trade tariffs. Although Domhoff's conclusions are controver-

In the United States, a mere 0.5 percent of the population owns over a quarter of the nation's wealth. Very few minorities are numbered among this 0.5 percent. An outstanding exception is Oprah Winfrey, whose ultra-successful career in entertainment, bringing her over $250 million a year, has made her one of the 400 richest Americans. Winfrey is shown here as she launched the premiere issue of *O, The Oprah Magazine,* at a press breakfast in New York City. Oprah has given millions of dollars to benefit minority children.

sial—and alarming—they certainly follow logically from the principle that wealth brings power, and extreme wealth brings extreme power.

Prestige

Occupations and Prestige What are you thinking about doing after college? Chances are you don't have the option of lolling under palm trees at the beach. Almost all of us have to choose an occupation and go to work. Look at Table 8.1 to see how the one you are considering stacks up in terms of **prestige** (respect or regard). Because we are moving toward a global society, this table also shows how the rankings given by Americans compare with those of the residents of sixty other countries.

Why do people give more prestige to some jobs than to others? If you look at Table 8.1, you will notice that the jobs at the top share four elements:

1. They pay more.
2. They require more education.
3. They entail more abstract thought.
4. They offer greater autonomy (freedom, or self-direction).

If we turn this around, we can see that people give less prestige to jobs that are low paying, require less preparation or education, involve more physical labor, and are closely supervised. In short, the professions and white-collar jobs are ranked at the top of the list, blue-collar jobs at the bottom.

One of the more interesting aspects of these rankings is how consistent they are across countries and over time. For example, people in every country rank college

Table 8.1

OCCUPATIONAL PRESTIGE: HOW THE UNITED STATES COMPARES WITH 60 COUNTRIES

Occupation	United States	Average of 60 Countries	Occupation	United States	Average of 60 Countries
Supreme court judge	85	82	Professional athlete	51	48
College president	82	86	Undertaker	51	34
Physician	82	78	Social worker	50	56
Astronaut	80	80	Electrician	49	44
College professor	78	78	Secretary	46	53
Lawyer	75	73	Real estate agent	44	49
Dentist	74	70	Farmer	44	47
Architect	71	72	Carpenter	43	37
Psychologist	71	66	Plumber	41	34
Airline pilot	70	66	Mail carrier	40	33
Electrical engineer	69	65	Jazz musician	37	38
Civil engineer	68	70	Bricklayer	36	34
Biologist	68	69	Barber	36	30
Clergy	67	60	Truck driver	31	33
Sociologist	65	67	Factory worker	29	29
Accountant	65	55	Store sales clerk	27	34
Banker	63	67	Bartender	25	23
High school teacher	63	64	Lives on public aid	25	16
Author	63	62	Bill collector	24	27
Registered nurse	62	54	Cab driver	22	28
Pharmacist	61	64	Gas station attendant	22	25
Chiropractor	60	62	Janitor	22	21
Veterinarian	60	61	Waiter or waitress	20	23
Classical musician	59	56	Bellhop	15	14
Police officer	59	40	Garbage collector	13	13
Actor or actress	55	52	Street sweeper	11	13
Athletic coach	53	50	Shoe shiner	9	1
Journalist	52	55			

Sources: Treiman 1977, Appendices A and D; Nakao and Treas 1991.

professors higher than nurses, nurses higher than social workers, and social workers higher than janitors. Similarly, the occupations that were ranked high back in the 1970s still rank high today—and likely will rank high in the years to come.

Displaying Prestige To get a sense of payoff, people want others to acknowledge their prestige. In times past, in some countries only the emperor and his family could wear purple. In France, only the nobility could wear lace. In England, no one could sit while the king was on his throne. Some kings and queens required that subjects walk backward as they left the room—so no one would "turn their back" on the "royal presence."

Concern with displaying prestige has not let up. For some, it is almost an obsession. The military has manuals that specify precisely who must salute whom. The U.S. president enters a room only after others are present (to show that *he* isn't the one waiting for *them*). They must also be standing when he enters. In the courtroom, bailiffs, sometimes armed, make certain that everyone stands when the judge enters.

The display of prestige permeates society. In Los Angeles, some people list their address as Beverly Hills and then add their correct ZIP code. When the town of East Detroit changed its name to East Pointe to play off its proximity to swank Grosse Pointe, property values shot up (Fletcher 1997). Many pay more for clothing that bears a "designer" label. Prestige is often a primary factor in deciding which college to attend. Everyone knows how the prestige of a generic sheepskin from Regional State College compares with a degree from Harvard, Princeton, Yale, or Stanford.

Interestingly, status symbols vary with social class. Clearly, only the wealthy can afford certain items, such as yachts. But beyond affordability lies a class-based preference in status symbols. For example, Yuppies (young upwardly mobile professionals) are quick to flaunt labels and other material symbols to show that they have "arrived," while the rich, who are more secure in their status, often downplay such images. The wealthy see designer labels of the more "common" classes as cheap and showy. They, of course, flaunt their own status symbols, such as $30,000 Rolex watches.

Status Inconsistency

Ordinarily a person has a similar rank on all three dimensions of social class—wealth, power, and prestige. The homeless men in the opening vignette are an example. Such people are **status consistent.** Sometimes the match is not there, however, and someone has a mix-

Acceptable display of prestige and high social position varies over time and from one culture to another. Shown here is Elisabeth d'Autriche, queen of France from 1554 to 1592. It certainly would be difficult to outdress her at a party.

ture of high and low ranks, a condition called **status inconsistency.** This leads to some interesting situations.

Sociologist Gerhard Lenski (1954, 1966) pointed out that each of us tries to maximize our **status,** our social ranking. Thus individuals who rank high on one dimension of social class but lower on others expect people to judge them on the basis of their highest status. Others, however, trying to maximize their own position, may respond to them according to their lowest status.

A classic study of status inconsistency was done by sociologist Ray Gold (1952). He found that after apartment house janitors unionized, they made more money than some of the tenants whose garbage they carried out. Tenants became upset when they saw their janitors driving more expensive cars than they did. Some attempted to "put the janitor in his place" by making "snotty" remarks to him. For their part, the janitors took secret pride in knowing "dirty" secrets about the tenants, gleaned from their garbage.

Individuals with status inconsistency, then, are likely to confront one frustrating situation after another. They claim the higher status, but are handed the lower. The sociological significance of this condition, said Lenski, is that such people tend to be more politically radi-

Status discrepancy is common for lottery winners, whose new wealth is vastly greater than their education and occupational status. Shown here are John and Sandy Jarrell of Chicago, after they learned that they were one of 13 families to share a $295 million jackpot. How do you think their $22 million will affect their lives?

cal. An example is college professors. Their prestige is very high, as we saw in Table 8.1, but their incomes are relatively low. Hardly anyone in U.S. society is more educated, and yet college professors don't even come close to the top of the income pyramid. In line with Lenski's prediction, the politics of most college professors are left of center. This hypothesis may also hold true among academic departments; that is, the higher a department's pay, the less radical are its politics. Teachers in departments of business and medicine, for example, are among the most highly paid in the university—and they also are the most politically conservative.

SOCIOLOGICAL MODELS OF SOCIAL CLASS

The question of how many social classes there are is a matter of debate. Sociologists have proposed several models, but no model has gained universal support. There are two main models: one that builds on Marx, the other on Weber.

Updating Marx

Marx argued that there are just two classes—capitalists and workers—with membership based solely on a person's re-

lationship to the means of production. Sociologists have criticized this view because these categories are too broad. For example, executives, managers, and supervisors are technically workers because they do not own the means of production. But what do they have in common with assembly-line workers? Similarly, the category of "capitalist" takes in too many types. For example, the decisions of someone who employs a thousand workers directly affect a thousand families. Compare this with a man I know in Godfrey, Illinois. Working on cars out of his own back yard, he gained a following, quit his regular job, and in a few years put up a building with five bays and an office. This mechanic is now a capitalist, for he employs five or six other mechanics and owns the tools and the building (the "means of production"). But what does he have in common with a factory owner who controls the lives of one thousand workers? Not only is his work different, but so are his lifestyle and the way he looks at the world.

Sociologist Erik Wright (1985) resolved this problem by regarding some people as members of more than one class at the same time. They have what he called **contradictory class locations.** By this, Wright means that people's position in the class structure can generate contradictory interests. For example, the automobile-mechanic-turned-business-owner may want his mechanics to have higher wages since he, too, has experienced their working conditions. At the same time, his current interests—making profits and remaining competitive with other repair shops—lead him to resist pressures to raise wages.

Because of such contradictory class locations, Wright modified Marx's model. As summarized in Table 8.2, Wright identified four classes: (1) *capitalists,* business owners who employ many workers; (2) *petty bourgeoisie,* small business owners; (3) *managers,* who sell their own labor but also exercise authority over other employees; and (4) *workers,* who simply sell their labor

Table 8.2	SOCIAL CLASS AND THE MEANS OF PRODUCTION	
Marx's Class Model (based on the means of production)	**Wright's Modification of Marx's Class Model (to account for contradictory class locations)**	
1. Capitalists (bourgeoisie)	1. Capitalists	
2. Workers (proletariat)	2. Petty bourgeoisie	
	3. Managers	
	4. Workers	

Sociologists use income, education, and occupational prestige to measure social class. For most people, this classification works well. But not for everyone. Entertainers sometimes are difficult to fit in. To what social class does Christine Aguilera belong?

to others. As you can see, this model allows finer divisions than the one Marx proposed, yet it maintains the primary distinction between employer and worker.

Updating Weber

Sociologists Joseph Kahl and Dennis Gilbert (Gilbert and Kahl 1993; Gilbert 1997) developed a six-class model to portray the class structure of the United States and other capitalist countries. Think of this model, illustrated in Figure 8.4, as a ladder. Our discussion will start with the highest rung and move downward. In line with Weber, on each lower rung you find less wealth, less power, and less prestige. Note that in this model education is also a primary criterion of class.

The Capitalist Class Only about 1 percent of the population occupies the top rung of the class ladder. As mentioned, this 1 percent is so wealthy that its members are worth more than the entire bottom 90 percent of the

nation. Their power is so great that their decisions open or close jobs for millions of people. They also have direct access to top politicians. This small elite even helps to shape the consciousness of the nation: They own our newspapers, magazines, radio and television stations, and control the boards of directors of our colleges and universities. The super-rich perpetuate themselves in privilege by passing to their children their assets and influential social networks.

The capitalist class can be divided into "old" and "new" money. The longer that wealth has been in a family, the more it adds to the family's prestige. Their children seldom mingle with "common" folk—instead, they attend exclusive private schools where they learn views of life that support their privileged position. They don't work for wages; instead, many study business or enter the field of law so they can manage the family fortune. These old-money capitalists (also called "blue-bloods") wield vast power as they use their extensive political connections to protect their huge economic empires (Persell et al. 1992; Domhoff 1990, 1999).

At the lower end of the capitalist class are those who have "new money" (also called the *nouveau riche*). They are outsiders to this upper class. Although they have made fortunes in business, the stock market, inventions, entertainment, or sports, they have not attended the "right" schools, and they lack the influential social networks that come with old money. Not a blue blood, they aren't trusted to have the right orientations to life. Donald Trump, for example, is not listed in the *Social Register,* the "White Pages" of the blue bloods that lists the most prestigious and wealthy one-tenth of 1 percent of the U.S. population. Trump says he "doesn't care," but he reveals his true feelings by adding that his heirs will be in it (Kaufman 1996). He probably is right, for the children of the new-moneyed can ascend into the top part of the capitalist class—if they go to the right schools *and* marry old money.

Many in the capitalist class are philanthropic. They establish foundations and give huge sums to "causes." Their motivations vary. Some feel guilty because they have so much while others have so little. Others feel a responsibility—even a sense of fate or purpose—to use their money for doing good. Still others seek prestige, acclaim, or fame.

The Upper Middle Class Of all the classes, the upper middle class is the one most shaped by education. Almost all members of this class have at least a bachelor's degree, and many have postgraduate degrees in business, management, law, or medicine. These people man-

Social Class	Education	Occupation	Income	Percentage of Population
Capitalist	Prestigious university	Investors and heirs, a few top executives	$500,000+	1%
Upper Middle	College or university, often with postgraduate study	Professionals and upper managers	$100,000+	15%
Lower Middle	At least high school; perhaps some college or apprenticeship	Semiprofessionals and lower managers, craftspeople, foremen	About $50,000	34%
Working Class	High school	Factory workers, clerical workers, low-paid retail sales, and craftspeople	About $30,000	30%
Working Poor	Some high school	Laborers, service workers, low-paid salespeople	About $16,000	16%
Underclass	Some high school	Unemployed and part-time, on welfare	Under $10,000	4%

Figure 8.4 THE U.S. SOCIAL CLASS LADDER

Source: Based on Gilbert and Kahl 1997 and Gilbert 1997; income estimates are modified from Duff 1995.

age the corporations owned by the capitalist class or else operate their own business or profession. As Gilbert and Kahl (1982) say, these positions

> may not grant prestige equivalent to a title of nobility in the Germany of Max Weber, but they certainly represent the sign of having "made it" in contemporary America.... Their income is sufficient to purchase houses and cars and travel that become public symbols for all to see and for advertisers to portray with words and pictures that connote success, glamour, and high style.

Consequently, parents and teachers push children to prepare for upper-middle-class jobs. About 15 percent of the population belong to this class.

The Lower Middle Class About 34 percent of the population belong to the lower middle class. Members

of this class have jobs that call for them to follow orders given by those who have upper-middle-class credentials. Their technical and lower-level management positions bring them a good living—albeit one threatened by taxes and inflation—and they enjoy a comfortable, mainstream lifestyle. They usually feel secure in their positions and anticipate being able to move up the social class ladder.

The distinctions between the lower middle class and the working class on the next lower rung are more blurred than those between other classes. In general, however, members of the lower middle class work at jobs that have slightly more prestige, and their incomes are generally higher.

The Working Class About 30 percent of the U.S. population belong to this class of relatively unskilled blue-collar and white-collar workers. Compared with the lower middle class, they have less education and lower incomes. Their jobs are also less secure, more routine, and more closely supervised. One of their greatest fears is being laid off during a recession. With only a high school diploma, the average member of the working class has little hope of climbing up the class ladder. Job changes usually bring "more of the same," so most concentrate on getting ahead by achieving seniority on the job rather than by changing their type of work.

The Working Poor Members of this class, about 16 percent of the population, work at unskilled, low-paying, temporary and seasonal jobs, such as sharecropping, migrant farm work, housecleaning, and day labor. Most are high school dropouts. Many are functionally illiterate, finding it difficult to read even the want ads. They are not likely to vote (Gilbert and Kahl 1993; Beeghley 2000), for they feel that no matter what party is elected to office their situation won't change.

About 6 million of the working poor work full time (O'Hare 1996b), but still must depend on help such as food stamps to supplement their meager incomes. It is easy to see how one can work full time and still be poor. Suppose that you are married and have a baby 3 months old and another child 3 years old. Your spouse stays home to care for them, so earning the income is up to you. But as a high-school dropout, all you can get is a minimum wage job. At $5.15 an hour, you earn $206 for 40 hours. In a year, this comes to $10,712 before deductions. Your nagging fear—and daily nightmare—is of ending up "on the streets."

The Underclass On the lowest rung, and with next to no chance of climbing anywhere, is the **underclass.** Concentrated in the inner city, this group has little or no connection with the job market. Those who are employed, and some are, do menial, low-paying, temporary work. Welfare, if it is available, along with food stamps and food pantries, are their main support. Most members of other classes consider these people the "ne'er-do-wells" of society. About 4 percent of the population fall into this class.

The homeless men described in the opening vignette of this chapter, and the women and children like them, are part of the underclass. These are the people who most Americans wish would just go away. Their presence on our city streets bothers passersby from the more privileged social classes—which includes just about everyone. "What are those obnoxious, dirty, foul-smelling people doing here, cluttering up my city?" appears to be a common response. Some people respond with sympathy and a desire to do something. But what? Almost all of us just shrug our shoulders and look the other way, despairing of a solution and somewhat intimidated by their presence.

The homeless are the "fallout" of industrialization, especially our developing postindustrial economy. In another era, they would have had plenty of work. They would have tended horses, worked on farms, dug ditches, shoveled coal, and run the factory looms. Some would have explored and settled the West. Others would have been lured to California, Alaska, and Australia by the prospect of gold. Today, however, with no frontiers to settle, factory jobs scarce, and farms that are becoming technological marvels, we have little need for unskilled labor.

Social Class in the Automobile Industry

The automobile industry illustrates the social class ladder. The Fords, for example, own and control a manufacturing and financial empire whose net worth is truly staggering. Their power matches their wealth, for through their multinational corporation their decisions affect production and employment in many countries. The family's vast fortune, and its accrued power, are now several generations old. Consequently, Ford children go to the "right" schools, know how to spend money in the "right" way, and can be trusted to make family and class interests paramount in life. They are without question at the top level of the *capitalist* class.

Next in line come top Ford executives. Although they may have an income of several hundred thousand dollars a year (and some, with stock options and bonuses, earn several million dollars annually), most are new to wealth and power. Consequently, they would be classified at the lower end of the capitalist class.

A husband and wife who own a Ford agency are members of the *upper middle class.* Their income clearly sets them apart from the majority of Americans, and their reputation in the community is enviable. More than likely they also exert greater-than-average influence in their community, but their capacity to wield power is limited.

A Ford salesperson, as well as the people who work in the dealership office, belongs to the *lower middle class.* Although there are some exceptional salespeople—even a few who make a lot of money selling prestigious, expensive cars to the capitalist class—salespeople at a run-of-the-mill local Ford agency are lower middle class. Compared with the owners of the agency, their income is less, their education is likely to be less, and their work is less prestigious.

Mechanics who repair customers' cars are members of the *working class*. A mechanic who is promoted to supervise the repair shop joins the lower middle class.

Those who "detail" used cars (making them appear newer by washing and polishing the car, painting the tires, spraying "new car scent" into the interior, and so on) belong to the *working poor*. Their income and education are low, the prestige accorded their work minimal. They are laid off when selling slows down.

Ordinarily, the *underclass* is not represented in the automobile industry. It is conceivable, however, that the agency might hire a member of the underclass to do a specific job such as raking the grass or cleaning up the used car lot. In general, however, personnel at the agency do not trust members of the underclass and do not want to associate with them—even for a few hours. They prefer to hire someone from the working poor for such jobs.

CONSEQUENCES OF SOCIAL CLASS

Each social class can be thought of as a broad subculture with distinct approaches to life. Of the many ways that social class affects people's lives, we will briefly review its impact on family life, education, religion, politics, and health. We will also look at how the consequences of the new technology depend on social class.

Family Life

Social class plays an especially significant role in family life. It even affects our choice of spouse and our chances of getting divorced.

Choice of Husband or Wife The capitalist class places strong emphasis on family tradition. They stress the family's ancestors, history, and even a sense of purpose or destiny in life (Baltzell 1979; Aldrich 1989). Children of this class learn that their choice of husband or wife affects not just themselves but the entire family, that their spouse will have an impact on the "family line." Because of these background expectations, the field of "eligible" marriage partners is much narrower than it is for the children of any other social class. In effect, parents in this class play a strong role in their children's mate selection.

Divorce The more difficult life of the lower social classes, especially the many tensions that come from insecure jobs and inadequate incomes, leads to higher marital friction and the greater likelihood of divorce. Consequently, children of the poor are more likely to grow up in broken homes.

Education

As we saw in Figure 8.4, education increases as one goes up the social class ladder. It is not just the amount of education that changes, but also the type of education. Children of the capitalist class bypass public schools. They attend exclusive private schools where they are trained to take a commanding role in society. Prep schools such as Phillips Exeter Academy, Groton School, and Woodberry Forest School teach upper-class values and prepare their students for prestigious universities (Beeghley 2000; Higley 2001). Aspiring members of the upper middle class, aware of the significance of this private school system, attempt to enroll their children in prestigious preschools by eliciting letters of recommendation for their 2- and 3-year-olds. Such differences in parental expectations and resources are a major reason why children from the more privileged classes do better in school and are more likely to enter and to graduate from college.

Religion

One area of social life that we might think would be unaffected by social class is religion. ("People are just religious, or they are not. What does class have to do with it?") As we shall see in Chapter 13, the classes tend to cluster in different denominations. Episcopalians, for example, are more likely to recruit from the middle and upper classes, Baptists draw heavily from the lower classes, and Methodists are more middle class. Patterns of worship also follow class lines: Those that attract the lower classes have more spontaneous worship services and louder music, while the middle and upper classes prefer more "subdued" worship.

Politics

As has been stressed throughout this text, symbolic interactionists emphasize that people see events from their own corner in life. Political views are no exception to this principle, and the rich and the poor walk different political paths. The higher people are on the social class ladder, the more likely they are to vote for Republicans. In contrast, most members of the working class believe that the government should intervene in the economy to make citizens financially secure, and most are Democrats. Although the working class is more liberal on *economic* issues (policies that increase government spending), it is more conservative on *social* issues (such as opposing abortion and the Equal Rights Amendment) (Lipset 1959; Houtman 1995). People toward the bottom of the class structure are also less likely to be politically active—to campaign for candidates, or even to vote (Gans 1991; Gilbert and Kahl 1993; Beeghley 2000).

Physical Health

Social class even affects our physical health. As shown in Figure 8.5, the lower people's income, the more often they are sick. Even our chances of living and dying are related to social class. The principle is simple: The lower a person's social class, the more likely that individual is to die before the expected age. This principle holds true at all ages: Infants born to the poor are more likely than other infants to die before their first birthday. In old age—whether 75 or 95—a larger proportion of the poor die each year than do the wealthy. Part of the reason for these death rates is unequal access to medical care. Consider this example:

> Terry Takewell (his real name) was a 21-year-old diabetic who lived in a trailer park in Somerville, Tennessee. When Zettie Mae Hill, Takewell's neighbor, found the unemployed carpenter drenched with sweat from a fever, she called an ambulance. Takewell was rushed to nearby Methodist Hospital, where, it turned out, he had an outstanding bill of $9,400. A notice posted in the emergency room told staff members to alert supervisors if Takewell ever returned.
>
> When the hospital administrator was informed of the admission, Takewell was already in a hospital bed. The administrator went to Takewell's room, helped him to his feet, and escorted him to the parking lot. There, neighbors found him under a tree and took him home.
>
> Takewell died about twelve hours later.
>
> Zettie Mae Hill is still torn up about it. She wonders if Takewell would be alive today if she had directed his ambulance to a different hospital. She said, "I didn't think a hospital would just let a person die like that for lack of money." (Based on Ansberry 1988)

Why was Terry Takewell denied medical treatment and his life cut short? The fundamental reason is that

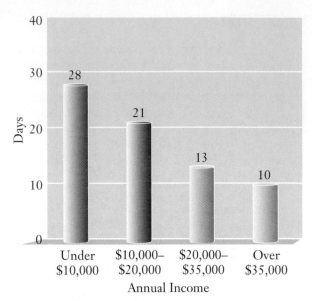

Note: Number of days people were so sick or injured that they cut down on their usual activities for more than half a day; includes days off work and school.

 **NUMBER OF DAYS SICK**

Source: *Statistical Abstract* 1999:Table 222.

in the United States health care is not a citizens' right, but a commodity for sale. The result is a two-tier system of medical care—superior care for those who can afford the cost, and inferior care for those who cannot. Unlike the middle and upper classes, few poor people have a personal physician, and they often spend hours waiting in crowded public health clinics. After waiting most of a day, some don't even get to see a doctor. Instead, they are told to come back the next day (Fialka 1993). And when the poor are hospitalized, they are likely to find themselves in understaffed and underfunded public hospitals, where they are treated by rotating interns who do not know them and cannot follow up on their progress.

Mental Health

Social class also affects our mental health. From the 1930s until now, sociologists have found that the mental health of the lower classes is worse than that of the higher classes (Faris and Dunham 1939; Srole et al. 1978; Lundberg 1991; Miller 1994). Greater mental problems are part of a stress package that comes with poverty. Compared with middle- and upper-class Americans, the poor have less job security, lower wages, more unpaid bills, more divorce, more alcoholism, greater vulnerability to crime, more physical illnesses—often accompanied by the threat of eviction hanging over their heads. Such conditions deal severe blows to people's emotional well-being.

People higher up the social class ladder experience stress in daily life, of course, but their stress is generally less and their coping resources greater. Not only can they afford vacations, psychiatrists, and counselors, but *their class position gives them greater control over their lives, a key to good mental health.*

Social class is also a deciding factor in mental health care, a topic of the following Thinking Critically section.

Thinking Critically

MENTAL ILLNESS AND INEQUALITY IN HEALTH CARE

Standing among the police, I watched as the elderly, nude man, looking confused, struggled to put on his clothing. The man had ripped the wires out of the homeless shelter's main electrical box, and then led the police on a merry chase as he ran from room to room.

I asked the officers where they were going to take the man, and they replied, "To Malcolm Bliss" (the state hospital). When I commented, "I guess he'll be in there for quite a while," they replied, "Probably just a day or two. We picked him up last week—he was crawling under cars at a traffic light—and they let him out in two days."

The police explained that a person must be a danger to others or to oneself to be admitted as a long-term patient. Visualizing this old man crawling under cars in traffic and the possibility of electrocuting himself by ripping out electrical wires with his bare hands, I marveled at the definition of "danger" that the hospital psychiatrists must be using.

Stripped of its veil, the two-tier system of medical care is readily visible. The poor—such as this confused naked man—find it difficult to get into mental hospitals. If they are admitted, they are sent to the dreaded state hospitals. In contrast, private hospitals serve the wealthy and those who have good insurance. The rich are likely to be treated with "talk therapy" (forms of psychotherapy), the poor with "drug therapy" (tranquilizers to make them docile, sometimes known as "medicinal straitjackets"). ■

For Your Consideration

How can we improve the treatment of the mentally ill poor? Take into consideration that the public does not want higher taxes. What about the broader, more fundamental issue—that of inequality in health care? Should medical care be a commodity that is sold to those who can afford it? Or do all citizens possess some fundamental right that should guarantee them high-quality health care?

Social Class and the New Technology

Effects of the new technology also follow social class lines. For the capitalist class, the new technology is a dream come true: By minimizing the obstacles of national borders, capitalists can locate factories in countries with cheap labor and maximize profits through global integration. A product's components can be produced in several countries, assembled in another country, and the product then marketed throughout the world. The new technology also benefits the upper middle class. Their education prepares them to take a leading role in managing this global system for the capitalist class, or for using the new technology to advance in their chosen professions.

Below these two classes, however, the new technology adds to the insecurity to life. As the new technology transforms the workplace, it eliminates jobs and makes workers' skills outdated. People in lower management can transfer their skills from one job to another, although in shifting job markets the periods of unemployment can create a precarious situation. Those who work at specialized crafts are even less secure, for their training is more specific and the new technology can reduce or even eliminate the need for their narrower, more specialized skills.

From this middle point on the ladder down, technology hits people the hardest. The working class is ill prepared for the changes the new technology brings, and they are haunted by the specter of unemployment. The working poor are even more vulnerable, for they have even less to offer in the new job market. As unskilled jobs dry up, many are consigned to the industrial garbage bin. The underclass, of course, with no technical skills, is bypassed entirely.

In short, the new technology opens and closes opportunities for people largely by virtue of where they are located on the social class ladder, a topic discussed in the Sociology and the New Technology box on the next page.

Sociology & the New Technology

CLOSING THE DIGITAL DIVIDE:
THE TECHNOLOGY GAP FACING THE POOR AND MINORITIES

Digital divide refers to the technology gap between the poor and the middle and upper classes. It also has a racial-ethnic component. Because a larger proportion of minorities are poor, compared with whites a smaller percentage of African Americans, Latinos, and Native Americans have access to computers and the Internet (Meeks 1999).

Sociologists focus on the *structural* basis of wealth and poverty. That is, they examine how advantage and disadvantage are *built into society*. This does not mean that children who are born into poverty cannot overcome this disadvantage. A lot of them do. In fact, the opportunities of this country are why so many people want to live in the United States. But because of structural reasons, some people face many obstacles because of their birth, while others face few.

The question, then, is not how we can destroy the advantages that some have, but, rather, how we can reduce the disadvantages that others face. What can we do to increase opportunities for those who are born into a world of huge obstacles? Or, at the very least, how can we prevent those obstacles from growing?

These questions take us to the digital divide. If the children who

live in poverty have less access to computers and the Internet, their disadvantage in our new technological world will grow. If computers were only for playing cyber games, this would not be an issue. But the Internet has become a major source of information. Think of the Internet as a gigantic library that spans the globe. As a practical example, in writing this text I used to make frequent trips to libraries. Now I do most of my research on the Internet. Not only do I have instant access to the latest government reports, but the Internet also provides e-mail connections with people around the world who can help me track down bits of arcane data.

Using the Internet to access information is a skill, much of it learned by trial and error. If children in poverty have less access to computers and the Internet, their skills in this vital area will be weak—and this will affect their future economic well-being. This disadvantage will be one more hurdle to keep them from advancing economically. No one wants middle- and upper-class children to relinquish this skill—the issue

is how to help level the playing field by enabling the children of the poor to increase their skills. ■

For Your Consideration

What do you think can be done to overcome the digital divide? For example, do you think the government should pay to connect every U.S. home to the Internet and buy a computer for every child, beginning in kindergarten? Why or why not?

Let's look at the problem this way: Would we ever allow libraries to grant entrance to white Americans and ban some minorities? Let in the wealthy, but close the door on some people because they are poor? Is it fair to draw this analogy, given that libraries are funded by tax dollars and computers and Internet access are paid for by individuals?

SOCIAL MOBILITY

No aspect of life, then—from marriage to education—goes untouched by social class. Because life is so much more satisfying in the more privileged classes, people strive to climb the social class ladder. What affects their chances?

Three Types of Social Mobility

There are three basic types of social mobility: intergenerational, structural, and exchange. **Intergenerational mobility** refers to a change that occurs between generations—when grown-up children end up on a different rung of the social class ladder than the one occupied by their parents. If the child of someone who sells used cars graduates from college and buys a Toyota dealership, that person experiences **upward social mobility.** Conversely, if a child of the dealer's owner parties too much, drops out of college, and ends up selling cars, he or she experiences **downward social mobility.**

We like to think that individual efforts are the reason people move up the social class ladder—their faults the reason they move down. In these examples, we can identify hard work, sacrifice, and ambition on the one hand, versus indolence and alcohol abuse on the other. Although individual factors such as these do underlie social mobility, sociologists consider **structural mobility** to be the crucial factor. This second basic type of mobility refers to changes in society that cause large numbers of people to move up or down the class ladder.

To better understand structural mobility, think of how opportunities opened when computers were invented. New types of jobs appeared overnight. Huge numbers of people took workshops and crash courses, switching from blue-collar to white-collar work. Although individual effort certainly was involved—for some seized the opportunity while others did not—the underlying cause was a change in the *structure* of work. Consider the opposite—how opportunities close during a depression, and millions of people are forced downward on the class ladder. In this instance, too,

The term *structural mobility* refers to changes in society that push large numbers of people either up or down the social class ladder. A remarkable example was the stock market crash of 1929, when thousands of people suddenly lost immense amounts of wealth. People who once "had it made" found themselves standing on street corners selling apples or, as depicted here, selling their possessions at fire-sale prices.

their changed status is due less to individual behavior than to *structural* changes in society.

The third type of social mobility, **exchange mobility,** occurs when large numbers of people move up and down the social class ladder, but, on balance, the proportions of the social classes remain about the same. Suppose that a million or so working-class people are trained in computers, and they move up the social class ladder. Suppose also that due to a vast surge in imports about a million skilled workers have to take lower-status jobs. Although millions of people change their social class, there is, in effect, an *exchange* among them. The net result more or less balances out, and the class system remains basically untouched.

Those who experience social mobility, regardless of its type, have to make huge adjustments to their new world. Even upward social mobility brings an uncomfortable adjustment, the topic of our Down-to-Earth Sociology box on the next page.

Women in Studies of Social Mobility

The United States is famous worldwide for its intergenerational mobility. That children can pass up their parents on the social class ladder is one of the attractions of this country. To find out how extensive this mobility is, sociologists used to study only men. In classic studies, they concluded that about half of sons passed their fathers; about one-third stayed at the same level, and only about one-sixth fell down the class ladder (Blau and Duncan 1967; Featherman and Hauser 1978; Featherman 1979).

Fathers and sons? How about the other half of the population? Feminists pointed out this obvious omission (Davis and Robinson 1988). They also objected to the assumption that women had no class position of their own and were simply assigned the class of their husbands. The defense was that too few women were in the labor force to make a difference.

With huge numbers of women now working for pay, more recent studies include women (Breen and Whelan 1995; Beeghley 2000). Sociologists Elizabeth Higginbotham and Lynn Weber (1992), for example, studied 200 women from working-class backgrounds who became professionals, managers, and administrators in Memphis. They found that almost without exception, the women's parents had encouraged them while they were still little girls to postpone marriage and get an education.

Sociology

LIVING IN TWO WORLDS:
MOVING UP THE SOCIAL CLASS LADDER

I want to begin this Down-to-Earth Sociology feature on a personal note. As you will read in the Down-to-Earth Sociology box on page 201, I was born in poverty. Education was my way out; it opened up a new world for me and led to the writing of this textbook. I was touched when I read sociologist David Croteau's account of his change in social class. Like me, Croteau was born into a blue-collar family and was the first in his family to attend college. He describes his experience of upward social mobility as only someone who has gone through it could. What he says resonates, matching what I experienced so well that I want to share his account with you.

After brief periods as a logger and as a shipworker, my father worked in a paper mill.... My mother, after stints as a domestic and factory worker, toiled at home raising four children....

That paper mill played a central role in my life, not only because my father and other family members worked there, but because it served as a source of motivation for me. As long as I can remember, I was determined not to work in the mill....

Neither of my parents had attended high school, let alone college, so I was left rudderless in choosing schools. The two part-time guidance counselors at my regional high school of more than seven hundred students were not helpful. One had suggested to me that perhaps, despite my excellent grades, welding would be more "practical" for someone with my "background." After applying to what in retrospect was an eclectic collection of schools, I made the only logical choice: the one that offered me the most scholarship money. It was an elite private college in the Boston area.

From the very first day, my college education brought with it a new awareness of how different cultures could be. I have a vivid memory of the awkwardness and discomfort on my parents' faces when they met my assigned roommate and his obviously wealthy parents (both doctors) in the totally alien environment of a college dorm (I was not feeling any better.) Cultures rarely confront each other so poignantly.

I shared my parents' discomfort as I learned lessons that would make it increasingly difficult for me to return to my working-class community. In both my formal and informal education, I was immersed in middle-class culture. Employment expectations ("careers," not jobs), food ("ethnic," not meat-and-potatoes), dress (natural fibers, not synthetic), music (folk and progressive/alternative rock, not heavy metal), entertainment and leisure (something other than television and hockey)—it was all different from what I was accustomed to.

Perhaps the most striking difference I encountered was the sense of entitlement shared by other students. For most of my middle-class peers, college seemed to be little more than a nuisance and an unexceptional part of their lives. Often choreographed by their parents, college was an expected step towards a larger world of broad opportunity. But for me school always seemed a luxury, and I had a strange sense that one day I would be told some terrible administrative error had been made and I would be sent packing back home to serve my time in the mill where I *really* belonged. (Years later, when I was a graduate student on a full scholarship, the feeling still lingered.)

On the whole, my experiences confirmed my earlier sense of the vast distance between "ordinary" people and the more privileged classes with whom I now interacted. Having strayed further and further from home, I saw and felt class differences more sharply than ever. The feelings were often unpleasant. During my first disorienting year at school, I found solace by making friends with local working-class "townies' and frequently drinking to excess....

But as I was learning to better analyze and understand the world in which I lived, I was drifting away from the world from which I had come. My education had equipped me with middle-class skills and had introduced me to middle-class values, attitudes, and ways of thinking....

In a study of social mobility, David Karp has commented that "Class background does not fall away like a snake's old skin once professional status is achieved." The image is a good one and it holds true for my travels to the middle-class Left. I found myself straddling a fence. I had a full set of middle-class educational credentials and was part of a middle-class movement ["peace-and-justice" organizations], but I still had strong attachments to my roots and to my working-class family and friends. I had a foot in each world but was completely comfortable in neither of them. Having been socialized into two different classes, I was constantly aware—sometimes painfully so—of the differences between these cultures....

I was confronted with the undeniable reality of a class divide that separated the cultures of the working-class from which I had come from that of the middle-class, political Left to which I had traveled.... Such a confrontation of cultures is fertile ground for sociological analysis. That is what my professional training has taught me. My lived experience of this class divide has, for me, made it more than an academic question. ■

Source: David Croteau. *Politics and the Class Divide: Working People and the Middle-Class Left.* Philadelphia: Temple University Press, 1995:xxiv-xxviii.

This study confirms findings that the family is of utmost importance in the socialization process and that the primary entry to the upper middle class is a college education. At the same time, note that if there had not been a structural change in society, the millions of new positions that women occupy would not exist.

The New Technology and Fears of the Future

The ladder also leads down, of course, which is precisely what strikes fear in the hearts of many workers. If the United States does not keep pace with global change and remain competitive by producing low-cost, quality goods, its economic position will decline. The result will be dwindling opportunities—fewer jobs and shrinking paychecks.

To compete in this global economic race, the United States is incorporating advanced technology in all spheres of life. While this means good jobs for many, it also means that the technologically illiterate are being left behind. This point was driven home to me when I saw the homeless sitting dejected in the shelters. There were our school dropouts, our technological know-nothings. Of what value are they to this new society that is now undergoing its piercing birth pains? They simply have no productive place. Their base of social belonging and self-esteem has been pulled out from under them.

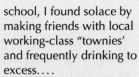

POVERTY

Many Americans find the "limitless possibilities" on which the American dream is based to be elusive. As illustrated in Figure 8.4 on page 187, the working poor and underclass together form about one-fifth of the U.S. population. This percentage translates into a huge number, about 55 million people. Who are these people?

Drawing the Poverty Line

To administer its programs for the poor, the U.S. government must determine who is eligible for them. Based on observations that poor people spend about one-third of their incomes on food, the government figures out a low-cost food budget and multiplies it by 3. This it calls the **poverty line**. You can see how arbitrary the poverty line is: Those whose incomes are less than this amount are classified as poor; those whose incomes are higher—even by a dollar—are determined to be "non-poor." As sociologists observe, the poverty line is also unrealistic. Some mothers work, and some don't, but both are treated the same even though one has to pay for child care. The poverty line is also the same dollar total across the nation, even though the cost of living is much higher in some states (Michael 1995; Corbett 1999).

It is part of the magical sleight-of-hand of government bureaucracy that a change in this official measure of poverty instantly makes millions of people poor—or takes away their poverty. This would almost be humorous, if it weren't for the consequences being so serious: The government uses the poverty line to decide who will receive help and who will not. Using this very arbitrary, but official, definition of poverty, let's see who in the United States is poor. Before we do this, though, compare your ideas of the poor with the myths explored in the Down-to-Earth Sociology box below.

Who Are the Poor?

Geography As you can see from the Social Map on the next page, the poor are not evenly distributed among the states. This map also shows a clustering of poverty in the South, a pattern that has prevailed for 100 years or so.

A second aspect of geography is also significant. About 56 million Americans live in rural areas. Of these, 9 million are poor. At 16 percent, their rate of poverty is higher than the national average of 13 percent. The rural poor are less likely to be single parents, and more likely to be married and to have jobs. Compared with urban Americans, the rural poor are less skilled and less educated, and the jobs available to them pay less than similar jobs in urban areas (Dudenhefer 1993).

The greatest predictor of whether Americans are poor is not geography, however, but race-ethnicity, education, and the sex of the person who heads the family. Let's look at these three factors.

Sociology

Down-to-Earth

EXPLORING MYTHS ABOUT THE POOR

Myth 1 Most poor people are lazy. They are poor because they do not want to work.

Half of the poor are either too old or too young to work. About 40 percent are under age 18, and another 10 percent are age 65 or older. About 30 percent of the working-age poor work at least half the year.

Myth 2 Poor people are trapped in a cycle of poverty that few escape.

The U.S. poverty population is *dynamic*. Most poverty lasts less than a year (Gottschalk et al. 1994). Only 12 percent remain in poverty for five or more consecutive years (O'Hare 1996a). Most children who are born in poverty are not poor as adults (Ruggles 1989).

Myth 3 Most of the poor are African Americans and Latinos.

As shown on Figure 8.8 (on page 198), the poverty rates of African Americans and Latinos are much higher than that of whites. Because there are so many more whites in the U.S. population, however, *most poor Americans are white*. Fifty-six percent of the poor are white, 21 percent African American, 19 percent Latino, 3 percent Asian American, and 1 percent Native American (*Statistical Abstract* 1999:Tables 54, 760).

Myth 4 Most of the poor are single mothers and their children.

Although about 38 percent of the poor do match this stereotype, 34 percent of the poor live in married-couple families, 22 percent live

alone or with nonrelatives, and 6 percent live in other settings.

Myth 5 Most of the poor live in the inner city.

This one is close to fact, as about 42 percent do live in the inner city. But 36 percent live in the suburbs, and 22 percent live in small towns and rural areas.

Myth 6 The poor live on welfare.

About half of the income of poor adults comes from wages and pensions, about 25 percent from welfare, and about 22 percent from Social Security. ■

Sources: Primarily O'Hare 1996a and O'Hare 1996b, but other sources as indicated.

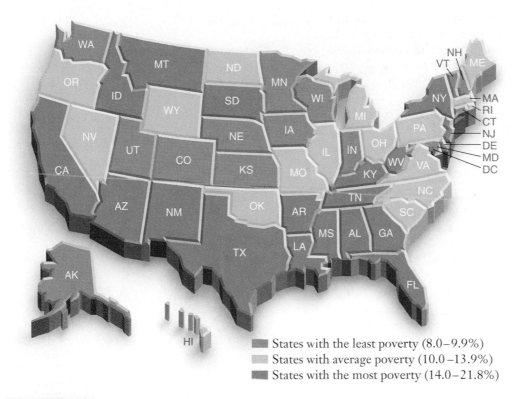

States with the least poverty (8.0–9.9%)
States with average poverty (10.0–13.9%)
States with the most poverty (14.0–21.8%)

Figure 8.6 PATTERNS OF POVERTY

Source: Statistical Abstract 1999:Table 765.

Race-Ethnicity One of the strongest factors in poverty is race-ethnicity. As Figure 8.7 on the next page shows, only 11 percent of white Americans are poor, but 27 percent of African Americans and Latinos live in poverty. Although white Americans are less likely to be poor than members of most other racial-ethnic groups, because there are so many more white Americans, most poor people are white.

Beyond the awareness of most Americans are the rural poor, such as this family in Louisiana. This family is typical of the rural poor: white and headed by a woman. What do you think the future holds for these children?

POVERTY IN THE UNITED STATES, BY AGE AND RACE-ETHNICITY

Note: The poverty line on which this figure is based is $16,400 for a family of four.

Source: Statistical Abstract 1999:Tables 760, 763.

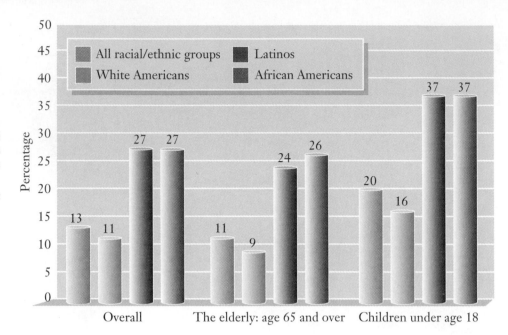

Education As you know, education is also a vital factor in poverty, but you may not have known just how powerful it is. From Figure 8.8, you can see that only 2 of 100 people who finish college end up in poverty, but one of every four people who drop out of high school is poor. As you can see, the chances of someone being poor decrease with each higher level of education. Although this principle applies regardless of race-ethnicity, you can see how race-ethnicity makes an impact at every level of education.

The Feminization of Poverty The other major predictor of poverty is the sex of the person who heads the family. Compared with men, women are more likely to be poor (*Statistical Abstract* 1999:Tables 756, 766). Women who head families average only two-thirds the income of men who head families (*Statistical Abstract* 1999:Table 754). The three major causes of this phenomenon, called **the feminization of poverty,** are divorce, births to single women, and the lower wages paid to women.

WHO ENDS UP POOR? POVERTY BY EDUCATION AND RACE-ETHNICITY

Source: Statistical Abstract 1999:Table 769.

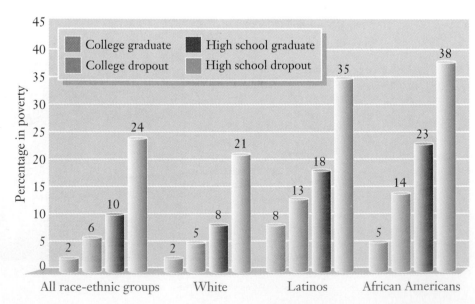

Old Age As Figure 8.7 shows, the elderly are less likely than the general population to be poor. It used to be that growing old increased people's chances of being poor, but government policies to redistribute wealth—Social Security and subsidized housing, food, and medical care—slashed the rate of poverty among the elderly. As you can see, the prevailing racial-ethnic patterns carry over into old age; an elderly African American or Latino is almost three times as likely to be poor as an elderly white person.

Children of Poverty

Children are more likely to live in poverty than are adults or the elderly. This holds true regardless of race, but from Figure 8.7 you can see how much greater poverty is among Latino and African American children. That about 14 million U.S. children are reared in poverty is shocking when one considers the wealth of this country and the supposed concern for the well-being of children. This tragic aspect of poverty is the topic of the following Thinking Critically section.

Thinking *Critically*

THE NATION'S SHAME: CHILDREN IN POVERTY

One of the most startling statistics in sociology is shown in Figure 8.7. One of every five U.S. children lives in poverty. One of six white children and one of three Latino and African American children are poor. These figures translate into incredible numbers—approximately *14 million* children live in poverty: 6 million white children, 4 million Latino children, and 4 million African American children.

Sociologist and former U.S. Senator Daniel Moynihan says that the main cause for this high rate of child poverty is the sharp increase in births outside marriage. He points out that in 1960, only one of twenty U.S. children was born to a single woman. Today that figure is *six times higher,* and single women now account for one of three (32 percent) of all U.S. births. The relationship to social class is striking, for as Table 8.3 shows, births to single women are not distributed evenly across the social classes. For women above the poverty line, only 6 percent of births are to single women, but for women below the poverty line this rate jumps to 44 percent.

Regardless of the causes of childhood poverty—and there are many—what is most significant are its far-reaching consequences. Poor children are more likely to die in infancy, to go hungry and become malnourished, to develop more slowly, and to have more health problems. They also are more likely to drop out of school, to become involved in criminal activities, and to have children while still in their teens—thus perpetuating the cycle of poverty. ■

For Your Consideration

Many social analysts are alarmed at this increase in child poverty. They emphasize that it is time to stop blaming the victim, and, instead, to focus on the *structural* factors that underlie child poverty. To relieve this problem, they say, we must take immediate steps to establish national programs of child nutrition and health care. Solutions will require at least three fundamental changes: (1) removing obstacles to employment; (2) improving education; and (3) strengthening the family. To achieve these changes, what specific programs would *you* recommend?

Sources: Moynihan 1991; Murray 1993; Sandefur 1995; *Statistical Abstract* 1997:Table 1338; 1999:Tables 22, 92, 760, 763.

The Dynamics of Poverty

Some analysts have suggested that the poor get trapped in a **culture of poverty** (Harrington 1962; Lewis 1966a). They assume that the values and behaviors of the poor "make them fundamentally different from other Americans, and that these factors are largely responsible for their continued long-term poverty" (Ruggles 1989:7).

Lurking behind this concept is the idea that the poor are lazy people who bring poverty on themselves. Certainly there are individuals and families who match this stereotype—many of us have known them. But is a self-perpetuating culture that is transmitted across generations, which "locks" people in poverty, the basic reason for U.S. poverty?

Table 8.3

U.S. BIRTHS TO SINGLE AND MARRIED WOMEN

Births to Women Above the Poverty Line		Births to Women Below the Poverty Line	
Married	Single	Married	Single
94%	6%	56%	44%

Note: Figures were available only for white women.

Source: Murray 1993.

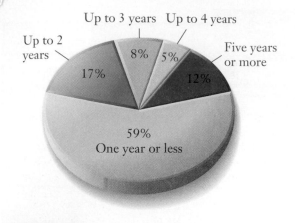

Figure 8.9 — HOW LONG DOES POVERTY LAST?

Source: Gottschalk et al 1994:89.

Researchers who followed 5,000 U.S. families uncovered some rather surprising findings. Contrary to common stereotypes, most poverty is short, lasting only a year or less. Most poverty comes about due to a dramatic life change such as divorce, sudden unemployment, or even the birth of a child (O'Hare 1996a). As Figure 8.9 shows, only 12 percent of poverty lasts five years or longer. Contrary to the stereotype of lazy people who are content to live off the government, the vast majority of poor people don't like poverty, and they do what they can *not* to be poor.

Yet from one year to the next, the number of poor people remains about the same. This means that the people who move out of poverty are replaced by people who move *into* poverty. The vast majority of these newly poor also will move out of poverty within a year. Some people even bounce back and forth, never quite making it securely out of poverty. Poverty, then, is dynamic, touching a lot more people than the official figures indicate. Although 13 percent of Americans may be poor at any one time, twice that number, about one-fourth of the U.S. population, is or has been poor for at least a year.

Welfare Reform

After decades of criticism, U.S. welfare was restructured in 1996. A federal law—the Personal Responsibility and Work Opportunity Reconciliation Act—requires states to place a lifetime cap on welfare assistance and to require welfare recipients to look for work and to take available jobs. The maximum length someone can collect welfare is two years. Many states made it shorter. They also required unmarried teen parents to attend school and to live at home or in some other adult-supervised setting.

This law set off a storm of criticism, with some calling it an attack on the poor. Defenders said that the new rules would rescue people from poverty—transforming them into self-supporting and hard-working citizens—and reduce welfare costs (Cohen 1997; Guiliani 1999). Some states put up new signs, changing "Welfare Center" to "Job Placement Center." Welfare rolls plummeted, in Wisconsin by 90 percent. Overall, national welfare rolls dropped by 44 percent (Dervarics 1998; Associated Press 1999; DeParle 1999). This is only the rosy part of the picture, however. Apparently, about one-fifth to one-sixth of former welfare recipients have no jobs, and having used up their allotted time to collect welfare, are worse off than before (Goldberg 1999; DeParle 1999).

Conflict theorists point out that the welfare system has a different purpose than we ordinarily realize—to maintain an army of reserve workers. It is designed to keep the unemployed alive during economic downturns until they are needed during the next economic boom. Reducing the welfare rolls through the 1996 law does fit this model, as it occurred during the longest economic boom in U.S history. During our next recession, which is inevitable, unemployment will surge. In line with conflict theory, we can predict that welfare rules will be softened—in order to keep the reserve army of the unemployed ready for the next time they are needed.

Why Are People Poor?

Two explanations for poverty compete for our attention. The first, which sociologists adopt, focuses on *social structure*. Sociologists stress that *features of society* deny some people access to education or learning job skills. They emphasize racial-ethnic, age, and gender discrimination, as well as changes in the job market—the closing of plants, drying up of unskilled jobs, and an increase in marginal jobs that pay poverty wages.

A competing explanation focuses on *characteristics of individuals* that are assumed to contribute to poverty. Individualistic explanations that sociologists reject outright as worthless stereotypes are laziness and lack of intelligence. Individualistic explanations that sociologists reluctantly acknowledge include dropping out of school, bearing children at younger ages, and averaging more children than women in other social classes. Most sociologists are reluctant to speak of such factors in this context, for they appear to blame the victim, something that sociologists bend over backward not to do.

In the Down-to-Earth Sociology box on the next page, in which I share my personal experiences with

Sociology

Down-to-Earth

POVERTY: A PERSONAL JOURNEY

I was born in poverty. My parents, who could not afford to rent a house or apartment, rented the tiny office in their minister's house. That is where I was born.

My father began to slowly climb the social class ladder. His fitful odyssey took him from laborer to truck driver to the owner of a series of small businesses (tire shop, bar, hotel), then to vacuum cleaner salesman, and back to bar owner. He converted a garage into a house. Although it had no indoor plumbing or insulation (in northern Minnesota!), it was a start. Later, he bought a house, and then he built a new home. After that we moved into a trailer, and then back to a house. My father's seventh grade education was always an obstacle. Although he never became wealthy, poverty did become a distant memory for him.

My social class took a leap—from working to upper middle—when, after attending college and graduate school, I became a university professor. I entered a world that was unknown to my parents, a world much more pampered and privileged. I had opportunities to do research, to publish, and to travel to exotic places. My reading centered on sociological research, and I read books in Spanish as well as in English. My father, in contrast, never read a book in his life, and my mother read only detective stories and romance paperbacks. One set of experiences isn't "better" than the other, just significantly different in determining what windows of perception it opens onto the world.

My interest in poverty, which was rooted in my own childhood experiences, stayed with me. I traveled to a dozen or so skid rows across the United States and Canada, talking to the homeless and staying in their shelters. In my own town, I spent considerable time with people on welfare, observing how they lived. I constantly marveled at the connections between *structural* causes of poverty (lack of education, the drying up of unskilled jobs, the lack of transportation) and its *personal* causes (the *culture of poverty*—alcohol and drug abuse, multiple out-of-wedlock births, frivolous spending, all-night partying, and a seeming incapacity to keep appointments—except to pick up the welfare check).

Sociologists haven't unraveled this connection, and as much as we might *like* for only the structural causes to apply, clearly *both* are at work. The situation can be illustrated by looking at the perennial health problems I observed among the poor—the constant colds, runny noses, back aches, and injuries. The health problems stemmed from the *social structure* (little access to medical care, lesser trained or less capable physicians, drafty houses, lack of education regarding nutrition, and more dangerous jobs). At the same time, *personal* characteristics—hygiene, eating habits, and overdrinking—caused health problems. Which was the cause and which the effect? Both, of course, for one fed into the other. The medical problems (which were based on both personal and structural causes) fed into the poverty these people experienced, making them less able to perform their jobs successfully—or even to show up at work regularly.

What an intricate puzzle for sociologists! ■

poverty, you will see the tension between these two explanations.

Where Is Horatio Alger?
The Social Functions of a Myth

In the early 1900s, Horatio Alger was one of the country's most talked-about fictional heroes. The rags-to-riches exploits of this national character, and his startling successes in overcoming severe odds, motivated thousands of boys of that period. Although he has disappeared from U.S. literature, Horatio Alger remains alive and well in the psyche of Americans. From abundant real-life examples of people from humble origins who climbed far up the social class ladder, Americans know that anyone can get ahead by really trying. In fact, they believe that most Americans, including minorities and the working poor, have an average or better than average chance of getting ahead—obviously a statistical impossibility (Kluegel and Smith 1986).

The accuracy of the **Horatio Alger myth** is less important than the belief that limitless possibilities exist for everyone. Functionalists would stress that this belief is functional for society. On the one hand, it encourages people to compete for higher positions, or, as the song says, "to reach for the highest star." On the other hand, it places blame for failure squarely on the individual. If you don't make it—in the face of ample opportunities to get ahead—the fault must be your own. The Horatio Alger myth helps to stabilize society, then, for since the fault is viewed as the individual's, not society's, current social arrangements can be re-

garded as satisfactory. This reduces pressures to change the system.

As Marx and Weber pointed out, social class penetrates our consciousness, shaping our ideas of life and our "proper" place in society. When the rich look at the world around them, they sense superiority and anticipate control over their own destiny. When the poor look around them, they are more likely to sense defeat, and to anticipate that their lives will be buffeted by unpredictable forces. Each knows the dominant ideology, that their particular niche in life is due to their own efforts, that the reasons for success—or failure—lie solely with the self. Like the fish that don't notice the water, people tend not to perceive the effects of social class on their own lives.

SUMMARY AND REVIEW

■ What Is Social Class?

Most sociologists have adopted Weber's definition of **social class** as a large group of people who rank closely to one another in terms of wealth, power, and prestige. **Wealth**, consisting of property and income, is concentrated in the upper classes. The distribution of wealth in the United States has changed little since World War II, but the changes that have occurred have been toward greater inequality. **Power** is the ability to get your way, even though others resist. C. Wright Mills coined the term **power elite** to refer to the small group that holds the reins of power in business, government, and the military. **Prestige** is often linked to occupational status. Pp.178–183.

People's rankings of occupational prestige have changed little over the decades and are similar from country to country. Globally, occupations that pay more, require more education and abstract thought, and offer greater autonomy bring greater prestige. P. 183.

What is meant by the term *status inconsistency*?

Status is social ranking. Most people are **status consistent**; that is, they rank high or low on all three dimensions of social class. People who rank higher on some dimensions than on others are status inconsistent. The frustrations of **status inconsistency** tend to produce political radicalism. Pp. 184–185.

■ Sociological Models of Social Class

What models are used to portray the social classes?

Erik Wright developed a four-class model based on Marx: (1) capitalists or owners; (2) petty bourgeoisie or small business owners; (3) managers; and (4) workers. Kahl and Gilbert developed a six-class model based on Weber. At the top is the

capitalist class. In descending order are the upper middle class, the lower middle class, the working class, the working poor, and the **underclass**. Pp. 185–189.

■ Consequences of Social Class

How does social class affect people's lives?

Social class leaves no aspect of life untouched. It affects our chances of living and dying, of getting sick, of receiving good health care, of getting divorced, of getting an education, of participating in politics. It even affects our religious affiliation and whether or not we benefit from the new technology. Pp. 189–192.

■ Social Mobility

What are the three types of social mobility?

The term **intergenerational mobility** refers to changes in social class from one generation to the next. **Exchange mobility** is the movement of large numbers of people from one class to another with the net result that the relative proportions of the population in the classes remain about the same. The term **structural mobility** refers to changes in society that affect the social class membership of large numbers of people. Pp. 192–195.

■ Poverty

Who are the poor?

Poverty is unequally distributed in the United States. Latinos, African Americans, Native Americans, children, women-headed households, and rural Americans are more likely than others to be poor. The poverty rate of the elderly is less than that of the general population. Pp. 195–200.

Why Are People Poor?

Some social analysts believe that characteristics of *individuals* cause poverty. Sociologists, in contrast, examine *structural* features of society, such as employment opportunities, to find the causes of poverty. Sociologists generally conclude that life orientations are a consequence, not the cause, of people's position in the social class structure. Pp. 200–201.

How is the Horatio Alger myth functional for society?

The **Horatio Alger myth**—the belief that anyone can get ahead if only he or she tries hard enough—encourages people to strive to get ahead. It also deflects blame for failure from society to the individual. Pp. 201–202.

Where can I read more on this topic?

Suggested readings for this chapter are listed on page SR-5.

YOUR INTERACTIVE COMPANION WEB SITE

Your Interactive Companion Web Site includes practice tests, with feedback, and online learning activities with video, audio, and Weblinks. Your access code for this Web site is provided with this text.

GLOSSARY

contradictory class locations Erik Wright's term for a position in the class structure that generates contradictory interests (p. 185)

culture of poverty the values and behaviors of the poor that are assumed to make them fundamentally different from other people; these factors are assumed to be largely responsible for their poverty, and parents are assumed to perpetuate poverty across generations by passing these characteristics on to their children (p. 199)

downward social mobility movement down the social class ladder (p. 193)

exchange mobility about the same numbers of people moving up and down the social class ladder, such that in the end the social class system shows little change (p. 193)

(the) feminization of poverty a trend in U.S. poverty whereby most poor families are headed by women (p. 198)

Horatio Alger myth a belief that anyone can get ahead if only he or she tries hard enough; encourages people to strive to get ahead and deflects blame for failure from society to the individual (p. 202)

intergenerational mobility the change that family members make in social class from one generation to the next (p. 192)

poverty line the official measure of poverty; calculated as three times a low-cost food budget (p. 195)

power the ability to get your way, even over the resistance of others (p. 182)

power elite C. Wright Mills' term for the top leaders of corporations, military, and politics who make the nation's major decisions (p. 182)

prestige respect or regard (p. 182)

social class a large number of people with similar amounts of income and education who work at jobs that are roughly comparable in prestige (p. 178)

status the position that someone occupies in society or a social group; one's social ranking (p. 184)

status consistency people ranking high or low on all three dimensions of social class (p. 184)

status inconsistency a contradiction or mismatch between statuses; a condition in which someone ranks high on some dimensions of social class and low on others (p. 184)

structural mobility movement up or down the social class ladder that is due to changes in the structure of society, not to individual efforts (p. 193)

underclass a small group of people for whom poverty persists year after year and across generations (p. 188)

upward social mobility movement up the social class ladder (p. 193)

wealth property and income (p. 178)

Chapter 9

Kerry James Marshall, Watts 1963, 1995

Inequalities of Race and Ethnicity

"My brother-in-law was a religious man," said Edmond. "When the militia came for him, he asked if he could pray first. They let him pray. After his prayers, he said he didn't want his family dismembered. They said he could throw his children down the latrine holes

instead. He did. Then the militia threw him and my sister on top."

Shining a flashlight into the 40-foot-deep hole, Edmond said, "Look You can still see the bones."

Between 800,000 and 1 million Rwandans died in the slaughter. Although the killings were low-tech—most were done with machetes—it took just 100 days in the summer of 1994 to complete the state-sanctioned massacres (Gourevitch 1995; 1998).

Rwanda has two major ethnic groups. The Hutus outnumber the Tutsis six to one. Hutus are stocky and round-faced, dark-skinned, flat-nosed, and thick-lipped. The Tutsis are lankier and longer-faced, lighter-skinned, narrow-nosed, and thin-lipped. But the two groups, who speak the same language, have intermarried for so long that they have difficulty telling Hutu from Tutsi.

The Hutus, who controlled the government, called on all Hutus to kill all Tutsis. It was a national duty, said the Hutu leaders. Obediently, neighbors hacked neighbors to death in their homes. Colleagues hacked colleagues to death at work. Even teachers killed their students.

Local Hutu officials opened stadiums and churches, offering refuge to Tutsis. It was there that the largest massacres occurred, supervised by these same local officials.

While radio announcers urged their listeners to disembowel pregnant Tutsi women, the government passed out machetes, guns, and alcohol—and bused men from massacre to massacre. ■

205

These bodies of Tutsis were discarded as so much trash after the slaughter described in the opening vignette. Because this photo is so gruesome, I debated whether to include it in the book. I even asked for advice from a couple of people whose opinion I respect. I chose to include it when one said, "It illustrates the massiveness of the horror and the cavalier attitude of those who did it without identifying any one person. This photo is not unlike the one of the Jews in the concentration camp (on the next page) and says to me, 'See, it does happen again'."

When, and if, the world ever changes, such photos can be relegated to musty museums, a reminder of a grisly past. For now, they serve as a harsh reminder of a continuing danger that plagues humanity.

LAYING THE SOCIOLOGICAL FOUNDATION

Seldom do race and ethnic relations degenerate to the brutal degree they did in Rwanda, but in our own society troubled race relations confront us in newspaper headlines and TV news. Sociology can contribute greatly to our understanding of this aspect of social life. To begin, let's consider to what extent race itself is a myth.

Race: Myth and Reality

With its 6 billion people, the world offers a fascinating variety of human shapes and colors. People see one another as black, white, red, yellow, and brown. Eyes come in various shades of blue, brown, and green. Lips are thick and thin. Hair is straight, curly, kinky, black, blonde, and red—and, of course, all shades of brown.

As humans spread throughout the world, their adaptations to diverse climates and other living conditions resulted in this profusion of complexions, colors, and shapes. Genetic mutations added distinct characteristics to the peoples of the globe. In this sense, the concept of

race—a group with inherited physical characteristics that distinguish it from another group—is a reality. Humans do, indeed, come in a variety of colors and shapes.

In two senses, however, race is a myth, a fabrication of the human mind. The *first* fabrication is the idea that any race is superior to others. All races have their geniuses—and their idiots. As with language, no race is superior to another.

Ideas of racial superiority, however, abound. They are not only false, but also dangerous. Adolf Hitler, for example, believed that the Aryans were a superior race, responsible for the cultural achievements of Europe. The Aryans, he said, were destined to establish a higher culture and institute a new world order. This destiny required them to avoid the "racial contamination" that would come from breeding with inferior races, and to isolate or destroy races that might endanger Aryan culture.

When Hitler's views were put into practice, the world was left an appalling legacy—the Nazi slaughter of those they deemed inferior: Jews, Slavs, gypsies, homosexuals, and people with mental and physical disabilities. Dark images of gas ovens and emaciated bodies stacked like cordwood haunted the world's nations. At Nuremberg, the Allies, flush with victory, put the top Nazi officials on trial, exposing their heinous deeds to a shocked world. Their public executions, everyone assumed, marked the end of such grisly acts. Obviously, they didn't, as the "ethnic cleansing" by the Serbs in Bosnia and the events recounted in our opening vignette sadly attest. **Genocide,** the attempt to destroy a people because of their presumed race or ethnicity, remains alive and well. Although the killings may not be accompanied by swastikas and goose-stepping, and machetes may replace poison gas and ovens, the goal is the same.

The *second* myth is that "pure" races exist. Humans show such a mixture of physical characteristics—in skin color, hair texture, nose shape, head shape, eye color, and so on—that there are no "pure" races. Instead of falling into distinct types that are clearly separate from one another, human characteristics flow endlessly together. The mapping of the human genome system shows that humans are strikingly homogenous, that so-called racial groups differ from one another only once in a thousand subunits of the genome (Angler 2000). As with Tiger Woods (discussed in the Cultural Diversity box on the next page), these minute gradations make any attempt to draw lines purely arbitrary.

Although large groupings of people can be classified by blood type and gene frequencies, even these classifications do not uncover "race." Rather, they are so arbitrary that biologists and anthropologists cannot even agree on how many races there are. They have drawn up many lists, each containing a different number of "races." Ashley Montagu (1964), a physical anthropologist, pointed out that some scientists have classified humans into only two "races" while others have found as many as two thousand. Montagu (1960) himself classified humans into forty "racial" groups.

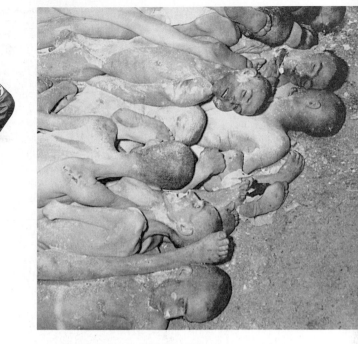

Although this strange-looking person could be a cartoon character, this is a serious photo of Adolf Hitler taken in 1924. Hitler is wearing lederhosen, traditional clothing of Bavaria, Germany.

The reason I selected this photo is to illustrate how seriously we must take all preaching of hatred and of racial supremacy, even though it seems to come from harmless or even humorous sources. This comical-appearing man caused the *Holocaust,* the attempted annihilation of all of Europe's Jews. When the victorious U.S. Army liberated the Ohrdrup concentration camp in 1945, it found this pile of emaciated corpses.

The *idea* of race, of course, is far from a myth. Firmly embedded in our culture, it is a powerful force in our everyday lives. That no race is superior and that even experts cannot decide how people should be biologically classified into races is not what counts. "I know what I see, and you can't tell me any different" seems to be the common attitude. As noted in Chapter 4, sociologist W. I. Thomas observed that "if people define situations as real, they are real in their consequences." In other words, people act on beliefs, not facts. As a result, we always have people like Hitler, the Hutu leaders, and the Serbs in Bosnia. While few people hold such extreme views, most people appear to be ethnocentric enough to believe, at least just a little, that their own race is superior to others.

Ethnic Groups

Whereas people use the term *race* to refer to supposed biological characteristics that distinguish one people from another, **ethnicity** and **ethnic** apply to cultural

CULTURAL DIVERSITY In the United States

TIGER WOODS AND THE EMERGING MULTIRACIAL IDENTITY: MAPPING NEW ETHNIC TERRAIN

Tiger Woods, one of the top golfers of all time, calls himself Cablinasian (Leland and Beals 1997). Woods invented this term as a boy to try to explain to himself just who he was—a combination of Caucasian, Black, Indian, and Asian. Woods wants to embrace both sides of his family. To be known by a racial identity that applies to just one of his parents is to deny the other parent.

Like many of us, Tiger Woods' racial-ethnic heritage is difficult to specify. Some, who like to count things, put Woods at one-quarter Thai, one-quarter Chinese, one-quarter white, an eighth Native American, and an eighth African American. From this chapter, you know how ridiculous such computations are, but the sociological question is why many consider Tiger Woods an African American. The U.S. racial scene is indeed complex, but a good part of the reason is simply that this is the label the media chose. "Everyone has to fit somewhere" seems to be our attitude. If they don't, we grow uncomfortable. And for Tiger Woods, the media chose African American.

The United States once had a firm "color line"—barriers between racial-ethnic groups that you didn't dare cross, especially in dating or marriage. This invisible barrier has bro-ken down, and today such marriages are common (Pollard and O'Hare 1999). Several campuses have interracial student organizations. Harvard has two, one just for students who have one African American parent (Leland and Beals 1997).

As we march into unfamiliar ethnic terrain, our classifications are bursting at the seams. Kwame Anthony Appiah, of Harvard's Philosophy and Afro-American Studies Departments, says, "My mother is English; my father is Ghanaian. My sisters are married to a Nigerian and a Norwegian. I have nephews who range from blond-haired kids to very black kids. They are all first cousins. Now according to the American scheme of things, they're all black—even the guy with blond hair who skis in Oslo" (Wright 1994).

Until recently, the U.S. census, which is taken every ten years, made everyone choose from Caucasian, Negro, Indian, and Oriental. Everyone was sliced and diced and packed into one of these restrictive classifications.

After years of complaints, the list was expanded. In the year 2000 census, everyone had to declare that they were or were not "Spanish/Hispanic/Latino." Then they had to mark "one or more races" that they "consider themselves to be." They could choose from White; Black, African American, or Negro; American Indian or Alaska Native; Asian Indian, Chinese, Filipino, Japanese, Korean, Vietnamese, Native Hawaiian, Guamanian or Chamorro, Samoan, and other Pacific Islander. Finally, if these didn't do it, you could check a box called "Some Other Race" and then write whatever you wanted.

Perhaps the census should list Cablinasian. Of course there should be GASH for the German-African-Swedish-Hispanic Americans, BITE for those of Botswanian-Indonesian-Turkish-English descent, and STUDY for the Swedish-Turkish-Uruguayan-Danish-Yugoslavian Americans. As you read farther in this chapter, you will see why these terms make as much sense as the categories we currently use. ■

For Your Consideration

Just why do we count people by "race" anyway? Why not eliminate race from the U.S. census? (Race became a factor in the census during slavery when five blacks were counted the same as three whites to determine how many representatives a state could send to Congress!) Why is race so important to some people? Perhaps you can use the materials in this chapter to answer these questions.

Tiger Woods, after hitting a hole-in-one on the fourteenth hole at the Greater Milwaukee Open.

characteristics. Derived from the word *ethnos* (a Greek word meaning "people" or "nation"), ethnicity and ethnic refer to people who identify with one another on the basis of common ancestry and cultural heritage. Their sense of belonging may center on nation of origin, distinctive foods, dress, language, music, religion, or family names and relationships.

People often confuse the terms *race* and *ethnicity*. For example, many people, including many Jews, consider the Jews a race. Jews, however, are more properly considered an ethnic group, for it is their cultural characteristics, especially religion, that bind them together. Wherever Jews have lived in the world, they have intermarried. Consequently, Jews in China may look mongoloid, while some Swedish Jews are blue-eyed blondes. This matter is strikingly illustrated in the case of Ethiopian Jews, who look so different from European Jews that when they immigrated to Israel many European Israelis felt that they could not be *real* Jews.

Minority and Dominant Groups

Sociologist Louis Wirth (1945) defined a **minority group** as people who are singled out for unequal treatment and who regard themselves as objects of collective discrimination. Worldwide, minorities share several conditions: Their physical or cultural traits are held in low esteem by the dominant group, which treats them unfairly, and they tend to marry within their own group (Wagley and Harris 1958). These conditions tend to create a shared sense of identity among minorities (a feeling of "we-ness"). In many instances, a sense of common destiny emerges (Chandra 1993b).

Surprisingly, a minority group is not necessarily a *numerical* minority. For example, before India's independence in 1947, a handful of British colonial rulers discriminated against millions of Indians. Similarly, when South Africa practiced apartheid, a small group of Dutch discriminated against the black majority. And all over the world, females are a minority group. Accordingly, sociologists refer to those who do the discriminating not as the *majority* but, rather, as the **dominant group**, for they have the greatest power, most privileges, and highest social status.

Possessing political power and unified by shared physical and cultural traits, the dominant group uses its position to discriminate against those with different—and supposedly inferior—traits. The dominant group considers its privileged position to be the result of its own innate superiority.

Emergence of Minority Groups A group becomes a minority in one of two ways. The *first* is through the expansion of political boundaries. With the exception of females, tribal societies contain no minority groups; everyone shares the same culture, including the same language, and belongs to the same physical stock. When a group expands its political boundaries, however, it produces minority groups if it incorporates people with different customs, languages, values, and physical characteristics into the same political entity and discriminates against them. For example, after defeating Mexico in war, the United States annexed the Southwest. The Mexicans living there, who had been the dominant group, were transformed into a minority group, a master status that has influenced their lives ever since. Referring to his ancestors, one Latino said, "We didn't move across the border—the border moved across us."

A *second* way in which a group becomes a minority is by migration. This can be voluntary, as with the millions of people who have chosen to move from Mexico to the United States, or involuntary, as with the millions of Africans forcibly transported to the United States. (The way females became a minority group represents a third way, but as will be reviewed in the next chapter, no one knows just how this occurred.)

How People Construct Their Racial-Ethnic Identity

Some of us have a greater sense of ethnicity than others. Some of us feel firm boundaries between "us" and "them." Others have assimilated so extensively into the mainstream culture that they are only vaguely aware of their ethnic origins. With interethnic marrying common, some do not even know the countries from which their families originated—nor do they care. If asked to identify themselves ethnically, they respond with something like "I'm Heinz 57—German and Irish, with a little Italian and French thrown in—and I think someone said something about being one-sixteenth Indian, too."

Why do some people feel an intense sense of ethnic identity, while others feel hardly any? Figure 9.1 on the next page portrays four factors, identified by sociologist Ashley Doane (1997), that heighten or reduce our sense of ethnic identity. From this figure, you can see that the keys are relative size, power, appearance, and discrimination. If your group is relatively small, has little power, looks different from most people in society, and is an object of discrimination, you will

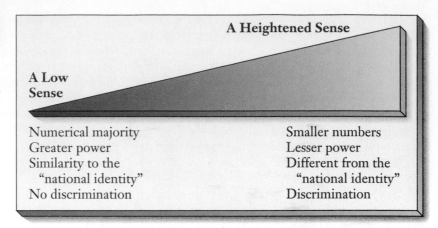

A SENSE OF ETHNICITY

Source: Based on Doane 1997.

A Heightened Sense

A Low Sense

Numerical majority
Greater power
Similarity to the
   "national identity"
No discrimination

Smaller numbers
Lesser power
Different from the
   "national identity"
Discrimination

have a heightened sense of ethnic identity. In contrast, if you belong to the dominant group that holds most of the power, looks like most people in the society, and feel no discrimination, you are likely to experience a sense of "belonging"—and wonder why ethnic identity is such a big deal.

We can use the term **ethnic work** to refer to how people construct their ethnicity. For people who have a strong ethnic identity, this term refers to how they enhance and maintain their group's distinctions—from clothing, food, and language to religion and holidays. For people whose ethnic identity is not as firm, it refers to their attempts to recover their ethnic heritage, such as trying to trace family genealogies. Millions of Americans are engaged in ethnic work, which has confounded the experts who thought that the United States would be a **melting pot,** its many groups quietly blending into a sort of ethnic stew. In recent years, however, Americans have become fascinated with their "roots," increasingly proud of their ethnic backgrounds, and, some, very assertive of their ethnicity. Consequently, some analysts think that "tossed salad" is more appropriate than "melting pot."

Prejudice and Discrimination

Prejudice and discrimination are common throughout the world. In Mexico, Hispanic Mexicans discriminate against Native American Mexicans; in Israel, Ashkenazi Jews, primarily of European descent, discriminate against Sephardi Jews from the Muslim world; and in Japan, the Japanese discriminate against just about anyone who isn't Japanese, especially immigrant Koreans

and the descendants of the Eta caste. The Eta, now renamed the Burakumin, still bear a stigma because they used to do the society's dirty work—handling dead animals (stripping the hides and tanning the leather) and serving as Japan's executioners and prison guards (Mander 1992). In some places the elderly discriminate against the young, in others the young against the elderly. And all around the world men discriminate against women.

As you can see from this list, **discrimination** is an *action*—unfair treatment directed against someone. When the basis of discrimination is race, it is known as **racism,** but discrimination can be based on many characteristics other than race—including age, sex, height, weight, income, education, marital status, sexual orientation, disease, disability, religion, and politics. Discrimination is often the result of an *attitude* called **prejudice**—a prejudging of some sort, usually in a negative way. There is also positive prejudice, which exaggerates the virtues of a group, as when people think that some group (usually their own) is more capable than others. Most prejudice, however, is negative, and involves prejudging a group as inferior.

The Extent of Prejudice Sociologists have found that ethnocentrism is so common that each racial or ethnic group views other groups as inferior in at least some ways. In a random sample of adults in the Detroit area, sociologists Maria Krysan and Reynolds Farley (1993) found that whites and African Americans tend to judge Latinos as less intelligent than themselves. Using a probability sample (from which we can generalize), sociologists Lawrence Bobo and James Kluegel (1991) found

U.S. race relations have gone through many stages, some of them very tense. They sometimes have even exploded into violence, as with the many lynchings in the South in the earlier part of this century. This photo was taken in Rayston, Georgia, on April 28, 1936. Earlier in the day, the 40-year-old victim, Lint Shaw, accused of attacking a white girl, had been rescued from a mob by National Guardsmen. After the National Guard left, the mob forced their way into the jail.

that older and less educated whites are not as willing to have close, sustained interaction with other groups as are younger and more educated whites. Details of their findings are shown in Figure 9.2. We must await matching studies to test the prejudices of Latinos, Asian Americans, and Native Americans.

Not everyone of the same age and education has the same amount of prejudice, of course. At the University of Alabama, sociologist Donal Muir (1991) measured racial attitudes of white students who belonged to fraternities and sororities and compared them to those of nonmembers. He asked a variety of questions—from their ideas about dating African Americans to their views on attending classes together. On all measures, fraternity members were more prejudiced than the nonfrats. Research on other campuses supports this finding (Morris 1991). Let's take a closer look at race relations on U.S. campuses.

Percentage of white Americans, by education, who believe that different races should live in segregated housing.

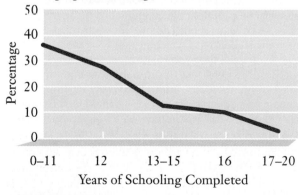

Years of Schooling Completed

Percentage of white Americans, by age, who believe that interracial marriage should be banned.

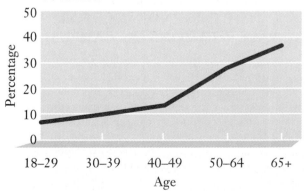

Age

Figure 9.2 **A MEASURE OF PREFERRED SOCIAL DISTANCE**

Source: Bobo and Kluegel 1991.

In the 1920s and 1930s, the Ku Klux Klan was a powerful political force in the United States. To get a sense of the prevailing mood at the time, consider the caption that accompanied this photo of the Ku Klux Klan women from Freeport, New York, when it appeared in the papers: "Here's the Ladies in Their Natty Uniforms Marching in the Parade." Which theories would be most useful to explain this upsurge in racism among mainstream whites of the time?

Thinking Critically

SELF-SEGREGATION: HELP OR HINDRANCE FOR RACE RELATIONS ON CAMPUS?

Only after a long, bitter, and violent struggle was federal civil rights legislation prohibiting racial segregation on college campuses passed in the 1960s. These laws did not mark the end of *self*-segregation, however; certain practices continued, such as an area of a cafeteria or lounge being used almost exclusively by a particular group. In recent years, minority students have requested separate dormitories and campus centers. At Brown University, an Ivy League school located in Providence, Rhode Island, the old rows of fraternity and sorority houses have been replaced by Harambee House (for African Americans), Hispanic House, Slavic House, East Asian House, and German House. Cornell University offers "theme dorms" for African Americans, Hispanics, and Native Americans.

Intense controversy surrounds this self-segregation. On one side is William H. Gray, III, the head of the United Negro College Fund. Both African American and Latino students drop out of college at a much higher rate, Gray says, so colleges should do everything they can to make minority students feel welcome and accepted.

Critics call the trend toward separate housing a "separatist movement" that divides students into "small enclaves." Administrators at the University of Pennsylvania appointed a commission to study campus life. The committee concluded that when students self-segregate, they lose opportunities for wider interaction with diverse groups of students. Since students tend to socialize with the people they live with, separate housing inhibits the mixing of different groups, depriving students of the rich experiences that come through intercultural contacts.

Joshua Lehrer, a Brown University student who is white, says that some racial and ethnic groups "are separating themselves from everybody else, yet complain when society separates them. Can you really have it both ways?" he asks. ■

For Your Consideration

Compare separate racial-ethnic housing on college campuses with three patterns discussed in this chapter: segregation, assimilation, and multiculturalism. Should self-segregation be permitted if minority students desire it, but not permitted if white students desire it? Explain your position.

Sources: Bernstein 1993; Jordon 1996.

Individual and Institutional Discrimination

Sociologists stress that we need to move beyond thinking in terms of **individual discrimination**, the negative treat-

ment of one person by another. Although such behavior creates problems, it is primarily a matter of one individual treating another badly. With their focus on the broader picture, sociologists encourage us to examine **institutional discrimination,** that is, to see how discrimination is woven into the fabric of society. Let's look at two examples.

Home Mortgages Mortgage lending provides an excellent illustration. As shown in Figure 9.3 below, race-ethnicity is a significant factor in getting a mortgage. When bankers looked at the statistics shown in this figure, they cried foul. They said that it might *look* like discrimination, but the truth was that whites had better credit histories. To see if this were true, researchers went over the data again, comparing the credit histories of applicants. Not only did they check for late payments, but they also compared the applicants' debts,

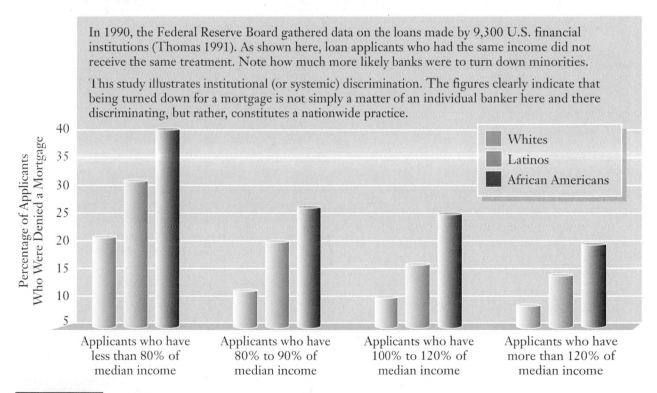

In 1990, the Federal Reserve Board gathered data on the loans made by 9,300 U.S. financial institutions (Thomas 1991). As shown here, loan applicants who had the same income did not receive the same treatment. Note how much more likely banks were to turn down minorities.

This study illustrates institutional (or systemic) discrimination. The figures clearly indicate that being turned down for a mortgage is not simply a matter of an individual banker here and there discriminating, but rather, constitutes a nationwide practice.

Figure 9.3 RACE-ETHNICITY AND MORTGAGES: AN EXAMPLE OF INSTITUTIONAL DISCRIMINATION

Note: The totals refer to applicants for conventional mortgages. Although applicants for government-backed mortgages had lower overall rates of rejection, the identical pattern showed up for all income groups. Median income is the income of each bank's local area.

loan size relative to income, and even characteristics of the property they wanted to buy. The lending gap did narrow a bit, but the bottom line was that even when applicants were identical in these areas, African Americans and Latinos were *60 percent* more likely to be rejected than whites (Thomas 1992; Passell 1996). In short, the results do not show that a banker here and there is discriminating; rather, they show that discrimination is built into the country's financial institutions.

Health Care Discrimination does not have to be deliberate. It can occur without the awareness of either those doing the discriminating or those being discriminated against. An example is coronary bypass surgery. Physicians Mark Wenneker and Arnold Epstein (1989) studied all patients admitted to Massachusetts hospitals for circulatory diseases or chest pain. After comparing their age, sex, race, and income, they found that whites were 89 percent more likely to be given coronary bypass surgery. A national study of Medicare patients showed an even higher discrepancy—that whites were three times as likely as blacks to receive this surgery (Winslow 1992). Another national study showed that for every 100 whites who are treated by drugs or surgery to clear their blocked blood vessels after a heart attack, only 85 blacks get this life-saving treatment (Emery 2000).

The particular interracial dynamics that cause medical decisions to be made on the basis of race are unknown at present. It is likely that physicians *do not intend* to discriminate, but that in ways we do not yet fully understand, discrimination is built into the medical delivery system. There race serves as a subconscious motivation for giving or denying access to advanced medical procedures.

Institutional discrimination, then, is much more than a matter of inconvenience, for it even translates into life and death. Table 9.1 also illustrates this point. Here you can see that an African American baby has *twice* the chance of dying in infancy as does a white baby, that an African American mother is *four* times as likely to die in childbirth as a white mother, and that African Americans live six to eight years less than whites. The reason for these differences is not biology, but *social* factors, in this case largely income—the key factor in determining who has access to better nutrition, housing, and medical care.

Table 9.1

	RACE AND HEALTH			
			Life Expectancy	
	Infant Deaths	*Maternal Deaths*	*Males*	*Females*
White Americans	6.6	5.1	73.9	79.7
African Americans	13.5	20.3	66.1	74.2

Note: The national data base used for this table does not list these figures for other racial-ethnic groups. *White* refers to non-Hispanic whites. Infant deaths refers to the number of deaths per year of infants under 1 year old per 1,000 live births; for maternal deaths, it is the number per 100,000.

Source: Statistical Abstract 1999:Tables 129, 133.

THEORIES OF PREJUDICE

Why are people prejudiced? The commonsense explanation is that some member of a group has done something negative to them or to someone they know, and they transfer their feelings to other members of the group. In some cases, this may be true, but a classic piece of research shows that much more is involved. Psychologist Eugene Hartley (1946) asked people how they felt about several racial and ethnic groups. Besides blacks, Jews, and so on, he included the Wallonians, Pireneans, and Danireans—names he had made up. Most people who expressed dislike for Jews and blacks also expressed dislike for these three fictitious groups. Hartley's study shows that prejudice does not depend on negative experiences with others. It also reveals that people who are prejudiced against one racial or ethnic group tend to be prejudiced against other groups. People can be, and are, prejudiced against people they have never met—and even against groups that do not exist!

Social scientists have developed several theories to explain prejudice. Let's look first at psychological theories, then at sociological explanations.

Psychological Perspectives

Frustration and Scapegoats In 1939, psychologist John Dollard suggested that prejudice is the result of frustration. People who are unable to strike out at the real source of their frustration (such as low wages) find someone to blame. This **scapegoat**, often a racial, ethnic, or religious minority that they unfairly blame for their troubles, becomes a target on which they vent their frustrations. Gender and age also provide common bases for scapegoating.

Even mild frustration can increase prejudice. Psychologists Emory Cowen, Judah Landes, and Donald Schaet (1959) measured the prejudice of a sample of students. They then gave the students two puzzles to solve, making sure they did not have enough time to solve them. After the students had worked furiously on the puzzles, the experimenters shook their heads in disgust and said they couldn't believe they hadn't finished such simple tasks. They then retested the students; their scores on prejudice had increased. The students had directed their frustrations outward, onto people who had nothing to do with their problem.

The Authoritarian Personality Have you ever wondered if personality is a cause of prejudice? Maybe some people are more inclined to be prejudiced, and others more fair-minded. For psychologist Theodor Adorno, who had escaped from the Nazis, this was no idle speculation. With the horrors he had observed still fresh in his mind, Adorno wondered if there might be a certain type of person who is more likely to fall for the racist utterances and policies of people like Hitler, Mussolini, and the Ku Klux Klan.

To find out, Adorno (1950) tested about two thousand people, ranging from college professors to prison inmates. He used tests he had developed to measure ethnocentrism, anti-Semitism, and support for strong, authoritarian leaders. Adorno found that people who scored high on one test also scored high on the other two. For example, people who agreed with anti-Semitic statements also agreed that governments should be authoritarian and that foreign ways of life posed a threat to the "American" way.

Adorno concluded that highly prejudiced people are insecure, conformist, submissive to superiors, and have deep respect for authority. He termed this the **authoritarian personality.** These people believe that things are either right or wrong. Ambiguity disturbs them, especially in matters of religion or sex. They become anxious when they confront norms and values that differ from their own. To define people who differ from themselves as inferior assures them that their own positions are right.

Adorno's research stirred the scientific community, stimulating more than a thousand research studies. In general, the researchers found that people who are older, less educated, less intelligent, and from a lower social class are more likely to be authoritarian. Critics say that this doesn't indicate a particular personality, just that the less educated are more prejudiced—which we already knew (Yinger 1965; Ray 1991).

Sociological Perspectives

Sociologists find psychological explanations inadequate. They stress that the key to understanding prejudice is not an individual's *internal* state, but factors *outside* the individual. Thus, sociological theories focus on how some environments foster prejudice, while others discourage it. This topic is explored in the Mass Media box on the next page. With this background, let's compare functionalist, conflict, and symbolic interactionist perspectives on prejudice.

Functionalism In a telling scene from a television documentary, journalist Bill Moyers interviewed Fritz Hippler, a Nazi intellectual who at age 29 was put in charge of the entire German film industry. Hippler said that when Hitler came to power the Germans were no more anti-Semitic than the French, probably less so. He was told to create anti-Semitism, which he did by producing movies that contained vivid scenes comparing Jews to rats—their breeding threatening to infest the population.

Why was Hippler told to create hatred? Prejudice and discrimination were functional for the Nazis; they helped the Nazis come to power. The Jews provided a convenient scapegoat, a common enemy against which the Nazis could unite a Germany weakened by defeat in World War I and bled by war reparations and rampant inflation. In addition, the Jews owned businesses, bank accounts, and other property that the Nazis could confiscate. They also held key positions (university professors, reporters, judges, and so on), which the Nazis could fill with their own flunkies. In the end hatred also showed its dysfunctional side, as the Nazi officials who were hanged at Nuremberg discovered.

When state machinery is harnessed to hatred as it was by the Nazis—who used the schools, police, courts, mass media, and almost all aspects of the government—prejudice becomes practically irresistible. Recall the identical twins featured in the Down-to-Earth Sociology box on page 59. Oskar and Jack had been separated as babies. Jack was brought up as a Jew in Trinidad, while Oskar was reared as a Catholic in Czechoslovakia.

Authoritarian personality = Things are "right" or "wrong", highly prejudiced Less educated, older, lower social class.

Mass Media in Social Life

PREACHING HATRED:
CRIME OR INALIENABLE RIGHT?

The Internet is a marvelous source of information—and misinformation. Anyone can put up a Web site and fill it with distortions of truth or with outright lies. People of all ages, from all walks of life, can nurse grudges, seek revenge for perceived wrongs, and fan hatred.

Such negative communications can be upsetting, especially those that champion hatred. Consider these statements:

Civil Rights come out of the barrel of a gun, and we mean to give the niggers and Jews all the civil rights they can handle.... Our security team will see that no live targets escape from the range. Any who refuse to run or can't for any reason will be fed to the dogs. The dogs appreciate a good feed as much as we do.

—An invitation to a summer conference held by the Aryan Nations at Hayden Lake, Idaho. The group's founder, Richard Butler, is a former Lockheed executive. (Quoted in Murphy 1999)

Who's pimping the world? The hairy hands of the Zionist.... The so-called Jew claims that there were six million in Nazi Germany. I am here today to tell you that there is absolutely no...evidence to substantiate,

to prove that six million so-called Jews lost their lives in Nazi Germany.... Don't let no hooked-nose, bagel-eating, lox-eating, perpetrating-a-fraud so-called Jew who just crawled out of the ghettoes of Europe just a few days ago...

—Khalid Abdul Muhammad (Quoted in Herbert 1998)

Hatred knows no racial-ethnic boundaries; the first statement was made by a white, the second by an African American.

The issue of what to do about hate speech is perplexing. Some want to ban it, while others say that censorship of any speech threatens the free speech of us all. Canada has taken action. Ingrid Rimland of San Diego runs a Web site on which she sells anti-Semitic literature and features the views of Ernst Zundel. Zundel, an immigrant from Germany who has lived in Canada for forty years, denies the Holocaust took place and preaches anti-Semitism. Canadian authorities accused Zundel of controlling the San Diego Web site and charged him under laws that prohibit the use of telephone lines to spread hate messages based on race, religion, or ethnic origin ("Canada Tries to..." 1998).

The technological solution may be at hand. The Anti-

Defamation League, a human rights group, has developed a "hate filter" (Mendels 1998). When this software is installed on a computer, it blocks access to Web sites that promote intolerance: the Ku Klux Klan, skinheads, and neo-Nazis, as well as those that spew hatred for homosexuals or other groups. ■

For Your Consideration

Should we ban statements of hate from the mass media? Should we perhaps make such statements illegal and punish their authors for breaking the law? Or should we allow the promotion of hatred in the mass media, regardless of its inflammatory nature, regardless of how it twists the facts and incites prejudice and hatred? Is there a middle ground, perhaps installing hate filters in grade and middle schools?

Do you think that censorship of this one type of speech can threaten free speech itself? Could it be one step toward banning other kinds of speech? If the government prohibits this speech, what is to stop it from censoring speech that it finds irritating, such as criticism of its leadership, perhaps claiming that it is a threat to "national security"?

Under the Nazi regime, Oskar learned to hate Jews, although, unknown to himself, he was a Jew.

That prejudice is functional and is shaped by the social environment was demonstrated by psychologists Muzafer and Carolyn Sherif (1953). In a boys' summer camp, they assigned friends to different cabins and then had the cabins compete in sports. In just a few days, strong in-groups had formed, and even former lifelong friends were calling one another "crybaby" and "sissy" and showing intense dislike for one another.

Conflict < Reserve labor force : to use during economic boom
theory < Split Labor Market : workers divided along racial -ethnic gender line

Sherif's study illustrates four major points. First, we can arrange the social environment to generate positive and negative feelings about people. Second, prejudice can be produced by pitting group against group in an "I win, you lose" situation. Third, prejudice is functional in that it creates in-group solidarity. Fourth, prejudice is dysfunctional in that it destroys human relationships.

Conflict Theory The common interests of all groups include good nutrition, health care, housing, and education. For all these, jobs are the central issue. If workers were united, they could demand higher wages and better working conditions. It is in the interest of capitalists to keep workers divided. To do so, capitalists use two weapons.

The first is insecurity, especially the fear of unemployment. Workers know they can lose their jobs, and they fear eviction and the repossession of their goods. Keeping some people unemployed produces a **reserve labor force** for the capitalists. They draw on this group to expand production during economic booms, and, when the economy contracts, they release these workers to rejoin the ranks of the unemployed. The lesson is not lost on those who still have jobs—they know they are just one paycheck from ending up "on the streets."

The second weapon is to exploit racial and ethnic strife. To pit worker against worker weakens their bargaining power. Sowing fear and suspicion among racial-ethnic groups—such as by letting whites know that blacks are ready to take their jobs, or by getting blacks to view Latinos as a threat to theirs—produces docile workers. The result is a **split labor market,** workers divided along racial-ethnic and gender lines (Du Bois 1935/1992; Reich 1972; Brueggemann 2000).

The consequences are devastating, say conflict theorists. Just like the boys in the Sherif experiment, African Americans, Latinos, whites, and so on see themselves as able to make gains only at one another's expense. This rivalry shows up along even finer racial-ethnic lines, such as that between Miami's Haitians and Miami's African Americans, who distrust each other as competitors. Divisions among workers deflect anger and hostility away from the capitalists and direct these powerful emotions toward other racial and ethnic groups. Instead of recognizing their common class interests and working for their mutual welfare, workers learn to fear and distrust one another.

Symbolic Interactionism While conflict theorists focus on the role of the capitalist class in exploiting racial and ethnic inequalities, symbolic interactionists examine how labels affect perception and produce prejudice.

How Labels Create Prejudice Symbolic interactionists stress that *the labels we learn color the way we see people.* Labels cause **selective perception;** that is, they lead us to see certain things and blind us to others. If we apply a label to a group, we tend to see its members as all alike. We shake off evidence that doesn't fit (Simpson and Yinger 1972). Racial and ethnic labels are especially powerful. They are shorthand for emotionally laden stereotypes. The term *nigger,* for example, is not neutral. Nor are *honky, spic, mick, kike, limey, kraut, dago,* or any of the other scornful words people use to belittle ethnic groups. Such words overpower us with emotions, blocking out rational thought about the people to whom they refer (Allport 1954).

Stereotypes and Discrimination: The Self-Fulfilling Prophecy Some stereotypes not only justify prejudice and discrimination—they even produce the behavior depicted in the stereotype. Let's consider Group X. Negative stereotypes characterize Group X as lazy. If they are lazy, they don't deserve good jobs. ("They are lazy and undependable and wouldn't do well.") This attitude creates a *self-fulfilling prophecy.* Because they are denied jobs that require high dedication and energy, most members of Group X are limited to doing "dirty work," the kind of work thought appropriate for "that kind" of people. Since much dirty work is sporadic, members of Group X are often seen standing around street corners. The sight of their idleness reinforces the original stereotype of laziness. The discrimination that created the "laziness" in the first place passes unnoticed.

Symbolic interactionists stress that we are not born with prejudice. Instead, we learn prejudice through interaction with others. At birth each of us joins some particular family and racial or ethnic group, where we learn beliefs and values. There, as part of our basic orientations to the world, we learn to like—or dislike—members of other groups and to perceive them positively or negatively. If discrimination is common, we learn to practice it routinely. Just as we learn any other attitudes and customs, then, so we learn prejudice and discrimination.

One aspect of racism that has gained national attention and concern from citizens and government alike is the rise of neo-Nazi and Ku Klux Klan organizations. To understand the racist mind—and the appeal it has to some—see the Down-to-Earth Sociology box on the next page.

Sociology

THE RACIST MIND

Sociologist Raphael Ezekiel wanted to get a close look at the racist mind. As a Jew, he faced a unique problem. The best way to study racism from the inside is to do participant observation (see pp. 26–27). Would this be possible for him? Openly identifying himself as a Jew, Ezekiel asked Ku Klux Klan and neo-Nazi leaders if he could interview them and attend their meetings. Surprisingly, they agreed. Ezekiel published his pathbreaking research in a book, *The Racist Mind* (1995). Here are some of the insights he gained during his fascinating sociological adventure:

[The leader] builds on mass anxiety about economic insecurity and on popular tendencies to see an Establishment as the cause of the economic threat; he hopes to teach people to identify that Establishment as the puppets of a conspiracy of Jews. [He has a] belief in exclusive categories. For the white racist leader, it is profoundly true...that the socially defined collections we call races represent fundamental categories. A man is black or a man is white; there are no in-betweens. Every human belongs to a racial category, and all the members of one category are radically different from all the members of other categories. Moreover, race represents the essence of the person. A truck is a truck, a car is a car, a cat is a cat, a dog is a dog, a black is a

black, a white is a white.... These axioms have a rock-hard quality in the leaders' minds; *the world is made up of racial groups*. That is what exists for them.

Two further beliefs play a major role in the minds of leaders. First, life is war. The world is made of distinct racial groups; life is about the war between those groups. Second, events have secret causes, are never what they seem superficially.... Any myth is plausible, as long as it involves intricate plotting.... It does not matter to him what others say.... He lives in his ideas and in the little world he has created where they are taken seriously.... Gold can be made from the tongues of frogs; Yahweh's call can be heard in the flapping of the swastika banner. (pp. 66–67)

Who is attracted to the neo-Nazis and Ku Klux Klan? Here is what Ezekiel discovered:

[There is a] ready pool of whites who will respond to the racist signal.... This population [is] always hungry for activity—or for the talk of activity—that promises dignity and meaning to lives that are working poorly in a highly competitive world.... Much as I don't want to believe it, [this] movement brings a sense of meaning—at least for a while—to some of the discontented. To struggle in a cause that transcends the individual lends meaning

to life, no matter how ill-founded or narrowing the cause. For the young men in the neo-Nazi group...membership was an alternative to atomization and drift; within the group they worked for a cause and took direct risks in the company of comrades....

When interviewing the young neo-Nazis in Detroit, I often found myself driving with them past the closed factories, the idled plants of our shrinking manufacturing base. The fewer and fewer plants that remain can demand better educated and more highly skilled workers. These fatherless Nazi youths, these high-school dropouts, will find little place in the emerging economy... a permanently underemployed white underclass is taking its place alongside the permanent black underclass. The struggle over race merely diverts youth from confronting the real issues of their lives. Not many seats are left on the train, and the train is leaving the station. (pp. 32–33) ■

For Your Consideration

Use functionalism, conflict theory, and symbolic interactionism to explain (1) why some people are attracted to the message of hate, and (2) how the leaders and followers of these hate groups view the world.

Savage = Native American

GLOBAL PATTERNS OF INTERGROUP RELATIONS

Sociologists have studied racial-ethnic relations around the world. They have found that in any society that contains minorities, basic patterns develop between the dominant group and the minorities. These patterns are shown in Figure 9.4 below. Let's look at each.

Genocide

Last century's most notorious examples of genocide were Hitler's attempt to destroy all Jews and, as depicted in our opening vignette, the Hutus' attempt to destroy all Tutsis. One of the horrifying aspects of these slaughters is that those who participated did not crawl out from under a rock someplace. Rather, they were ordinary citizens whose participation was facilitated by labels that singled out the victims as enemies worthy of death (Huttenbach 1991; Browning 1993; Simmons 1998).

To better understand how ordinary people can participate in genocide, let's focus on an example from the 1800s. The U.S. government and white settlers chose the label "savages" to refer to Native Americans. To define the Native Americans as less than human made it easier to justify killing them in order to take over their resources and to slaughter those who resisted their advance toward the West. Most Native Americans, however, did not die from bullets but from diseases that the whites brought with them. The Native Americans had

no immunity against these diseases, such as measles and the flu (Dobyns 1983; Schaefer 2000). The settlers also ruthlessly destroyed the Native Americans' food supply (buffalo, crops). As a result, about *95 percent* of Native Americans died (Garbarino 1976; Thornton 1987).

The same thing was happening in other places. In South Africa, the Boers, or Dutch settlers, viewed the native Hottentots as jungle animals and totally wiped them out. In Tasmania, the British settlers stalked the local aboriginal population, hunting them for sport and sometimes even for dog food.

Labels are powerful forces in human life. Labels that dehumanize others help people to **compartmentalize**—to separate their acts from their sense of being good and moral people. If some group is less than human, it is okay to treat them inhumanely. Thus people can kill—and still retain a good self-concept (Bernard et al. 1971; Markhusen 1995). In short, *labeling the targeted group as less than fully human facilitates genocide.*

Population Transfer

Population transfer is of two types, indirect and direct. *Indirect* population transfer is achieved by making life so unbearable for members of a minority that they leave "voluntarily." Under the bitter conditions of czarist Russia, for example, millions of Jews made this "choice." *Direct transfer* occurs when a dominant group expels a minority. Examples include the relocation of Native Americans to reservations and the transfer of Americans of Japanese descent to relocation camps during World War II.

Inhumanity					Humanity
Rejection					Acceptance
Genocide	**Population Transfer**	**Internal Colonialism**	**Segregation**	**Assimilation**	**Multiculturalism (Pluralism)**
The dominant group tries to destroy the minority (e.g., Germany and Rwanda)	The dominant group expels the minority (e.g., reservations for Native Americans)	The dominant group exploits the minority (e.g., low-paid, menial work)	The dominant group structures the social institutions to maintain minimal contact with the minority (e.g., the U.S. South before the 1960s)	The dominant group absorbs the minority (e.g., American Czechoslovakians)	The dominant group encourages racial and ethnic variation; when fully successful, there is no longer a dominant group (e.g., Switzerland)

Figure 9.4 PATTERNS OF INTERGROUP RELATIONS: A CONTINUUM

Amid hysterical fears that Japanese Americans were "enemies within" who would sabotage industrial and military installations on the West Coast, in the early days of World War II Japanese Americans were transferred to "relocation camps." Many returned home after the war to find that their property had been vandalized.

In the 1990s, a combination of genocide and population transfer occurred in Bosnia and Kosovo, parts of the former Yugoslavia. A hatred nurtured for centuries had been kept under wraps during Tito's iron-fisted rule. After the breakup of communism, these suppressed, smoldering hatreds broke to the surface and Yugoslavia split into warring factions. When the Serbs gained power, Muslims rebelled and began engaging in guerilla warfare. The Serbs vented their hatred by what they termed **ethnic cleansing:** They terrorized villages with killing and rape, forcing survivors to flee in fear.

Internal Colonialism

In Chapter 7, the term *colonialism* was used to refer to one way that the Most Industrialized Nations exploit the Least Industrialized Nations (p. 170). Conflict theorists use the term **internal colonialism** to refer to how a country's dominant group exploits minority groups for its economic advantage. The dominant group manipulates the social institutions to suppress minorities and deny them access to the society's benefits. Slavery, reviewed in Chapter 7, is an extreme example of internal colonialism, as was the South African system of *apartheid*. Although the dominant Afrikaaners despised the minority, they found its presence necessary. As Simpson and Yinger (1972) put it, who else would do the hard work?

Segregation

Internal colonialism is often accompanied by **segregation**—the formal separation of racial or ethnic groups. Segregation allows the dominant group to maintain social distance from the minority and yet to exploit their labor as cooks, cleaners, chauffeurs, housekeepers, nannies, factory workers, and so on. In the U.S. South until the 1960s, by law African Americans and whites had to use separate public facilities such as hotels, schools, swimming pools, bathrooms, and even drinking fountains. In thirty-eight states, laws prohibited marriage between blacks and whites. Violators could be put in prison (Mahoney and Kooistra 1995). In Israel, Palestinians who worked for the dominant Israelis had to carry passes and go through armed checkpoints in the morning and return to their own areas at the end of the day.

Assimilation

- Forced.
- Permssible

Assimilation is the process by which a minority group is absorbed into the mainstream culture. There are two types. In *forced assimilation* the dominant group refuses to allow the minority to practice its religion, speak its language, or follow its customs. Prior to the fall of the Soviet Union, for example, the dominant group, the Russians, required that Armenian schoolchildren attend schools where they were taught in Russian. Armenians could honor only Russian, not Armenian, holidays. *Permissible assimilation,* in contrast, permits the minority to adopt the dominant group's patterns in its own way and at its own speed. In Brazil, for example, an ideology favoring the eventual blending of the country's diverse racial types into a "Brazilian stock" encourages its racial and ethnic groups to intermarry.

Multiculturalism (Pluralism)

A policy of **multiculturalism,** also called **pluralism,** permits or even encourages racial and ethnic variation. The minority groups are able to maintain their separate identities, yet freely participate in the country's social institutions, from education to politics. Switzerland provides an outstanding example of multiculturalism. The Swiss are made up of four ethnic groups—French, Italians, Germans, and Romansh. These groups have kept their own languages, and they live peacefully in political and economic unity. Multiculturalism has been so successful that none of these groups can properly be called a minority.

RACE AND ETHNIC RELATIONS IN THE UNITED STATES

As I have stressed, racial classifications are arbitrary and changing. Nevertheless, as a part of everyday life, we classify one another as belonging to distinct racial-ethnic groups. (Figure 9.5 below summarizes how Americans classify themselves.) Most of us also have strong racial-ethnic self-identities. Let's explore some of the implications of those memberships and identities.

White Europeans

Perhaps the single event that best crystallizes the racial view of the nation's founders occurred at the first Continental Congress of the United States. There they passed

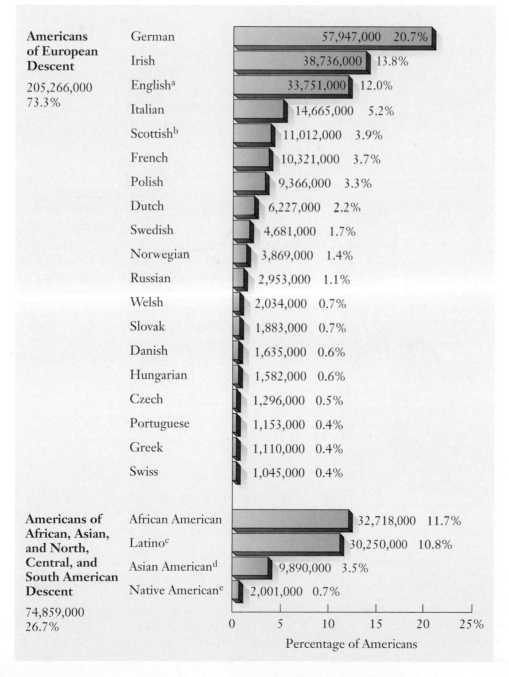

Figure 9.5

U.S. RACIAL AND ETHNIC GROUPS

To compute percentages, the population totals of the individual groups listed in the source were added, and the groups' totals were divided by this sum. To obtain the groups' population, these percentages were multiplied by the official U.S. population count.

[a] Includes "British."

[b] Includes "Scottish-Irish."

[c] Most Latinos trace at least part of their ancestry to Europe.

[d] In descending order, the largest six groups of Asian Americans are Chinese, Filipinos, Japanese, Asian Indians, Koreans, and Vietnamese.

Source: Statistical Abstract 1999:Tables 19, 23, 32, 59.

Americans of European Descent

205,266,000
73.3%

Group	Population	Percentage
German	57,947,000	20.7%
Irish	38,736,000	13.8%
English[a]	33,751,000	12.0%
Italian	14,665,000	5.2%
Scottish[b]	11,012,000	3.9%
French	10,321,000	3.7%
Polish	9,366,000	3.3%
Dutch	6,227,000	2.2%
Swedish	4,681,000	1.7%
Norwegian	3,869,000	1.4%
Russian	2,953,000	1.1%
Welsh	2,034,000	0.7%
Slovak	1,883,000	0.7%
Danish	1,635,000	0.6%
Hungarian	1,582,000	0.6%
Czech	1,296,000	0.5%
Portuguese	1,153,000	0.4%
Greek	1,110,000	0.4%
Swiss	1,045,000	0.4%

Americans of African, Asian, and North, Central, and South American Descent

74,859,000
26.7%

Group	Population	Percentage
African American	32,718,000	11.7%
Latino[c]	30,250,000	10.8%
Asian American[d]	9,890,000	3.5%
Native American[e]	2,001,000	0.7%

Percentage of Americans

WASP.

the Naturalization Act of 1790, declaring that only white immigrants could apply for citizenship. Their sense of superiority was not limited to their views of race. These **WASPs** (white Anglo-Saxon Protestants) also viewed white Europeans from countries other than England as inferior. They greeted **white ethnics**—immigrants from Europe whose language and other customs differed from theirs—with negative stereotypes. They especially despised the Irish, viewing them as dirty, lazy drunkards, but they also painted Germans, Poles, Jews, Italians, and so on with similarly broad brush strokes.

The cultural and political dominance of the WASPs placed pressure on immigrants to blend into the mainstream culture. The children of most immigrants embraced the new way of life and quickly came to think of themselves as Americans rather than as Germans, French, Hungarians, and so on. They dropped their distinctive customs, especially their language, often viewing them as symbols of shame. This second generation of immigrants was sandwiched between two worlds, that of their parents from "the old country" and their new home. Their children, the third generation, had an easier

JUST SO.

HOODLUM. " 'Tain't their color I mind s'much—(hic) it's their (hic) habits I 'bject to."

Almost all racial-ethnic groups, including white ethnics, have experienced prejudice and discrimination. The objects of scorn in this cartoon, which appeared in U.S. newspapers in 1879, are Irish immigrants. The Irish were despised at the time and were often depicted drunk. In a surprising twist, the Chinese immigrants in this cartoon are portrayed positively as hard workers.

adjustment, for they had fewer customs to discard. As immigrants from other parts of Europe assimilated into this Anglo culture, the meaning of WASP expanded to include people of this descent.

Because the English settled the colonies, they established the culture to which later immigrants had to conform—from the dominant language to the dominant religion. Highly ethnocentric, they considered the customs of any group that differed from theirs as inferior. In short, it was the European colonists who, taking power and determining the national agenda, controlled the destiny of the nation and dominated and exploited other ethnic groups. Throughout the years, other ethnic groups have had to react to this institutional and cultural dominance of western Europeans, which still sets the stage for current ethnic relations.

African Americans

After slavery was abolished, in a practice known as *Jim Crow,* the South passed laws to segregate blacks and whites. In 1896, the Supreme Court ruled in *Plessy v. Ferguson* that state laws requiring "separate but equal" accommodations for blacks were a reasonable use of state power. Whites used this ruling to strip blacks of the political power they had gained after the Civil War. They prohibited blacks from voting in "white" primaries. It was not until 1944 that the Supreme Court ruled that African Americans could vote in southern primaries, and not until 1954 that they had the legal right to attend the same public schools as whites (Schaefer 2000). Well into the 1960s, the South was still openly—and legally—practicing segregation.

The Struggle for Civil Rights

It was 1955, in Montgomery, Alabama. As specified by law, whites took the front seats of the bus, while blacks went to the back. As the bus filled up, blacks had to give up their seats to whites.

When Rosa Parks, a 42-year-old African American woman and secretary of the Montgomery NAACP, was told she would have to stand so white folks could sit, she refused (Bray 1995). She stubbornly sat there while the bus driver raged and whites felt insulted. Her arrest touched off mass demonstrations, led fifty thousand blacks to boycott the city's buses for a year, and thrust an otherwise unknown preacher into a historic role.

Rev. Martin Luther King, Jr., who had majored in sociology at Morehouse College in Atlanta, Georgia, took control. He organized car pools and preached nonviolence. Incensed at this

Until the 1960s, public facilities in the South were racially segregated. Some were reserved for whites only, others for blacks only. This *apartheid* was broken by blacks and whites who worked together and risked their lives to bring about a fairer society. Shown here is a 1963 sit-in at a Woolworth's lunch counter in Jackson, Mississippi. Sugar, ketchup, and mustard are being poured over the heads of the demonstrators.

radical organizer and at the stirrings in the normally compliant black community, segregationists also put their beliefs into practice—by bombing homes and dynamiting churches.

Rising Expectations and Civil Strife The barriers came down, but they came down slowly. Not until 1964 did Congress pass the Civil Rights Act, making it illegal to discriminate in restaurants, hotels, theaters, and other public places. Then in 1965, Congress passed the Voting Rights Act, banning the fraudulent literacy tests that the South had used to keep African Americans from voting.

Encouraged by these gains, African Americans experienced what sociologists call **rising expectations**; that is, they believed better conditions would soon follow. The lives of the poor among them, however, changed little, if at all. Frustrations built, finally exploding in Watts in 1965, when people living in that African American ghetto of central Los Angeles took to the streets in the first of what have been termed "the urban revolts." When King was assassinated by a white supremacist on April 4, 1968, ghettos across the nation again erupted in fiery violence. Under threat of the destruction of U.S. cities, Congress passed the sweeping Civil Rights Act of 1968.

Continued Gains Since then, African Americans have made remarkable political, educational, and economic gains. At 9 percent, African Americans have *quadrupled* their membership in the U.S. House of Representatives in the past 25 years (Rich 1986; *Statistical Abstract* 1999:Table 473). College enrollment increased, and the middle class expanded. Today, one of every four African American families makes more than $50,000 a year. One of ten makes more than $75,000 (*Statistical Abstract* 1999:Table 749).

The extent of African American political prominence was highlighted when Jesse Jackson (another sociology major) competed for the Democratic presidential nomination in 1984 and 1988. This progress was further confirmed in 1989 when L. Douglas Wilder of Virginia became the nation's first elected African American governor. The political prominence of African Americans came to the nation's attention again in 2000 when Alan Keyes competed for the Republican presidential nomination.

Current Losses Despite these gains, African Americans continue to lag behind in politics, economics, and education. No U.S. Senator is African American, when by ratio in the population we would expect 12. As Table 9.2 on the next page shows, African Americans average only 61 percent of white income, have much more unemployment and poverty, and are much less likely to own their home. As Table 9.3 shows, only 15 percent have graduated

Table 9.2

RACE-ETHNICITY AND COMPARATIVE WELL-BEING

	Median Family Income	Percentage of White Income	Percentage Unemployed	Percentage of White Unemployment	Percentage Below Poverty Line	Percentage of White Poverty	Percentage Owning Their Homes	Percentage of White Home Ownership
White Americans	$46,754	—	2.6%	—	11.0%	—	70%	—
African Americans	$28,602	61%	5.9%	227%	26.5%	241%	46%	66%
Latinos	$28,141	60%	4.9%	188%	27.1%	246%	45%	64%
Country of origin								
Mexico	$27,088	58%	5.0%	192%	27.9%	254%	49%	70%
Puerto Rico	$23,729	51%	5.0%	192%	34.2%	311%	34%	49%
Cuba	$37,537	80%	3.7%	142%	19.6%	178%	56%	80%
Central and South America	$32,030	69%	4.4%	169%	21.5%	195%	32%	46%
Asian Americans[a]	$51,850	111%	3.1%	119%	14.0%	127%	53%	76%
Native Americans	$25,000[b]	53%	NA[c]	NA	29.0%	264%	NA	NA

Note: The racial and ethnic groups are listed from largest to smallest.
[a]Includes Pacific Islanders.
[b]Author's estimate, based on the changes made by the other groups between 1990 and 1998.
[c]Not available.

Source: Statistical Abstract 1999:Tables 51, 52, 54, 55.

from college. That one in four African American families have an income over $50,000 is only part of the story. The other part is that about one of every six families makes less than $10,000 a year (*Statistical Abstract* 1999:Table 749).

Race or Social Class? A Sociological Debate This division of African Americans into "haves" and "have-nots" has fueled a sociological controversy. Sociologist William Julius Wilson (1978, 1987), argues that social class is now more important than race in determining the life chances of African Americans. Prior to civil rights legislation, he says, the African American experience was dominated by race. Throughout the United States, African Americans were systematically excluded from avenues of economic advancement—from good schools and good jobs. When civil rights legislation opened new opportunities, middle-class African Americans seized them. Following the path taken by other ethnic groups, as they advanced economically they, too, moved out of the inner city. Just as legal remedies began to open

doors to African Americans, however, manufacturing jobs dried up and many blue-collar jobs were moved to the suburbs. As a result, while better-educated African Americans were able to obtain middle-class, white-collar jobs, a large group of African Americans—those with poor education and lack of skills—was left behind, trapped by poverty in the inner city.

The result, says Wilson, is two worlds of African American experience. One group is stuck in the inner city, lives in poverty, attends poor schools, faces dead-end jobs or welfare, and is filled with hopelessness and despair, combined with apathy or hostility. In contrast, those who have moved up the social class ladder live in comfortable housing in secure neighborhoods, work at well-paid jobs, and send their children to good schools. Their middle-class experiences and lifestyle have changed their views on life. Their aspirations and values no longer have much in common with those of African Americans who remain poor. According to Wilson, then, social class—not race—

Table 9.3

	Less than High School Education	High School Education	1–3 Years of College	College Graduate	Number of Doctorates Awarded	Percentage of all Doctorates Awarded
EDUCATION AND RACE-ETHNICITY						
White Americans	16%	34%	25%	25%	23,860	78%
African Americans	24%	36%	25%	15%	1,530	5%
Latinos	34%[a]	55%	NA	11%	1,224	4%
Asian Americans	15%	23%	20%	42%	3,060	10%
Native Americans	22%[a,b]	68%	NA	10%	306	1%

Note: NA = Not Available. Totals except for doctorates refer to persons 25 years and over.
[a]Totals for Latinos and Native Americans are not listed in the same way in the source as they are for other groups.
[b]Author's estimate, based on the changes made by the other groups between 1990 and 1998.

Source: Statistical Abstract 1999: Tables 51, 54, 55, 1004.

has become the most significant factor in the lives of African Americans.

Many sociologists point out that this analysis overlooks the discrimination that continues to underlie the African American experience (Feagin 1997). Sociologist Charles Willie (1991), for example, notes that even when they do the same work, whites average higher pay than of African Americans. This, he argues, points to racial discrimination, not to social class.

As discussed in the text, sociologists disagree about the relative significance of race and social class in determining social and economic conditions of African Americans. William Julius Wilson, shown here, is an avid proponent of the social class side of this debate.

What is the answer to this debate? Wilson would reply that it is not an either-or question. My book is titled *The **Declining** Significance of Race,* he would say, not *The **Absence** of Race.* Certainly racism is still alive, he would add, but today social class is more central to the African American experience than is racial discrimination. The answer, then, is to provide jobs—for the availability of work offers hope, and work provides an anchor to a responsible life (Wilson 1996; 2000).

Continued Discrimination and Social Class African Americans who occupy higher statuses and enjoy greater opportunities face less discrimination. What they do face, however, is no less painful. Many middle-class and wealthy African Americans, for example, report being pulled over in traffic by police who assume their expensive cars must be stolen. Christopher Darden (1997), an African American prosecutor in the O. J. Simpson case, says that the police stop him about five times a year:

> I know the rules of the game, and I put them to work instinctively. Don't move. Don't turn around. Don't give some rookie an excuse to shoot you. Don't ask questions, no matter how badly you might want to know the answer to "Why are you stopping us, but no other cars on the street? Why aren't you stopping any of those white people?"
>
> "You've got a bad tail light," the cop would say. Or, "You were weaving a little." But you know what the real crime was: suspicion of being black.

The Down-to-Earth Sociology box on the next page reports on one aspect of the ongoing racism experienced by African Americans.

Sociology

WHAT YOU REVEAL BY YOUR VOICE: RACISM IN THE RENTAL MARKET

Blatant expressions of discrimination have become a thing of the past. There was a time when whites could burn crosses at the homes of blacks with impunity. Some even lynched African and Asian Americans without fear of the law. Today cross burning and lynching will be investigated and prosecuted. If local officials don't make an arrest, the FBI will step in. Similarly, discrimination in public accommodations was once standard. Today, no hotel, restaurant, or gas station would refuse service on the basis of race-ethnicity. This, too, has become a criminal matter.

With times so changed, some may think that racism is a thing of the past. Although overt racism has been relegated to the back shelves of social life, racism is alive and well, as sociologist Douglas Massey (Massey and Lundy 2001) of the University of Pennsylvania documents. In his undergraduate course in research methods were some whites who spoke what is called White Middle Class English, some African Americans who spoke a dialect known by sociolinguists as Black English Vernacular, and other African Americans who spoke middle-class English with a black accent.

As you know, Americans often identify one another racially by their speech. Massey used this feature of everyday life to test discrimination in the housing market. He and his students designed standard iden-

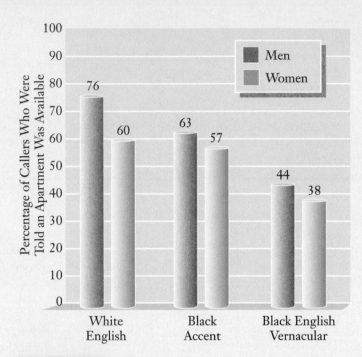

Figure 9.6 CALLERS WHO WERE TOLD AN APARTMENT WAS AVAILABLE

Source: Massey and Lundy 2001.

tities for members of these linguistic groups (assigning similar income, for example). They also developed a standard script, the one group translating it into Black English Vernacular. The students called on 79 apartments that were advertised for rent in newspapers. The study was done blindly, with the white and black students not knowing how the others were being treated.

Compared with whites, African Americans were less likely to speak to rental agents, who often used answering machines to screen calls. They also were

less likely to be told that a rental unit was available, more likely to have to pay an application fee, and more likely to have credit mentioned. Figure 9.6 shows the percentage of callers who were told that an apartment was available. Students who posed as lower-class blacks (speakers of Black English Vernacular) had the least access to apartments.

As you can see from this figure, in all instances, for both whites and blacks, discrimination was worse against women. We'll pick up this topic in the next chapter. ■

Latinos

A Note on Terms To write on race-ethnicity is like stepping into a mine field: One never knows where to expect the next explosion. Even basic terms are controversial. Some, for example, prefer the term *Hispanic Americans,* while others reject it, saying that it ignores the Indian side of their heritage. Similarly, although the term *Chicanos* is commonly used to refer to Americans from Mexico, some would limit this term to Americans from Mexico who have a sense of oppression and ethnic unity. They would not use it to refer to those who have assimilated. As you read this chapter, keep in mind that *Latino* and *Hispanic* do not refer to a race, but to ethnic groups. Latinos may identify themselves racially as black, white, or Native American.

Numbers, Origin, and Location When birds still nestled in the trees from which the *Mayflower* was made, Latinos had already established settlements in Florida and New Mexico (Bretos 1994). Today, Latinos are the second-largest minority group in the United States. As shown in Figure 9.7, about 20 million people trace their origins to Mexico, almost 3 million to Puerto Rico, 1 million to Cuba, and 4 million to Central or South America. Officially tallied at 31 million, the actual number of Latinos is considerably higher, perhaps 35 million. No one knows for certain because, although most Latinos are legal residents, several million have entered the country illegally. Each year, more than 1 million people are apprehended at the border or at points inland and are deported to Mexico (*Statistical Abstract* 1999:Table 362).

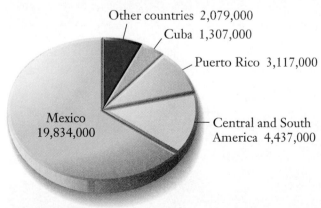

Other countries 2,079,000

Cuba 1,307,000

Puerto Rico 3,117,000

Mexico 19,834,000

Central and South America 4,437,000

COUNTRY OF ORIGIN OF U.S. LATINOS

Source: Statistical Abstract 1999:Table 55.

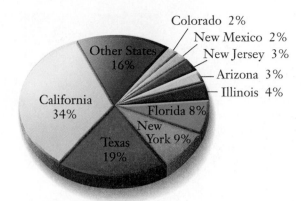

Colorado 2%

New Mexico 2%

New Jersey 3%

Arizona 3%

Illinois 4%

Other States 16%

California 34%

Florida 8%

New York 9%

Texas 19%

WHERE U.S. LATINOS LIVE

Source: Statistical Abstract 1999:Table 38.

Latino immigration has been so extensive that today there are more Latinos in the United States than there are Canadians in Canada (30 million). To Midwesterners, such a comparison often comes as a surprise, for Latinos are absent from vast stretches of mid-America. As shown in Figure 9.8, 70 percent are concentrated in just four states: California, Texas, New York, and Florida. By the year 2004, the U.S. government expects Latinos to become the largest minority group (*Statistical Abstract* 1999: Table 19). Some think that the 2000 census shows that this has already occurred (Porter 2001; Schmitt 2001).

Spanish Language The Spanish language distinguishes most Latinos from other U.S. ethnic groups. With 17 million people speaking Spanish at home, the United States has become one of the largest Spanish-speaking nations in the world (*Statistical Abstract* 1999:Table 60). Because about half of Latinos are unable to speak English, or can do so only with difficulty, many face a major obstacle to getting good jobs.

Diversity For Latinos, country of origin is highly significant. Those from Puerto Rico, for example, feel little in common with people from Mexico, Venezuela, or El Salvador—just as earlier immigrants from Germany, Sweden, and England felt they had little in common with one another. A sign of these divisions is the preference many have to refer to themselves by country of origin, such as Puerto Rican or Cuban American, rather than as Latino or Hispanic.

As with other ethnic groups, Latinos, too, are separated by social class. The half-million Cubans who fled Castro's rise to power in 1959, for example, were mostly well-educated, well-to-do professionals or

In reaction to the millions of recent Latino immigrants who speak Spanish, an "English-only" movement has developed in the United States. Twenty-three states have passed laws declaring that English is their official language (Schaefer 2000). One wonders which version of English the legislators had in mind.

businesspeople who feared reprisal for resisting the revolution. In contrast, the 100,000 "boat people" who fled Cuba in 1980 were mostly lower-class refugees, people with whom the earlier arrivals would not have associated in Cuba. The earlier arrivals, who are firmly established in Florida and control many businesses and financial institutions, distance themselves from the more recent immigrants.

These divisions of national origin and social class are a major obstacle to political unity. One consequence is an underrepresentation in politics. Although Latinos make up 11 percent of the U.S. population, they hold only 4 percent of the seats in the U.S. Congress and 1 percent of the elected local offices (*Statistical Abstract* 1999:Tables 473, 481).

Fragmented among themselves, Latinos also find that a huge gulf separates them from African Americans. With highly distinct histories and cultures, these two minorities often avoid each other. As Latinos have become

When the U.S. government took control of what is now the southwestern United States, Mexicans living there were transformed from the *dominant group* into a *minority group*. These children in Austin, Texas, dancing at a Cinco de Mayo festival, are learning to appreciate their ethnic identity, with its rich cultural heritage.

more visible in U.S. society and more vocal in their demands for equality, they have come face to face with African Americans who fear that Latino gains in jobs and at the ballot box will come at their expense.

Comparative Conditions Table 9.2 on page 224 shows how Latinos compare with other groups. You can see that Latinos are worse off than European Americans and Asian Americans on all indicators of well-being shown on this table. Their rankings on these indicators are similar to those of African Americans. This table also illustrates the significance of country of origin. You can see that Cuban Americans score higher on these indicators of well-being, while Puerto Rican Americans score far worse. Table 9.3 on page 225 shows that almost half of Latinos do not complete high school, and only 11 percent graduate from college. In a postindustrial society that increasingly stresses advanced skills, these figures indicate that a large number of Latinos will be left behind.

Asian Americans

I have stressed in this chapter that our racial-ethnic categories are based more on social considerations than on biological ones. This point is again obvious when we examine the category Asian American. As Figure 9.9 shows, those who are called Asian Americans came to the United States from many nations. With no unifying culture or "race," why should they ever be clustered together in a single category? Think about it. What culture or race-ethnicity do Samoans and Vietnamese have in common? Or Laotians and Pakistanis? Or Native Hawaiians and Chinese? Or people from India and those from Guam? Yet all these groups—and more—are lumped together and called Asian American. Apparently the U.S. government is not satisfied until it is able to pigeonhole everyone into a racial-ethnic group.

Since Asian American is a standard term, however, let's look at the characteristics of the 10 million people who are lumped together and assigned this label.

A Background of Discrimination From the time of their first arrival on these shores, Asian Americans met discrimination. Lured by gold strikes in the West and a vast need for unskilled workers to build the railroads, 200,000 Chinese immigrated between 1850 and 1880. Feeling threatened by competing cheap labor, Anglos formed mobs and vigilante groups to intimidate the Chinese. In 1850, California passed the Foreign Miner's Act, which required Chinese (and Latinos) to pay a fee of $20 a month—when wages were a dollar a day. When the famous golden spike was driven at Promontory, Utah, in 1869 to mark the completion of the railroad to the West Coast, white workers prevented Chinese workers from being in the photo—even though Chinese made up 90 percent of Central Pacific Railroad's labor force (Hsu 1971). The California Supreme Court ruled that Chinese testimony against whites was inadmissible in court (Carlson and Colburn 1972). In 1882, Congress passed the Chinese Exclusion Act, suspending all Chinese immigration for 10 years. Four years later, the Statue of Liberty was dedicated. The tired, the poor, and the huddled masses it was to welcome were obviously not Chinese.

When immigrants from Japan arrived, they met *spillover bigotry,* a stereotype that lumped Asians together, depicting them as sneaky, lazy, and untrustworthy. After Japan attacked Pearl Harbor in 1941, conditions grew worse for the 110,000 Japanese Americans who called the United States their home. U.S. authorities feared that Japan would invade the United States and that the Japanese Americans would fight on Japan's side. They also feared that Japanese Americans would sabotage military installations on the West Coast. Although no Japanese American had been involved in even a single act of sabotage, on February 19, 1942, President Franklin D. Roosevelt ordered that everyone who was *one-eighth Japanese or more* be placed in special prisons (called "relocation camps"). They were charged with no crime, and they had no trials. Japanese ancestry was sufficient cause for being imprisoned.

Figure 9.9 **THE ETHNIC BACKGROUND OF ASIAN AMERICANS**

Source: Lee 1998.

[a]Includes people from Cambodia, Guam, Hawaii, Laos, Pakistan, Samoa, Thailand, and elsewhere

Asian Americans   **Total U.S. Population**

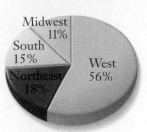 

 **RESIDENCE OF ASIAN AMERICANS**

Source: Statistical Abstract 1999:Table 32.

A World of Striking Contrasts Today, Asian Americans are the fastest-growing minority in the United States. Most Asian Americans live in the West, as can be seen in Figure 9.10. The three largest groups of Asian Americans—of Chinese, Filipino, and Japanese descent—are concentrated in Los Angeles, San Francisco, Honolulu, and New York City. From Table 9.2 (page 224), you can see that Asian Americans have a higher annual income than any other racial-ethnic group listed in this table. This has led to the stereotype that all Asian Americans are successful, a stereotype that masks huge ethnic differences. Look at the poverty rate of Asian Americans shown in this table. Although 14 percent is much less than that of other minority groups, it means that about one and a half million Asian Americans live in poverty. Their poverty is not evenly distributed. Although poverty is unusual among Chinese and Japanese Americans, it clusters among Americans from Southeast Asia.

Reasons for Success The general success of Asian Americans can be traced to three major factors: family life, educational achievement, and assimilation into mainstream culture.

Of all ethnic groups, including whites, Asian American children are the most likely to grow up with two parents and the least likely to be born to a single mother (Lee 1998; *Statistical Abstract* 1999:Table 99). Most grow up in close-knit families that stress self-discipline, thrift, and hard work (Suzuki 1985; Bell 1991). This early socialization provides strong impetus for the other two factors.

The second factor is their high rate of college graduation. As Table 9.3 on page 225 shows, 42 percent of Asian Americans complete college. To realize how stunning this is, compare this with the other groups shown in this table. Their educational achievement, in turn, opens doors to economic success.

Assimilation, the third factor, is indicated by several measures. With about two of five marrying someone of another race-ethnic group, Asian Americans have the highest intermarriage rate of any minority. They also are the most likely to live in integrated neighborhoods (Lee 1998). Japanese Americans, the financially most successful of Asian Americans, are the most assimilated (Bell 1991; Schaefer 2000). About 73 percent say that their best friend is not a Japanese American.

Asian Americans are becoming more prominent in politics. With 63 percent of its citizens being Asian American, Hawaii has elected Asian American governors and sent several Asian American senators to Washington (Lee 1998; *Statistical Abstract* 1999:Table 34). The first Asian American governor outside of Hawaii is Gary Locke, who in 1996 was elected governor of Washington, a state in which Asian Americans make up less than 6 percent of the population.

Native Americans

Diversity of Groups Thanks to countless grade B Westerns, many Americans hold stereotypes of Native Americans who lived on the frontier. They see them as wild, uncivilized savages, a single group of people subdivided into separate tribes. The European immigrants to the Colonies, however, encountered diverse groups of people with a variety of cultures—from nomadic hunters and gatherers to people living in wooden houses in settled agricultural communities. Altogether, they spoke over 700 languages (Schaefer 2000). Each group had its own norms and values—and the usual ethnocentric pride in its own culture. Consider what happened in 1744 when the colonists of Virginia offered college scholarships for "savage" lads. The Iroquois replied:

> "Several of our young people were formerly brought up at the colleges of Northern Provinces. They were instructed in all your sciences. But when they came back to us, they were bad runners, ignorant of every means of living in the woods, unable to bear either cold or hunger, knew neither how to build a cabin, take a deer, or kill an enemy.... They were totally good for nothing."
>
> They added, "If the English gentlemen would send a dozen or two of their children to Onondaga, the great Council would take care of their education, bring them up in really what was the best manner and make men of them." (Nash 1974; in McLemore 1994)

Native Americans, who numbered between 5 and 10 million, had no immunity to the diseases the Europeans brought with them. With deaths due to disease—and warfare, a much lesser cause—their number was reduced to about *one-twentieth* its original size. A hundred years ago, the Native American population reached a low point of a half million. Native Americans, who now number about 2 million (see Figure 9.5 on page 221), speak 150 different languages. Like Latinos and Asian Americans, they do not think of themselves as a single people that justifies a single label (McLemore 1994).

From Treaties to Genocide and Population Transfer At first, relations between the European settlers and the Native Americans were by and large peaceful. The Native Americans accommodated the strangers, as there was plenty of land for both. As wave after wave of settlers continued to arrive, however, Pontiac, an Ottawa chief, saw the future—and didn't like it. He convinced several tribes to unite in an effort to push the Europeans into the sea. He almost succeeded, but failed when the English were reinforced by fresh troops (McLemore 1994).

A pattern developed. The U.S. government would make treaties to buy some of a tribe's land, with the promise to honor forever the tribe's right to what it had not sold. European immigrants, who continued to pour into the United States, would disregard these boundaries. The tribes would resist, with death tolls on both sides. Washington would then intervene—not to enforce the treaty, but to force the tribe off its lands. In its relentless drive westward, the U.S. government embarked on a policy of genocide. It assigned the U.S. cavalry the task of "pacifica-

tion," which translates as slaughtering Native Americans who "stood in the way" of this territorial expansion.

The acts of cruelty perpetrated by the Europeans against Native Americans appear endless, but two were especially grisly. The first was the distribution of blankets contaminated with smallpox—under the guise of a peace offering. The second was the Trail of Tears, a forced march of a thousand miles from the Carolinas and Georgia to Oklahoma. Fifteen thousand Cherokees were forced to make this midwinter march in light clothing. Conditions were so bad that 4,000 died. The symbolic end to Native American resistance came in 1890 with a massacre at Wounded Knee, South Dakota. Of 350 men, women, and children, the U.S. cavalry gunned down 300 and buried them in a mass grave (Thornton 1987; Lind 1995; Johnson 1998). These acts took place after the U.S. government changed its policy from genocide to population transfer and began to confine Native Americans to specified areas called *reservations.*

The Invisible Minority and Self-Determination Native Americans can truly be called the invisible minority. Because about 50 percent live in rural areas and one-third in just three states—Oklahoma, California, and Arizona—most other Americans are hardly conscious of a Native American presence in the United States. The isolation of two of every five Native Americans on reservations further reduces their visibility (Thornton 1987; *Statistical Abstract* 1999:Table 53).

Of all the oppressive acts perpetrated against the Native Americans by the dominant Anglos, it is difficult to choose a single example. Among the most brutal, however, is the Trail of Tears. This painting is a sanitized depiction: Most victims walked, some were barefoot (although it was winter), and dead bodies were left strewn along the trail. Also, it is unlikely that any Native American was allowed to possess a rifle.

The systematic attempts of European Americans to destroy the Native Americans' way of life and their resettlement onto reservations continue to have deleterious effects. Of all U.S. minorities, Native Americans are the worst off. Table 9.2 on page 224 shows their high rate of poverty. Their rates of suicide and alcoholism are also higher, while their life expectancy is lower than that of the nation as a whole (U.S. Department of Health and Human Services 1990; Lester 1997). Table 9.3 on page 225 also shows that their education lags behind the nation's, that only 10 percent graduate from college.

These negative conditions are the consequence of Anglo domination. In the 1800s, U.S. courts determined that Native Americans did not own the land on which they had been settled and had no right to develop their resources. Native Americans were made wards of the state and treated like children by the Bureau of Indian Affairs (Mohawk 1991). Then, in the 1960s, Native Americans won a series of legal victories that restored their control over the land and their right to determine economic policy. As a result, several Native American tribes have opened businesses on their lands—ranging from industrial parks serving metropolitan areas to fish canneries.

It is the casinos, though, that have attracted the most attention. In 1988, the federal government passed a law allowing Native Americans to operate gambling establishments on reservations. Tribal gambling has created 120,000 jobs, bringing a taste of prosperity to more than 200 tribes (McLemore 1994; Johnson 1999). Some tribes have struck it rich. The Mdewakanton Dakota Sioux in Minnesota, which has just 270 members, owns a casino that nets $900,000 a year for each man, woman, and child (Farney 1998; "Reservations..." 2000). The most successful tribe, however, is the Pequot of Connecticut. With only 310 members, they bring in more than $2 million a day (Zielbauer 1999).

A highly controversial issue is *separatism.* Because Native Americans were independent peoples when the Europeans arrived and they never willingly joined the United States, many tribes maintain the right to remain separate from the U.S. government and U.S. society. The chief of the Onondaga tribe in New York, a member of the Iroquois Federation, summarizes the issue this way:

> For the whole history of the Iroquois, we have maintained that we are a separate nation. We have never lost a war. Our government still operates. We have refused the U.S. government's reorganization plans for us. We have kept our language and our traditions, and when we fly to Geneva to UN meetings, we carry Hau de no sau nee passports. We made some treaties that lost some land, but that also confirmed our separate-nation status. That the U.S. denies all this doesn't make it any less the case. (Mander 1992)

One of the most significant changes is **pan-Indianism.** This emphasis on common elements that run through Native American cultures is an attempt to develop an identity that goes beyond the tribe. Whether Native Americans wish to work together as in pan-Indianism or to stress

Like families, groups in societies also retell their past—with the retelling representing a particular point of view. The victors of wars gain a tremendous advantage in such retelling, for their versions become official history. As this photo depicts, even art is part of history. And like official history, art is also far from neutral, as this painting illustrates. Supposedly this is an authentic depiction of the Battle at Little Bighorn, but note that the artist uses the perspective of those who lost the battle but won the war. The U.S. cavalry is dominantly portrayed, not the Native Americans. Also note Custer's exaggerated bravery. In the artist's rendering, Custer remains a symbol of "glorious" defeat.

separatism and to identify solely with their own tribe, to assimilate into the dominant culture or to remain apart from it, to move to cities or to remain on reservations, to operate casinos or to engage only in traditional activities—"Such decisions must be ours," say the Native Americans. "We are sovereign, and we will not take orders from the victors of past wars."

LOOKING TOWARD THE FUTURE

Back in 1903, sociologist W. E. B. Du Bois said, "The problem of the twentieth century is the problem of the color line—the relation of the darker to the lighter races of men." Incredibly, a hundred years later, the color line remains one of the most volatile topics facing the nation.

In another hundred years, will yet another sociologist lament that the color of people's skin still affects human relationships? Granted our past, it seems that although racial walls will diminish, even crumble at some points, the color line is not likely to disappear. Two issues we are currently grappling with are immigration and affirmative action.

The Immigration Debate

Throughout its history, the United States has both welcomed immigration and feared its consequences. The gates opened wide (numerically, if not in attitude) for a massive wave of immigrants in the late nineteenth and early twentieth centuries. During the past 20 years, a second great wave of immigration has brought about a million new residents to the United States each year (*Statistical Abstract* 1999:Table 4). Unlike the first wave, which was almost exclusively from western Europe, this second wave is much more diverse. In fact, it is changing the U.S. racial-ethnic mix. If current trends in immigration (and birth) persist, in a little over 50 years the "average" American will trace his or her ancestry to Africa, Asia, South America, the Pacific Islands, the Middle East—to almost anywhere but white Europe. See Figure 9.11.

In some states, the future is arriving much sooner than this. In California, ethnic and racial minorities already constitute the majority. California has 17 million minorities and 16 million whites (*Statistical Abstract* 1999:Table 38). Californians who request new telephone service from Pacific Bell can speak to customer service representatives in Spanish, Korean, Vietnamese, Mandarin, Cantonese—or in English.

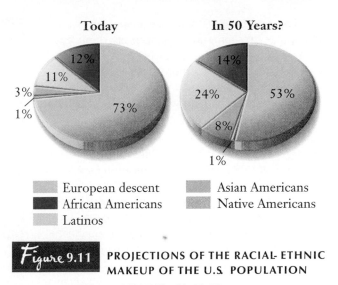

Today / **In 50 Years?**

- European descent
- African Americans
- Latinos
- Asian Americans
- Native Americans

Figure 9.11 **PROJECTIONS OF THE RACIAL-ETHNIC MAKEUP OF THE U.S. POPULATION**

Source: Statistical Abstract 1999:Tables 19, 23, 59.

As in the past, there is concern that "too many" immigrants will alter the character of the United States. "Throughout the history of American immigration," write sociologists Alejandro Portés and Ruben Rumbaut (1990), "a consistent thread has been the fear that the 'alien element' would somehow undermine the institutions of the country and would lead it down the path of disintegration and decay." A widespread fear held by native-born European Americans in the early 1900s was that immigrants from southern Europe would subvert the democratic system in favor of communism. Today, some fear that Spanish-speaking immigrants threaten the primacy of the English language. In addition, the age-old fear that immigrants will take jobs away from native-born Americans remains strong. Finally, minority groups that struggled for political representation fear that newer groups will gain political power at their expense.

Affirmative Action

The role of affirmative action in our multicultural society lies at the center of a national debate about race and ethnic relations. In this policy, goals based on race (and sex) are used in hiring, promotion, and college admission. Sociologist Barbara Reskin (1998) examined the results of affirmative action. In agreement with earlier studies (Badgett and Hartmann 1995), she concluded that, although it is difficult to separate the results of affirmative action from economic booms and busts and the increased number of women in the work force, affirmative action has had a modest impact.

The results may have been modest, but the reaction to this program has been anything but modest. Affirmative action has been the source of intense controversy for more than a generation, Liberals, both white and minority, say that this program is the most direct way to level the playing field of economic opportunity. If whites are passed over, this is an unfortunate cost we must pay if we are to make up for past discrimination. Conservatives, in contrast, both white and minority, agree that opportunity should be open to all, but claim that putting race (or sex) ahead of people's training and ability to perform a job is reverse discrimination. Because of their race (or sex), qualified people who had nothing to do with past discrimination are discriminated against. They add that affirmative action stigmatizes the people who benefit from it, because it suggests that they hold their jobs because of race (or sex), rather than merit.

This national debate crystallized with several controversial rulings. Perhaps the most significant was *Proposition 209*, an amendment to the California state constitution that banned preferences to minorities and women in hiring, promotion, and college admission. Despite appeals by a coalition of civil rights groups, the U.S. Supreme Court upheld this California law. The issue of the proper role of affirmative action in a multicultural society is likely to remain center stage for quite some time.

Toward a True Multicultural Society

The potential is for the United States to become a society in which different racial-ethnic groups not only co-exist, but also respect one another and work for mutually beneficial goals. In a true multicultural society, the minority groups that make up the United States will participate fully in the nation's social institutions while maintaining their cultural integrity. To reach this goal will require that we understand that "the biological differences that divide one race from another add up to a drop in the genetic ocean." For a long time, we have given racial categories an importance they never merited. Now we need to figure out how to reduce them to the irrelevance they deserve. In short, we need to make real the abstraction called equality that we profess to believe (Cose 2000).

If we are to have a true multicultural society, U.S. citizens—especially those who belong to the group that has taken its dominance for granted since the founding of the nation—must grapple with their traditional beliefs and national symbols. As is apparent from the Thinking Critically section that concludes this chapter, this is a global issue.

The United States is the most racially-ethnically diverse society in the world. This can be our central strength, with our many groups working together to build a harmonious society, a stellar example for the world. Or it can be our Achilles heel, with us breaking into feuding groups, a Balkanized society that marks an ill-fitting end to a grand social experiment. Our reality will probably fall somewhere between these extremes

Thinking *Critically*

WHOSE HISTORY?

As symbolic interactionists stress, the events of life do not come with built-in meanings. Instead, we place them within a framework of thought, which lends them a certain interpretation. It is no wonder, then, that the victors and the vanquished look at the same events in remarkably different ways.

The victors have the advantage of writing the textbooks that recount those events.

In Israel, schoolchildren are taught about the 1948 War of Independence, in which Israel defeated five Arab nations. The textbooks used to portray the early Zionists as peace-loving pioneers who fell victim to Arab hatred. Now, since Israel and the Palestinians have pursued a peaceful solution, Israel is rewriting its texts. Consider these two accounts of the same event—both from official Israeli history textbooks for ninth graders (Bronner 1999):

The old text: The Jewish community numbered about 650,000. The Arab states together came to 40 million.

The chances of success were doubtful, and the Jewish community had to draft every possible fighter for the defense of the community.

The new text: On nearly every front and in nearly every battle, the Jewish side had the advantage over the Arabs in terms of planning, organization, operation of equipment and also in the number of trained fighters who participated in the battle.

Such a drastic change does not come without resistance. Says one Israeli, a well-known novelist: "This is an act of moral suicide that deprives our children of everything that makes people proud of Israel. Why not just translate the Palestinian books for our children and be done with it?"

The United States has similar controversies. Consider the Battle of Little Bighorn. Children's history books usually recount the massacre of an outnumbered, brave band of cavalrymen, with Gen. George Custer going down to a sad but somehow glorious defeat. When Joe Marshall, a Lakota Sioux, heard this version as a fourth-grader, he mustered all the courage he could, raised his hand, and told the class the version he had learned from the descendants of the victors of that battle. This version describes armed soldiers who invade Sioux lands (Charlier 1992). When the young boy finished, his teacher smiled indulgently and said, "That's nice, but we'll stick to the real story."

The U.S. history books say there were no survivors of this battle. Think about this for a moment, and the point about perspectives in history will become even more obvious. For the Native Americans, there were many survivors. Indeed, those survivors kept the memory of the battle alive, using what is called "oral tradition" to pass on from one generation to the next an account of the battle.

In U.S. schools, the question of what should be taught used to be a moot point, for the school boards, teachers, and textbook writers were united by a background of shared assumptions. It was assumed, for example, that George Washington was the general-hero-founder of the nation. No question was raised about whether school curricula should mention that he owned slaves. Most white school board members, teachers, and textbook writers were ignorant of this aspect of Washington's life. If they learned of it, they thought it irrelevant.

But no longer. Information is more available than it used to be, and the issue now is one of balance. How do we make certain that the accomplishments of both genders and our many racial-ethnic groups are included? This issue, called *multiculturalism,* presents teachers, administrators, school boards, and publishers with a slew of difficult questions. How much space should be given to Harriet Tubman in comparison to George Washington? Is enough attention paid to discrimination against Asian Americans? Against Latinos? Is the attempted genocide of Native Americans sufficiently acknowledged? What about the contributions of women to U.S. society? How about those of white ethnics—Jews, Poles, Russians, and so on?

And there are other issues. Thomas Jefferson—prophet of freedom and owner of slaves—apparently fathered children by his slave, Sally Hemings. At first, Jefferson's white descendants vigorously denied this accusation. Then came DNA tests, as well as records showing that Hemings' pregnancies coincided with Jefferson's returns to Monticello and that at his death Jefferson freed Hemings and her children—but not his other slaves. In the face of this evidence, the white descendants acknowledged that the Hemings, too, are Jefferson's descendants (Breaux 2000). ■

For Your Consideration

How would you resolve this issue? How would you get more objectivity into history books? Can history be told from all perspectives? What place should the Jefferson-Hemmings relationship play in our history texts?

The answers to such questions will give birth to new images of history. Like the images that preceded them, will they, too, not be myth making? Is there such a thing as objectivity?

SUMMARY AND REVIEW

■ Laying the Sociological Foundation

How is race both a reality and a myth?

In the sense that different groups inherit distinctive physical traits, race is a reality. There is, however, no agreement regarding what constitutes a particular race, or how many races there are. In the sense of one race being superior to another, and of there being pure races, race is a myth. The *idea* of race is powerful, shaping basic relationships among people. Pp. 206–207.

How do race and ethnicity differ?

Race refers to inherited biological characteristics, **ethnicity** to cultural ones. Members of ethnic groups identify with one another on the basis of common ancestry and cultural heritage. Pp. 207–209.

What are minority and dominant groups?

Minority groups are people singled out for unequal treatment by members of the **dominant group**, the group with more power, privilege, and social status. Minorities originate with migration, or the expansion of political boundaries. P. 209.

What heightens racial-ethnic identity, and what is "ethnic work"?

A group's size, power, physical characteristics, and amount of discrimination heighten or reduce ethnic identity. **Ethnic work** is the process of constructing an ethnic identity. For people with strong ties to their culture of origin, ethnic work involves enhancing and maintaining group distinctions. For those without a firm ethnic identity, ethnic work is an attempt to recover one's ethnic heritage. Pp. 209–210.

Are prejudice and discrimination the same thing?

Prejudice is an attitude, **discrimination** an act. Some people who are prejudiced do not discriminate, while others who are not prejudiced, do. Pp. 210–213.

How do individual and institutional discrimination differ?

Individual discrimination is the negative treatment of one person by another, while **institutional discrimination** is discrimination built into social institutions. Institutional discrimination often occurs without the awareness of either the perpetrator or the object of discrimination. Referral rates for coronary bypass surgery are but one example. Pp. 213–214.

■ Theories of Prejudice

How do psychologists explain prejudice?

Psychological theories of prejudice stress **authoritarian personalities** and frustration displaced toward **scapegoats**. Pp. 214–215.

How do sociologists explain prejudice?

Sociological theories focus on how different social environments increase or decrease prejudice. Functionalists stress the benefits and costs that come from discrimination. Conflict theorists look at how the groups in power exploit racial and ethnic divisions in order to hold down wages and otherwise maintain power. Symbolic interactionists stress how labels create **selective perception** and self-fulfilling prophecies. Pp. 215–218.

■ Global Patterns of Intergroup Relations

What are the major patterns of minority and dominant group relations?

Beginning with the least humane, they are **genocide, population transfer, internal colonialism, segregation, assimilation,** and **multiculturalism (pluralism)**. Pp. 219–220.

■ Race and Ethnic Relations in the United States

What are the major ethnic groups in the United States?

From largest to smallest, the major ethnic groups are European Americans, African Americans, Latinos, Asian Americans, and Native Americans. P. 221.

What are some issues in race-ethnic relations and characteristics of minority groups?

African Americans are increasingly divided into middle and lower classes, with two sharply contrasting worlds of experience. Latinos are divided by social class and country of origin. On many measures, Asian Americans are better off than white Americans, but their well-being varies with country of origin. For Native Americans, the primary issues are poverty, nationhood, and settling treaty obligations. The overarching issue for minorities is overcoming discrimination. Pp. 221–233.

■ Looking Toward the Future

What main issues dominate race-ethnic relations?

The main issues are immigration, affirmative action, and how to develop a true multicultural society. The answers affect our future. Pp. 233–235.

Where can I read more on this topic?

Suggested readings for this chapter are listed on page SR-6.

YOUR INTERACTIVE COMPANION WEB SITE

Your Interactive Companion Web Site includes practice tests, with feedback, and online learning activities with video, audio, and Weblinks. Your access code for this Web site is provided with this text.

GLOSSARY

assimilation the process of being absorbed into the mainstream culture (p. 220)

authoritarian personality Adorno's term for people who are prejudiced and rank high on scales of conformity, intolerance, insecurity, respect for authority, and submissiveness to superiors (p. 215)

compartmentalize to separate acts from feelings or attitudes (p. 219)

discrimination act of unfair treatment directed against an individual or a group (p. 210)

dominant group the group with the most power, greatest privileges, and highest social status (p. 209)

ethnic cleansing a policy of population elimination, including forcible expulsion and genocide (p. 220)

ethnic work activities designed to discover, enhance, or maintain ethnic and racial identification (p. 210)

ethnicity (and ethnic) distinctive cultural characteristics (p. 207)

genocide the systematic annihilation or attempted annihilation of a race or ethnic group (p. 207)

individual discrimination the negative treatment of one person by another on the basis of that person's perceived characteristics (p. 213)

institutional discrimination negative treatment of a minority group that is built into a society's institutions (p. 213)

internal colonialism the systematic economic exploitation of a minority group (p. 220)

melting pot the idea that Americans of various backgrounds would melt (or merge), leaving behind their distinctive ethnic identities and forming a new ethnic group (p. 210)

minority group people who are singled out for unequal treatment on the basis of their physical and cultural characteristics, and who regard themselves as objects of collective discrimination (p. 209)

multiculturalism (also called pluralism) a policy that permits or encourages groups to express their individual, unique racial and ethnic identities (p. 220)

pan-Indianism an emphasis on the welfare of all Native Americans (p. 232)

pluralism another term for multiculturalism (p. 220)

population transfer causing a minority group to relocate (p. 219)

prejudice an attitude of prejudging, usually in a negative way (p. 210)

race a group whose inherited physical characteristics distinguish it from other groups (p. 206)

racism discrimination on the basis of race (p. 210)

reserve labor force the term used by conflict theorists for the unemployed, who can be put to work during times of high production and then discarded when no longer needed (p. 217)

rising expectations the sense that better conditions are soon to follow, which, if unfulfilled, creates mounting frustration (p. 223)

scapegoat an individual or group that is unfairly blamed for someone else's troubles (p. 214)

segregation the policy of keeping racial or ethnic groups apart (p. 220)

selective perception seeing certain features of an object or situation, but remaining blind to others (p. 217)

split labor market a term used by conflict theorists for the practice of weakening the bargaining power of workers by splitting them along racial, ethnic, sex, age, or any other lines (p. 217)

WASP white *Anglo-Saxon Protestant;* narrowly, an American of English descent; broadly, an American of western European ancestry (p. 222)

white ethnics white immigrants to the U.S. whose culture differs from that of WASPs (p. 222)

Chapter 10

Phoebe Beasley, Holding Court, 1989

Inequalities of Age
and Gender

In Tunis, the capital of Tunisia, on Africa's northern coast, I met some U.S. college students with whom I spent a couple of days. When they said that they wanted to see Tunis' red light district, I wondered if it would be worth the trip. I already had seen other red light districts, including the unusual one in Amsterdam where the state licenses the women, requires medical exams (certificates must be posted so customers can check them), sets the prices, and pays the prostitutes' social security benefits upon retirement. The women sit behind lighted picture windows while customers stroll along the canalside streets and browse from the outside.

This time the sight turned my stomach.

We ended up on a wharf that extended into the Mediterranean. Each side was lined with a row of one-room wooden shacks, each one crowded up against the next. In front of each open door stood a young woman. Peering from outside into the dark interiors, I could see that each door led to a tiny room with a well-worn bed.

The wharf was crowded with men who were eyeing the women. Many of them wore sailor uniforms from countries that I couldn't identify.

As I looked more closely, I could see that some of the women had runny sores on their legs. Incredibly, with such visible evidence of their disease, customers still entered. Evidently the low price (at that time $2) was too much to resist.

[handwritten top margin: Gender: refers to masculinity & femmity (Society sees.) Sex refers to Male & femal.]

With a sickening feeling in my stomach and the desire to vomit, I kept a good distance between myself and the beckoning women. One tour of the two-block area was more than sufficient.

Out of sight, I knew, was a group of men whose wealth derived from exploiting these women who were condemned to live short lives punctuated by fear and misery. ■

[handwritten left margin: form into]

In the previous chapter, we considered how race and ethnicity affect people's well-being and their position in society. In this chapter, we examine how being classified by sex and age makes significant differences in people's lives. Our primary focus is **gender stratification**—males' and females' unequal access to power, prestige, and property on the basis of sex—but we also examine the prejudice, discrimination, and hostility directed against people because of their age.

Gender and age are especially significant because they are master statuses that cut across all aspects of social life. No matter what we may attain in life, such as our education, *we are labeled male or female and are assigned some age category*. These labels and categories carry images and expectations about how we should act. They not only guide our behavior but also serve as the basis of power and privilege.

INEQUALITIES OF GENDER

Let's begin by considering the distinction between sex and gender.

*I*SSUES OF SEX AND GENDER

When we consider how females and males differ, the first thing that usually comes to mind is **sex,** the *biological characteristics* that distinguish males and females. *Primary sex characteristics* consist of a vagina or a penis and other organs related to reproduction. *Secondary sex characteristics* are the physical distinctions between males and females that are not directly connected with reproduction. Secondary sex characteristics become clearly evident at puberty, when males develop more muscles, a lower voice, and more hair and height while females form more fatty tissue, broader hips, and larger breasts.

Gender, in contrast, is a *social,* not a biological characteristic. **Gender** consists of whatever traits a group considers proper for its males and females. Consequently, gender varies from one society to another. Whereas *sex* refers to male or female, *gender* refers to masculinity or femininity. In short, you inherit your sex, but you learn your gender as you are socialized into the behaviors and attitudes thought appropriate for your sex. As the photo montage on the next page illustrates, these expectations vary around the world.

The sociological significance of gender is that it is a device by which society controls its members. Gender sorts us, on the basis of sex, into different life experiences. It opens and closes doors to power, property, and even prestige. Like social class, gender is a structural feature of society.

Before examining inequalities of gender, let's consider why the behaviors of men and women differ.

Gender Differences in Behavior: Biology or Culture?

Why are most males more aggressive than most females? Why do women enter "nurturing" occupations such as nursing in far greater numbers than men? To answer such questions, many people respond with some variation of "They're just born that way."

Is this the correct answer? Certainly biology plays a significant role in our lives. Each of us begins as a fertilized egg. The egg, or ovum, is contributed by our mother, the sperm that fertilizes the egg by our father. At the very moment the egg is fertilized, our sex is determined. Each of us receives twenty-three pairs of chromosomes from the ovum and twenty-three from the sperm. The egg has an X chromosome. If the sperm that fertilizes the egg also has an X chromosome, we become a girl (XX). If the sperm has a Y chromosome, we become a boy (XY).

That's the biology. Now, the sociological question is, Does this biological difference control our behavior? Does it, for example, make females more nurturing and submissive, and males more aggressive and domineering? Almost all sociologists take the side of "nurture" in this "nature versus nurture" controversy, but a few do not. The dominant sociological position is that social factors, not biology, are the reasons we do what we do.

India

Brazil

Standards of beauty vary so greatly from one culture to another that what one group finds attractive, another may not. Yet, in its ethnocentrism, each group thinks that its standards are the best—that its preferences reflect what beauty "really" is. As indicated here, around the world men and women aspire to their group's standards of gender. To make themselves appealing to others, they make certain that their appearance reflects those standards.

Republic of Georga

Mexico

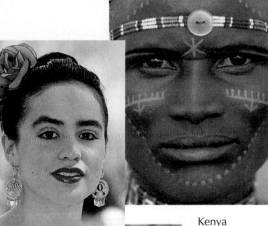

Kenya

Peru

Ivory Coast

Tibet

The visible differences of sex do not come with meanings built into them. Rather, each human group makes its own interpretation of these physical differences, and on that basis assigns males and females to separate groups. There people learn what is expected of them and are given different access to their society's privileges.

Most sociologists find the argument compelling that if biology were the principal factor in human behavior, all around the world we would find women to be one sort of person and men another. In fact, however, ideas of gender vary greatly from one culture to another—and, as a result, so do male-female behaviors. The Tahitians in the South

Pacific stand in remarkable contrast to our usual expectations of gender. They don't give their children names that are identifiable as male or female, and they don't divide their labor on the basis of gender. They expect *both* men and women to be passive, yielding, and to ignore slights. Neither males nor females are competitive in trying to attain material possessions (Gilmore 1990).

Opening the Door to Biology

The matter of "nature" versus "nurture" is not so easily settled, however, and some sociologists acknowledge that biological factors are involved in some human behavior other than reproduction and childbearing (Udry 2000). Alice Rossi, a feminist sociologist and former president of the American Sociological Association, has suggested that women are better prepared biologically for "mothering" than are men. She (1977, 1984) says that women are more sensitive to the infants' soft skin and to their nonverbal communications. Rossi stresses that the issue is not either biology or society. It is that nature provides biological predispositions, which are then overlaid with culture.

To see why the door to biology is opening, just slightly, in sociology, let's consider a medical accident and a study of Vietnam veterans.

A Medical Accident The drama began in 1963, when 7-month-old identical twins were taken to a doctor for a routine circumcision (Money and Ehrhardt 1972). The inept physician, who was using electrocautery (a heated needle), turned the electric current too high and accidentally burned off the penis of one of the boys. You can imagine the parents' reaction of disbelief, followed by horror, as the truth sank in.

What can be done in a situation like this? The damage was irreversible. The parents were told that the child could never have sexual relations. After months of soul-searching and tearful consultations with experts, the parents decided that their son should have a sex-change operation. When he was 17 months old, surgeons castrated the boy, using the skin to construct a vagina. The parents then gave the child a new name, Brenda, dressed him in frilly clothing, let his hair grow long, and began to treat him as a girl. Later, physicians gave Brenda female steroids to promote female pubertal growth.

At first, the results were extremely promising. When the twins were 4 years old, the mother said (remember that the children are biologically identical),

One thing that really amazes me is that she is so feminine. I've never seen a little girl so neat and tidy. She likes for me to wipe her face. She doesn't like to be dirty, and yet my son is quite different. I can't wash his face for anything. She is very proud of herself, when she puts on a new dress, or I set her hair. She seems to be daintier. (Money and Ehrhardt 1972)

About a year later, the mother described how their daughter imitated her while their son copied his father:

I found that my son, he chose very masculine things like a fireman or a policeman. He wanted to do what daddy does, work where daddy does, and carry a lunch kit. [My daughter] didn't want any of those things. She wants to be a doctor or a teacher.... But none of the things that she ever wanted to be were like policeman or a fireman, and that sort of thing never appealed to her. (Money and Ehrhardt 1972)

If the matter were this clear-cut, we could use this case to conclude that gender is entirely up to nurture. Seldom are things in life so simple, however, and a twist occurs in this story. Despite this promising start and her parents' coaching, Brenda did not adapt well to femininity. She preferred to mimic her father shaving rather than her mother putting on makeup. She rejected dolls and insisted on urinating standing up. Classmates teased her and called her a "cavewoman" because she walked like a boy. At age 14, she was expelled from school for beating up a girl who teased her. Despite estrogen treatment, she was not attracted to boys, and, at age 14, in despair over her inner turmoil, she was thinking of suicide. In a tearful confrontation, her father told her about the accident and her sex change.

"All of a sudden, everything clicked. For the first time things made sense, and I understood who and what I was," is what this twin (now Bruce) says of this revelation. He then requested male hormone shots and later had surgery to partially reconstruct a penis. At age 25 he married a woman and adopted her children (Diamond and Sigmundson 1997).

The Vietnam Veterans Study Time after time, researchers have found that boys and men who have higher levels of testosterone tend to be more aggressive. Some of the findings are intriguing. In one study, researchers compared the testosterone levels of college men in a "rowdy" fraternity with those of men in a fraternity that had a reputation for academic success and social responsibility. Men in the "rowdy" fraternity had higher levels of testosterone (Dobbs et al. 1996). The samples researchers used

Sociologists stress the social factors that underlie human behavior, the experiences that mold us, funneling us into different directions in life. The study of Vietnam veterans discussed in the text is one indication of how the sociological door is slowly opening to also consider biological factors in human behavior. Shown here are men of the 173rd Airborne Brigade in a "search and destroy" patrol in Tuy Province, Vietnam, in June 1966.

were small, however, and you never knew if the findings of a particular study were due to chance.

Then in 1985, the U.S. government began a health study of Vietnam veterans. To be certain the study was representative, the researchers chose a random sample of 4,462 men. Among the data they collected was a measurement of testosterone for each veteran. Now, unexpectedly, sociologists had a large random sample available, and the sample is turning out to hold surprising clues about human behavior.

This sample supports earlier studies showing that men who have higher levels of testosterone tend to be more aggressive and to have more problems as a consequence. When the veterans with higher testosterone levels were boys, they were more likely to get in trouble with parents and teachers and to become delinquents. As adults, they are more likely to use hard drugs, to get into fights, to end up in lower-status jobs, and to have more sexual partners. Knowing this, you probably won't be surprised to learn that they also are less likely to marry. Certainly their low-paying jobs and trouble with authorities make them less appealing candidates for marriage. Those who do marry are less likely to share problems with their wives. They also are more likely to have af-

fairs, to hit their wives, and, it follows, to get divorced (Dabbs and Morris 1990; Booth and Dabbs 1993).

Fortunately for us sociologists, the Vietnam veterans study does not leave us with biology as the sole basis for behavior. Not all men with high testosterone get in trouble with the law, do poorly in school, or mistreat their wives. A chief difference, in fact, is social class. High-testosterone men from higher social classes are less likely to be involved in antisocial behaviors than are high-testosterone men from lower social classes (Dabbs and Morris 1990). *Social* factors (socialization, life goals, self-definitions), then, also play a part. Uncovering the social factors and discovering how they work in combination with testosterone will be of high sociological interest.

In Sum We shall have to await further studies, but the initial findings are intriguing. They indicate that some behavior that we sociologists usually assume to be due entirely to socialization is, in fact, also influenced by biology. The findings are preliminary but extremely significant. In the years to come, this should prove to be an exciting—and controversial—area of sociological research. One level of research will be to determine if there are behaviors that are due only to biology. The second level will be to discover how social factors modify biology. The third level will be, in sociologist Janet Chafetz's (1990:30) phrase, to determine how "different" becomes translated into "unequal."

How Females Became a Minority Group

Around the world, gender is *the* primary division between people. Every society sets up barriers to provide unequal access to power, property, and prestige on the basis of sex. Consequently, sociologists classify females as a *minority group*. Since females outnumber males, you may think this strange, but because this term refers to people who are discriminated against on the basis of physical or cultural characteristics, this concept applies to females (Hacker 1951). For an overview of gender discrimination in a changing society, see the Cultural Diversity box on the next page.

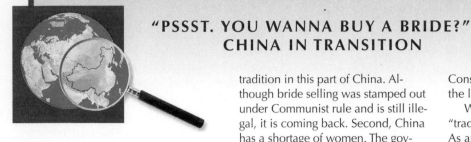

CULTURAL DIVERSITY Around the World

"PSSST. YOU WANNA BUY A BRIDE?"
CHINA IN TRANSITION

Nguyen Thi Hoan, age 22, thanked her lucky stars. A Vietnamese country girl, she had just arrived in Hanoi to look for work, and while she was still at the bus station a woman offered her a job in a candy factory.

It was a trap. After Nguyen had loaded a few sacks of sugar, the woman took her into the country to "get supplies." There some men took her to China, which was only 100 miles away. Nguyen was put up for sale at an auction, along with a 16-year-old Vietnamese girl. Each sold for $350, a small fortune in China. After being traded from one bride dealer to another, Nguyen was sold to a man for $700. She is now his wife (Marshall 1999).

What's behind this kidnapping and sale of brides? Apparently two factors. First, bride selling is a centuries-long

tradition in this part of China. Although bride selling was stamped out under Communist rule and is still illegal, it is coming back. Second, China has a shortage of women. The government enforces a "one-couple-one-child" policy. Since sons are preferred, female infanticide has become common (a topic explored on page 371). This has created a shortage of women of marriageable age.

Actually, Nguyen was lucky. Many kidnapped women are sold to brothel owners.

As you might infer from these practices, women in China have low status. Although their situation apparently improved under Communist rule, it is deteriorating under China's embryonic capitalism. Factory managers used to be assigned production goals and then given the resources to meet those goals. Profit was not a factor. Now it is. Maternity leaves, child care centers, and rooms for nursing mothers—all requirements under Chinese law—make women workers more expensive than men.

Consequently, women have become the last hired and first fired.

Women are encouraged to enter "traditional" women's occupations. As an official with the Buding Labor Bureau said, being "nurses, nursery school teachers, grade school teachers, and street sweepers is more appropriate for women." Because these are among the least skilled of occupations, they pay little.

Women's bodies are being "Westernized," too. A new cosmetic surgery industry has sprung up to give Chinese women Western-looking eyes, stenciled eyebrows, and bigger breasts. Even advertising has begun to follow a Western model: Scantily clad women now perch on top of sports cars (Sun 1993; Chen 1995).

China in transition...It is a country that is bringing back the old, bride selling, and moving toward new, Westernized ideas of beauty. In both the old and new, women are commodities for the consumption of men. ■

Have females always been a minority group? Some analysts speculate that in some earlier societies women and men may have been social equals. Apparently the horticultural and hunting and gathering societies reviewed in Chapter 4 had less gender discrimination than we have today. In these societies, women may have been equal partners with men, and they may have contributed about 60 percent of the group's total food (Lerner 1986).

How did it happen, then, that around the world women came to be systematically discriminated against? Let's consider the primary theory that has been developed.

The Origins of Patriarchy

This theory points to social consequences of the biology of human reproduction (Lerner 1986; Friedl 1990).

In early human history, life was short, and in order to reproduce the human group many children had to be born. Because only females get pregnant, carry a child for nine months, give birth, and nurse, women were limited in their activities for a considerable part of their lives. To survive, an infant needed a nursing mother. With a child at her breast or in her uterus, or one carried on her hip or on her back, women were physically encumbered. Consequently, around the world women assumed tasks that were associated with the home and child care, while men took over the hunting of large animals and other tasks that required greater speed and longer absence from the base camp (Huber 1990).

As a consequence, men became dominant. It was they who left camp to hunt animals, who made contact with other tribes, who traded with these other groups,

Patriarchy := men become head of household/tribe.

One theory about the origin of *patriarchy* is that because of childbirth women assumed tasks associated with home and child care, while men hunted and performed other tasks requiring greater strength, speed, and absence from home. Shown here is a woman on her way to work in the fields at Lake Inec, Myanmar.

had different origins in different places. And, of course, we cannot rule out biology altogether.

Whatever its origins, a circular system of thought evolved. Men developed notions of their own inherent superiority—based on the evidence of their dominant position in society. They surrounded many of their activities with secrecy and constructed elaborate rules and rituals to avoid "contamination" by females, whom they now openly deemed inferior. Even today, patriarchy is always accompanied by cultural supports designed to justify male dominance—such as certain activities not being "appropriate" for women.

As tribal societies developed into larger groups, men, who enjoyed their power and privileges, maintained their dominance. Long after hunting and hand-to-hand combat ceased to be routine, and even after large numbers of children were no longer needed in order to reproduce the

and who quarreled and waged war with them. It was also the men who made and controlled the instruments of death, the weapons used for hunting and warfare. It was they who accumulated possessions in trade, and gained prestige by triumphantly returning with prisoners of war or with large animals to feed the tribe. In contrast, little prestige was given to the ordinary, routine, taken-for-granted activities of women—who were not seen as risking their lives for the group. Eventually, men took over society. Their weapons, items of trade, and knowledge gained from contact with other groups became sources of power. Women became second-class citizens, subject to men's decisions.

Is this theory correct? Remember that the answer lies buried in human history, and there is no way of testing it. Male dominance may be due to some entirely different cause. For example, anthropologist Marvin Harris (1977) proposed that because most men are stronger than most women and hand-to-hand combat was necessary in tribal groups, men became the warriors and women the reward to entice them to do battle. Frederick Engels proposed that **patriarchy** (male dominance of a society) developed with the origin of private property (Lerner 1986). He could not explain why private property should have produced patriarchy, however. Gerda Lerner (1986) suggests that patriarchy may even have

Foot binding, a form of violence against women, was practiced in China. This photo of a woman in Canton, China, is from the early 1900s. The woman's tiny feet, which made it difficult for her to walk, were a "marker" of status, indicating that her husband was wealthy and did not need her labor. It also made her dependent on him.

SUffrage: right to vote

human group, men held on to their power. Male dominance in contemporary societies, then, is a continuation of a millennia-old pattern whose origin is lost in history.

GENDER INEQUALITY IN THE UNITED STATES

Gender inequality is not some accidental, hit-or-miss affair. Rather, the institutions of each society work together to maintain the group's particular forms of inequality. Customs, often venerated throughout history, both justify and maintain these arrangements. Although men have resisted sharing their privileged positions with women, change has come.

Fighting Back: The Rise of Feminism

To see how far we have come, it is useful to see where we used to be. In early U.S. society, the second-class status of women was taken for granted. A husband and wife were legally one person—him (Chafetz and Dwor-

kin 1986). Women could not serve on juries, nor could they vote, make legal contracts, or hold property in their own name. How could times have changed so much that these examples sound like fiction?

A central lesson of conflict theory is that power yields privilege; like a magnet, it draws society's best resources to the elite. Because men held tenaciously onto their privileges and used social institutions to maintain their position, basic rights for women came only through prolonged and bitter struggle.

Feminism, the view that biology is not destiny and that stratification by gender is wrong and should be resisted, met with strong opposition—both by men who had privilege to lose and by women who accepted their status as morally correct. In 1916, feminists, then known as *suffragists,* founded the National Women's Party. In January 1917, they formed a picket line around the White House. After picketing continuously for six months, the picketers were arrested. Hundreds were sent to prison, including Lucy Burns and Alice Paul, two leaders of the National Women's Party. The extent to which these women had threatened male privilege is demonstrated by their treatment in prison.

The women's struggle for equal rights has been long and hard. Shown here is a 1919 photo from the "first wave" of the U.S. women's movement. Only against enormous opposition from men did U.S. women win the right to vote. They first voted in national elections in 1920.

Two men brought in Dorothy Day [the editor of a periodical that espoused women's rights], twisting her arms above her head. Suddenly they lifted her and brought her body down twice over the back of an iron bench. They had been there a few minutes when Mrs. Lewis, all doubled over like a sack of flour, was thrown in. Her head struck the iron bed and she fell to the floor senseless. As for Lucy Burns, they handcuffed her wrists and fastened the handcuffs over [her] head to the cell door. (Cowley 1969)

This "first wave" of the women's movement had a radical branch that wanted to reform all the institutions of society, and a conservative branch that concentrated on winning the vote for women (Chafetz and Dworkin 1986). The conservative branch dominated, and after the vote was won in 1920 the movement basically dissolved.

The "second wave" began in the 1960s. Sociologist Janet Chafetz (1990) points out that up to this time most women thought of work as a temporary activity intended to fill the time between completing school and getting married. As more women took jobs, however, many began to think of them as careers. Women then started to compare their working conditions with those of men. This shift in their reference group radically changed how they viewed conditions at work. The result was a "second wave" of protest and struggle against gender inequalities. The goals of this second wave (which continues today) are broad—they range from changing women's work roles to changing policies on violence against women.

This second wave of the women's movement also has its liberal and conservative branches. Although each holds a different view of what gender equality should look like, the two share several goals, including equality in job opportunities and pay. Both liberals and conservatives have a radical wing. The radicals on the liberal side call for hostility toward men; radicals on the conservative side favor a return to traditional family roles. All factions—whether radical or conservative—claim to represent the "real" needs of today's women. It is from these claims and counterclaims that the women's movement will continue to take shape and affect public policy.

Although women enjoy fundamental rights today, gender inequality continues to play a central role in social life. Let's look at gender relations in education, in medicine, and at work.

Gender Inequality in Education

Gender inequality in education is not readily apparent. More women than men are enrolled in U.S. colleges and universities, women earn 56 percent of all bachelor's degrees, and they also complete their bachelor's degrees faster than men (*Statistical Abstract* 1999:Table 328). A closer look, however, reveals *gender tracking;* that is, degrees tend to follow gender, which reinforces male-female distinctions. Here are two extremes: Men earn 84 percent of bachelor's degrees in the "masculine" field of engineering, while women are awarded 86 percent of bachelor's degrees in the "feminine" field of library "science" (*Statistical Abstract* 1999:Table 331). Because socialization gives men and women different orientations to life, they enter college with sex-linked aspirations. It is their socialization—not some presumed innate characteristics—that channels men and women into different educational paths.

If we follow students into graduate school, we see that with each passing year the proportion of women decreases. Table 10.1 gives us a snapshot of doctoral programs in the sciences. Note how aspirations (enrollment) and accomplishments (doctorates earned) are sex

Table 10.1

DOCTORATES IN SCIENCE, BY SEX

Field	Students Enrolled		Doctorates Conferred		Completion Ratio* (Higher or Lower Than Expected)	
	Women	Men	Women	Men	Women	Men
Computer sciences	27%	73%	16%	84%	−41	+15
Engineering	19%	81%	12%	88%	−37	+9
Agriculture	38%	62%	26%	74%	−32	+19
Mathematics	34%	66%	23%	77%	−32	+17
Physical sciences	28%	72%	22%	78%	−21	+8
Social sciences	49%	51%	39%	61%	−20	+20
Biological sciences	50%	50%	43%	57%	−14	+12
Psychology	69%	31%	67%	33%	−3	+6

*The formula for the completion ratio is X minus Y divided by X, where X is the proportion enrolled in a program and Y is the proportion granted doctorates.
Source: Statistical Abstract 1999:Tables 1002, 1004.

linked. In six of these doctoral programs, men outnumber women, in one they are even, and in one women outnumber men. In *all* of them, women are less likely to complete the doctorate.

If we follow those who earn doctoral degrees to their teaching careers at colleges and universities, we find gender stratification in rank and pay. Throughout the United States, women are less likely to be awarded the rank of full professor, the highest-paying and most prestigious rank. Professors are paid more than the lower ranks (instructor, assistant professor, and associate professor). In both private and public colleges, professors average more than twice the salary of instructors (*Statistical Abstract* 1999:Table 320). Even when women do become full professors, they average less pay than men who are full professors (DePalma 1993).

Figure 10.1 illustrates a remarkable change in education. Note how sharply the proportion of professional degrees earned by women has increased. The greatest change is in dentistry: Across the entire United States, in 1970 only 34 women earned this degree. Today about 1,400 women become dentists each year (*Statistical Abstract* 2000:Table 322).

Gender Inequality in Health Care

Medical researchers were perplexed. Reports were coming in from all over the country: Women were twice as likely as men to die after coronary bypass surgery. Researchers at Cedars-Sinai Medical Center in Los Angeles checked their own records. They found that of 2,300 coronary bypass patients, 4.6 percent of the women died as a result of the surgery, compared with 2.6 percent of the men.

These findings presented a sociological puzzle. To solve it, researchers first turned to biology (Bishop 1990). In coronary bypass surgery, a blood vessel is taken from one part of the body and stitched to a coronary artery on the surface of the heart. Perhaps this operation was more difficult to perform on women because of their smaller coronary arteries. To find out, researchers measured the amount of time that surgeons kept patients on the heart-lung machine while they operated. They were surprised to learn that women spent less time on the machine than men. This indicated that the operation was not more difficult to perform on women.

As the researchers probed, a surprising answer unfolded—unintended sexual discrimination. Physicians had not taken the chest pains of their women patients as seriously as they took the complaints of their men patients. They were *ten* times more likely to give men exercise stress tests and radioactive heart scans. They also sent men to surgery on the basis of abnormal stress tests, but waited until women showed clear-cut symptoms of coronary heart disease before sending them to surgery. Having surgery after the disease is further along reduces the chances of survival.

You obviously are also more likely to die if you are sent home from a hospital emergency room when you are having a heart attack. Researchers have also found that when people with heart pain go to emergency rooms, doctors are

Figure 10.1

	Women	Men
Medicine (M.D.) 1970	8	92
Medicine (M.D.) 1996	41	59
Dentistry (D.D.S., D.M.D.) 1970	1	99
Dentistry (D.D.S., D.M.D.) 1996	37	63
Law (L.L.B., J.D.) 1970	5	95
Law (L.L.B., J.D.) 1996	44	56

GENDER CHANGES IN PROFESSIONAL DEGREES

Source: Statistical Abstract 2000:Table 322.

more likely to admit the men and to send the women home (Seiker and Pope 2000).

Women's Organs as Causes of Disease—and Sources of Profit Sociologist Sue Fisher (1986), who did participant observation in a hospital, was surprised to hear surgeons recommend total hysterectomy (removal of both the uterus and the ovaries) *when no cancer was present.* When she asked why, the men doctors explained that the uterus and ovaries are "potentially disease producing." They also said that they are unnecessary after the childbearing years, so why not remove them?

Surgical sexism is reinforced by another powerful motive—greed. Surgeons make money by performing this surgery. But they have to "sell" the operation, for women, to understate the matter, are reluctant to part with these organs. Here is how one resident explained the "hard sell" to sociologist Diana Scully (1994):

> You have to look for your surgical procedures; you have to go after patients. Because no one is crazy enough to come and say, "Hey, here I am. I want you to operate on me." You have to sometimes convince the patient that she is really sick—if she is, of course [laughs], and that she is better off with a surgical procedure.

To "convince" a woman to have this surgery, the doctor tells her that, unfortunately, the examination has turned up fibroids in her uterus—and they *might* turn into cancer. This statement is often sufficient, for it frightens women, who picture themselves dying from cancer. To clinch the sale, the surgeon withholds the rest of the truth—that the fibroids probably will *not* turn into cancer and that she has several nonsurgical alternatives.

Gender Inequality in the Workplace

One of the chief characteristics of the U.S. work force is a steady growth in the numbers of women who work outside the home for wages. Figure 10.2 shows that in 1900 one of five U.S. workers was a woman. By 1940, this ratio had grown to one of four, by 1960 to one of three, and today it is almost one of two.

Because the changes have been so gradual and the implications so profound, sociologists use the term **quiet revolution** to refer to the many women who have joined the ranks of paid labor. This trend, shown in Figure 10.3 on the next page, has been accompanied by a transformation in consumer patterns, relations at work, self-concepts, and relationships with boyfriends, husbands, and children. One of the most significant aspects of the quiet revolution is indicated by Figure 10.3d. Note that since 1960 the percentage of married women who have preschool children and work for wages has

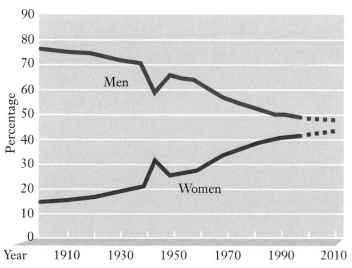

Figure 10.2

WOMEN'S AND MEN'S PROPORTION OF THE U.S. LABOR FORCE

Sources: 1969 Handbook on Women Workers, 1969:10; *Manpower Report to the President,* 1971:203, 205; Mills and Palumbo, 1980:6, 45: *Statistical Abstract* 1999:Table 652.

Note: Pre-1940 totals include women age 14 and over. Totals for 1940 and after are for women age 16 and over. Broken lines indicate the author's projections.

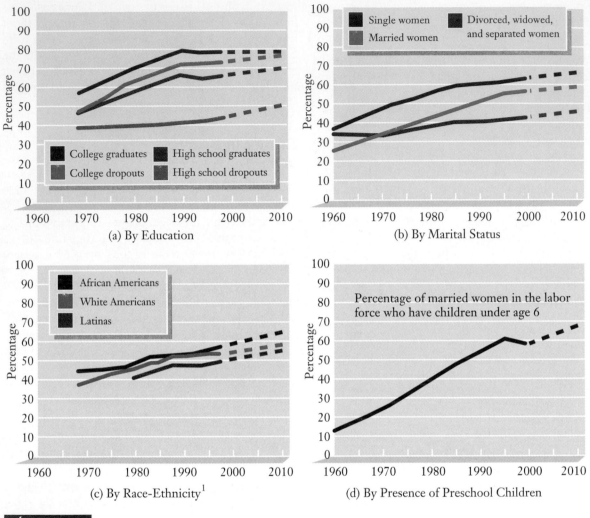

Figure 10.3 WOMEN IN THE U.S. LABOR FORCE

[1]Data for other racial-ethnic groups unavailable in the source; no data for Latinas for 1970–1980.

Source: Statistical Abstract 1995:Tables 627, 629, 637, 639; 1999:Tables 650, 653, 657, 659. Broken lines indicate the author's projections.

tripled. It now equals the average percentage of all U.S. women. From the Social Map on the next page, you can see that where a woman lives makes a difference in how likely she is to work outside the home. This map apparently reflects regional-subcultural differences of which we currently have little understanding.

These materials provide a background of historical change, but they do not illustrate inequality. For that, let's look at the pay gap.

The Gender Pay Gap Chances are, you are going to go to work after you complete college. How would you like to earn an extra $950,000 on your job? If this sounds appealing, read on. I'm going to reveal how you

can make an extra $2,000 a month between the ages of 25 and 65.

Is this hard to do? Actually, it is simple for some, but impossible for others. All you have to do is be born a male and graduate from college. As Figure 10.5 shows, if we compare full-time workers, this is how much more the *average male* college graduate earns over the course of his career. Hardly any single factor pinpoints gender discrimination better than this total. From this figure, you can also see that the pay gap shows up at all levels of education.

The pay gap is so great that women who work full time average only two-thirds (67 percent) of what men are paid (*Statistical Abstract* 1999:Table 758). As Figure 10.6 on page 252 shows, the pay gap used to be even worse. This

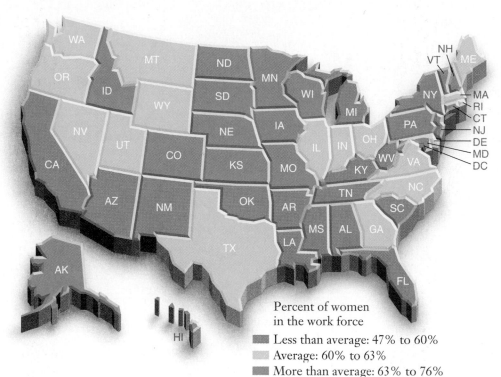

Figure 10.4

SOCIAL MAP: HOW LIKELY IS A WOMAN TO WORK FOR WAGES?

Note: The state with the lowest percentage of women in the work force is West Virginia (47.8%); the state with the highest percentage of women in the work force is Wisconsin (69.7%). This refers to women who are 16 years old and over who are in the civilian labor force, commonly called the *labor force participation rate.*

Sources: Statistical Abstract 1999:Table 654.

Percent of women in the work force

■ Less than average: 47% to 60%
■ Average: 60% to 63%
■ More than average: 63% to 76%

gap does not occur only in the United States. All industrialized nations have it, although only in Japan is the gap larger than in the United States (Blau and Kahn 1992).

What logic can underlie the gender pay gap? Earlier we saw that college degrees are gender linked, so perhaps this gap is due to career choices. Maybe women are more likely to choose lower-paying jobs, such as teaching grade school, whereas men are more likely to go into better-paying fields, such as business, law, and engineering. Actually, this is true, and researchers have found that about *half* the pay gap is due to such factors. The balance, however, is due to gender discrimination (Kemp 1990).

Depending on your sex, then, you are likely either to benefit from gender discrimination—or to be its victim.

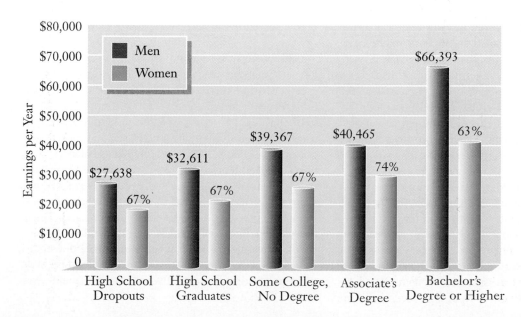

Figure 10.5

THE GENDER PAY GAP BY EDUCATION[1]

[1]Full-time workers in all fields.

Source: Statistical Abstract 1999:Table 266.

THE GENDER PAY GAP OVER TIME: THE ANNUAL INCOME OF FULL-TIME WORKERS AND THE PERCENTAGE OF THE MEN'S INCOME EARNED BY WOMEN

Note: The income jump from 1990 to 1995 is probably due to a statistical procedure. The 1995 source (for 1990 income) uses "median income," while the 1997 source (for 1995 income) says "average earnings." How the "average" is computed is not stated. For a review of this distinction, see Table 1.3 on page 23. Broken lines indicate the author's estimates.

Source: Beeghley 1989:239; *Statistical Abstract* 1995:Table 739; 1999:Table 758.

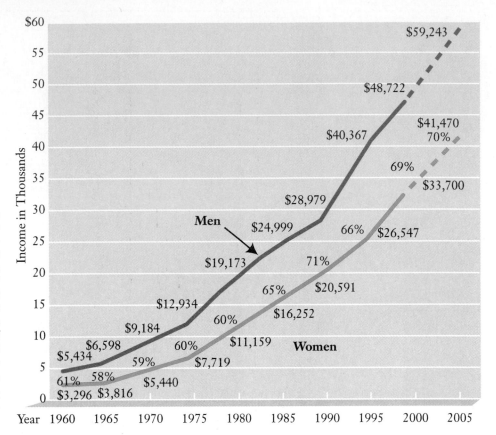

Because the pay gap will be so important in your own work life, let's follow some college graduates to see how it actually comes about. Economists Rex Fuller and Richard Schoenberger (1991) examined the starting salaries of the business majors at the University of Wisconsin, of whom 47 percent were women. They found that the women's starting salaries averaged 11 percent ($1,737) less than the men's.

You might be able to think of valid reasons for this initial pay gap. For example, the women might have been less qualified. Perhaps their grades were lower. Or maybe they completed fewer internships. If so, they would deserve lower salaries. To find out, Fuller and Schoenberger reviewed the students' college records. To their surprise, they found that the women had *higher* grades and *more* internships. In other words, if women were equally qualified, they were offered lower salaries—and if they were more qualified, they were offered lower salaries—a classic lose-lose situation.

What happened after these graduates had been on the job awhile? Did things tend to even out, so that after a few years the women and men earned about the same? Fuller and Schoenberger checked their salaries five years later. Instead of narrowing, the pay gap had grown even wider. By this time, the women earned 14 percent ($3,615) less than the men.

As a final indication of the extent of the U.S. gender pay gap, consider this. I examined the names of the CEOs of the 350 largest U.S. corporations, and *not one of them is a woman.* Your best chance to reach the top is to be named (in this order) John, Robert, James, William, or Charles. Edward, Lawrence, and Richard are also advantageous. Amber, Katherine, Leticia, and Maria, however, apparently draw a severe penalty.

The Glass Ceiling and the Glass Escalator What keeps women from breaking through the *glass ceiling,* the mostly invisible barrier that keeps women from reaching the executive suite? Researchers have identified a "pipeline" that leads to the top—the marketing, sales, and production positions that directly affect the corporate bottom line (Reich 1995). Stereotyped as better at "support," women tend to be steered into human resources or public relations. There, successful projects are not appreciated the same way as those that bring in corporate profits—and bonuses for their managers. Felice Schwartz, founder of Catalyst, an organization that focuses on women's issues in the workplace, put it this way: Men, who dominate the executive suite, stereotype potential leaders as people who look like themselves (Lopez 1992).

One of the frustrations felt by many women in the labor force is that no matter what they do, they hit a glass ceiling. Another is that to succeed they feel forced to abandon characteristics they feel are essential to their self.

Another reason the glass ceiling is so powerful is that women lack mentors, successful executives who take an interest in them and teach them the ropes. Some men executives fear gossip and charges of sexual harassment if they get close to a woman in a subordinate position. Others don't mentor women because they stereotype women as being weak (Lancaster 1995; Reich 1995). Lack of a mentor is no trivial matter, for supposedly all top executives have had a coach or mentor (Lancaster 1995).

The glass ceiling is cracking, however, and more women are reaching the executive suite (Parker-Pope 1998). A look at women who have broken through the glass ceiling reveals highly motivated women with a fierce competitive spirit who are willing to give up sleep and recreation for the sake of career advancement. They also learn to play by "men's rules," developing a style that makes men comfortable. In the background of about three-fourths of women at the top is a supportive husband who shares household duties and adapts his career to the needs of his executive wife (Lublin 1996).

Sociologist Christine Williams (1995) interviewed men and women who worked as nurses, elementary school teachers, librarians, and social workers. She found that the men in these traditionally women's occupations, instead of bumping into a glass ceiling, had climbed aboard a *glass escalator.* That is, compared with women, the men were accelerated into higher-level positions, given more desirable work assignments, and paid higher salaries. The motor that drives the glass escalator is gender—the stereotype that because someone is male he is more capable.

Sexual Harassment

Sexual harassment—unwelcome sexual attention at work or at school, which may affect a person's job performance or create a hostile work environment—was not

recognized as a problem until the 1970s. Before this, women considered unwanted sexual comments, touches, looks, and pressure to have sex to be a personal matter.

With the prodding of feminists, women began to see unwanted sexual advances at work and school as part of a *structural* problem. That is, they began to see them not simply as a man here and there doing obnoxious things because he was attracted to a woman, but, rather, as men abusing their positions of authority in order to force unwanted sexual activities on women. Since women have moved into positions of authority, they, too, have become sexual harassers (Lawlor 1994). With most authority vested in men, however, most sexual harassers are men.

Shown here is Martha Stewart, an entrepreneur. In 1999, Stewart went public with her company, Omnimedia Inc., a provider of household products and services. This initial public offering on the New York Stock exchange brought in $315 million.

As symbolic interactionists stress, terms affect our perception. Because we have the term *sexual harassment*, we see acts in a different light than did our predecessors. The meaning of sexual harassment is vague and shifting, however, and court cases constantly change what it does and does not include. For example, originally sexual desire was an element of sexual harassment, but this is no longer true in a legal sense. A homosexual who had been tormented by his supervisors and fellow workers when he was working on an oil rig sued his employer. The Court ruled that sexual desire is not necessary, that sexual harassment laws also apply to homosexuals who are harassed by heterosexuals on the job (Felsenthal 1998).

Gender and Violence

The high rate of violence in the United States shocks foreigners and frightens Americans. Only a couple of generations back, many Americans left their homes and cars unlocked. Today, fearful of carjackings, they lock their cars even while driving, and, fearful of rape and kidnappings, they escort their children to school. Lurking behind these fears is gender inequality of violence—the fact that females are much more likely to be victims of males, not the other way around. Let's briefly review this almost one-way street in gender violence.

In the Cultural Diversity box on the next page, we examine violence against women in other cultures, and in Chapter 12 we shall examine violence in the home. Here, due to space limitations, we can review only briefly the primary features of violence against U.S. women.

Forcible Rape Being raped is a common fear of U.S. women. And this fear is far from groundless. Rape is so common that each year between 2 and 3 of every 1,000 females age 12 and over in the entire United States are raped. The official rate is 8.4 per 10,000. Surveys of crime victims, however, show that only one-third (32 percent) of rapes are reported, giving us a real rate of 26 per 10,000. Females of all ages are victims, but the typical rape victim is 16 to 19 years old. Although rapists may be in their early teens or over age 65, the typical rapist is under age 30. Contrary to stereotypes, most rape victims know their assailant; only one-third of rapes are committed by strangers (*Statistical Abstract* 1999:Tables 349, 354, 355, 358, and page 212).

Date Rape What has shocked so many about date rape (also known as acquaintance rape) is studies showing that it does not consist of a few isolated events. For example, in a survey of the introductory psychology courses at Texas A&M University, about 21 percent of the women students reported that they had been forced to have sexual intercourse. (Keep in mind what we reviewed on sampling in Chapter 1. Students taking a

specific course at a particular university are *not* representative of college students in general. We obviously need better studies.) Apparently, date rape most commonly occurs not between relative strangers on first dates, but between couples who have known each other about a year (Muehlenhard and Linton 1987). Most date rapes go unreported. Those that are reported are difficult to prosecute, for juries tend to believe that if a woman knows the accused she wasn't "really" raped.

Some rapists use a variety of drugs (rohypnol, GHB, Ketamine, Versed) that put their victims into a hazy state, make them incapable of resisting, and in some cases make them forget what happened to them. Because these rapists often slip a drug into their victim's drink at bars or parties, this is known as "chemically assisted date rape." The term "date," however, often does not apply, for some women have found themselves victims of total strangers.

Murder Table 10.2 summarizes how gender fits into U.S. patterns of murder. Note that although females make up a little over 51 percent of the U.S. population, they don't even come close to making up 51 percent of the nation's killers. Note also that almost one-fourth of all murder victims are female—and nine times out of ten the killer is a male.

Violence in the Home Women are also the typical victims of family violence. Spouse battering, marital rape, and incest are discussed in Chapter 12, while genital circumcision is the focus of the Cultural Diversity box on the next page.

Feminism and Gendered Violence Feminist sociologists have been especially effective in bringing violence against women to the public's attention. Some use symbolic interactionism, pointing out that to associate strength and virility with violence—as is done in so many areas of U.S. culture—is to promote violence. Others use conflict theory. They argue that as gender relations change males lose power, and that some males become violent against females as a way to reassert their declining power and status. Perhaps this is the underlying reason for the violence featured in the Mass Media box on page 256.

Table 10.2 — KILLERS AND THEIR VICTIMS

The Victims		The Killers	
Male	*Female*	*Male*	*Female*
77%	23%	89%	11%

Source: FBI Uniform Crime Reports 1998:Table 33; Statistical Abstract 1999:Table 347.

CULTURAL DIVERSITY Around the World

FEMALE CIRCUMCISION

Female circumcision is common in parts of Muslim Africa and in some parts of Malaysia and Indonesia. This custom, often called female genital mutilation FGM) by Westerners, is also known as clitoral excision, clitoridectomy, infibulation, and labiadectomy, depending largely on how much of the tissue is removed. Worldwide, between 100 million and 200 million females have been circumcised.

In some cultures only the girl's clitoris is cut off, in others the clitoris and both the labia majora and the labia minora. The Nubia in the Sudan cut away most of the girl's genitalia, then sew together the remaining outer edges with silk or catgut. The girl's legs are bound from ankles to waist for several weeks while scar tissue closes up the vagina almost completely. They leave a small opening the size of a matchstick or a pencil for the passage of urine and menstrual fluids. In East Africa the vaginal opening is not sutured shut, but the clitoris and both sets of labia are cut off.

Among most groups, the surgery takes place between the ages of 4 and 8. In some cultures it occurs seven to ten days after birth, while in others it is not performed until girls reach adolescence. Because the surgery is often done without anesthesia, the pain is so excruciating that adults must hold the girl down. In urban areas, the operation is sometimes performed by physicians; in rural areas, it is usually performed by a neighborhood woman.

Some of the risks are shock, extensive bleeding, infection, infertility, and death. Ongoing complications include vaginal spasms, painful intercourse, and lack of orgasms. The tiny opening makes urination and menstruation difficult. Frequent urinary tract infections result from urine and menstrual flow building up behind the little opening.

When the woman marries, the opening is cut wider to permit sexual intercourse. In some groups, this is the husband's responsibility. Before a woman gives birth, the opening is enlarged further. After birth, the vagina is again sutured shut, a cycle of surgically closing and opening that begins anew with each birth.

One woman, circumcised at 12, described it this way:

"Lie down there," the excisor suddenly said to me, pointing to a mat stretched out on the ground. No sooner had I laid down than I felt my frail, thin legs tightly grasped by heavy hands and pulled wide apart. I lifted my head. Two women on each side of me pinned me to the ground. My arms were also immobilized. Suddenly I felt some strange substance being spread over my genital area. It was supposed to facilitate the excision. I would have given anything at that moment to be a thousand miles away; then a shooting pain brought me back to reality. I underwent the ablation of the labia minor and then of the clitoris. The operation seemed to go on forever. I was in the throes of agony, torn apart both physically and psychologically. It was the rule that girls of my age did not weep in this situation. I broke the rule. I reacted immediately with tears and screams of pain.... Never have I felt such excruciating pain!

[After the operation] they forced me not only to walk back to join the other girls who had already been excised, but to dance with them.... I was doing my best...then I fainted. It was a month before I was completely healed. When I was better, everyone mocked me, as I hadn't been brave, they said. (Walker and Parmar 1993:107–108)

What are the reasons for this custom? Some groups believe that it reduces female sexual desire, thus making it more likely that a woman will be a virgin at marriage, and, afterward, will remain faithful to her husband. Others believe that it enhances female fertility, prevents the clitoris from getting infected, and enhances vaginal cleanliness.

Feminists, who call female circumcision a form of ritual torture to control female sexuality, point out that the societies that practice it are male dominated. Mothers cooperate with the circumcision because in these societies an unmarried woman has virtually no rights, and an uncircumcised woman is considered impure and is not allowed to marry. Grandmothers insist that the custom continue out of concern that their granddaughters marry well.

Some immigrants to the United States have taken their daughters back to the homeland for the operation, while others pool their money and fly in an excisor who performs the surgery on several girls. In 1997, the United States passed a law that makes arranging or performing female circumcision punishable by up to five years in prison. ■

(continued)

CULTURAL DIVERSITY Around the World

FEMALE CIRCUMCISION *(Continued)*

For Your Consideration

Do you think that Western nations should try to make African nations stop this custom? Or would this be ethnocentric, the imposition of Western values on other cultures? As one Somali woman said, "The Somali woman doesn't need an alien woman telling her how to treat her private parts." What legitimate basis do you think there is for members of one culture to interfere with another?

Sources: Based on Mahran 1978, 1981; Ebomoyi 1987; Lightfoot-Klein 1989; Merwine 1993; Walker and Parmar 1993; Welsh 1995; "Egipto..." 1996; Chalkley 1997.

Mass Media in Social Life

BEAUTY AND PAIN: HOW MUCH IS AN AD WORTH?

The studio audience at *Super Jockey,* a popular television program in Japan, waits expectantly. They've seen it before, and they can't get enough. A young woman, clad in a revealing bikini, walks onto the stage. Cringing with fear, she is lowered into a glass tank of scalding hot water.

The studio audience eagerly watches the woman through the glass. The national audience watches at home. Both break into laughter as the girl writhes in pain.

To make sure the young woman gets the full treatment, a man standing behind the tank ladles hot water over the woman's chest— just as though he were basting a chicken. As her flesh quickly reddens, the television camera zooms in for a close-up shot of her breasts.

Most women last only three or four seconds.

The camera follows as the young woman scrambles out of the tub. The audience howls with glee as she jumps up and down in pain and rubs ice over her body.

Why do the women do it? For every second they stay in the hot water, they get one second on the program to advertise any product they wish. Most advertise their place of employment, their pain a favor to their boss (Strauss 1998).

It is often difficult to understand other cultures. *Super Jockey* wouldn't be tolerated in the United States. If some television station tried to air a U.S. version, protests would erupt. The studio would be picketed, its sponsors boycotted.

Instead of trying to explain the intricacies of a culture that finds such behavior amusing (*Super Jockey* is a comedy show), we might wish to turn the focus onto our own culture. Why do we find the rape of women a source of entertainment? How can I say that we do? It is apparent from our television. I'm not talking about some dry, historical documentary on Public Television. I'm referring to TV "dramas," police shows, detective shows, and other programs in which the story line centers on women who are raped. Some of these programs focus on serial rapists, others on rape victims. Of course, in order to make sure this kind of entertainment gets a seal of approval, producers see to it that the rapist is apprehended and punished. As further evidence that this kind of meritorious entertainment carries a moral message, the rapist may commit suicide, get shot by the police, or get run down by a car as he tries to escape into his netherworld.

Our society also finds the murder of women to be highly entertaining. The Halloween shocker-thriller-slasher films serve as outstanding examples. Audiences that are simultaneously thrilled and terror-stricken watch, riveted, as crazed, masked killers hunt down college coeds with knives, axes, even chain saws. Audiences seem to find the screams of the victims especially entertaining. And the prettier, shapelier, and more skimpily clad the victim, the higher the entertainment value. ■

For Your Consideration

It is difficult to understand cultures, especially to explain why people find certain things amusing or entertaining. Why would Japanese and Americans find the victimization of women to be a scintillating source of entertainment?

Solutions There is no magic bullet for this problem of gendered violence, but to be effective any solution must break the connection between violence and masculinity. This would require an educational program that incorporates schools, churches, homes, and the media. Given the gun-slinging heroes of the Wild West and other American icons, as well as the violent messages so prevalent in today's mass media and throughout our culture, it is difficult to be optimistic that a change will come any time soon.

Our next topic, women in politics, however, gives us much more reason for optimism.

THE CHANGING FACE OF POLITICS

Why don't women, who outnumber men, take political control of the nation? Eight million more women than men are of voting age (*Statistical Abstract* 1999:Table 487). As Table 10.3 shows, however, men greatly outnumber women in political office. Despite the gains women have made in recent elections, since 1789 over 1,800 men have served in the U.S. Senate, but only 28 women, including 13 current senators. Not until 1992 was the first African American woman (Carol Moseley-Braun) elected to the U.S. Senate (National Women's Political Caucus 1998; *Statistical Abstract* 1999:Table 473). No Latina or Asian American woman has yet been elected to the Senate.

Why are women underrepresented in U.S. politics? First, women are still underrepresented in law and business, the careers from which most politicians come. Further, most women do not perceive themselves as belonging to a class of people who need to organize politically in order to overcome domination. Most women also find that the irregular hours kept by those who run for office are incompatible with their role as mother. Fathers, in contrast, whose ordinary roles are more likely to take them away from home, do not feel this same conflict. Women are also less likely to have a supportive spouse who is willing to play an unassuming background role while providing solace, encouragement, child care, and voter appeal. Finally, preferring to hold on tightly to their positions of power, men have been reluctant to incorporate women into

Table 10.3	U S. WOMEN IN POLITICAL OFFICE*	
	Percentage and Number Held by Women	
	Percentage	**Number**
National Office		
U.S. Senate	13	13
U.S. House of Representatives	17%	59
State Office		
Governors	8%	4
Lt. Governors	16%	8
Attorneys general	16%	8
Secretaries of state	26%	13
Treasurers	22%	11
State auditors	12%	6
State controllers	8%	4
Local Office		
Mayors[a]	18%	177

*These totals, from 2000, do not include women elected to the judiciary, appointed to state cabinet-level positions, elected to executive posts by the legislature, or members of a university board of trustees.
[a]Of cities with a population over 30,000.

Source: National Women's Political Caucus 1998, *Statistical Abstract* 1999:Tables 473, 478, 482; online election results from election 2000; Center for American Women and Politics, 2000; Center for American Women and Politics, 2001.

centers of decision making or to present them as viable candidates.

These factors are changing, however, and we can expect more women to seek and gain political office. As we saw in Figure 10.1 (on page 248), more women are going into law. The same is true for business. There they are doing more traveling and making statewide and national contacts. Increasingly, child care is seen as a mutual responsibility of both mother and father. This generation, then, is likely to mark a fundamental change in women's political participation, and it appears to be only a matter of time until a woman occupies the Oval Office.

Glimpsing the Future— with Hope

By playing a fuller role in the decision-making processes of our social institutions, women are going against the

"Covering up"

stereotypes and role models that lock males into exclusively male activities and push females into roles that are considered feminine. As structural barriers fall and more activities are degendered, both males and females will be free to pursue activities that are more compatible with their abilities and desires as individuals.

As females and males develop a new consciousness of themselves and of their own potential, relationships between them will change. Certainly distinctions between the sexes will not disappear. There is no reason, however, for biological differences to be translated into social inequalities. The reasonable goal is to have an appreciation of sexual differences coupled with equality of opportunity—which may well lead to a transformed society (Gilman 1911/1971; Offen 1990). If this happens, as sociologist Alison Jaggar (1990) observed, gender equality can become less a goal than a background condition for living in society.

INEQUALITIES OF AGING

In 1928, Charles Hart, who was working on his Ph.D. in anthropology, did fieldwork with the *Tiwi*, who lived on an island off the northern coast of Australia. Because every Tiwi belonged to a clan, they assigned Hart to the bird (Jabijabui) clan and told him that a particular woman was his mother. Hart described the woman as "toothless, almost blind, withered," and as "physically quite revolting and mentally rather senile." He then described this remarkable event:

> [T]oward the end of my time on the islands an incident occurred that surprised me because it suggested that some of them had been taking my presence in the kinship system much more seriously than I had thought. I was approached by a group of

about eight or nine senior men, all of whom I knew. They were all senior members of the Jabijabui clan and they had decided among themselves that the time had come to get rid of the decrepit old woman who had first called me son and whom I now called mother. As I knew, they said, it was Tiwi custom, when an old woman became too feeble to look after herself, to "cover her up." This could only be done by her sons and her brothers and all of them had to agree beforehand, since once it was done they did not want any dissension among the brothers or clansmen, as that might lead to a feud. My "mother" was now completely blind, she was constantly falling over logs or into fires, and they, her senior clansmen, were in agreement that she would be better out of the way. Did I agree?

I already knew about "covering up." The Tiwi, like many other hunting and gathering peoples, sometimes got rid of their ancient and decrepit females. The method was to dig a hole in the ground in some lonely place, put the old woman in the hole and fill it in with earth until only her head was showing. Everybody went away for a day or two and then went back to the hole to discover, to their surprise, that the old woman was dead, having been too feeble to raise her arms from the earth. Nobody had "killed" her; her death in Tiwi eyes was a natural one. She had been alive when her rela-

Central to a group's culture are ways of viewing reality. Living for centuries in isolation on Bathurst and Melville Islands off the northern coast of Australia, the Tiwi, featured in the vignette on "covering up," developed a unique culture. Shown here is Wurabuti, who has prepared himself to lead his uncle's funeral dance. To be certain that his late uncle's ghost will not recognize him, Wurabuti is wearing a "shirt" painted with ocher and clay, a topknot of cockatoo feathers, and a beard of goose feathers.

tives last saw her. I had never seen it done, though I knew it was the custom, so I asked my brothers if it was necessary for me to attend the "covering up."

They said no and they would do it, but only after they had my agreement. Of course I agreed, and a week or two later we heard in our camp that my "mother" was dead, and we wailed and put on the trimmings of mourning. (Hart 1970:154)

We won't deal with the question of research ethics, of Hart agreeing that the old woman should be "covered up." What is of interest for our purpose is how the Tiwi treated their frail elderly—or, more specifically, their frail *female* elderly. You may have noticed that they "covered up" only their old women. As noted earlier, throughout the world females are discriminated against. As this case makes evident, in some places that discrimination extends even to death.

AGING IN GLOBAL PERSPECTIVE

Every society must deal with the problem of people growing old, and of some elderly becoming very frail. Although few societies choose to bury them alive, all must decide how to allocate limited resources among their citizens. As the proportion of the population that is old increases, as is happening in many nations, those decisions generate tensions among the generations.

The Social Construction of Aging

The way the Tiwi treated their frail elderly women reflects one extreme of how societies cope with aging. Another extreme, one that reflects an entirely different attitude, is illustrated by the Abkhasians, an agricultural people who live in a mountainous region of Georgia, a republic of the former Soviet Union. Rather than "covering up" their elderly, the Abkhasians pay them high respect and look to them for guidance. They would no more dispense with one of their elderly in this manner than we would "cover up" a sick child.

The Abkhasians may be the longest-lived people on earth. Many claim to live past 100—some beyond 120 and even 130 (Benet 1971). Although it is difficult to document the accuracy of these claims (Haslick 1974; Harris 1990), government records indicate that

an extraordinary number of Abkhasians do live to a very old age.

Three main factors appear to account for their long lives. The first is their diet, which consists of little meat, much fresh fruit, vegetables, garlic, goat cheese, cornmeal, buttermilk, and wine. The second is their lifelong physical activity. They do slow down after age 80, but even after the age of 100 they still work about four hours a day. The third factor—a highly developed sense of community—goes to the very heart of Abkhasian culture. From childhood, each individual is integrated into a primary group, and remains so throughout life. There is no such thing as a nursing home, nor do the elderly live alone. Because they continue to work and contribute to the group's welfare, the elderly aren't a burden to anyone. They don't vegetate, nor do they feel the need to "fill time" with bingo and shuffleboard. In short, the elderly feel no sudden rupture between what they "were" and what they "are."

The examples of the Tiwi and the Abkhasians reveal an important sociological principle—that, like gender, aging is *socially constructed*. That is, nothing in the nature of aging summons forth any particular set of attitudes. Rather, attitudes toward the aged are rooted in society, and therefore differ from one social group to another.

Effects of Industrialization

As noted in previous chapters, industrialization is a worldwide trend. Along with a higher standard of living, industrialization also brings more food, better public health practices (especially a purer water supply), and more effective ways of fighting the diseases that kill children. Consequently, when a country industrializes, more of its people reach older ages. The Social Map on the next two pages shows the percentage of elderly in the world's nations. The range is broad, from just 1 of 45 citizens in Cote d'Ivoire to almost 1 of 5 in Italy. You can see that no industrialized country is among the nations with the lowest percentage of elderly.

As a nation's elderly population increases, so does the bill that the younger citizens pay to provide for their needs. This bill has become a major social issue. Although Americans complain that they pay 14 percent of their wages to Social Security, the U.S. rate is comparatively low. Workers in Holland and Italy pay 39 percent of their wages to social security, while those in Germany and Greece pay 34 percent of theirs. French workers are hit the hardest—43 percent of their pay goes to social security (*Statistical Abstract* 1999:Table 1384). In contrast, workers in the Least Industrialized Nations pay no social security taxes. There, families are expected to take care of their own elderly, with no help from the government.

The cost to provide for the elderly in the Most Industrialized Nations has alarmed analysts. An outstanding case is Germany. By the year 2020, about 30 percent of Germans will be over the age of 60. In order to continue to furnish them the high level of care they now receive, Germany will have to tax nearly *all* the lifetime income of its future workers (Wessel 1995). Obviously, this is impossible, but no one has yet come up with a workable solution to the problem. Similar problems loom for all the Most Industrialized Nations.

The Graying of America

The number of elderly is growing rapidly in the United States. Figure 10.8 explains why. It shows how U.S. **life expectancy,** the number of years people can expect to live, has increased since 1900. To me, and perhaps to you, it is startling to realize that a hundred years ago the average American could not even expect to see age 50. Since then, we've added about 30 years to our life expectancy, and Americans born today can expect to live into their 70s or 80s.

The term **graying of America** refers to this increasing proportion of older people in the U.S. population. Look at Figure 10.9 on page 262. In 1900, only 4 percent of Americans were age 65 and over. Today almost 13 percent are. The average 65-year-old can expect to live another eighteen years (*Statistical Abstract* 1999:Table 129). U.S. society has become so "gray" that the median age has *doubled* since 1850, and today we have seven million more elderly than we have teenagers (*Statistical Abstract* 1999:Table 22). Despite this change, on a global scale Americans rank just seventeenth in life expectancy (*Statistical Abstract* 1999:Table 1352).

As anyone who has ever visited Florida has noticed, the elderly population is not evenly distributed around the country. (As Jerry Seinfeld sardonically noted, "There's a law that when you get old you've got to move to Florida.") The Social Map on page 262 shows how uneven this distribution is expected to be in a couple of decades.

It is important to keep in mind that although more people are living to old age, the maximum length of life possible, the **life span,** has not increased. Experts disagree, however, on what that maximum is. It is at least 122, for this was the well-documented age of Jeanne Louise Calment of France at her death in 1998. If the reports on the Abkhasians are correct (and this is a matter of controversy), the human life span may exceed even this number by a comfortable margin.

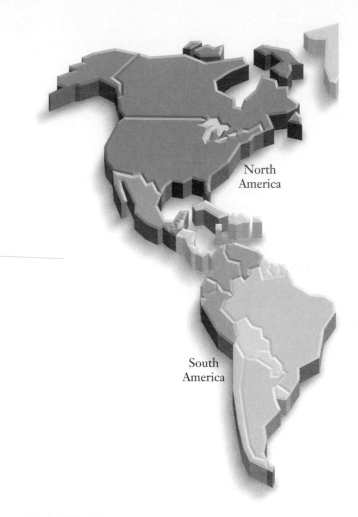

North America

South America

Figure **10.7** SOCIAL MAP: THE GRAYING OF THE GLOBE

Source: Statistical Abstract 1999:Table 1350.

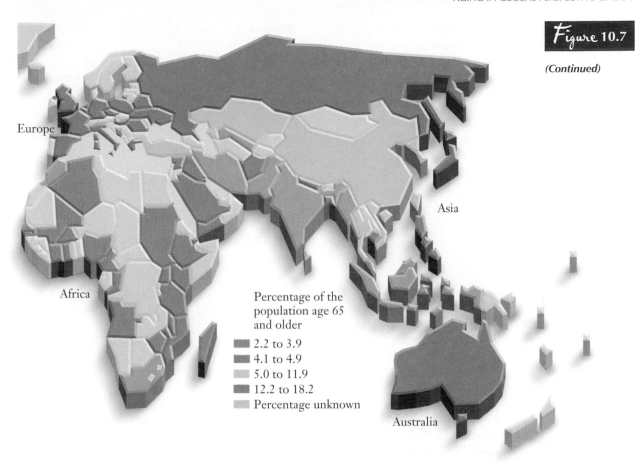

Figure 10.7

(Continued)

Percentage of the population age 65 and older

- 2.2 to 3.9
- 4.1 to 4.9
- 5.0 to 11.9
- 12.2 to 18.2
- Percentage unknown

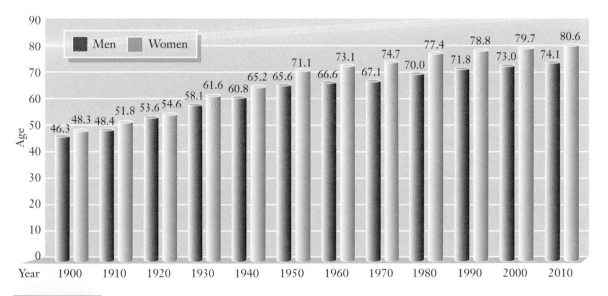

Figure 10.8   **U.S. LIFE EXPECTANCY BY YEAR OF BIRTH**

Sources: Historical Statistics of the United States, Colonial Times to 1970, Bicentennial Edition, Part 1, Series B, 107–115; *Statistical Abstract* 1999:Table 127.

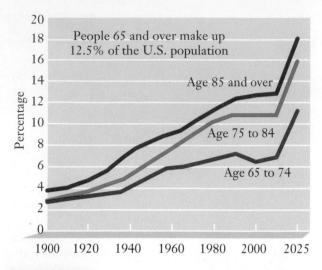

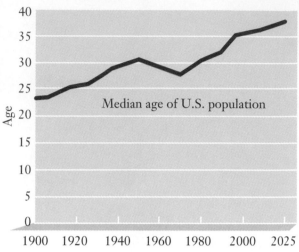

Figure 10.9 THE GRAYING OF AMERICA

Sources: Statistical Abstract, various editions, and 1999:Tables 13, 24.

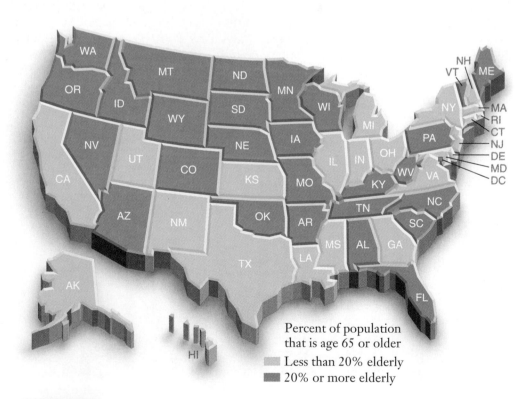

Percent of population
that is age 65 or older
Less than 20% elderly
20% or more elderly

Figure 10.10 AS FLORIDA GOES, SO GOES THE NATION: THE YEAR 2025

Note: The growing proportion of the elderly in the U.S. population is destined to have profound effects on U.S. society. By the year 2025, one-fifth of the population of 27 states is expected to be 65 or older. Today, at 19 percent, only Florida comes close to this.

Source: U.S. Bureau of the Census, 1996, U.S. Department of Commerce, PPL-47.

THE SYMBOLIC INTERACTIONIST PERSPECTIVE

To apply symbolic interactionism, let's consider ageism and how negative stereotypes of the elderly developed.

Ageism: The Concept

At first, the audience sat quietly as the developers explained their plans to build a high-rise apartment building. After a while, people began to shift uncomfortably in their seats. Now they were showing open hostility.

"That's too much money to spend on those people," said one.

"You even want them to have a swimming pool?" asked another incredulously.

Finally, one young woman put their attitudes in a nutshell when she asked, "Who wants all those old people around?"

When physician Robert Butler (1975, 1980) heard these responses to plans to build an apartment building for senior citizens, he began to realize how deeply feelings against the elderly can run. He coined the term **ageism** to refer to prejudice, discrimination, and hostility that are directed against people because of their age. Let's see how ageism developed in U.S. society.

Shifting Meanings

As we have seen, there is nothing inherent in old age to summon forth negative attitudes. Some researchers even suggest that in early U.S. society old age had positive meanings (Cottin 1979; Kart 1990; Clair et al. 1993). Due to high death rates, they point out, not many people made it to old age. Consequently, growing old was seen as an accomplishment, and the younger generation listened to the elderly's advice about how to live a long life. With no pensions (this was before industrialization), the elderly continued to work at jobs that changed little over time, making them a storehouse of knowledge about work skills.

The coming of industrialization, however, eroded these bases of respect. With improved sanitation and medical care, more people reached old age, and it was no longer a distinction to be elderly. Then, too, the new forms of mass production made young workers as productive as the elderly. This development, coupled with mass education, stripped away the elderly's superior knowledge (Cowgill 1974). A sign of this shift in meanings is a change in how people lie about their age (Clair et al. 1993): They used to claim they were older than they were, but now they say they are younger than they are.

Because most U.S. elderly can take care of themselves financially—and many are very well off—the meaning of old age is changing once again. In addition,

PEANUTS® by Charles M. Schulz

Stereotypes, which play such a profound role in social life, are a basic area of sociological investigation. In contemporary society, the mass media are a major source of stereotypes.

the baby boom generation, the first of whom are now in their 50s, has begun to confront the realities of aging. With their vast numbers and better health and finances, they are destined to positively affect our images of the elderly. The next step in this symbolic change, now in process, is to celebrate old age as a time of renewal—not simply as a period that precedes death but, rather, as another stage of growth.

The Mass Media: Powerful Source of Symbols

In Chapter 3 (pages 66–67), we noted how the mass media help to shape our ideas about gender and about relationships between men and women. As a powerful source of symbols, the media also influence our ideas of the elderly, the topic of the following Mass Media box.

Mass Media in Social Life

SHAPING OUR PERCEPTIONS OF THE ELDERLY

The mass media profoundly influence our lives. What we hear and see on television and in the movies, the songs we listen to, the books and magazines we read—all become part of our world view. Without our knowing it, the media shape our images of people. They influence how we view minorities, the dominant group, men, women, and children, people with disabilities, people from other cultures—and the elderly.

The shaping is subtle, so much so that it is usually beneath our awareness. The elderly, for example, are underrepresented on television and in most popular magazines. The covert message is that the elderly are of little consequence and can be safely ignored. Or consider how the media reflect and reinforce stereotypes of gender age. Older male news anchors are likely to be retained, while female anchors who turn the same age are more likely to be transferred to less visible positions. Similarly, in movies older men are more likely to play romantic leads—and opposite much younger rising stars.

Then there is advertising. The American Association of Retired

As emphasized in the text, age is much more than biology. The point at which old age begins, for example, differs from one culture to another. In some cultures, Tom Selleck, at age 50, would be considered an old man, but on the television show *Friends* he portrayed the romantic lead opposite Courteney Cox, age 31.

Persons (AARP) points out that television ads often depict the elderly as being feeble or foolish, or as passing their time in rocking

chairs (Goldman 1993). The reason for this, claims the AARP, is that younger people dominate advertising firms, and their ads reflect their negative images of older people. They pick out the "worst traits of the group, making everyone believe that old is something you don't want to be."

The message is not lost. As we add years, we go to great lengths to deny that we are growing old. This plays into advertisers' hands, who exploit our fears of losing our youth so they can sell us their hair dyes, skin creams, and other products that supposedly conceal even the appearance of old age (Vernon et al. 1990; Vasil and Wass 1993; Ryan and Wentworth 1999).

As discussed in the text, the elderly's affluence is growing. This translates into economic power, something that advertisers and producers must take into consideration. It is inevitable, then, that the media's images of the elderly will change. An indication of that change is shown in the photo in this box. We might also note the sexism that still clings to these changing images—the primary depiction is that of older men and younger women. ■

Cohort=group

THE CONFLICT PERSPECTIVE ■ 265

THE FUNCTIONALIST PERSPECTIVE

Functionalists analyze how the parts of society work together. We can consider an **age cohort,** people who were born at roughly the same time and who pass through the life course together, as a component of society. This component affects other parts. For example, if the age cohort nearing retirement is large (a "baby boom" generation), many jobs will open at roughly the same time. If it is small (a "baby bust" generation), fewer jobs will open. For large numbers of people to retire from their jobs, an adjustment must take place between that age cohort and other parts of society. Let's examine disengagement theory and activity theory, which focus on these adjustments.

Disengagement Theory

Elaine Cumming and William Henry (1961) developed **disengagement theory** to explain how society prevents disruption when the elderly leave (or disengage from) their positions of responsibility. It would be disruptive if the elderly left their positions only when they died or became incompetent. Consequently, societies use pensions to entice the elderly to hand over their positions to younger people. Thus, disengagement is a mutually beneficial agreement between two parts of society; it facilitates a smooth transition between the generations.

Cumming (1976) also examined disengagement from the individual's perspective. She pointed out that disengagement begins during middle age, long before retirement, when someone senses that the end of life is closer than its start. The individual does not immediately disengage, however, but, realizing that time is limited, begins to assign priority to goals and tasks. Disengagement begins in earnest when children leave home, then increases with retirement and eventually widowhood.

Evaluation of the Theory Disengagement theory has come under attack. Anthropologist Dorothy Jerrome (1992) points out that it contains an implicit bias against older people—assumptions that the elderly disengage from productive social roles, and then sort of sink into oblivion. Her own research shows that, instead of disengaging, the elderly *exchange* one set of roles for another. The new roles, which center around friendship, are no less satisfying than the earlier roles. They are less visible to researchers, however, who tend to have a youth-

ful orientation—and who show their bias by assuming that productivity is the measure of self-worth.

Retirement, too, is changing. The explosion in communications and types of work means that the dividing line between the working years and the retirement years is growing fuzzy. Less and less, retirement means to hit a wall at a certain age and to abruptly stop working. Instead, many workers just slow down. They may continue at their job, but put in fewer hours. Some may move to another area, taking their work with them, but they do not "retire"—at least not in the sense of sinking into a recliner, or being forever on the golf course. Disengagement theory has not yet come to grips with this fundamental change.

Activity Theory

Are retired people less satisfied with life? Are intimate activities more satisfying than formal ones? Such questions are the focus of **activity theory,** which assumes that the more activities elderly people engage in, the more they find life satisfying. Although we could consider this theory from other perspectives, because its focus is how disengagement is functional or dysfunctional, it can be considered from the functionalist perspective.

Evaluation of the Theory The research results are mixed. In general, researchers have found that more active people are more satisfied. But not always. For example, a study of retired people in France found that some people are happier when they are very active, others when they are less involved (Keith 1982). Similarly, most people find more informal activities, such as spending time with friends, to be more satisfying than formal activities. But not everyone. In one study, 2,000 retired U.S. men reported formal activities to be as important as informal ones. Even solitary activities, such as doing home repairs, had about the same impact as intimate activities on these men's life satisfaction (Beck and Page 1988). Researchers must take into account what activities *mean* to people, not simply count their activities.

■ **In Sum** The broader perspective of the functionalists is how society's parts work together to keep society functioning smoothly. Although it is inevitable that younger workers replace the elderly, this could lead to disruptions. Retirement and pensions are used to smooth the way in this inevitable transition. The narrower perspective of the functionalists is how the elderly adjust to their retirement.

As the numbers of U.S. elderly grow, a new emphasis is being placed on their well-being. Researchers are exploring the elderly's mental and social development, as well as the causes of physical well-being. As research progresses, do you think we will reach the point where the average old person will be in this man's physical condition?

THE CONFLICT PERSPECTIVE

From the conflict perspective, the guiding principles of social life are competition, disequilibrium, and change. So it is with society's age groups. Whether the young and old recognize it or not, they are part of a basic struggle that threatens to throw society into turmoil. The passage of Social Security legislation is an example of this struggle.

Social Security Legislation

In the 1920s, before Social Security provided an income for the aged, two-thirds of all citizens over 65 had no savings and could not support themselves (Holtzman 1963; Hudson 1978). The Great Depression made matters even worse, and in 1930 Francis Townsend, a physician, started a movement to rally older citizens. He soon had one-third of all Americans over 65 enrolled in his Townsend clubs. They demanded that the federal government impose a national sales tax of 2 percent to provide $200 a month for every person over 65 (more than $2,000 a month in today's money). In 1934, the Townsend Plan went before Congress. Because it called for such high payments and many were afraid that it would destroy people's incentive to save for the future, Congress looked for a way to reject the plan without appearing to oppose old age pensions. When President Roosevelt announced his own, more modest Social Security plan in 1934, Congress embraced it (Schottland 1963; Amenta et al. 1997).

This legislation required that workers retire at 65. It did not matter how well people did their work, nor how much they needed an income. For decades, the elderly protested. Finally, in 1978 Congress raised the mandatory retirement age to 70, and in 1986 eliminated it altogether. Today, almost 90 percent of Americans retire by age 65, but they do so voluntarily. No longer can they be forced out of their jobs simply because of their age.

Conflict theorists point out that Social Security did not come about because the members of Congress had generous hearts. Social Security, rather, emerged from a struggle between competing interest groups. As conflict theorists stress, equilibrium is only a temporary balancing of social forces, one that can be upset at any time. Perhaps, then, more direct conflict may emerge in the future. Let's consider that possibility.

Intergenerational Conflict

Will the future bring conflict between the elderly and the young? Although violence is not likely, the grumbling is increasing—complaints that the elderly are getting more than their share of society's resources (Brownstein and Rosenblatt 1999). The huge costs of Social Security and Medicare have become a national concern. These two programs alone account for one of every three tax dollars (*Statistical Abstract* 1999:Table 548). As Figure 10.11 shows, Social Security taxes were $781 million in 1950; now they run *500* times higher.

Some form of conflict seems inevitable. The graying of the United States leaves proportionately fewer working people to pay for the benefits received by the increasing millions who collect Social Security. Some see this shift in the **dependency ratio**—the number of workers who collect Social Security compared with the number of workers who contribute to it—as especially troubling. As Figure 10.12 shows, sixteen workers used to support each person who was drawing Social Security. Now the dependency ratio has dropped to four to one. As this ratio continues to shrink, will younger workers be willing to pay the huge sums it will take to support the older generation?

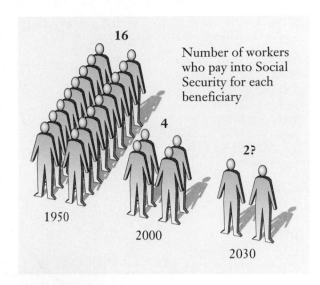

Number of workers who pay into Social Security for each beneficiary

Figure 10.12 **FEWER WORKERS ARE SUPPORTING A LARGER NUMBER OF RETIREES**

Source: Social Security Administration; *Statistical Abstract* 1999:Tables 614, 616.

As Figure 10.13 on the next page shows, medical costs for the elderly have also soared. Because of this, some fear that the health care of children is being shortchanged and Congress will be forced to "choose between old people and kids." What especially alarms some are the data shown in Figure 10.14. As the condition of the elderly has improved, that of children has worsened. Although critics are pleased that the elderly are better off than they were, they are bothered that this improvement has come at the cost of the nation's children.

But has it really? Conflict sociologists Meredith Minkler and Ann Robertson (1991) say that while the figures themselves are true, the comparison is misleading. The money that went to the elderly did *not* come from the children. Would anyone say that the money the government gives to flood victims or that the money the government spends on national parks comes from the children? Of course not. The government makes choices about where to spend its income, and it could very well have decided to increase spending on *both* the elderly and the children. It simply has not done so. As conflict theorists point out, framing the issue as a case of money going to one group at the expense of another is an attempt to divide the working class. If the working class can be made to think that it must choose between pathetic children and suffering old folks,

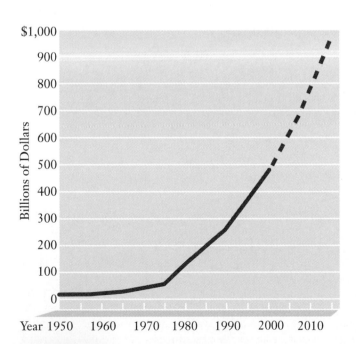

Figure 10.11 **COSTS OF SOCIAL SECURITY**

Source: Statistical Abstract 1997:Table 518; 1999:Table 543. Broken line indicates the author's projections.

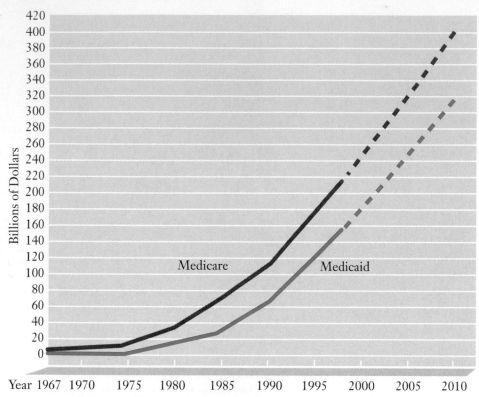

Note: Medicare is intended for the elderly and disabled, Medicaid for the poor. About 31 percent of Medicaid payments ($38 billion) goes to the elderly.

Figure 10.13 **HEALTH CARE COSTS FOR THE ELDERLY AND DISABLED**

Source: Statistical Abstract, various years, and 1999:Tables 177, 181.

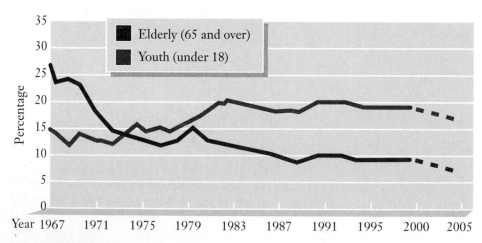

Note: For some years the government totals for youth refer to people under 18, for other years to people under 16 or 15. Broken lines indicate the author's projections.

Figure 10.14 **TRENDS IN POVERTY**

Source: Congressional Research Service, *Statistical Abstract* 1999:Table 763.

it will be divided and unable to work together to improve U.S. society.

LOOKING TOWARD THE FUTURE

We have reviewed several key issues in aging. To close the chapter, I would like you to reflect on some exciting and, perhaps, disturbing scientific breakthroughs that may have a direct impact on your own life.

Thinking Critically

HOW LONG DO YOU WANT TO LIVE? PUSHING PAST THE LIMITS OF BIOLOGY

How would you like to live to 150? to 200?

Such a question may strike you as absurd. But with our new and still developing technology, science may stretch the life span to limits unheard of since biblical days.

We are just at the beginning stages of genetic engineering, and ahead of us may lie a brave new world. Predictions are that technicians will be able to snip out our bad DNA and replace it with more compliant bits. The caps at the end of our chromosomes, the telomeres, shrink as we age, causing the cells to die. An enzyme called telomerase may be able to modify this process, allowing cells to reproduce many more times then they do now (Nuland 1999).

Already—just by manipulating a gene or two—scientists have been able to double the life span of worms, flies, and mice. Humans have these same genes (Kolata 1999;

Recer 2000). A doubled human life span would take the longest living people past 200.

We are only peering over the edge of the future, only glimpsing what might be possible. Some optimistic molecular biologists predict that we will find ways to grow spare body parts. From the same stem cells we will grow livers, hearts, kidneys, fingers—whatever you need.

Spare body parts? Apparently they're on the way. If the growing of body parts becomes routine, I can envision the day when the organ and limb salespeople take over. Can't you just hear it now? "Such a deal! I got a new kidney coming in Tuesday. Everybody's gonna want it, but for some reason I like you, and I'm gonna give you a special price."

Back in grade school, my teachers told me stories about Ponce de Leon, an explorer from Spain who searched for the fountain of youth. He eventually "discovered" Florida, but the fountain of youth eluded him. In our perpetual search for immortality, could we, finally, have found what eluded Ponce de Leon? ■

For Your Consideration

Let's assume that biomedical science does stretch the human life span, that living to be 200 or so becomes common. If people retired at age 65, how could society afford to support them for 135 years? They can't work a lot longer, for—and this may be the basic flaw in this brave new world scenario—even with new body parts, the world would not be filled with 200-year-olds who functioned as though they were 25. They would be old people, subject to the diseases and debilities that come with advancing age. If Medicare costs are bulging at the seams now, what would they be like in such a world?

Finally, how would you answer this question (Nuland 1999): Is the real issue how we can live longer, or how we can live better?

SUMMARY AND REVIEW

■ Issues of Sex and Gender

What is gender stratification?

The term **gender stratification** refers to unequal access to power, prestige, and property on the basis of sex. Each society establishes a structure that, on the basis of sex and gender, opens and closes doors to its privileges. P. 240.

How do sex and gender differ?

Sex refers to biological distinctions between males and females. It consists of both primary and secondary sex characteristics. **Gender**, in contrast, is what a society considers proper behaviors and attitudes for its male and female members. Sex physically distinguishes males from females; gender defines what is "masculine" and "feminine." P. 240.

Why do the behaviors of males and females differ?

The "nature versus nurture" debate refers to whether differences in the behaviors of males and females are caused by inherited (biological) or learned (cultural) characteristics. Almost all sociologists take the side of nurture. In recent years, how-

XX = girl
XY = boy

Sociology = nurture

ever, sociologists have begun to cautiously open the door to biology. Pp. 240–243.

■ How Females Became a Minority Group

How did females become a minority group?
Patriarchy, or male dominance, appears to be universal. The origin of discrimination against females is lost in history, but the primary theory of how females became a minority group in their own societies focuses on the physical limitations imposed by childbirth. Pp. 243–246.

■ Gender Inequality in the United States

Is the feminist movement new?
1920 In what is called the "first wave," feminists made demands for social change in the early 1900s—and were met with hostility and even violence. The "second wave" began in the 1960s and *1960* continues today. Pp. 246–247.

What forms does gender stratification take?
Formed into, become
Although more women than men attend college, each tends to select "feminine" or "masculine" fields. Women are underrepresented in most doctoral programs in science, and they are less likely to complete these programs. Fundamental change is indicated by the growing numbers of women in law and medicine. Pp. 247–248. *56% bachelor degree*

How are women discriminated against in health care?
Women are referred for heart surgery later than men, resulting in higher surgical death rates. *utilize* Exploiting women's fears, surgeons also perform unnecessary hysterectomies. Pp. 248–249.

How does gender inequality show up in the workplace?
Over the last century, women have made up an increasing proportion of the work force. Nonetheless, all occupations show a gender gap in pay. For college graduates, the lifetime pay gap runs almost a million dollars in favor of men. **Sexual harassment** also continues to be a reality of the workplace. Pp. 249–254.

What forms does violence against women take?
The victims of battering, rape, incest, and murder are overwhelmingly females. Female circumcision is a special case of violence against females. Conflict theorists point out that men use violence to maintain their power and privilege. Pp. 254–257.

■ The Changing Face of Politics

What is the trend in gender inequality in politics?
A traditional division of gender roles—women as child care providers and homemakers, men as workers outside the home—used to keep women out of politics. Women continue to be underrepresented in politics, but the trend toward greater political equality is firmly in place. P. 257.

What progress has been made in reducing inequality?
In the United States, women are playing a fuller role in the decision-making processes of our social institutions. The rea-

sonable goal is appreciation of sexual differences coupled with equality of opportunity. Pp. 257–258.

■ Aging in Global Perspective

How are the elderly treated around the world?
No single set of attitudes, beliefs, or policies regarding the aged characterizes the world's nations. Rather, they vary from exclusion and killing to integration and honor. The global trend is for more people to live longer. Pp. 258–259.

What does the social construction of aging mean?
Nothing in the nature of aging summons forth any particular set of attitudes. Rather, attitudes toward the elderly are rooted in society and differ from one social group to another. Pp. 259–262.

■ The Symbolic Interactionist Perspective

What factors influence perceptions of aging?
Symbolic interactionists stress the social construction of aging, emphasizing that no age has any particular built-in meaning. **Ageism,** negative reactions to the elderly, is based on stereotypes. Pp. 263–264.

■ The Functionalist Perspective

How is retirement functional for society?
Functionalists focus on how the withdrawal of the elderly from positions of responsibility benefits society. **Disengagement theory** examines retirement as a device for ensuring that a society's positions of responsibility will be passed smoothly from one generation to the next. **Activity theory** examines how people adjust when they disengage from productive roles. P. 265.

■ The Conflict Perspective

Is there conflict among different age groups?
Social Security legislation is an example of one generation making demands on another generation for limited resources. As the number of retired people grows, there are relatively fewer workers to support them. This can create resentment. The argument that benefits to the elderly come at the cost of benefits to children is fallacious. Pp. 265–268.

■ Looking Toward the Future

What technological developments can be a wild card in social planning for the aged?
Technological breakthroughs may stretch the human life span. If so, it is difficult to see how younger workers would be able to support retired people for 100 years or so. Pp. 268–269.

Where can I read more on these topics?
Suggested readings for this chapter are listed on page SR-7.

YOUR INTERACTIVE COMPANION WEB SITE

Your Interactive Companion Web Site includes practice tests, with feedback, and online learning activities with video, audio, and Weblinks. Your access code for this Web site is provided with this text.

GLOSSARY

activity theory the view that satisfaction during old age is related to a person's level and quality of activity (p. 265)

age cohort people born at roughly the same time who pass through the life course together (p. 265)

ageism prejudice, discrimination, and hostility directed against people because of their age; can be directed against any age group, including youth (p. 263)

dependency ratio the number of workers required to support one person on Social Security (p. 267)

disengagement theory the view that society prevents disruption by having the elderly vacate their positions of responsibility so the younger generation can step into their shoes (p. 265)

feminism the philosophy that men and women should be politically, economically, and socially equal; organized activity on behalf of this principle (p. 246)

gender the social characteristics that a society considers proper for its males and females; masculinity or femininity (p. 240)

gender stratification males' and females' unequal access to power, prestige, and property on the basis of their sex (p. 240)

graying of America older people making up an increasing proportion of the U.S. population (p. 260)

life expectancy the age that someone can be expected to live to (p. 260) *80 yrs*

life span the maximum possible length of life (p. 260) *120 yrs*

patriarchy a society in which authority is vested in men; control by men of a society or group (p. 245)

quiet revolution the fundamental changes in society that follow when vast numbers of women enter the work force (p. 249)

sex biological characteristics that distinguish females and males, consisting of primary and secondary sex characteristics (p. 240)

sexual harassment unwanted sexual advances, usually within an occupational or educational setting (p. 253)

Chapter 11

Franklin McMahon, Voting, 1976

Politics and the Economy: Leadership and Work in the Global Village

In 1949, George Orwell wrote *1984*, a book about a future in which the government, known as "Big Brother," dominates society, dictating almost every aspect of each individual's life. Even to love someone is considered a sinister activity, a betrayal of the supreme love and total allegiance that all citizens owe Big Brother.

Despite the danger, Winston and Julia fall in love. They meet furtively, always with the threat of discovery hanging over their heads. When informers turn them in, interrogators separate Julia and Winston, and proceed swiftly to quash their affection in order to restore their loyalty to Big Brother.

Then follows a remarkable account of Winston and his tormentor, O'Brien. Winston is strapped into a chair so tightly that he can't even move his head. O'Brien explains that although inflicting pain is not always enough to break a person's will, everyone has a breaking point. There is some worst fear that will push anyone over the edge.

O'Brien tells Winston that he has discovered his worst fear. Then he sets a cage with two giant, starving sewer rats on the table next to Winston. O'Brien picks up a hood connected to the door of the cage and places it over Winston's head. He then explains that when he presses the lever, the door of the cage will slide up, and the rats will shoot out like bullets and bore straight into Winston's face. Winston's eyes, the only part of his body that he can move, dart back and forth, revealing his terror. Speaking so quietly that Winston has to strain to hear him, O'Brien adds that the rats sometimes attack the eyes first, but sometimes they burrow through the cheeks and devour the tongue. When O'Brien places his hand on the lever, Winston realizes that the only way out is for someone else to take his place. But who? Then he hears his own voice screaming,

"Do it to Julia!... Tear her face off. Strip her to the bones. Not me! Julia! Not me!"

Orwell does not describe Julia's interrogation, but when Julia and Winston see each other later they realize that each has betrayed the other. Their love is gone. Big Brother has won.

Winston's misplaced loyalty had made him a political heretic, for every citizen had the duty to place the state above all else in life. To preserve the state's dominance over the individual, Winston's allegiance had to be taken away from Julia. As you see, it was. ■

Although seldom this dramatic, politics is always about power and authority.

POLITICS: ESTABLISHING LEADERSHIP

To exist, every society must have a system of leadership. Some people must have power over others. Let's explore this topic that is so significant for our lives.

*P*OWER, AUTHORITY, AND VIOLENCE

As Max Weber (1913/1947) pointed out, we perceive **power**—the ability to get your way, even over the resistance of others—as either legitimate or illegitimate. Legitimate power is called **authority**. This is power that people accept as right. In contrast, illegitimate power—called **coercion**—is power that people do not accept as just.

Imagine that you are on your way to buy a DVD player on sale for $250. As you approach the store, a man jumps out of an alley and shoves a gun in your face. He demands your money. Frightened for your life, you hand over the $250. After filing a police report, you head back to college to take a sociology exam. You are running late, so you step on the gas. As the needle hits 85, you see flashing blue and red lights in your rearview mir-

ror. Your explanation about the robbery doesn't faze the officer—nor the judge who hears your case a few weeks later. She first lectures you on safety and then orders you to pay $50 court costs plus $10 for every mile an hour over 65. You pay the $250.

The mugger, the police officer, and the judge—each has power, and in each case you part with $250. What, then, is the difference? The difference is that the mugger has no authority. His power is *illegitimate*—he has no *right* to do what he did. In contrast, you acknowledge that the officer has the right to stop you and that the judge has the right to fine you. They have authority, or legitimate power.

Authority and Legitimate Violence

As sociologist Peter Berger observed, it makes little difference whether you willingly pay the fine that the judge levies against you, or refuse to pay it. The court will get its money one way or another.

> There may be innumerable steps before its application [violence], in the way of warnings and reprimands. But if all the warnings are disregarded, even in so slight a matter as paying a traffic ticket, the last thing that will happen is that a couple of cops show up at the door with handcuffs and a Black Maria (billy club). Even the moderately courteous cop who hands out the initial traffic ticket is likely to wear a gun—just in case. (Berger 1963)

The *government,* then, also called the **state,** claims a monopoly on legitimate force or violence. This point,

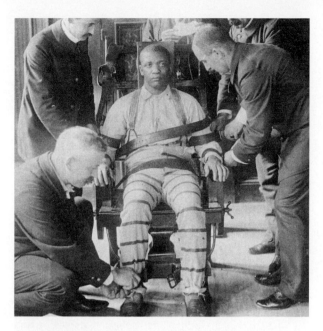

The ultimate foundation of any political order is violence. Nowhere is this more starkly demonstrated than when a government takes a human life. Shown in this 1910 photo from New York's Sing Sing Prison is a man who is about to be executed.

made by Max Weber (1946, 1922/1968)—that the state claims the exclusive right to use violence and the right to punish everyone else who does—is crucial to our understanding of politics. If someone owes you a debt, you cannot imprison that person or even forcibly take the money. The state, however, can. The ultimate proof of the state's authority is that you cannot kill someone because he or she has done something that you consider absolutely horrible—but the state can. As Berger (1963) summarized this matter, *"Violence is the ultimate foundation of any political order."*

Why do people accept power as legitimate? Max Weber (1922/1968) identified three sources of authority: traditional, rational-legal, and charismatic. Let's examine each.

Traditional Authority

Throughout history, the most common basis for authority has been tradition. **Traditional authority,** which is based on custom, is the hallmark of preliterate groups. In these societies, custom dictates basic relationships. For example, birth makes a particular individual the chief, king, or queen. As far as members

of that society are concerned, this is the right way to determine who shall rule, because "we've always done it this way."

Traditional authority declines with industrialization, but it never dies out. In postindustrial societies, for example, parents exercise authority over their children *because* parents always have had such authority. From generations past, we inherit the idea that parents should discipline their children, choose their doctors and schools, and teach them religion and morality.

Rational-Legal Authority

The second type of authority, **rational-legal authority,** is not based on custom, but on written rules. *Rational* means reasonable, and *legal* means part of law. Thus *rational-legal* refers to matters agreed to by reasonable people and written into law (or regulations of some sort). The matters agreed to may be as broad as a constitution that specifies the rights of all members of a society or as narrow as a contract between two individuals. Because bureaucracies are based on written rules, rational-legal authority is sometimes called *bureaucratic authority.*

Rational-legal authority comes from the position that someone holds, not from the person who holds the position. In a democracy, for example, the president's authority comes from the office, as specified in a written constitution, not from custom or the individual's personal characteristics. In rational-legal authority, everyone—no matter how high the office—is subject to the organization's written rules. In governments based on traditional authority, the ruler's word may be law, but in those based on rational-legal authority, the ruler's word is subject to that law.

Charismatic Authority

A few centuries back, in 1429, the English controlled large parts of France. When they prevented the coronation of a new French king, a farmer's daughter heard a voice telling her that God had a special assignment for her—that she should put on men's clothing, recruit an army, and go to war against the English. Inspired, Joan of Arc raised an army, conquered cities, and defeated the English. Later that year, her visions were fulfilled as she stood next to Charles VII while he was crowned king of France. (Bridgwater 1953)

Joan of Arc is an example of **charismatic authority,** the third type of authority Weber identified. (*Charisma* is a

One of the best examples of charismatic authority is Joan of Arc. She is shown here at the coronation of Charles VII, whom she was instrumental in making king. Uncomfortable at portraying Joan of Arc wearing only a man's coat of armor, the artist has made certain she is wearing plenty of makeup and also added a ludicrous skirt.

Charismatic authorities can be of any morality, from the saintly to the most bitterly evil. Like Joan of Arc, Adolf Hitler attracted throngs of people, providing the stuff of dreams and arousing them from disillusionment to hope. This poster from the 1930s entitled *Es Lebe Deutschland* ("Long Live Germany") illustrates the qualities of leadership that Germans of that period saw in Hitler.

Greek word that means a gift freely and graciously given [Arndt and Gingrich 1957].) A charismatic individual is someone people are drawn to because they believe that person has been touched by God or has been endowed by nature with exceptional qualities (Lipset 1993). The armies did not follow Joan of Arc because it was the custom to do so, as in traditional authority. Nor did they risk their lives alongside her because she held a position defined by written rules, as in rational-legal authority. Instead, people followed her because they were drawn to her outstanding traits. They saw her as a messenger of God fighting on the side of justice, and they accepted her leadership because of these appealing qualities.

The Threat Posed by Charismatic Leaders A king owes allegiance to tradition, and a president to written laws. To what, however, does a charismatic leader owe allegiance? Because their authority is based on their personal ability to attract followers, charismatic leaders pose a threat to the established political system. They lead their followers according to personal inclination, not according to the paths of tradition or the regulations of law. Accordingly, they can inspire followers to disregard—or even to overthrow—traditional and rational-legal authorities.

This means that charismatic leaders pose a threat to the established order. Consequently, traditional and rational-legal authorities are often quick to oppose charismatic leaders. If they are not careful, however, their opposition may arouse even more positive sentiment in favor of the charismatic leader, causing him or her to be viewed as a martyr. Occasionally the Roman Catholic church faces such a threat, as when a priest claims miraculous powers that appear to be accompanied by amazing healings. As people flock to this individual, they bypass parish priests and the formal ecclesiastical structure. This transfer of allegiance from the organization to an individual threatens the church bureaucracy. Consequently, the church hierarchy may encourage the priest to withdraw from the public eye, perhaps to a monastery, to rethink matters. Thus the threat is defused, rational-legal authority reasserted, and the stability of the organization maintained.

The Transfer of Authority

The orderly transfer of authority from one leader to another is crucial for social stability. Under traditional authority, people know who is next in line. Under rational-legal authority, people may not know who the next leader will be, but they do know how that person will be selected. In both traditional and rational-legal systems of authority, the rules of succession are firm.

Charismatic authority, however, has no such rules of succession, which makes it less stable than either traditional or rational-legal authority. Because charismatic authority is built around a single individual, the death or incapacitation of a charismatic leader can mean a bitter struggle for succession. Consequently, some charismatic leaders make arrangements for an orderly transition of power by appointing a successor. This does not guarantee orderly succession, of course, for the followers may not perceive the designated heir in the same way as they did the charismatic leader. A second strategy is for the charismatic leader to build an organization, which then develops a system of rules or regulations, thus transforming itself into a rational-legal leadership. Weber used the term **routinization of charisma** to refer to the transfer of authority from a charismatic leader to either traditional or rational-legal authority.

*T*YPES OF GOVERNMENT

How do the various types of government—monarchies, democracies, dictatorships, and oligarchies—differ? As we compare them, let's also look at how the institution of the state arose, and how the idea of citizenship was revolutionary.

Monarchies: The Rise of the State

Early societies were small and needed no extensive political system. They operated more like an extended family, with decisions being made as they became necessary. As surpluses developed and societies grew larger, cities evolved—perhaps around 3500 B.C. (Fischer 1976). **City-states** then came into being, with power radiating outward from a city like a spider's web. Although the city controlled the immediate area around it, the areas between cities remained in dispute. Each city-state had its own **monarchy,** a king or queen whose right to rule was passed on to the children.

City-states often quarreled, and wars were common. The victors extended their rule, and eventually a single city-state was able to wield power over an entire region. As the size of these regions grew, the people slowly began to identify with the larger region. That is, they began to see distant inhabitants as "we" instead of "they." What we call the **state**—the political entity that claims a monopoly on the use of violence within a territory—came into being.

Democracies: Citizenship as a Revolutionary Idea

The United States had no city-states. Each colony, however, like a city-state, was small and independent. After the American Revolution, the colonies united. With the greater strength and resources that came from political unity, they conquered almost all of North America, bringing it under the power of a central government.

The government formed in this new country was called a **democracy.** (Derived from two Greek words—*kratos* [power] and *demos* [common people]—*democracy* literally means "power to the people.") Because of the bitter antagonisms associated with the revolution against the British king, the founders of the new country were distrustful of monarchies. They wanted to put political decisions into the hands of the people. This was not the first democracy the world had seen, but such a system had been tried before only with smaller groups. Athens, a city-state of Greece, practiced democracy two thousand years ago, with each free male above a certain age having the right to be heard and to vote. Members of some Native American tribes also elected their chiefs, and in some, women were able to vote and to hold the office of chief. (The Incas and Aztecs of Mexico and Central America had monarchies.)

Because of their small size, tribes and cities were able to practice **direct democracy.** That is, they were small enough for the eligible voters to meet together, express their opinions, and then vote publicly—much

It is said that money is the mother's milk of politics. Because running for high political office is costly, U.S. politicians spend a good deal of time raising money instead of developing social policy. This preoccupation with campaign funds—and the ethical violations it sometimes leads to—is what this cartoonist is satirizing.

like a town hall meeting today. As populous and spread out as the United States was, however, direct democracy was impossible, and **representative democracy** was invented. Certain citizens (at first only male white landowners) voted for men to represent them in Washington. Later the vote was extended to nonowners of property, to African American men, then to women, and to others. Our new communications technologies, which make "electronic town meetings" possible, may also allow a new form of direct democracy. This issue is explored in the Mass Media in Social Life box on the next page.

Today we take the idea of citizenship for granted. What is not evident to us is that the idea had to be conceived in the first place. There is nothing natural about citizenship—it is simply one way in which people choose to define themselves. Throughout most of human history, people were thought to *belong* to a clan, to a tribe, or even to a ruler. The idea of **citizenship**—that by virtue of birth and residence people have basic rights—is quite new to the human scene (Turner 1990).

The concept of representative democracy based on citizenship, perhaps the greatest gift the United States has given to the world, was revolutionary. Power was to be vested in the people themselves, and government was to flow from the people. That this concept was revolutionary is generally forgotten, but its implementation meant *the reversal of traditional ideas, for the government was to be responsive to the people's wishes, not the people to*

the wishes of the government. To keep the government responsive to the needs of its citizens, people not only had the right, but the obligation, to express dissent. In a widely quoted statement, Thomas Jefferson observed that

A little rebellion now and then is a good thing.... It is a medicine necessary for the sound health of government.... God forbid that we should ever be twenty years without such a rebellion.... The tree of liberty must be refreshed from time to time with the blood of patriots and tyrants. (In Hellinger and Judd 1991)

The idea of **universal citizenship**—of *everyone* having the same basic rights by virtue of being born in a country (or by immigrating and becoming a naturalized citizen)—flowered very slowly, and came into practice only through fierce struggle. When the United States was founded, for example, this idea was still in its infancy. Today it seems inconceivable to us that anyone's gender or race-ethnicity should deny that person the right to vote, hold office, make a contract, testify in court, or own property. For earlier generations of Americans, however, it seemed just as inconceivable that women, African Americans, Native Americans, Asian Americans, and the poor should be allowed such rights.

Dictatorships and Oligarchies: The Seizure of Power

If an individual seizes power and then dictates his will onto the people, the government is known as a **dictatorship.** If a small group seizes power, the government is called an **oligarchy.** The frequent coups in Central and South America, in which a few military leaders seize control of a country, are examples of oligarchies. Although one individual may be named president, often it is a group of high-ranking officers, working behind the scenes, that makes the decisions. If their designated president becomes uncooperative, they remove him from office and designate another.

Monarchies, dictatorships, and oligarchies vary in the amount of control they exert over their people. **Totalitarianism** is almost *total* control of a people by a government. As our opening vignette demonstrated, totalitarian regimes tolerate no opposing opinion. In Nazi Germany, for example, Hitler organized a ruthless secret police force, the Gestapo, that searched for any sign

Mass Media in Social Life

POLITICS AND DEMOCRACY IN A TECHNOLOGICAL SOCIETY

"Politics is just like show business."
—Ronald Reagan

Is the new technology a threat to democracy? Politicians use computers, telephone link-ups, faxes, e-mail, and Web sites to take the pulse of the public—and to convey their platforms and their biases. Instead of tuning in and passively listening to a politician's speech, we now can talk back to candidates and leaders via chat rooms, "electronic town meetings," and call-in radio and TV talk shows.

This shift to interactive communication lies at the heart of a debate over the health and future of our democracy. Critics charge that when those who are elected to govern use the new technology to constantly "take the public's temperature," they give more attention to minute shifts in public opinion than they do to the business of governing. When politicians use poll results to "fine tune" their public posturing, the positions they take on issues are not based on personal conviction. In other words, politicians now campaign nonstop.

A major issue is the role of the Internet. "Televoting" could replace our representational democracy with a form of direct democracy. Voters could sign petitions with digital signatures, and then online decide issues that politicians now decide for them. They could even make laws online.

Some fear that the Internet isn't safe for voting. With no poll watchers, undue influence (threats, promises, or gifts in return for votes) would go undetected. Others raise a more fundamental issue: Direct democracy might detour the U.S. Constitution's system of checks and balances, which was designed to safeguard us from the "tyranny of the majority." To determine from a poll that 51 percent of adults hold a certain opinion on an issue is one thing—that information can guide our leaders. But to have 51 percent of televoters determine a

Crucial for society is the orderly transfer of power. Under its constitutional system, the United States is remarkably stable: Power is transferred peacefully—even when someone of an unusual background wins an election. Jesse Ventura, shown here, is now governor of Minnesota.

law is not the same as having elected representatives publicly argue the merits of a proposed law and then try to balance the interests of the many groups that make up their constituents.

Some point with alarm to the election of Jesse Ventura as governor of Minnesota. He ran as an independent, and for much of his campaign Ventura had no physical headquarters. Ventura fans sent e-mail to their personal contacts, encouraging them to pass on the message. Even two-thirds of Ventura's fund-raising pledges arrived by e-mail. ■

For Your Consideration

Do you think direct democracy would be superior to representative democracy? What is wrong with emphasizing image over substance? So what if we are replacing reasoned leadership with nonstop campaigning? How does an e-mail campaign compare with 30-second "sound bites"? Do you think Ventura's election breathed fresh air into the stale world of politics—or does it indicate that the Internet poses a danger to U.S. politics? Or is it something else entirely? How can we use the mass media to improve government?

Sources: "Democracy and Technology" 1995; Diamond and Silverman 1995; Grossman 1995; Fineman 1999; Raney 1999; Seib 2000.

of dissent. Spies even watched moviegoers' reactions to newsreels, reporting those who did not respond "appropriately" (Hippler 1987). Today, Saddam Hussein acts as ruthlessly toward Iraqis.

People around the world find the ideas of citizenship and representative democracy appealing. Those who have no say in their government's decisions, or who face prison or even death for expressing dissent, find in these ideas the hope for a brighter future. With today's electronic communications, people no longer remain ignorant of whether they are more or less privileged politically than others. This knowledge produces pressure for greater citizen participation in government. As electronic communications develop further, this pressure will increase.

THE U.S. POLITICAL SYSTEM

With this global background, let's examine the U.S. political system. We shall consider the two major political parties, voting patterns, and the role of lobbyists and PACs.

Political Parties and Elections

After the founding of the United States, numerous political parties emerged, but by the time of the Civil War, two parties dominated U.S. politics (Burnham 1983): the Democrats, who in the public mind are associated with the working class, and the Republicans, who are associated with wealthier people. Each party nominates candidates, and in pre-elections, called *primaries,* the voters decide which candidates will represent their party. Each candidate then campaigns, trying to appeal to the most voters. The Social Map below shows how Americans align themselves with political parties.

Although the Democrats and Republicans represent different philosophical principles, each party appeals to such a broad membership that it is difficult to distinguish a conservative Democrat from a liberal Republican. The extremes, however, are easy to discern. Deeply committed Democrats support legislation that transfers income from one group to another or that controls wages, working conditions, and competition. Dyed-in-the-wool Republicans oppose such legislation.

Those elected to Congress may cross party lines. That is, some Democrats vote for legislation proposed by Republicans, and *vice versa.* This happens because officeholders support their party's philosophy but not necessarily its specific proposals. Thus when it comes to a particular bill, such as raising the minimum wage, some

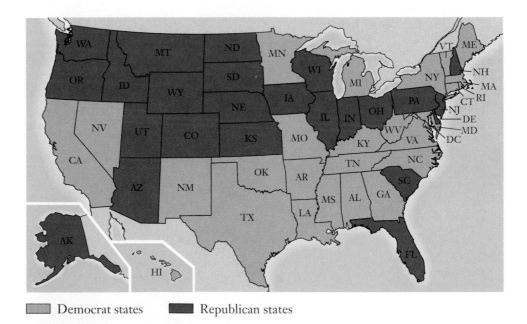

☐ Democrat states ■ Republican states

Figure 11.1 **POLITICAL PARTIES IN THE UNITED STATES: WHICH PARTY DOMINATES, DEMOCRAT OR REPUBLICAN?**

Note: Based on the composition of the state legislatures. In the case of Delaware, Nevada, New York, N. Carolina, S. Carolina, and Texas, whose lower and upper houses are dominated by different parties, the percentage of the legislators was used. For Nebraska, whose legislators are elected with no party designation, percentage vote for president was used. The most recent available data in the source is 1996.

Source: Statistical Abstract 2000:Table 469.

conservative Democrats may view the measure as unfair to small employers, or too costly, and vote with the Republicans against the bill. At the same time, liberal Republicans—feeling that the proposal is just, or sensing a dominant sentiment in voters back home—may side with its Democratic backers.

Regardless of their differences, however, the Democrats and Republicans represent *different slices of the center.* Although each may ridicule its opposition and promote different legislation, each party firmly supports such fundamentals of U.S. political philosophy as free public education, a strong military, freedom of religion, speech, assembly, and, of course, capitalism—especially the private ownership of property.

Third parties also play a role in U.S. politics, but to have any influence they, too, must support these centrist themes. Any third party that advocates radical change is doomed to a short life of little political consequence. Because most Americans consider a vote for a third party a waste, third parties do notoriously poorly at the polls. Two exceptions are the Bull Moose party, whose candidate, Theodore Roosevelt, won more votes in 1912 than Taft, the Republican presidential candidate, and the United We Stand (now Reform) party, founded by billionaire Ross Perot, which won 19 percent of the vote in 1992, but only 8 percent in 1996 and less than 1 percent in 2000 (Bridgwater 1953; *Statistical Abstract* 1995:Table 437; 1999:Table 466; election 2000 reports).

Voting Patterns

Year after year, Americans show consistent voting patterns. From Table 11.1, you can see that the percentage of people who vote increases with age. The exception is those ages 21 to 24. This table also shows the significance of race-ethnicity. Non-Hispanic whites are more likely to vote than are African Americans, while Latinos are the least likely to vote. The significance of race-ethnicity is so great that non-Hispanic whites are more than twice as likely to vote as are Latinos.

Table 11.1 also shows that voting increases with education. College graduates are more than twice as likely to vote as those who don't complete high school. Employment and income are also significant. People who make over $35,000 a year are twice as likely to vote as those who make less than $5,000. Finally, note that women are more likely to vote than men.

Table 11.1

WHO VOTES IN U.S. PRESIDENTIAL ELECTIONS?					
	1980	**1984**	**1988**	**1992**	**1996**
Overall					
Americans Who Vote	59%	60%	57%	61%	54%
Age					
18–20	36	37	33	39	31
21–24	38	44	46	33	24
25–34	55	58	48	53	43
35–44	64	64	61	64	55
45–64	69	70	68	70	64
65 and up	65	68	69	70	67
Sex					
Male	59	59	56	60	53
Female	59	61	58	62	56
Race/Ethnicity[a]					
Whites	61	61	59	64	56
African Americans	51	56	52	54	51
Latinos	30	33	29	29	27
Education					
Grade school only	43	43	37	35	28
High school dropout	46	44	41	41	34
High school graduate	59	59	55	58	49
College dropout	67	68	65	69	61
College graduate	80	79	78	81	73
Labor Force					
Employed	62	62	58	64	55
Unemployed	41	44	39	46	37
Income					
Under $5,000	38	39	35	NA	NA
$5,000 to $9,999	46	49	41	NA	NA
$10,000 to $14,999	54	55	48	NA	NA
$15,000 to $19,999	57	60	54	NA	NA
$20,000 to $24,999	61	67	58	NA	NA
$25,000 to $34,999	67	74	64	NA	NA
$35,000 and over	74	74	70[b]	NA	NA

[a]Other race-ethnic groups are not listed in the sources.
[b]For 1988, the percentage is an average of $35,000 to $49,900 and over $50,000.
Sources: Statistical Abstract 1991:Table 450; 1997:Table 462; *Current Population Reports,* Series P-20, vols. 440, 446, 504.

Social Integration How can we explain the voting patterns shown in Table 11.1? The people most likely to vote are older, more educated, affluent, employed whites, while those least likely to vote are poor, younger, less educated, unemployed Latinos. From these patterns, we can draw this principle: *The more that people feel they have a stake in the political system, the more likely they are to vote.* They have more to protect and feel that voting can make a difference. In effect, people who have been rewarded by the political system feel more socially integrated. They vote because they perceive that elections directly affect their own lives and the type of society in which they and their children live.

Alienation and Apathy In contrast, those who gain less from the system—in terms of education, income, and jobs—are more likely to feel alienated from politics. Looking at themselves as outsiders, many feel hostile to the government. Some feel betrayed, believing that politicians have sold out to special-interest groups. They are convinced that all politicians are liars. Minorities who feel the U.S. political system is a "white" system are less likely to vote.

From Table 11.1, we see that many highly educated people with good incomes also stay away from the polls. Many people do not vote because of **voter apathy,** or indifference. Their view is that "next year will just bring more of the same, regardless of who is president." A common attitude of those who are apathetic is "What difference will my one vote make when there are millions of voters?" Many see little difference between the two major political parties.

Alienation and apathy are so common that *half* of the eligible voters do not vote for president, and *two-thirds* of the nation's eligible voters don't bother to vote for candidates for Congress (*Statistical Abstract* 1999:Table 490).

The Gender Gap in Politics Historically, men and women have voted the same way. Now when they go to the ballot box, they are somewhat more likely to vote for different presidential candidates. Women vote about two to one for the Democratic candidate, while men are about evenly split between the parties (*Statistical Abstract* 1999:Table 464).

Lobbyists and Special-Interest Groups

Suppose you are president of the United States, and you want to make milk and bread more affordable for the poor. You discover that prices are high because the government is paying farmers millions of dollars a year in price supports (*Statistical Abstract* 1996:Table 1091; 1999:Tables 1109, 1110). You propose to eliminate these subsidies.

Immediately, large numbers of people leap into action. They send telegrams and e-mail to your office, contact their senators and representatives, and call reporters for news conferences. The Associated Press distributes pictures of a farm family—their Holsteins grazing contentedly in the background—and informs readers how this hard-working, healthy, happy family of good Americans who are struggling to make a living will be destroyed by your harsh proposal. President or not, you have little chance of getting your legislation passed.

What happened? The dairy industry went to work to protect its special interests. A **special-interest group** consists of people who think alike on a particular issue and who can be mobilized for political action. The dairy industry is just one of thousands of such groups that employ **lobbyists,** people who are paid to influence legislation on behalf of their clients. Special-interest groups and lobbyists have become a major force in U.S. politics. Members of Congress who want to be reelected must pay attention to them, for they represent blocs of voters who share a vital interest in the outcome of specific bills. Well financed and able to contribute huge sums, lobbyists can deliver votes to you—or to your opponent.

To prevent special-interest groups from unduly influencing legislation, the law limits the amount that any individual, corporation, or special-interest group can give a candidate, and requires all contributions over $1,000 to be reported. Special-interest groups get around the law by forming **political action committees (PACs).** These organizations solicit contributions from many donors—each contribution being within the allowable limit—and then use the large total to influence legislation.

PACs are powerful, for they bankroll lobbyists and legislators. About 4,000 PACs shell out about $220 million a year (*Statistical Abstract* 1999:Table 499). A few PACs represent broad social interests such as environmental protection, but most stand for narrow financial concerns, such as the dairy, oil, banking, and construction industries.

Criticism of Lobbyists and PACs The major criticism leveled against lobbyists and PACs is that their money, in effect, buys votes. Rather than representing the people who elected them, legislators support the special interests of groups that have the ability to help them stay in power. Those PACs with the most clout in terms of money and votes gain the ear of Congress. To politicians, the sound of money talking apparently sounds like the voice of the people.

Even if the United States were to outlaw PACs, special-interest groups would not disappear from the U.S. political scene. Lobbyists walked the corridors of the Senate long before PACs, and for good or ill, they play an essential role in the U.S. political system.

WHO RULES THE UNITED STATES?

With lobbyists and PACs so influential, just whom do U.S. senators and representatives really represent? This question has led to a lively debate among sociologists.

The Functionalist Perspective: Pluralism

Functionalists view the state as having arisen out of the basic needs of the social group. To protect themselves from oppressors, people formed a government and gave it the monopoly on violence. The risk is that the state can turn that force against its own citizens. To return to the example used earlier, states have a tendency to become muggers. Thus, people must find a balance between having no government—which would lead to **anarchy,** a condition of disorder and violence—and having a government that protects them from violence, but that also may itself turn against them. When functioning well, then, the state is a balanced system that protects its citizens—from one another *and* from government.

What keeps the U.S. government from turning against its citizens? Functionalists say that **pluralism,** a diffusion of power among many interest groups, prevents any one group from gaining control of the government and using it to oppress the people (Polsby 1959; Huber and Form 1973; Dahl 1961, 1982). To keep the government from coming under the control of any one group, the founders of the United States set up three branches of government: the executive branch (the president), the judiciary branch (the courts), and the legisla-

tive branch (the Senate and House of Representatives). Each is sworn to uphold the Constitution, which guarantees rights to citizens, and each can nullify the actions of the other two. This system, known as **checks and balances,** was designed to ensure that no one branch of government dominates.

Our pluralist society has many parts—women, men, racial-ethnic groups, farmers, factory and office workers, religious groups, bankers, bosses, the unemployed, the retired, as well as such broader categories as the rich, middle class, and poor. As each group pursues its own interests, it is balanced by other groups pursuing theirs. As special-interest groups negotiate with one another and reach compromises, conflict is minimized, and the resulting policies gain wide support. Consequently, say functionalists, no one group rules, and the political system is responsive to the people.

The Conflict Perspective: The Power Elite, or Ruling Class

Conflict theorists disagree. If you focus on the lobbyists scurrying around Washington, they say, you get a blurred image of superficial activities. What really counts is the big picture, not its fragments. The important question is who holds the power that determines the overarching policies of the United States. For example, who determines how many Americans will be out of work by raising or lowering interest rates? Who sets policies that transfer jobs from the United States to countries with low-cost labor? And the ultimate question of power: Who is behind the decision to go to war?

C. Wright Mills (1956) took the position that the most important matters are not decided by lobbyists or even by Congress. Rather, the decisions that have the greatest impact on the lives of Americans—and people across the globe—are made by a **power elite.** As depicted in Figure 11.2 on the next page, the power elite consists of the top leaders of the largest corporations, the most powerful generals and admirals of the armed forces, and certain elite politicians—the president, his cabinet, and select senior members of Congress who chair the major committees. It is they who wield power, who make the decisions that direct the country and shake the world.

Are the three groups that make up the power elite—the top corporate, political, and military leaders—equal in power? Mills said they were not, but he

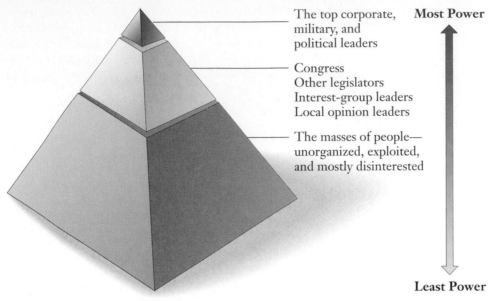

The top corporate, military, and political leaders — **Most Power**

Congress
Other legislators
Interest-group leaders
Local opinion leaders

The masses of people—
unorganized, exploited,
and mostly disinterested

Least Power

Source: Based on Mills 1956.

 11.2   **POWER IN THE UNITED STATES:
THE MODEL PROPOSED BY C. WRIGHT MILLS**

didn't point to the president and his staff or even to the generals and admirals as the most dominant group. The most powerful group, he said, is the corporate heads. Because all three segments of the power elite view capitalism as essential to the welfare of the country, business interests, he said, come foremost in setting national policy.

Sociologist William Domhoff (1990, 1998) uses the term *ruling class* to refer to the power elite. He focuses on the 1 percent of Americans who belong to the super-rich, the powerful capitalist class analyzed in Chapter 8. Members of this class control our top corporations and foundations, even the boards that oversee our major universities. It is no accident, says Domhoff, that from this group the president chooses most members of his cabinet and appoints ambassadors to the most powerful countries of the world.

Conflict theorists point out that we should not think of the ruling class (or power elite) as a group that meets together in order to agree on specific matters. Rather, it consists of people whose backgrounds and orientations to life are so similar—they attend prestigious private schools, belong to exclusive private clubs, and are millionaires many times over—that they share the same values and goals. Their behavior stems not from some grand con-

spiracy to control the country, but, from a mutual interest in solving the problems that face big business (Useem 1984). With their political connections extending to the top centers of power, this elite determines the economic and political conditions under which the rest of the country operates (Domhoff 1990, 1998).

Which View Is Right?

The functionalist and conflict views of power in U.S. society cannot be reconciled. Either competing interests block the dominance of any single group, as functionalists assert, or a power elite oversees the major decisions of the United States, as conflict theorists maintain. Perhaps at the middle level of Mills' model, depicted in Figure 11.2, the competing interest groups do keep each other at bay, and none is able to dominate. If so, the functionalist view would apply to this middle level, as well as to the lowest level of power. Perhaps functionalists have not looked high enough, however, and activities at the peak remain invisible to them. If so, on that level lies the key to U.S. power, the dominance by an elite whose members are following their mutual interests.

The answer, however, is not yet conclusive. For that, we must await more research.

THE ECONOMY: WORK IN THE GLOBAL VILLAGE

If you are like most students, you are wondering how changes in the economy are going to affect your chances of getting a good job. Let's see if we can shed some light on this question. Let's begin with this story:

> The sound of her alarm rang in Kim's ears. "Not Monday already," she groaned. "There must be a better way of starting the week." She pressed the snooze button on the clock (from Germany) to sneak another ten minutes' sleep. In what seemed like just thirty seconds, the alarm shrilly insisted she get up and face the week.

> Still bleary-eyed after her shower, Kim peered into her closet and picked out a silk blouse (from China), a plaid wool skirt (from Scotland), and leather shoes (from India). She nodded, satisfied, as she added a pair of simulated pearls (from Taiwan). Running late, she hurriedly ran a brush (from Mexico) through her hair. As Kim wolfed down a bowl of cereal (from the United States) topped with milk (from the United States), bananas (from Costa Rica), and sugar (from the Dominican Republic), she turned on her kitchen television (from Korea) to listen to the weather forecast.

> Gulping the last of her coffee (from Brazil), Kim grabbed her briefcase (from Wales), purse (from Spain), and jacket (from Malaysia), left her house, and quickly climbed into her car (from Japan). As she glanced at her watch (from Switzerland), she hoped the traffic would be in her favor. She muttered to herself as she pulled up at a stop light (from Great Britain) and eyed her gas gauge. She muttered again when she pulled into a station and paid for gas (from Saudi Arabia), for the price had risen over the weekend. "My paycheck never keeps up with prices," she moaned.

> When Kim arrived at work, she found the office abuzz. Six months ago, New York headquarters had put the company up for sale, but there had been no takers. The big news this Monday was that both a German and a Canadian corporation had put in bids over the weekend. No one got much work done that day, as the whole office speculated about how things might change.

> As Kim walked to the parking lot after work, she saw a tattered "Buy American" bumper sticker on the car next to hers. "That's right," she said to herself. "If people were more like me, this country would be in better shape."

THE TRANSFORMATION OF ECONOMIC SYSTEMS

Although this vignette may be slightly exaggerated, many of us are like Kim—we use a multitude of products from around the world, and yet we're concerned about our country's ability to compete in global markets. Today's **economy**—a system of producing and distributing goods and services—differs radically from those in all but our most recent past. The products Kim uses make it apparent that today's economy knows no national boundaries. To better understand how global forces affect the U.S. economy, let's begin with an overview of sweeping historical changes.

Preindustrial Societies: The Birth of Inequality

The earliest human groups, *hunting and gathering societies,* had a **subsistence economy.** Groups of perhaps twenty-five to forty people lived off the land. They gathered what they could find and moved from place to place as their food supply ran low. Because there was little or no excess food or other items, they did little trading with other groups. With no excess to accumulate, everybody possessed as much (or, really, as little) as everyone else.

Then people discovered how to breed animals and cultivate plants. This produced a surplus and ushered in social inequality. Due to the more dependable food supply in *pastoral and horticultural societies,* humans settled down in a single place. Their groups grew larger, and for the first time some individuals could devote their energies to tasks other than producing food. Some people became leather workers, others weapon makers, and so on. This new division of labor produced a surplus, and groups traded items with one another. The primary sociological significance of surplus and trade is this: They fostered *social inequality,* for some people accumulated more possessions than others. The effects of that change remain with us today.

The plow brought the next major change. It made land much more productive, allowing *agricultural societies* to develop. Even more people were freed from food production, and more specialized divisions of labor followed. Trade expanded, and trading centers developed. As trading centers turned into cities, power passed from the heads of families and clans to a ruling elite. The result was even greater social, political, and economic inequality.

One of the negative consequences of early industrialization in the West was the use of child labor. In the photo on the left, of the U.S. textile industry in the 1800s, you can see spindle boys at work in a Georgia cotton mill. Today's Least Industrialized Nations are experiencing the same negative consequence as they industrialize. The photo on the right shows boys at work in a contemporary textile factory in Varanas, India. About the only improvement is that the child workers in India are able to sit down as they exhaust their childhood.

Industrial Societies: The Birth of the Machine

The steam engine, invented in 1765, ushered in *industrial societies*. Based on machines powered by fuels, these societies created a surplus unlike anything the world had seen. This, too, stimulated trade among nations and brought even greater social inequality. A handful of individuals opened factories and exploited the labor of many.

As machines improved, surpluses increased, and the emphasis changed from producing goods to consuming them. In 1912, sociologist Thorstein Veblen coined the term **conspicuous consumption** to describe this fundamental change in people's orientations. By this term, Veblen meant that the Protestant ethic identified by Weber—an emphasis on hard work, savings, and a concern for salvation (discussed in Chapter 13)—was being replaced by an eagerness to show off wealth by the "elaborate consumption of goods."

Postindustrial Societies: The Birth of the Information Age

In 1973, sociologist Daniel Bell noted that *a new type of society was emerging*. This new society, which he called the *postindustrial society*, has six characteristics: (1) a service sector so large that most people work in it; (2) a vast surplus of goods; (3) even more extensive trade among nations; (4) a wider variety and quantity of goods available to the average person; (5) an information explosion; and (6) a "global village"—that is, the world's nations are linked by fast communications, transportation, and trade.

Figure 11.3 illustrates our transition to this new society, a change without parallel in human history. In the 1800s, most U.S. workers were farmers. Today, farmers make up only about 2 percent of the work force. To see why this transition came about, we can note that using the technology of the 1800s a typical farmer produced enough food for only five people. With today's powerful machinery and hybrid seeds, he or she now feeds about eighty. In 1940, about half of U.S. workers wore a blue collar; then changing technology shrank the market for blue-collar jobs. White-collar work continued its ascent, reaching the dominant position it holds today. This figure illustrates nothing less than the transition to a new society.

This change affects you directly. Because of the information explosion, for example, when you graduate from college, you will do some form of "knowledge

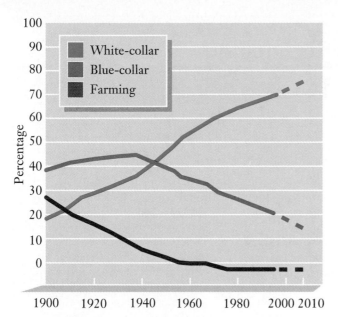

Note: From 1900 to 1940, "workers" refers to people age 14 and over, from 1970 to people age 16 and over. Broken lines are the author's projections.

 THE REVOLUTIONARY CHANGE IN THE U.S. WORK FORCE

Source: Statistical Abstract, various years, and 1999:Table 677.

work"—managing information, or designing, selling, or servicing products. Doing a different type of work has profound implications, for it produces different social networks, attitudes, and even ways of viewing the world.

Our new global village also has deep implications for your life. Think of the globe as divided into three large neighborhoods—the three worlds of industrialization we reviewed in Chapter 7. Due to political and economic arrangements, some nations are located in the poor part of the village. Their citizens barely eke out a living from menial work. Some even starve to death—while fellow villagers in the rich neighborhood feast on the best that the globe has to offer. It's the same village, but what a difference the neighborhood makes.

Now visualize any one of the three neighborhoods. Again you will see gross inequalities. Not everyone who lives in the poor neighborhood is poor, and some areas of the rich neighborhood are packed with poor people. Because the United States is the global economic leader, occupying the most luxurious mansion in the best neighborhood, let's look at U.S. trends.

Ominous Trends in the United States

The global village also means fierce global competition. Nike soccer balls and sports shoes can be made by U.S. workers at $20 an hour or by workers in a Least Industrialized Nation who earn $5 a day. To remain competitive in the global marketplace, U.S. multinational firms assign work where it is the cheapest (or most "cost effective," as they put it). Sometimes this means using child labor in India, but other times powerful U.S. machinery can spew out those same products even more cheaply.

The implications for U.S. workers (and those of Canada, Germany, France, and so on) are ominous. Waiting impatiently on the sidelines are millions upon millions of men, women, and children who are ready to work for a pittance. To reduce costs, U.S. firms are *"downsizing"* (a nice word for firing workers). In their place, they hire temporary workers, who can be released at will. This allows firms to bypass costly "frills," such as vacation pay and retirement sbenefits. Some analysts are concerned that these patterns may be permanent, that they foreshadow an era of easily discharged workers who live with insecurity, low pay, and few benefits. Related issues are explored in the Sociology and the New Technology box on the next page.

With cost, not education, their chief concern, even colleges and universities are following this pattern. When their full-time, better-paid teachers retire, they replace them with part-timers. Hired only to teach specific courses a semester at a time, these instructors are exempt from tenure, promotion, sick leave, and retirement benefits. Some of them are not even given offices where they can meet with their students. This might interfere with education, but it does cut down on the utility bill.

Another disturbing event is that many Americans find that their standard of living is stagnating or even declining. Social analysts Bennett Harrison and Barry Bluestone (1988) call this change the great American U-turn. Look at Figure 11.4 on page 289. The purple bars show current dollars, the dollars the average worker finds in his or her paycheck. From this, it appears that U.S. workers are making a lot more than they used to. They bring home *four* times as many dollars as workers did in 1970. Back in 1970 workers averaged only a little over $3 an hour; now it is over $13. The green bars, which show the *buying power* of these paychecks, strip away the illusion. They show that inflation has whittled

Sociology & the New Technology

NEW TECHNOLOGY AND THE RESTRUCTURING OF WORK: WHAT TYPE OF NEW SOCIETY?

The fear of being automated out of a job plagues many workers. They have seen machines displace people who worked at their side, the lucky ones getting "early retirement," the others nothing.

But does technology actually take away jobs? On the one hand, there is no doubt that technology causes job after job to become obsolete. On this score, the workers' fears are not irrational. The automobile industry makes about as many cars as it did 30 years ago, but it employs less than half as many production workers. The number of workers at U.S. Steel has dropped from 120,000 to just 20,000—yet production remains the same (Volti 1995). Computerized automation will continue to erase millions of U.S. manufacturing jobs.

But there is another side to the story, for technology also creates jobs. The automobile industry wiped out the livelihood of bicycle workers and stable hands, but it put tens of thousands more to work in the new steel and gasoline industries. These jobs are in addition to mechanics, salespeople, and advertisers, as well as the work done in the body shops that dot our landscape.

Each new technology, then, both destroys old jobs and creates new ones. Some of these jobs—as with the gasoline stations that automobiles require—are readily visible. Others are less evident. The technology that went into airplanes, for example, not only spawned pilots, mechanics, and reservation clerks, but also stimulated global tourism. To put this in a nutshell: *Most* of us work at jobs that did not even exist a hundred years ago.

And the future? New technologies are inevitable. The basic question is whether they will destroy jobs faster than they create them. In the past, when one sector shrank, another absorbed its displaced workers. Today, growth is in the knowledge sector. But can this elite of entrepreneurs, scientists, technicians, computer programmers, educators, and consultants absorb the hundreds of millions of workers worldwide who will lose their jobs due to the information revolution (Rifkin 1995)? Even that staunch defender of U.S. and global capitalism, the *Wall Street Journal,* reported that the U.S. economy isn't producing enough well-paying jobs to replace those lost to technology and trade (Davis 1996).

Although of fundamental significance for our welfare, the answer to this issue remains hidden in the future. For certain, we can't turn back the clock. The new technology is here to stay, and more will rapidly follow on its heels. Each will transform the shape of work—and, with it, our lives. Perhaps, as the optimists stress, the adjustment will be painful, but technology will see us through.

The reply of the pessimists, however, is haunting—that this time will be different. They see growing divisions in society. The technologically prepared will inhabit a technoparadise of abundance and leisure, while impoverished workers who have been dispossessed from the work force will survive in despair. Their children, seeing a hopeless future with bleak job opportunities, will produce a violent subculture. ■

For Your Consideration

What future do you think the country faces? In answering this, refer to the discussion in this chapter about the effects of the new technologies on work, the globalization of capitalism, and the growing power of the multinational corporations.

away the value of those dollars. Today's workers can't buy as much with their $13 as workers in 1970 could with their "measly" $3. The question is not "How could anyone live on just $3 an hour back in 1970?" but, rather, "How can you live on just $13 an hour today?"

As mentioned in the New Technology box above, an ominous trend is a growing gap between the "haves" and the "have-nots." The inverted pyramid shown in

Figure 11.5 provides a snapshot of how the nation's income is divided. Each rectangle represents a fifth of the U.S. population. At the top of the inverted pyramid is the proportion of the nation's income that goes to the nation's wealthiest fifth. The bottom shows the proportion going to the poorest fifth. Note that *47 percent* of the whole country's income goes to just one-fifth of Americans, while only *4 percent* goes to the poorest fifth.

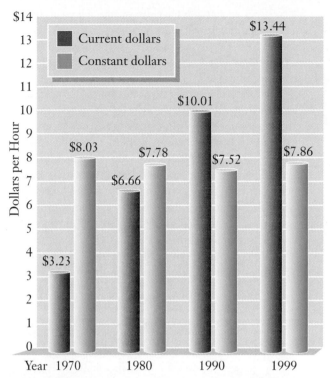

Note: "Constant dollars" means inflation-adjusted dollars.

 11.4

AVERAGE HOURLY EARNINGS OF U.S. WORKERS IN CURRENT AND CONSTANT (1982) DOLLARS

Source: Statistical Abstract 2000:Table 692; Bureau of Labor Statistics 2000: Table B4.

This gap is now greater than it has been in generations. Rather than bringing equality, then, the postindustrial economy has perpetuated the income inequalities of the industrial economy.

Another ominous trend is the U.S. national debt. The United States used to sell (export) more than it purchased (imported). Now, feeding a voracious, uncontrolled appetite, it imports much more than it exports (*Statistical Abstract* 1999:Table 1323). In addition, Americans are saving less. In 1980, Americans saved 7 percent of their income. Today it has dropped to just 1/2 percent (*Statistical Abstract* 1990:Table 700; 1999:Table 730).

Like an individual, if a nation spends more each year than it takes in, economic problems are inevitable. The United States used to be the world's largest creditor—now it is the world's largest debtor. The national debt is so huge that the U.S. government spends *more* on interest payments than it spends for all these programs: job training, science, education, space exploration, urban development, housing credits for the poor, environmental protection, and the entire justice system (*Statistical Abstract* 1999:Tables 543, 547). Paying these billions of dollars in interest leaves less money to invest in wages, education, factories, parks, or any of the things that increase a people's quality of life.

Some fear that we may end up with a *"two-thirds society"* (Glotz 1986). An upper third would consist of well-educated and prosperous technocrats who would be in charge. In the middle third would be workers who, though insecure in their jobs, earn an adequate income. At the bottom would be the unemployed and underemployed. This third of the population would consist of migrant workers, the physically and mentally handicapped, teenagers who can't find their way into the job market, and older people who have been pushed out of their jobs. Minorities would make up a disproportionate share of this bottom third.

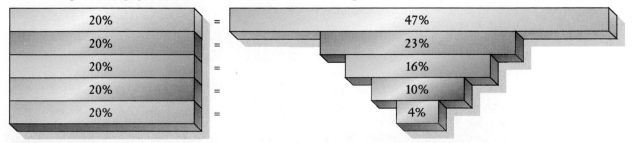

 11.5

THE INVERTED INCOME PYRAMID: THE PROPORTION OF INCOME RECEIVED BY EACH FIFTH OF THE U.S. POPULATION

Source: Statistical Abstract 1999:Table 751.

Table 11.2	
COMPARING SOCIALISM AND CAPITALISM	
Socialism	**Capitalism**
1. The public owns the means of production	1. Individuals own the means of production
2. Central committees plan production, no competition	2. The owners determine production, based on competition
3. No profit motive in the distribution of goods and services	3. The pursuit of profit is the reason for distributing goods and services.

World Economic Systems

To understand where the United States stands in the world economic order, let's compare capitalism and socialism, the two main economic systems in force today. (See Table 11.2 above.)

Capitalism

People who live in a capitalist society may not understand its basic tenets, though they see them reflected in their local shopping malls and fast-food chains. If we distill the many businesses of the United States to their basic components, we see that **capitalism** has three essential features: (1) *private ownership of the means of production* (individuals own the land, machines, and factories, and decide what they will produce); (2) *market competition* (an exchange of items between willing buyers and sellers); and (3) the pursuit of *profit* (selling something for more than it costs).

Many people believe that the United States is an example of pure capitalism. Pure capitalism, however, known as **laissez-faire capitalism** (literally, "hands off" capitalism), means that the government doesn't interfere in the market. Such is not the case in the United States. The current form of U.S. capitalism is **welfare** or **state capitalism.** Private citizens own the means of production and pursue profits, but they do so within a vast system of laws designed to protect the welfare of the population.

Suppose that you have discovered what you think is a miracle tonic: It will grow hair, erase wrinkles, and dissolve excess fat. If your product works, you will become an overnight sensation—not only a millionaire, but also the toast of the television talk shows.

Before you count your money—and your fame—you must reckon with **market restraints,** the laws and regulations of welfare capitalism that limit your capacity to produce and sell. First, you must comply with local and state rules. You must obtain a business license and a state tax number that allows you to buy your ingredients without paying sales taxes. Then come the federal regulations. You cannot simply take your product to local stores and ask them to sell it; you first must seek approval from federal agencies that monitor compliance with the Pure Food and Drug Act. This means you must prove that your product will not

This advertisement from 1885 represents an earlier stage of capitalism when individuals were free to manufacture and market products with little or no interference from the government. Today, the production and marketing of goods take place under detailed, complicated government laws and regulations.

cause harm to the public. In addition, you must be able to substantiate your claims—or else face being shut down by state and federal agencies that monitor the market for fraud. Your manufacturing process is also subject to state and local laws concerning cleanliness and to state and federal rules for the disposal of hazardous wastes.

Suppose that you overcome these obstacles, and your business prospers. Other federal agencies will monitor your compliance with regulations concerning racial, sexual, and disability discrimination, minimum wages, and Social Security taxes. State agencies will examine your records to see if you have paid unemployment taxes and sales taxes. Finally, the Internal Revenue Service will look over your shoulder and demand a share of your profits (up to 39.6 percent). In short, the highly regulated U.S. economic system is far from an example of laissez-faire capitalism.

Socialism

Socialism also has three essential components: (1) the public ownership of the means of production; (2) central planning; and (3) the distribution of goods without a profit motive.

In socialist countries, the government owns the means of production—not only the factories, but also the land, railroads, oil wells, and gold mines. Unlike capitalism, in which **market forces**—supply and demand—determine what will be produced and the prices that will be charged, a central committee decides that the country needs X number of toothbrushes, Y toilets, and Z shoes. The committee decides how many of each will be produced, which factories will produce them, what price will be charged for the items, and where they will be distributed.

Socialism is designed to eliminate competition, for goods are sold at predetermined prices regardless of the demand for an item or the cost to produce it. Profit is not the goal, nor is encouraging consumption of goods in low demand (by lowering the price), nor limiting the consumption of hard-to-get goods (by raising the price). Rather, the goal is to produce goods for the general welfare and to distribute them according to people's needs, not their ability to pay.

In a socialist economy, *everyone* in the economic chain works for the government. The members of the central committee who determine production goals are government employees, as are the supervisors who im-

plement their plans, the factory workers who produce the merchandise, the truck drivers who move it, and the clerks who sell it. Those who buy the items may work at different jobs—in offices, on farms, in day care centers—but they, too, are government employees.

Just as capitalism does not exist in a pure form, neither does socialism. Although the ideology of socialism calls for resources to be distributed according to need and not position, in line with the functionalist argument of social stratification presented in Chapter 8, socialist countries found it necessary to offer higher salaries for some jobs in order to entice people to take greater responsibilities. For example, in socialist countries factory managers always earned more than factory workers. By narrowing the huge pay gaps that characterize capitalist nations, however, socialist nations established considerably greater equality of income.

Dissatisfied with the greed and exploitation of capitalism and the lack of freedom and individuality of socialism, Sweden and Denmark developed **democratic socialism** (also called welfare socialism). In this form of socialism, both the state and individuals produce and distribute goods and services. The government owns and runs the steel, mining, forestry, and energy concerns, as well as the country's telephones, television stations, and airlines; remaining in private hands are the retail stores, farms, manufacturing concerns, and most service industries.

Ideologies of Capitalism and Socialism

Not only do capitalism and socialism have different approaches to producing and distributing goods, but also they represent distinct ideologies. *Capitalists* believe that market forces should determine both products and prices. They also believe that greed is good. It is healthy for people to strive after profits, for this stimulates them to develop new products. The Mass Media box on the next page examines how capitalists create demand for their products.

Socialists, in contrast, believe that profits are immoral. Karl Marx said that an item's value is based on the work that goes into it. Profit, then, is the *excess value* withheld from workers. The government should protect workers from this exploitation. To do so, it should own the means of production, using them not for profit, but to produce and distribute items according to people's needs, not their ability to pay.

Mass Media in Social Life

GREED IS GOOD—
SELLING THE AMERICAN DREAM

Advertising is such an integral part of our lives that being deluged with ads almost appears to be our natural state. We open a newspaper or magazine and expect to find pages that proclaim the virtues of products and firms. We turn on the television and are assailed with commercials for ten minutes of every half hour. Some social analysts even claim that the purpose of television is to round up an audience to watch the commercials, that the programs are mere diversions from the medium's real objective of selling products!

Advertising is so powerful that it can produce the desire to consume products for which we previously felt no need whatsoever. U.S. kitchens, filled with gadgets that slice and dice, attest to this power.

Advertising's power to make people gluttons goes beyond kitchen gadgets that are soon con-

signed to back drawers and garage sales. Many Americans would not think of going out in public without first shampooing, rinsing, conditioning, and blow-drying their hair. Many feel the need to apply an underarm deodorant so powerful that it overcomes the body's natural need to sweat. For many women, public appearance also demands the application of foundation, lipstick, eye shadow, mascara, rouge, powder, and perfume. For many men, after-shave lotion is essential. And only after covering the body with clothing that displays designer labels do Americans feel that they are presentable to the public.

Advertising influences not only what we put on our bodies, what we eat, and what we do for recreation, but also how we feel about ourselves. Our ideas of whether we are too fat, too skinny, too hippy, too buxom, whether our hair is too oily or too dry, our

body too hairy, or our skin too rough are largely a consequence of advertising. As we weigh our self-image against the idealized images that bombard us in our daily fare of commercials, we conclude that we are lacking something. Advertising assures us that there is salvation—some new product that promises to deliver exactly what we lack.

The approach is ingenious in its simplicity: Create discontent by presenting ideal images that are impossible to attain. And it works. We become dissatisfied with ourselves. And we snatch the advertisers' solution: We strive to consume more of the never-ending products that the corporations offer us, those they have decided we need.

The American Dream...built on greed, discontent, enticing images, and the promise of redemption. Of course, dreams often strangely juxtapose realities. ■

Adherents to these ideologies paint each other in such stark colors that *each sees the other as a system of exploitation.* Capitalists see socialists as violating basic human rights of freedom of decision and opportunity, while socialists see capitalists as violating the basic human right of freedom from poverty. With each side claiming moral superiority while viewing the other as a threat to its very existence, the last century witnessed the world split into two main blocs.

Criticisms of Capitalism and Socialism

The primary criticism leveled against capitalism is that it leads to social inequality. Capitalism, say its critics,

produces a tiny top layer of wealthy, powerful people who exploit a vast bottom layer of poorly paid workers. Those few who own the means of production reap huge profits, accrue power, and get legislation passed that goes against the public good.

The primary criticism leveled against socialism is that it does not respect individual rights (Berger 1991). Others (in the form of some government body) decide where people will work, live, and go to school. In China, they even decide how many children women may bear (Mosher 1983). Critics also argue that central planning is grossly inefficient and that socialism is not capable of producing much wealth. They say that its greater equality really amounts to giving almost everyone an equal chance to be poor.

The Convergence of Capitalism and Socialism

Regardless of the validity of these mutual criticisms, as nations industrialize they grow alike. They urbanize, produce similar divisions of labor (such as professionals and skilled technicians), and encourage higher education. Even similar values emerge (Kerr 1960, 1983). By itself, this tendency would make capitalist and socialist nations grow more alike, but another factor also brings them closer to one another (Form 1979): Despite their incompatible ideologies, both capitalist and socialist systems have adopted features of the other.

That capitalism and socialism are growing similar is known as **convergence theory.** This view points to a possible hybrid or mixed economy for the future. Convergence theory is supported by a fundamental change in socialist countries. Suffering from shoddy goods and plagued by shortages, their standard of living severely lagging behind the West, in the 1980s and 1990s Russia and China reinstated market forces. Making a profit—which had been a crime—was encouraged. Private ownership of property became respectable, and the state auctioned off many of its industries. They even invited their former archenemies, Western corporations, to open up shop.

Changes in capitalism also support this theory. The United States has adopted many socialist practices including extracting money from some to pay for benefits it gives to others. Examples include unemployment compensation (taxes paid by workers are distributed to those who no longer produce a profit); subsidized housing (shelter, paid for by the many, is given to the poor and elderly, with no motive of profit); welfare (taxes from the many are distributed to the needy); a minimum wage (the government, not the employer, determines the minimum that workers receive); and Social Security (the retired do not receive what they paid into the system, but, rather, money that the government collects from current workers). Such embrace of socialist principles means that the United States has produced its own version of a mixed type of economy.

Perhaps, then, convergence is unfolding before our very eyes. On the one hand, capitalists now assume that their system should provide workers at least minimal support during unemployment, extended illness, and old age. On the other hand, socialist leaders have reluctantly admitted that profit does motivate people to work harder.

$\mathcal{C}$APITALISM IN A GLOBAL ECONOMY

To understand today's capitalism, we need to consider the corporation within the context of a global economy.

Corporate Capitalism

The dominance of capitalism, which is driving today's global interdependence, is rooted in a social invention called the corporation. A **corporation** is a business that is treated in law as a person. It can make contracts, incur debts, sue and be sued. Its liabilities and obligations, however, are separate from those of its owners. For example, each shareholder of Ford Motor Company—whether he or she has 1 or 100,000 shares—owns a portion of the company. Ford, however, not its individual owners, is responsible for fulfilling its contracts and paying its debts. To indicate how corporations now dominate the economy, sociologists use the term **corporate capitalism.**

One of the most significant aspects of corporations is the *separation of ownership and management.* Unlike most businesses, it is not the owners, those who own the company's stock, who run the day-to-day affairs of the company (Walters 1995). Instead, managers run the corporation, and they are able to treat it *as though it were their own.* The result is the "ownership of wealth without appreciable control, and control of wealth without appreciable ownership" (Berle and Means 1932). Sociologist Michael Useem (1984) put it this way:

> When few owners held all or most of a corporation's stock, they readily dominated its board of directors, which in turn selected top management and ran the corporation. Now that a firm's stock [is] dispersed among many unrelated owners, each holding a tiny fraction of the total equity, the resulting power vacuum allow[s] management to select the board of directors; thus management [becomes] self-perpetuating and thereby acquire[s] de facto control over the corporation.

Because of this power vacuum, at their annual meeting stockholders ordinarily rubber-stamp management's recommendations. It is so unusual for this *not* to happen that when it does not it is called a **stockholders' revolt.** The irony of this term is generally lost, but remember that in such cases it is not the workers but the owners who are rebelling!

Interlocking Directorates The wealthy expand their power through **interlocking directorates**; that is, they serve as directors of several companies. Their fellow members on those boards also sit on the boards of other companies, and so on. Like a spider's web that starts at the center and then fans out in all directions, the top companies are interlocked into a network (Mintz and Schwartz 1985). The chief executive officer of a firm in England, who sits on the board of directors of half a dozen other companies, noted,

> If you serve on, say, six outside boards, each of which has, say, ten directors, and let's say out of the ten directors, five are experts in one or another subject, you have a built-in panel of thirty friends who are experts who you meet regularly, automatically each month, and you really have great access to ideas and information. You're joining a club, a very good club. (Useem 1984)

Multinational Corporations

The two Social Maps on these pages illustrate how corporations have outgrown their national boundaries. The world map shows the investments that U.S. corporations have made in other countries. Cross-border investments are not a one-way street, however, as the U.S. map shows: About 1 of every 20 U.S. businesses is owned by people in other countries.

As **multinational corporations**—corporations that operate across national borders—do business, they become more and more detached from the interests and values of their country of origin. A U.S. executive made this revealing statement, "The United States does not have an automatic call on our resources. There is no mind-set that puts the country first" (Kennedy 1993). These global giants move investments and production from one part of the globe to another—with no concern for consequences other than profits. How their adding—or withdrawing—investments affects workers is of no concern to them. With profit their moral guide, the conscience of multinational corporations is dominated by dollar signs.

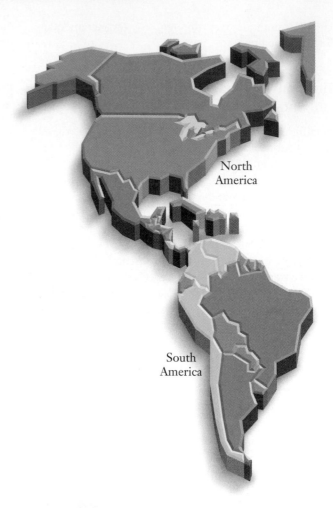

North America

South America

SOCIAL MAP: THE GLOBALIZATION OF CAPITALISM: U.S. OWNERSHIP IN OTHER COUNTRIES

Source: Statistical Abstract 1999:Table 1317.

Multinational corporations have become a powerful political force, one that is reshaping the globe as no army has ever been able to do. Although we have started to take the presence of multinational corporations for granted—as well as their cornucopia of products—their power and presence are new to the world scene. It is possible that an unintended consequence of the globalization of capitalism will be a New World Order. Let's consider this possibility.

A New World Order?

Today we see the world's nations almost frantically embracing capitalism. Underlying this fury is the worldwide

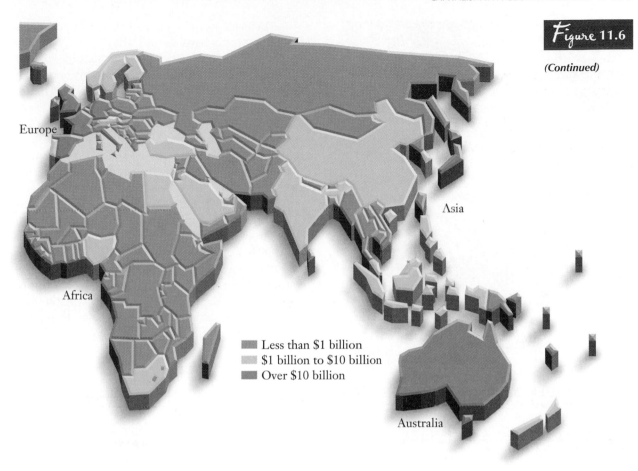

Figure 11.6

(Continued)

Europe

Asia

Africa

Less than $1 billion
$1 billion to $10 billion
Over $10 billion

Australia

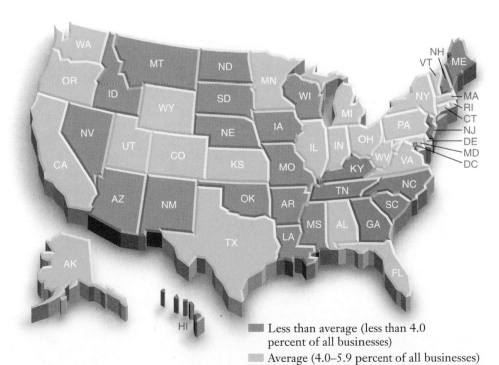

Figure 11.7

**SOCIAL MAP:
THE GLOBALIZATION
OF CAPITALISM:
FOREIGN OWNERSHIP
OF U.S. BUSINESS**

Source: Statistical Abstract 1999:
Table 1314.

Less than average (less than 4.0
percent of all businesses)
Average (4.0–5.9 percent of all businesses)
More than average (6 percent or
more of all businesses)

As capitalism globalizes, it is not just the products but also the cultures of the dominant capitalist nations that are exported around the world. As the premier producer and exporter of images, Hollywood makes a global impact. Shown here in Xian, China, is what has become a global icon.

flow of information, capital, and goods that we have been discussing. Perhaps the most significant consequence of this frenzied pursuit of profits, however, will be an unintended bonus: world peace.

Let's consider firm trends. The United States, Canada, and Mexico have formed the North American Free Trade Association (NAFTA), to which all of South America may eventually belong. Argentina and some other South American countries have adopted the dollar as an official currency, even as their national currency coexists alongside it. In a giant and unprecedented step, most European countries have formed an economic and political unit (the European Union, or EU). They have adopted a cross-national currency, the Euro, which will replace their marks, francs, liras, and pesetas. A single military appears on the horizon. Already, the EU has established a "rapid reaction force" of 60,000 troops under a unified command (Krauthammer 1999).

Underlying these economic and political events is the triumph of capitalism. As the multinational corporations expand, the pressure for profits will stimulate more trade agreements. To forge them, and to solidify their interlocking interests, the corporate elites court national elites, those who wield power within a country. In exchange for access to a country's workers, natural resources, and markets, the corporate elites give the national elites cash, credit, and armaments that help them to stay in power. This process of mutual back rubbing may ultimately interlace the business and political elites of the world's nations into a single cooperative system. If so, far removed from the tribal loyalties of national boundaries, the regional—and eventually global—trade agreements forged by the multinational corporations may well become a force for peace.

With the world yearning for peace, such economic and political unity carries strong seductive surface appeal. It is likely to come at a high price, however. If our new world order is dominated by a handful of corporate leaders, our everyday life with Big Brother could be like that of Winston and Julia in our opening vignette.

ＳUMMARY AND ＲEVIEW

■ Power, Authority, and Violence

How are authority and coercion related to power?

Authority is **power** that people view as legitimately exercised over them, while **coercion** is power they consider unjust. The

state is a political entity that claims a monopoly on violence over some territory. Pp. 274–275.

What kinds of authority are there?

Max Weber identified three types of authority. Power in **traditional authority** derives from custom—patterns set down in the past are the rules for the present. Power in **rational-legal authority** (also called *bureaucratic authority*) is based on law and written procedures. In **charismatic authority,** power is based on loyalty to an individual to whom people are attracted. Charismatic authority, which undermines traditional and rational-legal authority, has built-in problems in transferring authority to a new leader. Pp. 275–277.

■ Types of Government

How are the types of government related to power?

In a **monarchy,** power is based on hereditary rule; in a **democracy,** power is given to the ruler by citizens; and in a **dictatorship,** power is seized by an individual or small group. Pp. 277–280.

■ The U.S. Political System

What are the main characteristics of the U.S. political system?

The United States has two main political parties, each trying to win the center of the political spectrum. Voter turnout is higher among people who are more socially integrated, those who sense a greater stake in the outcome of elections, such as the more educated and well-to-do. **Lobbyists** and **special-interest groups,** such as **political action committees (PACs),** play a significant role in U.S. politics. Pp. 280–283.

■ Who Rules the United States?

Is the United States controlled by a ruling class?

In a view known as **pluralism,** functionalists say that no one group holds power, that the country's many competing interest groups balance one another. Conflict theorists, who focus on the top level of power, say that the United States is governed by a **power elite,** a ruling class made up of the top corporate, military, and political leaders. At this point, the matter is not settled. Pp. 283–284.

■ The Transformation of Economic Systems

How are economic systems linked to types of societies?

The earliest societies (hunting and gathering) were subsistence economies: Small groups lived off the land and produced little or no surplus. Economic systems grew more complex as people discovered how to domesticate and cultivate (pastoral and horticultural societies), farm (agricultural societies), and manufacture (industrial societies). Each of these methods allowed people to produce a surplus, which fostered trade. Trade, in turn, brought social inequality as some people began to accumulate more than others. Pp. 285–289.

■ World Economic Systems

How do the major economic systems differ?

The world's two major economic systems are capitalism and socialism. In **capitalism,** private citizens own the means of production and pursue profits. In **socialism,** the state owns the means of production and determines production with no goal of profit. Adherents of each have developed ideologies that defend their own system and paint the other as harmful. Following **convergence theory,** in recent years each system has adopted features of the other. Pp. 290–293.

■ Capitalism in a Global Economy

What is the role of the corporation in global capitalism?

The term **corporate capitalism** indicates that giant corporations dominate capitalism. The profit goal of **multinational corporations** removes their allegiance from any particular nation. The global expansion of capitalism due to new technology, accompanied by the trend toward larger political unions, may indicate that a world political order is developing. This may bring world peace, but perhaps at a high cost of personal freedom. Pp. 293–296.

Where can I read more on this topic?

Suggested readings for this chapter are listed on page SR-8.

YOUR INTERACTIVE COMPANION WEB SITE

Your Interactive Companion Web Site includes practice tests, with feedback, and online learning activities with video, audio, and Weblinks. Your access code for this Web site is provided with this text.

GLOSSARY

anarchy a condition of lawlessness or political disorder caused by the absence or collapse of governmental authority (p. 283)

authority power that people accept as rightly exercised over them (p. 274)

capitalism an economic system characterized by the private ownership of the means of production, the pursuit of profit, and market competition (p. 290)

charismatic authority authority based on an individual's outstanding traits, which attract followers (p. 275)

checks and balances separation of powers among the three branches of U.S. government—legislative, executive, and judicial—so that each is able to nullify the actions of the others, thus preventing the domination of any single branch (p. 283)

citizenship the concept that birth (and residence) in a country impart basic rights (p. 278)

city-state an independent city whose power radiates outward, bringing the adjacent area under its rule (p. 277)

coercion power that people do not accept as just (p. 274)

conspicuous consumption Thorstein Veblen's term for a change from the Protestant ethic to an eagerness to show off wealth by the elaborate consumption of goods (p. 286)

convergence theory the view that as both capitalist and socialist economic systems adopt features of the other, a hybrid (or mixed) economic system will emerge (p. 293)

corporate capitalism the domination of the economic system by giant corporations (p. 293)

corporation the joint ownership of a business enterprise, whose liabilities and obligations are separate from those of its owners (p. 293)

democracy a system of government in which authority derives from the people (p. 277)

democratic socialism a hybrid economic system in which capitalism is mixed with state ownership (p. 291)

dictatorship a form of government in which power is seized by an individual (p. 278)

direct democracy a form of democracy in which voters meet together to discuss and decide issues (p. 277)

economy a system of distribution of goods and services (p. 285)

interlocking directorates individuals serving on the board of directors of several companies (p. 294)

laissez-faire capitalism unrestrained manufacture and trade (literally "hands off" capitalism) (p. 290)

lobbyists people who try to influence legislation on behalf of their clients or interest groups (p. 282)

market forces the law of supply and demand (p. 291)

market restraints laws and regulations that govern the manufacture and sale of products (p. 290)

monarchy a form of government headed by a king or a queen (p. 277)

multinational corporations companies that operate across national boundaries (p. 294)

oligarchy a form of government in which power is held by a small group; the rule of the many by the few (p. 278)

pluralism diffusion of power among many interest groups, preventing any single group from gaining control of the government (p. 283)

political action committees (PACs) an organization formed by one or more special-interest groups to solicit and spend funds for the purpose of influencing legislation (p. 282)

power the ability to get your way, even over the resistance of others (p. 274)

power elite C. Wright Mills' term for the top leaders of U.S. corporations, military, and politics who make the nation's major decisions (p. 283)

rational-legal authority authority based on law or written rules and regulations (also called bureaucratic authority) (p. 275)

representative democracy a form of democracy in which voters elect representatives to make decisions on their behalf (p. 278)

routinization of charisma the transfer of authority from a charismatic leader to either a traditional or a rational-legal form of authority (p. 277)

socialism an economic system characterized by the public ownership of the means of production, central planning, and the distribution of goods without a profit motive (p. 291)

special-interest group people who share views on a particular issue and who can be mobilized for political action (p. 282)

state a government; the political entity that claims a monopoly on the use of violence within a territory (pp. 274, 277)

stockholders' revolt the refusal of a corporation's stockholders to rubber-stamp decisions made by its managers (p. 294)

subsistence economy a type of economy in which human groups live off the land with little or no surplus (p. 285)

totalitarianism a form of government that exerts almost total control over the people (p. 278)

traditional authority authority based on custom (p. 275)

universal citizenship the idea that everyone has the same basic rights by virtue of being born in a country (or by immigrating and becoming a naturalized citizen) (p. 278)

voter apathy indifference and inaction with respect to the political process (p. 282)

welfare (or state) capitalism an economic system in which individuals own the means of production but the state regulates many economic activities for the welfare of the population (p. 290)

Chapter 12

Ralph Fasanella, Family Supper, 1972

Marriage and Family

"**H**old still. We're going to be late," said Sharon as she tried to put shoes on 2-year-old Michael, who kept squirming away.

Finally succeeding with the shoes, Sharon turned to 4-year-old Brittany, who was trying to pull a brush through her hair. "It's stuck, Mom," Brittany said.

"Well, no wonder. Just how did you get gum in your hair? I don't have time for this, Brittany. We've got to leave."

Getting to the van fifteen minutes behind schedule, Sharon strapped the kids in and then herself. Just as she was about to pull away, she remembered that she had not checked the fridge for messages.

"Just a minute, kids. I'll be right back."

Running into the house, she frantically searched for a message from Tom. She vaguely remembered him mumbling something about being held over at work. She grabbed the Post-It and ran back to the van.

"He's picking on me," complained Brittany when her mother climbed back in.

"Oh, shut up, Brittany," Sharon said. "He's only 2. He can't pick on you."

"Yes, he did," Brittany said, crossing her arms defiantly, as she stretched out her foot to kick her brother's seat.

"Oh, no! How did Mikey get that smudge on his face? Did you do that, Brit?"

Polygyny = more than one wife
Polyyandry = more than one husband

Brittany crossed her arms again, pushing out her lips in her classic pouting pose.

As Sharon drove to the day care center, she tried to calm herself. "Only two more days of work this week, and then the weekend. Then I can catch up on housework and have a little relaxed time with the kids. And Tom can finally cut the lawn and buy the groceries," she thought. "And maybe we'll even have time to make love. Boy, that's been a long time."

At a traffic light, Sharon found time to read Tom's note. "Oh, no. That's what he meant. He has to work Saturday. Well, there go those plans."

What Sharon didn't know was that her boss also had made plans for Sharon's Saturday. And that their emergency Saturday babysitter wouldn't be available. And that the van would break down on the way home from work. That Michael was coming down with chicken pox. That Brittany would follow next. That... ■

Marriage and Family in Global Perspective

To better understand U.S. patterns of marriage and family, let's first look at how customs differ around the world. This will give us a context for interpreting our own experiences in this vital social institution.

What Is a Family?

"What is a family, anyway?" asked William Sayres (1992) at the beginning of an article on this topic. By this question, he meant that although the family is so significant to humanity that it is universal—every human group in the world organizes its members in families—the world's cultures display so much variety that the term *family* is difficult to define. For example, although the Western world regards a family as a husband, wife, and children, other groups have family forms in which men have more than one wife (**polygyny**) or women more than one husband (**polyandry**). How about the obvious? Can we define the family as the approved group into which children are born? This would overlook the Banaro of New Guinea. In this group a young woman must give birth before she can marry, and she *cannot* marry the father of her child (Murdock 1949).

And so it goes. For just about every element you might consider essential to marriage or family, some group has a different custom. Even the sex of the bride and groom may not be what you expect. Although in almost every instance the bride and groom are female and male, there are exceptions. In some Native Ameri-

Often one of the strongest family bonds is that of mother–daughter. The young artist, an eleventh grader, wrote: "This painting expresses the way I feel about my future with my child. I want my child to be happy and I want her to love me the same way I love her. In that way we will have a good relationship so that nobody will be able to take us apart. I wanted this picture to be alive; that is why I used a lot of bright colors."

can tribes, for example, a man or woman who wanted to be a member of the opposite sex went through a ceremony (*berdache*) and was *declared* a member of the opposite sex. Not only did the "new" man or woman do the tasks associated with his or her new sex, but also the individual was allowed to marry. In this instance, the husband and wife were of the same biological sex. In the contemporary world, Denmark (in 1989), Norway (in 1993), Sweden (in 1995), and Holland (in 1998) have legalized same-sex marriages.

Such remarkable variety means settling for a broad definition. A **family** consists of people who consider themselves related by blood, marriage, or adoption. A **household,** in contrast, consists of all people who occupy the same housing unit—a house, apartment, or other living quarters.

We can classify families as **nuclear** (husband, wife, and children) and **extended** (including people such as grandparents, aunts, uncles, and cousins in addition to the nuclear unit). Sociologists also refer to the **family of orientation** (the family in which an individual grows up) and the **family of procreation** (the family formed when a couple have their first child). Finally, regardless

of its form, **marriage** can be viewed as a group's approved mating arrangements—usually marked out by a ritual of some sort (the wedding) to indicate the couple's new public status.

Common Cultural Themes

Despite this diversity, several common themes do run through the concepts of marriage and family. As Table 12.1 illustrates, all societies use marriage and family to establish patterns of mate selection, descent, inheritance, and authority. Let's look at these patterns.

Mate Selection Each human group establishes norms to govern who marries whom. Norms of **endogamy** specify that people should marry within their own group. Groups may prohibit interracial marriages, for example. In contrast, norms of **exogamy** specify that people must marry outside their group. The best example is the **incest taboo,** which prohibits sex and marriage among designated relatives. In some societies these norms are written into law, but in most cases they are informal. For example, in the United States most whites marry whites

Table 12.1

COMMON CULTURAL THEMES:
MARRIAGE IN TRADITIONAL AND INDUSTRIALIZED SOCIETIES

Characteristic	Traditional Societies	Industrialized (and Postindustrialized) Societies
What is the structure of marriage?	*Extended* (marriage embeds spouses in a large kinship network of explicit obligations)	*Nuclear* (marriage brings fewer obligations toward the spouse's relatives)
What are the functions of marriage?	Encompassing (see the six functions listed on p. 304)	More limited (many functions are fulfilled by other social institutions)
Who holds authority?	Highly *patriarchal* (authority is held by males)	Although some patriarchal features remain, authority is more evenly divided
How many spouses at one time?	Most have one spouse (*monogamy*), while some have several (*polygamy*)	One spouse
Who selects the spouse?	The spouse is selected by the parents, usually the father	Individuals choose their own spouse
Where does the couple live?	Couples most commonly reside with the groom's family (*patrilocal residence*), less commonly with the bride's family (*matrilocal residence*)	Couples establish a new home (*neolocal residence*)
How is descent figured?	Most commonly figured from male ancestors (*patrilineal* kinship), less commonly from female ancestors (*matrilineal* kinship)	Figured from male and female ancestors equally (*bilateral kinship*)
How is inheritance figured?	Rigid system of rules; usually patrilineal, but may be matrilineal	Highly individualistic; usually bilateral

nuclear = husband + wife + children

In 1937, Mary Frances Grimes, an 11-year-old bride, and her 67-year-old husband, William H. Grimes, received national publicity. Married "in the woods" near Neelyville, Missouri, the bride said that she regretted the marriage and did not "love anyone but my doll." Is this an example of gender age, as symbolic interactionists might say? Or, as conflict theorists would say, of gender exploitation?

and most African Americans marry African Americans—not because of any laws but because of informal norms.

Descent How are you related to your father's father or to your mother's mother? The explanation is found in your society's **system of descent,** the way people trace kinship over generations. To us, a **bilateral system** seems logical—and natural—for we think of ourselves as related to *both* our mother's and father's side of the family. "Doesn't everyone?" you might ask. Interestingly, this is only one logical way to reckon descent. In a **patrilineal system,** descent is traced only to the father's side, and children are not considered related to their mother's relatives. In a **matrilineal system,** descent is figured only on the mother's side, and children are not considered related to their father's relatives.

Inheritance Marriage and family—in whatever form is customary in a society—are also used to compute rights of inheritance. In the bilateral system, property is passed to both males and females, in the patrilineal system only to males, and in the matrilineal system (the

rarest form) only to females. Each system matches a people's ideas of justice and logic.

Authority Historically, some form of **patriarchy,** a social system in which men dominate women, has formed a thread that runs through all societies. Contrary to what many think, there are no historical records of a true **matriarchy,** a social system in which women as a group dominate men as a group. Our marriage and family customs, then, developed within a framework of patriarchy. Although U.S. family patterns are becoming more *egalitarian,* or equal, many of today's customs still point to their patriarchal origin. Naming patterns, for example, reflect patriarchy. Despite recent trends, the typical bride still takes the groom's last name; children, too, usually receive the father's last name.

MARRIAGE AND FAMILY IN THEORETICAL PERSPECTIVE

A global perspective reveals that human groups have chosen many forms of mate selection, ways to trace descent, and so on. Although these patterns are arbitrary, each group sees its own forms of marriage and family as natural. Now let's see what picture emerges when we apply the three sociological theories.

The Functionalist Perspective: Functions and Dysfunctions

Functionalists stress that to survive, a society must meet certain basic needs, or functions. When functionalists look at family, they examine how it is related to other parts of society, especially how the family contributes to the well-being of society.

Why the Family Is Universal Functionalists note that although the form of marriage and family varies from one group to another, the family is universal because it fulfills six needs that are basic to the survival of every society. These needs, or functions, are (1) economic production, (2) socialization of children, (3) care of the sick and aged, (4) recreation, (5) sexual control, and (6) reproduction. To make certain that these functions are performed, every human group has adopted some form of the family.

Functions of the Incest Taboo Functionalists note that the incest taboo helps families avoid *role confusion.* This, in turn, facilitates the socialization of children. For example, if father-daughter incest were allowed, how should a wife treat her daughter—as a daughter, as a subservient second wife, or even as a rival? Should the daughter act toward her mother as her mother, as the first wife, or as a rival? Would her father be a father or a lover? And would the wife be the husband's main wife, a secondary wife—or even the "mother of the other wife" (whatever role that might be)? Maternal incest would also lead to complications every bit as confusing as these.

Another function of the incest taboo is to force people to look outside the family for marriage partners. Anthropologists theorize that *exogamy* was especially functional in tribal societies, for it forged alliances between tribes that otherwise might have killed each other off. Today, exogamy extends a bride's and groom's social networks beyond the nuclear family by building relationships with the spouse's family.

Isolation and Emotional Overload Functionalists also analyze dysfunctions that arise from the relative isolation of the nuclear family. Unlike extended families, which are enmeshed in kinship networks, members of nuclear families can count on fewer people for material and emotional support. This makes nuclear families vulnerable to "emotional overload." That is, the stress that comes with crises such as the loss of a job—or even the routine pressures of a harried life, as depicted in our opening vignette—is spread around fewer people. This places greater strain on each family member. In addition, the relative isolation of the nuclear family makes it vulnerable to a "dark side"—incest and various other forms of abuse, matters we examine later in this chapter.

The Conflict Perspective: Gender and Power

As you recall, central to conflict theory is the struggle over scarce resources. The recurring struggle over who does housework is actually a struggle over limited resources—time, energy, and the leisure to pursue interesting activities.

Most men resist doing housework. As Figure 12.1 shows, even wives who work outside the home full time end up doing most of it. The lesser effort that husbands make seems so great to them, however, that even when his wife does almost all the cooking and cleaning, the husband is likely to see himself as splitting the work fifty-fifty (Galinsky et al. 1993). Things are so one-sided that wives are *eight* times more likely to feel that the division of housework is unfair (Sanchez 1994).

And no wonder. Wives who put in an eight-hour day of working for wages average eleven hours more child care and housework each week than their husbands (Bianchi and Spain 1996). *Incredibly, this is the equivalent of twenty-four 24-hour days a year.* Sociologist Arlie Hochschild (1989) calls this the working wife's "second shift." To stress the one-sided nature of the second shift, she quotes this satire by Garry Trudeau in the *Doonesbury* comic strip:

> A "liberated" father is sitting at his word processor writing a book about raising his child. He types, "Today I wake up with a heavy day of work ahead of me. As Joannie gets Jeffry ready for day care, I ask her if I can be relieved of my usual household responsibilities for the day. Joannie says, 'Sure, I'll make up the five minutes somewhere.'"

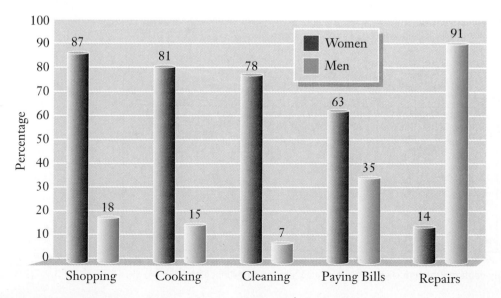

Figure 12.1

IN TWO-PAYCHECK MARRIAGES, WHO HAS MORE RESPONSIBILITY FOR HOUSEWORK?

Source: Galinsky et al. 1993.

Not surprisingly, the burden of the second shift creates deep discontent among wives (Risman 1998). These problems, as well as how wives and husbands cope with them, are discussed in the following Thinking Critically section.

Thinking *Critically*

THE SECOND SHIFT— STRAINS AND STRATEGIES

To find out what life is like in two-paycheck families, for nine years sociologist Arlie Hochschild (1989) and her research associates interviewed and reinterviewed fifty-some families. Hochschild also did participant observation with a dozen of them. She "shopped with them, visited friends, watched television, ate with them, and came along when they took their children to day care."

Hochschild notes that women have no more time in a day now than when they stayed home, but now there is twice as much to get done. Most wives and husbands in her sample felt that the *second shift*—the household duties that follow the day's work for pay—is the wife's responsibility. But as they cook, clean, and take care of the children after their job at the office or factory, many wives feel tired, emotionally drained, and resentful. Not uncommonly, these feelings show up in the bedroom, where the wives show a lack of interest in sex.

It isn't that men do nothing around the house. But since they see household responsibilities as the wife's duty, they "help out" when they feel like it—or when they get nagged into it. And since most of us prefer to tend to our children than to clean house, men are more likely to "help out" on the second shift by taking children to do "fun" things—to see movies, or to go for outings in the park. In contrast, the woman's time with the children is more likely to be "maintenance"—feeding and bathing them, taking them to the doctor, and so on.

The strains from working the second shift affect not only the marital relationship, but also the wife's self-concept. Here is how one woman tried to lift her flagging self-esteem:

> After taking time off for her first baby, Carol Alston felt depressed, "fat," and that she was "just a housewife." For a while she became the supermarket shopper who wanted to call down the aisles, "I'm an MBA! I'm an MBA!"

Most wives feel strongly that the second shift should be shared, but many feel it is hopeless to try to get their husbands to change. They work the second shift, but they resent it. Others have a "showdown" with their husbands. Some even give an ultimatum, "It's share the second shift, or it's divorce." Still others try to be the "supermom" who can do it all.

Some men cooperate and cut down on their commitment to a career. Others cut back on movies, seeing friends, doing hobbies. Most men, however, engage in what Hochschild describes as "strategies of resistance." She identified the following:

Waiting it out. Many men never volunteer to do housework. Since many wives dislike asking because it feels like "begging," this strategy often works. Some men make this strategy even more effective by showing irritation or becoming glum when they are asked, discouraging the wife from asking again.

Playing dumb. When they do housework, some men become incompetent. They can't cook rice without burning it; when they go to the store, they forget grocery lists; they can never remember where the broiler pan is. Hochschild did not claim that husbands do these things on purpose, but, rather, by withdrawing their mental attention from the task, they "get credit for trying and being a good sport"—but in such a way that they are not chosen next time.

ARLO & JANIS ® by Jimmy Johnson

The cartoonist has beautifully captured the reduction of needs strategy discussed by Hochschild.

Needs reduction. An example of this strategy is a father of two who explained that he never shopped because he didn't "need anything." He didn't need to iron his clothes because he "[didn't] mind wearing a wrinkled shirt." He didn't need to cook because "cereal is fine." As Hochschild observed, "Through his reduction of needs, this man created a great void into which his wife stepped with her 'greater need' to see him wear an ironed shirt…and cook his dinner."

Substitute offerings. Expressing appreciation to the wife for being so organized that she can handle both work for wages and the second shift at home can be a substitute for helping—and subtle encouragement for her to keep on working the second shift. ■

For Your Consideration

Hochschild (1991) is confident such problems can be resolved. Based on the materials just presented,

1. Identify the underlying *structural* causes of the problem of the second shift.
2. Based on your answer to number 1, identify *structural* solutions to this problem.
3. Determine how a working wife and husband might best reconcile this problem.

The Symbolic Interactionist Perspective: Gender and Housework

As noted in Chapter 1, symbolic interactionists focus on the meanings that people give their experiences. Let's apply this perspective to some surprising findings about husbands and housework.

The first finding is probably what you expect—the closer a husband's and wife's earnings, the more likely they are to share housework. Although husbands in such marriages don't share housework equally, they share more than other husbands. This finding, however, may be surprising: When husbands get laid off, most *decrease* their housework. *And husbands who earn less than their wives do the least housework.*

How can we explain this? It would seem that husbands who get laid off or who earn less than their wives would want to balance things out by doing more around the house, not less. Researchers suggest that the key is gender role. If a wife earns more than her husband, it threatens his masculinity—he takes it as a sign that he has failed in his traditional gender role of provider. To do housework—"women's work" in his eyes—threatens it even further. By avoiding housework, he "reclaims" his masculinity (Hochschild 1989; Brines 1994).

THE FAMILY LIFE CYCLE

Thus far we have seen that the forms of marriage and family vary widely, and we have examined marriage and family from the three sociological perspectives. Now let's discuss love, courtship, and the family life cycle.

Love and Courtship in Global Perspective

Until recently, social scientists thought that romantic love originated in western Europe during the medieval period (Mount 1992). When anthropologists William Jankowiak and Edward Fischer (1992) surveyed the data available on 166 societies around the world, they found that this was not so. **Romantic love**—people being sexually attracted to one another and idealizing the other—showed up in 88 percent (147) of these groups. The role of love, however, differs sharply from one society to another. As the Cultural Diversity box on the next page details, for example, Indians don't expect love to occur until *after* marriage—if then.

Because love plays such a significant role in Western life—and often is thought to be the *only* proper basis for marriage—social scientists have probed this concept

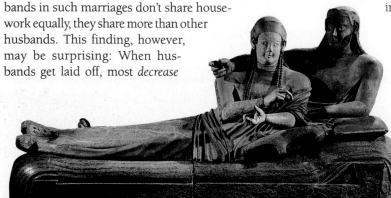

Romantic love reaches far back into history, as illustrated by this Etruscan sarcophagus. The Etruscans, who reached their peak of civilization in 500 B.C. in what is now Italy, were conquered by Rome about one hundred years later. The artist has portrayed the couple's mutual affection and satisfaction.

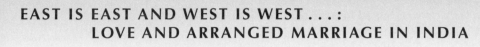

CULTURAL DIVERSITY Around the World

EAST IS EAST AND WEST IS WEST . . . : LOVE AND ARRANGED MARRIAGE IN INDIA

After Arun Bharat Ram returned to India with a degree from the University of Michigan, his mother announced that she wanted to find him a wife. Arun would be a good "catch" anywhere: 27 years old, well educated, well mannered, handsome, and—incidentally—heir to a huge fortune.

Arun's mother already had someone in mind. Manju came from a solid, middle-class family and was also a college graduate. Arun and Manju met in a coffee shop in a luxury hotel—along with both sets of parents. He found her pretty and quiet. He liked that. She was impressed that he didn't boast about his background.

After four more meetings, one where the two young people met by themselves, the parents asked their children if they were willing to marry. Neither had any major objections.

The Prime Minister of India and fifteen hundred other guests came to the wedding.

"I didn't love him," Manju says. "But when we talked, we had a lot of things in common." She then adds,

"But now I couldn't live without him. I've never thought of another man since I met him."

Although India has undergone extensive social change, Indian sociologists estimate that about 95 percent of marriages are still arranged by the parents. Today, however, as with Arun and Manju, couples have veto power over their parents' selection. Another innovation is that the couple are allowed to talk to each other before the wedding—unheard of just a generation ago.

Why does India have arranged marriages, and why does this practice persist today, even among the educated and upper classes? We can also ask why the United States has such an individualistic approach to marriage. A search for the answer to these questions takes us to a basic sociological principle: *A group's marriage practices match its values and patterns of social stratification.* Individual mate selection matches U.S. values of individuality and independence, while arranged marriages match the Indian value of children's deference to parental authority. Arranged marriages also reaffirm caste lines by channeling marriage within the same caste.

To Indians, to practice unrestricted dating would be to trust important matters to inexperienced young people. It would encourage premarital

sex, which, in turn, would break down family lines. (Virginity at marriage assures the upper castes that they know the fatherhood of the children.) Consequently, Indian young people are socialized to think that parents have cooler heads and superior wisdom in these matters. In the United States, family lines are less important, and caste is an alien concept.

Even ideas of love differ. For Indians, love is a peaceful emotion, based on long-term commitment and devotion to family. Indians also think of love as something that can be "created" between two people. To do so, one needs to arrange the right conditions. Marriage is one of those right conditions.

Thus, Indian and U.S. cultures have produced different approaches to love and marriage. *For Indians, marriage produces love—while for Americans, love produces marriage.* Americans see love as having a mysterious element, a passion that suddenly seizes an individual. Indians see love as a peaceful feeling that develops when a man and a woman are united in intimacy and share common interests and goals in life. ■

Source: Based on Cooley 1962; Gupta 1979; Weintraub 1988; Bumiller 1992; Sprecher and Chandak 1992; Whyte 1992; Dugger 1998.

---

with the tools of the trade: laboratory experiments, questionnaires, interviews, and systematic observations. One of the more interesting experiments was conducted by psychologists Donald Dutton and Arthur Aron, who discovered that fear breeds love (Rubin 1985). Across a rocky gorge, about 230 feet above the Capilano River in North Vancouver, a rickety footbridge sways in the wind. Another footbridge, a solid structure, crosses only ten feet

above a shallow stream. An attractive woman approached men who were crossing these bridges and told them she was studying "the effects of exposure to scenic attractions on creative expression." She showed them a picture, and they wrote down their associations. The sexual imagery in their stories showed that the men on the unsteady, frightening bridge were more sexually aroused than the men on the solid bridge. More of these men also called the young woman afterward—supposedly to get information about the study.

This research, of course, was really about sexual attraction, not love. The point, however, is that romantic love usually begins with sexual attraction. We find ourselves sexually attracted to someone and spend time with that person. If we discover mutual interests, we may label our feelings "love." Apparently, then, romantic love has two components. The first is emotional, a feeling of sexual attraction. The second is cognitive, a label that we attach to our feelings. If we do attach this label, we describe ourselves as being "in love."

Marriage

In the typical case, marriage in the United States is preceded by "love," but contrary to folklore, whatever love is, it certainly is not blind. That is, love does not hit anyone willy-nilly, as if Cupid had shot darts blindly into a crowd. If it did, marital patterns would be unpredictable. An examination of who marries whom, however, reveals that love is socially channeled.

The Social Channels of Love and Marriage The most highly predictable social channels are age, education, social class, race, and religion. For example, a Latina with a college degree whose parents are both physicians is likely to fall in love with and marry a Latino slightly older than herself who has graduated from college. Similarly, a female high school dropout whose parents are on welfare is likely to fall in love with and marry a man who comes from a background similar to hers.

Sociologists use the term **homogamy** to refer to the tendency of people with similar characteristics to marry one another. Homogamy occurs largely as a result of *propinquity,* or spatial nearness. That is, we tend to "fall in love" and marry people who live near us or whom we meet at school, church, or work. The people with whom we associate are far from a random sample of the population, for social filters produce neighborhoods, schools, and churches that follow racial-ethnic and social class lines.

As with all social patterns, there are exceptions. Although 94 percent of Americans who marry choose someone of their same race, 6 percent do not. Because there are 55 million married couples in the United States, those 6 percent add up, totaling three and a half million couples.

One of the more dramatic changes in U.S. marriage is a sharp increase in interracial marriages. We can trace this change back to the norm-shattering 1960s. Among the many changes ushered in during this period was a

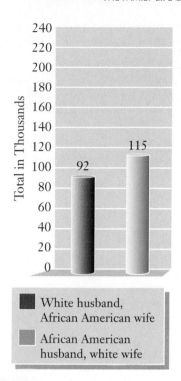

Figure 12.2

THE RACIAL BACKGROUND OF HUSBANDS AND WIVES IN MARRIAGES BETWEEN WHITES AND AFRICAN AMERICANS

Source: Statistical Abstract 2000:Table 54.

breaking of the "color line" in courtship. As you can see from Figure 12.2, interracial marriages also show distinct patterns.

Childbirth

Marital Satisfaction Sociologist Martin Whyte (1992), who interviewed wives in the Detroit area, found that marital satisfaction usually *decreases* with the birth of a child. To understand why, recall from Chapter 5 that a dyad (just two persons) provides greater intimacy than a triad (after adding a third person, interaction must be shared). To move from the theoretical to the practical, think about the implications for marriage of coping with a fragile newborn's 24-hour-a-day needs of being fed, soothed, and diapered—while having less sleep, less free time, and heavier expenses.

Social Class Sociologist Lillian Rubin (1976, 1992b) compared fifty working-class couples with twenty-five middle-class couples. She found that social class made a significant difference in how couples adjust to the arrival of children. For the average working-class couple, the first baby arrived just nine months after marriage. They hardly had time to adjust to being husband and wife before they were thrust into the demanding roles of mother and father. The result was financial problems, bickering, and interference from in-laws. The young husbands weren't ready to "settle down," and they resented getting less attention from their wives. A working-class husband who became a father just five months after getting married made a telling remark to Rubin when he said, "There I was, just a kid myself, and I finally had someone to take care of me. Then suddenly, I had to take care of a kid, and she was too busy with him *to take care of me*" (italics added).

In contrast, the middle-class couples postponed the birth of their first child, which gave them more time to adjust to each other. On average, their first baby arrived three years after marriage. Their greater financial resources also worked in their favor, making life a lot easier and marriage more pleasant.

Child Rearing

Who's minding the kids while the parents are at work? A while back such a question would have been ridiculous, for the mother was at home taking care of the chil-

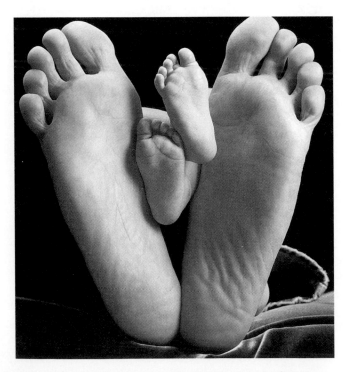

No adequate substitute has been found for the family. Although its form and functions vary around the world, the family remains the primary socializer of children.

dren. As with Sharon in our opening vignette, however, that assumption no longer holds. With three of five U.S. mothers working for wages, who is taking care of the children?

Married Couples and Single Mothers Figure 12.3 compares the child care arrangements of married couples and single mothers. As you can see, their overall child care arrangements are similar. For each group, about one of three preschoolers is cared for in the child's home. The main difference is the role of the child's father while the mother is at work. For married couples, almost one of four children is cared for by the father, while for single mothers this plummets to only one of fourteen. As you can see, grandparents step in to help fill the gap left by the absent father.

Day Care As Figure 12.3 shows, about one of six children is in day care. The broad conclusions of research on day care were reported in Chapter 3. Apparently, only a minority of U.S. day care centers offer high-quality care as measured by stimulating learning activities, safety, and emotional warmth (Bergmann 1995). A primary reason for this dismal situation is the abysmal salaries paid to day care workers, which average less than $10,000 a year (Casper and O'Connell 1997; *Statistical Abstract* 1999:Table 1300).

It is difficult for parents to judge the quality of day care, since they don't know what takes place when they are not there. The Internet is providing an innovative solution to some parents' nagging fears that their children might be neglected or even abused. Closed circuit television cameras pipe images onto the Web. Parents at work can visit via cyberspace each room of the day care center, monitoring their toddler's activities and care (Rabinovitz 1997).

Social Class Social class makes a huge difference in child rearing. Sociologist Melvin Kohn (1963, 1977; Kohn and Schooler 1969) found that parents socialize their children into the norms of their work worlds. Because members of the working class are more closely supervised and are expected to follow explicit rules, their concern is less with their children's motivation and more with their outward conformity. They are more apt to use physical punishment. In contrast, middle-class parents, who are expected to take more initiative on the job, are more concerned that their children develop curiosity, self-expression, and self-control. They are also more likely to withdraw privileges or affection than to use physical punishment.

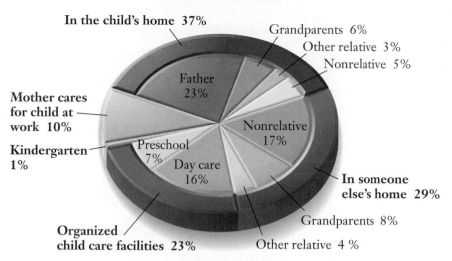

MARRIED COUPLES

In the child's home 37%
Grandparents 6%
Other relative 3%
Nonrelative 5%
Father 23%
Mother cares for child at work 10%
Kindergarten 1%
Preschool 7%
Day care 16%
Nonrelative 17%
In someone else's home 29%
Grandparents 8%
Other relative 4 %
Organized child care facilities 23%

Figure 12.3

WHO TAKES CARE OF PRESCHOOLERS WHILE THEIR MOTHERS ARE AT WORK?

Source: O'Connell 1993.

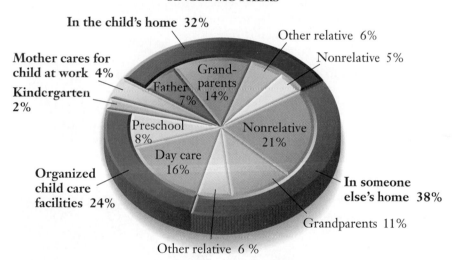

SINGLE MOTHERS

In the child's home 32%
Other relative 6%
Nonrelative 5%
Mother cares for child at work 4%
Kindergarten 2%
Father 7%
Grand-parents 14%
Preschool 8%
Day care 16%
Nonrelative 21%
Organized child care facilities 24%
In someone else's home 38%
Grandparents 11%
Other relative 6 %

Birth Order Birth order is also important. Parents tend to discipline their firstborns more than their later children, and to give them more attention. When the second child arrives, the firstborn competes to remain the focus of attention. Researchers suggest that this instills in firstborns a greater drive for success, which is why they are more likely than their siblings to earn higher grades in school, to go to college, and to go further in college. Firstborns are even more likely to become astronauts, to appear on the cover of *Time* magazine, and to become president of the United States. Although subsequent children may not go as far, most are less anxious about being successful, and more relaxed in their relationships (Snow et al. 1981; Goleman 1985; Storfer 2000). Firstborns are also more likely

to defend the status quo and to support conservative causes, laterborns to upset the apple cart and to support liberal causes (Sulloway 1997).

Although such tendencies are strong, they are only that—tendencies. Some firstborns are liberal, while others are conservative on some issues and liberal on others (Freese et al. 1999). *There are no inevitable outcomes of birth order, social class, or any other social characteristic.*

The Family in Later Life

The later stages of family life bring their own pleasures to be savored and problems to be solved. Let's look at the empty nest and widowhood.

The Empty Nest When the last child leaves home, the husband and wife are left, as at the beginning of their marriage, "alone together." This situation, sometimes called the **empty nest,** is thought to signal a difficult time of adjustment for women, because they have devoted so much energy to a child-rearing role that is now gone. Sociologist Lillian Rubin (1992a), who interviewed both career women and homemakers, found that this picture is largely a myth. Contrary to the stereotype, she found that women's satisfaction generally *increases* when the last child leaves home. A typical statement was made by a 45-year-old woman, who leaned forward in her chair as though to tell Rubin a secret:

> To tell you the truth, most of the time it's a big relief to be free of them, finally. I suppose that's awful to say. But you know what, most of the women I know feel the same way. It's just that they're uncomfortable saying it because there's all this talk about how sad mothers are supposed to be when the kids leave home.

Similar findings have come from other researchers, who report that most mothers feel relieved at being able to spend more time on themselves. Many couples also report a renewed sense of intimacy at this time (Mackey and O'Brien 1995). This closeness appears to stem from four causes: The couple is free of the many responsibilities of child rearing, they have more leisure, their income is at its highest, and they have fewer financial obligations.

The Not-So-Empty Nest An interesting twist on leaving home has taken place in recent years. With prolonged education and the higher cost of establishing a household, U.S. children are leaving home later. In addition, many who strike out on their own find the cost or responsibility too great and return to the home nest. As a result, 53 percent of all U.S. 18- to 24-year-olds live with their parents, and one of eight 25- to 34-year-olds is still living at home (*Statistical Abstract* 1997:Table 65).

Widowhood Women are more likely than men to become widowed and to have to face the wrenching problems this entails. Not only does the average wife live longer than her husband, but also she has married a man older than herself. The death of a spouse tears at the self, clawing at identities that had merged through the years. Now that the one who had become an essential part of the self is gone, the survivor, as in adolescence, is forced once again to wrestle with the perplexing question "Who am I?"

When death is unexpected, the adjustment is more difficult (Hiltz 1989). Survivors who know that death is impending make preparations that smooth the transition—from arranging finances to psychologically preparing themselves for being alone. Saying good-bye and cultivating treasured last memories help them to adjust to the death of an intimate companion.

Diversity in U.S. Families

It is important to note that there is no such thing as *the* American family. Rather, family life varies widely throughout the United States. The significance of social class, noted earlier, will continue to be evident as we examine diversity in U.S. families.

African American Families

Note that the heading reads "African American *families,*" not "*The* African American family." There is no such thing as *the* African American family, any more than there is *the* white family or *the* Latino family. The primary distinction is not between African Americans and

There is no such thing as *the* African American family, any more than there is *the* Native American, Asian American, Latino, or Irish American family. Rather, each racial-ethnic group has different types of families, with the primary determinant being social class.

This African American family is observing Kwanzaa, a new festival that celebrates their African heritage. Can you explain how Kwanzaa is an example of *ethnic work,* a concept introduced in Chapter 9?

other groups, but between social classes. Because African Americans who are members of the upper class follow the class interests reviewed in Chapter 8—preservation of privilege and family fortune—they are especially concerned about the family background of those whom their children marry (Gatewood 1990). To them, marriage is viewed as a merger of family lines. Children of this class marry later than children of other classes.

Middle-class African American families focus on achievement and respectability. Both husband and wife are likely to work outside the home. Their concerns are that the family stay intact and that their children go to college, get good jobs, and marry well—that is, marry people like themselves, respectable and hardworking, who want to get ahead in school and pursue a successful career.

African American families in poverty face all the problems that cluster around poverty (Wilson 1996; Liebow 1999; Anderson 2001). Because the men are likely to have few skills and to be unemployed, it is difficult for them to fulfill the cultural roles of husband and father. Consequently, these families are likely to be headed by a woman and to have a high rate of births to single women. Divorce and desertion are also more common than among other classes. Sharing scarce resources and

"stretching kinship" are primary survival mechanisms. That is, people who have helped out in hard times are considered brothers, sisters, or cousins, to whom one owes obligations as though they were blood relatives (Stack 1974). Sociologists use the term *fictive kinship* to refer to this stretching of kinship.

From Figure 12.4, you can see that, compared with other groups, African American families are less likely to be headed by married couples and more likely to be headed by women. Because of a *marriage squeeze*—an imbalance in the sex ratio, in this instance fewer unmarried men per 100 unmarried women—African American women are more likely than other racial-ethnic groups to marry men who are less educated than themselves, who are unemployed, or who are divorced (South 1991).

Latino Families

As Figure 12.4 shows, the proportion of Latino families headed by married couples and women falls in between that of whites and African Americans. The effects of social class on families, just sketched, also apply to Latinos. In addition, families differ by country of origin. Families from Cuba, for example, are more likely to be headed

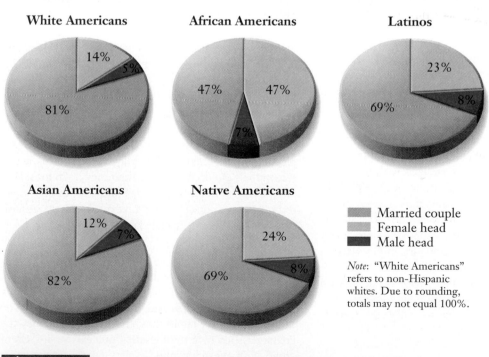

Figure 12.4 **FAMILY STRUCTURE: THE PERCENTAGE OF U.S. HOUSEHOLDS HEADED BY MEN, WOMEN, AND MARRIED COUPLES**

Source: Statistical Abstract 1999:Tables 54, 74.

Although there is no such thing as *the* Latino family, in general, Latinos place high emphasis on extended family relationships.

by a married couple than are families from Puerto Rico (*Statistical Abstract* 1999:Table 55).

What really distinguishes Latino families, however, is culture—especially the Spanish language, the Roman Catholic religion, and a strong family orientation coupled with a disapproval of divorce. Although there is some debate among the experts, another characteristic seems to be **machismo**—an emphasis on male strength and dominance. In Chicano families (those originating from Mexico), the husband-father plays a stronger role than in either white or African American families (Vega 1990). Machismo apparently decreases with each generation in the United States (Hurtado et al. 1992). In general, however, the wife-mother makes most of the day-to-day decisions for the family and does the routine disciplining of the children. She usually is more family centered than her husband, displaying more warmth and affection for her children.

Generalizations have limits, of course, and as with other ethnic groups individual Latino families vary considerably from one another (Baca Zinn 1994; Carrasquillo 1994).

Asian American Families

As you can see from Figure 12.4 on the previous page, the structure of Asian American families is almost identi-

cal to that of white families. Apart from this broad characteristic, because Asian Americans come from twenty countries, their family life varies considerably, reflecting their many cultures. In addition, as with Latino families, the more recent their immigration, the closer their family life reflects the family life of their country of origin (Kibria 1993; Glenn 1994).

Despite such differences, sociologist Bob Suzuki (1985), who studied Chinese American and Japanese American families, identified several distinctive characteristics. Although Asian Americans have adopted the nuclear family, they have retained Confucian values that provide a distinct framework for family life: humanism, collectivity, self-discipline, hierarchy, respect for the elderly, moderation, and obligation. Obligation means that each individual owes respect to other family members and is responsible to never bring shame on the family. Asian Americans tend to be more permissive than Anglos in child rearing and more likely to use shame and guilt rather than physical punishment to control their children's behavior.

Native American Families

Perhaps the single most significant issue that Native American families face is whether to follow traditional values or to assimilate (Yellowbird and Snipp 1994). This primary distinction makes for vast differences among families. The traditionals speak native languages and emphasize distinctive Native American values and beliefs. Those who have assimilated into the broader culture do not.

Figure 12.4 (on page 313) depicts the structure of Native American families. You can see how it is almost identical to that of Latinos. In general, Native American parents are permissive with their children and avoid physical punishment. Elders play a much more active role in their children's families than they do in most U.S. families: They not only provide child care, but they also teach and discipline children. Like others, Native American families differ by social class.

■ **In Sum** From this brief review, you can see that race-ethnicity signifies little for understanding family life. Rather, social class and culture hold the keys. The more resources a family has, the more it assumes the characteristics of a middle-class nuclear family. Compared with the poor, middle-class families have fewer children, have fewer unmarried mothers, and place greater emphasis on educational achievement and deferred gratification.

One-Parent Families

One-parent families have become a matter of general concern. They are discussed by TV talk show hosts and politicians alike. The increase in the number of one-parent families is no myth. Since 1970, the number of one-parent families has tripled, while the number of two-parent families has decreased by 250,000 (*Statistical Abstract* 1995:Table 71; 1999:Table 77). Two primary reasons underlie this change. The first is the high divorce rate, which each year forces a million children from two-parent homes to one-parent homes (*Statistical Abstract* 1999:Table 159). The second is the sharp increase in births to women who are not married. Overall, 32 percent of U.S. children are born to unmarried women (*Statistical Abstract* 1999:Table 99).

The primary reason for the concern, however, may have less to do with children being reared by one parent than with most one-parent families being poor. This poverty is not a coincidence. Most one-parent families are headed by women. Although 90 percent of children of divorce live with their mothers, most divorced women earn less than their former husbands. And most mothers who have never married have little education and few marketable skills, which condemns them to bouncing from one minimum-wage job to another, with welfare sandwiched in between.

To understand the typical one-parent family, then, we need to view it through the lens of poverty; for that is its primary source of strain. The results are serious, not just for these parents and their children, but for society as a whole. Children from single-parent families are more likely to drop out of high school, to get arrested, to have emotional problems, and to get divorced (McLanahan and Sandefur 1994; Menaghan et al. 1997). If female, they are more likely to bear children while still unmarried teenagers. The cycle of poverty is so powerful that *nearly half* of all welfare recipients are current or former teenage parents (Corbett 1995).

Families Without Children

Overall, about 14 percent of U.S. married couples never have children (*Statistical Abstract* 1999:Table 109). The percentage varies by education. The more education a woman has, the more likely she is to expect to bear no children. Race-ethnicity is also significant, and Latinas are much less likely to expect to remain childless than are white and African American women.

Why do some couples choose to not have children? Sociologist Kathleen Gerson (1985) found that some women see their marriage as too fragile to withstand the strains that a child would bring. Other women believe they would be stuck at home—bored, lonely, with dwindling career opportunities. Many couples see a child as too expensive. Perhaps the most common reason, though, is summarized by this statement in a newsletter:

> We are DINKS (dual incomes, no kids). We are happily married. I am 43, my wife is 42. We have been married for almost twenty years. . . . Our investment strategy has a lot to do with our personal philosophy. "You can have kids—or you can have everything else."

With trends firmly in place—more education and careers for women; abortion; technological advances in contraception; the high cost of rearing children; and an emphasis on possessing more and more material things—the proportion of women who never bear children is likely to increase.

Many childless couples, however, are not childless by choice. Some adopt, while a few turn to the solutions featured in the New Technology box on the next page.

Blended Families

An increasingly significant type of family in the United States is the **blended family,** one whose members once were part of other families. Two divorced people who marry and each bring their children into a new family unit become a blended family. With divorce common, millions of children spend some of their childhood in blended families. One result is more complicated family relationships. Consider this description written by one of my students:

> I live with my dad. I should say that I live with my dad, my brother (whose mother and father are also my mother and father), my half sister (whose father is my dad, but whose mother is my father's last wife), and two stepbrothers and stepsisters (children of my father's current wife). My father's wife (my current stepmother, not to be confused with his second wife, who, I guess, is no longer my stepmother) is pregnant, and soon we all will have a new brother or sister. Or will it be a half brother or half sister?
>
> If you can't figure this out, I don't blame you. I have trouble myself. It gets very complicated around Christmas. Should we all stay together? Split up and go to several other homes? Who do we buy gifts for, anyway?

Gay and Lesbian Families

In 1989, Denmark became the first country to legalize marriage between people of the same sex. Since then, Holland, Norway, and Sweden have made same-sex marriages

Sociology & the New Technology

THE BRAVE NEW WORLD OF HIGH-TECH REPRODUCTION: WHERE TECHNOLOGY OUTPACES LAW AND SOMETIMES COMMON SENSE

Jaycee has five parents—or none, depending on how you look at it. The story goes like this. Luanne and John Buzzanca were infertile. Although they spent more than $100,000 on treatments, nothing worked. Then a fertility clinic mixed an anonymous donor's sperm with an egg that had been surgically removed from a woman, who also remained anonymous. A surgeon implanted the feritilized egg in Pamela Snell, who gave birth to Jaycee (Davis 1998a; Foote 1998).

Her job as surrogate mother completed, Pamela handed Jaycee over to Luanne, who was waiting at her beside. Luanne's husband, John, would have been there, but he had filed for divorce just a month before.

Luanne asked John for child support. John refused, and Luanne sued. The judge ruled that John didn't have to pay. He said that because Jaycee had been conceived in a petri dish with an egg and sperm from anonymous donors, John wasn't the baby's father. The judge added that Luanne wasn't the baby's mother either.

Five parents—or none? Welcome to the brave—and very real—new world of high-tech reproduction. Although most children conceived with the aid of high-tech procedures claim only two parents, reproductive technologies have made such scenarios a nightmare for the unsuspecting. ■

For Your Consideration

In our new, high-tech world, what's a mother? Is Pamela Snell, who gave birth to Jaycee, a mother? Strangely, she is not. Is the donor of the egg a mother? Biologically, yes, but legally, no. Is Luanne a mother? Fortunately, for Jaycee's sake, a higher court ruled that she is.

What's a father? Consider this case. Elizabeth Higgins of Jacksonville, Indiana, had difficulty conceiving. She gave eggs to Memorial Hospital. Her husband gave sperm. A hospital technician mixed someone else's sperm with Mrs. Higgins' eggs. The fertilized eggs were implanted in Mrs. Higgins, who gave birth to twin girls. Mrs. Higgins is white, her husband black. Mr. Higgins was bothered because the girls had only Caucasian features, and he couldn't bond with them. Mr. and Mrs. Higgins separated. They sued the hospital for child support, arguing that the hospital, not Mr. Higgins, is the father (Davis 1998b).

If a hospital can be a father in this brave new world, then what's a grandparent? A man in New Orleans donated sperm to a fertility clinic. He died, and his girlfriend decided to be artificially inseminated with his sperm. The grieved parents of the man were upset that their son, although dead, could still father children. They also feared that those children, who would be their grandchildren, would have a legal claim to their estate (Davis 1998b).

How would you apply common sense to these many cases?

The McCaughey septuplets of Carlisle, Iowa, with their parents, Bobby and Kenny, and their three-year-old sister, Mikayla.

legal. In 2000, Vermont became the first state to legalize what they call "gay unions." Except for the name, "gay unions" are marriages. Partners are treated as married couples for purposes of inheritance, property transfers, medical decisions, insurance, and state income taxes. If they want to split up, they must go through "dissolution" proceedings in Family Court. By retaining the term "marriage" for heterosexual couples, Vermont legislators hoped to soften criticism of its pathbreaking law. This didn't work, and across the state Vermonters protested. If other states follow Vermont's lead, it seems inevitable that some will use the term marriage to refer to same-sex unions.

What are gay marriages like? As with everything else in life, same-sex couples cannot be painted with a single brush stroke. As with opposite-sex couples, social class is significant, and orientations to life differ according to education, occupation, and income. Sociologists Blumstein and Schwartz (1985) interviewed same-sex couples and found their main struggles to be housework, money, careers, problems with relatives, and sexual adjustment—the same problems that face heterosexual couples. Same-sex couples are more likely to break up, however, and one argument for legalizing gay marriages is that these relationships will become more stable.

TRENDS IN U.S. FAMILIES

As is apparent from this discussion, patterns of marriage and family life in the United States are undergoing a fundamental shift. Other indicators of this change, which we shall now examine, include the postponement of marriage, cohabitation, single motherhood, divorce, and remarriage.

Postponing Marriage

Figure 12.5 below illustrates one of the most significant trends in U.S. marriages. As you can see, the average age of first-time brides and grooms declined from 1890 to about 1950. In 1890 the typical first-time bride was 22, but by 1950 she had just left her teens. For about twenty years there was little change. Then in 1970 the average age started to increase sharply. *Today's average first-time bride is older than at any other time in U.S. history.* The average age of first-time grooms is back to where it was in 1890.

Since postponing marriage is today's norm, it may come as a surprise to many readers to learn that most U.S. women used to marry before they turned 25. Look

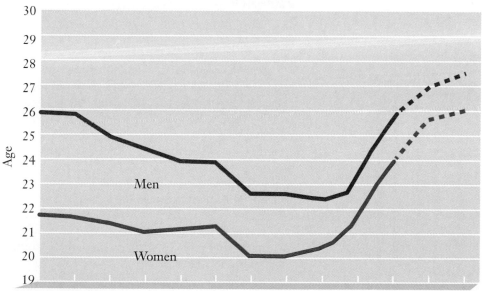

The broken lines are the author's estimates.

 THE MEDIAN AGE AT WHICH AMERICANS MARRY FOR THE FIRST TIME

Source: Statistical Abstract 1999:Table 158.

at Figure 12.6. You can see that the percentage of younger Americans who have not married has soared. The percentage of unmarried women is now about *double* what it was in 1970.

Why did this change occur? As sociologist Larry Bumpass points out, if we were to count cohabitation, we would find that this average age has changed little (Bumpass et al. 1991). Although Americans have postponed the age at which they first marry, they have *not* postponed the age at which they first set up housekeeping with someone of the opposite sex. Let's look at this trend in cohabitation.

Cohabitation

Figure 12.7 shows the remarkable increase in **cohabitation**, adults living together in a sexual relationship without being married. *Eight times* more Americans are cohabiting today than did so 30 years ago. Forty-one percent of U.S. women have cohabited (*Statistical Abstract* 1999:Table 66). (Although the source does not give totals for men, it must be similar.) With this change in behavior have come changed attitudes. For example, when hiring executives, some corporations now pay for live-in partners to attend orientation sessions.

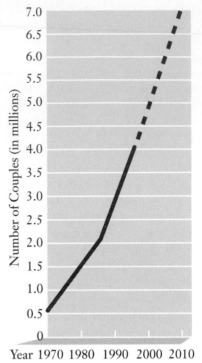

Note: Broken lines indicate the author's estimates.

Figure 12.7 **COHABITATION IN THE UNITED STATES**

Source: Statistical Abstract 1995:Table 60; 1999:Table 68.

Commitment is the essential difference between cohabitation and marriage. Whereas the assumption of marriage is permanence, cohabiting couples agree to remain together for "as long as it works out." Marriage requires public vows—and a judge to authorize its termination. Cohabitation requires only that a couple move in together; if the relationship sours, they can move out. Sociologists have found that couples who cohabit before marriage are more likely to divorce than couples who do not first cohabit (Bennett et al. 1988; Whyte 1992). The reason, they conclude, is that cohabiting couples have a weaker commitment to marriage and to relationships.

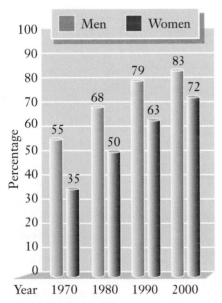

Year 2000 is the author's estimate.

Figure 12.6 **AMERICANS AGES 20–24 WHO HAVE NEVER MARRIED**

Source: Statistical Abstract 1993:Table 60; 1999:Table 63.

Unmarried Mothers

Earlier we discussed the steady increase in births to U.S. single women. To better understand this trend, we can place it in global perspective. As Figure 12.8 shows, the United States is not alone in this increase. Of the ten in-

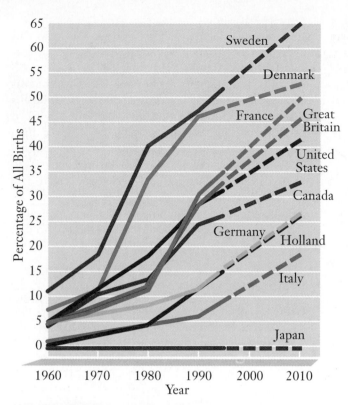

Figure 12.8 BIRTHS TO UNMARRIED WOMEN IN TEN INDUSTRIALIZED NATIONS

Source: Statistical Abstract 1993:Table 1380; 1998:Table 1347.

dustrial nations for which we have data, all except Japan have experienced sharp increases in births to unmarried mothers. Far from the highest, the U.S. rate falls in the middle third of these nations.

From this figure, it seems fair to conclude that industrialization sets in motion social forces that encourage out-of-wedlock births. There are several problems with this conclusion, however. Why was the rate so low in 1960? Industrialization had been in process for many decades prior to that time. Why are the rates in the bottom four nations only a fraction of those in the top two nations? Why does Japan's rate remain so consistently low? Why are Sweden's and Denmark's so high? With but a couple of minor exceptions, the ranking of these nations today is the same as in 1960. By itself, then, industrialization is too simple an answer. A fuller explanation must focus on customs and values embedded within these cultures. For that answer, we will have to await further research.

The Sandwich Generation and Elder Care

The *sandwich generation* refers to people who find themselves sandwiched between two generations, responsible for both their children and their own aging parents. Typically between the ages of 40 and 55, these people find themselves pulled in two strongly compelling directions. Feeling responsible for both their children and their parents, they are plagued with guilt and anger because they can be in only one place at a time (Shellenbarger 1994a).

Concerns about elder care have gained the attention of the corporate world, and about 25 percent of large companies offer elder care assistance to their employees (Hewitt Associates 1995). This assistance includes seminars, referral services, and flexible work schedules designed to help employees meet their responsibilities without missing so much work (Shellenbarger 1994b). Some experts believe that companies may respond more positively to the issue of elder care than to child day care. Why? Most CEOs are older men whose wives stayed home to take care of their children, so they don't understand the stresses of balancing work and child care. Nearly all have aging parents, however, and many have faced the turmoil of trying to cope with work, family, and aging parents.

With people living longer, this issue is likely to become increasingly urgent.

DIVORCE AND REMARRIAGE

The topic of family life would not be complete without considering divorce. Let's first try to determine how much divorce there really is.

Problems in Measuring Divorce

You probably have heard that the U.S. divorce rate is 50 percent, a figure that is popular with reporters. The statistic is true in the sense that each year about half as many divorces are granted as there are marriages performed. In 1999, for example, 2,334,000 U.S. couples married and 1,175,000 couples divorced ("Population Update" 2000, 2001).

With these statistics, what is wrong with saying that the divorce rate is 50 percent? The real question is why these two totals should be compared in the first place. The couples who divorced do not—with rare exceptions—come from the group who married that year. The one figure has *nothing* to do with the other, so these statistics in no way establish the divorce rate.

What figures should we compare, then? Couples who divorce are drawn from the entire group of married people in the country. Since the United States has 55,000,000 married couples, and only 1,135,000 of them obtained divorces in 1998, the divorce rate is 2.1 percent, not 50 percent. A couple's chances of still being married at the end of a year are 98 percent—not bad odds—and certainly much better odds than the mass media would have us believe. As the Social Map below shows, however, the "odds," if we want to call them that, change depending on where you live.

Over time, of course, those annual 2.1 percentages add up. A third way of measuring divorce, then, is to ask, "Of all U.S. adults, what percentage are divorced?"

Figure 12.10 shows the increase. You can see that divorce has risen among all the groups shown in this figure, but at a slower rate among Latinos. Again, a cross-cultural comparison helps to place U.S. statistics in perspective—but the news is not good. The United States has—by far—the highest divorce rate in the industrialized world (*Statistical Abstract* 1998:Table 1346). If current trends persist, half or even more of all U.S. marriages may end in divorce (Milbank 1996). But contrary forces are also at work, for the U.S. divorce rate peaked around 1980, and has declined since then.

The Down-to-Earth Sociology box on the next page reports some "curious" findings about divorce, while factors that make marriage successful are summarized at the end of this chapter.

Children of Divorce

Each year, over one million U.S. children discover that their parents are divorcing (*Statistical Abstract* 1999:Table 159). Most divorcing parents become so wrapped up in

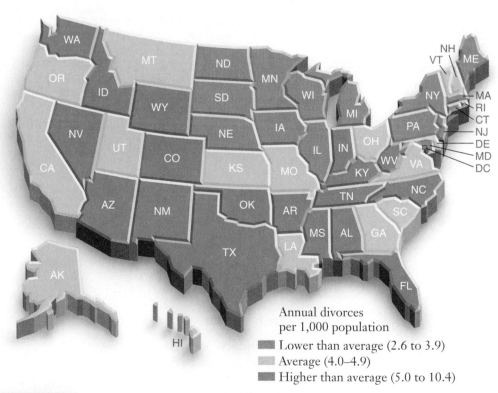

Annual divorces per 1,000 population
- ■ Lower than average (2.6 to 3.9)
- ■ Average (4.0–4.9)
- ■ Higher than average (5.0 to 10.4)

Figure 12.9 THE "WHERE" OF U.S. DIVORCE

Source: Statistical Abstract 1999:Table 162

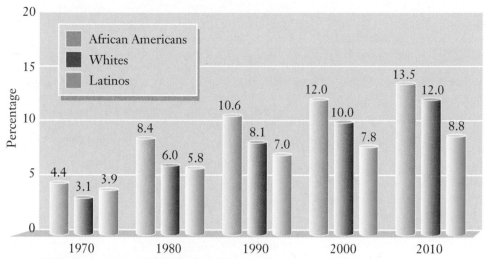

Note: Only these racial-ethnic groups are listed in the source. Years 2000 and 2010 are the author's estimate, based on totals for the late 90s.

Figure 12.10 **WHAT PERCENTAGE OF AMERICANS ARE DIVORCED?**

Source: Statistical Abstract 1995:Table 58; 1999:Table 62.

their own problems that they are unable to prepare their children for the divorce—even if they knew how to do so. When the break comes, children become confused and insecure. For security, many cling to the unrealistic idea that their parents will be reunited (Wallerstein and Kelly 1992). To help resolve this conflict, they may side with one parent and reject the other.

The effects of divorce follow children into adulthood. For example, compared with adults who grew up in intact families, grown-up children of divorced parents have less contact with either their father or their mother (Webster and Herzog 1995). They also are less likely to marry and more likely to divorce (Diekmann and Engelhardt 1999; Wallerstein, Lewis, and Blakeslee

Sociology

Down-to-Earth

YOU BE THE SOCIOLOGIST: CURIOUS DIVORCE PATTERNS

Sociologists Alex Heckert, Thomas Nowak, and Kay Snyder (1995) did secondary analysis (see page 27) of data gathered on a nationally representative sample of 5,000 U.S. households. Here are three of their findings:

1. If a wife earns more than her husband, the chances of di-

vorce increase. If a husband earns more than his wife, divorce is less likely.

2. If the wife's health is poorer than her husband's, the marriage is more likely to break up. If the husband's health is poorer than his wife's, divorce is less likely.

3. The more housework a wife does, the less likely a couple is to divorce.

Can you explain these findings? You be the sociologist. Please develop your explanations before looking at the box on the next page. ■

(continued)

Sociology (continued)

Heckert, Nowak, and Snyder suggest these explanations:

1. A wife who earns more than her husband has more alternatives to an unsatisfying marriage; a wife who earns less is more dependent.

2. Social pressure is greater for a wife to take care of a husband in poor health than it is for a husband to take care of a wife in poor health.

3. Who does the most housework is an indication of a husband's and wife's relative bargaining power. Wives with the most bargaining power are the least likely to put up with unsatisfying marriages. ■

2000). Their apparently greater difficulty in romance depends more on how they were reared, however, than it does on their parents' divorce. Those who have the most difficulty are those whose mothers did not remarry, who remarried and then divorced again, or who interfered with their relationship with their father. Those whose mothers established a single, stable relationship after the divorce build more stable intimate relationships. For a controversial solution to this problem of children of divorce, see the Down-to-Earth Sociology box on the next page.

Researchers have identified several factors that help children adjust to divorce. Adjustment is better if (1) both parents show understanding and affection; (2) the child lives with a parent who is making a good adjustment; (3) family routines are consistent; (4) the family has adequate money for its needs; and (5) at least according to preliminary studies, the child lives with the parent of the same sex (Lamb 1977; Clingempeel and Repucci 1982; Peterson and Zill 1986; Wallerstein and Kelly 1992). Sociologists have found that children adjust better if there is a second adult who can be counted on for support. Urie Bronfenbrenner (1992) says that this person makes the third leg of a stool, giving stability to the smaller family unit. Any adult can be the third leg, he says—a relative, friend, mother-in-law, or even coworker—but the most powerful stabilizing third leg is the father, the ex-husband.

The Absent Father and Serial Fatherhood

With divorce common and mothers usually granted custody of the children, a new fathering pattern has emerged. In this pattern, known as **serial fatherhood,** a

It is difficult to capture the anguish of the children of divorce, but when I read these lines by the fourth-grader who drew these two pictures, my heart was touched:

Me alone in the park . . .
All alone in the park.
My Dad and Mom are divorced
That's why I'm all alone.

This is me in the picture with my son.
We are taking a walk in the park.
I will never be like my father.
I will never divorce my wife and kid.

Serial fatherhood.

Sociology

Down-to-Earth

SHALL WE TIGHTEN THE TIES THAT BIND? ROLLING BACK NO-FAULT DIVORCE

It is not divorce, but the children of divorce, that bother people. What can you do about such a huge problem—a million kids a year? How about making it difficult to get a divorce? In 1997, the Louisiana legislature decided to take this approach, and passed law that created "covenant marriages." In a covenant marriage, vows are to be taken more seriously, and they can be broken only because of extreme circumstances.

This law has stirred up controversy. Conservatives applaud covenant marriages as a step in the right direction. The disintegration of the family, they point out, is at the root of what ails our society: crime, violence, even poor national test scores. Having children should mean pledging to remain together as husband-wife, mother-father, in order to nurture those children. Children deserve that kind of commitment. Personal goals, other relationships, even personal happiness, need to be put aside for the welfare of the children. If you want "Marriage Lite," then don't choose the covenant marriage. Otherwise, be prepared to follow through. It's your choice.

Liberals, in contrast, view covenant marriage through a different lens. They see it as a step backward, as a way of shackling women to their husbands. Covenant marriage will reduce women's choices and bind them to the home. Abuse and betrayal aren't the only signs of a bad marriage, and people—men as well as women—need the right to leave bad marriages. If someone is unhappy, he or she should be able to seek happiness elsewhere. ■

For Your Consideration

What do you think about covenant marriage? Can you explain what lens you are using to come to your conclusions?

---

divorced father tends to maintain high contact with his children during the first year or two after the divorce. As the man develops a relationship with another woman, he begins to play a fathering role with the woman's children and reduces contact with his own children. With another breakup, this pattern may repeat. Only about one-sixth of children who live apart from their fathers see their dad as often as every week. Actually, *most* divorced fathers stop seeing their children altogether (Ahlburg and De Vita 1992; Furstenberg and Harris 1992; Seltzer 1994). Apparently, for many men fatherhood has become a short-term commitment.

The Ex-Spouses

Anger, depression, and anxiety are common feelings at divorce. But so is relief. Women are more likely than men to feel that the divorce is giving them a "new chance" in life. A few couples manage to remain friends through it all—but they are the exception. The spouse who initiates the divorce usually gets over it sooner (Stark 1989; Kelly 1992).

After divorce, the ex-spouses' cost of living increases—two homes, two utility bills, and so forth. But the financial impact is different for men and for women. Divorce often spells economic hardship for women (Smock et al. 1999). This is especially true for mothers of small children, whose standard of living drops about 37 percent (Seltzer 1994). In contrast, the former husband's standard of living is likely to increase (Weitzman 1985). The higher a woman's level of education, the better prepared she is to survive financially after divorce (Dixon and Rettig 1994).

Remarriage

Despite the number of people who emerge from the divorce court swearing "Never again!" most do marry again. But they aren't remarrying as quickly as they used to. In the 1960s, the average woman remarried in about two years. Today she waits five years to remarry (*Statistical Abstract* 1999:Table 160). Comparable data are not available for men.

As Figure 12.11 shows, most divorced people marry other divorced people. You may be surprised that the

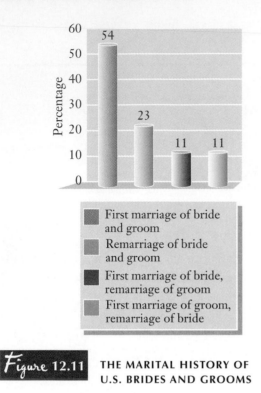

Figure 12.11 THE MARITAL HISTORY OF U.S. BRIDES AND GROOMS

Source: Statistical Abstract 1999:Table 156.

women most likely to remarry are young mothers and those who have not graduated from high school (Glick and Lin 1986). Apparently women who are more educated and more independent (no children) can afford to be more selective. Men are more likely than women to remarry, perhaps because they have a larger pool of potential mates.

How do remarriages work out? The divorce rate of remarried people *without* children is the same as that of first marriages. Those who bring children into a new marriage, however, are more likely to divorce again (MacDonald and DeMaris 1995). As sociologist Andrew Cherlin (1989) notes, we have not developed adequate norms for remarriages. For example, we lack satisfactory names for stepmothers, stepfathers, stepbrothers, stepsisters, stepaunts, stepuncles, stepcousins, and stepgrandparents. At the very least, these are awkward terms to use, but they also represent ill-defined relationships.

TWO SIDES OF FAMILY LIFE

Let's first look at situations in which marriage and family have gone seriously wrong and then try to answer the question of what makes marriage work.

The Dark Side of Family Life: Battering, Child Abuse, and Incest

The dark side of family life involves events that people would rather keep in the dark. We shall look at battering, child abuse, and incest.

Battering To study violence, sociologists have interviewed nationally representative samples of U.S. couples (Straus 1980; Straus, Gelles, and Steinmetz 1980; Straus and Gelles 1988; Straus 1992). Although not all sociologists agree (Dobash et al. 1992, 1993; Pagelow 1992), Murray Straus concludes that husbands and wives are about equally likely to attack one another. When it comes to the effects of violence, however, gender equality vanishes (Gelles 1980; Straus 1980, 1992). As Straus points out, even though *she* may throw the coffeepot first, it is generally *he* who lands the last and most damaging blow. Consequently, many more wives than husbands seek medical attention because of marital violence. A good part of the reason, of course, is that most husbands are bigger and stronger than their wives, putting women at a disadvantage in this literal battle of the sexes.

Violence against women is related to the sexist structure of society, which we reviewed in Chapter 10, and to the socialization we reviewed in Chapter 3. Because they grew up with norms that encouraged aggression and the use of violence, many men feel it is their right to control women. When frustrated in a relationship—or even by causes outside it—many men turn violent toward their wives and lovers. The basic sociological question is how to socialize males to handle frustration and disagreements without resorting to violence (Rieker et al. 1997). We do not yet have this answer.

Child Abuse

My wife and I answered an ad about a house in a middle-class neighborhood that was for sale by owner. As the woman showed us through the house, which was immaculate, we were surprised to see a plywood box in the youngest child's bedroom. About 3 feet high, 3 feet wide, and 6 feet long, the box was perforated with holes and had a little door with a padlock. Curious, I asked what it was. The woman matter-of-factly replied that her son had a behavior problem, and this was where they locked him for "time out." She added that at other times they would tie him to a float, attach a line to the dock, and put him in the lake.

We left as soon as we could. With thoughts of a terrorized child filling my head, I called the state child abuse hot line.

As you can tell, what I saw upset me. Most of us are bothered by child abuse—helpless children being victimized by their own parents, the very adults who are supposed to love, protect, and nurture them. The most gruesome of these cases make the evening news: The 4-year old girl who was beaten and raped by her mother's boyfriend, who passed into a coma and then three days later passed out of this life; the 6- to 10-year old children whose stepfather videotaped them engaging in sex acts. Unlike these cases, which made headlines in my area, most child abuse is never brought to our attention: the children who live in filth, who are neglected—left alone for hours or even days at a time—or who are beaten with extension cords. Cases like the little boy I learned about when I went house hunting.

We do know that child abuse is extensive. Each year, about 3 million U.S. children are reported to the authorities as victims of abuse or neglect. About 1 million of these cases are substantiated (*Statistical Abstract* 1999:Table 379).

Incest Sexual relations between relatives (for example, between brothers and sisters or between parents and children) constitute incest. Incest is most likely to occur in families that are socially isolated (Smith 1992). Sociological research has destroyed assumptions that incest is not common. Sociologist Diana Russell (n.d.), who interviewed women in San Francisco, found that incest victims who experience the most difficulty are those who were victimized the most often, over longer periods of time, and whose incest was "more intrusive"—for example, sexual intercourse as opposed to sexual touching.

Who are the offenders? Russell found that uncles are the most common offenders, followed by first cousins, fathers (stepfathers especially), brothers, and, finally, relatives ranging from brothers-in-law to stepgrandfathers. Other researchers report that brother-sister incest is several times more common than father-daughter incest (Canavan et al. 1992). Incest between mothers and sons is rare.

The Bright Side of Family Life: Successful Marriages

Successful Marriages After examining divorce and family abuse, one could easily conclude that marriages seldom work out. That would be far from the truth, however, for about two of every three married Americans report that they are "very happy" with their marriages (Cherlin and Furstenberg 1988; Whyte 1992). To find out what makes marriage successful, sociologists Jeanette and Robert Lauer (1992) interviewed 351 couples who had been married fifteen years or longer. Fifty-one of these marriages were unhappy, but the couples stayed together for religious reasons, family tradition, or

"for the sake of the children." Of the others, the 300 happy couples, all:

1. Think of their spouse as their best friend
2. Like their spouse as a person
3. Think of marriage as a long-term commitment
4. Believe that marriage is sacred
5. Agree with their spouse on aims and goals
6. Believe that their spouse has grown more interesting over the years
7. Strongly want the relationship to succeed
8. Laugh together

Sociologist Nicholas Stinnett (1992) used interviews and questionnaires to study 660 families from all regions of the United States and parts of South America. He found that happy families

1. Spend a lot of time together
2. Are quick to express appreciation
3. Are committed to promoting one another's welfare
4. Do a lot of talking and listening to one another
5. Are religious
6. Deal with crises in a positive manner

Symbolic Interactionism and the Misuse of Statistics Many of my students express concerns about their own marital future, a wariness born out of the divorce of their parents, friends, neighbors, relatives—even their pastors and rabbis. They wonder what chance they really have. Because sociology is not just about abstract ideas, but is really about our lives, it is important to stress that we are individuals, not statistics. That is, if the divorce rate were 33 percent or 50 percent, this would *not* mean that if we marry our chances of getting divorced are 33 percent or 50 percent. That is a misuse of statistics, and a very common one at that. Divorce statistics represent all marriages, and have absolutely *nothing* to do with any individual marriage. Our own chances depend on our own situation—especially the way we approach marriage.

To make this point clearer, let's apply symbolic interactionism. From a symbolic interactionist perspective, we create our own worlds. That is, experiences don't come with built-in meanings. Rather, we interpret our experiences, and act accordingly. Simply put, if we think of our marriage as likely to fail, we increase the likelihood that it will fail; if we think that our marriage will work out well, the chances of a good marriage increase. In other words, we tend to act according to our ideas, creating a sort of self-fulfilling prophecy. The folk saying "There are no guarantees in life" is certainly true, but it does help to have a vision that a good marriage is possible and that it is worth achieving.

THE FUTURE OF MARRIAGE AND FAMILY

What can we expect of marriage and family in the future? Despite its many problems, marriage is in no danger of becoming a relic of the past. Marriage is so functional that it exists in every society. Consequently, the vast majority of Americans will continue to find marriage vital to their welfare.

Certain trends are firmly in place. Cohabitation, births to single women, and age at first marriage will increase. More married women will join the work force, and they will continue to gain marital power. Equality in marriage, however, is not even on the horizon. The number of el-derly will continue to increase, and more couples will find themselves sandwiched between caring for their parents and their own children. The reduction in our divorce rate is another matter entirely. At this point we don't know if it is the prelude to a long-term decline, or merely a lull out of which an even higher rate will be launched.

Finally, our culture will continue to be haunted by distorted images of marriage and family: the bleak ones portrayed in the mass media and the rosy ones perpetuated by cultural myths. Sociological research can help correct these distortions and allow us to see how our own family experiences fit into the patterns of our culture. Sociological research also can help to answer the big question of how to formulate social policy that will support and enhance family life.

SUMMARY AND REVIEW

■ Marriage and Family in Global Perspective

What is a family—and what themes are universal?
Family is difficult to define. There are exceptions to every element one might consider essential. Consequently, **family** is defined broadly—as people who consider themselves related by blood, marriage, or adoption. Universally, **marriage** and family are mechanisms for governing mate selection, reckoning descent, and establishing inheritance and authority. Pp. 302–304.

■ Marriage and Family in Theoretical Perspective

What is the functionalist perspective on marriage and family?
Functionalists examine the functions and dysfunctions of family life. Examples include the **incest taboo** and how weakened family functions increase divorce. Pp. 304–305.

What is the conflict perspective on marriage and family?
Conflict theorists examine how marriage and family help perpetuate inequalities, especially the subservience of women. Power struggles in marriage, such as those over housework, are an example. Pp. 305–307.

What is a symbolic interactionist perspective on marriage and family?
Symbolic interactionists examine how the contrasting perspectives of men and women are played out in marriage. They stress that only by grasping the perspectives of wives and husbands can we understand their behavior. P. 307.

■ The Family Life Cycle

What are the major elements of the family life cycle?
The major elements are love and courtship, marriage, childbirth, child rearing, and the family in later life. Most mate selection follows predictable patterns of age, social class, race-ethnicity, and religion. Childbirth and child-rearing patterns also vary by social class. Pp. 307–312.

■ Diversity in U.S. Families

How significant is race-ethnicity in family life?
The primary distinction is social class, not race-ethnicity. Families of the same social class are likely to be similar, regardless of their racial or ethnic makeup. Pp. 312–314.

What other diversity in U.S. families is there?
Also discussed were one-parent, childless, **blended,** and gay families. Each has its unique characteristics, but social class is significant in determining their primary characteristics. Poverty is especially significant for one-parent families, most of which are headed by women. Pp. 315–317.

■ Trends in U.S. Families

What major changes characterize U.S. families?
Two changes are postponement of first marriage and an increase in **cohabitation.** With more people living longer, many middle-aged couples find themselves sandwiched between caring for their children and their parents. Pp. 317–319.

■ Divorce and Remarriage

What is the current divorce rate?
Depending on what figures you choose to compare, you can produce almost any rate you wish, from 75 percent to just 2.1 percent. However you figure it, the U.S. divorce rate is higher than in any other industrialized nation. Pp. 319–320.

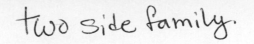
two side family.

How do children and their parents adjust to divorce?
Divorce is especially difficult for children, whose adjustment problems often continue into adulthood. Most divorced fathers do not maintain ongoing relationships with their children. Financial problems are usually greater for the former wives. Although most divorced people remarry, their rate of remarriage has slowed considerably. Pp. 320–324.

■ **Two Sides of Family Life** < *Dark abusement / Bright Satisfaction*

What are the two sides of family life?
The dark side is family abuse—spouse battering, child abuse, and **incest**—acts that revolve around the misuse of family power. The bright side is families that produce intense satisfaction for spouses and their children. Pp. 324–325.

■ **The Future of Marriage and Family**

What is the likely future of marriage and family?
We can expect **cohabitation**, births to unmarried single women, and age at first marriage to increase. The growing numbers of women in the work force will likely continue to shift the marital balance of power. P. 326.

Where can I read more on this topic?
Suggested readings for this chapter are listed on page SR-9.

YOUR INTERACTIVE COMPANION WEB SITE

Your Interactive Companion Web Site includes practice tests, with feedback, and online learning activities with video, audio, and Weblinks. Your access code for this Web site is provided with this text.

GLOSSARY

bilateral system a system of reckoning descent that counts both the mother's and the father's side (p. 304)

blended family a family whose members were once part of other families (p. 315)

cohabitation unmarried people living together in a sexual relationship (p. 318)

empty nest a married couple's domestic situation after the last child has left home (p. 312)

endogamy the practice of marrying within one's own group (p. 303)

exogamy the practice of marrying outside one's group (p. 303)

extended family a nuclear family plus other relatives—such as cousins and grandparents who live together (p. 303)

family people who consider themselves related by blood, marriage, or adoption (p. 303)

family of orientation the family in which a person grows up (p. 303)

family of procreation the family formed when a couple's first child is born (p. 303)

homogamy the tendency of people with similar characteristics to marry one another (p. 309)

household people who occupy the same housing unit (p. 303)

incest taboo rules specifying the degrees of kinship that prohibit sex or marriage (p. 303)

machismo an emphasis on male strength and dominance (p. 314)

marriage a group's approved mating arrangements, usually marked by a ritual of some sort (p. 303)

matriarchy a society or group in which authority is vested in women (p. 304)

matrilineal system a system of reckoning descent that counts only the mother's side (p. 304)

nuclear family a family consisting of a husband, wife, and child(ren) (p. 304)

patriarchy a society or group in which authority is vested in men (p. 304)

patrilineal system a system of reckoning descent that counts only the father's side (p. 304)

polyandry a marriage in which a woman has more than one husband (p. 302)

polygyny a marriage in which a man has more than one wife (p. 302)

romantic love feelings of erotic attraction accompanied by an idealization of the other (p. 307)

serial fatherhood a pattern of parenting in which a father, after divorce, reduces contact with his own children, serves as a father to the children of the woman he marries or lives with, then ignores his own children after moving in with or marrying another woman; this pattern repeats (p. 322)

system of descent how kinship is traced over the generations (p. 304)

Chapter 13

Sing-Fang Chen, Creative Mind, 1988

Education and Religion

There wasn't much for teenagers to do in Littleton, Colorado. Not much happened in this quiet town of 35,000, a middle-class suburb southwest of Denver. Some of the high school kids liked to draw attention to themselves by wearing black trenchcoats and black shirts with swastikas. They called themselves the Trenchcoat Mafia and tossed around a few phrases in German.

"Just kids. They'll grow out of it," was the typical adult response. "We all went through something ourselves."

The Trenchcoat Mafia had their own table in the cafeteria and their group picture in the yearbook. The caption: "Who says we're different? Insanity's healthy…. Stay alive, stay different, stay crazy! Oh, and stay away from CREAM SODA!!"

Just another high school group: jocks, Goths, stoners, deadbeats, geeks, preppies. Every school has some.

The jocks despised the Trenchcoat Mafia. They threw them into lockers and called them scumbags, faggots, and inbreeds. They threw rocks and bottles at them from moving cars.

Two seniors, Eric Harris and Dylan Klebold, honors students and members of the Trenchcoat Mafia, talked and dreamed about killing their classmates, especially the jocks. Eric even had his own Web page, where he described whom he wanted to kill and how he wanted to do it. As a class project, Eric and Dylan made a video in which they pretended to kill the classmates they didn't like. Just talk. But as the killing on *Doom,* the video game they both loved, no longer satisfied, the boys hatched a plan for real killing. It was risky. Maybe they would survive, maybe not. But if not, they would go out in a blaze of glory. Hitler's birthday would be perfect.

The carnage left Columbine High School seared into the national memory. TV viewers switched on their sets and found that a quiet Tuesday afternoon had been interrupted by stunning events. The drama was high as SWAT teams moved in and cautiously began to assess the situation. Bodies lay strewn on sidewalks. No one knew how many were dead inside the school. The nation watched transfixed as events unfolded.

Violence in U.S. schools has become a major concern of parents, the public, and politicians. Shown here is a scene outside Columbine High School in Littleton, Colorado, an upper-middle-class suburb of Denver, where two students went on a shooting rampage in 1999. They sought athletes, minorities, and Christians for victims. After wounding 23 students and killing 12 students and a teacher, the two killed themselves.

As bombs went off and shots rang out, students ran in terror, cowering in closets and under tables. Harris and Klebold went from room to room in search of victims. In the library, they found students hiding under a table. "Do you believe in God?" asked one of the shooters. "Yes," replied Cassie Bernall. "There is no God," the gunman retorted, as he placed a gun against her head and squeezed the trigger.

The boys killed twelve of their fellow students and one teacher before they turned their guns on themselves. They wounded twenty-three students.

Once again, the nation shook its head in collective disbelief. ■

—Based on Bai 1999; Gibbs 1999.

EDUCATION: TRANSFERRING KNOWLEDGE AND SKILLS

The events at Columbine High School have been seared into the nation's consciousness. School shootings have confused just about everyone. No one has the full explanation for why they are occurring, or what we can do to prevent them. When we return to this topic, we are going to find a surprise, but, first, let's take a broad look at education.

EDUCATION IN GLOBAL PERSPECTIVE

Sociologist Randall Collins (1979) observed that industrialized nations have become **credential societies,** with employers using diplomas and degrees to determine who is eligible for a job. In many cases the diploma or degree is irrelevant for the work that must be performed. Does anyone really need a high school diploma in order to pump gas or sell tacos? Yet employers routinely require such credentials. In fact, it is often on the job, not at school, that employees learn the specific knowledge

or skills that a job requires. Why, then, do employers insist on diplomas and degrees? Why don't they simply use on-the-job training?

Diplomas and degrees serve as sorting devices. Because employers in large, industrialized societies don't know potential workers, they depend on schools to weed out the capable from the incapable. College graduates, they assume, are responsible people, for they presumably have shown up on time for numerous classes, have turned in scores of assignments, and have demonstrated basic writing and thinking skills. The job skills a position requires can then be grafted onto this foundation, which has been certified by the college.

In some cases, job skills must be mastered before an individual is allowed to do certain work. On-the-job training was once adequate for physicians, engineers, and airline pilots, but with changes in knowledge and technology this is no longer the case. This is precisely why doctors display their credentials so prominently. They stand before you certified by an institution of higher learning, their framed degrees declaring that they have completed rigorous training programs and are licensed to work on your body.

Education, which varies widely around the world, is always related to a nation's economy. Let's look at education in three countries. Keep in mind that these are

In hunting and gathering societies, there is no separate social institution called *education*. As with this Eskimo child, children learn their adult economic roles from their parents and other kin.

just examples. No single nation represents the wide variety of education that characterizes these three levels of industrialization.

Education in the Most Industrialized Nations: Japan

A central sociological principle of education is that a nation's education reflects its culture. Because a core Japanese value is solidarity with the group, the Japanese discourage competition among individuals. Even in the work force, people who are hired together work as a team. They are not expected to compete with one another for promotions, but, instead, they are promoted as a group (Ouchi 1993). Japanese education reflects this group-centered ethic. Children in grade school work as a group, all mastering the same skills and materials. Teachers stress cooperation and respect for elders and others in positions of authority. By law, Japanese schools all use the same textbooks (Haynes and Chalker 1997).

In a fascinating cultural contradiction, college admission procedures in Japan are highly competitive (Cooper 1991). Like the Scholastic Assessment Test (SAT) required of U.S. college-bound high school seniors, Japanese seniors who want to attend college must take a national test. Only the top scorers in Japan, however—rich and poor alike—are admitted to college. In contrast, even U.S. high school graduates who perform poorly on these tests can find some college to attend—as long as their parents can pay the tuition.

Education in the Industrializing Nations: Russia

After the Revolution of 1917, the Soviet Communist party attempted to upgrade the nation's educational system. At that time, as in most countries, education was limited to children of the elite. Following the sociological principle that education reflects culture, the new central government made certain that socialist values dominated its schools, for it saw education as a means to undergird the new political system. As a result, schoolchildren were taught that capitalism was evil and that communism was the salvation of the world.

Education, including college, was free. Schools stressed mathematics and the natural sciences, and few courses in the social sciences were taught (Taylor and Mechitov 1994). Just as the economy was directed from central headquarters, so was education. With orders issued out of Moscow, schools throughout the country followed the same state-prescribed curriculum. All students in the same grade used the same textbooks. To prevent

the development of thinking that might be contrary to communism, students memorized the materials and were discouraged from discussing them (Bridgman 1994).

Post-Soviet Russians are in the midst of "reinventing" education. For the first time, private, religious, and even foreign-run schools are allowed, and teachers can encourage students to question and to think for themselves. The problems that the Russians confronted are mind-boggling. Not only did they have to retrain tens of thousands of teachers who were used to teaching pat political answers, but also school budgets shrank, while inflation spiraled upward. Teachers stampeded out of education into fields that, with the new capitalism, paid many times what teachers were paid.

Because it is true of education everywhere, we can safely predict that Russia will develop an educational system that reflects its culture. This system will glorify its historical exploits and reinforce its values and world views. One difficulty for Russians at this point is that their values and world views are changing rapidly. The transition to capitalism is transforming basic ideas about profit and private property—and their educational system is destined to reflect those changed values.

Education in the Least Industrialized Nations: Egypt

Education in the Least Industrialized Nations stands in sharp contrast to that in the industrialized world. Even if the Least Industrialized Nations have mandatory attendance laws, they are not enforced. Because most of their people work the land or take care of families, they find little need for education. In addition, most of these nations simply cannot afford extensive formal education. As we saw from Figure 7.2 (pp. 168–169), most people in the Least Industrialized Nations live on less than $1,000 a year. Consequently, in some nations most children do not go to school beyond the first couple of grades. As was once common around the globe, it is primarily the wealthy in the Least Industrialized Nations who have the means and the leisure for formal education—especially anything beyond the basics. As an example, let's look at education in Egypt.

Several centuries before the birth of Christ, Egypt's world-renowned centers of learning produced such acclaimed scientists as Archimedes and Eukleides. The primary areas of study during this classic period were physics, astronomy, geometry, geography, mathematics, philosophy, and medicine. The largest library in the world was at Alexandria. Fragments from the papyrus manuscripts of this library, which burned to the ground, have been invaluable in deciphering ancient manuscripts. After

functionalist Manifest function (+) thing intend
Latent function = (+) action result
THE FUNCTIONALIST PERSPECTIVE: PROVIDING SOCIAL BENEFITS ■ 333 NOT intend

The poverty of some of the Least Industrialized Nations defies the imagination of most people who have been reared in the industrialized world. Their educational systems are similarly marked by poverty. This photo shows an outdoor school in Hunza, Pakistan.

Egypt suffered defeat in war, however, education declined, never again to rise to its former prominence.

Although the Egyptian constitution guarantees five years of free grade school for all children, many poor children receive no education at all. For those who do, qualified teachers are few and classrooms are crowded. Only 39 percent of women and 64 percent of men can read and write ("Egypt," 1998). Those who go beyond the five years of grade school attend a preparatory school for three years. High school also lasts for three years. During the first two years, all students take the same required courses, but during the third year they specialize in arts, science, or mathematics. All high school students take a monthly examination and a national exam at the end of the senior year.

THE FUNCTIONALIST PERSPECTIVE: PROVIDING SOCIAL BENEFITS

A central position of functionalism is that when the parts of society are working properly, each contributes to the well-being or stability of that society. The positive things that people intend their actions to accomplish are known as **manifest functions.** The

positive consequences they did not intend are called **latent functions.**

Education's most obvious manifest function is to teach knowledge and skills—whether the traditional three *R*'s or their more contemporary counterparts, such as computer literacy. Each society must train the next generation to fulfill its significant positions. Because our postindustrial society needs highly educated people, the schools supply them.

Over the years, the functions of U.S. schools have expanded, and they now rival some family functions. Child care is an example. Grade schools do double duty as babysitters for parents who both work, or for single mothers in the work force. Child care always has been a latent function of formal education, for it was an unintended consequence of schooling. Now, however, because most families have two wage earners, child care has become a manifest function. Some schools even offer child care both before and after formal classes. Another function schools are performing is giving sex education and birth control advice. This has stirred controversy, for some families resent this function being taken from them.

Cultural Transmission of Values   Patriotism

Another manifest function of education is the **cultural transmission** of values, a process by which schools pass a society's core values from one generation to the next. Consequently, schools in a socialist society stress values of socialism, while schools in a capitalist society teach values that support capitalism. U.S. schools, for example, stress respect for private property, individualism, and competition.

Regardless of a country's economic system, loyalty to the state is a cultural value, and schools around the world teach patriotism. U.S. schools teach that the United States is the best country in the world; Russians learn that no country is better than Russia; and French, German, Japanese, Afghani, and Egyptian students all learn the same about their respective countries. To instill patriotism, grade school teachers in every country extol the virtues of the society's founders, their struggle for freedom from oppression, and the goodness of the country's basic social institutions.

Social Integration

Schools also perform the function of *social integration,* helping to mold students into a more cohesive unit. When students salute the flag and sing the national anthem, for example, they become aware of the "greater government," and their sense of national identity grows.

[handwritten at top: Gatekeeper → track and does social Placement according to merit]

One of the best indicators of how education promotes political integration is the millions of immigrants who have attended U.S. schools, learned mainstream ideas and values, and given up their earlier national and cultural identities as they became Americans (Violas 1978; Rodriguez 1995).

This integrative function of education goes far beyond similarities of appearance or speech. *To forge a national identity is to stabilize the political system.* If people identify with a society's social institutions and *perceive them as the basis of their welfare,* they have no reason to rebel. This function is especially significant when it comes to the lower social classes, from which most social revolutionaries are drawn. The wealthy already have a vested interest in maintaining the status quo, but to get the lower classes to identify with a social system *as it is* goes a long way toward preserving the system in its current state.

People with disabilities often have found themselves left out of the mainstream of society. To overcome this, U.S. schools have added a new manifest function, **mainstreaming**, or inclusion. This means that schools try to incorporate students with disabilities into regular social activities. As a matter of routine policy, students with disabilities used to be placed in special schools. There, however, they learned to adjust to a world of the disabled, leaving them ill prepared to cope with the dominant world. The educational philosophy then changed to one that encourages or even requires students with disabilities to attend regular schools. For people who cannot walk, wheelchair ramps are provided; for those who cannot hear, "signers" (interpreters who use their hands) may attend classes with them. Most students who are blind attend special schools, as do people with severe learning disabilities. Overall, one half of students with disabilities now attend school in regular classrooms ("State of American Education," 2000).

Gatekeeping

Gatekeeping, or determining which people will enter what occupations, is another function of education. One type of gatekeeping is credentialing, which opens the door of opportunity to some and closes it to others. Gatekeeping is often accomplished by **tracking**, sorting students into different educational programs on the basis of real or perceived abilities. U.S. high schools, for example, often funnel students into one of three tracks: general, college prep, or honors. Those in the lowest track are likely to go to work after high school, or perhaps take a vocational course at a community college. Those in the highest track usually enter the more prestigious colleges around the country. Those in between usually attend a local college or regional state university.

Gatekeeping sorts people on the basis of merit, say functionalists. Sociologists Talcott Parsons (1940) and Kingsley Davis and Wilbert Moore (1945), who pioneered this view, also known as **social placement,** argue that a major task of society is to fill its positions with capable people. Some positions, such as that of physician, require high intelligence and many years of advanced education. Consequently, to motivate capable people to postpone gratification and to submit to many years of demanding courses, high income and prestige are held out as rewards. Other jobs require fewer skills and can be performed by people of lesser intelligence. Thus, functionalists look on education as a system that, to the benefit of society, sorts people according to their abilities.

In recent years, social integration, a traditional function of public education, has been extended. In a process called *mainstreaming* (also known as *inclusion* by educators), children who used to be sent to special schools now attend regular schools. Shown here is a class in Highland Park, California (near Los Angeles). This child with disabilities is the victim of a drive-by shooting.

THE CONFLICT PERSPECTIVE: REPRODUCING THE SOCIAL CLASS STRUCTURE

Unlike functionalists, who see education as a social institution that performs functions for the benefit of society, conflict theorists see education as a tool used by the elite to maintain their dominance. Education, they stress, *reproduces the social class structure*. By this, they mean that education perpetuates a society's social divisions. For example, in high school, the more well-to-do are likely to be placed in college-bound tracks, the poor into vocational tracks, and both to inherit the corresponding life opportunities laid down before they were born. As a result, family background is more important than test scores in predicting who will attend college. If you rank families from the poorest to the richest, as the income increases the likelihood that children will attend college also increases (Bowles 1977; Manski 1992–1993).

Conflict theorists also stress that education helps to reproduce society's divisions of race-ethnicity. Look at Figure 13.1, which shows the *funneling effect* of education. You can see that compared with whites, African Americans and Latinos are less likely to complete high school, less likely to go to college, and if they go to college, less likely to graduate. Those without college degrees have less access to jobs with better pay and the potential for advancement. Thus education helps perpetuate across generations the existing inequality among racial-ethnic groups.

Let's look at three other ways that education reproduces the social class structure.

The Hidden Curriculum

The term **hidden curriculum** refers to the unwritten rules of behavior and attitudes, such as obedience to authority and conformity to mainstream norms, that schools teach in addition to the formal curriculum (Gillborn 1992). Conflict theorists note how this hidden curriculum helps to perpetuate social inequalities. For example, the elite need people to run their business empires, and they are more comfortable if their managers possess "refined" language and manners. Consequently, middle-class schools, whose teachers know where their pupils are headed, stress "proper" English and "good" manners. Because few children from inner-city schools will occupy managerial positions, however, their teachers allow ethnic and street language in the classroom. These children do not need "refined" speech and manners; they simply need to be taught to obey rules. The schools prepare them for the closely supervised, low-paying, low-status positions for which they are destined (Bowles and Gintis 1976; Olneck and Bills 1980).

Don't lose sight of the significance of how schools approach language and manners. It is one way that education helps children take positions similar to those of their parents, which helps to keep the social classes intact across generations.

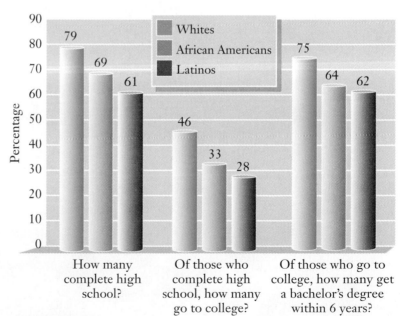

Figure 13.1 **THE FUNNELING EFFECTS OF EDUCATION: RACE AND ETHNICITY**

Source: Statistical Abstract 1999:Tables 304, 328.

Tilting the Tests: Discrimination by IQ

Even intelligence tests play a part in keeping the social class system intact. For example, how would you answer this question?

A symphony is to a composer as a book is to a(n) _____

___paper ___sculptor ___musician ___author ___man

You probably had no difficulty coming up with "author" as your choice. Wouldn't any intelligent person have done so?

In point of fact, this question raises a central issue in intelligence testing. Not all intelligent people would know the answer. This question contains *cultural biases*. Children from some backgrounds are more familiar with the concepts of symphonies, composers, sculptors, and musicians than are other children. Consequently, the test is tilted in their favor (Turner 1972; Ashe 1992).

Perhaps asking a different question will make the bias clearer. How would you answer this question?

If you throw dice and "7" is showing on the top, what is facing down?

___seven ___snake eyes ___box cars ___little Joes ___eleven

This question, suggested by Adrian Dove (n.d.), a social worker in Watts, is slanted toward a lower-class experience. It surely is obvious that this *particular* cultural bias tilts the test so that children from some social backgrounds will perform better than others.

It is no different with IQ (intelligence quotient) tests that use such words as *composer* and *symphony*. A lower-class child may have heard about rap, rock, hip hop, or jazz, but not about symphonies. In other words, IQ tests measure not only intelligence but also culturally acquired knowledge. Whatever else we can say, the cultural bias built into the IQ tests used in schools is clearly *not* tilted in favor of the lower classes. One consequence is that disproportionate numbers of minorities and the poor are assigned to noncollege tracks. This destines them for lower-paying jobs in adult life. Thus, conflict theorists view IQ tests as another weapon in an arsenal designed to maintain the social class structure across the generations.

Stacking the Deck: Unequal Funding

To see how funding for education differs by geography, look at the Social Map below. You can see that where

What states spend on each student per year

▬ The top spenders, more than $7,000 per student
▬ The average spenders, $6,000–$7,000 per student
▬ The low spenders, less than $6,000 per student

Figure 13.2 THE UNEQUAL FUNDING OF EDUCATION

Source: Statistical Abstract 1999:Table 286.

students live is significant for determining how much is spent on their education. Conflict theorists go beyond this observation, however. They stress that in all states the deck is stacked against the poor. Because public schools are largely supported by local property taxes, the richer communities (where property values are higher) have more to spend on their children. The poorer communities end up with much less. Consequently, the richer communities can offer higher salaries and take their pick of the most highly qualified and motivated teachers. They can afford to buy the latest textbooks, computers, and software, as well as to teach courses in foreign language, music, and so on.

■ **In Sum** Because U.S. schools so closely reflect the U.S. social class system, the children of the privileged emerge from grade school best equipped for success in high school. In turn, they come out of high school best equipped for success in college. This prepares them to maintain their dominance. The children of the poor are blown away in this competition, much as a one-legged runner would be in a race against Jackie Joyner-Kersee.

In short, because education's doors of opportunity swing wide open for some but have to be pried open by others, conflict theorists say that the educational system reproduces (or perpetuates) the social class structure. In fact, they add, this is one of its primary purposes.

THE SYMBOLIC INTERACTIONIST PERSPECTIVE: FULFILLING TEACHER EXPECTATIONS

Whereas functionalists look at how education benefits society and conflict theorists examine how education perpetuates social inequality, symbolic interactionists study face-to-face interactions inside the classroom. They have found that teacher expectations have profound consequences for their students.

The Rist Research → power of Lable

Symbolic interactionists have uncovered some of the dynamics of educational tracking. In what has become a classic study, sociologist Ray Rist did participant obser-

vation in an African American grade school with an African American faculty. Rist (1970) found that after only eight days in the classroom, the kindergarten teacher felt she knew the children's abilities well enough to assign them to three separate work tables. To Table 1, Mrs. Caplow assigned those she considered to be "fast learners." They sat at the front of the room, closest to her. Those whom she saw as "slow learners," she assigned to Table 3, located at the back of the classroom. She placed "average" students at Table 2, in between the other tables.

This seemed strange to Rist. He knew that the children had not been tested for ability, yet the teacher was certain she could differentiate between bright and slow children. Investigating further, Rist found that social class was the underlying basis for assigning the children to the different tables. Middle-class students were separated out for Table 1, children from poorer homes to Tables 2 and 3. The teacher paid the most attention to the children at Table 1, who were closest to her, less to Table 2, and the least to Table 3. As the year went on, children from Table 1 perceived that they were treated better and came to see themselves as smarter. They became the leaders in class activities and even ridiculed children at the other tables, calling them "dumb." Eventually, the children at Table 3 disengaged themselves from many classroom activities. Not surprisingly, at the end of the year only the children at Table 1 had completed the lessons that prepared them for reading.

This early tracking stuck. When these students entered the first grade, their new teacher looked at the work they had accomplished and placed students from Table 1 at her Table 1. She treated her tables much as the kindergarten teacher had, and the children at Table 1 again led the class. When they entered the second grade, their new teacher reviewed the children's scores, and assigned the highest performing children to a group called the "Tigers." Befitting their name, she gave them challenging readers. Not surprisingly, the Tigers came from the original Table 1 in kindergarten. The second group, called the "Cardinals," came from the original Tables 2 and 3. Her third group consisted of children she had failed the previous year, whom she called the "Clowns." The Cardinals and Clowns were given less advanced readers.

Rist concluded that *the child's journey through school was determined at the eighth day of kindergarten!* This research, as with that done on the Saints and the Roughnecks (reported in Chapter 6), demonstrates the power of labels: They can set people on courses of action that affect the rest of their lives.

How Do Teacher Expectations Work?

Sociologist George Farkas (1990a, 1990b, 1996) became interested in how teacher expectations affect students' grades. A fascinating finding emerged from his stratified sample of students in a large school district in Texas. *Even though they had the same test scores,* girls and Asian Americans averaged higher course grades than did boys, African Americans, Latinos, and whites.

At first, this may sound like more of the same old news—another case of discrimination. But this explanation doesn't fit, which is what makes this finding fascinating. Look who the victims are. It is most unlikely that the teachers would be prejudiced against boys and whites. To interpret these unexpected results, Farkas used symbolic interactionism. He observed that some students "signal" to their teachers that they are "good students." They show an eagerness to cooperate, and they quickly agree with what the teacher says. They also show that they are "trying hard." The teachers pick up these signals and reward these "good students" with better grades. Girls and Asian Americans, the researcher concludes, are better at displaying these characteristics so coveted by teachers.

We do not yet have enough information on how teachers form their expectations, or how they communicate them to students. Nor do we know much about how students "signal" messages to teachers. Perhaps you will become the educational sociologist who will shed more light on this significant area of human behavior.

PROBLEMS IN U.S. EDUCATION— AND THEIR SOLUTIONS

To conclude this section, let's examine two of the major problems facing U.S. education today—and consider their potential solutions.

Problems: Mediocrity and Violence

The Rising Tide of Mediocrity All Arizona high school sophomores took a math test. It covered the math that sophomores should know. One of ten passed. Meanwhile, in New York, to get its students to graduate, the state had to drop its passing grade to 55 out of 100

(Steinberg 1999). Perhaps nothing so captures what is wrong with U.S. schools as this event, reported by sociologist Thomas Sowell (1993b):

> [A]n international study of 13-year-olds...found that Koreans ranked first in mathematics and Americans last. When asked if they thought they were "good at mathematics," only 23 percent of the Korean youngsters said "yes"—compared to 68 percent of American 13-year-olds. The American educational dogma that students should "feel good about themselves" was a success in its own terms—though not in any other terms.

Scores on the Scholastic Assessment Test (SAT) indicate this same problem. As Figure 13.3 shows, the math scores have recovered, but the verbal scores are still much lower than they were years ago.

The president of the American Federation of Teachers has come up with a unique defense of the decline in SAT scores: The low test scores, he said, mean that teachers are doing a *better* job! They are getting more students to stay in high school and to go on to college. Students from poorer academic backgrounds, who used to drop out of high school, now become part of the test results (Sowell 1993b). Perhaps this is the reason. But if it is, it indicates not success, but a severe underlying problem—teachers giving infe-

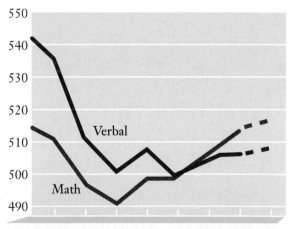

Note: Broken lines indicate the author's estimates.

 **Figure 13.3** NATIONAL RESULTS OF THE SCHOLASTIC ASSESSMENT TEST (SAT)

Source: Statistical Abstract 2000:Table 284.

rior education to disadvantaged students (Murray and Herrnstein 1992).

How to Cheat on the SATs If you receive poor grades this semester, wouldn't you like to use a magic marker to, presto! change them into higher grades? I suppose every student would. Now imagine that you had that power. Would you use it?

Some people in authority appear to have found such a magic marker, and they are using it to raise our embarrassingly low national SAT scores. Table 274 of the 1996 edition of the *Statistical Abstract of the United States* shows that in 1995 only 8.3 percent of students earned 600 or more on the verbal portion of the SAT test. The very next edition, in 1997, however, holds a pleasant surprise. Table 276 tells us that it was really 21.9 percent of students who scored 600 or higher in 1995. Later editions of this source retain the higher figure. What a magic marker!

In the twinkle of an eye, we get another bonus. It seems that between 1996 and 1997 the scores of *everyone* who took the test in previous years improved. Now that's the kind of power we all would like to have. Students, grab your report cards. Workers, change the numbers on your paycheck.

While all the explanations for this sleight-of-hand are not in, we do know that it is easier to give simpler tests than to do better teaching. And this is what the authorities have done with the SAT. The test is now shorter, students have more time to answer fewer questions, and the verbal part was made easier by dropping the antonym portion (Manno 1995; Stecklow 1995). This "dummying down" of the SAT is yet another form of grade inflation, to which we shall now turn.

Grade Inflation, Social Promotion, and Functional Illiteracy High school teachers used to give about twice as many *C's* as *A's*, but now there are more *A's* than *C's*. Since grades went up while learning went down, some of today's *A's* are the *C's* of years past. Another sign of **grade inflation** is that *one-third* of all college freshmen have an overall high school grade point average of A. This is *twice* what it was in 1970 (*Statistical Abstract* 1999:Table 324).

Grade inflation in the face of declining standards has been accompanied by **social promotion,** the practice of passing students from one grade to the next even though they have not mastered basic materials. One result is **functional illiteracy,** people having difficulty with reading and writing even though they have graduated from high school. Some high school graduates can-

not fill out job applications; others can't figure out if they've been given the right change at the grocery store.

Violence in Schools Many U.S. urban schools have deteriorated to the point that basic safety is an issue. Consequently, to get into some schools, students must pass through metal detectors, and uniformed guards have become a permanent fixture in them. Some grade schools even supplement their traditional fire drills with "drive-by shooting drills" (Toch 1993; Grossman 1995).

And school shootings, such as the event with which we opened this chapter? For a surprising analysis, read the Mass Media box on the next page.

Solutions: Safety and Standards

It is one thing to identify problems, quite another to find solutions for them. Let's consider solutions to the problems we just reviewed.

A Secure Learning Environment The first criterion for a good education is safety. Granted the high rate of violence in U.S. society, some violence is bound to spill over into the schools. To minimize that spillover, school administrators and teachers can expel all students who threaten the welfare of others. They can refuse to tolerate threats, violence, drugs, and weapons (Toby 1992). A zero tolerance policy for guns on school property is not unreasonable.

Higher Standards A study by sociologists James Coleman and Thomas Hoffer (1987) provides guidelines for improving the quality of education. They wanted to see why the test scores of students in Roman Catholic schools average 15 to 20 percent higher than those of students in public schools. Is it because Catholic schools attract better students, while the public schools have to put up with everyone? To find out, Coleman and Hoffer tested 15,000 students in public and Catholic high schools.

Their findings? From their sophomore through their senior years, students at Catholic schools pull ahead of public school students by a full grade in verbal and math skills. The superior test performance of students in Catholic schools, they concluded, is due not to better students, but to higher standards. Catholic schools have not watered down their curricula as have public schools. The researchers also found that parental involvement is important. Parents and teachers in Catholic schools reinforce each other's commitment to learning.

Mass Media in *Social Life*

SCHOOL SHOOTINGS: WHEN MYTH GIVES WAY TO PANIC

The media sprinkle their reports of school shootings with such dramatic phrases as "alarming proportions," "outbreak of violence," and "out of control." They give us the impression that schools all over the nation are set to erupt in gunfire. The public views the shootings as convincing evidence that something is seriously wrong with society. Parents used to consider schools safe havens, but no longer. Those naïve thoughts have been shattered by the bullets that have sprayed our schools—or at least by the media's portrayal of growing danger and violence in our schools.

Have our schools really become war zones, as the mass media would have us believe? Certainly events such as those at Columbine High School are disturbing, but we need to probe deeper than newspaper headlines and televised images in order to understand their social significance.

When we do, we find that the media's sensationalist reporting has created a myth. Contrary to "what everyone knows," there is no trend toward greater school violence. Despite the many dramatic school shootings that make headlines, as Table 13.1 shows, shooting deaths at schools are *not* increasing. As you can see, even during the 1998–1999 school year, when the Columbine killers went on their lethal rampage, the number of shooting deaths at U.S. schools was *below* the average for the 1990s. The total that year was half what it had been six years earlier.

This is not to say that school shootings are not a serious problem. Even one student being wounded or killed is one too

This picture was taken when Drew Golden was 6 years old. Five years later, when Drew was 11, he teamed up with 13-year-old Mitch Johnson. Together, they ambushed their middle school teachers and classmates in Jonesboro, Arkansas. They wounded nine students and one teacher and killed four girls and one teacher.

many. But, contrary to the impression fostered by the media, we are not seeing an escalation of school shooting deaths.

This is why we need sociology: to quietly, dispassionately search for facts so we can better understand the events that shape our lives. The first requirement for solving any problem is accurate data, for we do not want to create solutions based on hysteria. The information presented in this box may not make for sensational headlines, but it does serve to explode the myths that the media promulgate. ■

Table 13.1

			EXPLODING A MYTH: DEATHS AT U.S. SCHOOLS[a]		
School Year	Shooting Deaths	Other Homicides[b]	Total by Gender		Total
			Boys	Girls	
1992–1993	43	11	47	7	54
1993–1994	39	12	41	10	51
1994–1995	15	5	17	3	20
1995–1996	28	7	25	10	35
1996–1997	15	10	18	7	25
1997–1998	35	8	26	17	43
1998–1999	21	5	21	5	26
Mean, 1992–1999	28	8.3	27.9	8.4	36.3

[a]Includes all school-related homicides, even those that occurred on the way to or from school; includes suicides; includes school personnel killed at school by other adults; includes adults who had nothing to do with the school but who were found dead on school property.

[b]Beating, hanging, jumping, stabbing, and strangling.

Source: National School Safety Center, 2000.

These findings support the basic principle reviewed earlier about teacher expectations. Students perform better when they are expected to do well. This principle also means that we must expect (and require) more of teachers. These two expectations are combined in the following Thinking Critically section.

Thinking Critically

BREAKING THROUGH THE BARRIERS: RESTRUCTURING THE CLASSROOM

Jaime Escalante taught in an East Los Angeles inner-city school that was plagued with poverty, crime, drugs, and gangs. In this self-defeating environment, he taught calculus. His students scored so highly on national tests that officials suspected cheating. They asked his students to retake the test. They did. This time, they earned even higher scores.

How did Escalante do it?

First, Escalante had to open his students' minds to the possibility of success, that they *could* learn. Most Latino students were tracked into craft classes where they made jewelry and birdhouses. "Our kids are just as talented as anyone else. They just need the opportunity to show it," Escalante said. "They just don't think about becoming scientists or engineers."

Students also need to see learning as a way out of the barrio, as the path to good jobs. Escalante arranged for foundations to provide money for students to attend the colleges of their choice. Students learned that if they did well, their poverty wouldn't stop them.

Escalante also changed the system of instruction. He had his students think of themselves as a team, of him as the coach, and the national math exams as a sort of Olympics for which they were preparing. To foster team identity, students wore team jackets, caps, and T-shirts with logos that identified them as part of the math team. Before class, his students did "warm-ups" (hand clapping and foot stomping to a rock song).

Escalante's team had practice schedules as rigorous as a championship football team. Students had to sign a contract that bound them to participate in the summer program he developed, to complete the daily homework, and to attend Saturday morning and after-school study sessions. To remind students of the principle that self-discipline pays off, Escalante covered his walls with posters of sports figures—Michael Jordan, Babe Ruth, Jackie Joyner-Kersee, and Scottie Pippin.

The sociological point is this: The problem was not the ability of the students. Their failure to do well in school was not due to something *within* them. The problem was the *system,* the way classroom instruction was designed. When Escalante changed the system of instruction—*and* brought in hope—both attitudes and performance changed. ■

For Your Consideration

What principles discussed in this or earlier chapters did Escalante apply? What changes do you think we can make in education to bring about similar results all over the country? ■

Sources: Based on Barry 1989; Meek 1989; Escalante and Dirmann 1990; Hilliard 1991.

To say that today's schoolchildren can't learn as well as previous schoolchildren is a case of blaming the victim. As discussed in the text, Jaime Escalante (shown here) demonstrated that teachers can motivate even highly deprived students to study hard and to excel in learning. His experience challenges us to rethink our approach to education.

RELIGION: ESTABLISHING MEANING

Let's look at the main characteristics of a second significant social institution.

WHAT IS RELIGION?

Sociologists who do research on religion analyze the relationship between society and religion and study the role that religion plays in people's lives. They do not seek to prove that one religion is better than another. Nor is their goal to verify or disprove anyone's faith. As mentioned in Chapter 1, sociologists have no tools for deciding that one course of action is more moral than another, much less that one religion is "the" correct one. Religion is a matter of faith; sociologists deal with empirical matters, things they can observe or measure. Thus sociologists study the effects of religious beliefs and practices on people's lives. They also analyze how religion is related to stratification systems. Unlike theologians, however, sociologists cannot evaluate the truth of a religion's teachings.

In 1912 Emile Durkheim published an influential book, *The Elementary Forms of the Religious Life,* in which he tried to identify the elements common to all religions. After surveying religions around the world, Durkheim could find no specific belief or practice that all religions share. He did find, however, that all religions separate the sacred from the profane. By **sacred**, Durkheim referred to aspects of life having to do with the supernatural that inspire awe, reverence, deep respect, even fear. By **profane,** he meant aspects of life that are not concerned with religion or religious purposes but, instead, are part of the ordinary aspects of everyday life. Durkheim also found that all religions develop a community around their practices and beliefs. He (1912/1965) concluded:

> A religion is a unified system of beliefs and practices relative to sacred things, that is to say, things set apart and forbidden—beliefs and practices which unite into one single moral community called a Church, all those who adhere to them.

Thus, Durkheim said, a **religion** is defined by three elements:

1. *Beliefs* that some things are sacred (forbidden, set apart from the profane)
2. *Practices* (rituals) centering around the things considered sacred
3. *A moral community* (a church) resulting from a group's beliefs and practices

From his review of world religions, Durkheim concluded that all religions have beliefs, practices, and a moral community. Part of Hindu belief is that the Ganges is a holy river and bathing in it imparts spiritual benefits. Each year, millions of Hindus participate in this rite of ablution (purification).

Durkheim used the word **church** in an unusual sense, to refer to any "moral community" centered on beliefs and practices regarding the sacred. In Durkheim's sense, church refers to Buddhists bowing before a shrine, Hindus dipping in the Ganges River, and Confucianists offering food to their ancestors. Similarly, the term moral community does not imply morality in the sense familiar to most of us. A moral community is simply people who are united by their religious practices—and that would include sixteenth-century Aztec priests who each day gathered around an altar to pluck out the beating heart of a virgin.

To better understand the sociological approach to religion, let's see what pictures emerge when we apply the three theoretical perspectives.

THE FUNCTIONALIST PERSPECTIVE

Functionalists stress that religion is universal because it meets basic human needs. Let's look at some of the functions—and dysfunctions—of religion.

Functions of Religion

Around the world, religions provide answers to perplexing questions about ultimate meaning—such as the purpose of life, why people suffer, and the existence of an afterlife. Religion fosters social solidarity by uniting believers into a community that shares values and perspectives ("we Jews," "we Christians," "we Muslims"). The religious rituals that surround marriage, for example, link the bride and groom with a broader community that wishes them well. So do other religious rituals, such as those that celebrate birth and mourn death.

The teachings of religion help people adjust to life's problems and provide guidelines for daily life. Six of the Ten Commandments, for example, contain instructions on how to live everyday life, from how to get along with parents, employers, and neighbors to warnings about lying, stealing, and adultery. Religion also can help people adapt to new environments. For example, it isn't easy for immigrants to adjust to the customs of a new land. By keeping their native language alive and preserving familiar rituals and teachings, religion provides continuity with the immigrants' cultural past.

Just as education instills the value of patriotism, so do most religions. The most obvious example is the way so many churches prominently display the U.S. flag. For its part, governments reciprocate by supporting God—as witnessed by the inaugural speeches of U.S. presidents, who, believers or not, invariably ask God to bless the nation.

Although religion is often so bound up with the prevailing social order that it resists social change, occasionally religion spearheads change. In the 1960s, for example, the civil rights movement, which fought to desegregate public facilities and abolish racial discrimination at southern polls, was led by religious leaders, especially leaders of African American churches, such as Dr. Martin Luther King, Jr. Churches also served as centers at which demonstrators were trained and rallies were organized (Jones 1992).

Religion can promote social change, as was evident in the U.S. civil rights movement. Dr. Martin Luther King, Jr., a Baptist minister, shown here in his famous "I have a dream" speech, was the foremost leader of this movement. Many thought that Pope John Paul II's visit to communist Cuba in 1998 would stimulate social change in that island nation. Shown here is the Pope meeting with Fidel Castro, the communist revolutionary who has headed Cuba since 1957.

Woodcuts (engraved blocks of wood coated with ink to leave an impression on paper) were used to illustrate books shortly after the printing press was invented. This woodcut commemorates a dysfunction of religion, the burning of witches at the stake. This particular event occurred at Derneburg, Germany, in 1555.

Dysfunctions of Religion

Functionalists also examine ways in which religion can be *dysfunctional,* that is, how it can bring harmful results. Two main dysfunctions are war and religious persecution.

War History is filled with wars based on religion commingled with politics. Between the eleventh and fourteenth centuries, for example, Christian monarchs conducted nine bloody crusades in an attempt to wrest control of the Holy Land from the Muslims. Unfortunately, such wars are not just a relic of the past. Even in recent years we have seen Protestants and Catholics kill one another in Northern Ireland, while Jews and Muslims in Israel and Christians and Muslims in Bosnia have done the same thing.

Religion as Justification for Persecution Beginning in the 1200s and into the 1800s, in what has become known as the Inquisition, special commissions of the Roman Catholic church tortured women to elicit confessions that they were witches, and then burned them at the stake. In 1692, Protestant leaders in Salem, Massachusetts, executed 21 men and women who were accused of being witches. (The last execution for witchcraft was in Scotland in 1722 [Bridgwater 1953].) Similarly, it seems fair to say that the Aztec religion had its dysfunctions—at least for the virgins who were offered to appease angry gods. In short, religion has been used to justify oppression and any number of brutal acts.

THE SYMBOLIC INTERACTIONIST PERSPECTIVE

[handwritten notes: 1) Symbols (†) 2) ritual (pray) 3) experiences (feeling close, born again) also (Cosmology)]

Symbolic interactionists focus on the meanings that people give their experiences. They especially examine how people use symbols. Let's apply this perspective to religious symbols, rituals, and beliefs to see how they help forge a community of like-minded people.

Religious Symbols

Suppose that it is about two thousand years ago and you have just joined a new religion. You have come to believe that a recently crucified Jew named Jesus is the Messiah, the Lamb of God offered for your sins. The Roman leaders are persecuting the followers of Jesus. They hate your religion because you and your fellow believers will not acknowledge Caesar as God.

Cosmology: unified picture of the world. (one God)

THE SYMBOLIC INTERACTIONIST PERSPECTIVE ■ 345

Christians are few in number, and you are eager to have fellowship with other believers. But how can you tell who is a believer? Spies are all over. The government has sworn to destroy this new religion, and you do not relish the thought of being fed to the lions in the Coliseum.

You use a simple technique. While talking with a stranger, as though doodling absentmindedly in the sand or dust, you casually trace out the outline of a fish. Only fellow believers know the meaning—that, taken together, the first letter of the words in the Greek sentence "Jesus (is) Christ the Son of God" spell the Greek word for fish. If the other person gives no response, you rub out the outline and continue the interaction as usual. If there is a response, you eagerly talk about your new faith.

All religions use symbols to provide identity and social solidarity for their members. For Muslims, the primary symbol is the crescent moon and star, for Jews the Star of David, for Christians the cross. For members, these are not ordinary symbols, but sacred symbols that evoke feelings of awe and reverence. In Durkheim's terms, religions use symbols to specify what is sacred and to separate the sacred from the profane.

A symbol is a condensed way of communicating. Worn by a fundamentalist Christian, for example, the cross says, "I am a follower of Jesus Christ. I believe that He is the Messiah, the promised Son of God, that He loves me, that He died to take away my sins, that He rose from the dead and is going to return to earth, and that through Him I will receive eternal life."

That is a lot to pack into one symbol—and it is only part of what the symbol means to a fundamentalist believer. To people in other traditions of Christianity, the cross conveys somewhat different meanings—but to all Christians the cross is a shorthand way of expressing many meanings. So it is with the Star of David, the crescent moon and star, the cow (expressing to Hindus the unity of all living things), and the various symbols of the world's many other religions.

Rituals and Beliefs

Rituals, ceremonies or repetitive practices, are also symbols that help unite people into a moral community. Some rituals, such as the bar mitzvah of Jewish boys and Holy Communion of Christians, are designed to create in the devout a feeling of closeness with God and unity

with one another. Rituals include kneeling and praying at set times, bowing, crossing oneself, singing, lighting candles and incense, scripture readings, processions, baptisms, weddings, funerals, and so on.

Symbols, including rituals, develop from beliefs. The belief may be vague ("God is") or highly specific ("God wants us to prostrate ourselves and face Mecca five times each day"). Religious beliefs include not only *values* (what is considered good and desirable in life—how we ought to live) but also a **cosmology,** a unified picture of the world. For example, the Jewish, Christian, and Muslim belief that there is only one God, the Creator of the universe, who is concerned about the actions of humans and who will hold us accountable for what we do, is a cosmology. It presents a unifying picture of the universe.

Religious Experience

The term **religious experience** refers to a sudden awareness of the supernatural or a feeling of coming in contact with God. Some people undergo a mild version, such as feeling closer to God when they look at a mountain or listen to a certain piece of music. Others report a life-transforming experience; for example, St. Francis of Assisi became aware of God's presence in every living thing.

Some Protestants use the term **born again** to describe people who have undergone such a life-transforming religious experience. These people say they have come to the realization that they have sinned, that Jesus died for their sins, and that God wants them to live a new life. Their worlds become transformed. They look forward to the Resurrection and to a new life in heaven, and they see relationships with spouses, parents, children, and even bosses in a new light. They also report a need to make changes in how they interact with others so that their lives reflect their new, personal

Symbolic interactionists stress that a basic characteristic of humans is that they attach meaning to objects and events and then use representations of those objects or events to communicate with one another. Some religious symbols are used to communicate feelings of awe and reverence. Michaelangelo's Pietà, depicting Mary tenderly holding her son Jesus after his crucifixion, is one of the most acclaimed such symbols in the Western world, admired for its beauty by believers and nonbelievers alike.

commitment to Jesus as their "Savior and Lord." They describe a feeling of beginning life again, hence the term *born again*.

THE CONFLICT PERSPECTIVE

As we saw earlier, conflict theorists examine how education supports the status quo. They do the same in their analysis of religion.

Opium of the People

In general, conflict theorists are highly critical of religion. Karl Marx, an avowed atheist who believed that the existence of God was impossible, set the tone for conflict theorists with his most famous statement on this subject: "Religion is the sigh of the oppressed creature, the sentiment of a heartless world.... It is the opium of the people" (Marx 1844/1964). By this statement, Marx meant that oppressed workers escape into religion. For them, religion is like a drug that helps them forget their misery. By diverting their thoughts to future happiness in a coming world, religion takes their eyes off their suffering in this one, thereby greatly reducing the possibility that they will rebel against their oppressors.

A Legitimation of Social Inequalities

Just as they do with education, conflict theorists examine how religion legitimates the social inequalities of society. By this, they mean that religion teaches that the existing social arrangements of a society represent what God desires. For example, during the Middle Ages Christian theologians decreed the "divine right of kings." This doctrine meant that God determined who would become king and set him on the throne. The king ruled in God's place, and it was the duty of a king's subjects to be loyal to him (and to pay their taxes). To disobey the king was to disobey God.

In what was perhaps the supreme technique of legitimating the social order (and one that went even a step further than the "divine right of kings"), the religion of ancient Egypt held that the Pharaoh was a god. The Emperor of Japan was similarly declared divine. If this were so, who could even question his decisions? Today's politicians would give their right arm for such a religious teaching!

Conflict theorists point to many other examples of how religion legitimates the social order. In India, Hinduism supports the caste system by teaching that an individual who tries to change caste will come back in the next life as a member of a lower caste—or even as an animal. In the decades before the American Civil War, Southern ministers used Scripture to defend slavery, saying that it was God's will—while northern ministers legitimated their region's social structure and used Scripture to denounce slavery as evil (Ernst 1988; Nauta 1993; White 1995).

RELIGION AND THE SPIRIT OF CAPITALISM

Max Weber disagreed with the conflict perspective that religion impedes social change by encouraging people to focus on the afterlife. In contrast, Weber saw religion's focus on the afterlife as a source of profound social change.

Like Marx, Weber observed the industrialization of European countries. Weber became intrigued with the question of why some societies embraced capitalism, while others clung to their traditional ways. As he explored this problem, he concluded that religion held the key to **modernization**—the transformation of traditional societies into industrial societies.

To explain his conclusions, Weber wrote *The Protestant Ethic and the Spirit of Capitalism* (1904–1905/1958). He said that

1. Capitalism is not just a superficial change. Rather, capitalism represents a fundamentally different way of thinking about work and money. *Traditionally, people worked just enough to meet their basic needs, not so they would have a surplus to invest.* To accumulate money (capital) as an end in itself, not just to spend it, was a radical departure from traditional thinking. People even came to consider it a duty to invest money in order to make profits, which, in turn, they reinvested to make more profits. Weber called this new approach to work and money the **spirit of capitalism.**

2. Why did the spirit of capitalism develop in Europe, and not, for example, in China or India, where the people had similar material resources, education, and so on? According to Weber, *religion was the key.* The religions of China and India, and indeed Roman Catholicism in Europe, encouraged a traditional approach to life, not thrift and investment. Capitalism appeared when Protestantism came on the scene.

3. What was different about Protestantism, especially Calvinism? John Calvin taught that God had predestined some people to heaven, others to hell. People could depend neither on church membership nor on

feelings about their relationship with God to know they were saved. You wouldn't know your fate until after you died.

4. This doctrine made people anxious. "Am I predestined to hell or to heaven?" Calvinists wondered. As they wrestled with this question, they concluded that church members have a duty to prove that they are God's elect, and to live as though they are predestined to heaven—for good works are a demonstration of salvation.

5. This conclusion motivated Calvinists to lead moral lives *and* to work hard, to not waste time, and to be frugal—for idleness and needless spending were signs of worldliness. Weber called this self-denying approach to life the **Protestant ethic.**

6. As people worked hard and spent money only on necessities (a pair of earrings or a second pair of dress shoes would have been defined as sinful luxuries), they had money left over. Because it couldn't be spent, this capital was invested—which led to a surge in production.

7. Thus, a change in religion (from Catholicism to Protestantism, especially Calvinism) led to a fundamental change in thought and behavior (the *Protestant ethic*). The result was the *spirit of capitalism.* Thus capitalism originated in Europe, and not in places where religion did not encourage capitalism's essential elements: the accumulation of capital and its investment and reinvestment.

At this point in history, the Protestant ethic and the spirit of capitalism are not confined to any specific religion or even to any one part of the world. Rather, they have become cultural traits that have spread to societies around the world (Greeley 1964; Yinger 1970). U.S. Catholics have about the same approach to life as do U.S. Protestants. In addition, Hong Kong, Japan, Malaysia, Singapore, South Korea, and Taiwan—not exactly Protestant countries—have embraced capitalism (Levy 1992).

TYPES OF RELIGIOUS GROUPS

Sociologists have identified four types of religious groups: cult, sect, church, and ecclesia. The summary presented here is a modification of analyses by sociologists Ernst Troeltsch (1931), Liston Pope (1942), and Benton Johnson (1963). Figure 13.4 illustrates the relationship between each of these four types of groups.

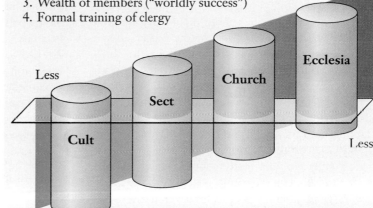

Characteristics of the Group
1. Number of members
2. Wealth of organization
3. Wealth of members ("worldly success")
4. Formal training of clergy

More

Less

Ecclesia

Church

Sect

Less

Cult

More

The Group Emphasizes
1. The need to reject society (the culture is a threat to true religion)
2. That it is rejected by society (the group feels hostility)
3. Hostility toward other religions
4. Hostility from other religions
5. Personal salvation
6. Emotional expression of religious beliefs
7. Revelation (God speaks directly to people)
8. God's direct intervention in people's lives (such as providing guidance or healing)
9. A duty to spread the message (evangelism)
10. A literal interpretation of scripture
11. A literal heaven and hell
12. That a conversion experience is necessary

Note: Any religious organization can be placed somewhere on this continuum, based on its having "more" or "less" of these characteristics.

 13.4 **A CONTINUUM OF RELIGIOUS GROUPS**

Sources: Based on Troeltsch 1931; Pope 1942; and Johnson 1963.

Cult

brings to mind

The word *cult* conjures up bizarre images—shaven heads, weird music, brainwashing—even ritual suicide may come to mind. Cults, however, are not necessarily weird, and few practice "brainwashing" or bizarre rituals. In fact, *all religions began as cults* (Stark 1989). A **cult** is simply a new or different religion, whose teachings and practices put it at odds with the dominant culture and religion. Cults often begin with the appearance of a **charismatic leader,** an individual who inspires people because he or she seems to have extraordinary qualities. **Charisma** refers to an outstanding gift or some exceptional quality. Finding something highly appealing about the individual—in some instances, almost a magnetic charm—people feel drawn to both the person and the message.

The most popular religion in the world began as a cult. Its handful of followers believed that an unschooled carpenter who preached in remote villages in a backwater country was the Son of God, that he was killed and came back to life. Those beliefs made the early Christians a cult, setting them apart from the rest of their society. Persecuted by both religious and political authorities, these early believers clung to one another for support. Many cut off associations with their unbelieving families and friends. To others, the early Christians must have seemed deluded and brainwashed.

Most cults fail. Not many people believe the new message, and the cult fades into obscurity. If the group recruits large numbers of people, however, the new religion changes from a cult to a sect.

Sect

A **sect** is larger than a cult. Its members still feel tension between their views and the prevailing beliefs and values of the broader society, but if a sect grows, that tension fades. To appeal to a broader base, the sect shifts some of its doctrines, redefining matters to remove some of the rough edges that created tension between it and the rest of society. As the members become more respectable in the eyes of society, they feel less hostility and little, if any, isolation. If a sect follows this course, as it grows and becomes more integrated into society it changes into a church.

Church

At this point, the religious group is highly bureaucratized—probably with national and international headquarters that direct the local congregations. The relationship with God has grown less intense. Worship services are likely to be more sedate, with less emphasis on personal salvation and emotional expression. Sermons become more formal, and written prayers may be read before the congregation. Most new members have not joined through conversion—after seeing the "new truth"—but are children born to existing members. To affirm their group's beliefs, the children, when older, may be asked to go through a ceremony such as a confirmation or bar mitzvah.

Ecclesia

Finally, some groups become so well integrated into a culture, and so strongly allied with their government, that it is difficult to tell where one leaves off and the other takes over. In these *state religions,* also called **ecclesia,** the government and religion work together to try to shape society. There is no recruitment of members, for citizenship makes everyone a member. The majority of the society, however, may belong to the religion in name only. The religion is part of cultural identification, not an eye-opening experience. In Sweden, for example, in the 1860s all citizens had to memorize Luther's *Small Catechism* and be tested on it yearly (Anderson 1995). Today, Lutheranism is still the state religion, but most Swedes come to church only for baptisms, marriages, and funerals.

Variations in Patterns

Obviously, not all religious groups go through all these stages—from cult to sect to church to ecclesia. Some die out because they fail to attract enough members. Others, such as the Amish, remain sects. And, as is evident from the few countries that have state religions, very few religions ever become ecclesias.

In addition, these classifications are not perfectly matched in the real world. For example, although the Amish are a sect, they place little or no emphasis on recruiting others. The early Quakers, another sect, shied away from emotional expressions of their beliefs. They would quietly meditate in church, with no one speaking until God gave someone a message to share with others. Finally, some groups that become churches may retain a few characteristics of sects, such as an emphasis on evangelism or a personal relationship with God.

Although all religions began as cults, not all varieties of a particular religion begin this way. For example, some denominations—"brand names" within a major religion, such as Methodism or Reform Judaism—may begin as splinter groups. A large group within a church may disagree with *some* aspects of the church's teachings (not its major message) and break away to form its own organization. An example is the Southern Baptist Convention, which was formed in 1845 to defend the right to own slaves.

Table 13.2

GROWTH IN RELIGIOUS MEMBERSHIP: THE PERCENTAGE OF AMERICANS WHO BELONG TO A CHURCH OR SYNAGOGUE	
	Percentage Who Claim Membership
1776	17%
1860	37%
1890	45%
1926	58%
1975	71%
1999	70%

Sources: Finke 1992; *Statistical Abstract* 2000:Table 75.

RELIGION IN THE UNITED STATES

Although many think religion is less important to Americans than it used to be, the growth in religious membership does not support such an assumption. As Table 13.2 shows, the proportion of Americans who belong to a church or synagogue is now *four* times higher than it was when the country was founded. Ninety-four percent of Americans believe there is a God, and 82 percent believe there is a life after death. On any given weekend, two of every five Americans report that they attend a church or synagogue (Woodward 1989; Gallup 1990; Greeley and Hout 1999; *Statistical Abstract* 1999:Table 89).

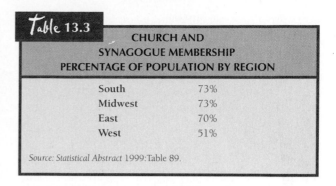

Table 13.3

CHURCH AND SYNAGOGUE MEMBERSHIP PERCENTAGE OF POPULATION BY REGION	
South	73%
Midwest	73%
East	70%
West	51%

Source: Statistical Abstract 1999:Table 89.

Characteristics of Members

Let's look at the characteristics of the 70 percent of Americans who belong to a church or synagogue. (The source does not contain information on members of mosques.)

Region Membership is not evenly distributed around the country. As Table 13.3 shows, membership is highest in the South and Midwest and not much lower in the East. Why is membership in the West so much lower? This may be due to the West being the newest region in the nation and having the highest net migration. If so, when its residents have put down firmer roots, the West's percentage of religious membership will increase.

Social Class Religion in the United States is stratified by social class. As Figure 13.5 illustrates, each religious group draws members from all social classes, but some are "top-heavy" and others "bottom-heavy." The most top-heavy are the Episcopalians and Jews, the most

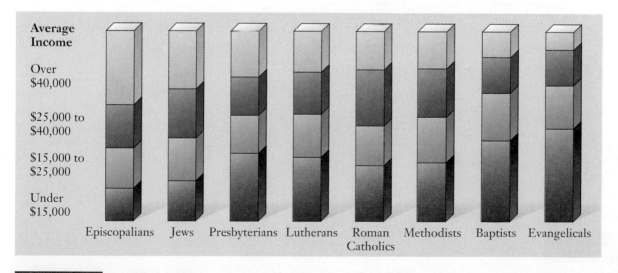

Figure 13.5 **INCOME AND RELIGIOUS AFFILIATION**

Source: Compiled from data in *Gallup Opinion Index,* 1987:20–27, 29.

bottom-heavy the Baptists and Evangelicals. This figure is further confirmation that churchlike groups tend to appeal more to the successful, while the more sectlike groups appeal to the less successful.

Race and Ethnicity All major religious groups draw from the nation's many racial and ethnic groups. Like social class, however, race and ethnicity tend to cluster. People of Latino or Irish descent are likely to be Roman Catholics, those of Greek origin to belong to the Greek Orthodox church. African Americans are likely to be Protestants, more specifically Baptists, or to belong to fundamentalist sects.

Although many churches are integrated, it is with good reason that Sunday morning between 10 and 11 A.M. has been called "the most segregated hour in the United States." African Americans tend to belong to African American churches, while most whites see only whites in theirs. The segregation of churches is based not on law, but on custom.

Age As shown in Table 13.4 , the chances that an American belongs to a church or synagogue increase with age. Possibly this is because people become more concerned about an afterlife as they age. Another explanation is that membership is seen as part of the adult role, and

Table 13.4	CHURCH OR SYNAGOGUE MEMBERSHIP, BY AGE	
Age	**Membership**	
18–29	63%	
30–49	66%	
50–64	71%	
65+	75%	

Source: Statistical Abstract 1999:Table 89.

as people marry, become parents, or become more established, they are more likely to join.

Characteristics of Religious Groups

Let's examine the major features of the religious groups in the United States.

Diversity With its 350,000 congregations and hundreds of denominations, no group even comes close to being a dominant religion in the United States (*Statistical Abstract* 1999:Table 88). As Figure 13.6 illustrates, however, there is a tendency for clustering to occur,

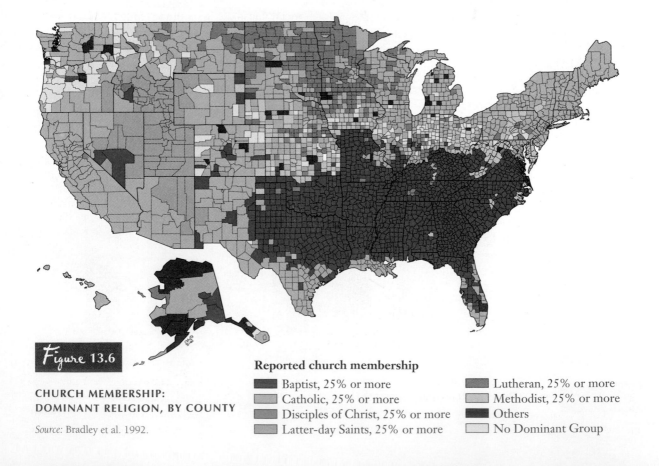

Figure 13.6

CHURCH MEMBERSHIP: DOMINANT RELIGION, BY COUNTY

Source: Bradley et al. 1992.

Reported church membership

- Baptist, 25% or more
- Catholic, 25% or more
- Disciples of Christ, 25% or more
- Latter-day Saints, 25% or more
- Lutheran, 25% or more
- Methodist, 25% or more
- Others
- No Dominant Group

CULTURAL DIVERSITY Around the World

THE NEW NEIGHBOR: ISLAM IN THE UNITED STATES

It is Sunday morning, and across the nation Americans are on their way to worship. Instead of going into a Baptist or a Roman Catholic church (or into a synagogue on Saturday), many Americans now enter mosques. In a scene that is growing increasingly familiar, they take off their shoes, face Mecca, and kneel with their faces to the floor.

Called by some the fastest growing religion in the United States, Islam is making its presence felt. Islam's growth is fueled by two main sources. The primary source is the millions of immigrants from the Middle East and Asia who have arrived in the United States since the 1980s. Like the immigrants before them, these refugees from Muslim countries brought along their religion as part of their culture. The second source is African Americans. Although believers represent a cross-section of African Americans, the call of Islam is heard most loudly in the inner city (Peart 1993). Overall, U.S. Muslims are about 42 percent African American, 25 percent South Asian, 12 percent Arab, and the remainder from a mix of backgrounds (Power 1998).

The appeal of Islam to African Americans is the message of black pride, self-improvement, and black power. Although U.S. Muslims are divided among twenty or so groups, the appeal is similar: morality (no drugs, crime, or extramarital sex), respect for women, and black empowerment. Among all groups, modest clothing is required. Among some, ultra-conservative codes govern behavior: Men and women sit apart in public, women wear robes that cover them from head to toe, and one-on-one dating is prohibited (Tapia 1994). Many men embrace the authority that Islam ascribes to them. For many, both men and women, Islam is a way to connect with African roots.

For many Americans, Louis Farrakhan is synonymous with U.S. Islam. Although he is the most visible and vocal Muslim leader, the group he heads, the Nation of Islam, has only about 10,000 members (Brooke 1995). The Chicago-based Muslim American Society, headed by W. Dean Mohammed, has 200,000 members (Miller 1999).

Just as their organizations are diverse, so their opinions are wideranging. With regard to race, for example, some believe the races are equal; others believe African Americans are superior and whites are devils. Similarly, some groups stress black separatism, while others emphasize the need to start businesses and run for office (Miller 1999).

Alarmed that Islam has gained so many converts, some African American Christians are counterattacking. They hold Muslim Awareness seminars in order to warn Christians away from Islam (Tapia 1994). A former Black Muslim who is now a Christian evangelist and who sees it as his duty to counter Islam, says the difference is grace. "Islam is a works-oriented religion, but Christianity is built on God's grace in Jesus."

"His is just a slave religion," retort some Muslims.

Despite tension and confrontation, it is apparent that the Muslim presence is not temporary, that the face of U.S. religion is being fundamentally altered. Mosques are taking their place in the midst of churches and synagogues, a sign of a maturing multicultural society. ■

Universally, children are socialized into the religion of their group. The kindergarten students shown here at the Al-Ghazaly Islamic school in Jersey City, New Jersey, are learning how to pray.

---

making some religious groups dominant in some regions. As the Cultural Diversity box above illustrates, with immigration from Muslim nations, the diversity is increasing.

Competition and Recruitment The many religious groups of the United States compete for clients. They even advertise in the Yellow Pages of the telephone directory and insert appealing advertising—under the guise of news—in the religious section of the Saturday or Sunday edition of the local newspapers.

Fundamentalist Revival The fundamentalist Christian churches are undergoing a revival. They teach that the Bible is literally true and that salvation comes only through a personal relationship with Jesus Christ. They also denounce what they see as the permissiveness of U.S. culture: sex on television and in movies, abortion, corruption in public office, premarital sex, cohabitation, and drugs. Their answer to these problems is firm, simple, and direct: People whose hearts are changed through religious conversion will change their lives.

The mainstream churches, which offer a remote God and a corresponding reduction in emotional involvement, fail to meet the basic religious needs of large numbers of Americans. Consequently, as Figure 13.7 shows, the mainstream churches are losing members, while the fundamentalists are gaining. The exception is the Roman Catholics, whose growth is due primarily to heavy immigration from Mexico and other Catholic countries.

The Electronic Church What began as a ministry to shut-ins and those who do not belong to a church has blossomed into its own type of church. Its preachers, called "televangelists," reach millions of viewers and raise millions of dollars. Some of its most famous ministries are those of Robert Schuller (the "Crystal Cathedral") and Pat Robertson (the 700 Club).

Many local ministers view the electronic church as a competitor. They complain that it competes for the attention and dollars of their members. The electronic church replies that its money goes to good causes and that through its conversions it feeds members into the local churches, strengthening, not weakening them.

The Internet and Religion As with so many aspects of life, the Internet has begun to have an impact on religion. The Mass Media box examines this theme.

Secularization and the Splintering of U.S. Churches

As the model, fashionably slender, paused before the head table of African American community leaders, her

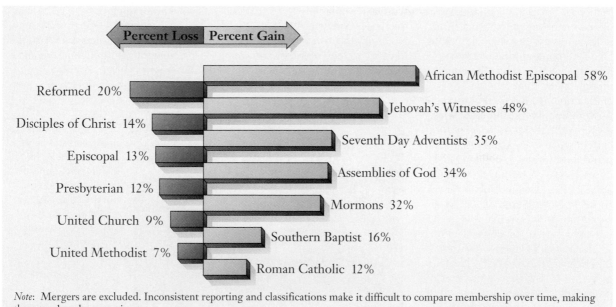

Note: Mergers are excluded. Inconsistent reporting and classifications make it difficult to compare membership over time, making these totals only approximate.

Figure 13.7 U.S. CHURCHES: GAINS AND LOSSES IN TEN YEARS

Sources: Yearbook of American and Canadian Churches 1993: Table 2; *Statistical Abstract* 1985:Table 74; 1995:Table 84.

gold necklace glimmering above the low-cut bodice of her emerald-green dress, the hostess, a member of the Church of God in Christ, said, "It's now OK to wear more revealing clothes—as long as it's done in good taste." Then she added, "You couldn't do this when I was a girl, but now it's OK—and you can still worship God." (Author's files)

When I heard these words, I grabbed a napkin and quickly jotted them down, my sociological imagination stirred at their deep implication. As strange as it may seem, this simple event pinpoints the essence of why the Christian churches in the United States have splintered. Let's see how this could possibly be.

The simplest answer to why Christians don't have just one church, or at most several, instead of the hundreds of sects and denominations that dot the U.S. landscape, is disagreements about doctrine (church teaching). As theologian and sociologist Richard Niebuhr pointed out, however, there are many ways of settling doctrinal disputes besides splintering off and forming another religious organization. Niebuhr (1929) suggested that the answer lies more in *social* change than it does in *religious* conflict.

The explanation goes like this. As noted earlier, when a sect becomes more churchlike, tension between it and the mainstream culture lessens. Quite likely, its founders and first members were poor, or at least not very successful in worldly pursuits. Feeling like strangers in the dominant culture, they derived a good part of their identity from their religion. Their services and customs stressed differences between their values and those of the dominant culture. Typically, their religion also stressed the joys of the coming afterlife, when they would be able to escape from their present pain.

As time passes, the group's values—such as frugality and the avoidance of gambling, alcohol, and drugs—help later generations become successful. As these later generations attain more education and become more middle

Mass Media in Social Life

GOD ON THE NET: THE ONLINE MARKETING OF RELIGION

Muslims in France download sermons and join an invisible community of worshippers at virtual mosques. Jews in Sweden type messages that fellow believers in Jerusalem download and insert in the Western Wall. Christians in California make digital donations to the Crystal Cathedral. Buddhists in Japan seek enlightenment online. The Internet helps to level the pulpit: On the Net, the leader of a pagan group can compete directly with the Pope.

The Internet is making religious rebellion easier, too. And it has become harder for organizations to punish those who do rebel. Jacques Gaillot is a French bishop who is critical of the Roman Catholic church. The church hierarchy ex-iled him to the Saharan desert of North Africa, a strategy that used to work. Instead of being silenced in his remote outpost, however, Gaillot logs onto the Internet, where he preaches to a virtual congregation via Real Audio (Huffstutter 1998).

No one knows the outcome, but the times, they are a' changin'. Some say that we are on the edge of a religious reformation as big as the one set off by Gutenberg's invention of the printing press (Huffstutter 1998).

Could be. Here are some of the developments in religion made possible by the Internet:

- New churches that exist only in cyberspace
- Online counseling for spiritual matters

- Chat rooms directed by rabbis
- Video and audio feeds of sermons
- Online forms for making donations by credit card
- Online stores that sell religious books and trinkets
- Mailing lists for those devoted to witchcraft

Will virtual religion satisfy? Will it prove to be an adequate replacement for the warm embrace of a fellow believer? Will it bring comfort to someone in mourning the way a sympathetic touch can? For some, not at all. For others, yes. We are gazing into the future. To what extent this new medium will affect our religious lives—and perhaps even alter the face of religion—remains to be seen. ■

class, they grow more respectable in the eyes of society. They no longer experience the alienation that was felt by the founders of their group. Life's burdens don't seem as heavy, and the need for relief through an afterlife doesn't seem as pressing. Similarly, the pleasures of the world no longer appear as threatening to the "true" belief. As illustrated by the woman at the fashion show, what follows is an attempt to harmonize religious beliefs with their changing ideas about the culture. This process is called the **secularization of religion**—shifting the focus from spiritual matters to the affairs of this world. (Secular means "belonging to the world and its affairs.")

Accommodation with the secular culture, however, displeases some of the group's members, especially those who have had less worldly success. They still feel a gulf between themselves and the broader culture. For them, tension and hostility continue to be real. They see secularization as a desertion of the group's fundamental truths, a "selling out" to the secular world. After futile attempts to bring the group back to its senses, they break away, forming a sect that once again stresses its differences from the world, the need for more personal, emotional religious experiences, and salvation from the pain of living in this world. The cycle then repeats itself.

THE FUTURE OF RELIGION

Religion thrives in even the most scientifically advanced nations. Humans are inquiring creatures, and one of the questions people develop as they reflect on life is, What is the purpose of it all? Why are we born? Is there an afterlife? If so, where are we going? Out of these concerns arises this question: If there is a God, what does God want of us in this life? Does God have a preference about how we should live?

Science, including sociology, cannot answer such questions. By its very nature, science cannot tell us about four main concerns that many people have: (1) the existence of God, (2) the purpose of life, (3) the existence of an afterlife, and (4) morality. About the first, science has nothing to say (no test tube has either isolated God or refuted God's existence). As to the second, although science can provide a definition of life and describe the characteristics of living organisms, it has nothing to say about ultimate purpose. As to the third, science can offer no information, for it has no tests that it can use to prove or disprove a "hereafter." As to the fourth, science can demonstrate the consequences of behavior but not the *moral* superiority of one action compared with another. This means that science cannot even prove that loving your family and neighbor is superior to hurting and killing them. Science can describe death and compute consequences, but it cannot dictate the moral superiority of any action, even in such an extreme example.

There is no doubt that religion will last as long as humanity lasts—for what could replace it? And if something did, and answered such questions, would it not be religion under another name?

SUMMARY AND REVIEW

■ **Education in Global Perspective**

What is a credential society, and how did it develop?
A **credential society** is one in which employers use diplomas and degrees to determine who is eligible for a job. One reason that credentialism developed is that large, anonymous societies lack the personal knowledge common to smaller groups; educational certification provides evidence of a person's ability. Pp. 331–332.

How does education compare among the Most Industrialized, Industrializing, and Least Industrialized Nations?
In general, formal education reflects a nation's economy. Education is extensive in the Most Industrialized Nations, under-going vast change in the Industrializing Nations, and spotty in the Least Industrialized Nations. Japan, Russia, and Egypt provide examples of education in countries at three levels of industrialization. Pp. 332–333.

■ **The Functionalist Perspective: Providing Social Benefits**

What is the functionalist perspective on education?
Among the functions of education are the teaching of knowledge and skills, **cultural transmission** of values, social integration, **gatekeeping**, and **mainstreaming**. Functionalists also note that education has replaced some traditional family functions. Pp. 333–334.

■ **The Conflict Perspective:
Reproducing the
Social Class Structure**

**What is the conflict perspective
on education?**

The basic view of conflict theorists is that education reproduces the social class structure; that is, through such mechanisms as unequal funding, education reinforces a society's basic
social inequalities. Pp. 335–337.

■ **The Symbolic Interactionist Perspective:
Fulfilling Teacher Expectations**

**What is the symbolic interactionist perspective
on education?**

Symbolic interactionists focus on face-to-face interaction. In
examining what occurs in the classroom, they have found a
self-fulfilling prophecy, that student performance tends to conform to teacher expectations, whether they are high or low.
Pp. 337–338.

■ **Problems in U.S. Education—
And Their Solutions**

**What are the chief problems that face
U.S. education?**

In addition to violence, the major problems are low achievement as shown by SAT scores, **grade inflation**, **social promotion**, and **functional illiteracy**. Pp. 338–339.

**What are the potential solutions to
these problems?**

The primary solution is to restore high educational standards, which can be done only after providing basic security for students. Any solution for improving quality must
be based on expecting more of *both* students and teachers.
Pp. 339–341.

■ **What Is Religion?**

Durkheim identified three essential characteristics of **religion**:
beliefs that set the **sacred** apart from the **profane**, **rituals**, and
a moral community (a **church**). P. 342.

■ **The Functionalist Perspective**

**What are the functions and dysfunctions
of religion?**

Among the functions of religion are answering questions about
ultimate meaning; providing social solidarity, guidelines for everyday life, adaptation, and support for the government; and
fostering social change. Among the dysfunctions of religion are
war and religious persecution. Pp. 343–344.

■ **The Symbolic Interactionist Perspective**

**What aspects of religion do symbolic
interactionists study?**

Symbolic interactionists focus on the meanings of religion for
its followers. They examine religious symbols, **rituals**, beliefs,
religious experiences, and the sense of community provided
by religion. Pp. 344–346.

■ **The Conflict Perspective**

What aspects of religion do conflict theorists study?

Conflict theorists examine the relationship of religion to social
inequalities, especially how religion reinforces a society's stratification system. P. 346.

■ **Religion and the Spirit of Capitalism**

**What does the spirit of capitalism have to do
with religion?**

Max Weber disagreed with Marx's conclusion that religion impedes social change. In contrast, Weber saw religion as a primary source of social change. He analyzed how Protestantism
gave rise to the **Protestant ethic**, which stimulated what he
called the **spirit of capitalism**. The result was capitalism,
which transformed society. Pp. 346–347.

■ **Types of Religious Groups**

What types of religious groups are there?

Sociologists divide religious groups into cults, sects, churches,
and ecclesias. All religions began as **cults**. Those that survive
tend to develop into **sects** and eventually into **churches**. Sects,
often led by **charismatic leaders**, are unstable. Some are perceived as threats and are persecuted by the state. **Ecclesias**, or
state religions, are rare. Pp. 347–348.

■ **Religion in the United States**

**What are the main characteristics of religion in the
United States?**

Membership varies by region, social class, age, and race or
ethnicity. Among the major characteristics are diversity, competition, a fundamentalist revival, and the electronic church.
Pp. 349–352.

**What is the connection between secularization of
religion and the splintering of churches?**

Secularization of religion, a change in a religious group's focus from spiritual matters to concerns of "this world," is the
key to understanding why churches divide. Basically, as a cult
or sect changes to accommodate its members' upward social
class mobility, it changes into a church. Left dissatisfied are
members who are not upwardly mobile. They tend to splinter

off and form a new cult or sect, and the cycle repeats itself. Pp. 352–354.

■ The Future of Religion

What is the future of religion?
Although industrialization led to the secularization of religion, this did not spell the end of religion. Because science cannot answer questions about ultimate meaning, the existence of God or an afterlife, or provide guidelines for morality, the need for religion will remain. In any foreseeable future, religion will prosper. P. 354.

Where can I read more on this topic?
Suggested readings for this chapter are listed on page SR-10.

YOUR INTERACTIVE COMPANION WEB SITE

Your Interactive Companion Web Site includes practice tests, with feedback, and online learning activities with video, audio, and Weblinks. Your access code for this Web site is provided with this text.

GLOSSARY

born again term describing Christians who have undergone a life-transforming religious experience so radical that they feel they have become a "new person" (p. 345)

charisma an extraordinary gift from God; more commonly, an outstanding, "magnetic" personality (p. 348)

charismatic leader someone to whom God has given an extraordinary gift; more commonly, someone who exerts extraordinary appeal to a group of followers (p. 348)

church to Durkheim, one of the three essential elements of religion—a moral community of believers (p. 342); used by other sociologists to refer to a highly bureaucratized religious organization (p. 348)

cosmology teachings or ideas that provide a unified picture of the world (p. 345)

credential society a group that uses diplomas and degrees to determine who is eligible for jobs, even though the diploma or degree may be irrelevant to the actual work (p. 331)

cult a new religion with few followers, whose teachings and practices put it at odds with the dominant culture and religion (p. 348)

cultural transmission in reference to education, the ways by which schools transmit culture, especially its core values (p. 333)

ecclesia a religious group so integrated into the dominant culture that it is difficult to tell where the one begins and the other leaves off (p. 348)

functional illiterate a high school graduate who has difficulty with basic reading and math (p. 339)

gatekeeping a process by which education opens and closes doors of opportunity; another term for the social placement function of education (p. 334)

grade inflation higher grades for the same work; a general rise in student grades without a corresponding increase in learning or test scores (p. 339)

hidden curriculum the unwritten goals of schools, such as teaching obedience to authority and conformity to cultural norms (p. 335)

latent functions unintended consequences of people's actions that help to keep a social system in equilibrium (p. 333)

mainstreaming helping people to become part of the mainstream of society (p. 334)

manifest functions the intended consequences of people's actions, designed to help some part of a social system (p. 333)

modernization the process by which a *Gemeinschaft* society is transformed into a *Gesellschaft* society; the transformation of traditional societies into industrial societies (p. 346)

profane Durkheim's term for common elements of everyday life (p. 342)

Protestant ethic Weber's term to describe the ideal of a self-denying moral life accompanied by hard work and frugality (p. 347)

religion to Emile Durkheim, beliefs and practices that separate the profane from the sacred and unite its adherents into a moral community (p. 342)

religious experience awareness of the supernatural or a feeling of coming in contact with God (p. 345)

rituals ceremonies or repetitive practices; in this context, religious observances or rites, often intended to evoke a sense of awe of the sacred (p. 345)

sacred Durkheim's term for things set apart or forbidden, that inspire fear, awe, reverence, or deep respect (p. 342)

sect a group larger than a cult whose members feel hostility from and toward society (p. 348)

secularization of religion the replacement of a religion's "other worldly" concerns with concerns about "this world" (p. 354)

social placement a function of education; funneling people into a society's various positions (p. 334)

social promotion promoting students to the next grade even though they have not mastered the basic materials (p. 339)

spirit of capitalism Weber's term for the desire to accumulate capital as a duty—not to spend it, but as an end in itself—and to constantly reinvest it (p. 346)

tracking sorting students into educational programs on the basis of real or perceived abilities (p. 334)

Chapter 14

Phoebe Beasley, Bus Stop in Beijing, 1983

Population and Urbanization

The image still haunts me. There stood Celia, age 30, her distended stomach visible proof that her thirteenth child was on its way. Her oldest was only 14 years old! A mere boy by our standards, he had already gone as far in school as he ever would.

Each morning, he joined the men to work in the fields. Each evening around twilight, we saw him return home, exhausted from hard labor in the subtropical sun.

My wife and I, who were living in Colima, Mexico, had eaten dinner in Celia's and Angel's home, which clearly reflected the family's poverty. A thatched hut consisting of only a single room served as home for all fourteen members of the family. At night, the parents and younger children crowded into a double bed, while the eldest boy slept in a hammock. As in many other homes in the village, the others slept on mats spread on the dirt floor.

The home was meagerly furnished. It had only a gas stove, a table, and a cabinet where Celia stored her few cooking utensils and clay dishes. There were no closets; clothes were hung on pegs in the walls. There also were no chairs, not even one. We were used to poverty in this village, but this really startled us. The family was so poor that they could not afford even a single chair.

Celia beamed as she told us how much she looked forward to the birth of her next child. Could she really mean it? It was hard to imagine that any woman would want to be in her situation.

Yet Celia meant every word. She was as full of delightful anticipation as she had been with her first child—and with all the others in between. ■

How could Celia have wanted so many children, especially when she lived in such poverty? That question bothered me. I couldn't let it go until I had the solution.

This chapter helps provide an answer.

POPULATION IN GLOBAL PERSPECTIVE

Celia's story takes us into the heart of **demography**, the study of the size, composition, growth, and distribution of human populations. It brings us face to face with the question of whether we are doomed to live in a world so filled with people that there will be practically no space for anybody. Will our planet be able to support its growing population? Or are chronic famine and mass starvation the sorry fate of most earthlings? Let's look at how

this concern first began, and then at what today's demographers say about it.

A PLANET WITH NO SPACE TO ENJOY LIFE?

The story begins with the lowly potato. When the Spanish Conquistadors found that people in the Andes ate this vegetable, which was unknown in Europe, they brought it home with them. Europeans viewed it suspiciously, but gradually the potato became the main food of the lower classes. With more abundant food, fertility increased, the death rate dropped and Europe's population soared, almost doubling during the 1700s (McKeown 1977; McNeill 1999).

Thomas Malthus (1766–1834), an English economist, saw this surging growth as a sign of doom. In 1798, he wrote a book that became world famous, *An*

In earlier generations, large farm families were common. (My own father came from a Minnesota farm family of ten children.) As the country industrialized and urbanized, having many children changed from a function (many hands to help with crops and food production) to a dysfunction (children were expensive non-producers). Consequently, the size of families shrank as we entered Stage 3 of the *demographic transition,* and today U.S. families of this size are practically nonexistent. This photo was taken of a Cajun family in Louisiana in 1938.

Essay on the Principle of Population. In it, Malthus proposed what became known as the **Malthus theorem.** He argued that while population grows geometrically (from 2 to 4 to 8 to 16 and so forth), the food supply increases only arithmetically (from 1 to 2 to 3 to 4 and so on). This meant, he claimed, that if births go unchecked, the population of a country, or even of the world, will outstrip its food supply.

The New Malthusians

Was Malthus right? This question has become a matter of heated debate among demographers. One group, which can be called the "New Malthusians," is convinced that today's situation is at least as grim, if not grimmer, than Malthus ever imagined. For example, *the world's population is growing so fast that in just the time it takes you to read this chapter, another fifteen thousand to twenty thousand babies will be born!* By this time tomorrow, the earth will have an additional quarter of a million people to feed. This increase goes on hour after hour, day after day, without letup. For an illustration of this growth, see Figure 14.1.

The New Malthusians point out that the world's population is following an **exponential growth curve.** This means that if growth doubles during approximately equal intervals of time, it suddenly accelerates. To illustrate the far-reaching implications of exponential growth, sociologist William Faunce (1981) told a parable about a poor man who saved a rich man's life. The rich man was grateful and said that he wanted to reward the man for his heroic deed.

The man replied that he would like his reward to be spread out over a four-week period, with each day's amount being twice what he received on the preceding day. He also said he would be happy to receive only one penny on the first day. The rich man immediately handed over the penny and congratulated himself on how cheaply he had gotten by. At the end of the first week, the rich man checked to see how much he owed and was pleased to find that the total was only $1.27. By the end of the second week he owed only $163.83. On the twenty-first day, however, the rich man was surprised to find that the total had grown to $20,971.51. When the twenty-eighth day arrived the rich man was shocked to discover that he owed $1,342,177.28 for that day alone and that the total reward had jumped to $2,684,354.56!

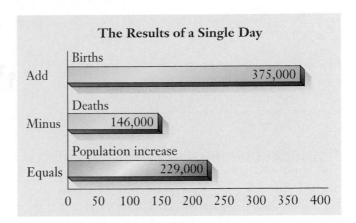

The Results of a Single Day

Add	Births — 375,000
Minus	Deaths — 146,000
Equals	Population increase — 229,000

0 50 100 150 200 250 300 350 400

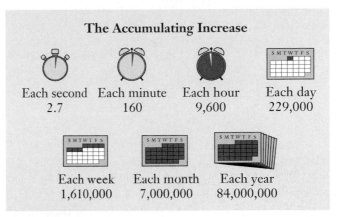

The Accumulating Increase

Each second	Each minute	Each hour	Each day
2.7	160	9,600	229,000

Each week	Each month	Each year
1,610,000	7,000,000	84,000,000

Figure 14.1   **HOW FAST IS THE WORLD'S POPULATION GROWING?**

Source: "Population Update" 2000.

This is precisely what alarms the New Malthusians. They claim that humanity has just entered the "fourth week" of an exponential growth curve. Figure 14.2 on the next page shows why they think the day of reckoning is just around the corner. They point out that it took all of human history for the world's population to reach its first billion. This happened about 1800. To add the second billion took only one hundred thirty years (1930). Just thirty years later (1960), the world population hit three billion. To reach the fourth billion took only fifteen years (1975). Then in just twelve years (1987) the total reached five billion, and in another twelve years it hit six billion (in 1999).

To illustrate this speeding increase, the New Malthusians have come up with some mind-boggling statistics. They note that before the Industrial Revolution it took 1,600 years for the world's population to double, but that

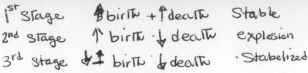

1st stage — ↑birth + ↑death — stable
2nd stage — ↑ birth ↓ death — explosion
3rd stage — ↓↑ birth ↓ death — · Stabelized

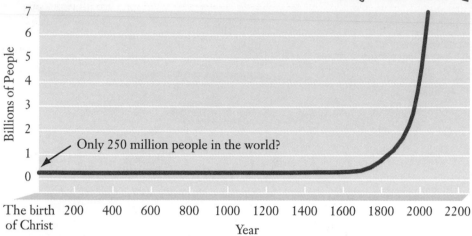

Only 250 million people in the world?

The birth of Christ

Year

Figure 14.2 WORLD POPULATION GROWTH OVER 2,000 YEARS

Source: Modified from Piotrow 1973:4.

the most recent doubling took just 40 years—40 times as fast (Cohen 1996). They also point out that between 8000 B.C. and A.D. 1750 the world added an average of only 67,000 people a year—but now that many people are being added *every seven hours* (Weeks 1994).

It is obvious, claim the New Malthusians, that there is going to be less and less for more and more.

Due to the Chinese government's policy of "one couple, one child," the birth rate of China has dropped sharply. As discussed in the text, this policy is carried out ruthlessly, including forcing abortions on protesting women.

The Anti-Malthusians

This does seem obvious, and no one wants to live shoulder-to-shoulder and fight for scraps. How, then, can anyone argue with the New Malthusians?

An optimistic group of demographers, whom we can call the "Anti-Malthusians", see things quite differently. They believe that Europe's **demographic transition** provides a more accurate picture of the future. This transition is diagrammed in Figure 14.3. During most of its history, Europe was in Stage 1. The population was stable, for high death rates offset the high birth rates. Then came Stage 2, the "population explosion" that so upset Malthus. Europe's population surged because birth rates remained high, while death rates went down. Finally, Europe made the transition to Stage 3: The population stabilized as people brought their birth rates into line with their lower death rates.

This, say the Anti-Malthusians, is precisely what will happen in the Least Industrialized Nations. Their current surge in growth simply indicates that they have reached Stage 2 of the demographic transition. Hybrid seeds and medicine imported from the Most Industrialized Nations have cut their death rates, but their birth rates remain high. When they move into Stage 3, as surely they will, we will wonder what all the fuss was about.

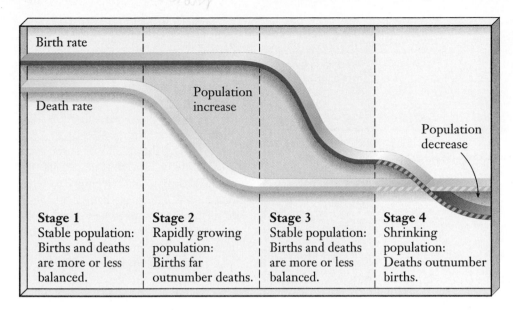

Figure 14.3

THE DEMOGRAPHIC TRANSITION

Note: The standard demographic transition is depicted by Stages 1–3. Stage 4 has recently been suggested by some Anti-Malthusians.

Who Is Correct?

As you can see, both the New Malthusians and the Anti-Malthusians have looked at historical trends and projected them onto the future. The New Malthusians project continued world growth and are alarmed. The Anti-Malthusians project Stage 3 onto the Least Industrialized Nations and are reassured.

There is no question that the Least Industrialized Nations are in Stage 2 of the demographic transition. The question is, will these nations enter Stage 3? After World War II, the West exported its hybrid seeds, herbicides, and techniques of public hygiene around the globe. Death rates plummeted in the Least Industrialized Nations as their food supply increased and health improved. Their birth rates stayed high, however, and their populations mushroomed. Just as Malthus had done 200 years before, demographers predicted worldwide catastrophe if something were not done immediately to halt the population explosion (Ehrlich and Ehrlich 1972, 1978).

We can use the conflict perspective to understand what happened when this message reached the leaders of the industrialized world. They saw the mushrooming populations of the Least Industrialized Nations as a threat to the balance of power they had so carefully worked out. With swollen populations, the poorer countries might demand a larger share of the earth's resources. The leaders found the United Nations to be a willing tool, and they used it to spearhead efforts to re-

duce world population growth. The results have been remarkable. The birth rates of the Least Industrialized Nations have dropped from an average of 2.1 percent a year in the 1960s to 1.4 percent today (Haub and Yinger 1994; Haub and Cornelius 1999).

The New Malthusians and Anti-Malthusians have greeted this news with significantly different interpretations. The New Malthusians stressed that the populations of the Least Industrialized Nations have not stopped growing—their growth had just slowed. A slower growth rate still spells catastrophe—it just takes a little longer for it to hit (Ehrlich and Ehrlich 1997). For the Anti-Malthusians, however, this slowing of the growth rate was the signal they had been waiting for—Stage 3 of the demographic transition was arriving. First the death rates of the Least Industrialized Nations fell—now, just as we predicted, they said, their birth rates are also falling.

The Anti-Malthusians also argue that our future will be the opposite of what the New Malthusians worry about. There will be too few children in the world, not too many. The world's problem will not be a population explosion, but **population shrinkage**—populations getting smaller. They point out that births in 65 of the world's nations have dropped so low that these countries no longer produce enough children to maintain their populations. Table 14.1 lists ten of those nations. As you look at this table, keep in mind that it

more deaTh Than birTh

Table 14.1

EXTREMES IN CHILDBIRTH

Where Do Women Give Birth to the Fewest Children?		Where Do Women Give Birth to the Most Children?	
Country	Number of Children	Country	Number of Children
1. Bulgaria	1.1	1. Niger	7.5
2. Latvia	1.1	2. Oman	7.1
3. Czech Republic	1.2	3. Ethiopia	7.0
4. Estonia	1.2	4. Gaza	7.0
5. Italy	1.2	5. Uganda	6.9
6. Macao	1.2	6. Angola	6.8
7. Russia	1.2	7. Somalia	6.8
8. San Marino	1.2	8. Western Sahara	6.8
9. Slovenia	1.2	9. Mali	6.7
10. Spain	1.2	10. Yemen	6.7

Note: The primary source also lists a fertility rate of 6.7 for Burkina Faso and the Marshall Islands. The secondary source lists these two countries as having a lower rate, so I have not included them in this table.

Sources: Primary, Haub and Cornelius 1999; Secondary, *Statistical Abstract* 1999:Table 1352.

takes an average of 2.1 children per couple to reproduce a population. (The extra .1 child makes up for those who die or fail to reproduce.) Due to immigration or to low death rates, these countries are continuing to grow slowly—but Germany and Italy already fill more coffins than cradles.

Some Anti-Malthusians even predict a "demographic free fall" (Mosher 1997). As more nations enter Stage 4 of the demographic transition the world's population will peak at about 7 or 8 billion, then begin to grow smaller. Two hundred years from now, they say, we will have a lot fewer people on earth.

Who is right? It simply is too early to tell. Like the proverbial pessimists who see the glass of water half empty, the New Malthusians interpret changes in world population growth negatively. And like the optimists who see the same glass half full, the Anti-Malthusians view the figures positively. Sometime during our lifetimes we should know the answer.

Why Are People Starving?

Pictures of starving children gnaw at our conscience. We live in such abundance, while these children and their parents starve before our very eyes. Why don't they have enough food? Is it because there are too many of them, or simply because the abundant food produced around the world does not reach them?

The Anti-Malthusians make a point that seems irrefutable. As Figure 14.4 shows, *the amount of food produced for each person in the world is now much more than it was in 1950.* Although the world's population has more

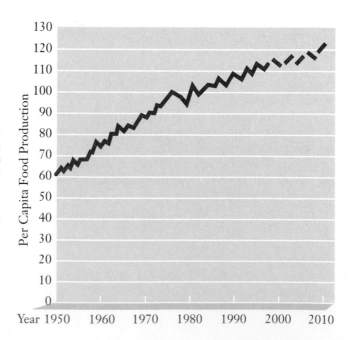

Figure 14.4

HOW MUCH FOOD DOES THE WORLD PRODUCE PER PERSON?

Note: 1979–1981 = 100

Years 1975 to 1991 are U.N. figures; years prior to 1975 have been recomputed from Simon to 1979–1981 base; years beyond 1998 are the author's projections.

Sources: Simon 1981:58; *United Nations Statistical Yearbook:* 1985–1986:Table 7; and 1990–1991: Table 4; *Statistical Abstract* 2000: Table 1396, and earlier years.

Photos of starving people, such as this mother and her child, haunt Americans and other members of the Most Industrialized Nations. Many of us wonder why, when others are starving, we should live in the midst of such abundance, often overeating and even casually scraping excess food into the garbage. The text discusses reasons for such unconscionable disparities.

than doubled during this time, improved seeds and fertilizers have made more food available for *each* person on earth. Even more food may be on the way, for scientists have found how to increase yields by planting more than one variety of a grain (Yoon 2000). Chemists have even discovered how to split nitrogen molecules. Since the earth's atmosphere is 78 percent nitrogen, we may be able to produce chemical compounds—including fertilizers—out of thin air (Naj 1995).

Then why do people die of hunger? From Figure 14.4, we can conclude that starvation does not occur because the earth produces too little food, but because particular places lack food. Some countries produce more food than their people can consume, others less than they need for survival. At the same time as famine ravishes West Africa, the U.S. government pays farmers to *reduce* their crops. The United States' problem is too much food; *theirs* too little.

The New Malthusians counter with the argument that the world's population is continuing to grow and that we do not know how long the earth will continue to produce enough food. They remind us of the penny doubling each day. It is only a matter of time, they say, until the earth no longer produces enough food—not "if," but "when."

Both the New Malthusians and the Anti-Malthusians have contributed significant ideas, but theories will not eliminate famines. Starving children are going to continue to peer out at us from our televisions and magazines, their tiny, shriveled bodies and bloated stomachs nagging at our conscience and calling for us to do some-

thing. Regardless of the underlying cause of this human misery, it can be alleviated by transporting food from nations that have a surplus.

These pictures of starving Africans leave the impression that Africa is overpopulated. Why else would all those people be starving? The truth, however, is far different. Africa has 22 percent of the earth's land, but only 10.5 percent of the earth's population (Nsamenang 1992). The reason for famines in Africa, then, *cannot* be too many people living on too little land. In fact, Africa contains some of the world's largest untapped lands suitable for agriculture (Bender and Smith 1997). Rather, these famines are due to three primary causes: drought, inefficient farming techniques, and wars that disrupt harvests and food distribution.

POPULATION GROWTH

Even if famines are due to a maldistribution of food rather than to world overpopulation, the fact remains that the Least Industrialized Nations are growing *fifteen times faster* than the Most Industrialized Nations—1.7 percent a year compared with 0.1 percent. (This looks like seventeen times faster because of rounding.) At these rates, it will take 583 years for the average Most Industrialized Nation to double its population, but just 40 years for the average Least Industrialized Nation to do so (Haub and Cornelius 1999). Why do the nations that can least afford it have so many children?

Why Do the Least Industrialized Nations Have So Many Children?

To understand why the population is growing so much faster in the Least Industrialized Nations, let's figure out why Celia is so happy about having her thirteenth child. To do this, we need to apply the symbolic interactionist perspective. We need to take the role of the other so we can understand the world of Celia and Angel as *they* see it. As our culture does for us, their culture provides a perspective on life that guides their choices. Celia's and Angel's culture tells them that twelve children are *not* enough, that they ought to have a thirteenth—as well as a fourteenth and fifteenth. How can this be? Let's consider three reasons that bearing many children plays a central role in their lives—and in the lives of millions of poor people around the world.

First is the status of parenthood. In the Least Industrialized Nations, motherhood is the most prized status a woman can achieve. The more children a woman bears, the more she is thought to have achieved the purpose for which she was born. Similarly, a man proves his manhood by fathering children. The more children he fathers, especially sons, the better—for through them his name lives on.

Second, the community supports this view. Celia and those like her live in *Gemeinschaft* communities, where people share values and closely identify with one another. Here children are seen as a sign of God's blessing. Accordingly, a couple should have many children. By producing children, people reflect the values of their community and achieve status. The barren woman, not the woman with a dozen children, is to be pitied.

These factors certainly provide strong motivations for bearing many children. Yet, there is a third incentive. For poor people in the Least Industrialized Nations, children are economic assets. These people have no social security or medical and unemployment insurance. This motivates them to bear *more* children, not fewer, for when parents become sick or too old to work—or when no work is to be found—they rely on their families to take care of them. The more children they have, the broader their base of support. Moreover, like the eldest son of Celia and Angel, children begin contributing to the family income at a young age. See Figure 14.5.

To those of us who live in the Most Industrialized Nations, it seems irrational to have many children. And *for us it would be.* Understanding life from the framework

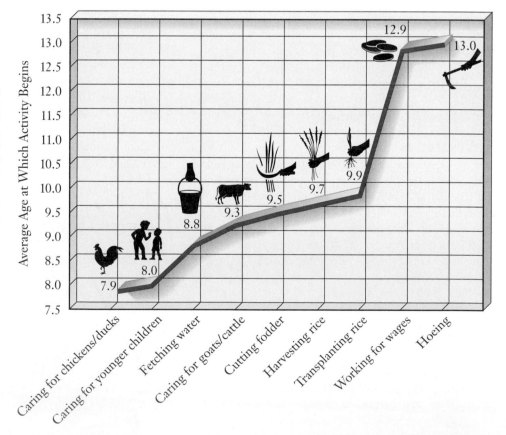

Figure 14.5

WHY THE POOR NEED CHILDREN

Surviving children are an economic asset in the Least Industrialized Nations. Based on a survey in Indonesia, this figure shows that boys and girls can be net income earners for their families by the age of 9 or 10.

Source: U.N. Fund for Population Activities.

of the people who are living it, however—the essence of the symbolic interactionist perspective—reveals how it makes perfect sense to have many children. Consider this report by a government worker in India:

> Thaman Singh (a very poor man, a water carrier) welcomed me inside his home, gave me a cup of tea (with milk and "market" sugar, as he proudly pointed out later), and said: "You were trying to convince me that I shouldn't have any more sons. Now, you see, I have six sons and two daughters and I sit at home in leisure. They are grown up and they bring me money. One even works outside the village as a laborer. *You told me I was a poor man and couldn't support a large family. Now, you see, because of my large family I am a rich man.*" (Mamdani 1973, italics added)

Conflict theorists offer a different view of why women in the poor nations bear so many children. They would argue that Celia has internalized values that support male dominance. In Latin America, *machismo*—an emphasis on male virility and dominance—is common. To father many children, especially sons, demonstrates virility, giving a man valued status in the community. From a conflict perspective, then, the reason poor people have so many children is that men control women's reproductive choices.

Implications of Different Rates of Growth

The result of Celia's and Angel's desire for many children—and of the millions of Celias and Angels like them—is that Mexico's population will double in thirty-six years. In contrast, Spain is growing so slowly that it will take 6,931 years to double (Haub and Cornelius 2000). To illustrate population dynamics, demographers use **population pyramids.** These depict a country's population by age and sex. Figure 14.6 compares the population pyramids of the United States, Mexico, and the world.

You can see how important age structure is. If by some miracle Mexico were transformed overnight into a nation as industrialized as the United States, and the average number of children per woman dropped to 2.0, the same as in the United States, the population of Mexico would continue to grow much faster—simply because a much higher percentage of Mexican women are in their childbearing years.

The implications of a doubling population are mind-boggling. *Just to stay even,* within thirty-six years Mexico must double its jobs, food production, and factories; hospitals and schools; transportation, communication, water, gas, sewer, and electrical systems; housing, churches, civic buildings, theaters, stores, and parks. If Mexico fails to double them, its already meager standard of living will drop even further.

Conflict theorists point out that a declining standard of living poses the threat of political instability—protests, riots, even revolution, and, in response, repression by the government. Political instability in one country can spill over into others, threatening an entire region's balance of power. Consequently, the leaders of

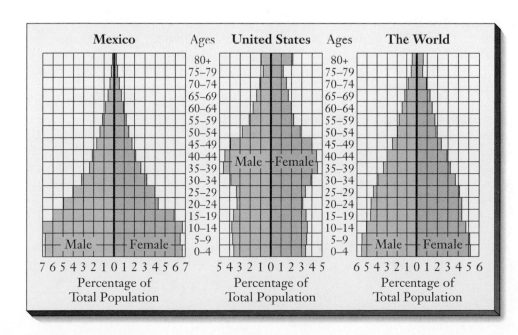

Figure 14.6

THREE POPULATION PYRAMIDS

Source: Population Today, 26, 9, September 1998:4, 5.

highest # Rate for birth & death – Niger: 24
Lowest Death Rate = Qatar, Kuwait (2)
highest for Migration = U.S.A.

the Most Industrialized Nations use the United Nations to direct a campaign of worldwide birth control. With one hand, they give agricultural aid, IUDs, and condoms to the masses in the Least Industrialized Nations—while, with the other, they sell weapons to the elites in these countries. Both actions, say conflict theorists, serve the same purpose of promoting political stability and the dominance of the Most Industrialized Nations in global stratification.

The Three Demographic Variables

How many people will live in the United States fifty years from now? What will the world's population be then? These are important questions. Educators want to know how many schools to build. Manufacturers want to anticipate changes in demand for their products. The government needs to know how many doctors, engineers, and executives to train. Politicians want to know how many people will be paying taxes—and how many young people will be available to fight a war.

To project the future of populations, demographers use three **demographic variables:** fertility, mortality, and migration. Let's look at each.

Fertility The **fertility rate** is the number of children the average woman bears. A term sometimes confused with fertility is *fecundity,* the number of children women are *capable* of bearing. The fecundity of women around the world is around twenty children each. Their fertility rate, however (the actual number of children they bear), is much lower. The world's overall fertility rate is 2.9, which means that the average woman in the world bears 2.9 children during her lifetime. At 2.0, the fertility rate of U.S. women is considerably less.

The region of the world that has the highest fertility rate is sub-Saharan Africa, where the average woman gives birth to 5.8 children; the lowest is Europe, where the average woman bears only 1.4 children. As you can see from Table 14.1 on page 364, Bulgaria and Latvia tie for the world's lowest fertility rate. There, the average woman gives birth to only 1.1 children. Niger in West Africa holds the record for the world's highest rate. There the average woman gives birth to 7.5 children, *seven* times as many children as the average woman in Bulgaria or Latvia.

To compute the fertility rate of a country, demographers analyze the government's records of births. From these, they figure the country's **crude birth rate,** the annual number of live births per 1,000 population. There may be considerable slippage here, of course. The birth records in many of the Least Industrialized Nations are haphazard.

Mortality The second demographic variable, **crude death rate,** refers to the number of deaths per 1,000 population. It, too, varies widely around the world. The highest death rate is 24, a record held by Niger in West Africa, the country that also has the world's highest birth rate. At 2, three oil-rich countries in the Mideast—Kuwait, Qatar, and United Arab Emirates—tie for the world's lowest death rate (Haub and Cornelius 1999).

Migration The third major demographic variable is the **net migration rate,** the difference between the number of *immigrants* (people moving in) and *emigrants* (people moving out) per 1,000 population. Unlike fertility and mortality, this rate does not affect the global population, for people are simply shifting their residence from one country or region to another.

As you know, immigrants are seeking a better life. They are willing to give up the security of their family and friends to move to a country with a strange language and unfamiliar customs. What motivates people to embark on such a venture? To understand migration, we need to look at both push and pull factors. The *push* factors are what people want to escape—poverty, the lack of religious and political freedoms, political persecution. The *pull* factors are the magnets that draw people to a new land, such as a chance for higher wages and better jobs.

Around the world, the flow of migration is from the Least Industrialized Nations to the industrialized countries. After "migrant paths" are established, immigration often accelerates as networks of kin and friends become additional magnets that attract more people from the same nation—and even from the same villages (Kalish 1994). As discussed in the Cultural Diversity box on the next page, immigration is contributing to a shifting U.S. racial-ethnic mix.

By far, the United States is the world's number one choice of immigrants. The United States admits more immigrants each year than all the other nations of the world

CULTURAL DIVERSITY In the United States

GLIMPSING THE FUTURE:
THE SHIFTING U.S. RACIAL-ETHNIC MIX

During the next twenty-five years, the population of the United States is expected to grow by about 22 percent. To see what the U.S. population will look like in twenty-five years, can we simply multiply the current racial-ethnic mix by 22 percent? The answer is a resounding no. As you can see from the figure below, some groups will grow much more than others, giving us a different-looking United States. Some of the changes in the U.S. racial-ethnic mix will be dramatic. In twenty-five years, one of every seventeen Americans is expected to have an Asian background, and one of every six a Latino background.

The basic cause of this fundamental shift is immigration. Because the racial-ethnic groups have different rates of immigration, their proportions of the U.S. population will change. As you can see, the proportion of non-Hispanic whites is expected to shrink, that of Native Americans to remain the same. Little immigration is expected from Africa, but because African Americans have a higher than average birth rate, their proportion of the overall population is expected to increase. Due to vast immigration, in twenty-five years Latinos will be, by far, the largest minority group, outnumbering African Americans by 16 million people. ■

For Your Consideration

This shifting racial-ethnic mix is one of the most significant events occurring in the United States. To better understand its implications, apply the three theoretical perspectives.

Use the conflict perspective to identify the groups likely to be threatened by this change. Over what resources are struggles likely to develop? What impact do you think this changing mix might have on European Americans? On African Americans? On Latinos? On Asian Americans? On Native Americans? What changes in immigration laws (or their enforcement) can you anticipate?

To apply the symbolic interactionist perspective, consider how groups might perceive one another differently as their proportion of the population changes. To apply the functionalist perspective, try to determine how each racial-ethnic group will benefit from this changing mix. How will other parts of society (such as businesses) benefit? What dysfunctions can you anticipate?

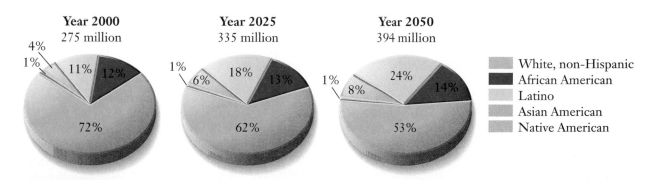

Year 2000
275 million
4%
1%
11%
12%
72%

Year 2025
335 million
1%
6%
18%
13%
62%

Year 2050
394 million
1%
8%
24%
14%
53%

- White, non-Hispanic
- African American
- Latino
- Asian American
- Native American

Figure 14.7 **LOOKING TOWARD THE FUTURE**

Source: U.S. Bureau of the Census. *Current Population Reports* P25–1130, 1996.

Table 14.2

PLACE OF BIRTH OF IMMIGRANTS TO THE UNITED STATES, BY REGION AND COUNTRY, 1981–1997

North America	6,173,000	Central and South America	1,698,000
Mexico	3,451,000	El Salvador	380,000
Dominican Republic	512,000	Colombia	219,000
Jamaica	341,000	Guatemala	167,000
Cuba	288,000	Guyana	159,000
Haiti	270,000	Peru	143,000
Canada	222,000	Ecuador	110,000
Trinidad and Tobago	88,000	Nicaragua	101,000
		Honduras	97,000
Asia	**5,025,000**	Brazil	62,000
Philippines	893,000	Panama	49,000
Vietnam	757,000	Argentina	45,000
China	699,000	Venezuela	38,000
India	537,000	Chile	37,000
Korea	467,000		
Iran	243,000	**Europe**	**1,701,000**
Laos	186,000	Former Soviet Union	487,000
Pakistan	145,000	Great Britain	248,000
Cambodia	130,000	Poland	240,000
Hong Kong	124,000	Germany	120,000
Thailand	105,000	Ireland	89,000
Taiwan	90,000	Romania	79,000
Japan	89,000	Yugoslavia	63,000
Lebanon	76,000	Portugal	60,000
Israel	62,000	Italy	50,000
Jordan	62,000	France	43,000
Iraq	52,000	Greece	41,000
Bangladesh	45,000		
Afghanistan	42,000	**Africa**	**453,000**
Syria	40,000	Nigeria	83,000
Turkey	40,000	Egypt	66,000
		Ethiopia	65,000
		Ghana	40,000

Note: Because only the countries with the largest emigration are listed, the total for an entire region is larger than the total of the countries from that region. When 1997 data was missing, 1996 data was doubled.

Source: Statistical Abstract 1999:Table 8.

ernment puts their number at 5 million. Most have come from Central and South America, especially Mexico (*Statistical Abstract* 1999:Table 10).

Experts cannot agree whether immigrants are a net contributor to or a drain on the U.S. economy. Economist Julian Simon (1986, 1993) claimed that they benefit the economy. After subtracting what immigrants collect in welfare and adding what they produce in jobs and taxes, he concludes that immigrants produce more than they cost. Other economists such as Donald Huddle (1993) use figures showing that immigrants are a drain on taxpayers. The fairest conclusion seems to be that the more educated immigrants produce more than they cost, while the less educated cost more than they produce ("Immigration's Costs" 1997).

Problems in Forecasting Population Growth

The total of the three demographic variables—fertility, mortality, and net migration—gives us a country's **growth rate**, the net change after people have been added to and subtracted from a population. What demographers call the **basic demographic equation** is quite simple:

$$\text{Growth rate} = \text{births} - \text{deaths} + \text{net migration}$$

If population increase depended only on biology, the demographer's job would be simple. But social factors—wars, economic booms and busts, plagues, and famines—push birth and death rates up or down. As shown in the Cultural Diversity box on the next page, even infanticide can affect population growth. Government programs also complicate projections. Some governments take steps to persuade women to bear more children. When Hitler decided that Germany needed more "Aryans," the German government outlawed abortion and offered cash bonuses for women who gave birth. The population increased.

Other countries take steps to reduce the number of children. None has been so draconian as China. As

combined. Twenty million—one of every twelve Americans—were born in another country. Table 14.2 shows where U.S. immigrants were born. To escape grinding poverty, such as that which surrounds Celia and Angel, people also enter the United States illegally. The U.S. gov-

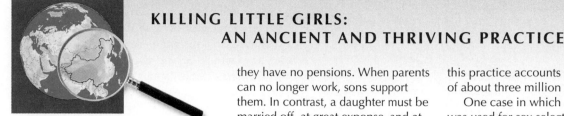

CULTURAL DIVERSITY Around the World

KILLING LITTLE GIRLS:
AN ANCIENT AND THRIVING PRACTICE

"The Mysterious Case of the Missing Girls" could have been the title of this box. Around the globe, for every 100 girls born, about 105 boys are born. In China, however, for every 100 baby girls, there are 111 baby boys. Given China's huge population, this means China has about 400,000 fewer baby girls than it should have. Why?

The answer is *female infanticide*, the killing of baby girls. When a Chinese woman goes into labor, village midwives sometimes grab a bucket of water. If the newborn is a girl, she is plunged into the water before she can draw her first breath.

At the root of China's infanticide is economics. The people are poor, and they have no pensions. When parents can no longer work, sons support them. In contrast, a daughter must be married off, at great expense, and at that point her obligations transfer to her husband and his family.

In the past few years, the percentage of baby boys has grown. The reason, again, is economics, but this time it has a new twist. As China opened the door to capitalism, travel and trade opened up—but primarily to men, for it is not thought appropriate for women to travel alone. Thus men find themselves in a better position to bring profits home to the family—and this is one more reason for parents to desire male children.

Female infanticide is also common in India. Many Indian women use ultrasound to learn the sex of their child, and then abort the fetus if it is a girl. Although the use of ultrasound for this purpose is illegal, this practice accounts for the abortion of about three million girls a year.

One case in which amniocentesis was used for sex selection led to a public outcry in India. The outrage was not about female infanticide, however; nor was it due to an antiabortion movement. Rather, the public became incensed when a physician mistakenly gave the parents wrong information and aborted a *male* baby!

It is likely that the preference for boys, and the resulting female infanticide, will not disappear until the social structures that perpetuate sexism are dismantled. This will not take place until women hold as much power as men, a development that, should it ever occur, apparently lies far in the future. ■

Sources: Lagaipa 1990; McGowan 1991; Polumbaum 1992; Renteln 1992; Greenhalgh and Li 1995; Jordan 2000.

---

you read these details, recall the Big Brother vignette that opened Chapter 11. What occurs in China goes beyond even Orwell's fertile imagination. China's "One couple, one child" national policy is well known, but few know how ruthlessly it is carried out. Steven Mosher, an anthropologist who did fieldwork in China, revealed that—whether she wants it or not—after the birth of her first child, each woman is fitted with an IUD (intrauterine device). If a woman has a second child, she is sterilized. If a woman gets pregnant without permission (yes, you read that right), she is aborted. If she does not consent to an abortion, one is performed on her anyway—even if she is nine months pregnant (Erik 1982). The government even has its agents check sanitary napkins to make sure that women are having their menstrual periods and are not pregnant.

Letting such policies pass without comment, we can see that a government's efforts to change a country's growth rate complicate the demographer's task of projecting future populations.

The primary factor that influences a country's growth rate is industrialization. *In every country that industrializes, the growth rate declines.* Not only does industrialization open up economic opportunities, but also it makes children more expensive. They require more education and remain dependent longer. Significantly, the basis for conferring status also changes—from having children to attaining education and displaying material wealth. People like Celia and Angel begin to see life differently, and their motivation to have many children drops sharply. Not knowing how rapidly industrialization will progress, or how quickly changes in values and reproductive behavior will follow, adds to the difficulty of making accurate projections.

Because of these many complications, demographers play it safe by making several projections of population growth. For example, what will the U.S. population be in the year 2050? Will there be **zero population growth,** with every 1,000 women giving birth to 2,100 children? (The extra 100 children make up for those

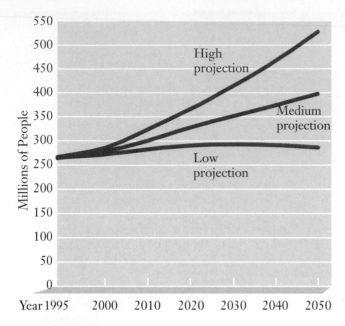

Figure 14.8   POPULATION PROJECTIONS OF THE UNITED STATES

Source: Statistical Abstract 1999:Table 17.

who do not survive or reproduce.) Will a larger proportion of women go to college? (The more education women have, the fewer children they bear.) How will immigration change during the coming years? Will AIDS rage out of control? Will some other devastating disease appear? What will happen to the new global economy? With such huge variables, it is easy to see why demographers make the three projections of the U.S. population shown in Figure 14.8.

URBANIZATION

Let's look at a different aspect of population: where people live. Because the world is rapidly becoming urban, we will concentrate on urban trends and urban life. To better understand urban life, let's first find out how the city itself came about.

THE DEVELOPMENT OF CITIES

Cities are not new to the world scene. Perhaps as early as seven to ten thousand years ago people built small cities with massive defensive walls, such as biblically famous Jericho (Homblin 1973). Cities on a larger scale originated about 3500 B.C., about the same time writing was invented (Chandler and Fox 1974; Hawley 1981). At that time, cities appeared in several parts of the world—first in Mesopotamia (Iran) and later in the Nile, Indus, and Yellow River valleys, in West Africa, around the Mediterranean, in Central America, and in the Andes (Fischer 1976; Flanagan 1990).

The key to the origin of cities is the development of more efficient agriculture (Lenski and Lenski 1987). Only when farming produces a surplus can some people stop being food producers and gather in cities to spend time in other pursuits. A **city**, in fact, can be defined as a place in which a large number of people are permanently based and do not produce their own food. The invention of the plow between five and six thousand years ago created widespread agricultural surpluses, stimulating the development of towns and cities (Curwin and Hart 1961).

Most early cities were tiny by comparison with those of today, merely a collection of a few thousand people in agricultural centers or on major trade routes. The most notable exceptions are two cities that reached one million for a brief period of time before they declined—Changan in China about A.D. 800 and Baghdad in Persia about A.D. 900 (Chandler and Fox 1974). Even Athens at the peak of its power in the fifth century B.C. had less than 200,000 inhabitants. Rome, at its peak, may have had a million or more (Flanagan 1990).

Even 200 years ago, the only city in the world that had a population of more than a million was Peking (now Beijing), China (Chandler and Fox 1974). Then in just 100 years, by 1900, the number of such cities jumped to sixteen. The reason was the Industrial Revolution, which drew people to cities by providing work. The Industrial Revolution also stimulated rapid transportation and communication, and allowed people, resources, and products to be moved efficiently—all essential factors (called *infrastructure*) on which large cities depend. Today about 300 cities have a million or more people (Frisbie and Kasarda 1988).

The Process of Urbanization

Although cities are not new to the world scene, urbanization is. **Urbanization** refers not just to masses of people moving to cities, but also to those cities having a growing influence on society. Urbanization is worldwide. In 1800, only 3 percent of the world's population lived in

Early cities were small economic centers surrounded by walls to keep out enemies. These cities had to be fortresses, for they were constantly threatened by armed, roving tribesmen and by nearby leaders of city-states who raised armies to enlarge their domain and enrich their coffers by sacking neighboring cities. Pictured here is Carcasonne, a restored medieval city in southern France.

cities (Hauser and Schnore 1965). Today 45 percent of the world's population lives in cities: about 75 percent of people in the industrialized world and 37 percent of those who live in the Least Industrialized Nations. Each year the world's urban population grows by about 0.5 percent, and soon most people will live in cities (Haub and Cornelius 1999). Without the Industrial Revolution this remarkable growth could not have taken place, for an extensive infrastructure is needed to support hundreds of thousands and even millions of people in a relatively small area.

To understand the city's attraction, we need to consider the "pulls" of urban life. Due to its exquisite division of labor, the city offers incredible variety—music ranging from rock and blues to country and classic, diets for vegetarians and diabetics as well as imported delicacies from around the world for everyone else. Cities also offer anonymity, which so many find refreshing in light of the much tighter controls of village and small-town life. And, of course, the city offers work.

Some cities have grown so large and have so much influence over a region that the term *city* is no longer adequate to describe them. The term **metropolis** is used instead. This term refers to a central city surrounded by smaller cities and their suburbs. They are linked by transportation and communication and connected ec-

onomically, and sometimes politically, through county boards and regional governing bodies.

St. Louis is an example. Although this name, St. Louis, properly refers to a city of fewer than 400,000 people in Missouri, it also refers to another two million people who live in more than a hundred separate towns in both Missouri and Illinois. Altogether, the region is known as the "St. Louis or Bi-State Area." Although these towns are independent politically, they form an economic unit. They are linked by work (many people in the smaller towns work in St. Louis, or are served by industries from St. Louis), by communications (they share the same area newspaper and radio and television stations), and by transportation (they use the same interstates, "Bi-State Bus" system, and international airport). As symbolic interactionists would note, a common identity also arises from the area's shared symbols (the Arch, the Mississippi River, Busch Brewery, the Cardinals, the Rams, the Blues—both the hockey team and the music). Most of the towns run into one another, and if you were to drive through this metropolis you would not know that you were leaving one town and entering another—unless you had lived here some time and were aware of the fierce small-town identifications and rivalries that exist side by side with this larger identification.

Some metropolises have grown so large and influential that the term **megalopolis** is used to describe them. This term refers to an overlapping area consisting of at least two metropolises and their many suburbs. Of the twenty or so megalopolises in the United States, the three largest are the eastern seaboard running from Maine to Virginia, the area in Florida between Miami, Orlando, and Tampa, and California's coastal area between San Francisco and San Diego. This California megalopolis extends into Mexico, and includes Tijuana and its southern suburbs.

This process of urban areas turning into a metropolis and a metropolis developing into a megalopolis occurs worldwide. Figure 14.9 shows the ten largest cities in the world. Note that most are located in the Least Industrialized Nations.

U.S. Urban Patterns

In its early years, the United States was almost exclusively rural. In 1790, only about 5 of every 100 Americans lived in cities. By 1920, this figure had jumped to 1 of 2. Urbanization has continued without letup, and today about 75 to 80 percent of Americans live in cities. As you can see from the Social Map on the next page, like our other social patterns, urbanization is uneven across the United States.

The U.S. Census Bureau has divided the country into 284 **metropolitan statistical areas (MSAs).** Each MSA consists of a central city of at least 50,000 people and the urbanized areas linked to it. About three of five Americans live in just fifty or so MSAs.

As Americans migrate in search of work and better lifestyles, some cities gain population while others shrink. Table 14.3 compares the fastest growing U.S. cities with those that are losing people. As you can see, ten of the fastest growing cities are in the West, and two are in the South. Of the declining cities, ten are in the Northeast, while the South and West have one each.

As Americans migrate, **edge cities** have developed. This term refers to clusters of shopping malls, hotels, office parks, and residential areas that are located near the intersection of major highways. Although these clusters may overlap the boundaries of several cities or towns, they provide a sense of place to those who live, work, or shop there.

Another major U.S. urban pattern is **gentrification**, the movement of middle-class people into rundown areas of a city. They are attracted by the low prices for quality housing that, though deteriorated, can be restored. One consequence is an improvement in the appearance of some urban neighborhoods—freshly painted buildings, well-groomed lawns, and the absence of boarded-up

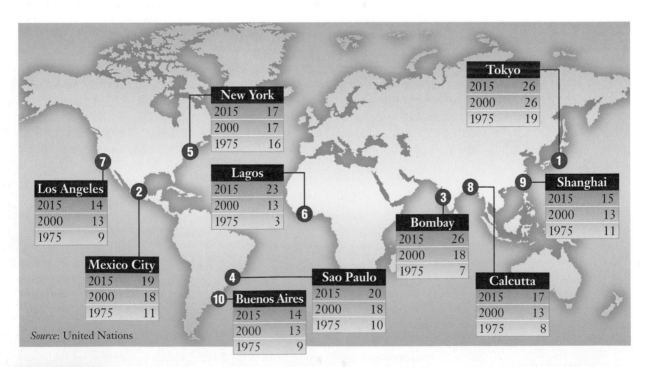

Figure 14.9 **THE URBAN GIANTS: THE POPULATION OF THE WORLD'S TEN LARGEST CITIES, IN MILLIONS**

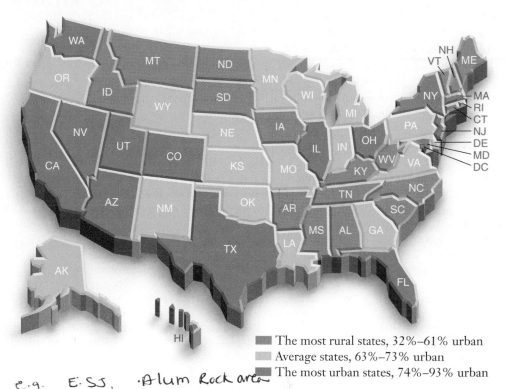

Figure **14.10**

HOW URBAN IS YOUR STATE? THE RURAL-URBAN MAKEUP OF THE UNITED STATES

Note: The most rural state is Vermont, where 2 of 3 residents (68 percent) live in rural areas. The most urban state is California, where only 1 of 14 residents (7 percent) lives in rural areas.

Source: Statistical Abstract 1999:Table 46.

■ The most rural states, 32%–61% urban
■ Average states, 63%–73% urban
■ The most urban states, 74%–93% urban

e.g. E·SJ. ·Alum Rock area

windows. Another consequence is that the poor residents are displaced as the more well-to-do newcomers move in. Tension often arises between these groups (Anderson 1990; 1999).

A common pattern is for the gentrifiers to be whites and the displaced to be minorities. As discussed in the Down-to-Earth Sociology box on the next page, in Harlem, New York, both the gentrifiers and the displaced

---

Table **14.3**

THE FASTEST-GROWING AND FASTEST-SHRINKING U.S. CITIES	
The Fastest-Growing Cities	**The Fastest-Shrinking Cities**
1. 40.9% Las Vegas, NV	1. −4.7% Salinas, CA
2. 29.2% McAllen-Edinburg-Mission, TX	2. −4.5% Utica-Rome, NY
3. 25.9% Boise City, ID	3. −3.9% Birmingham, NY
4. 23.7% Fayetteville-Springdale-Rogers, AR	4. −2.3% Charleston, SC
5. 23.1% Austin-San Marcos, TX	5. −1.9% Springfield, MA
6. 22.7% Phoenix-Mesa, AZ	6. −1.6% Scranton-Wilkes Barre, PA
7. 22.2% Olympia, WA	7. −1.5% Vineland-Millville-Bridgeton, NJ
8. 22.1% Bremerton, WA	8. −1.4% New London-Norwich, CT
9. 21.3% Provo-Orem, UT	9. −1.2% Buffalo-Niagara Falls, NY
10. 21.1% Brownsville-Harlingen-San Benito, TX	10. −1.2% New Haven-Meriden, CT
11. 19.4% Raleigh-Durham-Chapel Hill, NC	11. −1.1% Hartford, CT
12. 19.1% Colorado Springs, CO	12. −0.9% Providence, RI

Note: Figures indicate the percentage of population change from 1990–1996. A minus sign indicates a loss of population.

Source: Statistical Abstract 1999:Table 43.

urban ecology
human Ecology = people adaption to enviroment

Sociology

RECLAIMING HARLEM: "IT FEEDS MY SOUL"

The story is well known. The inner city is filled with crack, crime, and corruption. It reeks from foul, festering garbage strewn on the streets and piled up around burned-out buildings. Only those who have no choice live in this despairing, abandoned environment where danger lurks around every corner.

What is not so well known is that affluent African Americans are reclaiming some of these areas.

Howard Sanders was living the American Dream. After earning a degree from Harvard Business School, he took a position with a Manhattan investment firm. He lived in an apartment on exclusive Central Park West, but he missed Harlem, where he had grown up. He moved back, along with his wife and daughter.

African American lawyers, doctors, professors, and bankers are doing the same.

What's the attraction? The first is nostalgia, a cultural identification with the Harlem of legend and folklore. It was here that black writers and artists lived in the 1920s, here that the blues and jazz attracted young and accomplished musicians.

The second reason is a more practical one. Harlem offers housing value. Five bedroom homes with 6,000 square feet are available. Some feature Honduran mahogany. Some brownstones are only shells, and have to be renovated; others are in perfect condition. With the influx of the new professionals, prices have risen. A shell sells for $80,000; a house in mint condition goes for $450,000.

What is happening is the rebuilding of a community. Some people who "made" it want to be role models. They want children in the community to see them going to and returning from work.

When the middle class moved out of Harlem, so did its amenities. Now that young professionals are moving back in, the amenities are returning. There were no coffee shops, restaurants, jazz clubs, florists, copy centers, dentist and optometrist offices, art galleries—the types of things urbanites take for granted. Now there are.

The same thing is happening on Chicago's West Side and in other U.S. cities.

The drive to find community—to make a connection with others and with one's roots—is strong. As an investment banker who migrated to Harlem said, "It feeds my soul." ■

Source: Based on Cose 1999; McCormick 1999; Waldman 2000.

are African Americans. As middle-class and professional African Americans reclaim this and other urban areas, an infrastructure—which includes everything from Starbucks coffee houses to dentists—follows. So do soaring real estate prices.

Models of Urban Growth

In the 1920s, Chicago was a vivid mosaic of immigrants, gangsters, prostitutes, the homeless, the rich, and the poor—much as it is today. Sociologists at the University of Chicago studied these contrasting ways of life. One of these sociologists, Robert Park, coined the term **human ecology** to describe how people adapt to their environment (Park and Burgess 1921; Park 1936). (This concept is also known as *urban ecology.*) The process of urban growth is of special interest to human ecologists. Let's look at the three main models they developed.

The Concentric Zone Model To explain how cities expand, sociologist Ernest Burgess (1925) proposed a *concentric zone model.* As shown in part A of Figure 14.11, Burgess noted that a city expands outward from its center. Zone 1 is the central business district. Zone 2, which encircles this downtown area, is in transition. It contains rooming houses and deteriorating housing, which Burgess said breed poverty, disease, and vice. Zone 3 is the area to which thrifty workers have moved in order to escape the zone in transition and yet maintain easy access to their work. Zone 4 contains more expensive apartments, residential hotels, single-family dwellings, and exclusive areas where the wealthy live. Commuters live in Zone 5, which consists of suburbs or satellite cities that have grown up around transit routes.

Burgess intended this model to represent "the tendencies of any town or city to expand radially from

from the model by locating in outlying zones. This was in 1925, and Burgess was seeing the first stage of a major shift that led businesses away from downtown areas to suburban shopping malls. Today, these malls account for most of the country's retail sales.

The Sector Model Sociologist Homer Hoyt (1939, 1971) noted that a city's concentric zones do not form a complete circle, and he modified Burgess' model of urban growth. As shown in part B of Figure 14.11, a concentric zone can contain several sectors—one of working-class housing, another of expensive homes, a third of businesses, and so on, all competing for the same land.

What sociologists call an **invasion-succession cycle** is an example of this dynamic competition. When poor immigrants or rural migrants enter a city, they settle in the lowest-rent area they can find. As their numbers swell, they spill over into adjacent areas. Upset by their presence, the middle class moves out, which expands the sector of low-cost housing. The invasion-succession cycle is never complete, for later another group will replace this earlier one.

The Multiple-Nuclei Model Geographers Chauncey Harris and Edward Ullman noted that some cities have several centers or nuclei (Harris and Ullman 1945; Ullman and Harris 1970). As shown in part C of Figure 14.11, each nucleus is the focus of some specialized activity. A familiar example is the clustering of fast-food restaurants in one area and automobile dealerships in another. Sometimes similar activities are grouped together because they profit from cohesion; retail districts, for example, draw more customers if there are more stores. Other clustering occurs because some types of land use, such as factories and expensive homes, are incompatible with one another. Thus, push-pull factors separate areas by activities, and services are not spread evenly throughout an urban area.

The Peripheral Model More recently, Chauncey Harris (1997) developed the peripheral model shown in part D of Figure 14.11. This model portrays the impact of radial highways on the movement of people and services away from the central city to the city's periphery, or outskirts. It also show the development of industrial and office parks.

Critique of the Models These models tell only part of the story of how cities develop. They are time bound, for medieval cities didn't follow these patterns (see the photo on page 373). They also are geography bound, as Americans who have visited Europe can attest. England,

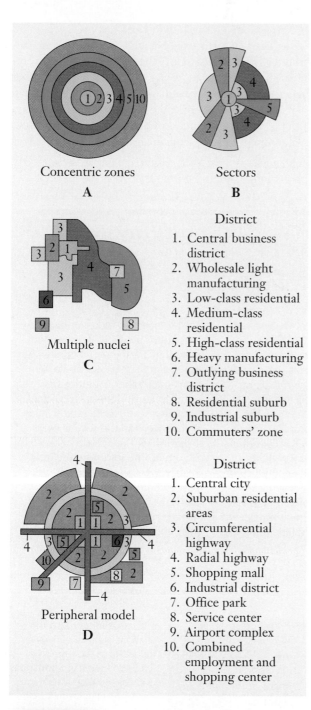

Concentric zones
A

Sectors
B

Multiple nuclei
C

District
1. Central business district
2. Wholesale light manufacturing
3. Low-class residential
4. Medium-class residential
5. High-class residential
6. Heavy manufacturing
7. Outlying business district
8. Residential suburb
9. Industrial suburb
10. Commuters' zone

Peripheral model
D

District
1. Central city
2. Suburban residential areas
3. Circumferential highway
4. Radial highway
5. Shopping mall
6. Industrial district
7. Office park
8. Service center
9. Airport complex
10. Combined employment and shopping center

Figure 14.11 **MODELS OF URBAN GROWTH**

Source: Cousins and Nagpaul 1970; Harris 1997.

its central business district." He noted, however, that no "city fits perfectly this ideal scheme." Some cities have physical obstacles, such as a lake, river, or railroad, which cause their expansion to depart from the model. Burgess also noted that businesses had begun to deviate

for example, has planning laws that preserve greenbelts (trees and farmlands) around the cities. This prevents urban sprawl. Wal-Mart cannot buy land outside the city and put up a store; instead, it must locate in the downtown area with the other stores. Norwich, for example, has 250,000 people; yet the city ends abruptly, and in its greenbelt pheasants skitter across plowed fields while sheep graze in verdant meadows (Milbank 1995b). The models, then, do not account for urban planning policies.

The models also fall short when it comes to the cities of the Least Industrialized Nations. U.S. visitors are surprised when they visit one of these cities. The wealthy often claim the inner city, where fine restaurants and other services are readily accessible. There, tucked behind tall walls and protected from public scrutiny, they enjoy luxurious homes and gardens. In contrast, the poor, especially rural migrants, settle in areas outside the city. This topic is discussed in the Cultural Diversity box below.

CULTURAL DIVERSITY Around the World

URBANIZATION IN THE LEAST INDUSTRIALIZED NATIONS

Images of the Least Industrialized Nations that portray serene pastoral scenes distort today's reality. In these nations, poor rural people have flocked to the cities in such numbers that, as we saw in Figure 14.9 on page 374, these nations now contain most of the world's largest cities. In general, industrialization has preceded urbanization, but here *urbanization is preceding industrialization*. The countries' limited technology makes it difficult to support their mushrooming urban populations.

When rural migrants and immigrants move to U.S. cities, they usually settle in areas of deteriorated housing near the city's center. In the Least Industrialized Nations, the wealthy live near the downtown area, and migrants establish squatter settlements outside the city. There they build shacks from scrap boards, cardboard, and bits of corrugated metal. Even flattened tin cans are used for building material. The squatters enjoy no city facilities—roads, transportation lines, water, sewers, or garbage pickup. After thousands of squatters

have settled in an area, the city acknowledges their right to live there by adding bus service and minimal water lines. Hundreds of people use a single spigot. About 5 *million* of Mexico City's residents live in such conditions.

Why this vast rush to live in the city under such miserable conditions? Basically, the rural way of life is breaking down. As the second leg of the demographic transition kicks in—low death rates and high birth rates—rural populations are multiplying. No longer is there enough land to divide up among descendants. "Pull" factors also draw people to the city—jobs, education, better housing—and even a more stimulating life.

Will the Least Industrialized Nations adjust to this vast, unwanted migration? They have no choice. Authorities in Brazil, Guatemala, Venezuela, and other countries have sent in the police and the army to evict the settlers. It doesn't work. It leads to violence, and the settlers keep streaming in. The adjustment will be painful. The infrastructure (roads, water, sewers, electricity, and so on) must be built, but these poor countries don't have the resources to build them. As the desperate flock to the cities, the problems will worsen. ■

For Your Consideration

What solutions do you see?

The Least Industrialized Nations are facing massive upheaval as they rapidly urbanize, resulting in disparities such as those depicted here. Lacking the infrastructure to support their many newcomers, cities in the Least Industrialized Nations, already steeped in poverty, face the daunting task of developing jobs, housing, sewage and electrical systems, roads, schools, and so on. This photo was taken in Bombay, India.

CITY LIFE: ALIENATION AND COMMUNITY

Just as cities provide opportunities, they also create problems. Humans have not only physical needs—food, shelter, and safety—but also a need for **community**, a feeling of belonging—the sense that others care what happens to us, and that we can depend on the people around us. Some people find this sense of community in the city; others find its opposite, **alienation**, a sense of not belonging, and a feeling that no one cares what happens to you:

> Twenty-eight-year-old Catherine Genovese, who was called Kitty by almost everyone in her Queens neighborhood, was returning home from work. After she had parked her car, a man grabbed her. She screamed, "Oh, my God, he stabbed me! Please help me! Please help me!"
>
> For more than half an hour, thirty-eight respectable, law-abiding citizens looked out their windows and watched as the killer stalked and stabbed Kitty in three separate attacks. Twice the sudden glow from their bedroom lights interrupted him and frightened him off. Each time he returned, sought her out, and stabbed her again. Not one person telephoned the police during the assault. (*New York Times*, March 26, 1964)

When the police interviewed them, some witnesses said, "I didn't want to get involved." Others said, "We thought it was a lovers' quarrel." Some simply said, "I don't know." People throughout the country were shocked. It was as though Americans awoke one morning to discover that the country had changed overnight. They took this event as a sign that people could no longer trust one another, that the city was a cold, lonely place.

Why should the city be alienating? In a classic essay, "Urbanism as a Way of Life," sociologist Louis Wirth (1938) argued that the city undermines kinship and neighborhood, which are the traditional sources of social control and social solidarity. Urban dwellers live in anonymity. As they go from one superficial encounter with strangers to another, they grow aloof from one another and indifferent to other people's problems—as did the neighbors of Kitty Genovese. In short, the personal freedom that the city provides comes at the cost of alienation.

Wirth built on ideas discussed in Chapter 4. As a society industrializes, *Gemeinschaft,* the sense of community that comes from everyone knowing everyone else, is ripped apart. What emerges is a new society based on *Gesellschaft,* secondary, impersonal relationships. Lack-

ing identification with one another, people develop the attitude "It's simply none of *my* business." The end result can be alienation so deep that people can sit by while someone else is being murdered.

The city, however, is more than a mosaic of strangers who feel disconnected and distrustful of one another. It also consists of a series of smaller worlds, within which people find community. People come to know the smaller areas of the city where they live, work, shop, and play. Even slums, which to outsiders seem so threatening, can provide a sense of belonging. In a classic study, sociologist Herbert Gans (1962:12) noted,

> After a few weeks of living in the West End (of Boston), my observations—and my perceptions of the area—changed drastically. The search for an apartment quickly indicated that the individual units were usually in much better condition than the outside or the hallways of the buildings. Subsequently, in wandering through the West End, and in using it as a resident, I developed a kind of selective perception, in which my eye focused only on those parts of the area that were actually being used by people. Vacant buildings and boarded-up stores were no longer so visible, and the totally deserted alleys or streets were outside the set of paths normally traversed, either by myself or by the West Enders...
>
> Since much of the area's life took place on the street, faces became familiar very quickly. I met my neighbors on the stairs and in front of my building. And, once a shopping pattern developed, I saw the same storekeepers frequently, as well as the area's "characters" who wandered through the streets every day on a fairly regular route and schedule. In short, the exotic quality of the stores and the residents also wore off as I became used to seeing them.

As he lived in the West End, Gans gradually gained an insider's perspective of the area. Despite the narrow streets, substandard buildings, and even piled-up garbage, most West Enders had chosen to live there: *To them the West End was a low-rent district, not a slum.* Within the deteriorated area was a community, people who visited back and forth with relatives and were involved in networks of friendships and acquaintances. Gans therefore titled his book *The Urban Villagers* (1962).

Then came well-intentioned urban planners, who drew up plans to get rid of the "slum." The residents of the West End were upset when they heard about the coming urban renewal, and distrustful that the improvements would benefit them. Their distrust proved well founded, for the urban renewal brought with it another invasion-succession cycle. Along with the gleaming new buildings came people with more money who took over the area. The former residents were dispossessed, their intimate patterns destroyed.

The city dwellers whom Gans identified as ethnic villagers find community in the city. Living in tightly knit neighborhoods, they know many other residents. Some first-generation immigrants have even come from the same village in the "old country."

Who Lives in the City?

Whether you find alienation or community in the city depends on many factors, but consider the five types of urban dwellers that Gans (1962, 1968, 1991) identified. Which type are you? How does this affect your chances of finding alienation or community?

The first three types live in the city by choice; they find a sense of community.

The Cosmopolites The cosmopolites are the city's students, intellectuals, professionals, musicians, artists, and entertainers. They have been drawn to the city because of its conveniences and cultural benefits.

The Singles Young, unmarried people come to the city seeking jobs and entertainment. Businesses and services such as singles bars, singles apartment complexes, and computer dating companies cater to their needs. Their stay in the city is often temporary, for most move to the suburbs after they marry and have children.

The Ethnic Villagers United by race-ethnicity and social class, these people live in tightly knit neighborhoods that resemble villages and small towns. Moving within a close circle of family and friends, the ethnic villagers try to isolate themselves from what they view as the harmful effects of city life.

The next two groups, the deprived and the trapped, have little choice about where they live. As alienated outcasts of industrial society, they are always skirting the edge of disaster.

The Deprived The deprived live in blighted neighborhoods that are more like urban jungles than urban villages. Consisting of the very poor and the emotionally disturbed, the deprived represent the bottom of society in terms of income, education, social status, and work skills. Some of them stalk their jungle in search of prey, their victims usually deprived people like themselves. Their future holds little chance for anything better in life.

The Trapped The trapped can find no escape either. Some could not afford to move when their neighborhood was "invaded" by another ethnic group. Others in this group are the elderly who are not wanted elsewhere, alcoholics and other drug addicts, and the downwardly mobile. Like the deprived, the trapped also suffer high rates of assault, mugging, robbery, and rape.

Men like this one, who has just drunk himself into a stupor, are not an unfamiliar sight in some parts of U.S. cities. The text describes various types of urban dwellers. What type is this man?

Urban Sentiment: Finding a Familiar World

Sociologists note that *the city is divided into little worlds* that people come to know down to their smallest details. City people create a sense of intimacy by *personalizing* their shopping (Stone 1954; Gans 1970). They shop in the same stores, and after a period of time customers and clerks greet each other by name. Certain bars, restaurants, and shops are more than just buildings in which they make purchases. They become places where neighborhood residents build social relationships with one another and share informal news about the community.

Spectator sports also help urban dwellers find a familiar world (Hudson 1991). When Mark McGwire of the Cardinals hit the 61st home run that broke Roger Maris' longstanding record, fans around the country celebrated, but in the St. Louis area the celebration was spe-

cial: It was for "our" man on "our" team—even though fewer than one in seven of the area's 2.5 million people live in the city. Sociologists David Karp and William Yoels (1990) note that such identification is so intense that long after moving to other parts of the country, many people maintain an emotional allegiance to the sports teams of the city in which they grew up.

The Norm of Noninvolvement and the Diffusion of Responsibility

Urban dwellers try to avoid intrusions from strangers. As they traverse everyday life in the city, they follow a *norm of noninvolvement.*

> To do this, we sometimes use props such as newspapers to shield ourselves from others and to indicate our inaccessibility for interaction. In effect, we learn to "tune others out." In this regard, we might see the Walkman as the quintessential urban prop in that it allows us to be tuned in and tuned out at the same time. It is a device that allows us to enter our own private world and thereby effectively to close off encounters with others. The use of such devices protects our "personal space," along with our body demeanor and facial expression (the passive "mask" or even scowl that persons adopt on subways). (Karp et al. 1991)

Recall Kitty Genovese, whose story was recounted on page 379. Her story troubled social psychologists John Darley and Bibb Latané (1968), who ran the series of experiments featured in Chapter 5, p. 120. Darley and Latané uncovered a *diffusion of responsibility.* They found that the *more* bystanders there are, the *less* likely people are to help. As a group grows, people's sense of responsibility becomes diffused, with each person assuming that *another* will do the responsible thing. "With these other people here, it is not *my* responsibility," they reason.

The diffusion of responsibility, along with the norm of noninvolvement, helps explain the response to Kitty Genovese's murder. The bystanders at her death were *not* uncaring people. They *did* care that a woman was being attacked. They simply were abiding by an urban norm, one that is helpful for getting them through everyday city life but, unfortunately, dysfunctional in some crucial situations. This norm, combined with killings, carjackings, muggings, and the generalized fear that the city now engenders in many Americans, underlies the desire many have to retreat to a safe haven. This topic is discussed in the Down-to-Earth Sociology box on the next page.

Sociology

Down-to-Earth

URBAN FEAR AND THE GATED FORTRESS

Gated neighborhoods—where wrought-iron gates open and close to allow or to prevent access to a neighborhood—are not new. They always have been available to the rich. What is new is the rush by the upper middle class to towns where they pay heavy taxes to keep all of the town's facilities, including its streets, private.

Towns cannot discriminate on the basis of religion or race-ethnicity, but they can—and do—discriminate on the basis of social class. Klahanie, Washington, is an excellent example. Begun in 1985, it was supposed to take twenty years to develop. With its safe streets, 300 acres of open space, and its ban on satellite dishes, flagpoles, and even basketball hoops on garages, demand for the $300,000-plus homes nestled by a lake in this private community exceeded supply (Egan 1995).

The future will bring many more such private towns as the upper middle class flees urban areas and attempts to build a bucolic dream. A strong sign of the future is Celebration, a planned town of 20,000 people built by the Walt Disney Com-

The U.S. economic system has proven highly beneficial to most citizens, but it also has left many in poverty. To protect themselves, primarily from the poor, the upper middle class increasingly seeks sanctuary behind gated residential enclaves.

pany just south of Orlando, Florida. With our new technology, the residents of private communities such as these will be able to communicate with the outside world while remaining securely locked within their gated fortresses. ■

For Your Consideration

Community always involves a sense of togetherness, a sense of identity with one another. Can you explain how this concept also contains the idea of separateness from others (not just in the example of gated communities)? What will our future be if we become a nation of gated communities, where middle-class homeowners withdraw into private domains, separating themselves from the rest of the nation?

Urban Problems and Social Policy

The primary problems of urban life today are poverty, decay, and a general decline of U.S. cities. Let's examine underlying reasons for these conditions and consider how to develop social policy to solve urban problems.

Suburbanization

Suburbanization, which refers to people moving from cities to **suburbs,** the communities located just outside a city, is not new. Many dream of a place of their own with green grass, a few trees, and kids playing in the yard. For the past hundred years or so, as transportation grew more efficient, especially with the development of automobiles, whites have moved to towns near the cities in which they work. Minorities joined this movement about 1970. The extent to which people have left the city in search of their dreams is remarkable. In 1957, about 20 percent of Americans lived in the suburbs (Karp et al. 1991). Today, over half of all Americans live in them (Rybczynski 1999).

The U.S. city has been the loser in this transition. As people moved out of the city, businesses and jobs followed. Now about two-thirds of people who live in the suburbs also work there (Gans 1991b). As the city's tax base shrank, it left a budget squeeze that affected not only parks, zoos, libraries, and museums, but also the city's basic services—its schools, streets, sewer and water systems, and police and fire departments.

This shift in population and resources left behind people who had no choice but to stay in the city. The net result, observes sociologist William Julius Wilson (1987), was to transform the inner city into a ghetto. Left behind were families and individuals who, lacking training and skills, were trapped by poverty, unemployment, and welfare dependency—along with people who prey on others through street crime. The term *ghetto,* says Wilson, "suggests that a fundamental social transformation has taken place…that groups represented by this term are collectively different from and much more socially isolated from those that lived in these communities in earlier years" (quoted in Karp et al. 1991).

City Versus Suburb Having made the move out of the city—or having been born in a suburb and preferring to live there—suburbanites want the city to keep its problems to itself. They reject proposals to share suburbia's revenues with the city and oppose measures that would allow urban and suburban governments joint control over what has become a contiguous mass of people and businesses. Suburban leaders generally see it as in their best interests to remain politically, economically, and socially separate from their nearby city. They do not mind going to the city to work, or venturing there on weekends for the diversions it offers, but they do not want to help shoulder the city's burdens.

It is likely that the mounting bill will come due ultimately, however, and that suburbanites will have to pay for their uncaring attitude toward the urban disadvantaged. Karp et al. (1991) put it this way:

> It may be that suburbs can insulate themselves from the problems of central cities, at least for the time being. In the long run, though, there will be a steep price to pay for the failure of those better off to care compassionately for those at the bottom of society.

Suburbs were once unplanned, taking irregular shapes as people moved from the city in search of bucolic dreams. Some are still unplanned as population spills over from the city. Others, however, as this photo of Sun City, Arizona, a suburb of Phoenix, shows, are precisely planned even before the first resident moves in.

Our occasional urban riots may be part of that bill—perhaps just the down payment.

Suburban Flight In some places, the bill is coming due quickly. As they age, some suburbs are becoming a mirror image of the city their residents so despise, with rising crime, flight of the middle class, a shrinking tax base, and eroding services. This, in turn, creates a spiraling sense of insecurity, more middle-class flight, and a further reduction of property values. Figure 14.12 on the next page illustrates this process, which is new to the urban-suburban scene.

Disinvestment and Deindustrialization

As the cities' tax base shrank and their services declined, neighborhoods deteriorated, and banks began **redlining:** Afraid of loans going bad, banks drew a line on a map around a problem area and refused to make loans for housing or businesses there. The **disinvestment** (withdrawal of investment) pushed these areas into further decline. Youth gangs, murders, and muggings are high in these areas, while education, employment, and income are low—factors that are not unconnected to this process of disinvestment.

The globalization of capitalism has also left a heavy mark on U.S. cities. As sociologist Victor Rodríguez (1994) points out, to compete in the global market, many U.S. industries abandoned local communities and

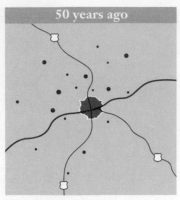

At first, the city and surrounding villages grew independently.

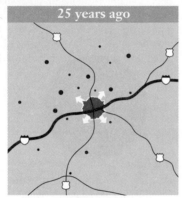

As city dwellers fled urban decay, they created a ring of suburbs.

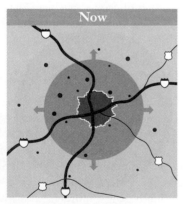

As middle-class flight continues outward, urban problems are arriving in the outer rings.

 14.12 URBAN GROWTH AND URBAN FLIGHT

moved their factories to countries where labor costs are lower. This process, called **deindustrialization**, made U.S. industries more competitive, but it eliminated millions of U.S. manufacturing jobs. Lacking training in the new information technologies, many poor people are locked out of the benefits of the postindustrial economy that is engulfing the United States. Left behind in the inner cities, many live in despair.

The Rural Rebound

The United States is now undergoing a trend that is without precedent in its history. In the 1970s, people began to move out of cities and suburbs and into rural areas. During the 1990s, seven of every ten U.S. rural counties grew in population. The only losses occurred in the Great Plains and the Mississippi Delta (Johnson 1999). Little farming towns are making a comeback, their boarded-up stores and schools once again open for business and learning.

The "push" factors for this fundamental shift are fears of urban crime and violence. The "pull" factors are safety, lower cost of living, recreation, and more space. Facilitating this movement are improvements in transportation and communication. Interstate highways make airports—and the city itself—accessible from longer distances. With satellite communications, mobile phones, fax machines, and the Internet, people can be connected with people in the city—and around the world—even though they live in what just a short time ago were remote areas.

Listen to the wife of a former student of mine describe why she and her husband moved to a rural area, three hours from the international airport that they fly out of each week:

> I work for a Canadian company. Paul works for a French company, with headquarters in Paris. He flies around the country doing computer consulting. I give motivational seminars to businesses. When we can, we drive to the airport together, but we often leave on different days. I try to go with my husband to Paris once a year.
>
> We almost always are home together on the weekends. We often arrange three- and four-day weekends, because I can plan seminars at home, and Paul does some of his consulting from here.
>
> Sometimes shopping is inconvenient, but we don't have to lock our car doors when we drive, and the new Wal-Mart superstore has most of what we need. E-commerce is a big part of it. I just type in www—whatever, and they ship it right to my door. I get make-up and books online. I even bought a part for my stove.

Why do we live here? Look at the lake. It's beautiful. We enjoy boating and swimming. We love to walk in this park-like setting. We see deer and wild turkeys. We love the sunsets over the lake. (author's files)

The Potential of Urban Revitalization

Social policy usually takes one of two forms. The first is to tear down and rebuild—something that is fancifully termed **urban renewal.** The result is the renewal of an area—but *not* for the benefit of its inhabitants. Stadiums, high-rise condos, luxury hotels, and expensive shops replace run-down, cheap housing. Outpriced, the area's inhabitants are displaced into adjacent areas.

The second is some sort of **enterprise zone,** economic incentives, such as reduced taxes, that are intended to encourage businesses to move into an area. Although the intention is good, failure is usually the result. Most businesses refuse to locate in high-crime areas. Those that do pay a high price for security and losses from crime, which can run higher than the tax savings. If workers are hired from within the problem area, and the jobs pay a decent wage, which most do not, the workers move to better neighborhoods—which doesn't help the area (Lemann 1994). After all, who chooses to live with the fear of violence?

Although urban renewal and enterprise zones have failed to solve the problems facing U.S. cities, a "nothing works" mentality will solve nothing. U.S. cities can be revitalized and made into safe and decent places to live. There is nothing in the nature of cities that turns them into dangerous, deteriorating slums. Most European cities, for example, are both safe and pleasant. If U.S. cities are to change, they must become top agenda items of the U.S. government, with adequate resources in terms of money and human talents focused on overcoming urban woes.

Given the deplorable condition of many U.S. cities and the flight of the middle classes—both whites and minorities—to greener pastures, an *urban Manhattan Project* seems in order. During World War II, the United States and the Allies faced a triumphant Hitler in Europe and a victorious Tojo in Asia. The United States gathered its top scientific minds and challenged them to produce the atomic bomb. "Manhattan Project" was the code name for that effort. It involved 37 installations across the country, at least 37 university laboratories, and more than 100,000 people, including several Nobel

Like the phoenix, luxury hotels and apartments, along with exclusive restaurants and shops, have arisen from the ashes of urban decay. *Urban renewal,* a benefit for the privileged, has displaced the poor, often shoving them into adjacent areas every bit as deprived as those in which they previously lived.

prize-winning physicists. Today, similar resources may be required to triumph over urban ills.

Sociologist William Flanagan (1990) suggests three guiding principles for working out the solutions to our pressing urban problems:

Scale. Regional and national planning is necessary. Local jurisdictions, with their many rivalries, competing goals, and limited resources, tend to implement a hodgepodge of mostly unworkable solutions. A positive example of regional planning is Portland, Oregon, where a regional government prohibits urban sprawl and ensures a greenbelt.

Livability. Cities must be appealing and meet human needs, especially the need of community we discussed earlier. This will attract the middle classes into the city and increase its tax base. In turn, this will help finance the services that make the city more livable.

demoghraphic = (death)—(Birth)—(migration) = population growth rate —

Social justice. In the final analysis, social policy must be evaluated by how it affects people. "Urban renewal" programs that displace the poor for the benefit of the middle class and wealthy do not pass this standard. The same would apply to solutions that create "livability" for select groups but neglect the poor and the homeless.

Unless we address the *root* causes of urban problems—poverty, housing, education, and jobs—any solutions we come up with will be, at best, only Band-Aids that cover up problems. Such fixes will be window dressings for politicians who want to *appear* as though they are doing something constructive about the problems that affect our quality of life.

SUMMARY AND REVIEW

■ A Planet with No Space to Enjoy Life?

What debate did Thomas Malthus initiate?

In 1798, Thomas Malthus analyzed the surge in Europe's population. His conclusion, called the **Malthus theorem**, was that because the population grows geometrically but the food supply increases only arithmetically, the world's population will outstrip its food supply. The debate between today's New Malthusians and those who disagree, the Anti-Malthusians, continues. Pp. 360–364.

Why are people starving?

Starvation is not due to a lack of food in the world, for there is now more food for each person in the entire world than there was fifty years ago. Starvation, rather, is due to a maldistribution of food, which is primarily due to drought and war. Pp. 364–365.

■ Population Growth

Why do the poor nations have so many children?

In the Least Industrialized Nations, children generally are viewed as gifts from God, cost little to rear, contribute to the family's income at an early age, and represent the parents' social security. Consequently, people are motivated to have large families. Pp. 365–368.

What are the three demographic variables?

To compute population growth, demographers use *fertility, mortality,* and *migration.* The **basic demographic equation** is births minus deaths plus net migration equals growth rate. Pp. 368–370.

Why is forecasting population growth difficult?

A nation's growth rate is affected by unanticipated variables—from economic cycles, wars, and famines to industrialization and government policies. Pp. 370–372.

■ The Development of Cities

What factors underlie the growth of cities?

Cities can develop only if there is a large agricultural surplus, which frees people from food production. The primary impetus to the development of cities was the invention of the plow about five or six thousand years ago. After the Industrial Revolution stimulated mechanical transportation and communica-

tion, the infrastructure on which modern cities depend, cities grew quickly and became much larger. P. 372.

Today, **urbanization** is so extensive that some cities have become **metropolises,** dominating the area adjacent to them. The areas of influence of some metropolises have merged, forming a **megalopolis.** Pp. 372–376.

What models of urban growth have been proposed?

The primary models are concentric zone, sector, multiple-nuclei, and peripheral. These models fail to account for medieval cities, many European cities, and those in the Least Industrialized Nations. Pp. 376–378.

■ City Life: Alienation and Community

Who lives in the city?

Some people experience **alienation** in the city; others find **community** in it. What people find depends largely on their background and urban networks. Five major types of people who live in cities are cosmopolites, singles, ethnic villagers, the deprived, and the trapped. Pp. 379–382.

■ Urban Problems and Social Policy

Why have U.S. cities declined?

Three primary reasons for their decline are **suburbanization** (as people moved to the suburbs, the tax base of cities eroded and services deteriorated), **disinvestment** (banks withdrawing their financing), and **deindustrialization** (which caused a loss of jobs). Pp. 382–384.

What is the rural rebound?

As people flee cities and suburbs, the population of most U.S. rural counties is growing. This is a fundamental departure from a trend that has been in place for a couple of hundred years. Pp. 384–385.

What social policy can salvage U.S. cities?

A Manhattan Project on Urban Problems could likely produce workable solutions. Three guiding principles for developing social policy are scale, livability, and social justice. Pp. 385–386.

Where can I read more on this topic?

Suggested readings for this chapter are listed on page SR-11.

YOUR INTERACTIVE COMPANION WEB SITE

Your Interactive Companion Web Site includes practice tests, with feedback, and online learning activities with video, audio, and Weblinks. Your access code for this Web site is provided with this text.

GLOSSARY

alienation a sense of not belonging, and a feeling that no one cares what happens to you (p. 379)

basic demographic equation growth rate = births – deaths + net migration (p. 370)

city a place in which a large number of people are permanently based and do not produce their own food (p. 372)

community a place people identify with, where they sense that they belong and that others care about what happens to them (p. 379)

crude birth rate the annual number of births per 1,000 population (p. 368)

crude death rate the annual number of deaths per 1,000 population (p. 368)

deindustrialization a process by which fewer people work in manufacturing; one reason is automation, while another is the globalization of capitalism, which moves manufacturing jobs to countries where labor costs less (p. 384)

demographic transition a three-stage historical process of population growth: first, high birth rates and high death rates; second, high birth rates and low death rates; and third, low birth rates and low death rates; a fourth stage of population shrinkage may be emerging (p. 362)

demographic variables the three factors that influence population growth: fertility, mortality, and net migration (p. 368)

demography the study of the size, composition, growth, and distribution of human populations (p. 360)

disinvestment the withdrawal of investments by banks, which seals the fate of an urban area (p. 383)

edge city a large clustering of service facilities and residences near a highway intersection that provides a sense of place to people who live, shop, and work there (p. 374)

enterprise zone the use of economic incentives in a designated area with the intention of encouraging investment there (p. 385)

exponential growth curve a pattern of growth in which numbers double during approximately equal intervals, thus accelerating in the latter stages (p. 361)

fertility rate the number of children that the average woman bears (p. 368)

gentrification the displacement of the poor as the relatively affluent purchase and renovate their homes (p. 374)

growth rate the net change in a population after adding births, subtracting deaths, and either adding or subtracting net migration (p. 370)

human ecology Robert Park's term for the relationship between people and their environment (natural resources, such as land); also called *urban ecology* (p. 376)

invasion-succession cycle the process of one group of people displacing a group whose racial-ethnic or social class characteristics differ from their own (p. 377)

Malthus theorem an observation by Thomas Malthus that although the food supply increases arithmetically, population grows geometrically (p. 361)

megalopolis an urban area consisting of at least two metropolises and their many suburbs (p. 374)

metropolis a central city surrounded by smaller cities and their suburbs (p. 373)

metropolitan statistical area (MSA) a central city and the urbanized counties adjacent to it (p. 374)

net migration rate the difference between the number of immigrants and emigrants per 1,000 population (p. 368)

population pyramid a graphic representation of a population, divided into age and sex (p. 367)

population shrinkage the process by which a country's population becomes smaller because its birth rate and immigration are too low to replace those who die and emigrate (p. 363)

redlining the officers of a bank refusing to make loans in a particular area (p. 383)

suburb a community adjacent to a city (p. 382)

suburbanization the movement from the city to the suburbs (p. 382)

urbanization an increasing proportion of a population living in cities and those cities having a growing influence on their society (p. 372)

urban renewal the rehabilitation of a rundown area of a city, which usually results in the displacement of the poor who are living there (p. 385)

zero population growth a demographic condition in which women bear only enough children to reproduce the population (p. 371)

New York Wall Painting Murals

Social Change: Technology, Social Movements, and the Environment

The morning of January 28, 1986, dawned clear but near freezing, strange weather for subtropical Florida. At the Kennedy Space Center, launch pad 39B was lined with three inches of ice. Icicles 6 to 12 inches long hung like stalactites from the pad's service structure.

Shortly after 8 A.M., the crew took the elevator to the white room, where they entered the crew module. By 8:36 A.M., the seven members of the crew were strapped in their seats. They were understandably disappointed when liftoff, scheduled for 9:38 A.M., was delayed because of the ice.

Due to a strong public relations campaign, public interest in the flight ran high. Attention focused on Christa McAuliffe, a 37-year-old high school teacher from Concord, New Hampshire, the first private citizen to fly aboard a space shuttle. Across the nation, schoolchildren watched with great anticipation, for Mrs. McAuliffe, selected from thousands of applicants (including the author of this text), was to give a televised lesson during the flight about life aboard a spacecraft.

At the viewing site, thousands of spectators had joined the families and friends of the crew awaiting the launch. After two hours of delay, they were delighted to see *Challenger*'s two solid-fuel boosters ignite, and they broke into cheers as this product of technical innovation thundered majestically into space. The time was 11:38 A.M.

Seventy-three seconds later, the *Challenger* was 7 miles from the launch site, racing skyward at 2,900 feet per second, when suddenly a brilliant glow appeared on one side of the external tank. In seconds, the glow blossomed into a gigantic fireball. Screams of horror arose from the crowd as the *Challenger,* now 19 miles away, exploded, and bits of debris began to fall from the sky.

In classrooms across the country, children burst into tears. Adult Americans stared at their televisions in stunned disbelief. (Based on Broad 1986; Magnuson 1986; Lewis 1988; Maier 1993.) ■

I f any characteristic describes social life today, it is rapid social change. As we shall see in this chapter, technology, such as that which made the *Challenger* first a reality and then a disaster, is a driving force behind this change. To understand social change is to better understand today's society—and our own lives.

How SOCIAL CHANGE TRANSFORMS SOCIETY

Social change, a shift in the characteristics of culture and society, is such a vital part of social life that it has been a theme throughout this book. To make this theme more explicit, let's review the main points about social change made in the preceding chapters.

The Four Social Revolutions

The rapid, far-reaching social change that the world is currently experiencing did not "just happen." Rather, it is the result of forces set in motion thousands of years ago, beginning with the domestication of plants and animals. This first social revolution allowed hunting and gathering societies to develop into horticultural and pastoral societies (see pages 85–90). The plow brought about the second social revolution, from which agricultural societies emerged. Then the invention of the steam engine ushered in the Industrial Revolution, and now we are witnessing the fourth social revolution, stimulated by the invention of the microchip.

From *Gemeinschaft* to *Gesellschaft*

Although our lives are being vitally affected by this fourth revolution, at this point we have seen only the tip of the iceberg. By the time this social revolution is full blown, little of our way of life will be left untouched. We can assume this because the first three social revolutions transformed society. For example, the change from agricultural to industrial society meant not only that people moved from villages to cities, but also that intimate, lifelong relationships were replaced by impersonal, short-term associations. Paid work, contracts, and money replaced the reciprocal obligations essential to kinship, social position, and friendship. As reviewed on page 90, sociologists use the terms *Gemeinschaft* and *Gesellschaft* to indicate this fundamental shift in society.

Capitalism, Modernization, and Industrialization

Just why did societies change from *Gemeinschaft* to *Gesellschaft*? Karl Marx pointed to a social invention called *capitalism*. He analyzed how the breakup of feudal society threw people off the land, creating a surplus of labor. These masses moved to cities, where they were exploited by the owners of the means of production (factories, machinery, tools). This set in motion antagonistic relationships between capitalists and workers that remain today.

Max Weber traced capitalism to the Protestant Reformation (see pages 346–347). He noted that the Reformation stripped Protestants of the assurance that church membership saved them. As they agonized over heaven and hell, they concluded that God did not want the elect to live in uncertainty. God would surely give a sign to assure them that they were predestined to heaven. That sign, they decided, was prosperity. An unexpected consequence of the Reformation, then, was to make Protestants work hard and be thrifty. This created an economic surplus, which stimulated capitalism. In this way, Protestantism laid the groundwork for the Industrial Revolution that transformed the world.

The Protestant Reformation ushered in not only religious change but also, as Max Weber analyzed, fundamental social-economic change. This painting by Hans Holbein, the Younger, shows the new prosperity of the merchant class. Previously only the nobility had such possessions.

The sweeping changes ushered in by the Industrial Revolution are called **modernization.** Table 15.1 on the next page reviews these changes. The features listed in this table are *ideal types* in Weber's sense of the term, for no society exemplifies to the maximum degree all the traits listed here. In addition, our new technology has created unevenness around the world. The elite in Uganda, for example, have computers. Thus the characteristics shown in Table 15.1 should be interpreted as "more" or "less" rather than "either-or."

When technology changes, societies change. Consider how the introduction of technology from the industrialized world is transforming traditional societies. When modern medicine was exported to the Least Industrialized Nations, for example, death rates dropped while birth rates remained high. As a result, the population exploded. This second stage of the demographic transition upset traditional balances of family, property, and inheritance. It also brought hunger and led to mass migration to cities with little industrialization. The Cultural Diversity box on page 378, discusses some of these problems.

Geopolitics and Ethnic Conflicts

With all the changes surrounding us, it is impossible to pinpoint the most significant one. Among the contenders, however, would be one that often lies below our vision— the interrelationship of power among nations. Already during the sixteenth century, today's global divisions had

Table 15.1

	COMPARING TRADITIONAL AND MODERN SOCIETIES	
Characteristics	**Traditional Societies**	**Modern Societies**
General Characteristics		
Social change	Slow	Rapid
Size of group	Small	Large
Religious orientation	More	Less
Formal education	No	Yes
Place of residence	Rural	Urban
Demographic transition	First stage	Third stage (or Fourth)
Family size	Larger	Smaller
Infant mortality	High	Low
Life expectancy	Short	Long
Health care	Home	Hospital
Temporal orientation	Past	Future
Material Relations		
Industrialized	No	Yes
Technology	Simple	Complex
Division of labor	Simple	Complex
Income	Low	High
Material possessions	Few	Many
Social Relationships		
Basic organization	*Gemeinschaft*	*Gesellschaft*
Families	Extended	Nuclear
Respect for elders	More	Less
Social stratification	Rigid	More open
Statuses	More ascribed	More achieved
Gender equality	Less	More
Norms		
View of reality, life, and morals	Absolute	Relativistic
Social control	Informal	Formal
Tolerance of differences	Less	More

ing to *dependency theory*, this made the nonindustrialized nations dependent and unable to develop their own resources (see page 171).

Today's information revolution will also have far-reaching consequences for global stratification. Those nations that make the fastest, most significant advances in computerized technology are destined to dominate in the coming generation. Obviously, this will be a continuation of the dominance of the Most Industrialized Nations.

Since World War II, a realignment of the world's powers (called *geopolitics*) has resulted in a triadic division of the globe: a Japan-centered East, a Germany-centered Europe, and a United States-centered western hemisphere. These three powers, along with four lesser ones—Canada, France, Great Britain, and Italy—dominate the globe today. Known as G7 (meaning *the* "Group of 7"), these industrial giants hold annual meetings at which they decide how to divide up the world's markets and regulate global economic policy, such as interest rates, tariffs, and currency exchanges. Their goal is to perpetuate their global dominance, which includes keeping prices down on the raw materials they buy from the Least Industrialized Nations. Cheap oil is essential for this goal, which requires that they dominate the Mideast—whether that be accomplished through peaceful means or by a joint war effort of the United Nations.

Because of Russia's nuclear arsenal, the G7 has courted Russia—giving Russia observer status at its annual summits and providing loans and expertise to help Russia make the transition to capitalism. The breakup of the Soviet Union has been a central consideration in G7's plans for a new world order. Events in Russia and in its former satellite nations will help determine the shape of future global stratification.

Threatening the global divisions so carefully constructed by G7 is the resurgence of ethnic conflicts. The breakup of the Soviet empire lifted the cover that had held in check the centuries-old hatreds and frustrated nationalistic ambitions of many ethnic groups. With the Soviet military and the KGB in disarray, these groups turned violently on one another. In Africa, similar seething hatreds brought warfare to groups that had been placed together in arbitrary political boundaries. In Europe, the former Yugoslavia split apart, with ethnic groups turning violently against one another. Ethnic conflicts threaten to erupt in Germany,

begun to emerge. Those nations that had the most advanced technology of the time (the swiftest ships and the most powerful cannons) became wealthy by conquering other nations and exploiting their resources. Then, as capitalism emerged, some nations industrialized. Those that did exploited the resources of those that did not. Accord-

Cultural Evolution

Two major types of evolutionary theories are unilinear and multilinear. *Unilinear* theories assume that all societies follow the same path. Each society evolves from simpler to more complex forms, and each goes through uniform sequences (Barnes 1935). Of the many versions of this theory, the one proposed by Lewis Morgan (1877) once dominated Western thought. Morgan said that all societies go through three stages: savagery, barbarism, and civilization. In Morgan's eyes, England, his own society, was the epitome of civilization. All others were destined to follow it.

Multilinear views of evolution replaced unilinear theories. Instead of assuming that all societies follow the same sequence, multilinear theorists proposed that different routes lead to the same stage of development. Although the path leads to industrialization, societies need not pass through the same sequence of stages on this journey (Sahlins and Service 1960; Lenski and Lenski 1987).

Central to evolutionary theories, whether unilinear or multilinear, is the assumption of *cultural progress*. Tribal societies are assumed to have a primitive form of human culture. As they evolve, they will reach a higher state—the supposedly advanced and superior form that characterizes modern societies. Growing appreciation of the rich diversity—and complexity—of tribal cultures has discredited this idea. In addition, Western culture is now in crisis (poverty, racism, discrimination, war, terrorism, alienation, sexual assaults, unsafe streets) and is no longer regarded as the apex of human culture. Consequently, the idea of cultural progress has been cast aside, and evolutionary theories have been rejected (Eder 1990; Smart 1990)

Natural Cycles

Cyclical theories attempt to account for the rise of entire civilizations. Why, for example, did Egypt, Greece, and Rome wield such power and influence, only to crest and fall into a decline? Cyclical theories assume that civilizations are like organisms: They are born, see an exuberant youth, come to maturity, then decline as they reach old age, and finally die (Hughes 1962).

Why do civilizations go through this cycle? Historian Arnold Toynbee (1946) said that each civilization faces challenges to its existence. The solutions to these challenges are not total, and oppositional forces remain. The ruling elite manages to keep these forces under control, but at a civilization's peak, when it has become an

Despite the vast social change that is occurring around the globe, race-ethnicity remains a fundamental distinction among human groups. Shown here is a Ukrainian being measured to see if he is really "full-lipped" enough to be called a Tartar.

France, Italy, the United States, and Mexico. At what point these resentments and hatreds will play themselves out, if ever, is unknown.

For the most part, the Most Industrialized Nations care little if the entire continent of Africa self-destructs in ethnic slaughter, but they cannot tolerate interethnic warfare in their own back yard. To let interethnic warfare in Bosnia and Kosovo go unchecked, for example, would be to tolerate conflict that could spread and engulf Europe. For global control, the G7 must be able to depend on political and economic stability in its own neighborhood, as well as in those countries that provide the raw materials essential for its industrial machine.

THEORIES AND PROCESSES OF SOCIAL CHANGE

Social change has fascinated theorists. Of the many attempts to explain why societies change, we shall consider just four: cultural evolution, cycles, conflict, and the pioneering views of sociologist William Ogburn.

empire, the ruling elite loses its capacity to keep the masses in line "by charm rather than by force." The fabric of society is eventually ripped apart. Force may hold the empire together for hundreds of years, but the civilization is doomed.

In a book that provoked widespread controversy, *The Decline of the West* (1926–1928), Oswald Spengler, a high school teacher in Germany, proposed that Western civilization had passed its peak and was in decline. Although the West succeeded in overcoming the crises provoked by Hitler and Mussolini, as Toynbee noted, civilizations don't end in sudden collapse. Because the decline can last hundreds of years, perhaps the crisis in Western civilization mentioned earlier (poverty, rape, murder, and so on) indicates that Spengler was right, and we are now in decline.

Conflict over Power

Long before Toynbee, Karl Marx identified a recurring process in human history. He said that each *thesis* (a current arrangement of power) contains its own *antithesis* (contradiction or opposition). A struggle develops between the thesis and its antithesis, leading to a *synthesis* (a new arrangement of power). This new social order, in turn, becomes a thesis that will be challenged by its own antithesis, and so on. Figure 15.1 gives a visual summary of this process.

According to Marx's view (called a **dialectical process** of history), each ruling group sows the seeds of its own destruction. Consider capitalism. Marx said that capitalism (the thesis) is built on the exploitation of workers (an antithesis, or built-in opposition). With workers and owners on a collision course, the dialectical process will not stop until workers establish a classless state (the synthesis).

The analysis of G7 in the previous section follows conflict theory. G7's current division of the globe's resources and markets is a thesis. Resentment on the part of have-not nations is an antithesis. If one of the Least Industrialized Nations gains in military power, that nation will press for a redistribution of resources. China, India, and Pakistan, with their nuclear weapons, fit this scenario. So do the efforts of Saddam Hussein to change the balance of power in the Mideast. Any new arrangement, or synthesis, will contain its own antitheses. They may be ethnic hostilities, or leaders feeling that their country has been denied its fair share of resources. These antitheses will haunt the arrangement of power and must at some point be resolved into a synthesis. The process repeats itself.

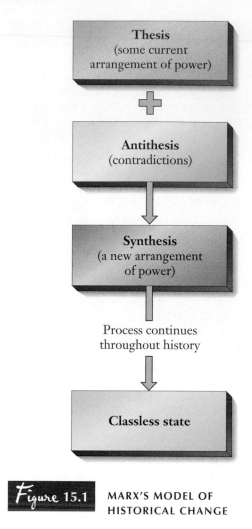

Figure 15.1 **MARX'S MODEL OF HISTORICAL CHANGE**

Ogburn's Theory

Sociologist William Ogburn (1922/1938, 1961, 1964) proposed a view of social change that is based on technology. Technology, he said, changes society by three processes: invention, discovery, and diffusion. Let's consider each.

Invention Ogburn defined **invention** as a combining of existing elements and materials to form new ones. We usually think of inventions as being only material, such as computers, but there are also *social inventions*. We have considered three social inventions in this text: capitalism (pages 346–347), bureaucracy (pages 111–116), and the corporation (pages 116–118, 293–294). As we saw in these instances, social inventions can have far-reaching consequences on society and people's relationship to one another.

Discovery Ogburn identified **discovery**, a new way of seeing reality, as a second process of change. The reality is already present, but people now see it for the first time. An example is Columbus' "discovery" of North America, which had consequences so huge that they altered the course of human history. This example also illustrates another principle: A discovery brings extensive change only when it comes at the right time. Other groups, such as the Vikings, had already "discovered" North America in the sense of learning that a new land existed—obviously no discovery to the Native Americans already living in it. Viking settlements disappeared into history, however, and Norse culture was untouched by the discovery.

Diffusion Ogburn stressed how **diffusion**, the spread of an invention or discovery from one area to another, can have extensive effects on people's lives. Consider a simple object such as the axe. When missionaries introduced steel axes to the Aborigines of Australia, it upset their whole society. Before this, the men controlled axe-making. They used a special stone available only in a remote region, and passed axe-making skills from father to son. Women had to request permission to use the axe. When steel axes became common, women also possessed them, and the men lost both status and power (Sharp 1995).

Diffusion also includes the spread of ideas. As we saw in Chapter 11, the idea of citizenship changed political structures around the world. It removed monarchs as an unquestioned source of authority. The concept of gender equality is now circling the globe. Although taken for granted in a few parts of the world, the idea that it is wrong to withhold rights on the basis of someone's sex is revolutionary. Like citizenship, this idea is destined to transform basic human relationships and entire societies.

Cultural Lag Ogburn coined the term **cultural lag** to refer to how some elements of a culture lag behind the changes that come from invention, discovery, and diffusion. Technology, he suggested, usually changes first, with culture lagging behind. In other words, we play catch-up with changing technology, adapting our customs and ways of life to meet its needs.

Technology underlies the rapid change that is engulfing us today. As we consider technology, let's focus on the computer, that powerful machine, which for good or ill, is transforming society and, with it, our way of life.

How Technology Changes Society

As you may recall from Chapter 2, **technology** has a double meaning. It refers both to *tools*, the items used to accomplish tasks, and to the skills or procedures needed to make and use those tools. Technology refers to tools as simple as a comb and those as complicated as a computer. Technology's second meaning—the skills or procedures needed to make and use tools—refers in this case not only to the procedures used to manufacture combs and computers but also to those required to "produce" an acceptable hairdo or to gain access to the Internet. Apart from its particulars, technology always refers to *artificial means of extending human abilities*.

All human groups make and use technology, but the chief characteristic of postindustrial societies (also called **postmodern societies**) is technology that greatly extends our abilities to analyze information, to communicate, and to travel. These *new technologies*, as they are called, allow us to do what had never been done in history: to probe space, to communicate almost instantaneously anywhere on the globe, to travel greater distances faster, and to store, retrieve, and analyze vast amounts of information.

This level of accomplishment, although impressive, is really superficial. Of much greater sociological significance is a deeper issue: how technology changes our way of life. *Technology is much more than the apparatus*. It is obvious, for example, that without automobiles, telephones, and televisions, our entire way of life would be strikingly different. The computer may be bringing about changes every bit as drastic as these.

The Impact of the Computer

The ominous wail seemed too close for comfort. Sally looked in her rear-view mirror and realized that the flashing lights and screaming siren might be for her. She felt confused. "I'm just on my way to Soc," she thought. "I'm not speeding or anything." After she pulled over, an angry voice over a loudspeaker ordered her out of the car.

As she got out, someone barked the command, "Back up with your hands in the air!" Bewildered, Sally stood frozen for a moment. "Put 'em up now! Right now!" She did as she was told.

The officer crouched behind his open door, his gun drawn. When Sally reached the police car—still backing up—the officer grabbed her, threw her to the ground, and handcuffed her hands behind her back. She heard words she

Culture contact is the source of *diffusion,* the spread of an invention or discovery from one area to another. Shown here are two children of the Huli tribe in Papua New Guinea, looking amused by a Polaroid photo of themselves.

would never forget. "You are under arrest for murder. You have the right to remain silent. Anything you say can and will be used against you in a court of law. You have the right to an attorney. If you cannot afford one, one will be provided for you."

Traces of alarm still flicker across Sally's face when she recalls her arrest. She had never even had a traffic ticket, much less been arrested for anything. The nightmare that Sally experienced happened because of a "computer error." With the inversion of two numbers, her car's license number had been entered into the police databank instead of the number belonging to a woman wanted for a brutal killing earlier that day.

None of us is untouched by the computer, but it is unlikely that many of us have felt its power as directly and dramatically as Sally did. For most of us, the computer's control lies quietly behind the scenes. Although the computer has intruded into our daily lives, most of us never think about it. Our grades are computerized, and probably our paychecks as well. When we buy groceries, a computer scans our purchases and presents a printout of the name, price, and quantity of each item.

Many people rejoice over the computer's capacity to improve their quality of life. They are pleased with the quality control of manufactured goods and the reduction of drudgery. Records are much easier to keep, and we can type just one letter and let the computer print and address it to ten individuals—or to ten thousand. If we use e-mail, those letters can be delivered in seconds.

Some people, however, worry about errors that can creep into computerized records, aware that something similar to Sally's misfortune could happen to them. Others are concerned about how easily computerized records can be manipulated to accomplish "identity theft." These are legitimate concerns, but space does not permit us to pursue them further.

At this point, let's consider how the computer is changing medicine, education, and the workplace. We'll then consider its likely effects on social inequality.

Computers in Medicine

The patient's symptoms were mystifying. After exercise, one side of his face and part of his body turned deep red, the other chalky white. He looked as though someone had taken a ruler and drawn a line down the middle of his body.

Stumped, the patient's physician consulted a medical librarian who punched a few words into a computer to search for clues in the world's medical literature. Soon, the likely answer flashed on the screen: Harlequin's disease. (Winslow 1994)

The computer was right, and a neurosurgeon was able to correct the patient's nervous system. With computers, physicians can peer within the body's hidden recesses to determine how its parts are functioning or to see if surgery is necessary. Surgeons can operate on previously inaccessible parts of the brain—even on unborn babies. In a few years, tiny devices—smaller than the diameter of a single human hair—will be inserted into the bloodstream to detect cancer cells (Kalb 2000). As the future rushes in, the microchip is bringing even more technological wonders. In what is called *tele-medicine,* data are transmitted by fiber-optic cable to remote locations. This allows doctors to use stethoscopes to check the hearts and lungs of patients who are hundreds of miles away (Richards 1996). Surgeons in Boston or San Francisco will soon be able to use remote-controlled robots and images relayed via satellite to operate on wounded soldiers in battlefield hospitals on the other side of the world (Associated Press 1995).

Will the computer lead to "doctorless" medical offices? Will we perhaps one day feed vital information about ourselves into a computer and receive a printout of what is wrong with us (and, of course, a prescription)? Many patients are likely to resist, for they would miss interacting with their doctors, especially the assurances and other emotional support that good physicians provide. Somehow "Take two aspirins and key me in the morning" doesn't sound comforting. Physicians, of course, will vigorously repel such an onslaught on their expertise. It is likely, then, that the computer will remain a diagnostic tool for physicians, not a replacement for them.

Computers in Education Almost every grade school in the United States introduces its students to the computer. Children learn how to type on it, as well as how to use mathematics and science software. Successful educational programs use a game-like format that makes students forget they are "studying." With classrooms wired to the Internet, students in schools that have no teachers knowledgeable in foreign languages are able to take courses in Russian, German, and Spanish. Even though they have no sociology instructors, they can take courses in the sociology of gender, race, or even sports.

The unequal funding we discussed in Chapter 13 is significant in this context. Schools that are able to afford the latest in computer technology are able to better prepare their students for the future. That advantage, of course, goes to students of private schools and to the richest public school districts, thus helping to perpetuate the social inequalities that arise from the chance of birth. At one point in our history, some schools could not afford textbooks. It is likely that, eventually, education's digital divide will also become a distant memory.

The computer will transform the college of the future. Each office and dormitory room and off-campus residence will be connected by fiber-optic cable. Professors will be able to transmit entire books directly from

In this 1905 photo, Henry Ford sits in the driver's seat of his latest model car. As is apparent, especially from the spokes on the car's wheels, new technology builds on existing technology. Only after supporting technology was developed, such as graveled and paved roads, did the automobile become a serious contender with other forms of transportation. At the time this photo was taken, who could have imagined that this vehicle would transform society?

their office to a student's room, or back the other way, in *less* time than it took you to read this sentence. To help students and professors do research or prepare reports, computers will search millions of pages of text. Digital textbooks will replace printed versions such as this one. You will be able to key in the terms *social interaction* and *gender,* select your preference of historical period and geographical area—and the computer will spew out text, maps, moving images, and sounds. You will be able to do the same with any topic: riots and Los Angeles, sexual discrimination in the military, or even the price of marijuana and cocaine. If you wish, the computer will give you a test—geared to the level of difficulty you choose—so you can check your mastery of the material.

Computers in the Workplace The computer is also transforming the workplace. At the simplest level, it affects how we do work. For example, I wrote the first two editions of this book on a computer, which commanded a printer to produce an immediate copy of the manuscript. Then, even in this electronic age, a series of archaic, precomputer processes followed: I sent the printed copy via the postal service to an editor, who

Technology, which drives much social change, is at the forefront of our information revolution. This revolution, based on the computer chip, allows reality to cross with fantasy, a merging that sometimes makes it difficult to tell where one ends and the other begins. Shown here is Liquid Metal Man morphing into a human in *Terminator 2.*

physically handled the manuscript and sent it to others who did the same. The manuscript, marked up in red pencil, was then sent to me, and I mailed back a corrected copy. The process was rather primitive, much the same as would have occurred during Benjamin Franklin's day.

Practice is finally catching up with potential. My editors and I now zap text back and forth electronically. I may be in the United States or in Spain, while they are in Oregon and Massachusetts. It makes no difference. I print nothing, and send no papers. Although the distances are greater, the time lapse has shrunk. For me, the process is marvelous testimony of our changing world—and unsettling confirmation of our steady steps into a brave new world.

The computer is also bringing changes on a deeper level, for it alters social relationships. For example, I used to bring my manuscript to a university secretary, wait several days for her to type it, and then retrieve it. Now, by making corrections directly at the computer and transmitting a revised electronic copy, the secretary

is bypassed entirely. In this instance, the computer enhanced social relationships, for I made fewer demands on the department secretary. This also eliminated the necessity of her making excuses when a manuscript was not ready on time—and the tensions that this brought to our relationship.

For some, including myself, the computer has also reversed the change in work location that industrialization ushered in. As discussed earlier, due to industrialization, work shifted from home to factory and office. Many workers now remain at home while computers and modems connect them with their bosses and fellow workers at locations around the country—or even on the other side of the globe. We may be seeing the beginning of another historical shift, one that may bring families closer together.

On the negative side are increased surveillance of workers and depersonalization. As a telephone information operator said,

The computer knows everything. It records the minute I punch in. It knows how long I take for each call.... I am supposed to average under eighteen seconds per call.... Everything I do is reported to my supervisor on his computer, and if I've missed my numbers I get a written warning. I rarely see the guy.... It's intense. It's me and the computer all day. I'm telling you, at the end of the day I'm wiped out. Working with computers is the coal mining of the nineties. (Mander 1992:57)

Computers in Business and Finance Not long ago, the advanced technology of businesses consisted of cash registers and adding machines. Connection to the outside world was by telephone. Today, those same businesses are electronically "wired" to suppliers, salespeople, and clients around the country—and around the world. Computers record changes in inventory and set in motion the process of reordering and restocking. They produce detailed reports of sales that alert managers to changes in their customers' tastes or preferences.

National borders have become meaningless as computers instantaneously transfer billions of dollars from one country to another. No "cash" changes hands in these transactions. The money consists of digits in computer memory banks, which update the accounts of businesses around the world. Governments are concerned. In a single day, this new type of digitized money can be transferred from the United States to Switzerland, from there to the Grand Cayman Islands, and then to the Isle of Mann, leaving few traces for government sleuths to follow. "Where's my share?" governments around the

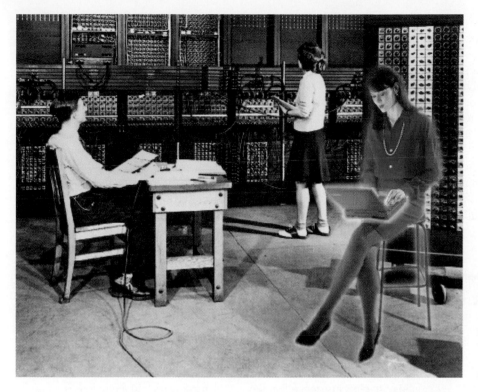

Most of us take computers for granted, but they are new to the world scene—as are their effects on our lives. This photo captures a significant change in the evolution of computers. The laptop held by the superimposed model has more power than the room-size ENIAC of 1946.

world are moaning, as they consider how to control—and tax—this new technology.

Cyberspace and Social Inequality

The term *information superhighway* conveys the idea of information traveling at a high rate of speed among homes and businesses. Just as a highway allows physical travel from one place to another, so the information superhighway allows homes and businesses to be connected by the rapid flow of information. Already about 200 million people around the world are able to communicate by Internet. Servers such as Prodigy, America Online, and Compuserve give them electronic access to libraries of information. Some programs sift, sort, and transmit images, sound, and video. Electronic mail (e-mail) allows people to zap messages around the globe. This is the future, a world linked by almost instantaneous communications, with information readily accessible around the globe, and few places that can be called "remote."

The implications of the information superhighway for national and global stratification are severe. On the national level, we can end up with information have-nots, primarily inner-city residents, which would perpetuate present inequalities. On the global level, the question is: Who will control the information superhigh-

way? The answer, of course, is obvious, for it is the Most Industrialized Nations that are developing this communications system. This leads to one of the more profound issues of the twenty-first century—will such control destine the Least Industrialized Nations to a perpetual pauper status? Or will their access to this new technology be their passport to affluence?

SOCIAL MOVEMENTS AS A SOURCE OF SOCIAL CHANGE

The contradictions (such as social inequality) that are built into arrangements of power create discontent. One result is **social movements,** large numbers of people who organize to promote or resist social change. Members of social movements hold strong ideas about what is wrong with the world—or some part of it—and how to make things right. Examples include the civil rights movement, the white supremacist movement, the women's movement, the animal rights crusade, the nuclear freeze movement, and the environmental movement.

At the heart of social movements lies a sense of injustice (Klandemans 1997). Some find a condition of society intolerable, and their goal is to *promote* social change. Theirs is called a **proactive social movement.** Others, in contrast, feel threatened because some condition of society is changing, and they organize to *resist* that change. Theirs is a **reactive social movement.**

To further their goals, people develop **social movement organizations.** Those whose goal is to promote social change develop such organizations as the National Association for the Advancement of Colored People (NAACP). In contrast, those who are trying to resist these particular changes form the Ku Klux Klan. To recruit followers and publicize their grievances, leaders of social movements use attention-getting devices, from marches and rallies to sit-ins and boycotts. Some stage "media events," sometimes quite effectively (see the Cultural Diversity box).

Social movements are like a rolling sea, observes sociologist Mayer Zald (1992). During one period, few social movements may appear, but shortly afterward a wave of them rolls in, each competing for the public's attention. Zald suggests that a *cultural crisis* can give birth to a wave of social movements. By this, he means that there are times when a society's institutions fail to keep up with social change. Then many people's needs go unfulfilled, massive unrest follows, and social movements spring into action to bridge the gap.

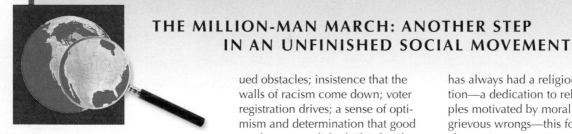

CULTURAL DIVERSITY In the United States

THE MILLION-MAN MARCH: ANOTHER STEP IN AN UNFINISHED SOCIAL MOVEMENT

The Civil Rights Movement of the 1950s and 1960s brought huge gains: integrated public facilities, schools, voting booths, housing, and workplaces. Or, rather, the movement affirmed that all Americans have the *right* to such aspects of social life; for many of the gains have been elusive, somehow disappearing just when they seemed on the verge of being realized. The inner city, with all of its ills, from unemployment to violent crime, has become the single most powerful symbol that this social movement is unfinished.

The Million-Man March—which consisted of several hundred thousand African American males from all over the country who gathered on the Mall in Washington, D.C., in the fall of 1995—picked up where this movement stalled. It had two essential features. The first was directed outward: protest at continued obstacles; insistence that the walls of racism come down; voter registration drives; a sense of optimism and determination that good can be accomplished. This first feature is a direct reflection of the old Civil Rights Movement.

The second feature, an inward turning, is a redirecting of the Civil Rights Movement. It is a conservative, proactive stance by African Americans who want to make changes in the African American community. As the organizers of the march stressed, this feature underscores the need to build greater respect between men and women, to reduce spouse abuse, and to assume the obligations of fatherhood—including marriage, nurturing and supporting one's children, and giving them a positive role model of responsible masculinity (Whetstone 1996).

This desire for inward change that is to be manifested in personal relationships reflects the religious orientation of the march's organizers. The emphases are on repentance, atonement, and changed behavior. Although the Civil Rights Movement has always had a religious orientation—a dedication to religious principles motivated by moral outrage over grievous wrongs—this focus on inner change is new.

The Million-Man March did not begin with a march to Washington, nor did it end with the departure of the buses. There may be other marches, but the specifics are not what is relevant. The march is but one facet of an ongoing social movement, a movement destined to stay with us, for grievances remain, and goals have been only partially reached. ■

For Your Consideration

What are these marches intended to accomplish? What do you think they accomplish? What other techniques might be more effective? What symbols did the organizers use? What messages are these marches intended to communicate? Who are the intended audiences? Look at Figure 15.2 on the next page; is this an alterative, redemptive, reformative, or transformative social movement?

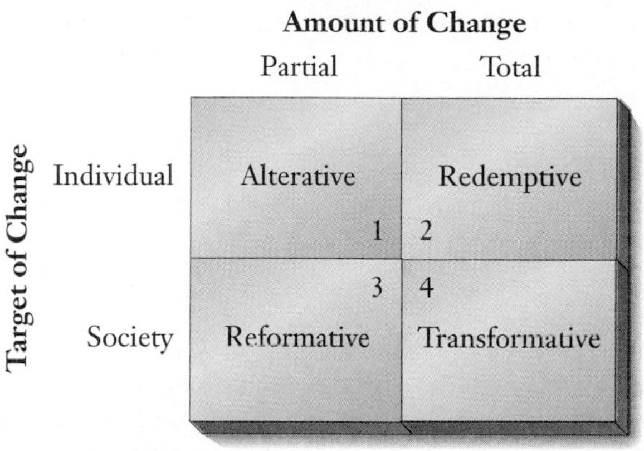

Amount of Change

Partial   Total

Figure 15.2   TYPES OF SOCIAL MOVEMENTS

Source: Aberle 1966.

Types of Social Movements

Since social change is their goal, we can classify social movements according to their *target* and the *amount of change* they seek. Figure 15.2 summarizes the classification developed by sociologist David Aberle (1966). If you read across, you will see that the target of the first two types of social movements is *individuals*. **Alterative social movements** seek only to *alter* some specific behavior. An example is the Women's Christian Temperance Union, a powerful social movement of the early 1900s. Its goal was to get people to stop drinking alcohol. Its members were convinced that if they could shut down the saloons, such problems as poverty and wife abuse would go away. **Redemptive social movements** also target individuals, but here the aim is for *total* change. An example is a religious social movement that stresses conversion. In fundamentalist Christianity, for example, when someone converts to Christ, the entire person is supposed to change, not just some specific behavior. Self-centered acts are to be replaced by loving behaviors toward others as the convert becomes, in their terms, a "new creation."

The target of the next two types of social movements is *society*. **Reformative social movements** seek to *reform* some specific aspect of society. The environmental movement, for example, seeks to reform the ways society treats the environment, from its disposal of garbage and nuclear wastes to its use of land and water. **Transformative social movements,** in contrast, seek to *transform* the social order itself. Its members want to replace it with their version of the good society. Revolutions, such as those in the American colonies, France, Russia, and Cuba, are examples.

Propaganda and the Mass Media

The leaders of social movements try to manipulate the mass media in order to influence **public opinion,** how people think about some issue. The right kind of publicity enables them to arouse the sympathetic public and to lay the groundwork for recruiting more members. Pictures of bloodied, dead baby seals, for example, go a long way toward getting a group's message across.

A key to understanding social movements, then, is **propaganda.** Although this word often evokes negative images, it actually is a neutral term. Propaganda is simply the presentation of information in the attempt to influence people. Its original meaning was positive. *Propaganda* referred to a committee of cardinals of the Roman Catholic church whose assignment was the care of foreign missions. (They were to *propagate* the faith.) The term has traveled a long way since then, however, and today it usually refers to a one-sided presentation of information that distorts reality.

Propaganda, in the sense of organized attempts to influence public opinion, is a regular part of everyday life. Advertisements, for example, are a form of propaganda, for they present a one-sided version of reality. Underlying effective propaganda are seven basic techniques, discussed in the Down-to-Earth Sociology box on the next page. Perhaps by understanding these techniques, you will be able to resist one-sided appeals—whether they come from social movements or from hawkers of jeans, sneakers, or perfume.

The mass media play such a crucial role in social movements that we can say they are the gatekeepers to social movements. If those who control and work in the mass media—from owners to reporters—are sympathetic to some particular "cause," you can be sure that it will receive sympathetic treatment. If the social movement goes against their own views, it will be ignored or will receive unfavorable treatment. If you ever get the impression that the media are trying to manipulate your opinions and attitudes on some particular social movement—or some social issue—you probably are right. Far from doing unbiased reporting, the media are under the control and influence of people who have an agenda to get across. To the materials in the Down-to-Earth Sociology box on propaganda, then, we need to add the biases of the media establishment, the issues to which it chooses to give publicity, those it chooses to ignore, and its favorable and unfavorable treatment of issues and movements.

Sociology can be a liberating discipline (Berger 1963/2001). It sensitizes us to the existence of *multiple*

Sociology

"TRICKS OF THE TRADE"—
THE FINE ART OF PROPAGANDA

Sociologists Alfred and Elizabeth Lee (1939) found that propaganda relies on seven basic techniques, which they termed "tricks of the trade." To be effective, the techniques should be subtle, with the audience unaware that their minds and emotions are being manipulated. If propaganda is effective, people will not know *why* they support something, only that they do—and they'll fervently defend it.

- *Name calling.* This technique aims to arouse opposition to the competing product, candidate, or policy by associating it with a negative image. By comparison, one's own product, candidate, or policy is attractive. Political candidates who call an opponent "soft on crime" are using this technique.

- *Glittering generality.* Essentially the opposite of the first technique, this one surrounds the product, candidate, or policy with phrases that arouse positive feelings. "She's a real Democrat" has little meaning, but it makes the audience feel that something substantive has been said. "He stands for individualism" is so general that it is meaningless, yet the audience thinks that it has heard a specific message about the candidate.

- *Transfer.* In its positive form, this technique associates the product, candidate, or policy with something the public respects or approves. You might not be able to get by with saying "Coors is patriotic," but surround a beer with images of the country's flag, and beer drinkers will get the idea that it is more patriotic to drink this brand of beer than to drink any other kind. In its negative form, this technique associates the product, candidate, or policy with something the public disapproves.

- *Testimonials.* Famous and admired individuals are used to endorse a product, candidate, or policy. Michael Jordan lends his name to cologne, Nike products, and even underwear, while Cindy Crawford does the same for Revlon. Candidates for political office solicit the endorsement of movie stars who may know next to nothing about the candidate or even politics. In the negative form of this technique, a despised person is associated with the competing product. If propagandists (called "spin doctors" in politics) could get by with it, they would show Saddam Hussein announcing support for an opposing candidate.

- *Plain folks.* Sometimes it pays to associate the product, candidate, or policy with "just plain folks." "If Mary or John Q. Public likes it, you will, too." A political candidate who kisses babies, puts on a hard hat, and has lunch at McDonald's while photographers "catch him (or her) in the act"—is using the "plain folks" strategy. "I'm just a regular person" is the message of the presidential candidate who poses for photographers in jeans and a work shirt—while making certain that the chauffeur-driven Mercedes does not show up in the background.

- *Card stacking.* The aim of this technique is to present only positive information about what you support, and only negative information about what you oppose. The intent is to make it sound as though there is only one conclusion a rational person can draw. Falsehoods, distortions, and illogical statements are often used.

- *Bandwagon.* "Everyone is doing it" is the idea behind this technique. Emphasizing how many others buy the product or support the candidate or policy conveys the message that anyone who doesn't join in is on the wrong track.

The Lees (1939) added, "Once we know that a speaker or writer is using one of these propaganda devices in an attempt to convince us of an idea, we can separate the device from the idea and see what the idea amounts to on its own merits." ■

The use of *propaganda* is popular among those committed to the goals of a *social movement*. They can see only one side to the social issue about which they are so upset. Do you think there is another side to this social issue?

realities; that is, for any single point of view on some topic, there are competing points of view, which some find equally compelling. Each represents reality as people see it, but different experiences lead to different perceptions. Consequently, although the committed members of a social movement are sincere, and perhaps even make sacrifices for "the cause," theirs is but one view of the world. If other sides were presented, the issue would look quite different.

The Stages of Social Movements

Sociologists have identified five stages in the growth and maturity of social movements (Lang and Lang 1961; Mauss 1975; Spector and Kitsuse 1977; Tilly 1978; Jaspar 1991). They are

1. *Initial unrest and agitation.* During this first stage, people are upset about some condition in society and want to change it. Leaders emerge who verbalize people's feel-

ings and crystallize issues. Most social movements fail at this stage. Unable to gain enough support, after a brief flurry of activity they quietly die.

2. *Mobilization.* A crucial factor that enables social movements to make it past the first stage is **resource mobilization.** By this term, sociologists mean the mobilization of resources—time, money, people's skills, and the ability to get the attention of the mass media. Technology and mailing lists are key resources: direct mailing, faxing, and e-mailing. In some cases, an indigenous leadership arises to mobilize resources. Other groups, having no capable leadership of their own, turn to outsiders, "specialists for hire." As sociologists John McCarthy and Mayer Zald (1977; Zald and McCarthy 1987) point out, even though large numbers of people may be upset over some condition of society, without resource mobilization they are only upset people, perhaps even agitators, but they do not constitute a social movement.

A social movement has developed around environmental concerns. Activists have protested the logging of the ancient redwood and sequoia groves in northern California; nuclear plants, weapons, and pollution; and the threatened extinction of animals, plants, and the rain forests. Shown here is a demonstration against the World Trade Organization (WTO) in Seattle, Washington. The demonstrators are wearing turtle suits to protest what they contend are animal-harming rulings by the WTO.

3. *Organization.* A division of labor is set up. The leadership makes policy decisions, and the rank and file carry out the daily tasks necessary to keep the movement going. There is still much collective excitement about the issue, the movement's focal point of concern.

4. *Institutionalization.* At this stage, the movement has developed a bureaucracy, the type of formal hierarchy described in Chapter 5. Control lies in the hands of career officers, who may care more about their own position in the organization than the movement for which the organization's initial leaders made sacrifices. The collective excitement diminishes.

5. *Organizational decline and possible resurgence.* During this phase, managing the day-to-day affairs of the organization dominates the leadership. A change in public sentiment may even have occurred, and there may no longer be a group of committed people who share a common cause. The movement is likely to wither away.

Decline is not inevitable, however. More idealistic and committed leaders may emerge and reinvigorate the movement. Or, as in the case of abortion, conflict between groups on opposite sides of the issue may continuously invigorate each side and prevent the movement's decline. The following Thinking Critically section contrasts two opposing groups in regard to abortion.

Thinking *Critically*

WHICH SIDE OF THE BARRICADES? PROCHOICE AND PROLIFE AS A SOCIAL MOVEMENT

No issue so divides Americans as abortion does. Although most Americans take a more moderate view, on one side are some who feel that abortion should be permitted under any circumstance, even during the last month of pregnancy. They are matched by some on the other side who are convinced that abortion should never be allowed for any circumstances, not even during the first month of pregnancy. This polarization constantly breathes new life into the movement.

When the U.S. Supreme Court decided in its 1973 decision, *Roe* v. *Wade,* that states could not restrict abortion, the prochoice side relaxed. Victory was theirs, and they thought their opponents would quietly disappear. Instead, large numbers of Americans were disturbed by what they saw as the legal right to murder unborn children.

The views of the two sides could not be more incompatible. Those who favor choice view the nearly 1.5 million abortions performed annually in the United States as examples of women exercising their basic reproductive rights. Those who gather under the prolife banner see these acts as legalized murder. To the prochoice side, those who oppose abortion are blocking women's rights—they would force women to continue pregnancies they want to terminate. To the prolife side, those who advocate choice are seen as condoning murder—they would put their own desires for school, career, or convenience ahead of the lives of their unborn children.

There is no way to reconcile these contrary views. Each sees the other as unreasonable and extremist. And each uses propaganda by focusing on worst-case scenar-

Activists in social movements become committed to "the cause." The social movement around abortion, currently one of the most dynamic in the United States, has split Americans, is highly visible, and has articulate spokespeople on both sides.

ios: prochoice images of young women raped at gunpoint, forced to bear the children of rapists; prolife images of women who are eight months pregnant killing their babies instead of nurturing them.

With no middle ground, these views remain in permanent conflict. As each side fights for what it considers basic rights, it reinvigorates the other. When in 1989 the U.S. Supreme Court decided in *Webster* v. *Reproductive Services* that states could restrict abortion, one side mourned it as a defeat, the other hailed it as a victory. Seeing the political battle going against them, the prochoice side regrouped for a determined struggle. The prolife side, sensing judicial victory within its grasp, gathered forces for a push to complete the overthrow of *Roe v. Wade*.

This goal of the prolife side almost became reality in *Casey* v. *Planned Parenthood*. On June 30, 1992, in a 6-to-3 decision the Supreme Court upheld the right of states to require women to wait 24 hours between the confirmation of pregnancy and abortion, to require girls under 18 to obtain the consent of one parent, and to require that women be informed about alternatives to abortion and that they be given materials that describe the fetus. In the same case, by a 5-to-4 decision, the Court ruled that a wife does not have to inform her husband if she intends to have an abortion.

Because the two sides do not see the same reality, this social movement cannot end unless the vast majority of Americans commit to one side or the other. Otherwise, every legislative and judicial outcome—including the extremes of a constitutional amendment that declares abortion to be either murder or a woman's right—are

victories to one and defeats to the other. To committed activists, then, no battle is ever complete. Rather, each action is only one small part of a hard-fought, bitter, moral struggle. ■

For Your Consideration

Typically, the last stage of a social movement is decline. Why hasn't this social movement declined? Under what conditions will it decline?

The longer the pregnancy in question, the fewer the Americans who approve abortion. How do you feel about abortion during the second month versus the eighth month? Or partial-birth abortion? What do you think about abortion in cases of rape and incest? Can you identify some of the *social* reasons that underlie your opinions?

Sources: Neikirk and Elsasser 1992; McKenna 1995; Williams 1995; *Statistical Abstract* 1999:Table 124; Henslin 2000.

$\mathcal{T}$HE GROWTH MACHINE VERSUS THE EARTH

Of all the changes swirling around us, perhaps those that affect the natural environment hold the most serious implications for human life.

Underlying today's environmental decay is the globalization of capitalism, which I have stressed throughout this text. To maintain their dominance and increase their wealth, the Most Industrialized Nations, spurred by the multinational corporations, continue to push for economic growth. At the same time, the Industrializing Nations, playing catch-up, are striving to develop their economies. Meanwhile, the Least Industrialized Nations are anxious to enter the race: Because they start from even farther behind, they have to push for even faster growth.

Many are convinced that the earth cannot withstand such an onslaught. Global economic production creates extensive pollution, and faster-paced production means faster-paced destruction of our environment. If the goal is a **sustainable environment,** a world system in which we use our physical environment to meet our needs without destroying humanity's future, we cannot continue to trash the earth. In short, the ecological message is incompatible with an economic message that it is OK to rape the environment for the sake of profits.

Before looking at the social movement that has grown around this issue, let's examine major environmental problems.

Environmental Problems in the Most Industrialized Nations

Although even tribal groups produced pollution, the frontal assault on the natural environment did not begin in earnest until nations industrialized. The more extensive its industrialization, the better it was considered for a nation's welfare. For the Most Industrialized Nations, the slogan has been "Growth at any cost."

Industrial growth did come, but at a high cost to the natural environment. Today, for example, formerly pristine streams are polluted sewers, and the water supply of many cities is unfit to drink. When Los Angeles announces "smog days" on radio and television, schoolchildren are kept inside during recess, and everyone is warned to stay indoors. The accumulation of hazardous wastes is a special problem. Despite the danger to people and the environment, in many cases the waste has simply been dumped. The Social Map below shows how the worst hazardous waste sites are distributed among the United States. The Down-to-Earth Sociology box on the next page discusses how *corporate welfare* contributes to pollution.

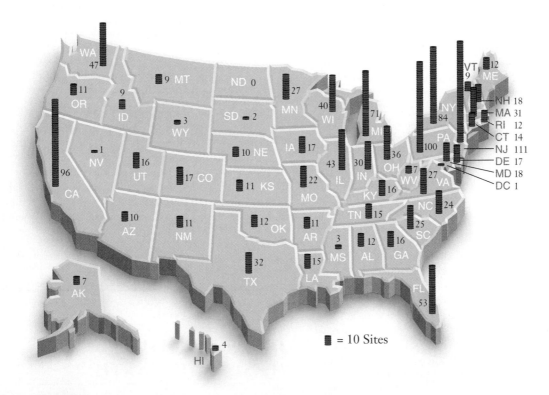

Figure 15.3   **WHERE ARE THE WORST HAZARDOUS WASTE SITES?**

Source: Statistical Abstract 1999:Table 414.

Sociology

CORPORATIONS AND BIG WELFARE BUCKS: HOW TO GET PAID TO POLLUTE

Welfare is one of the most controversial topics in the United States. It arouses the ire of many wealthy and middle-class Americans, who view the poor who collect welfare as parasites. But have you heard about *corporate welfare?*

Corporate welfare refers to handouts given to corporations. A state may offer a company tax breaks if it will locate within the state, or remain in the state if it has threatened to leave. A state may even provide land and factories at bargain prices. The reason: jobs.

Corporate welfare even goes to companies that foul the land, water, and air. Borden Chemicals in Louisiana has buried hazardous wastes without a permit and released hazardous chemicals so thick that to protect drivers the police have sometimes had to shut down the highway that runs near the plant. Borden even contaminated the groundwater be-

neath its plant, threatening the aquifer that provides drinking water for residents of Louisiana and Texas.

Borden's pollution has cost the company dearly: $3.6 million in fines, $3 million to clean up the groundwater, and $400,000 for local emergency response units. That's a hefty $7 million. But if we add corporate welfare, the company didn't make out so badly. With $15 million in reduced and canceled property taxes, Borden has enjoyed a net gain of $8 million (Bartlett and Steele 1998). And that's not counting the savings the company racked up by not having to properly dispose of its toxic wastes in the first place.

Louisiana has added a novel twist to corporate welfare. It offers an incentive to help start-up companies. This itself isn't novel; the owners of that little "mom and pop" grocery store on your corner may have gotten some benefits when they

first opened. Louisiana's twist is what it counts as a start-up operation. One of these little start-up companies is called Exxon Corp. Although Exxon opened for business about 120 years ago, it had $213 million in property taxes canceled under this program. Another little company that the state figured could use a nudge to help it get started was Shell Oil Co., which had $140 million slashed from its taxes (Bartlett and Steele 1998). Then there were International Paper, Dow Chemical, Union Carbide, Boise Cascade, Georgia Pacific, and another tiny one called Procter & Gamble. ■

For Your Consideration

Apply the functionalist, symbolic interactionist, and conflict perspectives to these materials. Which do you think provides the best interpretation of corporate welfare? Why?

Many aspects of pollution are worth discussing. Our follies include harming the ozone layer in order to have the convenience of spray bottles and air conditioners. With limited space, however, I would like to focus on an overarching aspect of our environment, the burning of fossil fuels.

Fossil Fuels and the Environment Burning fossil fuels for factories, motorized vehicles, and power plants has been especially harmful. Fish can no longer survive in some lakes in Canada and the northeastern United States because of **acid rain:** The burning of fossil fuels releases sulfur dioxide and nitrogen oxide, which react

with moisture in the air to become sulfuric and nitric acids (Luoma 1989). See Figure 15.4 on page 408.

An invisible but infinitely more serious consequence is the **greenhouse effect.** Like the glass of a greenhouse, the gases emitted from burning fossil fuels allow sunlight to enter the earth's atmosphere freely, but inhibit the release of heat. It is as though the gases have closed the atmospheric window through which our planet breathes. Scientists are increasingly convinced that we face **global warming.** They warn us that polar ice caps may melt and inundate the world's shorelines, the climate boundaries may move north about four hundred miles, and many animal and plant species may

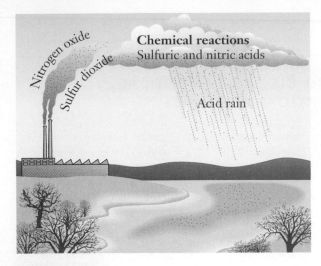

Chemical reactions
Sulfuric and nitric acids

Nitrogen oxide

Sulfur dioxide

Acid rain

Figure 15.4   **ACID RAIN**

become extinct (Weisskopf 1992; Begley 1997). They disagree, however, on whether the warming is due to natural or human causes (McFarling 2000). In 1997, 160 nations approved an environmental treaty to reduce "greenhouse gases."

The Energy Shortage and Multinational Corporations   If you ever read about an energy shortage, you can be sure that what you read is false. There is no energy shortage, nor can there ever be. We can produce unlimited low-cost power, which can help raise the living standards of humans across the globe. The sun, for example, produces more energy than humanity could ever use. Boundless energy is also available from the tides and the winds. In some cases, we need better technology to harness these sources of energy; in others, we need only to apply technology we already have.

We know that burning fossil fuels in internal combustion engines is the main source of pollution in the Most Industrialized Nations. With vast sources of alternative energy available to us, why don't we develop the technology to use them? From a conflict perspective, these abundant sources of energy present a threat to the multinational oil companies. It is in their interest to keep the gasoline-powered engine dominant. Competition is on the way, however, as the world's biggest auto makers will soon market cars powered by fuel cells, devices that convert hydrogen into electricity. Water, instead of carbon monoxide, will come out their exhaust pipes (Ball 1999).

Environmental Racism   Conflict and unequal power have led to what sociologists call **environmental racism**—minorities being the ones who suffer the most from the effects of pollution (Boone and Modarres 1999; Moberg 1999). Polluting industries locate where land is cheaper, which is where the wealthy do not live. Nor will the rich stand for factories to spew pollution near their homes. As a result, low-income communities, which are often inhabited by minorities, are exposed to more pollution. Sociologists have studied, formed, and joined environmental justice groups that fight to close polluting plants and to block construction of polluting industries.

Environmental Problems in the Industrializing and Least Industrialized Nations

Severe consequences of industrialization, such as ozone depletion, the greenhouse effect, and global warming, cannot be laid solely at the feet of the Most Industrialized Nations. With their rush to be contenders in the global competition, along with a lack of funds to pay for pollution controls, and few anti-pollution laws, the Industrializing Nations have made enormous contributions to this problem. Breathing the air of Mexico City, for example, is the equivalent of smoking two packs of cigarettes a day (Durbin 1995).

The former Soviet Union is a special case. Until this empire broke up, pollution had been treated as a state secret. Scientists and journalists were forbidden to mention pollution in public. Even peaceful demonstrations to call attention to pollution could net participants two years in prison (Feshbach 1992). With protest stifled and no environmental protection laws, pollution was rampant: Almost half of Russia's arable land has been made unsuitable for farming, about a third of Russians live in cities where air pollution is more than ten times greater than permissible levels in the United States, and half of Russia's tap water is unfit to drink. Pollution is so severe that the life expectancy of Russians has dropped, a lesson that should not be lost on the rest of us as we make decisions on how to treat our environment.

With their greater poverty and swelling populations, the Least Industrialized Nations have an even greater incentive to industrialize at any cost. These pressures, combined with almost nonexistent environmental regulations, may yet destine the Least Industrialized Nations to become the earth's major polluters.

Their lack of environmental protection laws has not gone unnoticed by opportunists in the Most Industrialized Nations, who use these countries as garbage dumps for hazardous wastes and for producing chemicals that their own people will no longer tolerate (Smith 1995; Englund and Cohn 1997). Alarmed at the growing environmental destruction, the World Bank, the monetary arm of the Most Industrialized Nations, has pressured the Least Industrialized Nations to reduce pollution and soil erosion (Lachica 1992). Understandably, the basic concern of these nations is to produce food and housing first, and to worry about the environment later.

Although the rain forests cover just 7 percent of the earth's land area, they are home to *one-third to one-half* of all plant and animal species. Despite our knowledge that the rain forests are essential for humanity's welfare, we seem bent on destroying them. For the sake of timber and farms,

we clear the rain forests at a rate of nearly *2,500 acres each hour* (McCuen 1993). In the process, we extinguish thousands of plant and animal species. Some estimate that we destroy 10,000 species each year—about 1 *per hour* (Durning 1990). Others say this number is conservative, that we extinguish 100 plant and animal species a day, 4 per hour (Wolfensohn and Fuller 1998). Whatever the number, as biologists remind us, a species once lost is gone forever.

As the rain forests are destroyed, so are the Indian tribes who live in them. With their extinction goes their knowledge of the environment, the topic of the Cultural Diversity box below. Like Esau who exchanged his birthright for a bowl of porridge, we exchange our future for some lumber, farms, and pastures.

CULTURAL DIVERSITY Around the World

THE RAIN FORESTS:
LOST TRIBES, LOST KNOWLEDGE

Since 1900, 90 of Brazil's 270 Indian tribes have disappeared. Other tribes have moved to villages as settlers have taken over their lands. With village life comes a loss of tribal knowledge.

Tribal groups are not just "wild" people who barely survive despite their ignorance. On the contrary, they have intricate forms of social organization and possess knowledge that has accumulated over thousands of years. The 2,500 Kayapo Indians, for example, belong to one of the Amazon's endangered tribes. The Kayapo use 250 types of wild fruit and hundreds of nut and tuber species. They cultivate thirteen types of bananas, eleven kinds of manioc (cassava), sixteen strains of sweet potato, and seventeen kinds of yams. Many of these varieties are unknown to non-Indians. The Kayapo also use thousands of

medicinal plants, one of which contains a drug that is effective against intestinal parasites.

Until recently, Western scientists dismissed tribal knowledge as superstitious and worthless. Now, however, the West is coming to realize that to lose tribes is to lose valuable knowledge. In the Central African Republic, a man whose chest was being eaten away by an amoeboid infection lay dying because he did not respond to drugs. Out of desperation, the Catholic nuns who were treating him sought the advice of a native doctor. He applied crushed termites to the open wounds. To the amazement of the nuns, the man made a remarkable recovery.

The disappearance of the rain forests means the destruction of plant species that may hold healing properties. Some of the discoveries from the rain forests have been astounding. The needles from a Himalayan tree in India contain taxol, a drug that is effective against ovarian cancer. A flower from Madagascar is used in the treatment of leukemia; a frog in

Peru produces a painkiller more powerful, but less addictive, than morphine (Wolfensohn and Fuller 1998).

On average, one tribe of Amazonian Indians has been lost each year for the past century—because of violence, greed for their lands, and exposure to infectious diseases against which they have little resistance. Ethnocentrism underlies much of this assault. Perhaps the extreme is represented by the cattle ranchers in Colombia who killed eighteen Cueva Indians. The cattle ranchers were perplexed when they were put on trial for murder. They asked why they should be charged with a crime, since everyone knew that the Cuevas were animals, not people. They pointed out that there was even a verb in Colombian Spanish, *cuevar*, which means "to hunt Cueva Indians." So what was their crime, they asked? The jury found them innocent because of "cultural ignorance." ■

Sources: Durning 1990; Gorman 1991; Linden 1991; Stipp 1992; Simons 1995; Nabhan 1998.

The Environmental Movement

Concern about environmental problems has produced a worldwide social movement. One result is *green parties*, political parties whose central issue is the environment. In some European countries, these parties are active and successful. Germany's Green Party has even won seats in the national legislature. Green parties have had little success in the United States, but in the 2000 election, a green party headed by Ralph Nader tipped the balance and gave the presidential election to George W. Bush. Activists in the environmental movement generally seek solutions in politics, education, and legislation. Despairing that pollution continues, that the rain forests are still being cleared, and that species are becoming extinct, some activists are convinced that the planet is doomed unless immediate steps are taken. Choosing a more radical course, they use extreme tactics to try to arouse indignation among the public and thus force the government to act. Convinced that they stand for true morality, many are willing to break the law and go to jail for their actions. Such activists are featured in the following Thinking Critically section.

Thinking *Critically*

ECOSABOTAGE

Chaining oneself to a giant Douglas fir slated for cutting; pouring sand down the gas tank of a bulldozer; tearing down power lines and ripping up survey stakes; driving spikes into redwood trees, and sinking whaling vessels—are these the acts of dangerous punks who are intent on vandalizing and who have little understanding of the needs of modern society? Or are they the acts of brave men and women who are willing to put their freedom, and even their lives, on the line on behalf of the earth itself?

To understand why **ecosabotage**—actions taken to sabotage the efforts of people thought to be legally harming the environment—is taking place, consider the Medicine Tree, a 3,000-year-old redwood in the Sally Bell Grove near the northern California coast. Georgia Pacific, a lumber company, was determined to cut down the Medicine Tree, the oldest and largest of the region's redwoods, which rests on a sacred site of the Sinkyone Indians. Members of Earth First! chained themselves to the tree. After they were arrested, the sawing began. Other protesters jumped over the police-lined barricade and planted themselves in front of the axes and chain saws. A logger swung an axe and missed a demonstrator. At that mo-

ment, the sheriff radioed a restraining order, and the cutting stopped.

Twenty-four-year-old David Chain's dedication cost him his life. The federal government and the state of California made a deal to purchase 10,000 acres of pristine redwoods for half a billion dollars. As last-minute negotiations dragged on, loggers from the Pacific Lumber Company kept felling trees, and Earth First! activists kept trying to stop them. David Chain died of a crushed skull when a felled tree struck him.

How many 3,000-year-old trees remain on this planet? Do fences and picnic tables for backyard barbecues justify cutting them down? It is questions like these, as well as the slaughter of seals, the destruction of the rain forests, and the drowning of dolphins in mile-long drift nets that spawned Earth First! and other organizations devoted to preserving the environment, such as Greenpeace, Sea Shepherds, and the Ruckus Society.

"We feel like there are insane people who are consciously destroying our environment, and we are compelled to fight back," explains a member of one of the militant groups. "No compromise in defense of Mother Earth!" says another. "With famine and death approaching, we're in the early stages of World War III," adds another.

Radical environmentalists represent a broad range of activities and purposes. They are united neither on tactics nor goals. Most espouse a simpler lifestyle that will consume less energy and reduce pressure on the earth's resources. Some want to stop a specific action, such as the killing of whales. Others want to destroy all nuclear weapons and dismantle nuclear power plants. Some want everyone to become vegetarians. Still others want the earth's population to drop to one billion, roughly what it was in 1800. Some even want humans to return to hunting and gathering societies. These groups are so splintered that the founder of Earth First!, Dave Foreman, quit his own organization when it became too confrontational for his tastes.

Radical groups have had some successes. They have brought a halt to the killing of dolphins off Japan's Iki Island, achieved a ban on whaling, established trash recycling programs in many communities, and saved hundreds of thousands of acres of trees, including, of course, the Medicine Tree. ■

For Your Consideration

Should we applaud ecosaboteurs or jail them? As symbolic interactionists stress, it all depends on how you view their actions. And as conflict theorists emphasize, your view likely depends on your location in the economic structure. That is, if you own a lumber company you will see ecosaboteurs differently from the way a camping enthusiast

As concern about the enviroment has grown, a social movement to try to change the course of events has developed. Protest groups have rallied around several issues, including whales and dolphins. Another is the destruction of the redwoods and sequoias in northern California.

will. How does your own view of ecosaboteurs depend on your life situation? What effective alternatives to ecosabotage are there for people who are convinced that we are destroying the very life support system of our planet?

Sources: Carpenter 1990; Eder 1990; Foote 1990; Parfit 1990; Reed and Benet 1990; Courtney 1995; Satchell 1998; Skow 1998; Nieves 1999.

Environmental Sociology

About 1970, a subdiscipline of sociology emerged called **environmental sociology.** Its focus is the relationship between human societies and the environment (Dunlap and Catton 1979, 1983; Buttel 1987; Freudenburg and Gramling 1989; Laska 1993; Redlift and Woodgate 1997). Its main assumptions are:

1. The physical environment is a significant variable in sociological investigation.
2. Human beings are but one species among many that depend on the natural environment.
3. Because of intricate feedback to nature, human actions have many unintended consequences.
4. The world is finite, so there are potential physical limits to economic growth.

5. Economic expansion requires increased extraction of resources from the environment.
6. Increased extraction of resources leads to ecological problems.
7. These ecological problems place restrictions on economic expansion.
8. Governments create environmental problems by trying to create conditions for the accumulation of capital.

The goal of environmental sociology is not to stop pollution or nuclear power, but, rather, to study how humans (their cultures, values, and behavior) affect the physical environment and how the physical environment affects human activities. Environmental sociologists, however, generally are also environmental activists, and the Section on Environment and Technology of the American Sociological Association tries to influence governmental policies (American Sociological Association n.d.).

Technology and the Environment: The Goal of Harmony It is inevitable that humans will continue to develop new technologies. But the abuse of our environment by those technologies is not inevitable. To understate the matter, the destruction of our planet is an unwise choice.

If we are to have a world that is worth passing on to coming generations, we must seek harmony between technology and the natural environment. This will not be easy. At one extreme are people who claim that to protect the environment we must eliminate industrialization and go back to a tribal way of life. At the other extreme are people who are blind to the harm being done to the natural environment, who want the entire world to industrialize at full speed. Somewhere, there must be a middle ground, one that recognizes not only that industrialization is here to stay but also that we *can* control it, for it is our creation. In-

dustrialization, controlled, can enhance our quality of life; uncontrolled, it will destroy us.

As a parallel to the development of technologies, then, we must develop systems to reduce or eliminate their harm to the environment. This includes mechanisms to monitor the production, use, and disposal of technology. The question, of course, is whether we have the resolve to take the steps to preserve the environment for future generations. What's at stake is nothing less than the welfare of the entire planet. Surely that is enough to motivate us to make the wise choices.

SUMMARY AND REVIEW

■ How Social Change Transforms Society

What major trends have transformed the course of human history?

The primary changes in human history are the four social revolutions (domestication, agriculture, industrialization, and information), the change from *Gemeinschaft* to *Gesellschaft* societies, capitalism and industrialization, **modernization,** and global stratification. Ethnic conflicts indicate cutting edges of social change. Pp. 390–393.

■ Theories and Process of Social Change

Besides technology, capitalism, modernization, and so on, what other theories of social change are there?

Evolutionary theories presuppose that societies move from the same starting point to some similar ending point. *Unilinear* theories, which assume the same path for everyone, were replaced with *multilinear* theories, which assume that different paths lead to the same stage of development. *Cyclical* theories view civilizations as going through a process of birth, youth, maturity, decline, and death. Conflict theorists view social change as inevitable, for each *thesis* (basically an arrangement of power) contains an *antithesis* (contradictions). A new *synthesis* develops to resolve these contradictions, but it, too, contains contradictions that must be resolved, and so on. This is called a **dialectical process.** Pp. 393–394.

What is Ogburn's theory of social change?

Ogburn identified technology as the basic cause of social change, which comes through three processes: **invention, discovery,** and **diffusion.** The term **cultural lag** refers to symbolic culture lagging behind changes in technology. Pp. 394–395.

■ How Technology Changes Society

How does new technology affect society?

Because **technology** is an organizing force of social life, changes in technology can have profound effects. The computer, for example, is changing the way we practice medicine, learn, work, and do business. The information superhighway is likely to perpetuate social inequalities both on a national and a global level. Pp. 395–399.

■ Social Movements as a Source of Social Change

What types of social movements are there?

Social movements consist of large numbers of people who organize to promote or resist social change. Depending on their target (individuals or society) and the amount of social change desired (partial or complete), social movements can be classified as **alterative, redemptive, reformative,** or **transformative.** Pp. 399–401.

How are the mass media related to social movements?

The mass media are gatekeepers for social movements. Leaders of social movements use **propaganda** to influence **public opinion.** Pp. 401–403.

What stages do social movements go through?

Sociologists have identified five stages of social movements: initial unrest and agitation, mobilization, organization, institutionalization, and, finally, decline. Resurgence is also possible, if, as in the case of the abortion clash, opposing sides revitalize one another. Pp. 403–405.

■ The Growth Machine Versus the Earth

What are the environmental problems of the Most Industrialized Nations?

The environmental problems of the Most Industrialized Nations are severe, ranging from smog and **acid rain** to the **greenhouse effect.** The greenhouse effect may cause **global warming** that will fundamentally affect our lives. Burning fossil fuels in internal combustion engines lies at the root of many environmental problems. It is in the interest of the oil companies to keep the internal combustion engine dominant, but alternatives are on the way. Due to the location of factories and hazardous waste sites, environmental problems have a greater impact on minorities and the poor. Pp. 405–406.

What are the environmental problems of the Industrializing and Least Industrialized Nations?

The worst environmental problems are found in the former Soviet Union, a legacy of the unrestrained exploitation of resources by the Communist party. The rush of the Least Industrialized Nations to industrialize is adding to our environmental decay. The world is facing a basic conflict between the lust for profits through the exploitation of the earth's resources and the need to produce a **sustainable environment.** Pp. 406–409.

What is the environmental movement?

The environmental movement is an attempt to restore a healthy environment for the world's people. This global movement takes many forms, from a peaceful attempt to influence the political process to **ecosabotage.** Pp. 410–411.

What is environmental sociology?

Environmental sociology is not an attempt to change the environment, but a study of the relationship between humans and the environment. Environmental sociologists are generally also environmental activists. Pp. 411–412.

Where can I read more on this topic?

Suggested readings for this chapter appear on page SR-11.

YOUR INTERACTIVE COMPANION WEB SITE

Your Interactive Companion Web Site includes practice tests, with feedback, and online learning activities with video, audio, and Weblinks. Your access code for this Web site is provided with this text.

GLOSSARY

acid rain rain that contains sulfuric and nitric acid; the result of burning fossil fuels (p. 407)

alterative social movement a social movement that seeks to alter only specific aspects of people's behavior (p. 401)

corporate welfare benefits (such as tax breaks or stadiums) given corporations to locate or to remain in an area (p. 407)

cultural lag William Ogburn's term for human behavior lagging behind technological innovations (p. 395)

dialectical process a view of history and power in which each arrangement, or thesis, contains contradictions, or antitheses, which must be resolved; the new arrangement, or synthesis, contains its own contradictions; and so on (p. 394)

diffusion the spread of an invention or discovery from one area to another; identified by William Ogburn as a major process of social change (p. 395)

discovery a new way of seeing reality; identified by William Ogburn as a major process of social change (p. 395)

ecosabotage actions taken to sabotage the efforts of people thought to be legally harming the environment (p. 410)

environmental racism the greater impact of pollution on the poor and racial minorities (p. 408)

environmental sociology a subdiscipline of sociology that examines how human activities affect the physical environment and how the physical environment affects human activities (p. 411)

global warming an increase in the earth's temperature due to the greenhouse effect (p. 407)

greenhouse effect the buildup of carbon dioxide in the earth's atmosphere that allows light to enter but inhibits the release of heat; believed to cause global warming (p. 407)

invention a combination of existing elements and materials to form new ones; identified by William Ogburn as a major process of social change (p. 394)

modernization the transformation of traditional societies into industrial societies (p. 391)

postmodern society another term for postindustrial society (p. 395)

proactive social movement a social movement that promotes some social change (p. 400)

propaganda in its broad sense, the presentation of information in an attempt to influence people; in its narrow sense, one-sided information used to try to influence people (p. 401)

public opinion how people think about some issue (p. 401)

reactive social movement a social movement that reacts to and resists some social change (p. 400)

redemptive social movement a social movement that seeks to change people totally (p. 401)

reformative social movement a social movement that seeks to reform some specific aspect of society (p. 401)

resource mobilization a theory that social movements succeed or fail based on their ability to mobilize resources such as time, money, and people's skills (p. 403)

social change the alteration of culture and societies over time (p. 390)

social movement large numbers of people who organize to promote or resist social change (p. 399)

social movement organization an organization developed to further the goals of a social movement (p. 400)

sustainable environment a world system in which we use our physical environment to meet the needs of humanity and leave a heritage of a sound environment to the next generation (p. 406)

technology often defined as the applications of science, but can be thought of as tools, items used to accomplish tasks, along with the skills or procedures needed to make and use those tools (p. 395)

transformative social movement a social movement that seeks to change society totally (p. 401)

dle Class - 30-35% - white collar jobs

Working Class - 30-35%
- blue collar positions. Jobs are more routine & closely supervised

Working Poor - 20-25%

- even when working, cannot make enough to pull out of poverty

Underclass - 1-3% ?

- chronic poverty, chronic unemployment

Consequences of Social Class

Wealth & Income Distribution in U.S.

Poverty in the U.S.

* Poverty Line - the official measure of poverty in the U.S.

* Relative poverty /Relative deprivation: compares what they have to others and decide they are poor or deprived.

* Absolute poverty/deprivation: when a person is truly living in poverty

* Feminization of poverty - a trend in U.S. poverty whereby most poor families are headed by women.

Who are the Poor in America?

* Racial minorities are over-represented

* However, most of the poor in America are White (56%)

* Women are more likely to be poor than men

* Most poverty in the U.S. is short, lasting one year or less

Theories of Stratification

Karl Marx - social class depends on a single factor - owning the means of production

- those who control the means of production exploit those who do not.

Max Weber - wealth & economic position is not the only factor in social class.

Social class is made of three components : Property (wealth), Power, and Prestige

Functionalist explanation - stratification is inevitable, and in part it is

Glossary

achieved statuses positions that are earned or accomplished, or that involve at least some effort or activity on the individual's part (p. 83)

acid rain rain that contains sulfuric and nitric acid; the result of burning fossil fuels (p. 407)

activity theory the view that satisfaction during old age is related to a person's level and quality of activity (p. 265)

age cohort people born at roughly the same time who pass through the life course together (p. 265)

ageism prejudice, discrimination, and hostility directed against people because of their age; can be directed against any age group, including youth (p. 263)

agents of socialization people and groups that influence our self-concept, emotions, attitudes, and behavior (p. 67)

aggregate people who temporarily share the same physical space but do not see themselves as belonging together (p. 106)

alienation Marx's term for the experience of being cut off from the product of one's labor, which results in a sense of powerlessness and normlessness; also refers to a sense of not belonging, and a feeling that no one cares what happens to you (pp. 114, 379)

alterative social movement a social movement that seeks to alter only specific aspects of people's behavior (p. 401)

anarchy a condition of lawlessness or political disorder caused by the absence or collapse of governmental authority (p. 283)

anticipatory socialization as we anticipate future roles, we learn aspects of them now (p. 70)

applied sociology sociology that is used to solve problems—from the micro level of family relationships to the macro level of war and pollution (p. 12)

ascribed statuses positions an individual either inherits at birth or receives involuntarily later in life (p. 83)

assimilation the process of being absorbed into the mainstream culture (p. 220)

authoritarian leader a leader who leads by giving orders (p. 121)

authoritarian personality Adorno's term for people who are prejudiced and rank high on scales of conformity, intolerance,

insecurity, respect for authority, and submissiveness to superiors (p. 215)

authority power that people accept as rightly exercised over them (p. 274)

background assumptions deeply embedded common understandings (basic rules or "codes") concerning our view of the world and how people ought to act (p. 97)

basic demographic equation growth rate = births − deaths + net migration (p. 370)

basic (or **pure**) **sociology** sociological research whose purpose is to make discoveries about life in human groups, not to make changes in those groups (p. 30)

bilateral system a system of reckoning descent that counts both the mother's and the father's side (p. 304)

blended family a family whose members were once part of other families (p. 315)

born again term describing Christians who have undergone a life-transforming religious experience so radical that they feel they have become a "new person" (p. 345)

bourgeoisie Karl Marx's term for capitalists, those who own the means of production (p. 159)

bureaucracies formal organizations with a hierarchy of authority, a clear division of labor, impersonality of positions, and emphasis on written rules, communications, and records (p. 111)

capitalism an economic system characterized by the private ownership of the means of production, the pursuit of profit, and market competition (p. 290)

capitalist class the wealthy who own the means of production and buy the labor of the working class (p. 145)

caste system a form of social stratification in which one's status is determined by birth and is lifelong (p. 156)

category people who have similar characteristics (p. 106)

charisma an extraordinary gift from God; more commonly, an outstanding, "magnetic" personality (p. 348)

charismatic authority authority based on an individual's outstanding traits, which attract followers (p. 275)

charismatic leader someone to whom God has given an extraordinary gift; more commonly, someone who exerts extraordinary appeal to a group of followers (p. 348)

checks and balances separation of powers among the three branches of U.S. government—legislative, executive, and judicial—so that each is able to nullify the actions of the others, thus preventing the domination of any single branch (p. 283)

church to Durkheim, one of the three essential elements of religion—a moral community of believers (p. 342); used by other sociologists to refer to a highly bureaucratized religious organization (p. 348)

citizenship the concept that birth (and residence) in a country impart basic rights (p. 278)

city-state an independent city whose power radiates outward, bringing the adjacent area under its rule (p. 277)

city a place in which a large number of people are permanently based and do not produce their own food (p. 372)

class conflict Karl Marx's term for the struggle between owners (the bourgeoisie) and workers (the proletariat) (p. 7)

class consciousness Karl Marx's term for awareness of a shared identity based on one's position in the means of production (p. 159)

class system a form of social stratification based primarily on the possession of money or material possessions (p. 158)

clique within a larger group, a cluster of people who choose to interact with one another; an internal faction (p. 110)

closed-ended questions questions followed by a list of possible answers to be selected by the respondent (p. 24)

coalition the alignment of some members of a group against others (p. 119)

coercion power that people do not accept as just (p. 274)

cohabitation unmarried people living together in a sexual relationship (p. 318)

colonialism the process by which one nation takes over another nation, usually for the purpose of exploiting its labor and natural resources (p. 170)

community a place people identify with, where they sense that they belong and that others care about what happens to them (p. 379)

compartmentalize to separate acts from feelings or attitudes (p. 219)

conflict theory a theoretical framework in which society is viewed as being composed of groups that compete for scarce resources (p. 17)

conspicuous consumption Thorstein Veblen's term for a change from the Protestant ethic to an eagerness to show off wealth by the elaborate consumption of goods (p. 286)

contradictory class locations Erik Wright's term for a position in the class structure that generates contradictory interests (p. 185)

control group the group of subjects not exposed to the independent variable (p. 28)

control theory the idea that two control systems—inner and outer controls—work against our tendencies to deviate (p. 135)

convergence theory the view that as both capitalist and socialist economic systems adopt features of the other, a hybrid (or mixed) economic system will emerge (p. 293)

corporate capitalism the domination of the economic system by giant corporations (p. 293)

corporate culture the orientations that characterize corporate work settings (p. 116)

corporate welfare benefits (such as tax breaks or stadiums) given corporations to locate or to remain in an area (p. 407)

corporation the joint ownership of a business enterprise, whose liabilities and obligations are separate from those of its owners (p. 293)

cosmology teachings or ideas that provide a unified picture of the world (p. 345)

counterculture a subculture whose values place its members in opposition to the values of the broader culture (p. 47)

credential society a group that uses diplomas and degrees to determine who is eligible for jobs, even though the diploma or degree may be irrelevant to the actual work (p. 331)

crime the violation of norms written into law (p. 130)

criminal justice system the system of police, courts, and prisons set up to deal with people who are accused of having committed a crime (p. 144)

crude birth rate the annual number of births per 1,000 population (p. 368)

crude death rate the annual number of deaths per 1,000 population (p. 368)

cult a new religion with few followers, whose teachings and practices put it at odds with the dominant culture and religion (p. 348)

cultural diffusion the spread of cultural characteristics from one group to another (p. 52)

cultural goals the legitimate objectives held out to the members of a society (p. 140)

cultural lag William Ogburn's term for a situation in which nonmaterial culture lags behind changes in the material culture (p. 52, 395)

cultural leveling the process by which cultures become similar to one another; especially refers to the process by which Western industrial culture is imported and diffused into other cultures (p. 53)

cultural relativism understanding a people from the framework of their own culture (p. 38)

cultural transmission in reference to education, the ways by which schools transmit culture, especially its core values (p. 333)

culture the language, beliefs, values, norms, behaviors, and even material objects that are passed from one generation to the next (p. 36)

culture of poverty the assumption that the values and behaviors of the poor perpetuate their poverty; parents are assumed to perpetuate poverty across generations by passing these characteristics on to their children (pp. 171, 199)

culture shock the disorientation that people experience when they come in contact with a fundamentally different culture and can no longer depend on their taken-for-granted assumptions about life (p. 37)

degradation ceremony a term coined by Harold Garfinkel to describe rituals that are designed to strip an individual of his or her identity as a group member; for example, a court martial or the defrocking of a priest (p. 70)

deindustrialization a process that reduces the number of people who work in manufacturing; one reason is automation, while another is the globalization of capitalism, which moves manufacturing jobs to countries where labor costs less (p. 384)

democracy a system of government in which authority derives from the people (p. 277)

democratic leader a leader who leads by trying to reach a consensus (p. 121)

democratic socialism a hybrid economic system in which capitalism is mixed with state ownership (p. 291)

demographic transition a three-stage historical process of population growth: first, high birth rates and high death rates; second, high birth rates and low death rates; and third, low birth rates and low death rates; a fourth stage of populaation shrinkage may be emerging (p. 362)

demographic variables the three factors that influence population growth: fertility, mortality, and net migration (p. 368)

demography the study of the size, composition, growth, and distribution of human populations (p. 360)

dependency ratio the number of workers required to support one person on Social Security (p. 267)

dependency theory the view that the Least Industrialized Nations have been unable to develop their economies because they grew dependent on the Most Industrialized Nations (p. 171)

dependent variable a factor that is changed by an independent variable (p. 28)

deviance the violation of rules or norms (p. 130)

dialectical process a view of history and power in which each arrangement (thesis) contains contradictions (antitheses) which must be resolved; the new arrangement (synthesis) contains its own contradictions; and so on (p. 394)

dictatorship a form of government in which power is seized by an individual (p. 278)

differential association Edwin Sutherland's term to indicate that associating with some groups results in learning an "excess of definitions" of deviance (attitudes favorable to committing deviant acts) and, by extension, in a greater likelihood that their members will become deviant (p. 134)

diffusion the spread of an invention or discovery from one area to another; identified by William Ogburn as a major process of social change (p. 395)

direct democracy a form of democracy in which voters meet together to discuss and decide issues (p. 277)

discovery a new way of seeing reality; identified by William Ogburn as a major process of social change (p. 395)

discrimination an act of unfair treatment directed against an individual or a group (p. 210)

disengagement theory the view that society prevents disruption by having the elderly vacate their positions of responsibility so the younger generation can step into their shoes (p. 265)

disinvestment the withdrawal of investments by banks, which seals the fate of an urban area (p. 383)

divine right of kings the idea that the king's authority comes directly from God (p. 164)

division of labor how work is divided among the members of a group (p. 90)

documents in its narrow sense, written sources that provide data; in its extended sense, archival material of any sort, including photographs, movies, and so on (p. 27)

dominant group the group with the most power, greatest privileges, and highest social status (p. 209)

downward social mobility movement down the social class ladder (p. 193)

dramaturgy an approach, pioneered by Erving Goffman, that analyzes social life in terms of drama or the stage (p. 93)

dyad the smallest possible group, consisting of two persons (p. 118)

ecclesia a religious group so integrated into the dominant culture that it is difficult to tell where the one begins and the other leaves off (p. 348)

economy a system of distribution of goods and services (p. 285)

ecosabotage actions taken to sabotage the efforts of people thought to be legally harming the environment (p. 410)

edge city a large clustering of service facilities and residences near a highway intersection that provides a sense of place to people who live, shop, and work there (p. 374)

ego Freud's term for a balancing force between the id and the demands of society (p. 64)

electronic community people who more or less regularly interact with one another on the Internet (p. 111)

empty nest a married couple's domestic situation after the last child has left home (p. 312)

endogamy the practice of marrying within one's own group (p. 156)

enterprise zone the use of economic incentives in a designated area with the intention of encouraging investment there (p. 385)

environmental racism the greater impact of pollution on the poor and racial minorities (p. 408)

environmental sociology a subdiscipline of sociology that examines how human activities affect the physical environment and how the physical environment affects human activities (p. 411)

ethnic cleansing a policy of population elimination, including forcible expulsion and genocide (p. 220)

ethnic work activities that are designed to discover, enhance, or maintain ethnic and racial identification (p. 210)

ethnicity (and **ethnic**) distinctive cultural characteristics (p. 207)

ethnocentrism the use of one's own culture as a yardstick for judging the ways of other individuals or societies, generally leading to a negative evaluation of their values, norms, and behaviors (p. 37)

ethnomethodology the study of how people use background assumptions to make sense of life (p. 96)

exchange mobility about the same numbers of people moving up and down the social class ladder, such that in the end the social class system shows little change (p. 193)

exogamy the practice of marrying outside one's group (p. 303)

experiment the use of control groups and experimental groups and dependent and independent variables to test causation (p. 28)

experimental group the group of subjects in an experiment who are exposed to the independent variable (p. 28)

exponential growth curve a pattern of growth in which numbers double during approximately equal intervals, thus accelerating in the latter stages (p. 361)

expressive leader an individual who increases harmony and minimizes conflict in a group; also known as a *socioemotional leader* (p. 121)

extended family a nuclear family plus other relatives: grandparents, uncles, and aunts, who live together (p. 303)

face-saving behavior techniques people use to salvage a performance that is going sour (p. 94)

false consciousness Karl Marx's term to refer to workers identifying with the interests of capitalists (p. 160)

family people who consider themselves related by blood, marriage, or adoption (p. 303)

family of orientation the family in which a person grows up (p. 303)

family of procreation the family formed when a couple's first child is born (p. 303)

feminism the philosophy that men and women should be politically, economically, and socially equal; organized activity on behalf of this principle (p. 246)

(the) feminization of poverty a trend in U.S. poverty whereby most poor families are headed by women (p. 198)

fertility rate the number of children that the average woman bears (p. 368)

folkways norms that are not strictly enforced (p. 45)

functional analysis a theoretical framework in which society is viewed as a whole unit, composed of interrelated parts, each with a function that, when fulfilled, contributes to society's equilibrium; also known as *functionalism* and *structural functionalism* (p. 15)

functional illiterate a high school graduate who has difficulty with basic reading and math (p. 339)

gatekeeping a process by which education opens and closes doors of opportunity; another term for the social placement function of education (p. 334)

Gemeinschaft village life; a type of society in which life is intimate; a community in which everyone knows everyone else and people share a sense of togetherness (p. 90)

gender the social characteristics that a society considers proper for its males and females; masculinity or femininity (p. 240)

gender socialization the ways in which society sets children onto different courses in life because they are male or female (p. 65)

gender stratification males' and females' unequal access to power, prestige, and property on the basis of their sex (p. 240)

generalized other taking the role of a large number of people (p. 62)

genetic predisposition inborn tendencies (p. 133)

genocide the systematic annihilation or attempted annihilation of a race or ethnic group (p. 207)

gentrification the displacement of the poor as the relatively affluent purchase and renovate their homes (p. 374)

Gesellschaft urban life; a type of society that is dominated by impersonal relationships, individual accomplishments, and self-interest (p. 90)

gestures the ways in which people use their bodies to communicate with one another (p. 39)

global warming an increase in the earth's temperature due to the greenhouse effect (p. 407)

globalization of capitalism the adoption of capitalism around the world (p. 171)

goal displacement the process in which one goal is displaced by another, such as when an organization adopts new goals (p. 113)

grade inflation higher grades for the same work; a general rise in student grades without a corresponding increase in learning or test scores (p. 339)

graying of America older people making up an increasing proportion of the U.S. population (p. 260)

greenhouse effect the buildup of carbon dioxide in the earth's atmosphere that allows light to enter but inhibits the release of heat; believed to cause global warming (p. 407)

group dynamics the ways in which individuals affect groups and groups influence individuals (p. 118)

group people who think of themselves as belonging together and who interact with one another in a general sense, people who have something in common and who believe that what they have in common is significant (pp. 85, 106)

groupthink Irving Janis' term for a narrowing of thought by a group of people, leading to the perception that there is only one correct answer; in groupthink, to suggest alternatives becomes a sign of disloyalty (p. 125)

growth rate the net change in a population after adding births, subtracting deaths, and either adding or subtracting net migration (p. 370)

hate crime a crime with more severe penalties attached because it is motivated by hatred (dislike, animosity) of someone's race-ethnicity, religon, sexual orientation, or disability (p. 148)

hidden curriculum the unwritten goals of schools, such as teaching obedience to authority and conformity to cultural norms (p. 335)

homogamy the tendency of people with similar characteristics to marry one another (p. 309)

Horatio Alger myth a belief that anyone can get ahead if only he or she tries hard enough; encourages people to strive to get ahead and deflects blame for failure from society to the individual (p. 202)

horticultural society a society based on cultivating plants by the use of hand tools (p. 88)

household people who occupy the same housing unit (p. 303)

human ecology Robert Park's term for the relationship between people and their environment (natural resources, such as land); also called *urban ecology* (p. 376)

hunting and gathering society a society that is dependent on hunting and gathering for survival (p. 87)

hypothesis a statement of the expected relationship between variables according to predictions from a theory (p. 190)

id Freud's term for the individual's inborn basic drives (p. 64)

ideal culture the ideal values and norms of a people: the goals held out for them (p. 51)

ideology beliefs that justify social arrangements (p. 156)

illegitimate opportunity structure opportunities for crimes that are woven into the texture of life (p. 141)

impression management the term used by Erving Goffman to describe people's efforts to control the impressions that others receive of them (p. 93)

in-groups groups toward which one feels loyalty (p. 108)

incest taboo rules that specify the degrees of kinship that prohibit sex or marriage (p. 303)

independent variable a factor that causes a change in another variable, called the *dependent variable* (p. 28)

individual discrimination the negative treatment of one person by another on the basis of that person's perceived characteristics (p. 213)

Industrial Revolution the third social revolution; it occurred when machines powered by fuels replaced most animal and human power (p. 89)

institutional discrimination negative treatment of a minority group that is built into a society's institutions (p. 213)

institutionalized means approved ways of reaching cultural goals (p. 140)

instrumental leader an individual who tries to keep the group moving toward its goals; also known as a *task-oriented leader* (p. 121)

intergenerational mobility the change that family members make in social class from one generation to the next (p. 192)

interlocking directorates individuals serving on the board of directors of several companies (p. 294)

internal colonialism the systematic economic exploitation of a minority group (p. 220)

invasion-succession cycle the process of one group of people displacing a group whose racial-ethnic or social class characteristics differ from their own (p. 377)

invention a combination of existing elements and materials to form new ones; identified by William Ogburn as a major process of social change (p. 394)

(the) iron law of oligarchy Robert Michel's term for the tendency of formal organizations to be dominated by a small, self-perpetuating elite (p. 108)

labeling theory the view, developed by symbolic interactionists, that the labels people are given affect their own and others' perceptions of them, thus channeling their behavior either into deviance or into conformity (p. 136)

laissez-faire capitalism unrestrained manufacture and trade (literally "hands off" capitalism) (p. 290)

laissez-faire leaders individuals who lead by being highly permissive (p. 121)

language a system of symbols that can be combined in an infinite number of ways to communicate abstract thought (p. 41)

latent functions unintended consequences of people's actions that help to keep a social system in equilibrium (p. 333)

leader someone who influences other people (p. 121)

leadership styles ways in which people express their leadership (p. 121)

life course the stages of our life as we go from birth to death (p. 72)

life expectancy the age that someone can be expected to live to (p. 260)

life span the maximum possible length of life (p. 260)

lobbyists people who try to influence legislation on behalf of their clients or interest groups (p. 282)

looking-glass self a term coined by Charles Horton Cooley to refer to the process by which our self develops through internalizing others' reactions to us (p. 62)

machismo an emphasis on male strength and dominance (p. 314)

macro-level analysis an examination of large-scale patterns of society (p. 17)

macrosociology analysis of social life that focuses on broad features of social structure, such as social class and the relationships of groups to one another; an approach usually used by functionalists and conflict theorists (p. 80)

mainstreaming helping people to become part of the mainstream of society (p. 334)

Malthus theorem an observation by Thomas Malthus that although the food supply increases arithmetically, population grows geometrically (p. 361)

manifest functions the intended consequences of people's actions, designed to help some part of a social system (p. 333)

marginal working class the most desperate members of the working class, who have few skills, have little job security, and are often unemployed (p. 145)

market forces the law of supply and demand (p. 291)

market restraints laws and regulations that govern the manufacture and sale of products (p. 290)

marriage a group's approved mating arrangements, usually marked by a ritual of some sort (p. 303)

mass media forms of communication directed to large audiences (p. 66)

master status a status that cuts across the other statuses that an individual occupies (p. 84)

material culture the material objects that distinguish a group of people, such as their art, buildings, weapons, utensils, machines, hairstyles, clothing, and jewelry (p. 36)

matriarchy a society or group in which authority is vested in women (p. 304)

matrilineal system a system of reckoning descent that counts only the mother's side (p. 304)

means of production the tools, factories, land, and investment capital used to produce wealth (p. 159)

mechanical solidarity Durkheim's term for the unity or shared consciousness that comes from being involved in similar occupations or activities (p. 90)

medicalization of deviance to make some deviance a medical matter, a symptom of some underlying illness that needs to be treated by physicians (p. 148)

megalopolis an urban area consisting of at least two metropolises and their many suburbs (p. 374)

melting pot the idea that Americans of various backgrounds would melt (or merge), leaving behind their distinctive ethnic identities and forming a new ethnic group (p. 210)

meritocracy a form of social stratification in which all positions are awarded on the basis of merit (p. 162)

metropolis a central city surrounded by smaller cities and their suburbs (p. 373)

metropolitan statistical area (MSA) a central city and the urbanized counties adjacent to it (p. 374)

micro-level analysis an examination of small-scale patterns of society (p. 17)

microsociology analysis of social life that focuses on social interaction; an approach usually used by symbolic interactionists (p. 80)

minority group people who are singled out for unequal treatment on the basis of their physical and cultural characteristics, and who regard themselves as objects of collective discrimination (p. 209)

modernization the process by which a *Gemeinschaft* society is transformed into a *Gesellschaft* society; the transformation of traditional societies into industrial societies (p. 346)

monarchy a form of government headed by a king or a queen (p. 277)

mores norms that are strictly enforced because they are thought to be essential to core values (p. 46)

multiculturalism (also called **pluralism**) a policy that permits or encourages groups to express their individual, unique racial and ethnic identities (p. 220)

multinational corporations companies that operate across national boundaries (p. 294)

negative sanction an expression of disapproval for breaking a norm, ranging from a mild, informal reaction such as a frown to severe formal reactions such as a prison sentence, banishment, or death (p. 45)

neocolonialism the economic and political dominance of the Least Industrialized Nations by the Most Industrialized Nations (p. 171)

net migration rate the difference between the number of immigrants and emigrants per 1,000 population (p. 368)

networking the process of consciously using or cultivating networks for some gain (p. 111)

new technology a technology introduced into a society that has a significant impact on that society (p. 51)

nonmaterial culture (also called **symbolic culture**) a group's ways of thinking (including its beliefs, values, and other assumptions about the world) and doing (its common patterns of behavior, including language and other forms of interaction) (p. 37)

nonverbal interaction communication without words through gestures, silence, use of space, and so on (p. 18)

norms the expectations, or rules of behavior, that develop out of values (p. 45)

nuclear family a family consisting of a husband, wife, and child(ren) (p. 303)

oligarchy a form of government in which power is held by a small group; the rule of the many by the few (p. 278)

open-ended questions questions that respondents are able to answer in their own words (p. 26)

operational definition the way in which a variable in a hypothesis is measured (p. 20)

organic solidarity Durkheim's term for the interdependence that results from people needing the skills, work, and products of one another; solidarity based on the division of labor (p. 90)

out-groups groups toward which one feels antagonism (p. 108)

pan-Indianism an emphasis on the welfare of all Native Americans (p. 232)

participant observation (or **fieldwork**) research in which the researcher *participates* in a research setting while *observing* what is happening in that setting (p. 26)

pastoral society a society based on the pasturing of animals (p. 88)

patriarchy a society in which authority is vested in men; control by men of a society or group (p. 245)

patrilineal system a system of reckoning descent that counts only the father's side (p. 304)

peer group a group of individuals of roughly the same age who are linked by common interests (p. 70)

personality disorders as a theory of deviance, the view that a personality disturbance of some sort causes an individual to violate social norms (p. 133)

pluralism diffusion of power among many interest groups, which prevents any single group from gaining control of the government; in an entirely different sense, a term for multiculturalism (pp. 220, 283)

pluralistic society a society made up of many different groups (p. 47)

political action committees (PACs) an organization formed by one or more special-interest groups to solicit and spend funds for the purpose of influencing legislation (p. 282)

polyandry a marriage in which a woman has more than one husband (p. 302)

polygyny a marriage in which a man has more than one wife (p. 302)

population the target group to be studied (p. 22)

population pyramid a graphic representation of a population, divided into age and sex (p. 367)

population shrinkage the process by which a country's population becomes smaller because its birth rate and immigration are too low to replace those who die and emigrate (p. 363)

population transfer causing a minority group to relocate (p. 219)

positive sanction a reward or positive reaction for following norms, ranging from a smile to a prize (p. 132)

positivism the application of the scientific method to the social world (p. 6)

postmodern society another term for postindustrial society (p. 395)

poverty line the official measure of poverty; calculated as three times a low-cost food budget (p. 195)

power the ability to get your way, even over the resistance of others (p. 182)

power elite C. Wright Mills' term for the top leaders of corporations, military, and politics who make the nation's major decisions (p. 182)

prejudice an attitude of prejudging, usually in a negative way (p. 210)

prestige respect or regard (p. 182)

primary group a group characterized by intimate, long-term, face-to-face association and cooperation (p. 106)

proactive social movement a social movement that promotes some social change (p. 400)

profane Durkheim's term for common elements of everyday life; see **sacred** (p. 342)

proletariat Karl Marx's term for workers (the exploited class that works for capitalists, those who own the means of production) (p. 159)

propaganda in its broad sense, the presentation of information in an attempt to influence people; in its narrow sense, one-sided information used to try to influence people (p. 401)

Protestant ethic Weber's term to describe the ideal of a self-denying moral life accompanied by hard work and frugality (p. 347)

public opinion how people think about some issue (p. 401)

quiet revolution the fundamental changes in society that follow when vast numbers of women enter the work force (p. 249)

race a group whose inherited physical characteristics distinguish it from other groups (p. 206)

racism discrimination on the basis of race (p. 210)

random sample a sample in which everyone in the target population has the same chance of being included in the study (p. 23)

rapport a feeling of trust between researchers and subjects (p. 26)

(the) rationalization of society the increasing influence of bureaucracies in society, which makes the "bottom line" all-important in social life (p. 114)

rational-legal authority authority based on law or written rules and regulations (also called *bureaucratic authority*) (p. 275)

reactive social movement a social movement that reacts to and resists some social change (p. 400)

real culture the norms and values that people actually follow (as opposed to *ideal culture*) (p. 51)

recidivism rate percent of people who are rearrested (p. 147)

redemptive social movement a social movement that seeks to change people totally (p. 401)

redlining the officers of a bank or other financial firm refusing to make loans in a particular area (p. 383)

reference group Herbert Hyman's term for a group whose standards we consider as we evaluate ourselves (p. 109)

reformative social movement a social movement that seeks to reform some specific aspect of society (p. 401)

reliability the extent to which data produce consistent results (p. 20)

religion to Emile Durkheim, beliefs and practices that separate the profane from the sacred and unite its adherents into a moral community (p. 342)

religious experience awareness of the supernatural or a feeling of coming in contact with God (p. 345)

replication repeating a study in order to test its findings (p. 30)

representative democracy a form of democracy in which voters elect representatives to make decisions on their behalf (p. 278)

research method (or *research design*) one of six procedures sociologists use to collect data: surveys, participant observation, secondary analysis, documents, unobtrusive measures, and experiments (p. 20)

reserve labor force the term used by conflict theorists for the unemployed, who can be put to work during times of high production and then discarded when no longer needed (p. 217)

resocialization the process of learning new norms, values, attitudes, and behaviors (p. 70)

resource mobilization a theory that social movements succeed or fail based on their ability to mobilize resources such as time, money, and people's skills (p. 403)

respondents people who respond to a survey, either in interviews or by self-administered questionnaires (p. 24)

rising expectations the sense that better conditions are soon to follow, which, if unfulfilled, creates mounting frustration (p. 223)

rituals ceremonies or repetitive practices; in the context of religion, observances or rites, often intended to evoke a sense of awe of the sacred (p. 345)

role the behaviors, obligations, and privileges attached to a status (p. 85)

role conflict conflicts that someone feels *between* roles because the expectations attached to one role are incompatible with the expectations of another role (p. 94)

role strain conflicts that someone feels *within* a role (p. 94)

romantic love feelings of erotic attraction accompanied by an idealization of the other (p. 307)

routinization of charisma the transfer of authority from a charismatic leader to either a traditional or a rational-legal form of authority (p. 277)

sacred Durkheim's term for things set apart or forbidden, that inspire fear, awe, reverence, or deep respect (p. 342)

sample the individuals who are intended to represent the population to be studied (p. 23)

sanction an expression of approval or disapproval given to people for upholding or violating norms (p. 45)

Sapir-Whorf hypothesis Edward Sapir and Benjamin Whorf's hypothesis that language creates ways of thinking and perceiving (p. 44)

scapegoat an individual or group unfairly blamed for someone else's troubles (p. 214)

secondary analysis the analysis of data already collected by other researchers (p. 27)

secondary group compared with a primary group, a larger, relatively temporary, more anonymous, formal, and impersonal group (p. 106)

sect a group larger than a cult whose members feel hostility from and toward society (p. 348)

secularization of religion the replacement of a religion's "other worldly" concerns with concerns about "this world" (p. 354)

segregation a policy designed to keep racial or ethnic groups apart (p. 220)

selective perception seeing certain features of an object or situation, but remaining blind to others (p. 217)

self the concept, unique to humans, of being able to see ourselves "from the outside"; our internalized perception of how others see us (p. 61)

serial fatherhood a pattern of parenting in which a father, after divorce, reduces contact with his own children, serves as a father to the children of the woman he marries or lives with, then ignores his own children after moving in with or marrying another woman; this pattern repeats (p. 322)

sex biological characteristics that distinguish females and males, consisting of primary and secondary sex characteristics (p. 240)

sexual harassment unwanted sexual advances, usually within an occupational or educational setting (p. 253)

significant other an individual who significantly influences someone else's life (p. 62)

slavery a form of social stratification in which some people own other people (p. 155)

small group a group small enough for everyone to interact directly with all the other members (p. 118)

social change the alteration of culture and societies over time (p. 390)

social class a large number of people who have similar amounts of income and education and who work at jobs that are roughly comparable in prestige (p. 83)

social cohesion the degree to which members of a group or a society feel united by shared values and other social bonds (p. 90)

social construction of reality the use of background assumptions and life experiences to define what is real (p. 97)

social control a group's formal and informal means of enforcing its norms (p. 132)

social environment the entire human environment, including direct contact with others (p. 58)

social institution the organized, usual, or standard ways by which society meets its basic needs (p. 85)

social integration the degree to which people are tied to their social groups (p. 7)

social interaction what people do when they are in one another's presence; this can be a virtual presence, such as the telephone or the Internet (p. 80)

social location the groups people belong to because of their location in history and society (p. 4)

social mobility movement up or down the social class ladder (p. 158)

social movement large numbers of people who organize to promote or resist social change (p. 399)

social movement organization an organization developed to further the goals of a social movement (p. 400)

social network the social ties radiating outward from the self that link people together (p. 110)

social order a group's customary social arrangements (p. 131)

social placement a function of education; funneling people into a society's various positions (p. 334)

social promotion promoting students to the next grade even though they have not mastered the basic materials (p. 339)

social stratification the division of people into layers according to their relative power, property, and prestige; applies to both a society and nations (p. 155)

social structure the relationship of people and groups to one another (p. 81)

socialism an economic system characterized by the public ownership of the means of production, central planning, and the distribution of goods without a profit motive (p. 291)

socialization the process by which people learn the characteristics of their group—the attitudes, values, and actions thought appropriate for them (p. 61)

society a group of people who share a culture and a territory (p. 85)

sociological perspective an approach that seeks to understand human behavior by placing it within its broader social context (p. 4)

sociology the scientific study of society and human behavior (p. 6)

special-interest group people who share views on a particular issue and who can be mobilized for political action (p. 282)

spirit of capitalism Weber's term for the desire to accumulate capital as a duty—not to spend it, but as an end in itself—and to constantly reinvest it (p. 346)

split labor market a term used by conflict theorists to refer to the practice of weakening the bargaining power of workers by splitting them along racial, ethnic, sex, age, or any other lines (p. 217)

state a government; the political entity that claims a monopoly on the use of violence within a territory (pp. 274, 277)

status the position that someone occupies; one's social ranking (p. 83)

status consistency a match between statuses; a condition in which people rank high or low on the dimensions of social class (p. 184)

status inconsistency a contradiction or mismatch between statuses; a condition in which a person ranks high on some dimensions of social class and low on others (p. 84)

status set all the statuses or positions that an individual occupies (p. 83)

status symbols items used to identify a status (p. 83)

stigma "blemishes" that discredit a person's claim to a "normal" identity (p. 130)

stockholders' revolt the refusal of a corporation's stockholders to rubber-stamp decisions made by its managers (p. 294)

strain theory Robert Merton's analysis of the strain engendered when a society socializes large numbers of people to desire a cultural goal (such as success) but withholds from many the approved means to reach that goal; one adaptation to the strain is deviance, including crime, the choice of an innovative means (one outside the approved system) to attain the cultural goal (p. 140)

stratified random sample a sample of specific subgroups of the target population in which everyone in the subgroups has an equal chance of being included in the study (p. 24)

street crime crimes such as mugging, rape, and burglary (p. 133)

structural mobility movement up or down the social class ladder that is due to changes in the structure of society, not to individual efforts (p. 193)

subculture the values and related behaviors of a group that distinguish its members from the larger culture; a world within a world (p. 46)

subsistence economy a type of economy in which human groups live off the land with little or no surplus (p. 285)

suburb a community adjacent to a city (p. 382)

suburbanization the movement from the city to the suburbs (p. 382)

superego Freud's term for the conscience, which consists of the internalized norms and values of our social groups (p. 64)

survey collecting data by having people answer a series of questions (p. 22)

sustainable environment a world system in which we use our physical environment to meet the needs of humanity and leave a heritage of a sound environment to the next generation (p. 406)

symbol something to which people attach meanings and then use to communicate with others (p. 38)

symbolic culture another term for nonmaterial culture (p. 38)

symbolic interactionism a theoretical perspective that focuses on how people use symbols to establish meaning, develop their views of the world, and communicate with one another (p. 13)

system of descent how kinship is traced over the generations (p. 304)

taboo a norm so strong that it brings revulsion if violated (p. 46)

taking the role of the other putting oneself in someone else's shoes; understanding how someone else feels and thinks and thus anticipating how that person will act (p. 62)

teamwork the collaboration of two or more persons who, interested in the success of a performance, manage impressions jointly (p. 94)

techniques of neutralization ways of thinking or rationalizing that help people deflect society's norms (p. 137)

technology often defined as the applications of science, but can be thought of as tools, items used to accomplish tasks, along with the skills or procedures needed to make and use those tools (p. 395)

theory a general statement about how some parts of the world fit together and how they work; an explanation of how two or more facts (or variables) are related to one another (p. 13)

Thomas theorem basically, that people live in socially constructed worlds; that is, people jointly build their own realities; summarized in William I. Thomas' statement, "If people define situations as real, they are real in their consequences." (p. 97)

total institution a place in which people are cut off from the rest of society and are almost totally controlled by the officials who run the place (p. 70)

totalitarianism a form of government that exerts almost total control over the people (p. 278)

tracking sorting students into educational programs on the basis of real or perceived abilities (p. 334)

traditional authority authority based on custom (p. 275)

transformative social movement a social movement that seeks to change society totally (p. 401)

triad a group of three people (p. 119)

underclass a small group of people for whom poverty persists year after year and across generations (p. 188)

universal citizenship the idea that everyone has the same basic rights by virtue of being born in a country (or by immigrating and becoming a naturalized citizen) (p. 278)

unobtrusive measures observing people in such a way that they do not know they are being studied (p. 27)

upward social mobility movement up the social class ladder (p. 193)

urban renewal the rehabilitation of a rundown area of a city, which usually results in the displacement of the poor who are living there (p. 385)

urbanization an increasing proportion of a population living in cities and those cities having a growing influence on their society (p. 372)

validity the extent to which an operational definition measures what it was intended to measure (p. 20)

value cluster a series of interrelated values that together form a larger whole (p. 49)

value contradiction values that contradict one another; to follow the one means to come into conflict with the other (p. 49)

value free the view that a sociologist's personal values or biases should not influence social research (p. 30)

values ideas about what is good or worthwhile in life; attitudes about the way the world ought to be; the standards by which people define what is desirable or undesirable, good or bad, beautiful or ugly (p. 30)

variable a factor thought to be significant for human behavior, which varies from one case to another (p. 19)

voluntary association a group made up of volunteers who organize on the basis of some mutual interest; the Girl Scouts, Baptists, and Alcoholics Anonymous are examples (p. 107)

voter apathy indifference and inaction with respect to the political process (p. 282)

WASP white *Anglo-Saxon* Protestant; narrowly, an American of English descent; broadly, an American of western European ancestry (p. 222)

wealth property and income (p. 178)

welfare (or **state**) **capitalism** an economic system in which individuals own the means of production but the state regulates many economic activities for the welfare of the population (p. 290)

white ethnics white immigrants to the U.S. whose culture differs from that of WASPs (p. 222)

white-collar crime Edwin Sutherland's term for crimes committed by people of respectable and high social status in the course of their occupations (p. 142)

working class people who sell their labor to the capitalist class (p. 145)

world system theory economic and political connections that tie the world's countries together (p. 170)

zero population growth a demographic condition in which women bear only enough children to reproduce the population (p. 371)

Suggested Readings

CHAPTER 1 The Sociological Perspective

Berger, Peter L. *Invitation to Sociology: A Humanistic Perspective.* New York: Doubleday, 1963. This delightful analysis of how sociology applies to everyday life is highly recommended.

Charon, Joel M. *Symbolic Interactionism: An Introduction, an Interpretation, an Integration,* 6th ed. Englewood Cliffs, N.J.: Prentice Hall, 1997. As it lays out the main points of symbolic interactionism, this book provides an understanding of why symbolic interactionism is important in sociology.

Henslin, James M., ed. *Down to Earth Sociology: Introductory Readings,* 11th ed. New York: Free Press, 2001. This collection of readings about everyday life is designed to broaden the reader's understanding of both society and the individual's place within it.

Mills, C. Wright. *The Sociological Imagination.* New York: Oxford University Press, 2000. Originally published in 1959. This classic work provides an overview of sociology from the framework of conflict theory.

Willis, Evans. *The Sociological Quest: An Introduction to the Study of Social Life,* 3rd ed. New Brunswick, N.J. Rutgers University Press, 1997. A user-friendly introduction to sociology.

Journals

Applied Behavioral Science Review, Clinical Sociology Review, International Clinical Sociology, Journal of Applied Sociology, The Practicing Sociologist, Sociological Practice: A Journal of Clinical and Applied Sociology, and *Sociological Practice Review* report the experiences of sociologists who work in applied settings, from peer group counseling and suicide prevention to recommending changes to school boards.

Humanity & Society, the official journal of the Association for Humanist Sociology, publishes articles that "serve to advance the quality of life of the world's people."

Sociological Theory and *Telos* publish theoretical articles.

Visual Sociology Review. A specialized journal in qualitative sociology that focuses on the analysis of social life through visual means such as photos, movies, and videos.

Research Methods in Sociology

Becker, Howard S. *Tricks of the Trade: How to Think about Your Research While You're Doing It.* Chicago: University of Chicago Press, 1998. Based on his extensive experience as a participant observer, the author shares insights into how to do research.

Klein, Ethel, Jacquelyn Campbell, and Esther Soler, eds. *Ending Domestic Violence: Changing Public Perceptions.* Beverly Hills, Calif.: Sage, 1998. A solution-oriented overview of domestic violence, with an emphasis on its relationship to gender, ethnicity, and social class.

Merton, Robert K., Albert E. Golin, and Patricia L. Kendall. *The Focused Interview: A Manual of Problems and Procedures,* 2nd ed. New York: Free Press, 1990. The interviewing techniques outlined here are of value primarily to more advanced students.

Newman, W. Lawrence. *Social Research Methods: Qualitative and Quantitative Approaches,* 4th ed. Boston: Allyn and Bacon, 2000. This "how-to" book of sociological research describes how sociologists gather data and the logic that underlies each of their methods.

Scully, Diana. *Understanding Sexual Violence: A Study of Convicted Rapists.* New York: Routledge, 1994. The author's examination of how rapists rationalize their acts helps us to understand why some men rape and what they gain from it.

Taylor, Stephen J., and Robert Bogdan. *Introduction to Qualitative Research Methods: A Guidebook and Resource,* 3rd ed. New York: John Wiley, 1998. This introduction to participant observation and in-depth interviewing contains many examples of qualitative research done by sociologists.

Webb, Eugene J., Donald T. Campbell, Richard D. Schwartz, Lee Sechrest, and Janet Below Grove. *Unobtrusive Measures: Nonreactive Research in the Social Sciences.* Boston: Houghton Mifflin, 1981. This overview of unobtrusive measures also contains concise summaries of a great deal of research.

Whyte, William Foote. *Creative Problem Solving in the Field: Reflections on a Career.* Lanham, Md:: AltaMira Press, 1997. Focusing on his extensive field experiences, the author provides insight into the crucial effects of the researcher in participant observation.

Writing Papers for Sociology

Cuba, Lee J. *A Short Guide to Writing about Social Science,* 3rd ed. Glenview, Ill.: Scott, Foresman, 1996. The author summarizes the types of social science literature, presents guidelines on how to organize and write a research paper, and explains how to prepare an oral presentation.

The Sociology Writing Group. *A Guide to Writing Sociology Papers,* 4th ed. New York: St. Martin's Press, 1998. Walks students through the steps in writing a sociology paper, from choosing the initial assignment to doing the research and turning in a finished paper. Also explains how to manage your time and correctly cite sources.

About a Career in Sociology

What can you do with sociology? You like the subject and would like to major in it, but.... The American Sociological Association (ASA) offers three pamphlets free of charge. You can obtain them from the ASA at 1307 New York Avenue NW, Suite 700, Washington, D.C. 20005–4701. Tel. (202) 383–9005. Fax (202) 638–0882. E-mail: ASA_Executive_Office@MCImail.com

The brochures are *Careers in Sociology, Majoring in Sociology: A Guide for Students,* and *The Sociology Major as Preparation for Careers in Business and Organizations.* The ASA also sells *Embarking Upon a Career with an Undergraduate Degree in Sociology* and *Mastering the Job Market with a Graduate Degree in Sociology.*

Ferris, Abbott L. *How to Join the Federal Workforce and Advance Your Sociological Career.* American Sociological Association. This pamphlet gives tips on how to find employment in the federal government, including information on how to prepare a job application.

Hess, Beth B. *Individual Voices, Collective Visions: Fifty Years of Women in Sociology.* Philadelphia: Temple University Press, 1995. During the past fifty years, women have played an increasingly larger role in sociology, which, like the other sciences, has been dominated by men. The author examines this change.

Steele, Stephen F., Annemarie Scarisbrick-Hauser, and William J. Hauser. *Solution-Centered Sociology: Addressing Problems Through Applied Sociology.* Beverly Hills, Calif.: Sage, 1999. From this book, you can gain not only a better idea of what applied sociology is but also of what careers are available in sociology.

Stephens, W. Richard. *Careers in Sociology,* 3rd ed. Boston: Allyn and Bacon, 1998. How can you make a living with a major in sociology? The author explores careers in sociology, from business and government to health care and the law.

CHAPTER 2 Culture

Chagnon, Napoleon A. *The Yanomamo,* 6th ed. New York: Harcourt College, 1997. This fascinating account of a tribal group whose customs are extraordinarily different from ours will help you to see the arbitrariness of choices that underlie human culture.

Cohen, Mark Nathan. *Culture of Intolerance: Chauvinism, Class, and Racism in the United States.* New Haven: Yale University Press, 2000. The author analyzes how ideas of race, intelligence, and competence permeate U.S. culture.

Edgerton, Robert B. *Sick Societies: Challenging the Myth of Primitive Harmony.* New York: Free Press, 1992. The author's thesis is that cultural relativism is misinformed, that we have the obligation to judge cultures that harm its members as inferior to those that do not.

Gitlin, Todd. *The Twilight of Common Dreams: Why America Is Wracked by Culture Wars.* New York: Metropolitan Books, 1997. "Culture wars" refers to fundamental disagreements about the way life should be lived and how some groups push their own agendas and disparage those of others. The author expresses hope that we can build "cultural bridges" so we once again can dream "common dreams."

Harris, Marvin. *Cannibals and Kings: The Origins of Cultures.* New York: Vintage Books, 1991.

Harris, Marvin. *Cows, Pigs, Wars, and Witches: The Riddles of Culture.* New York: Vintage Books, 1990.

Harris, Marvin. *Good to Eat: Riddles of Food and Culture.* New York: Simon & Schuster, 1986.

To read Harris's books is to read about cultural relativism. Using a functional perspective, this anthropologist analyzes cultural practices that often seem bizarre to outsiders. He interprets those practices within the framework of the culture being examined.

Jones, Steven G., ed. *Virtual Culture: Liberty and Communication in Cybersociety.* Beverly Hills, Calif.: Sage, 1997. The author's thesis is that the Internet will create vast social change and fundamentally affect our lives.

Rogers, Mary F. *Barbie Culture.* Beverly Hills, Calif.: Sage, 1999. As the author examines Barbie's gender, racial, sexual, and class identities, she explains how Barbie has been adapted to diverse cultures and subcultures.

Zellner, William W. *Countercultures: A Sociological Analysis.* New York: St. Martin's Press, 1995. The author's analysis of skinheads, the Ku Klux Klan, survivalists, satanists, the Church of Scientology, and the Unification Church (Moonies) helps us understand why people join countercultures.

Journal

Urban Life, which focuses on social interaction, contains studies of the cultures of small, off-beat groups.

CHAPTER 3 Socialization

Ariès, Philippe. *Centuries of Childhood: A Social History of Family Life.* New York: Vintage Books, 1965. This path-breaking study of childhood in Europe during the Middle Ages provides a sharp contrast to child-rearing patterns in modern society.

Cohen, Mark. *Lara Croft: The Art of Virtual Seduction.* New York: Prime Publishing, 2000. Interviews with the creators of Lara Croft and her programmers provide insight into Lara's popularity and the "cult" phenomenon centering around this virtual person.

Epstein, Jonathan S., ed. *Youth Culture: Identity in a Postmodern World.* Oxford, U.K.: Blackwell, 1998. Analysis of how youth find their identity in sexuality, music, politics, education, interaction, goals, and frustrations.

Gilmore, David D. *Manhood in the Making: Cultural Concepts of Masculinity.* New Haven, Conn.: Yale University Press, 1991. A survey of societies around the world aimed at determining if masculinity is constant; contains fascinating cross cultural data.

Mead, George Herbert. *Mind, Self and Society from the Standpoint of a Social Behaviorist,* Charles W. Morris, ed. Chicago: University of Chicago Press, 1974. First published in 1934. Put together from notes taken by Mead's students, this book presents Mead's analysis of how mind and self are products of society.

Mead, George Herbert. (Mary Jo Deegan, ed.) *Play, School, and Society.* New York: Peter Lang Publishing, 2000. The editor reorganizes notes taken by Mead's students, placing the focus on play as a central component in the formation of the human mind.

Rymer, Russ. *Genie: A Scientific Tragedy.* New York: Harper-Perennial Library, 1994. This moving account of Genie includes the battles over Genie among linguists, psychologists, and social workers, all of whom claimed to have Genie's best interests at heart.

Sociological Studies of Child Development: A Research Annual. Greenwich, Conn.: JAI Press, published annually. Along with theoretical articles, this publication reports on sociological research on the socialization of children.

Van Hoorn, Judith, Elzbieta Suchar, Akos Komlosi, and Doreen A. Samuelson, eds. *Adolescent Development and Rapid Social Change: Perspectives from Eastern Europe.* Albany: State University of New York Press, 2000. Based on the premise that when society changes, we change, this book examines the effects of social change on adolescents in eastern Europe.

CHAPTER 4 Social Structure and Social Interaction

Goffman, Erving. *The Presentation of Self in Everyday Life.* New York: Peter Smith, Publisher, 1999. First published in 1959. This classic statement of dramaturgical analysis provides a different way of looking at everyday life. As a student, this was one of the best books I read.

Helmreich, William B. *The Things They Say Behind Your Back: Stereotypes and the Myths Behind Them.* New Brunswick, N.J.: Transaction Books, 1984. Spiced with anecdotes and jokes, yet sensitively written, the book explores the historical roots of stereotypes. The author also illustrates how stereotypes help produce behaviors that reinforce the stereotypes.

Lennon, Sharron J., and Kim K. Johnson, eds. *Appearance and Power.* Oxford, England: Berg Publishers, Ltd., 2000. The authors of these articles analyze how significant appearance, especially clothing, is for what happens to us in social life.

Schellenberg, James A. *Exploring Social Behavior: Investigations in Social Psychology.* Boston: Allyn and Bacon, 1993. The author takes the reader on an intellectual journey, exploring such "mysteries" as identity, conscience, intelligence, attraction, and aggression.

Sobal, Jeffery, and Donna Maurer, eds. *Interpreting Weight: The Social Management of Fatness and Thinness.* New York: Aldine de Gruyter, 1999. The authors of these articles examine the strategies people use to give meaning to their weight, including how they interpret fatness and thinness and how they become involved in weight-related organizations.

Tönnies, Ferdinand. *Community and Society (Gemeinschaft und Gesellschaft).* New Brunswick, N.J.: Transaction Books, 1988. Originally published in 1887, this classic work, focusing on social change, provides insight into how society influences personality. Rather challenging reading.

Vinitzky-Seroussi, Vered. *After Pomp and Circumstance: High School Reunions as an Autobiographical Occasion.* Chicago: University of Chicago Press, 1998. In this analysis of high school reunions, the author examines the relationships between the self and the past and future.

Whyte, William Foote. *Street Corner Society: The Social Structure of an Italian Slum,* 4th ed. Chicago: University of Chicago Press, 1993. Originally published in 1943. The author's analysis of interaction in a U.S. Italian slum demonstrates how social structure affects personal relationships.

Journals

Qualitative Sociology, Symbolic Interaction, and *Urban Life* feature articles on symbolic interactionism and analyses of everyday life.

CHAPTER 5 Social Groups and Formal Organizations

Devereaux, James A. *Designing Bureaucracies: Institutional Capacity and Large-Scale Problem Solving.* Stanford, Calif.: Stanford University Press, 1995. Bureaucracies will remain part of the foreseeable future. The author explains how they can live up to their potential.

Drucker, Peter F. *The Frontiers of Management: Where Tomorrow's Decisions Are Being Shaped Today.* New York: Penguin, 1999. An analysis of global trends and management practices in business, including hostile takeovers and career gridlocks.

Fleisher, Mark S. *Beggars and Thieves: Lives of Urban Street Criminals.* Madison: University of Wisconsin Press, 1996. Based on years of participant observation, the author presents an insider's view of thieves, gangs, addicts, and lifelong criminals.

Forschi, Martha, and Edward J. Lawler, eds. *Group Processes: Sociological Analysis.* New York: Nelson-Hall, 1994. How do your associates, friends, family—and even strangers—influence you? Among other topics, these authors explore such influences.

Geneen, Harold. *Synergy and Other Lies: Downsizing, Bureaucracy, and Corporate Culture Debunked.* New York: St. Martin's Press, 1999. A scathing critique of the way U.S. business is done, and a defense of conglomerates, written by an acquisitive CEO.

Herkscher, Charles, and Anne Donnellon, eds. *The Post-Bureaucratic Organization.* Beverly Hills, Calif.: Sage, 1994. By any other name, is a bureaucracy still a bureaucracy? The authors of these articles explain how bureaucracies can be modified to better reach the organization's goals and to better meet human needs.

Homans, George. *The Human Group.* New York: Harcourt, Brace, 1950. In this classic work, Homans develops the idea that all human groups share common activities, interactions, and sentiments; he examines various types of social groups from this point of view.

Howard, Philip K. *The Death of Common Sense: How Law Is Suffocating America.* New York: Random House, 1996. One of the best examples of how bureaucracies can become impediments to the goals they are designed to achieve is the way law is practiced in the United States.

Hummel, Ralph P. *The Bureaucratic Experiment: A Critique of Life in the Modern Organization,* 4th ed. New York: St. Martin's Press, 1994. The author explores the perils and promises of bureaucracies, with an emphasis on how bureaucracies can become better tools for meeting human needs.

Janis, Irving. *Victims of Groupthink,* 2nd ed. Boston: Houghton Mifflin, 1982. Janis analyzes how groups can become cut off from alternatives, interpret evidence in light of their preconceptions, and embark on courses of action that should have been seen as obviously incorrect.

Kephart, William M., and William W. Zellner. *Extraordinary Groups: An Examination of Unconventional Lifestyles,* 6th ed. New York: St. Martin's Press, 1998. This sketch of the history and characteristics of eight groups (the Old Order Amish, Oneida Community, Gypsies, Shakers, Hasidim, Father Divine Movement, Mormons, and Jehovah's Witnesses) illustrates how groups can maintain unconventional beliefs and practices.

MacDonald, Keith M. *The Sociology of the Professions.* Newbury Park: Sage, 1996. Using a symbolic interactionist framework, the author analyzes how jobs are turned into professions.

Parkinson, C. Northcote. *Parkinson's Law.* Boston: Houghton Mifflin, 1997. Although this expose of the inner workings of bureaucracies is delightfully satirical, if Parkinson's analysis were generally true, bureaucracies would always fail.

Ritzer, George. *The McDonaldization of Society: An Investigation into the Changing Character of Contemporary Life,* 3rd ed. Thousand Oaks, Calif.: Pine Forge Press, 2000. The author examines how Durkheim's predictions about the rationalization of society are coming true in everyday life.

Yiannis, Gabriel, Stephen Fineman, and David Sims. *Organizing and Organizations: An Introduction.* Newbury Park, Calif.: Sage, 2nd ed, 2000. The authors draw on many first-hand accounts to help make the study of formal organizations come alive.

Wilson, Gerald L. *Groups in Context: Leadership and Participation in Small Groups,* 5th ed. New York: McGraw-Hill, 1998. An overview of principles and processes of interaction in small groups, with an emphasis on how to exercise leadership.

CHAPTER 6 Deviance and Social Control

Curra, John. *The Relativity of Deviance.* Beverly Hills, Calif.: Sage, 1999. The author uses provocative examples to illustrate the relativity of deviance, how it varies from place to place, time to time, and situation to situation.

Field, Barry C. *Bad Kids: Race and the Transformation of the Juvenile Court.* New York: Oxford University Press, 1999. In this overview of the juvenile court system, the author analyzes the trend to remove serious offenders from the juvenile system.

Fleisher, Mark. S. *Dead End Kids: Gang Girls and the Boys They Know.* Madison: University of Wisconsin Press, 2000. This fascinating participant observation study provides an insider's perspective on gang life.

Girshick, Lori B. *No Safe Haven: Stories of Women in Prison.* Boston: Northeastern University Press, 1999. Do women occupy a special status in the criminal justice system? The author analyzes the life stories of forty imprisoned women to help find the answer.

Goffman, Erving. *Stigma: Notes on the Management of Spoiled Identity.* New York: Simon & Schuster, 1986. A reprint of a 1968 classic that outlines the social and personal reactions to "spoiled identity," appearances that—due to disability, weight, ethnicity, birth marks, and so on—do not match dominant expectations.

Jankowski, Martín Sánchez. *Islands in the Street: Gangs and American Urban Society*. Berkeley: University of California Press, 1992. The author's extensive participant observation of street gangs makes a fascinating and insightful introduction to this topic.

Kleinknecht, William. *The New Ethnic Mobs: The Changing Face of Organized Crime in America*. New York: Free Press, 1996. Like ethnic groups before them, the predators among the new immigrants victimize both outsiders and their own groups.

LaFree, Gary. *Street Crime and the Decline of Social Institutions in America*. New York: Westview Press, 1998. The author's thesis is that the high rates of street crime in the United States indicate a decline of U.S. social institutions, a failure of the family, politics, and economics.

Lott, John R., Jr. *More Guns, Less Crime*. Chicago: University of Chicago Press, 2000. After reviewing state data on crime and right-to-carry gun laws, the author comes to the surprising conclusion that more guns means less crime.

Mann, Coramae Richey, and Marjorie S. Zatz, eds. *Images of Color, Images of Crime*. Los Angeles: Roxbury, 1998. This collection of twenty-two articles examines the relationship between racial stereotypes and crime.

Messner, Steven F., and Richard Rosenfeld. *Crime and the American Dream*, 3rd ed. Belmont, Calif.: Wadsworth, 2001. Explains how the "American Dream" produces a strong desire to make money but fails to instill adequate desires to play by the rules. Supports Merton's strain theory featured in this chapter.

Rafter, Nicole Hahn. *Creating Born Criminals*. Champaign: University of Illinois Press, 1998. Documents how our thinking about the cause of criminality has changed, with an emphasis on "born" criminals and the eugenics movement.

Reinarman, Craig, and Harry G. Levine, eds. *Crack in America: Demon Drugs and Social Justice*. Berkeley: University of California Press, 1998. Examines the consequences of a repressive drug policy and explores constructive alternatives.

Scott, Kody (Sanyika Shakur). *Monster: The Autobiography of an L.A. Gang Member*. New York: Addison Wesley, 1998. This intriguing insider's view of gang life provides a rare glimpse of the power of countercultural norms.

Journals

Contemporary Justice Review: Issues in Criminal, Social, and Restorative Justice, and *Journal of Law and Society* examine the social forces that shape law and justice.

CHAPTER 7 Social Stratification in Global Perspective

Carpenter, Ted Galen, ed. *NATO's Empty Victory*. Cato Institute, 2000. The author analyzes why NATO invaded Kosovo, although no NATO country had been attacked and the U.N. Security Council was divided on the issue.

Cotton, Samuel. *Silent Terror: A Journey into Contemporary African Slavery*. New York: Writers and Research, 1998. A vivid account of slavery in Mauritania, based on the author's observations.

Hajnal, Peter I., and Sian Meikle. *The G7/G8 System: Evolution, Role, and Documentation*. Burlington, Vermont: Ashgate Publishing, 1999. An analysis of the development of G7 and its role in world affairs.

Kempadoo, Mamala, ed. *Sun, Sex, and God: Tourism and Sex Work in the Caribbean*. Lanham, Md.: Rowman and Littlefield, 2000. The authors analyze connections between the global economy and the women, men, and children who sell sex; contains suggestions for changing the situation.

Miles, Rosalind. *The Woman's History of the World*. New York: HarperCollins, 1990. The author examines the importance of gender in human history.

Scheper-Hughes, Nancy. *Death without Weeping: The Violence of Everyday Life in Brazil*. Berkeley: University of California Press, 1993. As stressed in this chapter, global stratification leaves some nations in poverty—despite their possessing rich natural resources. The results can be a short and brutish life for the underprivileged of those nations, as documented in this report.

Thomas, Hugh. *The Slave Trade*. New York: Simon & Schuster, 1997. An overview of slavery from 1444, when slaves from Africa were first taken to Portugal, until the 1860s, when the last slave ships arrived in Cuba.

United Nations. *World Economic & Social Survey 1999*. New York: United Nations Publications, 1999. This survey of the economic characteristics of the world's nations provides a detailed contrast of the rich and poor nations.

Wilkins, David E. *American Indian Sovereignty and the U.S. Supreme Court: The Making of Justice*. Austin: University of Texas Press, 1998. The author traces the relationship of Native Americans and the U.S. government by analyzing fifteen decisions made by the U.S. Supreme Court.

Zakarta, Farred. *From Wealth to Power: The Unusual Origins of America's World*. Princeton, N.J.: Princeton University Press, 2000. The author analyzes how growing wealth and the passing of power from the states to the federal government allowed the United States to become a world power.

CHAPTER 8 Social Class in the United States

Dent, David J. *In Search of Black America: Discovering the African-American Dream*. New York: Simon and Schuster, 2000. The author, a journalist, examines the life of middle-class African Americans, who live in what is largely a segregated world.

Duncan, Greg J., and Jeanne Brooks-Gunn, eds. *Consequences of Growing Up Poor.* New York: Russell Sage, 2000. Examines how neighborhoods and families influence children's intellectual development and adolescent behavior.

Gatewood, Willard B. *Aristocrats of Color: The Black Elite, 1880–1920.* Fayetteville: University of Arkansas Press, 2000. Analyzing the rise and decline of the African American upper class that developed after the Civil War, the author focuses on marriage, occupations, education, religion, clubs, and relationships with whites and with African Americans of lower classes.

Hacker, Andrew. *Money: Who Has How Much and Why.* New York: Scribner's, 1997. An examination of how wealth is distributed in the United States, with a focus on what it means to be rich or poor.

Klepper, Michael, and Robert Gunther. *The Wealthy 100: A Ranking of the Richest Americans, Past and Present.* New York: Carol Publishing, 1997. The authors determine who the 100 richest Americans are by analyzing their fortunes relative to the country's gross national product. Only six living Americans made the list.

Kushnick, Louis, and James Jennings, eds. *A New Introduction to Poverty: The Role of Race, Power, and Politics..* New York: New York University Press, 1999. In this analysis of major causes and characteristics of U.S. poverty, the authors also analyze why poverty persists.

Liebow, Elliot. *Tally's Corner: A Study of Negro Streetcorner Men.* Boston: Little, Brown, 1999. This reprint of a 1968 classic of participant observation research of a group of Washington, D.C., African American men provides remarkable insight into the dynamics of decision making and relationships.

Newman, Katherine S. *Falling from Grace: Downward Mobility in the Age of Affluence.* Berkeley: University of California Press, 1999. The focus of this analysis of downward social mobility is on what happens to people who lose their jobs and are unable to find decent work.

Oliver, Melvin L., and Thomas M. Shapiro. *Black Wealth/White Wealth: A New Perspective on Racial Inequality.* New York: Routledge, 1997. This book, which makes the first comparison of the wealth (not income) of African Americans and whites, shows how deep the divide is.

Richardson, Chad. *Batos, Bolillos, Pochos, & Pelados: Class and Culture on the South Texas Border.* Austin: University of Texas Press, 1999. An analysis of class, conflict, cooperation, and identity among Mexican Americans, Anglos, African Americans, and immigrants in the Valley of South Texas.

Wilson, William Julius. *When Work Disappears: The World of the New Urban Poor.* New York: Knopf, 1997. The author analyzes consequences of the disappearance of unskilled jobs near the inner city: the destruction of inner-city businesses, the flight of the middle class, and the stranding of poor people who have few alternatives.

Zweigenhaft, Richard L., and G. William Domhoff. *Diversity in the Power Elite: Have Women and Minorities Reached the Top?* New Haven: Yale University Press, 1998. In answering the question asked in the subtitle, the authors explain how the recent arrival of minorities, including women, is affecting corporate culture.

Journal

Race, Gender, and Class publishes interdisciplinary articles on the topics listed in its title.

CHAPTER 9 Inequalities of Race and Ethnicity

Blea, Irene I. *U.S. Chicanas and Latinas within a Global Context.* New York: Praeger, 1998. By examining the global context, the author explains why Chicanas and Latinas sometimes feel that they have more in common with women of the Least Industrialized Nations than with feminists in their own country.

Browning, Christopher R. *Ordinary Men: Reserve Police Battalion 101 and the Final Solution in Poland.* New York: Harper-Perennial, 1993. A startling account of how a government turned ordinary men into mass murderers.

Chin, Ko-Lin, and Douglas S. Massey. *Smuggled Chinese: Clandestine Immigration to the United States.* Philadelphia: Temple University Press, 2000. Based on interviews with illegal immigrants, the authors analyze the conditions that illegal immigrants from China face on their journey and after their arrival; includes information on safe houses.

Du Bois, W. E. B. *Black Reconstruction in America: An Essay Toward a History of the Part Which Black Folk Played in the Attempt to Reconstruct Democracy in America, 1860–1880.* New York: Harcourt, Brace, 1935; London: Frank Cass, 1966. This analysis of the role of African Americans in the Civil War and in the years immediately following provides a glimpse into a neglected part of U.S. history.

Klinker, Philip A., and Roger M. Smith. *The Unsteady March: The Rise and Decline of Racial Equality in America.* Chicago: University of Chicago Press, 2000. Examines the conditions under which racial equality increases and decreases and proposes steps to increase racial equality.

Mander, Jerry. *In the Absence of the Sacred: The Failure of Technology and the Survival of the Indian Nations.* New York: Pete Smith, Publisher, 1999. With a focus on the impact of technology, the author analyzes past and present relations of Native Americans and the U.S. government.

Patillo-McCoy, Mary. *Black Picket Fences: Privilege and Peril among the Black Middle Class.* Chicago: University of Chicago Press, 1999. Based on participant observation of a black middle-class neighborhood in Chicago, the author examines the obstacles and pressures these families face and explains why they often produce outcomes different from those of the white middle class.

Press, Riv-Ellen. *Fighting to Become American: Jews, Gender, and the Anxiety of Assimilation.* Boston: Beacon Press, 1999. An analysis of the upward mobility of Jews in the U.S. racial-ethnic structure, and how their stereotypes reflect their aspirations and anxiety.

Reskin, Barbara F. *Realities of Affirmative Action in Employment.* Washington, D.C.: American Sociological Association, 1998. The author analyzes how affirmative action works, including its effects on employers and employees.

Rodriguez, Roberto. *Justice: A Question of Race.* Tempe, Arizona: Bilingual Review Press, 1997. The author was arrested and beaten by the police for taking photos of the police beating a mentally confused man. He recounts his own victimization and his subsequent trial against the Los Angeles Police Department.

Smith, Barbara E., ed. *Neither Separate nor Equal: Women, Race, and Class in the South.* Philadelphia: Temple University Press, 1999. A special focus of this anthology is the relationships among racial-ethnic groups and how a changing economy shapes those relationships.

Walker, Samuel, Cassia Spohn, and Miriam Delone. *The Color of Justice: Race, Ethnicity, and Crime in America,* 2nd ed. Belmont, CA: Wadsworth, 2000. The authors analyze racial, ethnic, and gender discrimination in the criminal justice system.

Wilson, William Julius. *The Bridge over the Racial Divide: Rising Inequality and Coalition Politics.* Berkeley: University of California Press, 2000. The author analyzes how monetary, trade, and tax policies increase social inequality; includes recommendations to increase multiracial political cooperation.

Friedman, Murray, and Nancy Isserman, eds. *The Tribal Basis of American Life: Racial, Religious, and Ethnic Groups in Conflict.* Westport, Conn.: Praeger, 1998. The book's focus is on why group assertiveness has increased and religious, racial, and ethnic conflicts have grown.

Journal

Ethnic and Racial Studies publishes multidisciplinary articles on ethnicity and nationalism.

CHAPTER 10 Inequalities of Gender and Age

Inequalities of Gender

Amott, Teresa. *Caught in the Crisis: Women and the U.S. Economy.* New York: Monthly Review Press, 2000. A short, readable overview of women's economic roles from a leftist perspective.

Anderson, Margaret L. *Thinking about Women: Sociological Perspectives on Sex and Gender,* 5th ed. New York: Allyn and Bacon, 1999. An overview of the main issues of sex and gender in contemporary society, ranging from sexism and socialization to work and health.

Driscoll, Dawn-Marie, and Carol R. Goldberg. *Members of the Club: The Coming of Age of Executive Women.* New York: Free Press, 1993. Based on interviews with senior women executives, the authors suggest strategies for climbing to the top of the corporate ladder.

Farganis, Sondra. *The Social Reconstruction of the Feminine Character,* 2nd ed. Lanham, Md: Rowman & Littlefield, 1996. An overview of feminist theory that emphasizes how views of women are shaped by concrete situations.

Ferree, Myra Marx, Judith Lorer, and Beth B. Hess, eds. *Revisioning Gender.* Thousand Oaks, Calif.: Sage, 1999. An analysis of changes occurring in gender roles with an emphasis on the potential for changing human relations.

Gilman, Charlotte Perkins. *The Man-Made World or, Our Androcentric Culture.* New York: Charlton, 1911. Reprinted in 1971 by Johnson Reprint. This early book on women's liberation provides an excellent view of female-male relations at the beginning of the last century.

Goldberg, Steven. *Why Men Rule: A Theory of Male Dominance.* Chicago: Open Court, 1994. An explanation of the author's theory of male dominance featured in this chapter.

Kimmel, Michael S., and Michael A. Messner, eds. *Men's Lives,* 5th ed. Boston: Allyn and Bacon, 2001. These authors examine major issues of sex and gender as they affect men. An excellent companion, and often counterpoint, to the Anderson book.

Lefkowitz, Bernard. *Our Guys: The Glen Ridge Rape and the Secret Life of the Perfect Suburb.* New York: Vintage Books, 1998. This account of a rape that made national news provides insight into how subcultures that center on competitive male athletics can encourage aggression, violence, and rape.

Lorber, Judith. *Gender and the Social Construction of Illness.* Thousand Oaks, Calif.: Sage, 1997. Taking the position that both gender and medicine are social institutions, the author examines their interrelationships.

Madriz, Esther. *Nothing Bad Happens to Good Girls: Fear of Crime in Women's Lives.* Berkeley: University of California Press, 1997. The author uses interviews to explain how women's fear of crime contributes to gender inequalities and the social control of women.

McKay, Jim, Michael A. Messner, and Donald F. Sabo, eds. *Masculinities, Gender Identities, and Sport.* Beverly Hills, Calif.: Sage, 2000. The authors of these articles provide an overview of major topics in gender relations, with a focus on the relationship between sport and gender.

Messner, Michael A., and Donald F. Sabo. *Sex, Violence, and Power in Sports: Rethinking Masculinity.* Freedom, Calif.: Crossing Press, 1994. The authors explore the connection between sports, pain, sexuality, and masculinity.

Proweller, Amira. *Constructing Female Identities: Meaning Making in an Upper Middle Class Youth Culture.* Albany: State

University of New York Press, 1998. The author analyzes what it means to be female in the United States and how class, race, and education merge in the formation of a female identity.

Tannen, Deborah. *The Argument Culture: Stopping America's War of Words.* New York: Ballantine, 1999. In this argument that Americans argue too much (including too much public debate), the author, a psycholinguist, also reviews basic differences in how boys and girls express agreement and aggression.

Williams, Christine L. *Still a Man's World: Men Who Do Women's Work.* Berkeley: University of California Press, 1995. Based on in-depth interviews with men and women in nursing, elementary school teaching, librarianship, and social work, the author concludes that, due to the high value placed on masculinity, men who work in traditionally women's occupations find a "glass escalator" instead of a "glass ceiling."

Witt, Linda, Karen M. Paget, and Glenna Matthews. *Running as a Woman: Gender and Power in American Politics.* New York: Macmillan, 1995. This history of women in politics includes successful strategies for running for political office as a woman.

Wymard, Ellie. *Conversations with Uncommon Women: Insights from Women Who've Risen above Life's Challenges to Achieve Extraordinary Success.* New York: AMACOM, 2000. The author, an English professor, interviewed 100 highly successful women to discover their understanding of how they overcame the obstacles they faced.

Journals

These journals focus on the role of gender in social life: *European Journal of Women's Studies, Feminist Studies; Gender and Society; Gender, Place and Culture: A Journal of Feminist Geography; Journal of Gender, Culture, and Health; Sex Roles;* and *Signs: Journal of Women in Culture and Society.*

Inequalities of Age

Blaikie, Andrew. *Ageing and Popular Culture.* Cambridge, England: Cambridge University Press, 1999. Examines how the extended leisure that has come with the growing numbers of elderly is breaking down the distinction between middle and old age.

Dychtwald, Ken. *Age Power: How the 21st Century Will Be Ruled by the New Old.* Los Angeles: J. P. Tarcher, 2000. Speculates on how the growing numbers of elderly will affect society and suggests how we should prepare for the coming change.

Gubrium, Jaber F. *Living and Dying at Murray Manor.* Charlottesville: University of Virginia Press, 1998. In this ethnography of a nursing home, the author analyzes how staff and patients relate to one another, how patients pass time, and how they react to death.

Quadrango, Jill S. *Aging and the Life Course: An Introduction to Social Gerontology.* New York: McGraw-Hill, 1999. As the author reviews the major issues in gerontology, she stresses that the quality of life people experience in old age is the result of their earlier choices, opportunities, and constraints.

Roszak, Theodore. *America the Wise: The Longevity Revolution and the True Wealth of Nations.* New York: Houghton Mifflin, 1999. The author's thesis is that as the numbers of elderly grow, they will have more wealth and political power, which will lead to a more compassionate and wise society.

Rubin, Lillian B. *Tangled Lives: Daughters, Mothers, and the Crucible of Aging.* Boston: Beacon Press, 2001. The author reflects on her own experiences with illness and death to try to come to grips with the meaning of growing old—and of life.

Stoller, Eleanor Palo, and Rose Campbell Gibson. *Worlds of Difference: Inequality in the Aging Experience,* 3rd ed. Thousand Oaks, Calif.: Pine Forge Press, 2000. The authors document extensive inequalities borne by the U.S. elderly and explain the social conditions that create those inequalities.

Journals

The Gerontologist, Journal of Aging and Identity, Journal of Aging and Social Policy, Journal of Aging Studies, Journal of Cross-Cultural Gerontology, Journal of Elder Abuse and Neglect, Journal of Gerontology, Journal of Women and Aging, and *Research on Aging* focus on issues of aging, while *Youth and Society* examines adolescent culture.

CHAPTER 11 Politics and the Economy: Leadership and Work in the Global Village

Politics

Allen, Oliver E. *The Tiger.* New York: Addison-Wesley, 1993. An entertaining account of Tammany Hall, the corrupt political group that controlled New York City from the 1800s to the middle of the last century.

Amnesty International. *Amnesty International Report.* London: Amnesty International Publications, published annually. Summarizes human rights violations around the world, naming names and listing specific instances country by country.

Castro, Fidel. *Capitalism in Crisis: Globalization and World Politics Today.* New York: Ocean Press, 2001. This collection of speeches by one of the few remaining communist rulers provides a conflict perspective on geopolitical change.

Chirot, Daniel. *Modern Tyrants: The Power and Prevalence of Evil in Our Age.* Princeton, N.J.: Princeton University Press, 1996. From Hitler and Stalin to Trujillo, Mao, and Pol Pot, the author analyzes the political expediency that underlies tyranny.

Domhoff, G. William. *Who Rules America? Power and Politics in the Year 2000,* 3rd ed. Mountain View, Calif.: Mayfield Publishing Company, 1998. An analysis of how multinational corporations dominate the U.S. government.

Ferguson, Thomas. *Golden Rule: The Investment Theory of Party Competition and the Logic of Money-Driven Political Systems.* Chicago: University of Chicago Press, 1995. The title, based on the statement "to discover who rules, follow the gold (money)," gives support to the conflict perspective of U.S. politics.

Mills, C. Wright. *The Power Elite,* 2nd ed. New York: Getty Center for Education in the Arts, 2000. Originally published in 1956. This classic analysis elaborates the conflict thesis summarized in this chapter—that U.S. society is ruled by the nation's top corporate leaders, together with an elite from the military and political institutions.

Porter, Bruce D. *War and the Rise of the State: The Military Foundations of Modern Politics.* New York: Free Press, 1994. The author presents an intriguing analysis of how war and the military underlie the creation of the state and of changed relations within it.

Simes, Dimitri K. *After the Collapse: Russia Seeks its Place as a Great Power.* New York: Simon and Schuster, 1999. The author, a Russian expatriate, analyzes the political turmoil in Russia and makes recommendations for U.S. policy toward Russia.

Zweigenhaft, Richard L., and G. William Domhoff. *Diversity in the Power Elite: Have Women and Minorities Reached the Top?* New Haven: Yale University Press, 2000. The author explores the extent to which Jews, women, blacks, Latinos, Asian Americans, and homosexuals have joined the power elite.

Journals

Most sociology journals publish articles on politics. Three that focus on this area of social life are *American Political Science Review, Journal of Political and Military Sociology,* and *Social Policy.*

Research in Political Sociology: A Research Annual. Greenwich, Conn.: JAI Press. This annual publication is not recommended for beginners, as the findings and theories are often difficult and abstract. It does, however, analyze political topics of vital concern to our well-being.

The Economy

Bales, Kevin. *Disposable People: New Slavery in the Global Economy.* Berkeley: University of California Press, 1999. The author documents the relationship between the globalization of capitalism and today's slavery in Brazil, India, Mauritania, Pakistan, and Thailand.

Bluestone, Barry, Bennett Harrison, and Richard C. Leone. *Growing Prosperity.* New York: Houghton Mifflin, 1999. An emphasis on how we can continue economic growth; also focuses on the need for a more just distribution of our wealth.

Blumenberg, Werner. *Karl Marx.* New York: VideoBooks, 1999. Written by a member of the underground that fought against Hitler, this biography of Marx explores both his personal and public life.

Bonilla, Frank, eds. *Borderless Borders: U.S. Latinos, Latin Americans, and the Paradox of Interdependence.* Philadelphia: Temple University Press, 1998. Analyzes how changes in politics and economics are affecting Latino Americans.

Harrison, Bennett. *Lean and Mean: Why Large Corporations Will Continue to Dominate the Global Economy.* New York: Guilford Press, 1998. As the author examines the role of the giant corporations in technological innovations and economic growth, he explains why a permanent workforce is threatened by the rise in part-time and temporary jobs.

Porter, Michael E. *The Competitive Advantage of Nations.* New York: Free Press, 1998. Based on research in ten countries, the author first examines how productivity is the key to a nation's competitive market position and then provides an explanation for the economic success of Japan and the decline of Great Britain.

Sennett, Richard, and Bob Sennett. *The Corrosion of Character: The Personal Consequences of Work in the New Capitalism.* New York: W. W. Norton, 2000. An examination of how the "new efficiencies" of the multinational corporations affect workers; contains case studies.

Journals

Two journals that focus on issues presented in this chapter are *Insurgent Sociologist* and *Work and Occupations.*

CHAPTER 12 Marriage and Family

Coontz, Stephanie, Maya Parson, and Gabrielle Raley, eds. *American Families: A Multicultural Reader.* Boston: Routledge, 1999. The articles in this anthology illustrate the diversity of U.S. family life, underscoring the point in the text that there is no such thing as *the* family.

Hackstaff, Karla B. *Marriage in a Culture of Divorce.* Philadelphia: Temple University Press, 2000. Through in-depth interviews with couples who married in the 1950s and 1970s, the author examines how the meaning of marriage and divorce has changed.

Hansen, Karen V., Anita Ilta Garey, and Ronnie J. Steinberg, eds. *Families in the U.S.: Kinship and Domestic Politics.* Philadelphia: Temple University Press, 1998. The authors of the sixty-two articles that make up this anthology cover the definition, structure, and economics of family, community, parenthood, kinship, marriage, divorce, caregiving, violence, and housework.

Hochschild, Arlie Russell. *The Time Bind: When Work Becomes Home and Home Becomes Work.* New York: Metropolitan Books,

1998. Do parents really want to spend more time with their families and less at work? Or do parents flee families, finding work a respite from family pressures? The author presents some surprising answers.

LaRossa, Ralph. *The Modernization of Fatherhood: A Social and Political History.* Chicago: University of Chicago Press, 1997. The author's exploration of how ideas of fatherhood have changed over time and varied from one group to another sheds light on our current ideas of fatherhood.

Rubin, Lillian. *Families on the Faultline: America's Working Class Speaks about the Family, the Economy, Race and Ethnicity.* New York: HarperCollins, 1996. Based on interviews, the author maps primary concerns of the working class, allowing us to better understand the tensions they face.

Staples, Robert, ed. *The Black Family: Essays and Studies,* 6th ed. Belmont Calif.: Wadsworth, 1999. The authors analyze black families—from the times of slavery to postindustrial society—reviewing gender roles, marriage and divorce, family life, parenthood, adolescence, health, violence, sexual relationships, and public policy.

Strasser, Mark. *The Challenge of Same-Sex Marriages: Federalist Principles and Constitutional Protection.* New York: Praeger, 2000. Based on challenges to state laws that limit marriage to people of the opposite sex, the author analyzes same-sex marriages in light of the U.S. Constitution.

Journals

Family Relations, International Journal of Sociology of the Family, Journal of Comparative Family Studies, Journal of Divorce, Journal of Family and Economic Issues, Journal of Family Issues, Journal of Family Violence, Journal of Marriage and the Family, and *Marriage and Family Review* publish articles on almost every aspect of marriage and family life.

CHAPTER 13 Education and Religion

Education

Garrod, Andrew, and Colleen Larimore, eds. *First Person, First Peoples: Native American College Graduates Tell Their Life Stories.* Ithaca, New York: Cornell University Press, 1997. Written by graduates of Dartmouth College, these essays recount the anguish that minority students feel when they attend a predominantly white college.

Kozol, Jonathan. *Ordinary Resurrections: Children in the Years of Hope.* New York: Crown Publishers, 2000. To listen as these children from a dismal neighborhood in South Bronx talk about life is to become aware of the potential of schools to transform the lives of children in poverty.

Matthews, Jay. *Class Struggle: What's Wrong (and Right) with America's Best Public High Schools.* New York: Times Books, 1999. As the author, a reporter, analyzes the experiences of students at Mamaroneck High School in New York, one of the best public schools in the nation, he focuses on how students from privileged and impoverished backgrounds are served by advanced classes.

Padilla, Felix M. *The Struggle of Latino/Latina University Students: In Search of a Liberating Education.* New York: Routledge, 1997. The author draws on his students' journal entries and his own educational experiences to analyze how Latino students construct the meaning of their education in a white university.

Reagin, Joe, Vera Hernan, and Imani Nikitah. *The Agony of Education: Black Students at a White University.* New York: Routledge, 1996. Based on interviews with African American students and their parents, the authors analyze the dilemmas these students face and the decisions they make.

Schiell, Timothy C. *Campus Hate Speech on Trial.* Lawrence: University of Kansas Press, 2000. An analysis of the limits of free speech, which lies at the heart of personal freedom.

Steinberg, Laurence, Stanford Dornbusch, and Bradford Brown. *Beyond the Classroom, Why Social Reform Has Failed and What Parents Need to Do.* New York: Simon & Schuster, 1996. Based on a study of 20,000 high school students, the authors conclude that the peer group is the most important factor in determining educational success or failure.

Weiler, Jeanne Drysdale. *Codes and Contradictions: Race, Gender Identity, and Schooling.* New York: State University of New York, 2000. After studying girls of African American, Latina, Puerto Rican, and European backgrounds who are at risk of failing in school, the author concludes that schools are able to reorient young women so they see educational success as crucial to their future well-being.

Journals

The following journals contain articles that examine almost every aspect of education: *Education and Urban Society, Harvard Educational Review,* and *Sociology of Education.*

Religion

Berger, Peter L. *A Far Glory: The Quest for Faith in an Age of Credulity.* New York: Free Press, 1992. A sociologist explains how faith is possible in an age of pluralistic relativism.

Csordas, Thomas J. *Language, Charisma, and Creativity: The Ritual Life of a Religious Movement.* Berkeley: University of California Press, 1997. The author analyzes the Charismatic Renewal (the emergence of Pentecostal groups) within the U.S. Roman Catholic Church; based on participant observation.

Finke, Roger, and Rodney Stark. *The Churching of America, 1776–1990: Winners and Losers in Our Religious Economy.* New Brunswick, N.J.: Rutgers University Press, 1992. The authors' account of why churches gain or lose members over the decades provides a sweeping view of religious change in U.S. history.

Galanter, Marc. *Cults: Faith, Healing, and Coercion.* New York: Oxford University Press, 1991. What do Alcoholics Anonymous, the Unification Church, and the mass suicide in Jonestown have in common? This book, rich in ethnographic materials on charismatic cults, provides answers, but the sociological reader will have to wade through some unacceptable psychiatric interpretations.

Helmreich, William B. *The Enduring Community: The Jews of Newark and Metrowest.* New Brunswick, N.J.: Transaction, 1999. An analysis of the subcultural forces that help Jews maintain their identity in the face of declining religiosity.

Lewis, David C. *After Atheism: Religion and Ethnicity in Russia and Central Asia.* New York: St. Martin's Press, 2000. The author reports on changes in religion since the downfall of communism in Russia.

Mazur, Eric Michael. *The Americanization of Religious Minorities: Confronting the Constitutional Order.* Baltimore: Johns Hopkins University Press, 2000. What happens when religious beliefs conflict with U.S. law? The author analyzes the experiences of Jehovah's Witnesses, Mormons, and Native Americans.

Thibodeau, David, and Leon Whiteson. *A Place Called Waco: A Survivor's Story.* New York: Public Affairs, 2000. A first-person account of life inside the Branch Davidians' compound, written by one of only four survivors of the fire who were not sentenced to prison

Williams, Miriam. *Heaven's Harlots: My Fifteen Years As a Sacred Prostitute in the Children of God Cult.* Deerfield, Mass.: Eagle Brook, 1999. A first-person account of membership in the Children of God, a pseudo-Christian group with international membership.

Journals

Journals that publish articles on the sociology of religion include *Journal for the Scientific Study of Religion, Review of Religious Research,* and *Sociological Analysis: A Journal in the Sociology of Religion.*

CHAPTER 14 Population and Urbanization

Anderson, Elijah. *Code of the Street: Decency, Violence, and the Moral Life of the Inner City.* New York: W. W. Norton & Co., 2000. An insider's perspective of how the need and demand for respect dominates social relationships in the inner city, and how this is related to violence, unemployment, and drugs.

Baxandall, Rosalyn Fraad, and Elizabeth Wewn. *Picture Window: How the Suburbs Happened.* New York: Basic Books, 1999. Analyzes how the suburbs were a response to the pivotal issues of U.S. life following World War II.

Benfield, F. Kaid, Donald D. T. Chen, and Matthew D. Raimi. *Once There Were Green Fields: How Urban Sprawl Is Undermin-*

ing America's Environment, Economy, and Social Fabric. New York: Natural Resource Defense, 1999. The authors' thesis is that urban sprawl is deteriorating our quality of life; they offer suggestions for what they call "smarter growth."

Danny, Andres, Elizabeth Plater-Zyberk, and Jeff Speck. *Suburban Nation: The Rise of Sprawl and the Decline of the American Dream.* San Francisco, Calif.: North Point Press, 2000. Lays out a vision of how to plan cities and suburbs so they meet human needs and become inviting places to live.

Department of Agriculture. *Yearbook of Agriculture.* Washington, D.C.: Department of Agriculture, published annually. This yearbook focuses on aspects of U.S. agribusiness, especially international economies and trade.

DeRosier, Linda Scott. *Creeker: A Woman's Journey.* Lexington: University Press of Kentucky, 2000. The author recounts her life growing up in the "hollers" of Appalachia; provides insight into a form of community and a way of rural life that are fast disappearing.

Mosher, Steven W. *A Mother's Ordeal: One Woman's Fight Against One-Child China.* New York: HarperCollins, 1994. This book puts a human face on China's coercive family planning policies.

Newman, Katherine S. *No Shame in My Game: The Working Poor in the Inner City.* New York: Knopf, 1999. Another look at the residents of the inner city, this time with a focus on the working poor, those who strive to get ahead but are held back by lack of opportunities and education.

Ross, Andrew. *The Celebration Chronicles: Life, Liberty, and the Pursuit of Property Values in Disney's New Town.* New York: Ballantine Books, 2000. An analysis of Disney's planned utopian community in Florida, written by a social scientist who lived in Celebration for a year.

Weeks, John R. *Population: An Introduction to Concepts and Issues,* 7th ed. Belmont, Calif.: Wadsworth Publishing Company, 1999. Focusing on both the U.S. and the world, the author analyzes major issues in population.

CHAPTER 15 Social Change: Technology, Social Movements, and the Environment

Breton, Mary Joy. *Women Pioneers for the Environment.* Boston: Northeastern University Press, 1999. The stories of forty women who stepped out of their traditional roles to spearhead environmental campaigns.

Brown, Lester R., ed. *State of the World.* New York: Norton, published annually. Experts on environmental issues analyze environmental problems throughout the world; a New Malthusian perspective.

Council on Environmental Quality. *Environmental Quality.* Washington, D.C.: U.S. Government Printing Office, published annually. Each report evaluates the condition of some aspect of the environment.

Gaard, Greta Claire. *Ecological Politics: Ecofeminists and the Greens.* Philadelphia: Temple University Press, 1998. Examines the ideological connections between feminist theory and social activism in the environmental movement, with a special emphasis on Green politics.

Gates, Bill. *Business @ the Speed of Thought: Using a Digital Nervous System.* New York: Warner Books, 1999. The premise is that the speed of business is increasing, and that to keep up businesses must develop a "digital nervous system" to gather, manage, and use information.

Guither, Harold. *Animal Rights: History and Scope of a Radical Social Movement.* Carbondale, Ill.: Southern Illinois Press, 1998. As the author recounts the history of the animal rights movement, he reviews the philosophies and debates of animal rights activists.

Hanagan, Michael P., and Leslie T. Moch, eds. *Challenging Authority: The Historical Study of Contentious Politics.* St. Paul: University of Minnesota Press, 1999. The authors of these articles analyze how social movements challenge the political order and lead to social change.

Jasper, James M. *The Art of Moral Protest: Culture, Biography, and Creativity in Social Movements.* Chicago: University of Chicago Press, 2000. A primary thrust of the author is how protest movements shape moral thinking.

Luker, Kristin. *Abortion and the Politics of Motherhood.* Berkeley: University of California Press, 2000. Based on documents and interviews with prochoice and prolife advocates, the author demonstrates how people's moral positions on abortion are related to their views on sexual behavior, the care of children, and family life.

Mercier, Jean. *Downstream and Upstream Ecologists: The People, Organizations, and Ideas Behind the Movement.* Westport, Conn.: Praeger, 1997. Based on interviews with leaders in the environmental and ecological movement, the author tries to analyze what unites people who have such diverse backgrounds and ideas.

Rensenbrink, John. *Against All Odds: The Green Transformation of American Politics.* Gray, Maine: Leopold Press, 1999. The thesis is that to have a "just and self-renewing society" the United States needs a new political system based on "ecological wisdom."

Rose, Fred. *Reclaiming the Environmental Debate: The Politics of Health in a Toxic Culture.* Ithaca, New York: Cornell University Press, 2000. The author's thesis is that to produce an environmentally sound society, the working and middle classes must unite.

Veltmeyer, Henry, and James F. Petras. *The Dynamics of Social Change in Latin America.* New York: St. Martin's Press, 2000. Analyzes the interrelationships of the globalization of capitalism, ideology, social class, politics, and the economy of Latin America.

Journals

Earth First! Journal and *Sierra,* magazines published by Earth First! and the Sierra Club respectively, are excellent sources for keeping informed of major developments in the environmental movement.

References

Aberle, David. *The Peyote Religion among the Navaho.* Chicago: Aldine, 1966.

Addams, Jane. *Twenty Years at Hull-House.* New York: Signet, 1981. First published in 1910.

Adler, Patricia A., and Peter Adler. *Peer Power: Preadolescent Culture and Identity.* New Brunswick, N.J.: Rutgers University Press, 1998.

Adler, Patricia A., Steven J. Kless, and Peter Adler. "Socialization to Gender Roles: Popularity among Elementary School Boys and Girls." *Sociology of Education, 65,* July 1992:169–187.

Adorno, Theodor W., Else Frenkel-Brunswick, D. J. Levinson, and R. N. Sanford. *The Authoritarian Personality.* New York: Harper & Row, 1950.

Aeppel, Timothy. "More Amish Women Are Tending to Business." *Wall Street Journal,* February 8, 1996:B1, B2.

Ahlburg, Dennis A., and Carol J. De Vita. "New Realities of the American Family." *Population Bulletin, 47,* 2, August 1992:1–44.

Akol, Jacob. "Slavery in Sudan." *New African,* September 1998.

Aldrich, Nelson W., Jr. *Old Money: The Mythology of America's Upper Class.* New York: Vintage Books, 1989.

Allport, Floyd. *Social Psychology.* Boston: Houghton Mifflin, 1954.

Alter, Joel. *Recidivism of Adult Felons.* St. Paul: State of Minnesota, January 1997.

Amenta, Edwin, Bruce G. Carruthers, and Yvonne Zylan. "A Hero for the Aged? The Townsend Movement, the Political Mediation Model, and U.S. Old-Age Policy, 1934–1950." *American Journal of Sociology, 98,* 2, September 1992:308–339. In *Social Movements: Readings on Their Emergence, Mobilization, and Dynamics,* Doug McAdam and David A. Snow, eds. Los Angeles: Roxbury Publishing, 1997:494–510.

American Sociological Association. "Code of Ethics." Washington, D.C.: American Sociological Association, August 14, 1989; Spring 1997.

American Sociological Association. "Section on Environment and Technology." Pamphlet, no date.

Anderson, Elijah. *A Place on the Corner.* Chicago: University of Chicago Press, 1978.

Anderson, Elijah. *Streetwise.* Chicago: University of Chicago Press, 1990.

Anderson, Elijah. "Streetwise." In *Down to Earth Sociology: Introductory Readings,* 10th ed., James M. Henslin, ed. New York: Free Press, 1999:193–202.

Anderson, Elijah. "Selling Crack." In *Down to Earth Sociology: Introductory Readings,* 11th ed. James M. Henslin, ed. New York: Free Press, 2001:247–256.

Anderson, Nels. *Desert Saints: The Mormon Frontier in Utah.* Chicago: University of Chicago Press, 1966. First published in 1942.

Anderson, Philip. "God and the Swedish Immigrants." *Sweden and America,* Autumn 1995:17–20.

Angler, Natalie. "Do Races Differ? Not Really, DNA Shows." *New York Times,* August 22, 2000.

Annin, Peter, and Kendall Hamilton. "Marriage or Rape?" *Newsweek,* December 16, 1996:78.

Ansberry, Clare. "Despite Federal Law, Hospitals Still Reject Sick Who Can't Pay." *Wall Street Journal,* November 29, 1988:A1, A4.

"Anybody's Son Will Do." National Film Board of Canada, KCTS, and Films, 1983.

Aptheker, Herbert. "W.E.B. Du Bois: Struggle Not Despair." *Clinical Sociology Review, 8,* 1990:58–68.

Ariés, Philippe. *Centuries of Childhood.* R. Baldick, trans. New York: Vintage Books, 1965.

Arlacchi, P. *Peasants and Great Estates: Society in Traditional Calabria.* Cambridge, England: Cambridge University Press, 1980.

Arndt, William F., and F. Wilbur Gingrich. *A Greek-English Lexicon of the New Testament and Other Early Christian Literature.* Chicago: University of Chicago Press, 1957.

Asch, Solomon. "Effects of Group Pressure upon the Modification and Distortion of Judgments." In *Readings in Social Psychology,* Guy Swanson, Theodore M. Newcomb, and Eugene L. Hartley, eds. New York: Holt, Rinehart and Winston, 1952.

Ashe, Arthur. "A Zero-Sum Game That Hurts Blacks." *Wall Street Journal,* February 27, 1992:A10.

Associated Press. "Future Medicine Looks Futuristic." December 2, 1995.

Associated Press. "Clinton Will Announce Welfare Rolls Are at Their Lowest Level in 30 Years." *Wall Street Journal,* January 25, 1999.

Ayittey, George B. N. "Black Africans Are Enraged at Arabs." *Wall Street Journal,* interactive edition, September 4, 1998.

Baca Zinn, Maxine. "Adaptation and Continuity in Mexican-Origin Families." In *Minority Families in the United States: A Multicultural Perspective,* Ronald L. Taylor, ed. Englewood Cliffs, N.J.: Prentice Hall, 1994:64–81.

Badgett, M. V. Lee, and Heidi Hartmann. "The Effectiveness of Equal Employment Opportunity Policies." In *Economic Perspectives in Affirmative Action,* Margaret C. Simms, ed. Washington, D.C.: Joint Center for Political and Economic Studies, 1995:55–83.

Bales, Robert F. *Interaction Process Analysis.* Reading, Mass.: Addison-Wesley, 1950.

Bales, Robert F. "The Equilibrium Problem in Small Groups." In *Working Papers in the Theory of Action,* Talcott Parsons et al., eds. New York: Free Press, 1953:111–115.

Ball, Jeffrey. "Auto Makers Race to Sell Cars Powered by Fuel Cells." *Wall Street Journal,* March 15, 1999.

Baltzell, E. Digby. *Puritan Boston and Quaker Philadelphia.* New York: Free Press, 1979.

Baltzell, E. Digby, and Howard G. Schneiderman. "Social Class in the Oval Office." *Society,* September–October 1988:42–49.

Barnes, Fred. "How to Rig a Poll." *Wall Street Journal,* June 14, 1995:A14.

Barnes, Harry Elmer. *The History of Western Civilization,* Vol. 1. New York: Harcourt, Brace, 1935.

Barry, Paul. "Strong Medicine: A Talk with Former Principal Henry Gradillas." *College Board Review,* Fall 1989:2–13.

Bartlett, Donald L., and James B. Steele. "Paying a Price for Polluters." *Time,* November 23, 1998:72–80.

Beck, Allen J., Susan A. Kline, and Lawrence A. Greenfeld. "Survey of Youth in Custody, 1987." Washington, D.C.: U.S. Department of Justice, September 1988.

Beck, Scott H., and Joe W. Page. "Involvement in Activities and the Psychological Well-Being of Retired Men." *Activities, Adaptation, & Aging, 11,* 1, 1988:31–47.

Becker, Howard S. *Outsiders: Studies in the Sociology of Deviance.* New York: Free Press, 1966.

Beckett, Paul. "Even Piñatas Sold in Mexico Seem to Originate in Hollywood Now." *Wall Street Journal,* September 11, 1996:B1.

Beeghley, Leonard. *The Structure of Social Stratification in the United States,* 3rd ed. Boston: Allyn and Bacon, 2000.

Begley, Sharon. "Twins: Nazi and Jew." *Newsweek, 94,* December 3, 1979:139.

Begley, Sharon. "Odds on the Greenhouse." *Newsweek,* December 1, 1997:72.

Bell, Daniel. *The Coming of Post-Industrial Society: A Venture in Social Forecasting.* New York: Basic Books, 1973.

Bell, David A. "An American Success Story: The Triumph of Asian-Americans." In *Sociological Footprints: Introductory Readings in Sociology,* 5th ed., Leonard Cargan and Jeanne H. Ballantine, eds. Belmont, Calif.: Wadsworth, 1991:308–316.

Belluck, Pam. "First Ever Criminal Conviction Levied in Food Poisoning Case." *New York Times,* July 24, 1998.

Benales, Carlos. "70 Days Battling Starvation and Freezing in the Andes: A Chronicle of Man's Unwillingness to Die." *New York Times,* January 1, 1973:3.

Bender, Sue. "Everyday Sacred: A Journey to the Amish." *Utne Reader,* September–October 1990:91–97.

Bender, William, and Margaret Smith. "Population, Food, and Nutrition." *Population Bulletin, 51,* 4, February 1997:1–47.

Benet, Sula. "Why They Live to Be 100, or Even Older, in Abkhasia." *New York Times Magazine, 26,* December 1971.

Bennett, Neil G., Ann Klimas Blanc, and David E. Bloo. "Commitment and the Modern Union: Assessing the Link between Premarital Cohabitation and Subsequent Marital Stability." *American Sociological Review, 53,* 1988:127–138.

Berger, Peter L. *Invitation to Sociology: A Humanistic Perspective.* New York: Doubleday, 1963.

Berger, Peter L. *The Capitalist Revolution: Fifty Propositions about Prosperity, Equality, and Liberty.* New York: Basic Books, 1991.

Berger, Peter L. "Invitation to Sociology." In *Down to Earth Sociology: Introductory Readings,* 11th ed. James M. Henslin, ed. New York: Free Press, 2001:3–7.

Bergmann, Barbara R. "The Future of Child Care." Paper presented at the 1995 meetings of the American Sociological Association.

Berk, Laura E. *Child Development,* 3rd ed. Boston: Allyn and Bacon, 1994.

Berle, Adolf, Jr., and Gardiner C. Means. *The Modern Corporation and Private Property.* New York: Harcourt, Brace and World, 1932. As cited in Useem 1980:44.

Bernard, Viola W., Perry Ottenberg, and Fritz Redl. "Dehumanization: A Composite Psychological Defense in Relation to Modern War." In *The Triple Revolution Emerging: Social Problems in Depth,* Robert Perucci and Marc Pilisuk, eds. Boston: Little, Brown, 1971:17–34.

Bernstein, Jonas. "How the Russian Mafia Rules." *Wall Street Journal,* October 26, 1994:A20.

Bernstein, Richard. "Play Penn." *New Republic,* August 2, 1993.

Besser, Terry L. "A Critical Approach to the Study of Japanese Management." *Humanity and Society, 16,* 2, May 1992:176–195.

Bianchi, Suzanne M., and Daphne Spain. "Women Work, and Family in America." *Population Bulletin, 51,* 3, December 1996:1–47.

Bishop, Jerry E. "Study Finds Doctors Tend to Postpone Heart Surgery for Women, Raising Risk." *Wall Street Journal,* April 16, 1990:B4.

Blau, Francine D., and Lawrence M. Kahn. "The Gender Earnings Gap: Some International Evidence." Working Paper No. 4224, National Bureau of Economic Research, December 1992.

Blau, Peter M., and Otis Dudley Duncan. *The American Occupational Structure.* New York: Wiley, 1967.

Blumstein, Alfred, and Jacqueline Cohen. "Characterizing Criminal Careers." *Science, 237,* August 1987:985–991.

Blumstein, Philip, and Pepper Schwartz. *American Couples: Money, Work, Sex.* New York: Pocket Books, 1985.

Bobo, Lawrence, and James R. Kluegel. "Modern American Prejudice: Stereotypes, Social Distance, and Perceptions of Discrimination toward Blacks, Hispanics, and Asians." Paper presented at the 1991 annual meeting of the American Sociological Association.

Boone, Christopher, and Ali Modarres. "Creating a Toxic Neighborhood in Los Angeles County: A Historical Examination of Environmental Inequity." *Urban Affairs Review, 35,* 2, November 1999:163–187.

Booth, Alan, and James M. Dabbs, Jr. "Testosterone and Men's Marriages." *Social Forces, 72,* 2, December 1993:463–477.

"The Boss's Pay." *Wall Street Journal,* April 6, 2000:R9.

Bourgois, Philippe. "Crack in Spanish Harlem." In *Haves and Have-Nots: An International Reader on Social Inequality,* James Curtis and Lorne Tepperman, eds. Englewood Cliffs, N.J.: Prentice Hall, 1994:131–136.

Bowles, Samuel. "Unequal Education and the Reproduction of the Social Division of Labor." In *Power and Ideology in Education,* J. Karabel and A. H. Halsey, eds. New York: Oxford University Press, 1977.

Bowles, Samuel, and Herbert Gintis. *Schooling in Capitalist America.* New York: Basic Books, 1976.

Brajuha, Mario, and Lyle Hallowell. "Legal Intrusion and the Politics of Fieldwork: The Impact of the Brajuha Case." *Urban Life, 14,* 4, January 1986:454–478.

Bray, Rosemary L. "Rosa Parks: A Legendary Moment, a Lifetime of Activism." *Ms. Magazine, 6,* 3, November–December 1995:45–47.

Breaux, Kia Shante. "Foundation Acknowledges Jefferson Fathered Heming's Child." Associated Press, January 27, 2000.

Breen, Richard, and Christopher T. Whelan. "Gender and Class Mobility: Evidence from the Republic of Ireland." *Sociology, 29,* 1, February 1995:1–22.

Bretos, Miguel A. "Hispanics Face Institutional Exclusion." *Miami Herald,* May 22, 1994.

Bridgman, Ann. "Report from the Russian Front." *Education Week, 13,* 28, April 6, 1994:22–29.

Bridgwater, William, ed. *The Columbia Viking Desk Encyclopedia.* New York: Viking Press, 1953.

Brines, Julie. "Economic Dependency, Gender, and the Division of Labor at Home." *American Journal of Sociology, 100,* 3, November 1994:652–688.

Broad, William J. "The Shuttle Explodes." *New York Times,* January 29, 1986:A1, A5.

Bronfenbrenner, Urie, as quoted in Diane Fassel. "Divorce May Not Harm Children." In *Family in America: Opposing Viewpoints,* Viqi Wagner, ed. San Diego, Calif.: Greenhaven Press, 1992:115–119.

Bronner, Ethan. "In Israel, New Grade School Texts for History Replace Myths With Facts." *New York Times,* August 14, 1999.

Brooke, James. "Amid U.S. Islam's Growth in the U.S., Muslims Face a Surge in Attacks." *New York Times,* August 28, 1995:A1, B7.

Brooks-Gunn, Jeanne, Greg. J. Duncan, and Lawrence Aber, eds. *Neighborhood Poverty, Volume 1: Context and Consequences for Children.* New York: Russell Sage Foundation, 1997.

Browne, Andrew. "Education Seen as the Solution." *Reuters On Line.* September 8, 1995.

Browning, Christopher R. *Ordinary Men: Reserve Police Battalion 101 and the Final Solution in Poland.* New York: HarperPerennial, 1993.

Brownstein, Ronald, and Robert A. Rosenblatt. "Extra Serving of Surplus to Elderly Raises Eyebrows." *Los Angeles Times,* February 2, 1999.

Brueggemann, John. "The Power and Collapse of Paternalism: The Ford Motor Company and Black Workers, 1937–1941." *Social Problems, 47,* 2, May 2000:220–240.

Bryant, Clifton D. "Cockfighting: America's Invisible Sport." In *Down to Earth Sociology: Introductory Readings,* 7th ed., James M. Henslin, ed. New York: Free Press, 1993:211–224.

Bullard, Robert D., ed. *Unequal Protection: Environmental Justice and Communities of Color.* San Francisco: Sierra Club, 1994.

Bumiller, Elisabeth. "First Comes Marriage—Then, Maybe, Love." In *Marriage and Family in a Changing Society,* 4th ed., James M. Henslin, ed. New York: Free Press, 1992:120–125.

Bumiller, Elisabeth. "Weekend Excursion: In Amish Land, Witnesses to Old and New." *New York Times,* June 26, 1998.

Bumpass, Larry L., James A. Sweet, and Andrew Cherlin. "The Role of Cohabitation in Declining Rates of Marriage." *Journal of Marriage and the Family, 53,* November 1991:913–927.

Burgess, Ernest W. "The Growth of the City: An Introduction to a Research Project." In *The City,* Robert E. Park, Ernest W. Burgess, and Roderick D. McKenzie, eds. Chicago: University of Chicago Press, 1925:47–62.

Burgess, Ernest W., and Harvey J. Locke. *The Family: From Institution to Companionship.* New York: American Book, 1945.

Burnham, Walter Dean. *Democracy in the Making: American Government and Politics.* Englewood Cliffs, N.J.: Prentice Hall, 1983.

Bush, Diane Mitsch, and Robert G. Simmons. "Socialization Processes over the Life Course." In *Social Psychology: Sociological Perspectives,* Morris Rosenberg and Ralph H. Turner, eds. New Brunswick, N.J.: Transaction Books, 1990:133–164.

Butler, Robert N. *Why Survive? Being Old in America.* New York: Harper & Row, 1975.

Butler, Robert N. "Ageism: Another Form of Bigotry." *Gerontologist, 9,* Winter 1980:243–246.

Buttel, Frederick H. "New Directions in Environmental Sociology." *Annual Review of Sociology, 13,* W. Richard Scott and James F. Short, Jr., eds. Palo Alto, Calif.: Annual Reviews, 1987:465–488.

Butterfield, Fox. "Number in Prison Population Grows Despite Crime Reduction." *New York Times,* August 10, 2000.

Canavan, Margaret M., Walter J. Meyer III, and Deborah C. Higgs. "The Female Experience of Sibling Incest." *Journal of Marital and Family Therapy, 18,* 2, 1992:129–142.

Cardoso, Fernando Henrique. "Dependent Capitalist Development in Latin America." *New Left Review, 74,* July–August 1972:83–95.

Carlson, Lewis H., and George A. Colburn. *In Their Place: White America Defines Her Minorities, 1850–1950.* New York: Wiley, 1972.

Carpenter, Betsy. "Redwood Radicals." *U.S. News & World Report, 109,* 11, September 17, 1990:50–51.

Carr, Deborah, Carol D. Ryff, Burton Singer, and William J. Magee. "Bringing the 'Life' Back into Life Course Research: A 'Person-Centered' Approach to Studying the Life Course." Paper presented at the 1995 meetings of the American Sociological Association.

Carrasquillo, Hector. "The Puerto Rican Family." In *Minority Families in the United States: A Multicultural Perspective,* Ronald L. Taylor, ed. Englewood Cliffs, N.J.: Prentice Hall, 1994:82–94.

Carrington, Tim. "Developed Nations Want Poor Countries to Succeed on Trade, But Not Too Much." *Wall Street Journal,* September 20, 1993:A10.

Cartwright, Dorwin, and Alvin Zander, eds. *Group Dynamics,* 3rd ed. Evanston, Ill.: Peterson, 1968.

Casper, Lynne M., and Martin O'Connell, "State Estimates of Organized Child Care Facilities." Annual meetings of the Population Association of America, March 1997, as contained in *Population Today, 25,* 5, May 1997:6.

Center for American Women and Politics, Eagleton Institute of Politics, Rutgers University, 2001.

Cerulo, Karen A., Janet M. Ruane, and Mary Chayko. "Technological Ties That Bind: Media-Generated Primary Groups." *Communication Research, 19,* 1, February 1992:109–129.

Chafetz, Janet Saltzman. *Gender Equity: An Integrated Theory of Stability and Change.* Newbury Park, Calif.: Sage, 1990.

Chafetz, Janet Saltzman, and Anthony Gary Dworkin. *Female Revolt: Women's Movements in World and Historical Perspective.* Totowa, N.J.: Rowman & Allanheld, 1986.

Chagnon, Napoleon A. *Yanomamo: The Fierce People,* 2nd ed. New York: Holt, Rinehart and Winston, 1977.

Chalkley, Kate. "Female Genital Mutilation: New Laws, Programs Try to End Practice." *Population Today, 25,* 10, October 1997:4–5.

Chambliss, William J. "The Saints and the Roughnecks." In *Down to Earth Sociology: Introductory Readings,* 11th ed. James M. Henslin, ed. New York: Free Press, 2001:257–271. First published in *Society, 11,* 1973.

Chandler, Tertius, and Gerald Fox. *3000 Years of Urban Growth.* New York: Academic Press, 1974.

Chandra, Vibha P. "Fragmented Identities: The Social Construction of Ethnicity, 1885–1947." Unpublished paper, 1993a.

Chandra, Vibha P. "The Present Moment of the Past: The Metamorphosis." Unpublished paper, 1993b.

Charlier, Marj. "Little Bighorn from the Indian Point of View." *Wall Street Journal,* September 15, 1992:A12.

Chavez, Linda. "Rainbow Collision." *New Republic,* November 19, 1990:14–16.

Chen, Edwin. "Twins Reared Apart: A Living Lab." *New York Times Magazine,* December 9, 1979:112.

Chen, Kathy. "China's Women Face Obstacles in Workplace." *Wall Street Journal,* August 28, 1995:B1, B5.

Chen, Kathy. "Chinese Are Going to Town as Growth of Cities Takes Off." *Wall Street Journal,* January 4, 1996: A1, A12.

Cherlin, Andrew. "Remarriage as an Incomplete Institution." In *Marriage and Family in a Changing Society,* 3rd ed., James M. Henslin, ed. New York: Free Press, 1989: 492–501.

Cherlin, Andrew, and Frank F. Furstenberg, Jr. "The American Family in the Year 2000." In *Down to Earth Sociology,* 5th ed., James M. Henslin, ed. New York: Free Press, 1988:325–331.

Chesnais, Jean-Claude. "The Demographic Sunset of the West?" *Population Today, 25,* 1, January 1997:4–5.

Chodorow, Nancy J. "What Is the Relation between Psychoanalytic Feminism and the Psychoanalytic Psychology of Women?" In *Theoretical Perspectives on Sexual Difference,* Deborah L. Rhode, ed. New Haven, Conn.: Yale University Press, 1990:114–130.

Clair, Jeffrey Michael, David A. Karp, and William C. Yoels. *Experiencing the Life Cycle: A Social Psychology of Aging,* 2nd ed. Springfield, Ill.: Thomas, 1993.

Clark, Candace. "Sympathy in Everyday Life." In *Down to Earth Sociology: Introductory Readings,* 6th ed., James M. Henslin, ed. New York: Free Press, 1991:193–203.

Clingempeel, W. Glenn, and N. Dickon Repucci. "Joint Custody after Divorce: Major Issues and Goals for Research." *Psychological Bulletin, 9,* 1982:102–127.

Cloward, Richard A., and Lloyd E. Ohlin. *Delinquency and Opportunity: A Theory of Delinquent Gangs.* New York: Free Press, 1960.

Cloud, John. "For Better or Worse." *Time,* October 26, 1998: 43–44.

Cnaan, Ram A. "Neighborhood-Representing Organizations: How Democratic Are They?" *Social Science Review,* December 1991:614–634.

Cohen, Adam. "The Great American Welfare Lab." *Time,* April 21, 1997:74–76, 78.

Cohen, Joel E. "How Many People Can the Earth Support?" *Population Today,* January 1996:4–5.

Coleman, James William. *The Criminal Elite: The Sociology of White Collar Crime.* New York: St. Martin's Press, 1989.

Coleman, James, and Thomas Hoffer. *Public and Private Schools: The Impact of Communities.* New York: Basic Books, 1987.

Collins, Randall. *Conflict Sociology: Toward an Explanatory Science.* New York: Academic Press, 1974.

Collins, Randall. *The Credential Society: An Historical Sociology of Education.* New York: Academic Press, 1979.

Collins, Randall. *Theoretical Sociology.* San Diego, Calif.: Harcourt Brace Jovanovich, 1988.

Cooley, Charles Horton. *Human Nature and the Social Order.* New York: Scribner's, 1902.

Cooley, Charles Horton. *Social Organization.* New York: Scribner's, 1909.

Cooley, Charles Horton. *Social Organization.* New York: Schocken, 1962.

Cooper, Kenneth J. "New Focus Sought in National High School Exams: NEH Backs Approach Used in Europe and Japan to Assess Knowledge Rather than Aptitude." *Washington Post,* May 20, 1991:A7.

Corbett, Thomas. "Welfare Reform in the 104th Congress: Goals, Options, and Tradeoffs." *Focus, 17,* 1, Summer 1995:29–31.

Corbett, Thomas. "Poverty: Improving the Measure After Thirty Years, A Conference." *Focus, 20,* 2, Spring 1999:51–55.

Cose, Ellis. "The Good News About Black America." *Newsweek,* June 7, 1999:29–40.

Cose, Ellis. "What's White Anyway?" *Newsweek,* September 18, 2000:64–65.

Coser, Lewis A. *Masters of Sociological Thought: Ideas in Historical and Social Context,* 2nd ed. New York: Harcourt Brace Jovanovich, 1977.

Cottin, Lou. *Elders in Rebellion: A Guide to Senior Activism.* Garden City, N.Y.: Anchor Doubleday, 1979.

Couch, Carl J. *Social Processes and Relationships: A Formal Approach.* Dix Hills, N.Y.: General Hall, 1989.

Courtney, Kelly. "Two Sides of the Environmental Movement: Radical Earth First! and the Sierra Club." Paper presented at the 1995 meetings of the American Sociological Association.

Cousins, Albert N., and Hans Nagpaul. *Urban Man and Society: A Reader in Urban Sociology.* New York: McGraw-Hill, 1970.

Cowen, Emory L., Judah Landes, and Donald E. Schaet. "The Effects of Mild Frustration on the Expression of Prejudiced Attitudes." *Journal of Abnormal and Social Psychology,* January 1959:33–38.

Cowgill, Donald. "The Aging of Populations and Societies." *Annals of the American Academy of Political and Social Science, 415,* 1974:1–18.

Cowley, Joyce. *Pioneers of Women's Liberation.* New York: Merit, 1969.

Croal, N'Gai, and Jane Hughes. "Lara Croft, the Bit Girl." *Newsweek,* November 10, 1997:82, 86.

Crosbie, Paul V., ed. *Interaction in Small Groups.* New York: Macmillan, 1975.

Crosette, Barbara. "Caste May Be India's Moral Achilles' Heel." *New York Times,* October 20, 1996, electronic version.

Crossen, Cynthia. *Wall Street Journal,* November 14, 1991:A1, A7.

Croteau, David. *Politics and the Class Divide: Working People and the Middle-Class Left.* Philadelphia: Temple University Press, 1995.

Cumming, Elaine. "Further Thoughts on the Theory of Disengagement." In *Aging in America: Readings in Social Gerontology,* Cary S. Kart and Barbara B. Manard, eds. Sherman Oaks, Calif.: Alfred Publishing, 1976:19–41.

Cumming, Elaine, and William E. Henry. *Growing Old: The Process of Disengagement.* New York: Basic Books, 1961.

Curwin, E. Cecil, and Gudmond Hart. *Plough and Pasture.* New York: Collier Books, 1961.

Cushman, John H., Jr. "Industries Press Plan for Credits in Emissions Control." *New York Times,* January 3, 1999.

Dabbs, James M., Jr., and Robin Morris. "Testosterone, Social Class, and Antisocial Behavior in a Sample of 4,462 Men." *Psychological Science, 1,* 3, May 1990:209–211.

Dahl, Robert A. *Who Governs?* New Haven, Conn.: Yale University Press, 1961.

Dahl, Robert A. *Dilemmas of Pluralist Democracy: Autonomy vs. Control.* New Haven, Conn.: Yale University Press, 1982.

Dahrendorf, Ralf. *Class and Class Conflict in Industrial Society.* Palo Alto, Calif.: Stanford University Press, 1959.

Darden, Christoper. *Contempt.* New York: HarperCollins, 1997.

Darley, John M., and Bibb Latané. "Bystander Intervention in Emergencies: Diffusion of Responsibility." *Journal of Personality and Social Psychology, 8,* 4, 1968.377–383.

Davis, Ann. "Artificial Reproduction Arrangers Are Ruled Child's Legal Parents." *Wall Street Journal,* March 11, 1998a:B2.

Davis, Ann. "High-Tech Births Spawn Legal Riddles." *Wall Street Journal,* January 26, 1998b:B1.

Davis, Fred. "The Cabdriver and His Fare: Facets of a Fleeting Relationship." *American Journal of Sociology, 65,* September 1959:158–165.

Davis, Kingsley. "Extreme Social Isolation of a Child." *American Journal of Sociology, 45,* 4 Jan. 1940:554–565.

Davis, Kingsley. "Extreme Isolation." In *Down to Earth Sociology: Introductory Readings,* 11th ed., James M. Henslin, ed. New York: Free Press, 11th ed., 2001: 129–137.

Davis, Kingsley, and Wilbert E. Moore. "Reply to Tumin." *American Sociological Review, 18,* 1953:394–396.

Davis, Kingsley, and Wilbert E. Moore. "Some Principles of Stratification." *American Sociological Review, 10,* 1945:242–249.

Davis, L. J. "Medscam." In *Deviant Behavior 96/97*, Lawrence M. Salinger, ed. Guilford, Conn.: Dushkin, 1996:93–97.

Davis, Nancy J., and Robert V. Robinson. "Class Identification of Men and Women in the 1970s and 1980s." *American Sociological Review, 53,* February 1988:103–112.

Deck, Leland P. "Buying Brains by the Inch." *Journal of the College and University Personnel Association, 19,* 1968:33–37.

Deegan, Mary Jo. "W. E. B. Du Bois and the Women of Hull-House, 1895–1899." *American Sociologist,* Winter 1988:301–311.

DeMause, Lloyd. "Our Forebears Made Childhood a Nightmare." *Psychology Today, 8,* 11, April 1975:85–88.

"Democracy and Technology." *The Economist,* June 17, 1995:21–23.

Denney, Nancy W., and David Quadagno. *Human Sexuality,* 2nd ed. St. Louis: Mosby Year Book, 1992.

Denzin, Norman K. *Interpretive Ethnography: Ethnographic Practices for the Twenty-first Century.* Thousand Oaks, Calif: Sage, 1997.

DePalma, Anthony. "Rare in Ivy League: Women Who Work as Full Professors." *New York Times,* January 24, 1993:1, 23.

DeParle, Jason. "Bold Effort Leaves Much Unchanged for the Poor." *New York Times,* December 30, 1999.

Dervarics, Charles. "Is Welfare Reform Reforming Welfare?" *Population Today, 26,* 10, October 1998:1–2.

Diamond, Edwin, and Robert A. Silverman. *White House to Your House: Media and Politics in Virtual America.* Cambridge, Mass.: MIT Press, 1995.

Diamond, Milton, and Keith Sigmundson. "Sex Reassignment at Birth: Long-term Review and Clinical Implications." *Archives of Pediatric and Adolescent Medicine, 151,* March 1997:298–304.

Diekmann, Andreas, and Henrietta Engelhardt. "The Social Inheritance of Divorce: Effects of Parent's Family Type in Postwar Germany." *American Sociological Review, 64,* December 1999:783–793.

Dixon, Celvia Stovall, and Kathryn D. Rettig. "An Examination of Income Adequacy for Single Women Two Years after Divorce." *Journal of Divorce and Remarriage, 22,* 1–2, 1994:55–71.

Doane, Ashley W., Jr. "Bringing the Majority Back In: Towards a Sociology of Dominant Group Ethnicity." Paper presented at the annual meetings of the Society for the Study of Social Problems, 1993.

Doane, Ashley W., Jr. "Dominant Group Ethnic Identity in the United States: The Role of 'Hidden' Ethnicity in Intergroup Relations." *The Sociological Quarterly, 38,* 3, Summer 1997:375–397.

Dobash, Russell P., R. Emerson Dobash, Margo Wilson, and Martin Daly. "The Myth of Sexual Symmetry in Marital Violence." *Social Problems, 39,* 1, February 1992:71–91.

Dobash, Russell P., R. Emerson Dobash, Margo Wilson, and Martin Daly. "Marital Violence Is Not Symmetrical: A Response to Campbell." *SSSP Newsletter, 24,* 3, Fall 1993:26–30.

Dobriner, William M. "The Football Team as Social Structure and Social System." In *Social Structures and Systems: A Sociological Overview.* Pacific Palisades, Calif.: Goodyear, 1969a:116–120.

Dobriner, William M. *Social Structures and Systems.* Pacific Palisades, Calif.: Goodyear, 1969b.

Dobyns, Henry F. *Their Numbers Became Thinned: Native American Population Dynamics in Eastern North America.* Knoxville: University of Tennessee Press, 1983.

Dollard, John, et al. *Frustration and Aggression.* New Haven, Conn.: Yale University Press, 1939.

Domhoff, G. William. *Who Rules America?* Englewood Cliffs, N.J.: Prentice Hall, 1967.

Domhoff, G. William. *Who Rules America Now? A View of the '80s.* Englewood Cliffs, N.J.: Prentice Hall, 1983.

Domhoff, G. William. *The Power Elite and the State: How Policy Is Made in America.* New York: Aldine de Gruyter, 1990.

Domhoff, G. William. *Who Rules America?: Power and Politics in the Year 2000,* 3rd ed. Mountain View, Calif.: Mayfield Publishing, 1998.

Domhoff, G. William. "The Bohemian Grove and Other Retreats." In *Down to Earth Sociology: Introductory Readings,* 10th ed., James M. Henslin, ed. New York: Free Press, 1999:391–403.

Dove, Adrian. "Soul Folk 'Chitling' Test or the Dove Counterbalance Intelligence Test." no date. (mimeo)

Du Bois, W. E. B. *The Souls of Black Folk: Essays and Sketches.* Chicago: McClurg, 1903.

Du Bois, W. E. B. *Black Reconstruction in America: An Essay Toward a History of the Part Which Black Folk Played in the Attempt to Reconstruct Democracy in America, 1860–1880.* New York: Cass, 1966. First published in 1935.

Du Bois, W. E. B. *The Autobiography of W. E. B. Du Bois: A Soliloquy on Viewing My Life from the Last Decade of Its First Century.* New York: International Press, 1968.

Du Bois, W. E. B. *Black Reconstruction in America, 1860–1889.* New York: Atheneum, 1992. First published in 1935.

Dudenhefer, Paul. "Poverty in the Rural United States." *Focus, 15,* 1, Spring 1993:37–46.

Dugger, Celia W. "Wedding Vows Bind Old World and New." *New York Times,* July 20, 1998.

Dunlap, Riley E., and William R. Catton, Jr. "Environmental Sociology." *Annual Review of Sociology, 5,* 1979:243–273.

Dunlap, Riley E., and William R. Catton, Jr. "What Environmental Sociologists Have in Common Whether Concerned with 'Built' or 'Natural' Environments." *Sociological Inquiry, 53,* 2/3, 1983:113–135.

Durbin, Stefanie. "Mexico." *Population Today,* July–August, 1995:7.

Durkheim, Emile. *The Division of Labor in Society.* George Simpson, trans. New York: Free Press, 1933. First published in 1893.

Durkheim, Emile. *The Rules of Sociological Method.* Sarah A. Solovay and John H. Mueller, trans.; George E. G. Catlin, ed. New York: Free Press, 1964. First published in 1893.

Durkheim, Emile. *The Elementary Forms of the Religious Life.* New York: Free Press, 1965. First published in 1912.

Durkheim, Emile. *Suicide: A Study in Sociology.* John A. Spaulding and George Simpson, trans. New York: Free Press, 1966. First published in 1897.

Durning, Alan. "Cradles of Life." In *Social Problems 90/91,* LeRoy W. Barnes, ed. Guilford, Conn.: Dushkin, 1990:231–241.

Ebomoyi, Ehigie. "The Prevalence of Female Circumcision in Two Nigerian Communities." *Sex Roles, 17, 3/4,* 1987:139–151.

Eder, Klaus. "The Rise of Counter-culture Movements against Modernity: Nature as a New Field of Class Struggle." *Theory, Culture & Society, 7,* 1990:21–47.

Edgerton, Robert B. *Deviance: A Cross-Cultural Perspective.* Menlo Park, Calif.: Benjamin/Cummings, 1976.

Edgerton, Robert B. *Sick Societies: Challenging the Myth of Primitive Harmony.* New York: Free Press, 1992.

Egan, Timothy. "Many Seek Security in Private Communities." *New York Times,* September 3, 1995:1, 22.

"Egipto prohibir la ablación femenina y adoptar medidas contra infractores." *El Pais,* July 19, 1996:22.

"Egypt." *Population Today,* December 1998:7.

Ehrlich, Paul R., and Anne H. Ehrlich. *Population, Resources, and Environment: Issues in Human Ecology,* 2nd ed. San Francisco: Freeman, 1972.

Ehrlich, Paul R., and Anne H. Ehrlich. "Humanity at the Crossroads." *Stanford Magazine,* Spring–Summer 1978:20–23.

Ekman, Paul, Wallace V. Friesen, and John Bear. "The International Language of Gestures." *Psychology Today,* May 1984:64.

Elder, Glen H., Jr. "Age Differentiation and Life Course." *Annual Review of Sociology, 1,* 1975:165–190.

Emery, Gene. "Blacks Less Likely to Get Clot-Busting Treatments." Reuters, April 12, 2000.

Englund, Will, and Gary Cohn. "A Third World Dump for America's Ships." *Baltimore Sun,* December 9, 1997.

Epstein, Cynthia Fuchs. *Deceptive Distinctions: Sex, Gender, and the Social Order.* New Haven, Conn.: Yale University Press, 1988.

Erik, John. "China's Policy on Births." *New York Times,* January 3, 1982: IV, 19.

Ernst, Eldon G. "The Baptists." In *Encyclopedia of the American Religious Experience: Studies of Traditions and Movements,* Vol. 1, Charles H. Lippy and Peter W. Williams, eds. New York: Scribner's, 1988:555–577.

Escalante, Jaime, and Jack Dirmann. "The Jaime Escalante Math Program." *Journal of Negro Education, 59,* 3, Summer 1990:407–423.

Ezekiel, Raphael S. *The Racist Mind: Portraits of American Neo-Nazis and Klansmen.* New York: Viking, 1995.

Famighetti, Robert, ed. *The World Almanac and Book of Facts.* Mahwah, N.J.: 1999.

Faris, Robert E. L., and Warren Dunham. *Mental Disorders in Urban Areas.* Chicago: University of Chicago Press, 1939.

Farkas, George. *Human Capital or Cultural Capital?: Ethnicity and Poverty Groups in an Urban School District.* New York: Walter DeGruyter, 1996.

Farkas, George, Robert P. Grobe, Daniel Sheehan, and Yuan Shuan. "Cultural Resources and School Success: Gender, Ethnicity, and Poverty Groups within an Urban School District." *American Sociological Review, 55,* February 1990a:127–142.

Farkas, George, Daniel Sheehan, and Robert P. Grobe. "Coursework Mastery and School Success: Gender, Ethnicity, and Poverty Groups within an Urban School District." *American Educational Research Journal, 27,* 4, Winter 1990b:807–827.

Farney, Dennis. "They Hold the Cards, But After All, They Do Own the Casino." *Wall Street Journal,* February 5, 1998: A1, A6.

Faunce, William A. *Problems of an Industrial Society,* 2nd ed. New York: McGraw-Hill, 1981.

FBI Uniform Crime Reports. Washington, D.C.: U.S. Government Printing Office, published annually.

Feagin, Joe R., "Death by Discrimination?" *SSSP Newsletter,* Winter 1997:15–16.

Featherman, David L., and Robert M. Hauser. *Opportunity and Change.* New York: Academic Press, 1978.

Featherman, David L. "Opportunities Are Expanding." *Society, 13,* 1979:4–11.

Feldman, Saul D. "The Presentation of Shortness in Everyday Life—Height and Heightism in American Society: Toward a Sociology of Stature." Paper presented at the 1972 meetings of the American Sociological Association.

Felsenthal, Edward. "Justices' Ruling Further Defines Sex Harassment." *Wall Street Journal,* March 5, 1998:B1, B2.

Ferguson, Thomas. *Golden Rule.* Chicago: University of Chicago Press, 1995.

Feshbach, Murray. "Russia's Farms, Too Poisoned for the Plow." *Wall Street Journal,* May 14, 1992:A14.

Feshbach, Murray, and Alfred Friendly, Jr. *Ecocide in the USSR: Health and Nature Under Siege.* New York: Basic Books, 1992.

Fialka, John J. "Demands on New Orleans's 'Big Charity' Hospital Are Symptomatic of U.S. Health-Care Problem." *Wall Street Journal,* June 22, 1993:A18.

Filkins, Dexter. "61 Slain as Violence Rocks the Caste System in India." *Seattle Times,* December 3, 1997, electronic version.

Finckenauer, James O., and Elin J. Waring. *Russian Mafia in America: Immigration, Culture, and Crime.* Boston: Northeastern University Press, 1999.

Fineman, Howard. "Pressing the Flesh Online." *Newsweek,* September 20, 1999:50–53.

Finke, Roger. *The Churching of America, 1776–1990: Winners and Losers in Our Religious Economy.* New Brunswick, N.J.: Rutgers University Press, 1992.

Fischer, Claude S. *The Urban Experience.* New York: Harcourt, 1976.

Fisher, Sue. *In the Patient's Best Interest: Women and the Politics of Medical Decisions.* New Brunswick, N.J.: Rutgers University Press, 1986.

Flanagan, William G. *Urban Sociology: Images and Structure.* Boston: Allyn and Bacon, 1990.

Flavell, John H., et al. *The Development of Role-Taking and Communication Skills in Children.* New York: Wiley, 1968.

Fletcher, June. "Address Envy: Fudging to Get the Best." *Wall Street Journal,* April 25, 1997:B10.

Foote, Donna. "And Baby Makes One." *Newsweek,* February 2, 1998:68–69.

Foote, Jennifer. "Trying to Take Back the Planet." *Newsweek, 115,* 6, February 5, 1990:20–25.

Form, William. "Comparative Industrial Sociology and the Convergence Hypothesis." In *Annual Review of Sociology, 5,* 1, 1979, Alex Inkeles, James Coleman, and Ralph H. Turner, eds.

Foster, J. Todd. "Russian Mafia Too Savvy for Deed." *The Oregonian,* March 21, 1998.

Fox, Elaine, and George E. Arquitt. "The VFW and the 'Iron Law of Oligarchy.'" In *Down to Earth Sociology: Introductory Readings,* 4th ed., James M. Henslin, ed. New York: Free Press, 1985:147–155.

Freese, Jeremy, Brian Powell, and Lala Carr Steelman. "Rebel Without a Cause or Effect: Birth Order and Social Attitudes." *American Sociological Review, 64,* April 1999:207–231.

Freudenburg, William R., and Robert Gramling. "The Emergence of Environmental Sociology: Contributions of Riley E. Dunlap and William R. Catton, Jr." *Sociological Inquiry, 59,* 4, November 1989:439–452.

Friedl, Ernestine. "Society and Sex Roles." In *Conformity and Conflict: Readings in Cultural Anthropology.* James P. Spradley and David W. McCurdy, eds. Glenview, Ill.: Scott, Foresman, 1990:229–238.

Frisbie, W. Parker, and John D. Kasarda. "Spatial Processes." In *Handbook of Sociology,* Neil J. Smelser, ed. Newbury Park, Calif.: Sage, 1988:629–666.

Fuller, Rex, and Richard Schoenberger. "The Gender Salary Gap: Do Academic Achievement, Internship Experience, and College Major Make a Difference?" *Social Science Quarterly, 72,* 4, December 1991:715–726.

Furstenberg, Frank F., Jr., and Kathleen Mullan Harris. "The Disappearing American Father? Divorce and the Waning Significance of Biological Fatherhood." In *The Changing American Family: Sociological and Demographic Perspectives,* Scott J. South and Stewart E. Tolnay, eds. Boulder, Colo.: Westview Press, 1992:197–223.

Furtado, Celso. *The Economic Growth of Brazil: A Survey from Colonial to Modern Times.* Westport, Conn.: Greenwood Press, 1984.

Galbraith, John Kenneth. *The Nature of Mass Poverty.* Cambridge, Mass.: Harvard University Press, 1979.

Galinsky, Ellen, James T. Bond, and Dana E. Friedman. *The Changing Workforce: Highlights of the National Study.* New York: Families and Work Institute, 1993.

Gallup, George, Jr. *The Gallup Poll: Public Opinion 1989.* Wilmington, Del.: Scholarly Resources, 1990.

Gallup Opinion Index. *Religion in America, 1987.* Report 259, April 1987.

Gans, Herbert J. *The Urban Villagers.* New York: Free Press, 1962.

Gans, Herbert J. *People and Plans: Essays on Urban Problems and Solutions.* New York: Basic, 1968.

Gans, Herbert J. "Urbanism and Suburbanism." In *Urban Man and Society: A Reader in Urban Ecology,* Albert N. Cousins and Hans Nagpaul, eds. New York: Knopf, 1970:157–164.

Gans, Herbert J. *People, Plans, and Policies: Essays on Poverty, Racism, and Other National Urban Problems.* New York: Columbia University Press, 1991.

Garbarino, Merwin S. *American Indian Heritage.* Boston: Little, Brown, 1976.

Garfinkel, Harold. "Conditions of Successful Degradation Ceremonies." *American Journal of Sociology, 61,* 2, March 1956:420–424.

Garfinkel, Harold. *Studies in Ethnomethodology.* Englewood Cliffs, N.J.: Prentice Hall, 1967.

Garreau, Joel. *Edge City: Life on the New Frontier.* New York: Doubleday, 1992.

Gatewood, Willard B. *Aristocrats of Color: The Black Elite, 1880–1920.* Bloomington: Indiana University Press, 1990.

Gelles, Richard J. "The Myth of Battered Husbands and New Facts about Family Violence." In *Social Problems 80–81,* Robert L. David, ed. Guilford, Conn.: Dushkin, 1980.

Gerbner, George. "Casting the American Scene." Screen Actors Guild, 1998.

Gerson, Kathleen. *Hard Choices: How Women Decide about Work, Career, and Motherhood.* Berkeley: University of California Press, 1985.

Gerth, H. H., and C. Wright Mills. *From Max Weber: Essays in Sociology.* New York: Galaxy, 1958.

Gilbert, Dennis L. *The American Class Structure: In an Age of Growing Inequality.* Belmont, Calif.: Wadsworth Publishing, 1997.

Gillborn, David. "Citizenship, 'Race' and the Hidden Curriculum." *International Studies in the Sociology of Education, 2,* 1, 1992:57–73.

Gilman, Charlotte Perkins. *The Man-Made World or, Our Androcentric Culture.* New York: Johnson Reprint, 1971. First published in 1911.

Gilmore, David D. *Manhood in the Making: Cultural Concepts of Masculinity.* New Haven, Conn.: Yale University Press, 1990.

Gitlin, Todd. *The Twilight of Common Dreams: Why America Is Wracked by Culture Wars.* New York: Metropolitan Books, 1997.

Giuliani, Rudolph W. "The Welfare Reform Battle Isn't Over Yet." *The Wall Street Journal Interactive Edition,* February 3, 1999.

Glenn, Evelyn Nakano. "Chinese American Families." In *Minority Families in the United States: A Multicultural Perspective,* Ronald L. Taylor, ed. Englewood Cliffs, N.J.: Prentice Hall, 1994:115–145.

Glick, Paul C., and S. Lin. "More Young Adults Are Living with Their Parents: Who Are They?" *Journal of Marriage and Family, 48,* 1986:107–112.

Glotz, Peter. "Forward to Europe." *Dissent, 33,* 3, Summer 1986:327–339. (As quoted in Harrison and Bluestone 1988.)

Glueck, Sheldon, and Eleanor Glueck. *Physique and Delinquency.* New York: Harper & Row, 1956.

Goble, Paul. "Russia: Analysis from Washington—Organized Crime's Three Faces." Radio Free Europe, November 5, 1996.

Goffman, Erving. *Asylums: Essays on the Social Situation of Mental Patients and Other Inmates.* Chicago: Aldine, 1961.

Goffman, Erving. *Stigma.* Englewood Cliffs, N.J.: Prentice Hall, 1963.

Gold, Ray. "Janitors versus Tenants: A Status–Income Dilemma." *American Journal of Sociology, 58,* 1952:486–493.

Goldberg, Carey. "Most Get Work After Welfare, Studies Suggest." *New York Times,* April 17, 1999.

Goldberg, Susan, and Michael Lewis. "Play Behavior in the Year-Old Infant: Early Sex Differences." *Child Development, 40,* March 1969:21–31.

Goldman, Kevin. "Seniors Get Little Respect on Madison Avenue." *Wall Street Journal,* September 20, 1993:B6.

Goleman, Daniel. "Spacing of Siblings Strongly Linked to Success in Life." *New York Times,* May 28, 1985:C1, C4.

Goleman, Daniel. "Pollsters Enlist Psychologists in Quest for Unbiased Results." *New York Times,* September 7, 1993:C1, C11.

Gordon, David M. "Class and the Economics of Crime." *The Review of Radical Political Economics, 3,* Summer 1971:51–57.

Gorman, Peter. "A People at Risk: Vanishing Tribes of South America." *The World & I,* December 1991:678–689.

Gottfredson, Michael R., and Travis Hirschi. *A General Theory of Crime.* Stanford, Calif.: Stanford University Press, 1990.

Gottschalk, Peter, Sara McLanahan, and Gary Sandefur, "The Dynamics and Intergenerational Transmission of Poverty and Welfare Participation." In *Confronting Poverty: Prescriptions for Change,* Sheldon H. Danziger, Gary D. Sandefur, and Daniel H. Weinberg, eds. Cambridge, Mass.: Harvard University Press, 1994.

Gourevitch, Philip. "After the Genocide." *New Yorker,* December 18, 1995:78–94.

Gourevitch, Philip. *We Wish to Inform You That Tomorrow We Will Be Killed with Our Families: Stories from Rwanda.* New York: Farrar, Straus, and Giroux, 1998.

Greeley, Andrew M. "The Protestant Ethic: Time for a Moratorium." *Sociological Analysis, 25,* Spring 1964:20–33.

Greeley, Andrew M., and Michael Hout. "Americans' Increasing Belief in Life After Death: Religious Competition and Acculturation." *American Sociological Review, 64,* December 1999:813–835.

Greenhalgh, Susan, and Jiali Li. "Engendering Reproductive Policy and Practice in Peasant China: For a Feminist Demography of Reproduction." *Signs, 20,* 3, Spring 1995:601–640.

Gross, Jane. "In the Quest for the Perfect Look, More Girls Choose the Scalpel." *New York Times,* November 29, 1998.

Grossman, Laurie. "Desolate Housing Project Provides Profit and Lessons." *Wall Street Journal,* April 5, 1995: B1, B7.

Grossman, Lawrence K. *The Electronic Republic: Reshaping Democracy in the Information Age.* New York: Viking, 1995.

Guha, Ramachandra. "Radical American Environmentalism and Wilderness Preservation: A Third World Critique." *Environmental Ethics, 11,* 1, Spring 1989:71–83.

Gupta, Giri Raj. "Love, Arranged Marriage, and the Indian Social Structure." In *Cross-Cultural Perspectives of Mate Selection and Marriage,* George Kurian, ed. Westport, Conn.: Greenwood Press, 1979.

Haas, Jack. "Binging: Educational Control among High-Steel Iron Workers." *American Behavioral Scientist, 16,* 1972: 27–34.

Hacker, Helen Mayer. "Women as a Minority Group." *Social Forces, 30,* October 1951:60–69.

Hall, Edward T. *The Silent Language.* New York: Doubleday, 1959.

Hall, Edward T. *The Hidden Dimension.* Garden City, N.Y.: Anchor Books, 1969.

Hall, G. Stanley. *Adolescence: Its Psychology and Its Relations to Physiology, Anthropology, Sociology, Sex, Crime, Religion, and Education.* New York: Appleton, 1904.

Hamermesh, Daniel S., and Jeff E. Biddle. "Beauty and the Labor Market." *American Economic Review, 84,* 5, December 1994:1174–1195.

Harlow, Harry F., and Margaret K. Harlow. "Social Deprivation in Monkeys." *Scientific American, 207,* 1962:137–147.

Harlow, Harry F., and Margaret K. Harlow. "The Affectional Systems." In *Behavior of Nonhuman Primates: Modern Research Trends,* Vol. 2, Allan M. Schrier, Harry F. Harlow, and Fred Stollnitz, eds. New York: Academic Press, 1965:287–334.

Harper, Charles L. "Time to Phase Out Fossil Fuels?" *Wall Street Journal,* December 26, 1995:A6.

Harrington, Michael. *The Other America: Poverty in the United States.* New York: Macmillan, 1962.

Harrington, Michael. *The Vast Majority: A Journey to the World's Poor.* New York: Simon & Schuster, 1977.

Harris, Chauncey, and Edward Ullman. "The Nature of Cities." *Annals of the American Academy of Political and Social Science, 242,* 1945:7–17.

Harris, Chauncey D. "The Nature of Cities and Urban Geography in the Last Half Century." *Urban Geography, 18,* 1997:15–35.

Harris, Diana K. *The Sociology of Aging.* New York: Harper, 1990.

Harris, Marvin. "Why Men Dominate Women." *New York Times Magazine,* November 13, 1977:46, 115, 117–123.

Harrison, Bennett, and Barry Bluestone. *The Great U-Turn: Corporate Restructuring and the Polarizing of America.* New York: Basic Books, 1988.

Harrison, Paul. *Inside the Third World: The Anatomy of Poverty,* 3rd ed. London: Penguin Books, 1993.

Hart, Charles W. M., and Arnold R. Pilling. *The Tiwi of North Australia.* New York: Holt, Rinehart, and Winston, 1970.

Hart, Paul. "Groupthink, Risk-Taking and Recklessness: Quality of Process and Outcome in Policy Decision Making." *Politics and the Individual, 1,* 1, 1991:67–90.

Hartley, Eugene. *Problems in Prejudice.* New York: King's Crown Press, 1946.

Haslick, Leonard. *Gerontologist, 14,* 1974:37–45.

Haub, Carl. "New UN Projections Depict a Variety of Demographic Futures." *Population Today, 25,* 4, April 1997:1–3.

Haub, Carl, and Diana Cornelius. "World Population Data Sheet." Washington, D.C.: Population Reference Bureau, 2000.

Haub, Carl, and Nancy Yinger. "The U.N. Long-Range Population Projections: What They Tell Us." Washington, D.C.: Population Reference Bureau, 1994.

Hauser, Philip, and Leo Schnore, eds. *The Study of Urbanization.* New York: Wiley, 1965.

Hauser, Robert M., Howard F. Taylor, and Troy Duster. "The Bell Curve." *Contemporary Sociology, 24,* March 1995:149–161.

Hawley, Amos H. *Urban Society: An Ecological Approach.* New York: Wiley, 1981.

Haynes, Richard M., and Donald M. Chalker. "World Class Schools." *American School Board Journal,* May 1997:20, 22–25.

Heckert, D. Alex, Thomas C. Nowak, and Kay A. Snyder. "The Impact of Husbands' and Wives' Relative Earnings on Marital Dissolution." Paper presented at the 1995 meetings of the American Sociological Association.

Heilbrun, Alfred B. "Differentiation of Death-Row Murderers and Life-Sentence Murderers by Antisociality and Intelligence Measures." *Journal of Personality Assessment, 64,* 1990:617–627.

Hellinger, Daniel, and Dennis R. Judd. *The Democratic Façade.* Pacific Grove, Calif.: Brooks/Cole, 1991.

Henley, Nancy, Mykol Hamilton, and Barrie Thorne. "Womanspeak and Manspeak." In *Beyond Sex Roles,* Alice G. Sargent, ed. St. Paul, Minn.: West, 1985.

Henslin, James M. *Introducing Sociology: Toward Understanding Life in Society.* New York: Free Press, 1975.

Henslin, James M. "Trust and Cabbies." In *Down to Earth Sociology: Introductory Readings,* 7th ed., James M. Henslin, ed. New York: Free Press, 1993:183–196.

Henslin, James M. *Social Problems,* 5th ed. Upper Saddle River, N.J.: Prentice Hall, 2000.

Henslin, James M. "On Becoming Male: Reflections of a Sociologist on Childhood and Early Socialization." In *Down to Earth Sociology: Introductory Readings,* 11th ed. James M. Henslin, ed. New York: Free Press, 2001:138–148.

Henslin, James M. "The Survivors of the F-227." In *Down to Earth Sociology: Introductory Readings,* 11th ed. James M. Henslin, ed. New York: Free Press, 2001:238–246.

Henslin, James M., and Mae A. Biggs. "Dramaturgical Desexualization: The Sociology of the Vaginal Examination." In *Studies in the Sociology of Sex,* James M. Henslin, ed. New York: Appleton-Century-Crofts, 1971:243–272.

Henslin, James M., and Mae A. Biggs. "Behavior in Pubic Places: The Sociology of the Vaginal Examination." In *Down to Earth Sociology: Introductory Readings,* 11th ed. James M. Henslin, ed. New York: Free Press, 2001:193–204.

Hentoff, Nat. "Fifth Grade Freedom Fighters." *Washington Post,* August 1, 1998:A15.

Hewitt Associates, *Summary of Work and Family Benefits Report.* Lincolnshire, Ill.: Hewitt Associates, 1995.

Hibbert, Christopher. *The Roots of Evil: A Social History of Crime and Punishment.* New York: Minerva, 1963.

Higginbotham, Elizabeth, and Lynn Weber. "Moving with Kin and Community: Upward Social Mobility for Black and White Women." *Gender and Society, 6,* 3, September 1992:416–440.

Higley, Stephen. "The U.S. Upper Class." In *Down to Earth Sociology: Introductory Readings,* 11th edition, James M. Henslin, ed. New York: The Free Press, 2001:338–349.

Hilliard, Asa, III. "Do We Have the *Will* to Educate All Children?" *Educational Leadership, 49,* September 1991:31–36.

Hiltz, Starr Roxanne. "Widowhood." In *Marriage and Family in a Changing Society,* 3rd ed., James M. Henslin, ed. New York: Free Press, 1989:521–531.

Hippler, Fritz. Interview in a television documentary with Bill Moyers in *Propaganda,* in the series "Walk through the 20th Century," 1987.

Hirschi, Travis. *Causes of Delinquency.* Berkeley: University of California Press, 1969.

Hochschild, Arlie Russell. "The Sociology of Feeling and Emotion: Selected Possibilities." In *Another Voice: Feminist Perspectives on Social Life and Social Science,* Marcia Millman and Rosabeth Moss Kanter, eds. Garden City, N.Y.: Anchor Books, 1975.

Hochschild, Arlie. *The Second Shift: Working Parents and the Revolution at Home.* New York: Viking, 1989.

Hochschild, Arlie. Note to the Author. 1991.

Hogan, Phyllis. "1990 Data on Interracial Households." Unpublished Paper, July 1994.

Holtzman, Abraham. *The Townsend Movement: A Political Study.* New York: Bookman, 1963.

Homblin, Dora Jane. *The First Cities.* Boston: Little, Brown, Time-Life Books, 1973.

Hornblower, Margot. "The Skin Trade." *Time,* June 21, 1993:45–51.

Horowitz, Ruth. *Honor and the American Dream: Culture and Identity in a Chicano Community.* New Brunswick, N.J.: Rutgers University Press, 1983.

Horowitz, Ruth. "Community Tolerance of Gang Violence." *Social Problems, 34,* 5, December 1987:437–450.

Horwitz, Tony. "Dinka Tribes Made Slaves in Sudan's Civil War." *Wall Street Journal,* April 11, 1989:A19.

Hostetler, John A. *Amish Society,* 3rd ed. Baltimore: Johns Hopkins University Press, 1980.

Houtman, Dick. "What Exactly Is a 'Social Class'?: On the Economic Liberalism and Cultural Conservatism of the 'Working Class.'" Paper presented at the 1995 meetings of the American Sociological Association.

Howells, Lloyd T., and Selwyn W. Becker. "Seating Arrangement and Leadership Emergence." *Journal of Abnormal and Social Psychology, 64,* February 1962:148–150.

Hoyt, Homer. *The Structure and Growth of Residential Neighborhoods in American Cities.* Washington, D.C.: Federal Housing Administration, 1939.

Hoyt, Homer. "Recent Distortions of the Classical Models of Urban Structure." In *Internal Structure of the City: Readings on Space and Environment,* Larry S. Bourne, ed. New York: Oxford University Press, 1971:84–96.

Hsu, Francis L. K. *The Challenge of the American Dream: The Chinese in the United States.* Belmont, Calif.: Wadsworth, 1971.

Huber, Joan, and William H. Form. *Income and Ideology.* New York: Free Press, 1973.

Huber, Joan. "Micro-Macro Links in Gender Stratification." *American Sociological Review, 55,* February 1990:1–10.

Huddle, Donald. "The Net National Cost of Immigration." Washington, D.C.: Carrying Capacity Network, 1993.

Hudson, James R. "Professional Sports Franchise Locations and City, Metropolitan and Regional Identities." Paper presented at the annual meetings of the American Sociological Association, 1991.

Hudson, Robert B. "The 'Graying' of the Federal Budget and Its Consequences for Old-Age Policy." *Gerontologist, 18,* October 1978:428–440.

Huffstutter, P. J. "God Is Everywhere on the Net." *Los Angeles Times,* December 14, 1998.

Huggins, Martha K. "Lost Childhoods: Assassinations of Youth in Democratizing Brazil." Paper presented at the annual meetings of the American Sociological Association, 1993.

Hughes, H. Stuart. *Oswald Spengler: A Critical Estimate,* rev. ed. New York: Scribner's, 1962.

Hughes, Kathleen A. "Even Tiki Torches Don't Guarantee a Perfect Wedding." *Wall Street Journal,* February 20, 1990:A1, A16.

Humphreys, Laud. *Tearoom Trade: Impersonal Sex in Public Places.* Chicago: Aldine, 1970.

Humphreys, Laud. "Impersonal Sex and Perceived Satisfaction." In *Studies in the Sociology of Sex,* James M. Henslin, ed. New York: Appleton-Century-Crofts, 1971:351–374.

Humphreys, Laud. *Tearoom Trade: Impersonal Sex in Public Places,* enlarged ed. Chicago: Aldine, 1975.

Hurtado, Aída, David E. Hayes-Bautista, R. Burciaga Valdez, and Anthony C. R. Hernández. *Redefining California: Latino Social Engagement in a Multicultural Society.* Los Angeles: UCLA Chicano Studies Research Center, 1992.

Huttenbach, Henry R. "The Roman *Porajmos:* The Nazi Genocide of Europe's Gypsies." *Nationalities Papers, 19,* 3, Winter 1991:373–394.

"Immigration's Costs and Benefits Weighted." *Population Today, 25,* 7/8, July/August 1997:3.

Jacobs, Charles. "Money Talks." *The Boston Globe,* February 19, 1999.

Jacobs, Margaret A. "'New Girl' Network Is Boon for Women Lawyers." *Wall Street Journal,* March 4, 1997:B1, B7.

Jaggar, Alison M. "Sexual Difference and Sexual Equality." In *Theoretical Perspectives on Sexual Difference,* Deborah L. Rhode, ed. New Haven, Conn.: Yale University Press, 1990:239–254.

Janis, Irving. *Victims of Groupthink.* Boston: Houghton Mifflin, 1972.

Jankowiak, William R., and Edward F. Fischer. "A Cross-Cultural Perspective on Romantic Love." *Journal of Ethnology, 31,* 2, April 1992:149–155.

Jankowski, Martín Sánchez. *Islands in the Street: Gangs and American Urban Society.* Berkeley: University of California Press, 1991.

Jaspar, James M. "Moral Dimensions of Social Movements." Paper presented at the annual meetings of the American Sociological Association, 1991.

Jerrome, Dorothy. *Good Company: An Anthropological Study of Old People in Groups.* Edinburgh, England: Edinburgh University Press, 1992.

Johnson, Benton. "On Church and Sect." *American Sociological Review, 28,* 1963:539–549.

Johnson, Cathryn. "The Emergence of the Emotional Self: A Developmental Theory." *Symbolic Interaction, 15,* 2, Summer 1992:183–202.

Johnson, Kenneth M. "The Rural Rebound." *Reports on America, 1,* 3, Population Reference Bureau, September 1999.

Johnson, Paul. *A History of the American People.* New York: HarperCollins, 1998.

Jones, Lawrence N. "The New Black Church." *Ebony,* November 1992:192, 194–195.

Jordan, Miriam. "Among Poor Villagers, Female Infanticide Still Flourishes in India." *Wall Street Journal,* May 9, 2000:A1, A12.

Jordon, Mary. "College Dorms Reflect Trend of Self-Segregation." In *Ourselves and Others,* 2nd ed., The Washington Post Writer's Group, eds. Boston: Allyn and Bacon, 1996:85–87.

Judis, John B. "The Japanese Megaphone." *New Republic, 202,* 4, January 22, 1990:20–25.

Kagan, Jerome. "The Idea of Emotions in Human Development." In *Emotions, Cognition, and Behavior,* Carroll E. Izard, Jerome Kagan, and Robert B. Zajonc, eds. New York: Cambridge University Press, 1984:38–72.

Kalb, Claudia. "The War on Disease Goes Miniature." *Newsweek,* January 1, 2000:89.

Kalichman, Seth C. "MMPI Profiles of Women and Men Convicted of Domestic Homicide." *Journal of Clinical Psychology, 44,* 6, November 1988:847–853.

Kalish, Susan. "International Migration: New Findings on Magnitude, Importance." *Population Today, 22,* 3, March 1994:1–2.

Kanter, Rosabeth Moss. *Men and Women of the Corporation.* New York: Basic Books, 1977.

Kanter, Rosabeth Moss. *The Change Masters: Innovation and Entrepreneurship in the American Corporation.* New York: Simon & Schuster, 1983.

Karp, David A., Gregory P. Stone, and William C. Yoels. *Being Urban: A Sociology of City Life,* 2nd ed. New York: Praeger, 1991.

Karp, David A., and William C. Yoels. "Sport and Urban Life." *Journal of Sport and Social Issues, 14,* 2, 1990:77–102.

Kart, Cary S. *The Realities of Aging: An Introduction to Gerontology,* 3rd ed. Boston: Allyn and Bacon, 1990.

Katz, Sydney. "The Importance of Being Beautiful." In *Down to Earth Sociology: Introductory Readings,* 11th ed. James M. Henslin, ed. New York: Free Press, 2001:297–303.

Kaufman, Joanne. "Married Maidens and Dilatory Domiciles." *Wall Street Journal,* May 7, 1996:A16.

Keith, Jennie. *Old People, New Lives: Community Creation in a Retirement Residence,* 2nd ed. Chicago: University of Chicago Press, 1982.

Kelly, Joan B. "How Adults React to Divorce." In *Marriage and Family in a Changing Society,* 4th ed., James M. Henslin, ed. New York: Free Press, 1992:410–423.

Kemp, Alice Abel. "Estimating Sex Discrimination in Professional Occupations with the *Dictionary of Occupational Titles.*" *Sociological Spectrum, 10,* 3, 1990:387–411.

Keniston, Kenneth. *Youth and Dissent: The Rise of a New Opposition.* New York: Harcourt Brace Jovanovich, 1971.

Kennedy, Paul. *Preparing for the Twenty-First Century.* New York: Random House, 1993.

Kephart, William M., and William W. Zellner. *Extraordinary Groups: An Examination of Unconventional Life-Styles,* 5th ed. New York: St. Martin's Press, 1994.

Kerr, Clark, et al. *Industrialism and Industrial Man: The Problems of Labor and Management in Economic Growth.* Cambridge, Mass.: Harvard University Press, 1960.

Kerr, Clark. *The Future of Industrialized Societies.* Cambridge, Mass.: Harvard University Press, 1983.

Kettl, Donald F. "The Savings-and-Loan Bailout: The Mismatch between the Headlines and the Issues." *PS, 24,* 3, September 1991:441–447.

Kibria, Nazli. *Family Tightrope: The Changing Lives of Vietnamese Americans.* Princeton, N.J.: Princeton University Press, 1993.

Kifner, John. "Building Modernity on Desert Mirages." *New York Times,* February 7, 1999.

Klandermans, Bert. *The Social Psychology of Protest.* Cambridge, Mass.: Blackwell, 1997.

Kluegel, James R., and Eliot R. Smith. *Beliefs about Inequality: America's Views of What Is and What Ought to Be.* Hawthorne, N.Y.: Aldine de Gruyter, 1986.

Kohlfeld, Carol W., and Leslie A. Leip. "Bans on Concurrent Sale of Beer and Gas: A California Case Study." *Sociological Practice Review, 2,* 2, April 1, 1991:104–115.

Kohn, Melvin L. "Social Class and Parental Values." *American Journal of Sociology, 64,* 1959:337–351.

Kohn, Melvin L. "Social Class and Parent–Child Relationships: An Interpretation." *American Journal of Sociology, 68,* 1963:471–480.

Kohn, Melvin L. "Occupational Structure and Alienation." *American Journal of Sociology, 82,* 1976:111–130.

Kohn, Melvin L. *Class and Conformity: A Study in Values,* 2nd ed. Homewood, Ill.: Dorsey Press, 1977.

Kohn, Melvin L., and Carmi Schooler. *Work and Personality: An Inquiry into the Impact of Social Stratification.* New York: Ablex Press, 1983.

Kohn, Melvin L., Kazimierz M. Slomczynski, and Carrie Schoenbach. "Social Stratification and the Transmission of Values in the Family: A Cross-National Assessment." *Sociological Forum, 1,* 1, 1986:73–102.

Kolata, Gina. "Pushing the Limits of the Human Life Span." *New York Times,* March 9, 1999.

Krauthammer, Charles. "A Second American Century." *Time,* December 27, 1999:186.

Kraybill, Donald B. *The Riddle of Amish Culture.* Baltimore: Johns Hopkins University Press, 1989.

Krysan, Maria, and Reynolds Farley. "Racial Stereotypes: Are They Alive and Well? Do They Continue to Influence Race Relations?" Paper presented at the 1993 meeting of the American Sociological Association.

Kurian, George Thomas. *Encyclopedia of the First World,* Vols. 1, 2. New York: Facts on File, 1990.

Kurian, George Thomas. *Encyclopedia of the Second World.* New York: Facts on File, 1991.

Kurian, George Thomas. *Encyclopedia of the Third World,* Vols. 1, 2, 3. New York: Facts on File, 1992.

Lacayo, Richard. "The 'Cultural' Defense." *Time,* Fall 1993:61.

Lachica, Eduardo. "Third World Told to Spend More on Environment." *Wall Street Journal,* May 18, 1992:A2.

Lagaipa, Susan J. "Suffer the Little Children: The Ancient Practice of Infanticide as a Modern Moral Dilemma." *Issues in Comprehensive Pediatric Nursing, 13,* 1990:241–251.

Lamb, Michael E. "The Effect of Divorce on Children's Personality Development." *Journal of Divorce, 1,* Winter 1977:163–174.

Lancaster, Hal. "Managing Your Career." *Wall Street Journal,* November 14, 1995:B1.

Landtman, Gunnar. *The Origin of the Inequality of the Social Classes.* New York: Greenwood Press, 1968. First published in 1938.

Lang, Kurt, and Gladys E. Lang. *Collective Dynamics.* New York: Crowell, 1961.

Langan, Patrick A., and Mark A. Cunniff. "Recidivism of Felons on Probation, 1986–89." Washington, D.C.: U.S. Department of Justice, February 1992.

Lannoy, Richard. *The Speaking Tree: A Study of Indian Culture and Society.* New York: Oxford University Press, 1975.

LaPiere, Richard T. "Attitudes versus Action." *Social Forces, 13,* December 1934:230–237.

Larson, Jeffry H. "The Marriage Quiz: College Students' Beliefs in Selected Myths about Marriage." *Family Relations,* January 1988:3–11.

Laska, Shirley Bradway. "Environmental Sociology and the State of the Discipline." *Social Forces, 72,* 1, September 1993:1–17.

Lauer, Jeanette, and Robert Lauer. "Marriages Made to Last." In *Marriage and Family in a Changing Society,* 4th ed., James M. Henslin, ed. New York: Free Press, 1992:481–486.

Lawlor, Julia. "Woman Gain Power, Means to Abuse It." *USA Today,* January 12, 1994:1A, 2A.

Lee, Alfred McClung, and Elizabeth Briant Lee. *The Fine Art of Propaganda: A Study of Father Coughlin's Speeches.* New York: Harcourt Brace, 1939.

Lee, Sharon M. "Asian Americans: Diverse and Growing." *Population Bulletin, 53,* 2, June 1998:1–39.

Leland, John, and Gregory Beals. "In Living Colors." *Newsweek,* May 5, 1997:58–60.

Lemann, Nicholas. *The Promised Land: The Great Black Migration and How It Changed America.* New York: Random House, 1991.

Lemann, Nicholas. "The Myth of Community Development." *New York Times Magazine,* January 9, 1994:27.

Lenski, Gerhard. "Status Crystallization: A Nonvertical Dimension of Social Status." *American Sociological Review, 19,* 1954:405–413.

Lenski, Gerhard. *Power and Privilege: A Theory of Social Stratification.* New York: McGraw-Hill, 1966.

Lenski, Gerhard, and Jean Lenski. *Human Societies: An Introduction to Macrosociology,* 5th ed. New York: McGraw-Hill, 1987.

Lerner, Gerda. *Black Women in White America: A Documentary History.* New York: Pantheon Books, 1972.

Lerner, Gerda. *The Creation of Patriarchy.* New York: Oxford University Press, 1986.

Lester, David. *Suicide in American Indians.* New York: Nova Science Publishers, 1997.

Levinson, D. J. *The Seasons of a Man's Life.* New York: Knopf, 1978.

Levy, Marion J., Jr. "Confucianism and Modernization." *Society, 24,* 4, May–June 1992:15–18.

Lewis, Oscar. "The Culture of Poverty." *Scientific American, 113,* October 1966a:19–25.

Lewis, Oscar. *La Vida.* New York: Random House, 1966b.

Lewis, Richard S. *Challenger: The Final Voyage.* New York: Columbia University Press, 1988.

Liben, Paul. "Farrakhan Honors African Slavers." *Wall Street Journal,* October 20, 1995:A14.

Liebow, Elliott. *Tally's Corner: A Study of Negro Streetcorner Men.* Boston: Little, Brown, 1999. Originally published in 1967.

Liebow, Elliot. "Tally's Corner." In *Down to Earth Sociology: Introductory Readings,* 9th ed., James M. Henslin, ed. New York: Free Press, 1997:330–339.

Lightfoot-Klein, A. "Rites of Purification and Their Effects: Some Psychological Aspects of Female Genital Circumcision and Infibulation (Pharaonic Circumcision) in an Afro-Arab Society (Sudan)." *Journal of Psychological Human Sexuality, 2,* 1989:61–78.

Lind, Michael. *The Next American Nation: The New Nationalism and the Fourth American Revolution.* New York: Free Press, 1995.

Linden, Eugene. "Lost Tribes, Lost Knowledge." *Time,* September 23, 1991:46, 48, 50, 52, 54, 56.

Linton, Ralph. *The Study of Man.* New York: Appleton-Century-Crofts, 1936.

Lippitt, Ronald, and Ralph K. White. "An Experimental Study of Leadership and Group Life." In *Readings in Social Psychology,* 3rd ed., Eleanor E. Maccoby, Theodore M. Newcomb, and Eugene L. Hartley, eds. New York: Holt, Rinehart and Winston, 1958:340–365. (As summarized in Olmsted and Hare 1978:28–31.)

Lipset, Seymour Martin. "Democracy and Working-Class Authoritarianism." *American Sociological Review, 24,* 1959:482–502.

Lipset, Seymour Martin, ed. *The Third Century: America as a Post-Industrial Society.* Stanford, Calif.: Hoover Institution Press, 1979.

Lipset, Seymour Martin. "The Social Requisites of Democracy Revisited." Presidential address to the American Sociological Association, Boston, Massachusetts, 1993.

Lipton, Michael. *Why Poor People Stay Poor: Urban Bias in World Development.* Cambridge, Mass.: Harvard University Press, 1979.

Lombroso, Cesare. *Crime: Its Causes and Remedies,* H. P. Horton, trans. Boston: Little, Brown, 1911.

Lopez, Julie Amparano. "Study Says Women Face Glass Walls as Well as Ceilings." *Wall Street Journal,* March 3, 1992:B1, B8.

Lublin, Joann S. "Women at Top Still Are Distant from CEO Jobs." *Wall Street Journal,* February 28, 1996:B1.

Lublin, Joann S. "Living Well." *Wall Street Journal,* April 8, 1999.

Lundberg, Olle. "Causal Explanations for Class Inequality in Health—An Empirical Analysis." *Social Science and Medicine, 32,* 4, 1991:385–393.

Luoma, Jon R. "Acid Murder No Longer a Mystery." In *Taking Sides: Clashing Views on Controversial Environmental Issues,* 3rd ed., Theodore D. Goldfarb, ed. Guilford, Conn.: Dushkin, 1989:186–192.

Mabry, Marcus. "The Price Tag on Freedom." *Newsweek,* May 3, 1999:50–51.

MacDonald, Heather. "Law School Humbug." *Wall Street Journal,* November 8, 1995:A23.

MacDonald, William L., and Alfred DeMaris. "Remarriage, Stepchildren, and Marital Conflict: Challenges to the Incomplete Institutionalization Hypothesis." *Journal of Marriage and the Family, 57,* May 1995:387–398.

Mackey, Richard A., and Bernard A. O'Brien. *Lasting Marriages: Men and Women Growing Together.* Westport, Conn.: 1995.

MacShane, Denis. "Lessons for Bosses and the Bossed." *New York Times,* July 19, 1993:A15.

Magnuson, E. "A Cold Soak, a Plume, a Fireball." *Time,* February 17, 1986:25.

Mahoney, John S., Jr., and Paul G. Kooistra. "Policing the Races: Structural Factors Enforcing Racial Purity in Virginia (1630–1930)." Paper presented at the 1995 meetings of the American Sociological Association.

Mahran, M. *Proceedings of the Third International Congress of Medical Sexology.* Littleton, Mass.: PSG Publishing, 1978.

Mahran, M. "Medical Dangers of Female Circumcision." *International Planned Parenthood Federation Medical Bulletin, 2,* 1981:1–2.

Maier, Mark. "Teaching from Tragedy: An Interdisciplinary Module on the Space Shuttle *Challenger.*" *T. H. E. Journal,* September 1993:91–94.

Mamdani, Mahmood. "The Myth of Population Control: Family, Caste, and Class in an Urban Village." New York: Monthly Review Press, 1973.

Mander, Jerry. *In the Absence of the Sacred: The Failure of Technology and the Survival of the Indian Nations.* San Francisco, Calif.: Sierra Club Books, 1992.

Manno, Bruno V. "The Real Score on the SATs." *Wall Street Journal,* September 13, 1995:A14.

Manski, Charles F. "Income and Higher Education." *Focus, 14,* 3, Winter 1992–1993:14–19.

Markhusen, Eric. "Genocide in Cambodia." In *Down to Earth Sociology: Introductory Readings,* 8th ed., James M. Henslin, ed. New York: Free Press, 1995:355–364.

Marshall, Samantha. "It's So Simple: Just Lather Up, Watch the Fat Go down the Drain." *Wall Street Journal,* November 2, 1995:B1.

Marshall, Samantha. "Vietnamese Women Are Kidnapped and Later Sold in China as Brides." *Wall Street Journal,* August 3, 1999.

Martin, Michael. "Ecosabotage and Civil Disobedience." *Environmental Ethics, 12,* 4, Winter 1990:291–310.

Marx, Karl. "Contribution to the Critique of Hegel's Philosophy of Right." In *Karl Marx: Early Writings,* T. B. Bottomore, ed. New York: McGraw-Hill, 1964:45. First published in 1844.

Marx, Karl, and Friedrich Engels. *Communist Manifesto.* New York: Pantheon, 1967. First published in 1848.

Massey, Douglas S., and Garvey Lundy. "Use of Black English and Racial Discrimination in Urban Housing Markets: New Methods and Findings." *Urban Affairs Review, 36,* 2001:451–468.

Mauss, Armand. *Social Problems as Social Movements.* Philadelphia: Lippincott, 1975.

McCall, Michael. "Who and Where Are the Artists?" In *Fieldwork Experience: Qualitative Approaches to Social Research,* William B. Shaffir, Robert A. Stebbins, and Allan Turowetz, eds. New York: St. Martin's, 1980:145–158.

McCarthy, John D., and Mayer N. Zald. "Resource Mobilization and Social Movements: A Partial Theory." *American Journal of Sociology, 82,* 6, 1977:1212–1241.

McCartney, Kathleen, et al. "Teacher-Child Interaction and Chid-Care Auspices as Predictors of Social Outcomes in Infants, Toddlers, and Preschoolers." *Merrill-Palmer Quarterly, 41,* 3, July 1997:426–450.

McCormick, John. "The Sorry Side of Sears." *Newsweek,* February 22, 1999:36–39.

McCormick, John. "Change Has Taken Place." *Newsweek,* June 7, 1999:34.

McCuen, Gary E., ed. *Ecocide and Genocide in the Vanishing Forest: The Rainforests and Native People.* Hudson, Wis.: GEM Publications, 1993.

McFarling, Usha Lee. "Climate Is Warming at Steep Rate, Study Says." *Los Angeles Times,* February 23, 2000.

McGowan, Jo. "Little Girls Dying: An Ancient & Thriving Practice." *Commonweal,* August 9, 1991:481–482.

McKenna, George. "On Abortion: A Lincolnian Position." *Atlantic Monthly,* September 1995:51–67.

McKeown, Thomas. *The Modern Rise of Population.* New York: Academic Press, 1977.

McLanahan, Sara, and Gary Sandefur. *Growing Up with a Single Parent: What Hurts, What Helps.* Cambridge, Mass.: Harvard University Press, 1995.

McLemore, S. Dale. *Racial and Ethnic Relations in America.* Boston: Allyn and Bacon, 1994.

McNeil, Donald G., Jr. "In Angola's Capital, Life Does Not Yet Imitate Art." *New York Times,* January 25, 1999.

McNeill, William H, "How the Potato Changed the World's History." *Social Research, 66,* 1, Spring 1999:67–83.

Mead, George Herbert. *Mind, Self and Society.* Chicago: University of Chicago Press, 1934.

Meek, Anne. "On Creating 'Ganas': A Conversation with Jaime Escalante." *Educational Leadership, 46,* 5, February 1989:46–47.

Menaghan, Elizabeth G., Lori Kowaleski-Jones, and Frank L. Mott. "The Intergenerational Costs of Parental Social Stressors: Academic and Social Difficulties in Early Adolescence for Children of Young Mothers." *Journal of Health and Social Behavior, 38,* March 1997:72–86.

Mendels, Pamela. "Rights Group Develops 'Hate' Filter." *New York Times,* November 11, 1998.

Menzel, Peter. *Material World: A Global Family Portrait.* San Francisco: Sierra Club, 1994.

Merton, Robert K. "The Social-Cultural Environment and Anomie." In *New Perspectives for Research on Juvenile Delinquency,* Helen L. Witmer and Ruth Kotinsky, eds. Washington, D.C.: U.S. Department of Health, Education, and Welfare, 1956:24–50.

Merton, Robert K. *Social Theory and Social Structure,* enlarged ed. New York: Free Press, 1968.

Merwine, Maynard H. "How Africa Understands Female Circumcision." *New York Times,* November 24, 1993.

Messner, Michael. "Boyhood, Organized Sports, and the Construction of Masculinities." *Journal of Contemporary Ethnography, 18,* 4, January 1990:416–444.

Meyrowitz, Joshua. "Shifting Worlds of Strangers: Medium Theory and Changes in 'Them' vs 'Us.'" Paper presented at the 1995 meetings of the American Sociological Association.

Michael, Robert T. "Measuring Poverty: A New Approach." *Focus, 17,* 1, Summer 1995:2–13.

Michalowski, Raymond J. *Order, Law, and Crime: An Introduction to Criminology.* New York: Random House, 1985.

Michels, Robert. *Political Parties.* Glencoe, Ill.: Free Press, 1949. First published in 1911.

Milbank, Dana. "Working Poor Fear Welfare Cutbacks Aimed at the Idle Will Inevitably Strike Them, Too." *Wall Street Journal,* August 9, 1995b:A10.

Milbank, Dana. "No Fault Divorce Law Is Assailed in Michigan, and Debate Heats Up." *Wall Street Journal,* January 5, 1996:A1, A6.

Milgram, Stanley. "Behavioral Study of Obedience." *Journal of Abnormal and Social Psychology, 67,* 4, 1963:371–378.

Milgram, Stanley. "Some Conditions of Obedience and Disobedience to Authority." *Human Relations, 18,* February 1965:57–76.

Milgram, Stanley. "The Small World Problem." *Psychology Today, 1,* 1967:61–67.

Miller, Dan E. "Milgram Redux: Obedience and Disobedience in Authority Relations." In *Studies in Symbolic Interaction,* Norman K. Denzin, ed. Greenwich, Conn.: JAI Press, 1986:77–106.

Miller, Lisa. "Son of Elijah Muhammad Preaches Gentler Islam in Tune With the Times." *Wall Street Journal,* July 9, 1999.

Miller, Michael W. "Survey Sketches New Portrait of the Mentally Ill." *Wall Street Journal,* January 14, 1994: B1, B10.

Miller, Walter B. "Lower Class Culture as a Generating Milieu of Gang Delinquency." *Journal of Social Issues, 14,* 3, 1958:5–19.

Mills, C. Wright. *The Power Elite.* New York: Oxford University Press, 1956.

Mills, C. Wright. *The Sociological Imagination.* New York: Oxford University Press, 1959.

Minkler, Meredith, and Ann Robertson. "The Ideology of 'Age/Race Wars': Deconstructing a Social Problem." *Ageing and Society, 11,* 1, March 1991:1–22.

Mintz, Beth A., and Michael Schwartz. *The Power Structure of American Business.* Chicago: University of Chicago Press, 1985.

Moberg, Mark. "Strategies of a Multiracial Environmental Coalition in Southern Alabama." *Enviro-Tech,* Spring 1999:4–8.

Mohawk, John C. "Indian Economic Development: An Evolving Concept of Sovereignty." *Buffalo Law Review, 39,* 2, Spring 1991:495–503.

Money, John, and Anke A. Ehrhardt. *Man and Woman, Boy and Girl.* Baltimore: Johns Hopkins University Press, 1972.

Montagu, M. F. Ashley. *Introduction to Physical Anthropology,* 3rd ed. Springfield, Ill.: Thomas, 1960.

Montagu, M. F. Ashley. *The Concept of Race.* New York: Free Press, 1964.

Morgan, Lewis Henry. *Ancient Society.* 1877.

Morris, J. R. "Racial Attitudes of Undergraduates in Greek Housing." *College Student Journal, 25,* 1, March 1991:501–505.

Mosca, Gaetano. *The Ruling Class.* New York: McGraw-Hill, 1939. First published in 1896.

Mosher, Steven W. "Why Are Baby Girls Being Killed in China?" *Wall Street Journal,* July 25, 1983:9.

Mosher, Steven W. "Too Many People? Not by a Long Shot." *Wall Street Journal,* February 10, 1997:A18.

Mount, Ferdinand. *The Subversive Family: An Alternative History of Love and Marriage.* New York: Free Press, 1992.

Moynihan, Daniel Patrick. "Social Justice in the Next Century." *America,* September 14, 1991:132–137.

Muehlenhard, Charlene L., and Melaney A. Linton. "Date Rape and Sexual Aggression in Dating Situations: Incidence and Risk Factors." *Journal of Counseling Psychology, 34,* 2, 1987:186–196.

Muir, Donal E. "'White' Fraternity and Sorority Attitudes Toward 'Blacks' on a Deep-South Campus." *Sociological Spectrum, 11,* 1, January–March 1991:93–103.

Murdock, George Peter. *Social Structure.* New York: Macmillan, 1949.

Murphy, Kim. "Last Stand of an Aging Aryan." *Los Angeles Times,* January 10, 1999.

Murray, Charles. "The Coming White Underclass." *Wall Street Journal,* October 29, 1993:A16.

Murray, Charles, and R. J. Hernstein. "What's Really Behind the SAT-Score Decline?" *Public Interest, 106,* Winter 1992:32–56.

Nabhan, Gary Paul. *Cultures in Habitat: On Nature, Culture, and Story.* New York: Counterpoint, 1998.

Naj, Amal Kumar. "Some Manufacturers Drop Efforts to Adopt Japanese Techniques." *Wall Street Journal,* May 7, 1993:A1, A12.

Naj, Amal Kumar. "MIT Chemists Achieve Goal of Splitting Nitrogen Molecules in the Atmosphere." *Wall Street Journal,* May 12, 1995:B3.

Nakao, Keiko, and Judith Treas. "Occupational Prestige in the United States Revisited: Twenty-Five Years of Stability and Change." Paper presented at the annual meetings of the American Sociological Association, 1990. (As referenced in Kerbo, Harold R. *Social Stratification and Inequality: Class Conflict in Historical and Comparative Perspective,* 2nd ed. New York: McGraw-Hill, 1991:181.)

Nash, Gary B. *Red, White, and Black.* Englewood Cliffs, N.J.: Prentice Hall, 1974.

Nathan, John. *Sony: The Private Life.* New York: Houghton Mifflin, 1999.

National Institute of Child Health and Human Development. "Child Care and Mother-Child Interaction in the First 3 Years of Life." *Developmental Psychology, 35,* 6, November 1999:1399–1413.

National School Safety Center. "The School Associated Violent Death Report," 2000.

National Women's Political Caucus. "Factsheet on Women's Political Progress." Washington, D.C., June 1998.

Naughton, Keith. "Cyberslacking." *Newsweek,* November 29, 1999:62–65.

Nauta, André. "That They All May Be One: Can Denominationalism Die?" Paper presented at the annual meetings of the American Sociological Association, 1993.

Neikirk, William, and Glen Elsasser. "Ruling Weakens Abortion Right." *Chicago Tribune,* June 30, 1992:1, 8.

Neugarten, Bernice L. "Middle Age and Aging." In *Growing Old in America,* Beth B. Hess, ed. New Brunswick, N.J.: Transaction Books, 1976:180–197.

Neugarten, Bernice L. "Personality and Aging." In *Handbook of the Psychology of Aging,* James E. Birren and K. Warren Schaie, eds. New York: Van Nostrand Reinhold, 1977: 626–649.

Newdorf, David. "Bailout Agencies Like to Do It in Secret." *Washington Journalism Review, 13,* 4, May 1991:15–16.

Niebuhr, H. Richard. *The Social Sources of Denominationalism.* New York: Holt, 1929.

Nieves, Evelyn. "Lumber Company Approves U.S. Deal to Save Redwoods." *New York Times,* March 3, 1999.

Nsamenang, A. Bame. *Human Development in Cultural Context: A Third World Perspective.* Newbury Park, Calif.: Sage, 1992.

Nuland, Sherwin B. "Immortality and Its Discontents." *Wall Street Journal,* July 2, 1999.

O'Brien, John E. "Violence in Divorce-Prone Families." In *Violence in the Family,* Suzanne K. Steinmetz and Murray A. Straus, eds. New York: Dodd, Mead, 1975:65–75.

O'Connell, Martin, "Where's Papa? Father's Role in Child Care." Population Trends and Public Policy no. 20. Washington, D.C.:Reference Bureau, September 1993.

Offen, Karen. "Feminism and Sexual Difference in Historical Perspective." In *Theoretical Perspectives on Sexual Difference,* Deborah L. Rhode, ed. New Haven, Conn.: Yale University Press, 1990:13–20.

Ogburn, William F. *Social Change, with Respect to Culture and Original Nature.* New York: Viking Press, 1938. First published in 1922.

Ogburn, William F. "The Hypothesis of Cultural Lag." In *Theories of Society: Foundations of Modern Sociological Theory,* Vol. 2, Talcott Parsons, Edward Shils, Kaspar D. Naegele, and Jesse R. Pitts, eds. New York: Free Press, 1961:1270–1273.

Ogburn, William F. *On Culture and Social Change: Selected Papers,* Otis Dudley Duncan, ed. Chicago: University of Chicago Press, 1964.

O'Hare, William P. "A New Look at Poverty in America." *Population Bulletin, 51,* 2, September 1996a:1–47.

O'Hare, William P. "U.S. Poverty Myths Explored: Many Poor Work Year-Round, Few Still Poor After Five Years." *Population Today: News, Numbers, and Analysis, 24,* 10, October 1996b:1–2.

Olmsted, Michael S., and A. Paul Hare. *The Small Group,* 2nd ed. New York: Random House, 1978.

Olneck, Michael R., and David B. Bills. "What Makes Sammy Run? An Empirical Assessment of the Bowles-Gintis Correspondence Theory." *American Journal of Education, 89,* 1980:27–61.

Orlans, Harold. "Members Comment on ASA's Publication on Affirmative Action." *Footnotes,* May–June 1999:8.

Orwell, George. *1984.* New York: Harcourt Brace, 1949.

Ouchi, William. *Theory Z: How American Business Can Meet the Japanese Challenge.* Reading, Mass.: Addison-Wesley, 1981.

Ouchi, William. "Decision-Making in Japanese Organizations." In *Down to Earth Sociology,* 7th ed., James M. Henslin, ed. New York: Free Press, 1993:503–507.

Pagelow, Mildred Daley. "Adult Victims of Domestic Violence: Battered Women." *Journal of Interpersonal Violence, 7,* 1, March 1992:87–120.

Palen, John J. *The Urban World,* 3rd ed. New York: McGraw-Hill, 1987.

Parfit, Michael, "Earth First!ers Wield a Mean Monkey Wrench." *Smithsonian, 21,* 1, April 1990:184–204.

Park, Robert Ezra. "Human Ecology." *American Journal of Sociology, 42,* 1, July 1936:1–15.

Park, Robert E., and Ernest W. Burgess. *Human Ecology.* Chicago: University of Chicago Press, 1921.

Parker-Pope, Tara. "Making a Stand." *Wall Street Journal,* April 9, 1998.

Parsons, Talcott. "An Analytic Approach to the Theory of Social Stratification." *American Journal of Sociology, 45,* 1940:841–862.

Passell, Peter. "Race, Mortgages and Statistics." *New York Times,* May 10, 1996:D1, D4.

Pasztor, Andy. "U.S., Grumman Reach Accord in Pentagon Case." *Wall Street Journal,* November 23, 1993:A3.

Pearlin, L. I., and Melvin L. Kohn. "Social Class, Occupation, and Parental Values: A Cross-National Study." *American Sociological Review, 31,* 1966:466–479.

Peart, Karen N. "Converts to the Faith." *Scholastic Update, 126,* 4, October 22, 1993:16–18.

Persell, Caroline Hodges, Sophia Catsambis, and Peter W. Cookson, Jr. "Family Background, School Type, and College Attendance: A Conjoint System of Cultural Capital Transmission." *Journal of Research on Adolescence, 2,* 1, 1992:1–23.

Peterson, James L., and Nicholas Zill. "Marital Disruption, Parent–Child Relationships, and Behavior Problems in Children." *Journal of Marriage and the Family, 48,* 1986:295–307.

Phillips, John L., Jr. *The Origins of Intellect: Piaget's Theory.* San Francisco: Freeman, 1969.

Piaget, Jean. *The Psychology of Intelligence.* London: Routledge & Kegan Paul, 1950.

Piaget, Jean. *The Construction of Reality in the Child.* New York: Basic Books, 1954.

Pines, Maya. "The Civilizing of Genie." *Psychology Today, 15,* September 1981:28–34.

Platt, Tony. " 'Street' Crime—A View from the Left." *Crime and Social Justice: Issues in Criminology, 9,* 1978:26–34.

Pollard, Kelvin M., and William P. O'Hare. "America's Racial and Ethnic Minorities." *Population Bulletin, 54,* 3, September 1999:3–47.

Polsby, Nelson W. "Three Problems in the Analysis of Community Power." *American Sociological Review, 24,* 6, December 1959:796–803.

Polumbaum, Judy. "China: Confucian Tradition Meets the Market Economy." *Ms.,* September–October 1992:12–13.

Pope, J. Hector, Tom P. Aufderheide, Robin Ruthazer, Robert H. Woolard, James A. Feldman, Joni R. Beshansky, John L. Griffith, and Harry P. Selker. "Missed Diagnoses of Acute Cardiac Ischemia in the Emergency Department." *New England Journal of Medicine, 342,* 16, April 20, 2000:1163–1170.

Pope, Liston. *Millhands and Preachers: A Study of Gastonia.* New Haven, Conn.: Yale University Press, 1942.

"Population Update." *Population Today, 28,* 1, January 2000.

"Population Update." *Population Today, 29,* 1, January 2001.

Porter, Eduardo. "U.S. Hispanic Population Is Close To Being Largest Minority Group." *Wall Street Journal.* March 8, 2001.

Portes, Alejandro, and Ruben G. Rumbaut. *Immigrant America.* Berkeley: University of California Press, 1990.

Power, Carla. "The New Islam." *Newsweek,* March 16, 1998:34–37.

Rabinovitz, Jonathan. "Working Parents Use Internet to Check on Children in Day Care." *New York Times,* December 9, 1997.

Ramo, Joshua Cooper. "Finding God on the Web." *Time,* December 16, 1996:60–67.

Raney, Rebecca Fairley. "Study Warns of Risks in Internet Voting." *New York Times,* March 8, 1999.

Ray, J. J. "Authoritarianism Is a Dodo: Comment on Scheepers, Felling and Peters." *European Sociological Review, 7,* 1, May 1991:73–75.

Raymond, Chris. "New Studies by Anthropologists Indicate Amish Communities Are Much More Dynamic and Diverse than Many Believed." *Chronicle of Higher Education,* December 19, 1990:A1, A9.

Read, Piers Paul. *Alive. The Story of the Andes Survivors.* Philadelphia: Lippincott, 1974.

Recer, Paul. "Gene Mutation Doubles Life Span." *New York Times,* December 14, 2000.

Reckless, Walter C. *The Crime Problem,* 5th ed. New York: Appleton, 1973.

Redclift, Michael, and Graham Woodgate, eds. *The International Handbook of Environmental Sociology.* Cheltenham, England: Edward Elgar, 1997.

Reed, Susan, and Lorenzo Benet. "Ecowarrior Dave Foreman Will Do Whatever It Takes in His Fight to Save Mother Earth." *People Weekly, 33,* 15, April 16, 1990:113–116.

Reich, Michael. "The Economics of Racism." In *The Capitalist System,* Richard C. Edwards, Michael Reich, and Thomas E. Weiskopf, eds. Englewood Cliffs, N.J.: Prentice Hall, 1972:313–321.

Reich, Robert B. *Good for Business: Making Full Use of the Nation's Human Capital, The Environmental Scan.* Washington, D.C.: U.S. Department of Labor, March 1995.

Reitman, Valerie, and Oscar Suris. "In a Cultural U-Turn, Mazda's Creditors Put Ford behind the Wheel." *Wall Street Journal,* November 21, 1994:A1, A4.

Renteln, Alison Dundes. "Sex Selection and Reproductive Freedom." *Women's Studies International Forum, 15,* 3, 1992:405–426.

"Reservations With Casinos Gain Ground on Poverty." *New York Times,* September 3, 2000.

Reskin, Barbara F. *The Realities of Affirmative Action in Employment.* Washington, D.C.: American Sociological Association, 1998.

Rich, Spencer. "Number of Elected Hispanic Officials Doubled in a Decade, Study Shows." *Washington Post,* September 19, 1986:A6.

Richards, Bill. "Doctors Can Diagnose Illnesses Long Distance, to the Dismay of Some." *Wall Street Journal,* January 17, 1996:A1, A8.

Ricks, Thomas E. " 'New' Marines Illustrate Growing Gap between Military and Society." *Wall Street Journal,* July 27, 1995:A1, A4.

Rieker, Patricia P., Chloe E. Bird, Susan Bell, Jenny Ruducha, Rima E. Rudd, and S. M. Miller, "Violence and Women's Health: Toward a Society and Health Perspective." Unpublished paper, 1997.

Riesman, David. "The Suburban Dislocation." In *Urban Man and Society: A Reader in Urban Ecology,* Albert N. Cousins and Hans Nagpaul, eds. New York: Knopf, 1970:172–184.

Rifkin, Jeremy. *The End of Work: The Decline of the Global Labor Force and the Dawn of the Post-Market Era.* New York: Putnam, 1995.

Risman, Barbara H. *Gender Vertigo: American Families in Transition.* New Haven, Conn.: Yale University Press, 1998.

Rist, Ray C. "Student Social Class and Teacher Expectations: The Self-Fulfilling Prophecy in Ghetto Education." *Harvard Educational Review, 40,* 3, August 1970:411–451.

Ritzer, George. *Sociological Theory,* 3rd ed. New York: McGraw-Hill, 1992.

Ritzer, George. *The McDonaldization of Society: An Investigation into the Changing Character of Contemporary Life.* Thousand Oaks, Calif.: Pine Forge Press, 1993.

Robertson, Ian. *Sociology,* 3rd ed. New York: Worth, 1987.

Rodriguez, Richard. "Searching for Roots in a Changing Society." In *Down to Earth Sociology: Introductory Readings,* 8th ed., James M. Henslin, ed. New York: Free Press, 1995:486–491.

Rodríguez, Victor M. "Los Angeles, U.S.A. 1992: 'A House Divided against Itself...'" *SSSP Newsletter,* Spring 1994:5–12.

Rogers, Joseph W. *Why Are You Not a Criminal?* Englewood Cliffs, N.J.: Prentice Hall, 1977.

Rosenblatt, Robert A. "Extra Serving of Surplus to Elderly Raises Eyebrows." *Los Angeles Times,* February 2, 1999.

Rosenthal, Elisabeth. "China's Chic Waistline: Convex to Concave." *New York Times,* December 9, 1999.

Rossi, Alice S. "A Biosocial Perspective on Parenting." *Daedalus, 106,* 1977:1–31.

Rossi, Alice S. "Gender and Parenthood." *American Sociological Review, 49,* 1984:1–18.

Rotundo, E. Anthony. "Changing Ideals of American Middle-Class Manhood, 1770–1920." *Journal of Social History, 16,* 4, Summer 1983:23–38.

Rubin, Lillian Breslow. *Worlds of Pain: Life in the Working-Class Family.* New York: Basic Books, 1976.

Rubin, Lillian Breslow. "The Empty Nest." In *Marriage and Family in a Changing Society,* 4th ed., James M. Henslin, ed. New York: Free Press, 1992a:261–270.

Rubin, Lillian Breslow. "Worlds of Pain." In *Marriage and Family in a Changing Society,* 4th ed., James M. Henslin, ed. New York: Free Press, 1992b:44–50.

Ruggles, Patricia. "Short and Long Term Poverty in the United States: Measuring the American 'Underclass.'" Washington, D.C.: Urban Institute, June 1989.

Russell, Diana E. H. "Preliminary Report on Some Findings Relating to the Trauma and Long-Term Effects of Intrafamily Childhood Sexual Abuse." Unpublished paper.

Ryan, John, and William M. Wentworth. *Media and Society: The Production of Culture in the Mass Media.* Boston: Allyn and Bacon, 1999.

Rybczynski, Witold. "The Virtues of Suburban Sprawl." *Wall Street Journal,* May 25, 1999.

Sahlins, Marshall D., and Elman R. Service. *Evolution and Culture.* Ann Arbor: University of Michigan Press, 1960.

Sampson, Robert J., Jeffrey D. Morenoff, and Felton Earls. "Beyond Social Capital: Spatial Dynamics of Collective Efficacy for Children." *American Sociological Review, 64,* October 1999:633–660.

Samuelson, Paul A., and William D. Nordhaus. *Economics,* 13th ed. New York: McGraw-Hill, 1989.

Sanchez, Laura. "Gender, Labor Allocations, and the Psychology of Entitlement within the Home." *Social Forces, 13,* 2, December 1994:533–553.

Sandberg, Jared. "Electronic Erotica: Too Much Traffic." *Wall Street Journal,* February 8, 1995:B1, B8.

Sandefur, Gary D. "Children in Single-Parent Families: The Roles of Time and Money." *Focus, 17,* 1, Summer 1995:44–45.

Sapir, Edward. *Selected Writings of Edward Sapir in Language, Culture, and Personality,* David G. Mandelbaum, ed. Berkeley: University of California Press, 1949.

Satchell, Michael. "A Whale of a Protest." *U.S. News Online,* October 5, 1998.

Savells, Jerry. "Social Change among the Amish." In *Down to Earth Sociology: Introductory Readings,* 11th ed., James M. Henslin, ed. New York: Free Press, 2001:507–515.

Saxe, G. B. "Candy Selling and Math Learning." *Educational Researcher, 17,* 6, 1995:14–21.

Sayres, William. "What Is a Family Anyway?" In *Marriage and Family in a Changing Society,* 4th ed., James M. Henslin, ed. New York: Free Press, 1992:23–30.

Scarr, Sandra, and Marlene Eisenberg. "Child Care Research: Issues, Perspectives, and Results." *Annual Review of Psychology, 44,* 1963:613–644.

Schaefer, Naomi. "Slavery in Africa Is Largely Ignored by U.S. Black Leaders and Major Media." *Massachusetts News,* May 12, 1999.

Schaefer, Richard T. *Sociology,* 3rd ed. New York: McGraw-Hill, 1989.

Schaefer, Richard T. *Racial and Ethnic Groups,* 8th ed. Upper Saddle River, N.J.: Prentice Hall, 2000.

Schellenberg, James A. *Conflict Resolution: Theory, Research, and Practice.* Albany: New York University Press, 1996.

Schottland, Charles I. *The Social Security Plan in the U.S.* New York: Appleton, 1963.

Scully, Diana. "Negotiating to Do Surgery." In *Dominant Issues in Medical Sociology,* 3rd ed., Howard D. Schwartz, ed. New York: McGraw-Hill, 1994:146–152.

Scully, Diana, and Joseph Marolla. "Convicted Rapists' Vocabulary of Motive: Excuses and Justifications." *Social Problems, 31,* 5, June 1984:530–544.

Scully, Diana, and Joseph Marolla. "'Riding the Bull at Gilley's': Convicted Rapists Describe the Rewards of Rape." *Social Problems, 32,* 3, February 1985:251–263.

Seabrook, Jeremy. *Travels in the Skin Trade: Tourism and the Sex Industry.* New York: Pluto Press, 1997.

Searle, John R. *The Construction of Social Reality.* New York: Free Press, 1995.

Seib, Gerald F. "Click Here for Democracy." *Wall Street Journal,* January 1, 2000:R45–R46.

Seltzer, Judith A. "Consequences of Marital Dissolution for Children." *Annual Review of Sociology, 20,* 1994:235–266.

Sharp, Deborah. "Miami's Language Gap Widens." *USA Today,* April 3, 1992:A1, A3.

Sharp, Lauriston. "Steel Axes for Stone-Age Australians." In *Down to Earth Sociology: Introductory Readings,* 8th ed., James M. Henslin, ed. New York: Free Press, 1995:453–462.

Sheldon, William. *Varieties of Delinquent Youth: An Introduction to Constitutional Psychiatry.* New York: Harper, 1949.

Shellenbarger, Sue. "The Aging of America Is Making 'Elder Care' a Big Workplace Issue." *Wall Street Journal,* February 16, 1994a:A1, A8.

Shellenbarger, Sue. "How Some Companies Help with Elder Care." *Wall Street Journal,* February 16, 1994b:A8.

Sherif, Muzafer, and Carolyn Sherif. *Groups in Harmony and Tension.* New York: Harper & Row, 1953.

Sherman, Spencer. "The Hmong in America." *National Geographic,* October 1988:586–610.

Shively, JoEllen. "Cultural Compensation: The Popularity of Westerns among American Indians." Paper presented at the annual meetings of the American Sociological Association, 1991.

Shively, JoEllen. "Cowboys and Indians: Perceptions of Western Films among American Indians and Anglos." *American Sociological Review, 57,* December 1992:725–734.

Signorielli, Nancy. "Television and Conceptions about Sex Roles: Maintaining Conventionality and the Status Quo." *Sex Roles, 21,* 5/6, 1989:341–360.

Signorielli, Nancy. "Children, Television, and Gender Roles: Messages and Impact." *Journal of Adolescent Health Care, 11,* 1990:50–58.

Sills, David L. *The Volunteers.* Glencoe, Ill.: Free Press, 1957.

Simmel, Georg. *The Sociology of Georg Simmel,* Kurt H. Wolff, ed. and trans. Glencoe, Ill.: Free Press, 1950. First published between 1902 and 1917.

Simmons, Ann M. "Survivors of Rwandan Genocide Fear Guilty Will Get Away With Murder." *Los Angeles Times,* December 26, 1998.

Simon, David R., and D. Stanley Eitzen. *Elite Deviance,* 4th ed. Boston: Allyn and Bacon, 1993.

Simon, Julian L. *The Ultimate Resource.* Princeton, N.J.: Princeton University Press, 1981.

Simon, Julian L. *Theory of Population and Economic Growth.* New York: Blackwell, 1986.

Simon, Julian L. "Population Growth Is Not Bad for Humanity." In *Taking Sides: Clashing Views on Controversial Social Issues,* Kurt Finsterbusch and George McKenna, eds. Guilford, Conn.: Dushkin, 1992:347–352.

Simon, Julian L. "The Nativists Are Wrong." *Wall Street Journal,* August 4, 1993:A10.

Simons, Marlise. "The Amazon's Savvy Indians." In *Down to Earth Sociology: Introductory Readings,* 8th ed., James M. Henslin, ed. New York: Free Press, 1995:463–470.

Simpson, George Eaton, and J. Milton Yinger. *Racial and Cultural Minorities: An Analysis of Prejudice and Discrimination,* 4th ed. New York: Harper & Row, 1972.

Simpson, Glenn R. "Now Showing on an E-Mail Screen Near You: Your Congressman." *Wall Street Journal,* January 7, 2000.

Skeels, H. M. *Adult Status of Children with Contrasting Early Life Experiences: A Follow-up Study.* Monograph of the Society for Research in Child Development, *31,* 3, 1966.

Skeels, H. M., and H. B. Dye. "A Study of the Effects of Differential Stimulation on Mentally Retarded Children." *Proceedings and Addresses of the American Association on Mental Deficiency, 44,* 1939:114–136.

Skow, John. "The Redwoods Weep." *Time,* September 28, 1998:70–72.

"Slavery in Sudan." *New African.* September 1998. Online.

Smart, Barry. "On the Disorder of Things: Sociology, Postmodernity and the 'End of the Social.'" *Sociology, 24,* 3, August 1990:397–416.

Smith, Beverly A. "An Incest Case in an Early 20th-Century Rural Community." *Deviant Behavior, 13,* 1992:127–153.

Smith, Craig S. "China Becomes Industrial Nations' Most Favored Dump." *Wall Street Journal,* October 9, 1995:B1.

Smock, Pamela J., Wendy D. Manning, and Sanjiv Gupta. "The Effect of Marriage and Divorce on Women's Economic Well-Being." *American Sociological Review, 64,* December 1999:794–812.

Snow, Margaret E., Carol Nagy Jacklin, and Eleanor E. Maccoby. "Birth-Order Differences in Peer Sociability at Thirty-Three Months." *Child Development, 52,* 1981:589–595.

Son, Johanna. "Changing Attitudes Key to Ending Child Sex Trade." InterPress Service, January 23, 1995.

Sourcebook of Criminal Justice Statistics. Washington, D.C.: U.S. Government Printing Office, published annually.

South, Scott J. "Sociodemographic Differentials in Mate Selection Preferences." *Journal of Marriage and the Family, 53,* November 1991:928–940.

Sowell, Thomas. *Inside American Education: The Decline, the Deception, the Dogmas.* New York: Free Press, 1993.

Spector, Malcolm, and John Kitsuse. *Constructing Social Problems.* Menlo Park, Calif.: Cummings, 1977.

Spencer, Herbert. *Principles of Sociology,* 3 vols. New York: Appleton, 1884.

Spengler, Oswald. *The Decline of the West,* 2 vols., Charles F. Atkinson, trans. New York: Knopf, 1926–1928. First published in 1919–1922.

Spitzer, Steven. "Toward a Marxian Theory of Deviance." *Social Problems, 22,* June 1975:608–619.

Sprecher, Susan, and Rachita Chandak. "Attitudes about Arranged Marriages and Dating among Men and Women from India." *Free Inquiry in Creative Sociology, 20,* 1, May 1992:59–69.

Srole, Leo, et al. *Mental Health in the Metropolis: The Midtown Manhattan Study.* New York: New York University Press, 1978.

Stack, Carol B. *All Our Kin: Strategies for Survival in a Black Community.* New York: Harper, 1974.

Stampp, Kenneth M. *The Peculiar Institution: Slavery in the Ante-Bellum South.* New York: Vintage Books, 1956.

Stark, Rodney. *Sociology,* 3rd ed. Belmont, Calif.: Wadsworth, 1989.

Starna, William A., and Ralph Watkins. "Northern Iroquoian Slavery." *Ethnohistory, 38,* 1, Winter 1991:34–57.

"State of American Education: A 5-Year Report Card on American Education." U.S. Department of Education, February 22, 2000.

Statistical Abstract. See U.S. Bureau of the Census.

Stecklow, Steve. "SAT Scores Rise Strongly after Test Is Overhauled." *Wall Street Journal,* August 24, 1995: B1, B12.

Steinberg, Jacques. "Academic Standards Eased as a Fear of Failure Spreads." *New York Times,* December 3, 1999.

Stinnett, Nicholas. "Strong Families." In *Marriage and Family in a Changing Society,* 4th ed., James M. Henslin, ed. New York: Free Press, 1992:496–507.

Stipp, David. "Himalayan Tree Could Serve as Source of Anti-Cancer Drug Taxol, Team Says." *Wall Street Journal,* April 20, 1992:B4.

Stodgill, Ralph M. *Handbook of Leadership: A Survey of Theory and Research.* New York: Free Press, 1974.

Stone, Gregory P. "City Shoppers and Urban Identification: Observations on the Social Psychology of City Life." *American Journal of Sociology, 60,* November 1954:276–284.

Stone, Michael H. "Murder." *Psychiatric Clinics of North America, 12,* 3, September 1989:643–651.

Storfer, Miles D. "Intelligence and Giftedness." In *Window on Society,* 5th ed., John W. Heeren, Marylee Requa, Robert H. Lauer, and Jeanette C. Lauer, eds. Los Angeles: Roxbury Publishing Company, 2000:27–32.

Straus, Murray A. "Victims and Aggressors in Marital Violence." *American Behavioral Scientist, 23,* May–June 1980:681–704.

Straus, Murray A. "Explaining Family Violence." In *Marriage and Family in a Changing Society,* 4th ed., James M. Henslin, ed. New York: Free Press, 1992:344–356.

Straus, Murray A., and Richard J. Gelles. "Violence in American Families: How Much Is There and Why Does It Occur?" In *Troubled Relationships,* Elam W. Nunnally, Catherine S. Chilman, and Fred M. Cox, eds. Newbury Park, Calif.: Sage, 1988:141–162.

Straus, Murray A., Richard J. Gelles, and Suzanne K. Steinmetz. *Behind Closed Doors: Violence in the American Family.* New York: Anchor/Doubleday, 1980.

Strauss, Neil. "Critic's Notebook: A Japanese TV Show That Pairs Beauty and Pain." *New York Times,* July 14, 1998.

Stryker, Sheldon. "Symbolic Interactionism: Themes and Variations." In *Social Psychology: Sociological Perspectives,* Morris Rosenberg and Ralph H. Turner, eds. New Brunswick, N.J.: Transaction Books, 1990.

Sullivan, Andrew. "What We Look Up to Now." *New York Times,* November 15, 1998.

Sulloway, Frank J. *Born to Rebel: Birth Order, Family Dynamics, and Creative Lives.* New York: Vintage Books, 1997.

Sumner, William Graham. *Folkways: A Study in the Sociological Importance of Usages, Manners, Customs, Mores, and Morals.* New York: Ginn, 1906.

Sun, Lena H. "A Great Leap Back: Chinese Women Losing Jobs, Status as Ancient Ways Subvert Socialist Ideal." *Washington Post,* February 16, 1993:A1.

Sutherland, Edwin H. *Criminology.* Philadelphia: Lippincott, 1924.

Sutherland, Edwin H. *Principles of Criminology,* 4th ed. Philadelphia: Lippincott, 1947.

Sutherland, Edwin H. *White Collar Crime.* New York: Dryden Press, 1949.

Sutherland, Edwin H., Donald R. Cressey, and David F. Luckenbill. *Principles of Criminology,* 11th ed. Dix Hills, N. Y.: General Hall, 1992.

Suzuki, Bob H. "Asian-American Families." In *Marriage and Family in a Changing Society,* 2nd ed., James M. Henslin, ed. New York: Free Press, 1985:104–119.

Sykes, Gresham M., and David Matza. "Techniques of Neutralization." In *Down to Earth Sociology: Introductory Readings,* 5th ed., James M. Henslin, ed. New York: Free Press, 1988:225–231.

Szasz, Thomas S. *The Myth of Mental Illness,* rev. ed. New York: Harper & Row, 1986.

Szasz, Thomas S. "Mental Illness Is Still a Myth." In *Deviant Behavior 96/97,* Lawrence M. Salinger, ed. Guilford, Conn.: Dushkin, 1996:200–205.

Szasz, Thomas S. *Cruel Compassion: Psychiatric Control of Society's Unwanted.* Syracuse: Syracuse University Press, 1998.

Tanouye, Elyse. "SmithKline to Pay $325 Million to Settle Federal Claims of Lab-Billing Fraud." *Wall Street Journal,* February 25, 1997:B8.

Tapia, Andres. "Churches Wary of Inner-City Islamic Inroads." *Christianity Today, 38,* 1, January 10, 1994:36–38.

Taylor, Chris. "The Man Behind Lara Croft." *Time,* December 6, 1999:78.

Taylor, Raymond G., and Alexander I. Mechitov. "Russian Schools and the Legacies of the Soviet Era." *Education, 115,* 2, Winter 1994:260–263.

Thomas, Paulette. "EPA Predicts Global Impact from Warming." *Wall Street Journal,* October 21, 1988:B5.

Thomas, Paulette. "U.S. Examiners Will Scrutinize Banks with Poor Minority-Lending Histories." *Wall Street Journal,* October 22, 1991:A2.

Thomas, Paulette. "Boston Fed Finds Racial Discrimination in Mortgage Lending Is Still Widespread." *Wall Street Journal,* October 9, 1992:A3.

Thornton, Russell. *American Indian Holocaust and Survival: A Population History since 1492.* Norman: University of Oklahoma Press, 1987.

Tilly, Charles. *From Mobilization to Revolution.* Reading, Mass.: Addison-Wesley, 1978.

Timerman, Jacobo. *Prisoner without a Name, Cell without a Number.* New York: Knopf, 1981.

Tobias, Andrew. "The 'Don't Be Ridiculous' Law." *Wall Street Journal,* May 31, 1995:A14.

Toby, Jackson. "To Get Rid of Guns in Schools, Get Rid of Some Students." *Wall Street Journal,* March 23, 1992:A12.

Toch, Thomas. "Violence in Schools." *U.S. News & World Report, 115,* 18, November 8, 1993:31–36.

Toffler, Alvin. *The Third Wave.* New York: Morrow, 1980.

Tolchin, Martin. "Mildest Possible Penalty Is Imposed on Neil Bush." *New York Times,* April 19, 1991:D2.

Tönnies, Ferdinand. *Community and Society (Gemeinschaft und Gesellschaft),* with a new introduction by John Samples New Brunswick, N J · Transaction Books, 1988. First published in 1887.

Tordoff, William. "The Impact of Ideology on Development in the Third World." *Journal of International Development, 4,* 1, 1992:41–53.

Toynbee, Arnold. *A Study of History,* D. C. Somervell, abridger and ed. New York: Oxford University Press, 1946.

Treiman, Donald J. *Occupational Prestige in Comparative Perspective.* New York: Academic Press, 1977.

Trice, Harrison M., and Janice M Beyer. "Cultural Leadership in Organization." *Organization Science, 2,* 2, May 1991: 149–169.

Troeltsch, Ernst. *The Social Teachings of the Christian Churches.* New York: Macmillan, 1931.

Tumin, Melvin M. "Some Principles of Stratification: A Critical Analysis." *American Sociological Review, 18,* 1953:387–394.

Turner, Bryan S. "Outline of a Theory of Citizenship." *Sociology, 24,* 2, May 1990:189–217.

Turner, Jonathan H. *American Society: Problems of Structure.* New York: Harper & Row, 1972.

Turner, Jonathan H. *The Structure of Sociological Theory.* Homewood, Ill.: Dorsey, 1978.

Udry, J. Richard. "Biological Limits of Gender Construction." *American Sociological Review, 65,* June 2000:443–457.

Ullman, Edward, and Chauncey Harris. "The Nature of Cities." In *Urban Man and Society: A Reader in Urban Ecology,* Albert N. Cousins and Hans Nagpaul, eds. New York: Knopf, 1970:91–100.

U.S. Bureau of the Census. *Statistical Abstract of the United States: The National Data Book.* Washington, D.C.: U.S. Government Printing Office. Published annually.

U.S. Department of Health and Human Services, Public Health Service. *Healthy People 2000.* Washington, D.C.: U.S. Government Printing Office, 1990.

Usdansky, Margaret L. "English a Problem for Half of Miami." *USA Today,* April 3, 1992:A1, A3, A30.

Useem, Michael. *The Inner Circle: Large Corporations and the Rise of Business Political Activity in the U.S. and U.K.* New York: Oxford University Press, 1984.

Vande Berg, Leah R., and Diane Streckfuss. "Prime-Time Television's Portrayal of Women and the World of Work: A Demographic Profile." *Journal of Broadcasting and Electronic Media,* Spring 1992:195–208.

Vasil, Latika, and Hannelore Wass. "Portrayal of the Elderly in the Media: A Literature Review and Implications for Educational Gerontologists." *Educational Gerontology, 19,* 1, January–February 1993:71–85.

Vega, William A. "Hispanic Families in the 1980s: A Decade of Research." *Journal of Marriage and the Family, 52,* November 1990:1015–1024.

Vernon, JoEtta A., J. Allen Williams, Jr., Terri Phillips, and Janet Wilson. "Media Stereotyping: A Comparison of the Way Elderly Women and Men Are Portrayed on Prime-Time Television." *Journal of Women and Aging, 2,* 4, 1990:55–58.

Violas, P. C. *The Training of the Urban Working Class: A History of Twentieth Century American Education.* Chicago: Rand McNally, 1978.

Volti, Rudi. *Society and Technological Change,* 3rd ed. New York: St. Martin's Press, 1995.

Von Hoffman, Nicholas. "Sociological Snoopers." *Transaction 7,* May 1970:4, 6.

Wagley, Charles, and Marvin Harris. *Minorities in the New World.* New York: Columbia University Press, 1958.

Waldholz, Michael. "'Computer Brain' Outperforms Doctors in Diagnosing Heart Attack Patients." *Wall Street Journal,* December 2, 1991:7B.

Waldman, Amy. "Homes and Shops to Rise on Abandoned Harlem Properties." *New York Times,* December 27, 2000.

Waldman, Peter. "Some Muslim Thinkers Want to Reinterpret Islam for Modern Times." *Wall Street Journal,* March 15, 1995a:A1, A8.

Walker, Alice, and Pratibha Parmar. *Warrior Marks: Female Genital Mutilation and the Sexual Blinding of Women.* New York: Harcourt Brace, 1993.

Wallerstein, Immanuel. *The Modern World System: Capitalist Agriculture and the Origins of the European World-Economy in the Sixteenth Century.* New York: Academic Press, 1974.

Wallerstein, Immanuel. *The Capitalist World-Economy.* New York: Cambridge University Press, 1979.

Wallerstein, Immanuel. *The Politics of the World-Economy: The States, the Movements, and the Civilizations.* Cambridge, England: Cambridge University Press, 1984.

Wallerstein, Immanuel. "Culture as the Ideological Battle-ground of the Modern World-System." In *Global Culture: Nationalism, Globalization, and Modernity,* Mike Feather-stone, ed. London: Sage, 1990:31–55.

Wallerstein, Judith S., and Joan B. Kelly. "How Children React to Parental Divorce." In *Marriage and Family in a Changing Society,* 4th ed., James M. Henslin, ed. New York: Free Press, 1992:397–409.

Wallerstein, Judith, Julia Lewis, and Sarah Blakeslee. *The Unexpected Legacy of Divorce: A 25 Year Landmark Study.* New York: Hyperion Press, 2000.

Walters, Alan. "Let More Earnings Go to Shareholders." *Wall Street Journal,* October 31, 1995:A23.

Warr, Mark. "Age, Peers, and Delinquency." *Criminology, 31,* 1, 1993:17–40.

Watson, J. Mark. "Outlaw Motorcyclists." In *Down to Earth Sociology: Introductory Readings,* 5th ed., James M. Henslin, ed. New York: Free Press, 1988:203–213.

Weber, Max. "Politics as a Vocation." In *From Max Weber: Essays in Sociology,* Hans Gerth and C. Wright Mills, eds. New York: Oxford University Press, 1946:77–128.

Weber, Max. *The Theory of Social and Economic Organization,* A. M. Henderson and Talcott Parsons, trans., Talcott Parsons, ed. Glencoe, Ill.: Free Press, 1947. First pub-lished in 1913.

Weber, Max. *The Protestant Ethic and the Spirit of Capitalism.* New York: Scribner's, 1958. First published in 1904–1905.

Weber, Max. *Economy and Society.* Ephraim Fischoff, trans. New York: Bedminster Press, 1968. First published in 1922.

Webster, Pamela S., and A. Regula Herzog. "Effects of Parental Divorce and Memories of Family Problems on Relationships between Adult Children and Their Parents." *Journal of Gerontology, 50B,* 1, 1995:S24–S34.

Weeks, John R. *Population: An Introduction to Concepts and Issues,* 5th ed. Belmont, Calif.: Wadsworth, 1994.

Wei, William. *The Asian American Movement.* Philadelphia: Temple University Press, 1993.

Weintraub, Richard M. "A Bride in India." *Washington Post,* February 28, 1988.

Weisburd, David, Stanton Wheeler, and Elin Waring. *Crimes of the Middle Classes: White-Collar Offenders in the Federal Courts.* New Haven, Conn.: Yale University Press, 1991.

Weisskopf, Michael. "Scientist Says Greenhouse Effect Is Set-ting In." In *Ourselves and Others: The Washington Post Sociology Companion,* Washington Post Writers Group, eds. Boston: Allyn and Bacon, 1992:297–298.

Weitzman, Lenore J. *The Divorce Revolution.* New York: Free Press, 1985.

Wells, Joseph. "Report to the Nation on Occupational Fraud and Abuse." Association of Certified Fraud Examiners, 1998.

Welsh, Stephanie. "A Dangerous Rite of Passage." *Nation,* May 7, 1995.

Wenneker, Mark B., and Arnold M. Epstein. "Racial Inequali-ties in the Use of Procedures for Patients with Ischemic Heart Disease in Massachusetts." *Journal of the American Medical Association, 261,* 2, January 13, 1989:253–257.

Wessel, David. "As Populations Age, Fiscal Woes Deepen." *Wall Street Journal,* September 11, 1995:A1.

Whetstone, Muriel L. "What Black Men and Women Should Do Now (about Black Men and Women)." *Ebony,* February 1996:135–138, 140.

White, Jack E. "Forgive Us Our Sins." *Time,* July 3, 1995:29.

Whorf, Benjamin. *Language, Thought and Reality.* Cambridge, Mass.: MIT Press, 1956.

Whyte, Martin King. "Choosing Mates—The American Way." *Society,* March–April 1992:71–77.

Whyte, William H. *The City: Rediscovering the Center.* New York: Doubleday, 1989.

Williams, Christine L. *Still a Man's World: Men Who Do Women's Work.* Berkeley: University of California Press, 1995.

Williams, Rhys H. "Constructing the Public Good: Social Movements and Cultural Resources." *Social Problems, 42,* 1, February 1995:124–144.

Williams, Robin M., Jr. *American Society: A Sociological Inter-pretation,* 2nd ed. New York: Knopf, 1965.

Willie, Charles V. "Caste, Class, and Family Life Experi-ences." *Research in Race and Ethnic Relations, 6,* 1991: 65–84.

Wilson, James Q. "Lock 'Em Up and Other Thoughts on Crime." *New York Times Magazine,* March 9, 1975:11, 44–48.

Wilson, James Q. "Is Incapacitation the Answer to the Crime Problem?" In *Taking Sides: Clashing Views on Controversial Social Issues,* 7th ed., Kurt Finsterbusch and George McKenna, eds. Guilford, Conn.: Dushkin, 1992:318–324.

Wilson, James Q., and Richard J. Herrnstein. *Crime and Hu-man Nature.* New York: Simon & Schuster, 1985.

Wilson, William Julius. *The Declining Significance of Race: Blacks and Changing American Institutions.* Chicago: Univer-sity of Chicago Press, 1978.

Wilson, William Julius. *The Truly Disadvantaged: The Inner City, the Underclass, and Public Policy.* Chicago: University of Chicago Press, 1987.

Wilson, William Julius. *When Work Disappears: The World of the New Urban Poor.* Chicago: University of Chicago Press, 1996.

Wilson, William Julius. *The Bridge over the Racial Divide: Ris-ing Inequality and Coalition Politics.* Berkeley: University of California Press, 2000.

Winslow, Ron. "Study Finds Blacks Get Fewer Bypasses." *Wall Street Journal,* March 18, 1992:B1.

Winslow, Ron. "More Doctors Are Adding On-Line Tools to Their Kits." *Wall Street Journal,* October 7, 1994:B4.

Wirth, Louis. "Urbanism as a Way of Life." *American Journal of Sociology, 44,* July 1938:1–24.

Wirth, Louis. "The Problem of Minority Groups." In *The Science of Man in the World Crisis,* Ralph Linton, ed. New York: Columbia University Press, 1945.

Wolfensohnn, James D., and Kathryn S. Fuller. "Making Common Cause: Seeing the Forest for the Trees." *International Herald Tribune,* May 27, 1998:11.

Wolfgang, Marvin E., and Franco Ferracuti. *The Subculture of Violence: Toward an Integrated Theory in Criminology.* London: Tavistock, 1967.

Wouters, Cas. "On Status Competition and Emotion Management: The Study of Emotions as a New Field." *Theory, Culture & Society, 9,* 1992:229–252.

Wright, Erik Olin. *Class.* London: Verso, 1985.

Wright, Lawrence. "One Drop of Blood." *New Yorker,* July 25, 1994:46–50, 52–55.

Wright, Lawrence. "Double Mystery." *New Yorker,* August 7, 1995:45–62.

Yearbook of American and Canadian Churches. Nashville, Tenn.: Abingdon. Various editions.

Yellowbird, Michael, and C. Matthew Snipp. "American Indian Families." In *Minority Families in the United States: A Multicultural Perspective,* Ronald L. Taylor, ed. Englewood Cliffs, N.J.: Prentice Hall, 1994:179–201.

Yinger, J. Milton. *Toward a Field Theory of Behavior: Personality and Social Structure.* New York: McGraw-Hill, 1965.

Yinger, J. Milton. *The Scientific Study of Religion.* New York: Macmillan, 1970.

Yoon, Carol Kaesuk. "Simple Method Found to Vastly Increase Crop Yields." *New York Times,* August 22, 2000.

Zachary, G. Pascal. "Behind Stocks' Surge Is an Economy in Which Big U.S. Firms Thrive." *Wall Street Journal,* November 22, 1995:A1, A5.

Zald, Mayer N. "Looking Backward to Look Forward: Reflections on the Past and the Future of the Resource Mobilization Research Program." In *Frontiers in Social Movement Theory,* Aldon D. Morris and Carol McClurg Mueller, eds. New Haven, Conn.: Yale University Press, 1992:326–348.

Zald, Mayer N., and John D. McCarthy, eds. *Social Movements in an Organizational Society.* New Brunswick, N.J.: Transaction Books, 1987.

Zellner, William W. *Countercultures: A Sociological Analysis.* New York: St. Martin's, 1995.

Zerubavel, Eviatar. *The Fine Line: Making Distinctions in Everyday Life.* New York: Free Press, 1991.

Zey, Mary. *Banking on Fraud: Drexel, Junk Bonds, and Buyouts.* Hawthorne, N.Y.: Aldine de Gruyter, 1993.

Name Index

Subject Index

A

Abkhasians, 259
Ablution, 158
Abortion, 362, 404–5
Abuse
    of children, 155–56, 157, 324–25
    of family, 324–25
    gender and, 254–56, 324
    social inequality and, 324
    spousal, research design example, 21–26
    of spouses, 27, 254, 324
Accents, 165, 226
Achievement, 22, 47
Acid rain, 407, 408
Activity theory, 265
Adolescence, 74
Adulthood, 75
Advertising
    and body image, 95–96
    and gender, 96
    and greed, 292
    as propaganda, 401–3
Affirmative action, 233–34
Africa
    culture of, 35–36
    ethnic conflicts in, 392, 393
    female circumcision in, 255–56
    and slavery today, 157–58
    starvation in, 365
African Americans. *See also* Slavery
    accents of, 226
    civil rights of, 222–23, 400
    and class, 224–25
    economic status of, 223–24
    and education, 10, 11–12, 222,
        223–24, 225, 335
    families, 312–13
    gains of, 223–24
    and Harlem, 376
    and health care, 214
    and housing, 213–14, 226
    interracial marriage, 211, 309

    life expectancy, 214
    lynching of, 10, 211
    middle class, 224–25
    Million Man March, 400
    in political office, 223, 257
    and population of U.S., 369
    race *versus* class, 224–25
    and racial caste system, 158
    racial-ethnic terminology, 45
    and religion, 351
    rising expectations of, 223
    segregation, 220
    U.S. race relations, 10–12, 222–24
    voting rights, 222
    W. E. B. Du Bois on, 10–12
    well-being of, 223–24
Age
    at first marriage, 317–18
    and religious affiliation, 350
    and voting patterns, 281
Age cohort, 265
Ageism, 263
Aggregate, 106
Aggression and testosterone, 242–43
Aging, 258–69
    activity theory of, 265
    changing sentiment about, 268
    conflict perspective on, 266–68
    costs of caring for, 260, 267, 268
    disengagement theory, 265
    functionalist perspective on, 265
    future of, 269
    and gender, 258–59, 264
    global aspects of, 259–62
    and health care, 267, 268
    and industrialization, 259–60, 263
    and life expectancy, 260–62
    in mass media, 263, 264
    and new technology, 269
    perceptions of, 264
    and poverty, 196, 199, 268
    social construction of, 259

    and Social Security, 259–60, 266–67,
        293
    and socialization, 75
    statistics on, 260–62
    symbolic interactionist perspective
        on, 263–64
    well-being of, 266
Agricultural revolution, 87, 88–89, 372
Agricultural societies, 87, 88–89, 285
Al-Ghazaly Islamic School, 351
Alcohol as a drug, 136
Alienation, 114–16, 379
Amazon, 87, 409
American Dream, 292, 376
American Federation of Teachers, 338
American Journal of Sociology, 9
American Sociological Association, 106,
    411
American Sociological Society, 10
Amish, 91, 348
Anarchy, 283
Angola, 170
Animal rights activism, 403
Animals
    deprived, 61
    domestication of, 87, 88
    extinction of, 409
    treatment of, 40
Anti-Malthusians, 362–64, 365
Anti-Semitism. *See under* Jews
Anticipatory socialization, 70
Antithesis and thesis, 394
Apathy, 282
Appearance, 39, 241
Applied sociology, 12–13
Arabs, 35–36, 132, 157, 234–35
Arkansas, 340
Aryan Nations, 216
Aryans, 207
Asian Americans. *See also* specific ethnic
    groups
    assimilation of, 230

Photo Credits

Chapter Opener Art Credits (*continued*)
Chapter 10: *Holding Court* by Phoebe Beasley, 1989. Collage, 36" × 36". © Phoebe Beasley/Omni-Photo Communications.
Chapter 11: *Voting, 1976* by Franklin McMahon, 1976. Pen (or Pencil) on Acrylic painting, 14" × 17". © Franklin McMahon/CORBIS.
Chapter 12: *Family Supper* by Ralph Fasanella, 1972. Oil on canvas, 70" × 50". Ellis Island Immigration Museum. Courtesy of ACA Galleries, New York and Eva Fasanella.

Chapter 13: *Creative Mind* by Tsing-Fang Chen, 1988. Acrylic on canvas, 66" × 48". © Lucia Gallery, New York City/TF Chen/SuperStock.
Chapter 14: *Bus Stop in Beijing* by Phoebe Beasley, 1983. Collage, 24" × 36". © Phoebe Beasley/Omni-Photo Communications.
Chapter 15: *New York Wall Painting Murals.* © SuperStock.

Photo Credits

p. 5 © Herve Collart Odinetz/Corbis Sygma; **p. 6** The Granger Collection, New York; **p. 7** (left) Mary Evans Picture Library; (center) North Wind Picture Archives; (right) © Bettmann/CORBIS; **pp. 8, 9** The Granger Collection, New York; **p. 10** (left) North Wind Picture Archives; (right) Photographs and Print Division, Schomburg Center for Research in Black Culture/The New York Public Library, Astor, Lenox, and Tilden Foundations; **p. 16** Master of Serrone (16th c.). Joseph's Workshop S. Maria Assunta, Serrone (Foligno), Italy. Photo © Alinari/Regione Umbria/Art Resource, NY; **p. 24** © Lash/Sipa Press; **p. 27** © Lannis Waters/The Palm Beach Post; **p. 39** (top/left to right) © SuperStock, Inc.; © Art Wolfe/All Stock/PictureQuest; (center/left to right) © Romano Cagnoni/Still Pictures; © SuperStock, Inc.; © Ben Mangor/SuperStock, Inc.; (bottom/left to right) © Gil Moti/Still Pictures; © Art Wolfe/All Stock/PictureQuest; © 2001 Stone/Stuart McClymont; **p. 40** © Charles Kennard/Stock, Boston; **p. 41** (top/left & center) © Craig M. Moore; (top/right—boy) Digital Imagery © 2001 PhotoDisc, Inc.; (top/right—hand) © Craig M. Moore; (bottom) © Liba Taylor/CORBIS; **p. 46** © Mirror Syndication International; **p. 47** © Owen Franken/Stock, Boston; **p. 48** Photofest, Inc.; **p. 49** © Esbin-Anderson/Photo Network/PictureQuest; **p. 50** © Clarke Memorial Museum, Eureka, California; **p. 51** © Moshe shai Photography; **p. 59** © Charlyn Zlotnik/Woodfin Camp & Associates; **p. 60** © Kate Brooks/SABA; **p. 61** © Harlow Primate Laboratory/ University of Wisconsin; **p. 62** © Marleen Ferguson/ PhotoEdit; **p. 63** © 2001 Stone/Charles Thatcher; **p. 66** © Bill Greenblatt/Gamma Liaison; **p. 68** (left) Universal/ MPTV; (right) Courtesy © Eidos Interactive; **p. 72** The Bridgeman Art Library; **p. 73** © Eddie Adams/Liaison Agency; **p. 74** © Michael MacIntyre/The Hutchison Library; **p. 81** AP/Wide World Photos; **p. 84** © Evan Agostini/Liaison Agency; **p. 87** © Carlos Humberto/ Contact Press Images; **p. 89** © The Museum of Modern Art/Film Stills Archive; **p. 91** © Jerry Irwin/Liaison Agency; **p. 92** (left) © Tim Thompson/CORBIS; (right) © Roberto Soncin Gerometta/Photo 20–20; **p. 93** (top/left to right) © Alain Evrard/Photo Researchers, Inc.; © Franz Lanting/Minden Pictures; (bottom) © Kevin Jones/MPTV; **p. 95** (left) © 2001 Stone/Robert Daly; (right) Photo © Richard Corkery/NY Daily News; **p. 97** © Heidi Levine/Sipa Press; **p. 100** (left) © Pictor International/ Pictor International, Ltd./PictureQuest; (right) © Brooks Kraft/Corbis Sygma; **p. 106** © Corbis Sygma; **p. 107** © Jean-Claude Coutasse/Contact Press Images; **p. 108** AP/Wide World Photos; **p. 109** © The New Yorker Collection 1979 Robert Weber from cartoonbank.com. All Rights Reserved. **p. 110** AP/Wide World Photos; **p. 111** The Granger Collection, New York; **p. 114** © March of Dimes; **p. 115** AP/Wide World Photos; **p. 118** © Michael Wolf/Visum/SABA; **p. 121** © Michael P. Manheim/Photo Network/PictureQuest; **p. 124** © 1965 by Stanley Milgram. From the film Obedience, distributed by Pennsylvania State University, Audio Visual Services;